**Advance Praise for Weaving Prayer**

"This engaging and erudite volume transforms the prayer experience. Not only is it of considerable intellectual interest to learn the history of prayers—how, when, and why they were composed—but this new knowledge will significantly help a person pray with intention (*kavvanah*). I plan to keep this volume right next to my siddur."

—**Rabbi Judith Hauptman** is the E. Billi Ivry Professor (emerita) of Talmud and Rabbinic Culture, Jewish Theological Seminary, author *Rereading the Rabbis: A Woman's Voice* and *The Stories They Tell: Halakhic Anecdotes in the Babylonian Talmud.*

"Jeffrey Hoffman is one of the few scholars specializing in the history and significance of Jewish prayer—and he is a good one. He is, equally, a superb teacher of his subject. His work thus combines academic credibility and lucid presentation; this book will make a significant addition to anyone's library."

—**Rabbi Lawrence A. Hoffman, PhD**, Professor Emeritus of Liturgy Worship and Ritual, Hebrew Union College, NY, author, *Beyond the Text: A Holistic Approach to Liturgy* and *The Way Into Jewish Prayer.*

"The inclusion of both a scholarly and spiritual commentary is a bringing together of two worlds often thought distant from one another. In going beyond and including contributions from all major modern approaches to Judaism, Rabbi Hoffman bridges the distances among them showing that each has something to offer the others. This book should appeal equally to those already familiar with Jewish prayer and to beginners. Difficult concepts are explained in accessible language and the footnotes provide valuable additions for those ready to go deeper.

"Rabbi Hoffman has provided a valuable addition to the literature on liturgy."

—**Rabbi Daniel Siegel,** editor of ALEPH's *Siddur Kol Koreh* project. He was the first person to receive rabbinic ordination from Rabbi Zalman Schachter-Shalomi.

"WEAVING PRAYER is a gift to the modern Jew—regardless of denomination or affiliation—seeking to find their place in the *siddur* and in the act of *tefillah* (prayer). Through Rabbi Dr. Hoffman's keen eye for literary structure and his expansive soul that humbly articulates the values and challenges of prayer today, this book illuminates and inspires. As much a resource for study as a companion to keep in hand in worship, WEAVING PRAYER is a much-needed contribution to our synagogues, schools, and homes.

—**Rav Steven Exler**, Senior Rabbi at Hebrew Institute of Riverdale-The Bayit.

"Few discussions of the Jewish prayer book carefully separate their historical, literary, and inspirational commentaries. Hoffman's offering, drawn from years of teaching liturgy in rabbinic seminaries and serving congregations, offers an accessible interdenominational perspective on American Jews' Ashkenazi heritage, both summarizing traditional and academic scholarship and addressing contemporary spiritual needs."

—**Rabbi Ruth Langer**, Professor of Jewish Studies, Theology Department, Boston College, author of *Liturgy in the Life of the Synagogue: Studies in the History of Jewish Prayer* and *Jewish Liturgy: A Guide to Research*

# Weaving Prayer

## *An Analytical and Spiritual Commentary on the Siddur*

Jeffrey Hoffman

**Ben Yehuda Press**
Teaneck, New Jersey

Published by Ben Yehuda Press
122 Ayers Court #1B
Teaneck, NJ 07666
http://www.BenYehudaPress.com

To subscribe to our monthly book club and support independent Jewish publishing, visit https://www.patreon.com/BenYehudaPress

Ben Yehuda Press books may be purchased at a discount by synagogues, book clubs, and other institutions buying in bulk. For information, please email markets@BenYehudaPress.com

ISBN13 978-1-953829-60-3 pb 978-1-963475-22-7 hc 978-1-963475-23-4 epub

Cover photo by Yossi Hoffman

24 25 26 / 10 9 8 7 6 5 4 3 2 1 20240607

*For Laurie*

Contents


**Introduction** xi
**Acknowledgements** xviii

## Services Throughout the Year

***Birkhot HaShaḥar*** 2

***Pesukei DeZimra*** 8
Overview 8
Outline of *Pesukei DeZimra* 15
Commentary on Select Units of *Pesukei DeZimra* 19
*Hodu L'YHVH Kir'u Vishmo* (I Chronicles 16:8-36)
Prayer from when David brought the Ark to Jerusalem 19
*Mizmor LeTodah,* A Psalm of Thanksgiving (Psalm 100) 20
*Ashrei (*Psalm 145) 22
Psalm 149 23
Psalm 150 25
Psalm 91 26

**The *Shema* and Its Blessings** 27
Introduction 27
The First Line of the *Shema* 30
First Paragraph of The *Shema, V'Ahavta* 39
The Second Paragraph of the *Shema, V'Haya Im Shamo'a* 42
The Third Paragraph of the *Shema* 44
The Blessings Surrounding the *Shema* 48
The First Blessing Before the *Shema* 49
The Second Blessing Before the *Shema* 57
The First Blessing After the *Shema* 61
The Second Blessing After the *Shema* (evening) 63
The Third Blessing After the *Shema* (evening) 65

**The Torah Service** 68

## Weekday Services

**The Weekday *Amidah* - Historical and Literary Introduction** 78
Blessing #1: *Magein Avraham,* Shield of Abraham 95
Blessing #2: *Meḥayei HaMeitim,* Reviver of the Dead 98
Blessing #3: *Ha'Eil HaKadosh,* Holy God 101
Blessing #4: *Ḥonein HaDa'at,* Gracious Giver of Knowledge 112
Blessing #5: *HaRotzeh BiTeshuvah,* Desirer of Repentance 114

Blessing #6: *Ḥanun HaMarbeh Lisloʾaḥ*
God Who Graciously and Abundantly Forgives 115
Blessing #7: *Goʾeil Yisrael,* Liberator of Israel 117
Blessing #8: *Rofei Ḥolei Amo Yisrael,* Healer of the Sick of his People Israel 122
Blessing #9: *Mevareikh HaShanim,* Blesser of the Years 127
Blessing #10: *Mekabeitz Nidḥei Amo Yisrael*
Gatherer of the Dispersed of his People Israel 128
Blessing #11: *Melekh Oheiv Tzedakah U'Mishpat*
King Lover of Righteousness and Justice 133
Blessing #12: *Shoveir Oyvim U'Makhniʾa Zeidim*
Breaker of enemies and Humbler of the arrogant 135
Blessing #13: *Mishʾan U'Mivtaḥ LaTzadikim*
Support and Trust of the Righteous 140
Blessing #14: *Boneh Yerushalayim,* Builder of Jerusalem 143
*Naḥeim,* Remembering Jerusalem on *Tisha B'Av* 144
Blessing #15: *Matzmiʾaḥ Keren Yeshua,* Grower of the Horn of Salvation 151
Blessing #16: *Shomeiʾa Tefillah,* Listener to Prayer 157
Blessing #17: *HaMaḥazir Shekhinato LeTzion*
Restorer of His Presence to Zion 159
Blessing #18: *HaTov Shimkha U'Lekha Naʾeh LeHodot*
Your Name is "Goodness" and to You it is
Pleasant to Offer Thanksgiving 162
Blessing #19: *HaMevareikh Et Amo Yisrael BaShalom*
The Blesser of Peace to His People Israel 165
Additions for Ḥanukkah and Purim *Al HaNissim,* For The Miracles 170
*Al HaNissim* for Ḥanukkah 170
*Al HaNissim* for *Purim* 178

***Taḥanun*—Supplication** 184

**Concluding Prayers of *Shaḥarit* (Morning Service)** 189
*Kedushah DeSidra* 189
*Kaddish* 191
*Aleinu* 203
*Adon Olam* 215

## Shabbat Services

***Kabbalat Shabbat*** 218
*Ana V'Khoʾaḥ* 226
*Lekhah Dodi* 227
Psalms 92 and 93 239

**Shabbat *Ma'ariv* (Evening Service)** 240
Shabbat Evening *Amidah*, Part 1 240
Shabbat Evening *Amidah*, Part 2 244
*Birkat Mei'ein Sheva* 252

**Shabbat *Shaḥarit* (Morning Service)** 259
*Nishmat Kol Ḥai* 259
*Eil Adon* 267
*La'Eil Asher Shavat* 277
The *Amidah* for Shabbat Morning 279

**Shabbat *Musaf*** 294
The *Musaf Amidah* for Shabbat 294

**Shabbat *Minḥah* (Afternoon Service)** 308
*Kedushah DeSidra* (*U'Va LeTzion*) 308
Shabbat *Amidah* of *Minḥah* 311

**Conclusion of Shabbat (*Havdalah*)** 316

## The Three Pilgrimage Festivals, *Shalosh Regalim*

**The Festival *Amidah*** 323
*Attah Veḥartanu*, You Have Chosen Us 324
*Ya'aleh VeYavo*, May We Be Remembered 326
*VeHasi'einu*, Grant to Us 327

**The Festival Torah Service** 331

***Hallel*** 336
***Yizkor*** 340
***Hoshanot*** 346
***Akdamut*** 352
***Tefillat Tal and Tefillat Geshem*** 357

**Afterword: A Medieval Kabbalist on the Upper West Side** 363

**Index** 387

**About the Author** 397

# Introduction

I have been teaching Jewish liturgy to rabbinical and cantorial students for almost forty years and this book represents a summary of the insights into the liturgy I discovered over that period. This book is meant for scholars, rabbis, cantors, Jewish educators, educated laypersons, and interested non-Jewish readers.

There are several unique features to this commentary:

**Two commentaries for each prayer or set of prayers**

The key characteristic of this book is that it includes both a scholarly "Analytical" commentary as well as a "Spiritual" commentary for each prayer or set of prayers. Several book-length commentaries on the siddur in English are currently available. However, they are either mainly scholarly or mainly spiritual/popular. There are none that feature both a scholarly commentary as well as a commentary that models how a modern Jew might apply the scholarly insights to an actual prayer experience. Scholarly books on the liturgy tend to be written with members of the academic community in mind, assume fluency in several languages, and often completely ignore any implications or relevance its content may have for the typical worshiper's prayer experience. The mainly spiritual or popular books on the liturgy tend to reflect the personal attitude of the author and often ignore many insights of either traditional or academic scholarship, or both. This book honors and cites both traditional and modern academic scholarship while also directly addressing the spiritual needs of the modern worshiper.

**The Analytical Commentary**

The Analytical Commentary subjects the liturgy to an historical and literary analysis and cites numerous primary sources to provide the necessary historical background. It also identifies the literary elements at work in the poetry of the prayerbook. This approach is known as the *peshat* interpretation. *Peshat* is often mistakenly translated literally as the "simple" interpretation, however it is anything but simple. A better way to describe it is as the "contextual" interpretation. It provides the historical and literary background necessary to place a text in its proper "context."

Since the Analytical Commentary answers the first questions about any prayer—what is this?—it is generally not specifically labeled.

The literary analysis in the Analytical Commentary pays attention to the use of alphabetic or other acrostics, alliteration, wordplays, intertextuality with the Bible and Rabbinic Literature, word- or root-repetition, rhyme, imagery, point of view, synecdoche, and motif, among others.

If the prayerbook contained text that was only meant to be read, perhaps the *peshat* approach of the Analytical Commentary would have been sufficient. However, the prayerbook is not meant to be read like any other book. It is meant to be prayed. For that reason, I've added the Spiritual Commentary.

**The Spiritual Commentary**

The Spiritual Commentary considers the conclusions of the Analytical Commentary and offers suggestions on how a given prayer might honestly be recited in worship by a contemporary Jew who is neither a fundamentalist nor an atheist. This approach is the way of *derash*, the more associative interpretation. The options offered in the Spiritual Commentary are by no means meant as the only ways to adapt the analyses of the Analytical Commentary for personal worship. Rather, they are meant as examples to stimulate the reader to grapple anew with each prayer in ways that lead to an authentic personal spiritual experience in worship.

Professor Neil Gillman was an important teacher of theology in my rabbinical training at The Jewish Theological Seminary. He often said that the question isn't so much whether one believes in God or not, but rather what one means when one uses the word "God." Since I wrote extensively in the Spiritual Commentary about how I might adapt the scholarly conclusions of the Analytical Commentary, let me explain what I mean when I use the word "God." I believe in the reality of God, so I am neither an atheist nor an agnostic. On the other hand, I am not a fundamentalist; while I take the language of the Bible and the prayerbook very seriously, I do not take it literally. I do not view God to simply be a highly improved version of a human being, a super-human who thinks and emotes the way people do.

I believe that God is the mysterious reality that stands behind all existence, behind the creation of the universe and all that is within it. And I believe that human beings have the capacity to connect to that reality through prayer. People can link themselves to God's presence when we consciously recite or chant words of prayer. The key word is "consciously." While God's presence is always available, conscious, intentional prayer can bring that presence into focus. And I believe that intentionally praying the words of the Jewish prayerbook can lead to profound spiritual experience.

How does prayer work? I do not believe that God can be "persuaded" to act directly in the world because of prayers that are recited because I do not believe that God functions like human beings. I don't believe that we need to draw God's attention to our needs or desires in order for us to access God's support or love nor that our praise of God fulfills a divine need. Rather, I believe that prayer works in a way similar to something I heard from the well-known Vietnamese Buddhist teacher, Thich Nhat Hanh (1926-2022). Some years ago, my wife and I attended an all-day seminar conducted by Thich Nhat Hanh at a Buddhist monastery in upstate New York. At one point, he told us that the nuns at the monastery—which was also a working farm—programmed an app on their smartphones to sound a gong once an hour. The gong was meant to remind the nuns to refocus on mindfulness, on being fully present and conscious, as they continued their daily tasks. He related this to assure us that staying mindful is challenging; even nuns at a monastery need hourly reminders.

I view the entire system of Judaism's thrice-daily prayer services, along with its myriad blessings (over food, drink, scents, bodily functions, etc.) as containing a similar purpose: They are all meant to remind us to refocus on the presence of God. How Jewish liturgy developed and how it is meant to continually recenter us on the presence of God is precisely what this book is about. Expressions of one's conception of God defy clear-cut definitions because God is, as Rabbi Abraham Joshua Heschel memorably put it, ineffable, meaning beyond utterance and speech. For that reason, I have written a short story that conveys more about my essential spiritual stance, using the medium of fiction to allude a little more intensely to what I believe. The story makes the case for integrating the contemporary scientific discoveries about the origin of the universe into our theology. For those interested in that kind of deeper dive—lightened by some humor—the story, "A Medieval Kabbalist on the Upper West Side," may be found in the Afterword beginning on page 363.

In this book, I have tried to avoid using male or female pronouns when referring to God because I don't believe that God carries gender. However, there were times when using pronouns regarding the divine were unavoidable, for example when translating biblical or prayer texts that explicitly use (almost invariably male) pronouns. I also did not capitalize pronouns relating to God, so readers will find, for example, "Blessed are you" and not "Blessed are You." Certainly, no disrespect is meant; I am simply following a more academic convention.

**Pluralistic Approach**

Another attribute of the book is its pluralistic approach. Regarding many prayers, the Commentaries compare the treatment given to them by the current prayer books of the major movements in North American Judaism: Orthodox, Conservative, Reform, and Reconstructing Judaism. Occasionally, interpretations from Renewal Judaism will be compared as well. The Analytical Commentary will often provide the theological context of the various movements' approaches to a given prayer. It will broaden the view of readers who are used to just one movement by exposing them to the versions and interpretations of prayers by the other major North American Jewish movements. As I mention in the Acknowledgements, my long association with The Academy for Jewish Religion (AJR) exposed me to the great benefits of not only recognizing, but embracing, pluralism in Jewish Studies and in Jewish life and I am happy to acknowledge my debt to AJR.

The main prayerbooks compared include:

Orthodox:

- Rabbi Nosson Scherman and Rabbi Meir Zlotowitz, eds., *The Complete Artscroll Siddur: Weekday, Sabbath, Festival* (Brooklyn, NY: Mesorah Publications, Ltd., 1984).

Conservative:

- Rabbi Edward Feld, Rabbi Jan Uhrbach, eds., *Siddur Lev Shalem for Shabbat & Festivals* (New York, NY: The Rabbinical Assembly, 2016).

Reform:

- Elyse D. Frishman, ed., *Mishkan T'filah: A Reform Siddur* (New York, NY: Central Council of American Rabbis, 2007).

Reconstructing Judaism:

- Rabbi David A. Teutsch, ed., *Kol Haneshamah: Shabbat Veḥagim* (Elkins Park, Pennsylvania: The Reconstructionist Press, 1994).
- Rabbi David A. Teutsch, ed., *Kol Haneshamah: Daily* (Wyncote, Pennsylvania: The Reconstructionist Press, 1996).

**Sensitivity to the Way the Non-Jewish Other is Portrayed in the Liturgy**

While my commentaries take a generally positive and "partisan" approach to Jewish tradition, they also attempt to maintain intellectual honesty. That means they will candidly identify and address the occasional xenophobic notes that appear in Jewish liturgy. Unfortunately, it is a very human tendency to praise one's in-group and to disparage the out-group. The liturgies of many faith communities reflect this tendency in some prayer texts, and Jewish liturgy is no exception. Happily, those instances are few, including, for example, *Aleinu* and *Birkat HaMinim* in the Weekday *Amidah* among a few others.

### *Ashkenazic* Rite and Key Commentaries

This book mainly takes the traditional Ashkenazic rite as the standard version of the liturgy as it reflects the prayer experience of the vast majority of North American Jews. I often delve into earlier versions of prayers and occasionally mention Sephardic or other rites. Among the earlier versions of, or commentaries on, the liturgy, there are several that are often cited and ought to be specifically introduced:

*Seder Rav Amram* (9th century, Babylonia), composed by Rabbi Amram ben Sheshet, is considered the first Jewish prayerbook even though in form it is more of a commentary than a prayerbook. It was written as a responsum (*teshuvah*) to the rabbis of Spain who wrote to Rav Amram as the reigning Gaon, the leader of the major Jewish community in Babylonia. *Seder Rav Amram* was the victim of its own success. Because it was revered as an authoritative source on the prayers, a copy was sought by many Jewish communities around the world. However, in the period before the printing press (15th century), often when the text of a prayer in *Seder Rav Amram* varied from local custom, the variant text was copied into the margin of *Seder Rav Amram*. When that community's copy of *Seder Rav Amram* was then itself copied, sometimes the text in the margin replaced the original version. As this proliferated over centuries, copies of *Seder Rav Amram* from, say, 13th-century France, differed in many ways from copies that originated in 14th-century Spain because each community ultimately "customized" their copy of *Seder Rav Amram* to resemble their own version of the prayerbook. For this reason, one can never be sure that a prayer in *Seder Rav Amram* actually reflects Rav Amram's own writing. The result is that one must be cautious and somewhat tentative when citing *Seder Rav Amram*. Still, as the first siddur in Jewish history, it cannot be ignored.

*Siddur Rav Saadia Gaon* (10th century, Babylonia). Rav Saadia ben Yosef was a Gaon who followed Rav Amram by about a century. He, too, composed a siddur and added a commentary in Arabic. While it was an important scholarly work, its layout was not user-friendly. For example, he set out all of the morning service, over many pages, for use when a *minyan* (quorum) was present, and then added the very same service, over additional pages, for use when a *minyan* was not present. Consequently, it was not very popular, and very few copies of *Siddur Rav Saadia Gaon* have reached us. Nevertheless, it remains an important source for early Jewish liturgy.

*Maḥzor Vitry* (11th-12th century, France), composed by Rabbi Simḥah ben Shmuel, remains a significant source for the Ashkenazic rite. (Even though these days, the term *maḥzor* tends to refer to prayerbooks specifically for the Days of Awe and/or for The Three Pilgrimage Festivals, in pre-modern times, the word was used synonymously with the word *siddur* to refer to any compendium of prayers.) Somewhat like *Seder Rav Amram*, the original version of *Maḥzor Vitry* was added to; in this case, by the generations that immediately followed the author's death. Therefore, the same prayer is often addressed in the book, as if anew, by several passages in a row, making this resource challenging reading. Yet, this compilation of prayers and commentaries forms a rich resource of interpretations of the emerging Ashkenazic liturgy.

*Arba'ah Turim* (14th century, Spain), composed by Rabbi Ya'akov ben Asher, is not a siddur but rather a work of Jewish law (*halakhah*) that covers all areas of practical law. I found his typically generous gathering of various opinions on prayer always interesting. Quite helpful was his familiarity with both Sephardic and Ashkenazic practice since he moved, along with his famous father, Rabbeinu Asher—the *Rosh*—from Germany to Spain.[1]

The Analytical Commentary routinely cites talmudic literature and often differentiates between talmudic teachings from the Tannaitic and Amoraic periods; this requires a brief explanation. The older, and more authoritative, stratum of talmudic literature derives from the Tannaitic Period, roughly the first century BCE through the early third century CE. The *Mishnah, Tosefta*, and Tannaitic Midrashim stem from this time. The scholars of the Amoraic Period reacted to, commented upon, and extended the teachings from the Tannaitic Period and were active roughly from the third century CE through the sixth century CE. The work of the Amoraic period, along with copious anonymous additional comments comprise the *Gemara* in the Babylonian Talmud. The anonymous comments actually make up the bulk of the Babylonian Talmud. This latest layer is the *Stam* ("anonymous"), or editorial, layer, sometimes identified with the *Savora'im*. The period of the *Stam* is

[1] For a fine brief treatment of the historical context of this code, see *Judah* D. *Galinsky*, "*Ashkenazim in Sepharad*: The Rosh and the Tur on the Codification of Jewish Law," *Jewish Law Annual*, vol. 16 (2006): 3-23.

roughly the seventh and eighth centuries CE. Basic knowledge of these three layers in the Babylonian Talmud, Tannaitic, Amoraic, and *Stam*, sometimes becomes important in the Analytical Commentary.

**Hebrew-English Source Sheets Available Online**

The interested reader may want to consult the more than 90 source sheets (the vast majority of which are related to the liturgy) that I have created on the Sefaria website (sefaria.org). These contain the original Hebrew and/or Aramaic—usually with an English translation—of many of the sources of the prayers that are cited in the Analytical Commentary. On the Sefaria website, type "Jeffrey Hoffman" into the search engine to access these source sheets.

Finally, it is my sincere hope that this book will enhance readers' knowledge about Jewish liturgy and will make it easier to engage in truly meaningful worship.

**About the Title of this Book**

The opening phrase of the title of this book, "Weaving Prayer," is loosely based on *VeShirim E'erog*, "(I will) weave hymns," from the first line of the prayer, *Anim Zemirot*. That prayer derives from the circle of the 12th-13th century mystical German community, *Ḥasidei Ashkenaz*. The idea of "weaving" hymns is related to the work of the liturgical poets who ingeniously "weave" allusions to biblical, talmudic, and midrashic teachings throughout the prayers they compose. One of the purposes of this book is to reveal the warp and woof of these allusions with the goal of enhancing worshipers' intellectual and spiritual experience of prayer.

**About the Cover of this Book**

The prayer book featured on the cover and spine of this book is a family heirloom. It was brought to the U.S. from Poland early in the 20th century by my maternal grandfather, Joseph (Yosef Shee'a) Baumgarten. The title page identifies the siddur as Sider Sifso Renones, published in Lublin, 1916.

The photo features the first page of the prayer *Anim Zemirot,* including the phrase *VeShirim E'erog*, "(I will) weave hymns," which inspired the title of this book. The photo was taken by my son, Yossi Hoffman, whose professional skills include photography. He also happens to share the same first name as my grandfather, his great-grandfather, which perhaps represents a kind of spiritual symmetry.

# Acknowledgements

I am happy to acknowledge my debt to several of the great contemporary scholars of Jewish liturgy whose published works and presentations at academic conferences have nurtured me for many years. These include Professors Joseph Heinemann, Ezra Fleischer, Reuven Hammer, Joseph Tabory,[2] Meir Bar-Ilan, and Uri Ehrlich in Israel; Lawrence Hoffman, Ruth Langer, Reuven Kimelman, Richard Sarason, and Tzvee Zahavy in the United States; and Stefan Reif in England. I had the great fortune to study with Professors Joseph Heinemann and Reuven Hammer—both of whom are now in the yeshivah *shel ma'alah* (on high)—during my three student years in Jerusalem. Professor Hammer honored me years later by asking me to review a draft of his *Or Ḥadash* commentary on the weekday liturgy. One of the suggestions I made was that he ought to add more expressly spiritual comments and his response was that I should write that commentary on my own. The present book was partly inspired by his encouragement. Lawrence Hoffman is a prolific scholar of liturgy, and I found the 10-volume *My People's Prayer Book* that he edited, along with his many other works on the liturgy, quite helpful. I had the privilege of introducing him when he spoke at a multi-day conference at The Academy for Jewish Religion where I have taught for many years. He presented brilliantly for two full days of lectures without any notes whatsoever.[3] I am indebted to Ruth Langer, not only for her many published studies of Jewish liturgy, but also for her stimulating challenge to me to expand my research in several fruitful ways on the prayer *Aleinu*.[4] I thank Professor Bezalel ("Buzzy") Porten—Professor Emeritus in the Department of Jewish History at The Hebrew University of Jerusalem—who long ago introduced me to an effective literary approach in studying and writing about the liturgy. In 1996, Marcia Falk published *The Book of Blessings: New Jewish Prayers for Daily Life, the Sabbath, and the New Moon Festival.* I confess that when it first appeared, I was shocked and overwhelmed by her daring proposed alterations to the liturgy. And yet, I was also intrigued because in a learned and erudite way, her book forced readers to come to terms with

---

[2] See Tabory's monumental "List of Articles Related to Prayer and Holidays," Appendix to vol. 64 of *Kiryat Sefer*, 1992-1993.

[3] See my very positive review of his *Beyond the Text: A Holistic Approach to Liturgy* by Lawrence A. Hoffman in *Conservative Judaism*, 46:3, spring, 1994, 89-91.

[4] She published my essay in her scholarly online journal. "The Image of the Other in Jewish Interpretations of *Aleinu*," *The Journal of Christian-Jewish Studies*, 10:1, February, 2015, 1-41. http://ejournals.bc.edu/ojs/index.php/scjr/article/view/5904/5230

the limitations of a fixed liturgy. The questions her book asked inform the book I have now written. I am grateful to her.

I wish to thank Professor Kenneth Berger who read and responded to large sections of the manuscript. I also wish to thank Professor Robert Scheinberg, Professor Judith Hauptman, Professor David Golinkin, and Rabbi Daniel Horwitz. Thanks are due to Yossi Hoffman who responded to a number of portions of the book with his sensitivity to many dimensions of life and literature. Thanks as well to writer and poet, Jay Franzel, who was a sounding board for a number of elements in this book. Thanks as well to Barry Mark, an expert in Kabbalah; he was always available for questions large and small. The wisdom of all of these gracious people enhanced my research, sharpened my argument, and improved my writing. I also wish to thank my editor, Laura Logan, for the suggestions she made that improved the writing in myriad locations throughout the manuscript. The remaining weaknesses in the book are, of course, my responsibility.

Among the many invaluable aids to my research, I want to especially acknowledge Ismar Elbogen's *Jewish Liturgy: A Comprehensive History* which was of constant help. Originally published in German more than a hundred years ago in 1913, updated and translated into Hebrew in 1972 by a team of scholars and, finally, translated into English in 1993, this work has still not been surpassed as a one-volume compendium of the most important historical sources for the study of Jewish liturgy. It is not without its problems, especially its devaluing of the role of mystical sources—not uncommon for Jewish academic scholars of Elbogen's era—and yet, it is an essential starting point for research in Jewish liturgy.[5] Several key pre-modern compendia and commentaries are described in the Introduction to this book. The many other sources I used—medieval and modern—are duly recorded in the footnotes.

I've had the privilege of teaching rabbinical, cantorial, and graduate students at The Academy for Jewish Religion (AJR) for nearly 40 years. I was also honored to teach at The Jewish Theological Seminary for five years, and more recently, at the Aleph Ordination Program and Hebrew Union College-Jewish Institute of Religion in New York. I served as rabbi for Congregation Beth Israel in Vancouver, BC for three years and Congregation

[5] The English translation was done by Professor Raymond P. Scheindlin, with whom I studied liturgy at the Jewish Theological Seminary in New York, and who remained a mentor after my graduation. Professor Scheindlin aptly notes in his foreword that Elbogen's work "impresses the contemporary reader with its sheer erudition, its delight in facts, and its bravura citation of sources." See Ismar Elbogen, *Jewish Liturgy: A Comprehensive History* (New York: The Jewish Publication Society and The Jewish Theological Seminary of America, 1993), xi.

Sons of Israel in Nyack, New York for 20 years. The interactions I had with students and congregants added to my understanding of Jewish liturgy. My long association with The Academy for Jewish Religion (AJR) sensitized me to the benefits of a pluralistic approach to Jewish life. I am especially grateful for AJR's influence in the many instances in which this book compares the *siddurim* of the several movements in North American Judaism.

I am so very grateful for the love of my family: Shaia and Tamar; Shulie, Jordan, Ziv and Edden; Yossi, Maddy, Ilan, and Tal. I thank my life companion, Laurie, for more than can be expressed here, and I dedicate this book to her. I am thankful for her constant spiritual and emotional support and her openness to my frequent raising of some obscure issue of liturgical exegesis. Often enough, her sensitivity to poetics in general, and to that of Jewish liturgy specifically, resulted in new insights which are represented in many more places than are formally acknowledged in the footnotes.

# Part One

# Services Throughout the Year

## *Birkhot HaShaḥar*

This is the first section of the *Shaḥarit*, "morning," service of every day of the year. While the core blessings of this section are recorded in the Talmud, these were meant to be recited at home, and not in the synagogue. This section developed as a synagogue service proper only after the talmudic period. Because of that, none of its prayers require a *minyan*, a "quorum," of ten people (except for the *Kaddish*, which is a special case; see the discussion on page 200). The blessings at the center of this service bring a spiritual consciousness to the typical routine followed at home as one awakens, opens one's eyes from sleep, descends from one's bed, gets dressed, etc.

Over the centuries, additional prayers were added to these blessings, as were a few short biblical and rabbinic study texts to allow each person to at least symbolically study Torah on a daily basis.[6] Here, I will only comment upon the blessings that comprise the core of this service.

The Talmud lists this series of blessings and connects each with one of the stages of awakening and preparing for a new day:

> Upon hearing the sound of the rooster, one should recite: "Blessed (are you, *YHVH*, Ruler of the Universe) who gave the rooster understanding to distinguish between day and night."
> Upon opening one's eyes, recite: "Blessed...who gives sight to the blind."
> Upon sitting up straight, recite: "Blessed...who sets captives free."
> Upon dressing, recite: "Blessed...who clothes the naked."
> Upon standing up straight, recite: "Blessed...who raises those bowed down."
> Upon descending (from one's bed) to the ground, recite: Blessed...who spreads the earth above the waters."

[6] Based on early liturgical manuscripts, Israel M. Ta-Shma theorized that while some of this section of the liturgy derived from the post-talmudic period, it also preserved some prayers from as early as the Second Temple Period. These prayers, he posited, came from the *Ma'amadot*, a service held in localities when their priests and Levites took their turn serving in the Temple in Jerusalem. I am skeptical about this theory, but Ta-Shma was a solid scholar and more needs to be researched about the issue. See Israel M. Ta-Shma, "Meqorah Umeqomah shel Tefillat 'Aleinu Leshabbe'aḥ' Basiddur Hatefillah: Seder Ha-ma'amadot U'she'elat Siyyum Hatefillah," in *Sefer Zikaron L'Efrayim Talmage*, ed. Barry Walfish (Haifa: Haifa University Press, 1992-1993), I; 85-98, reprinted with an abbreviated title in Ta-Shma's *The Early Ashkenazic Prayer: Literary and Historical Aspects* [Hebrew] (Jerusalem: Magnes, 2003), 139-153.

> Upon walking, recite: "Blessed...who makes firm the steps of a person."
> Upon putting on one's shoes, recite: "Blessed...who has provided me with all I need."
> Upon putting on one's belt, recite: "Blessed...who girds Israel with strength."
> Upon spreading a shawl upon one's head, recite: "Blessed... who crowns Israel with glory..."[7]

Another passage from early Rabbinic Literature adds another three blessings along with an explanation for each one:

> Rabbi Yehuda says: A person must say three blessings every day:
> "Blessed... who has not made me a non-Jew."
> "Blessed... who has not made me a woman."
> "Blessed... who has not made me an ignoramus."
> A non-Jew—"All the nations are as naught in His sight" (Isaiah 40:17).
> A woman—A woman is not obligated (to do) commandments.
> An ignoramus—Because he does not fear sin, and the unlearned is not pious.[8]

The first two of these blessings were, indeed, added to the traditional siddur (although the contemporary liberal movements have altered the wording; see below), but the third was not. The reason is found in the talmudic discussion of this teaching:

> Rav Aḥa bar Ya'akov heard his son reciting the blessing: "Who did not make me an ignoramus." He said to (his son): "What's all this?"
>
> (His son) said to him: "Rather, what blessing should I recite? If you will say that one should recite: 'Who did not make me a slave,' that is the same as a woman" (since neither are obligated to perform the commandments and why should one recite two blessings about the same matter?)

[7] Babylonian Talmud *Berakhot* 60b.
[8] *Tosefta Berakhot* 7:17.

> Rav Aḥa bar Ya'akov answered: "Nevertheless, a slave is lowlier (than a woman)."[9]

This passage calls for some commentary. Apparently, Rav Aḥa bar Ya'akov heard his son recite all three of the blessings mentioned above, thanking God for not having created him a non-Jew, a woman, or an ignoramus, and objected to the last blessing. Now, what did Rav Aḥa bar Ya'akov object to in hearing his son thanking God for not having created him as an ignoramus, i.e., a person ignorant of Torah teaching? Rashi offers two possible explanations. The first is that reciting such a blessing sounds like one is bragging about oneself. The second questions the logic of the third blessing. One can understand reciting the first two blessings: They express gratitude for the obligation to perform all the commandments, while non-Jews do not have that privilege and traditionally, women are only obligated to perform some, but not all, of the commandments. However, an unlearned man is still obligated to perform all the commandments, so why did the son recite that blessing? Either way, Rav Aḥa's son accepts that he should not recite that blessing. Instead, his father instructs him to recite the blessing thanking God for not making him a slave, with the explanation that although slaves have the same status as women in terms of the obligation to observe some, but not all, of the commandments, nevertheless, the status of a slave is "lowlier" than that of a woman. And therefore, one should add one's gratitude for not having been created a slave.

In the talmudic period, there was a Greek prayer that parallels versions of these three blessings, and which may have influenced the talmudic formulation. A version attributed to the ancient Greek philosopher Thales has him expressing gratitude to fate:

> For being made a human and not an animal
> A man and not a woman
> For being born a Greek and not a barbarian.[10]

During the early talmudic period, the New Testament records Paul addressing the Galatians in a way that may have been meant to critique both Greek and Jewish tradition:

---

[9] Babylonian Talmud *Menaḥot* 43b.

[10] See Ismar Elbogen, *Jewish Liturgy*, 78 and A.A. Halevy, *The Teachings of the Aggadah and the Ḥalakhah in the Light of Greek and Latin Sources* [Hebrew] (Tel Aviv, 1981), 3:157; the latter cited in Reuven Hammer, *Entering Jewish Prayer*, 108, n. 6.

> For you are—all of you—sons of God through the faith that is in Christ Jesus. For when all of you were baptized into Christ, you put on Christ as though he were your clothing. There is neither Jew nor Greek; there is neither slave nor free; there is no "male and female"; for all of you are One in Christ Jesus.[11]

The modern movements in North American Judaism all preserve the full list of these blessings, though the order varies slightly between their *siddurim*. The significant difference between them concerns the ways they present the final three blessings thanking God for not creating one a non-Jew, a woman, or a slave. The dominant Orthodox siddur preserves these *verbatim*, and, in its commentary, defends them. Regarding the blessing that men say thanking God for not having been created as a woman, it honestly admits that men "express gratitude that, unlike women, they were *not* freed from the obligation to perform time-related commandments." However, it then goes on to claim that "though women were not given the privilege of the challenge assigned to men, they were created closer to God's ideal of satisfaction. They express their gratitude in the blessing "(Blessed...) for having made me according to His will."[12] This defense of the alternative blessing women recite rings hollow given that Orthodox communities continue to prioritize the performance of all the commandments over women's supposed status of being "closer to God's ideal of satisfaction."

A more straightforward explanation for the women's version of the blessing is given in the law code, *Arba'ah Turim* (Germany/Spain, 14th c.) which is the earliest source for this blessing:

> The women have had the custom of blessing "who made me according to His will (*sheh'asani kirtzono*)" And it's possible that they have such a custom because it is like one who declares the justice of the evil decree.[13]

Here, the truth is not varnished as it is in the Orthodox prayer book. According to *Arba'ah Turim*, women understand that their status is lower than that of men. Status was gained in the community the more one was involved in

[11] J. Louis Martyn, ed., *Anchor Bible: The Epistle of Paul to the Galatians Or The Book of Galatians, A New Translation with Introduction and Commentary* (New York: Doubleday, 1997) 3:26-28. The citation in Galatians is recorded by Ismar Elbogen, *Jewish Liturgy*, 78, although he cites it as 3:19.

[12] *The Complete Artscroll Siddur*, 20-21.

[13] Rabbi Ya'akov ben Rabbi Asher, *Arba'ah Turim, Oraḥ Ḥayyim* 46:4.

the communal religious life of the community; in traditional Jewish society, that involvement was quite limited for women. Therefore, this law code explains, women are "like one who declares the justice of the evil decree." That phrase is used elsewhere to describe the obligation of mourners to accept the death of a loved one by reciting a blessing. In this way, mourners express that although they cannot explain why their loved one has died, they declare their faith in the justice of God's decree. Here, too, women express their acceptance that although being created a woman is "an evil decree," there is some elusive justice to that decree known only to God.

Over the last 150 years or so, the non-Orthodox movements have been uncomfortable with the images these blessings express of non-Jews, women, and slaves. Already in 1854, the early Reform siddur edited by Rabbi Abraham Geiger replaced the three blessings with the following single blessing:

> Blessed... who has made me to serve him.[14]

Since that time, non-Orthodox prayer books have offered alternate versions of these three blessings. The talmudic version of the version of the first of these blessings, "Blessed... who has not made me a non-Jew," is, in the standard, printed texts of the Talmud, phrased differently. It is presented in the positive, "Blessed... who has made me a Jew." However, the manuscript versions of this talmudic passage contain the blessing in in the negative formulation, making it clear that the positive version was the result of censorship (perhaps self-censorship) in order to avoid the guile of non-Jewish authorities. There are also versions of these blessings with several variations including both the positive and negative forms in prayer books recovered from the Cairo Genizah (ca. 10th-12th centuries):

> Blessed... who created me a human being and not an animal
> Blessed... who created me a man and not a woman
> Blessed... who created me a Jew and not a non-Jew
> Blessed... who created me free and not enslaved[15]

[14] Cited by David Ellenson in Lawrence A. Hoffman, *My People's Prayer Book*, Vol. 5, *Birkhot HaShachar* (Morning Blessings), 135.
[15] Jacob Mann, "Genizah Fragments of the Palestinian Order of Service," *Hebrew Union College Annual*, Vol. 2 (1925; Ktav Reprint, 1968), 277, cited in Reuven Hammer, *Entering Jewish Prayer*, 108, n. 5.

A Conservative Movement prayer book published in 1946 relied on both the printed talmudic text as well as the examples from the Genizah in rephrasing all three blessings only in the positive:

> Blessed... who hast made me in Thine image (instead of "who has not made me a woman")
> Blessed... who hast made me free (instead of "who has not made me a slave")
> Blessed... who hast made me an Israelite (instead of "who has not made me a non-Jew").[16]

This alternate version, with slight changes in the wording, has been adopted by all of the current prayer books produced by the liberal movements.

**Spiritual Commentary on *Birkhot HaShaḥar***

The blessings of this opening section of the morning service were surely composed to help us begin our day in a meditative and grateful frame of mind. We human beings tend to take many gifts in our lives for granted. Our eyesight, our ability to get out of bed, to stand up, and to walk are all capabilities which, if we are lucky enough to have them, we tend to miss only when we lose them through accident or illness. Similarly, we tend to not even think about the fact that we have clothes and shoes to wear, and for most of us, plenty of clothes and shoes. Reciting these blessings of gratitude with intention can help us appreciate all of these as the gifts that they are.

Once the printing press proliferated and prayer books became widely available, this section should have been removed from the opening of the synagogue morning service and, restored to its original location at home so that each blessing is actually joined to the appropriate action in real time. However, by then, *Birkhot HaShaḥar* had been recited as part of the synagogue service for several hundred years, and that kind of longstanding custom is difficult to change. And so, this section remains the opening to worship in the synagogue, and not at home, every morning.

Something is lost when the action that prompts each blessing is separated from the recitation of each blessing.

I have experimented with keeping a siddur by my bedside and have recited each of the blessings in the morning just before doing each of the actions to

[16] See *Sabbath and Festival Prayer Book* (New York: The Rabbinical Assembly of America and The United Synagogue of America, 1946), xi, 45. See also Robert Gordis, "'In His Image,': A New Blessing, an Old Truth," *Conservative Judaism* 40:1 (1987), 81-85.

which each blessing is linked. I have suggested this to students over many years as well. Their experience, as well as mine, confirms that recited this way, these blessings have much more life to them than they do when chanted in synagogue, divorced from their original purpose. This kind of practice has the effect of slowing down one's morning routine and imbuing it with a meditative flavor. Slowing down one's morning routine may be impractical for the busy, modern, lifestyle. However, on Shabbat, Sundays, and other holidays, it can be a bit more doable, and I highly recommend it.

## Pesukei DeZimra

### Overview

*Pesukei DeZimra*, literally, "Verses of Song," forms the second major section of the *Shaḥarit* service on every day of the year. In contemporary practice, it consists entirely of biblical poetry, mainly from the Book of Psalms, introduced and concluded by two rabbinic blessings. Those two blessings are *Barukh She'amar*, "Blessed Is The One Who Spoke," and *Yishtabaḥ*, "May (Your Name, God) Be Blessed." Most discussions of *Pesukei DeZimra* declare that this section was conceived as a kind of preliminary or introductory service, whose purpose it is to prepare the worshiper for the service proper which begins with the recitation of the *Shema* and its blessings. The preparation of the worshiper is said to be accomplished by having the worshiper chant this section's many praises of God as the creator of nature and as the savior of the Jewish people in history, thus forming the appropriate awe of God with which to commence the formal service which follows *Pesukei DeZimra*. Practically speaking, this section can, indeed, be viewed as just such a preliminary service. However, it was likely not conceived or planned this way. Its origin is quite interesting because the only place it is mentioned in the Talmud contains what is likely a misinterpretation of its origin. Let's examine that talmudic passage:

> Rabbi Yossi said:
> "Let my portion be among those who complete the *Hallel* every day."
> (The Talmud interjects here:) Is that so?! And didn't (another) master say: "One who recites *Hallel* every day blasphemes and reviles?"

> (The Talmud answers its own question:) When he (Rabbi Yossi) said that (i.e., when he praised those who complete the *Hallel* every day, he was not referring to *Hallel*, but rather to) *Pesukei DeZimra*.[17]

Rabbi Yossi here is Rabbi Yossi ben Ḥalafta, a *Tanna*, or Mishnaic Sage, of the second century CE. Therefore, nearly all commentaries on *Pesukei DeZimra* claim that this service derived no later than the second century. And the master historian of Jewish liturgy, Ismar Elbogen, was convinced that Rabbi Yossi was indeed referring to the six psalms, Psalms 145-150, which are part of all versions of *Pesukei DeZimra*.[18] However, I believe that the earliest that this service originated (albeit probably in a very different form than in contemporary *siddurim*) is about 500 years later in the seventh century.[19]

---

[17] Babylonian Talmud, *Shabbat* 118b. My translation is based upon the Munich manuscript of this passage which supports the rendering of "when he said (that)." The printed version reads "when we said (that)," which, while usually translated as something like "when we cited R. Yossi," is clumsier and probably reflects an incorrect fleshing out of the Aramaic abbreviation *ka'am'*.

[18] Ismar Elbogen, *Jewish Liturgy*, 73.

[19] Ruth Langer casts some doubt on whether this Rabbi Yossi is a *Tanna*: "There are several rabbis by this name. Most presume that this was the fourth generation tanna, Rabbi Yossi ben Ḥalafta. However, the Talmud does not introduce these texts using the technical language for tannaitic traditions, and this appears only in the Babylonian Talmud, opening the possibility it reflects a Babylonian reality." This thought appears in her forthcoming article, "The Early Medieval Emergence of Jewish Daily Morning Psalms Recitation, *Pesuqe de-Zimra*" in Claudia Bergmann, Tessa Rajak, Benedikt Kranemann, and Rebecca Sebbagh, eds., *The Psalms in Jewish Liturgy, Ritual and Community Formation from Antiquity to the Middle Ages: Biblical Texts in Dynamic, Pluralistic Contexts* (Brill, AJEC series, forthcoming), 5, n. 14. Professor Langer graciously shared an advance copy of her article with me. The presumption that Rabbi Yossi is indeed a *Tanna* is important enough to my thesis for me to address Professor Langer's doubt at some length. While she is correct that it is unusual for the Babylonian Talmud not to use the usual technical language introducing a tannaitic tradition regarding Rabbi Yossi's teaching, it is not unprecedented, and it is nevertheless more than likely that this Rabbi Yossi is, indeed, the *Tanna*, Rabbi Yossi ben Ḥalafta. There are several reasons for this. 1. There are no later Sages (i.e., *Amoraim*) who are identified in the Babylonian Talmud as "Rabbi Yossi" with no patronymic—See Ḥanokh Albeck, *Mavo LeTalmudim* (Tel Aviv: Devir, 1969), 674. 2. The larger passage within which this teaching is found deals with the importance of serving three meals on Shabbat; the connection to Rabbi Yossi's fifteen teachings is that the subject of his first teaching is the importance of the three Sabbath meals. Earlier in the larger passage, Rabbi Yoḥanan cites a Rabbi Yossi (Babylonian Talmud, Shabbat 118a, bottom) and here, there is almost no question that this Rabbi Yossi is a *Tanna*, for Rabbi Yoḥanan with no patronymic is the second-generation *Amora* who very often transmits tannaitic traditions (See Albeck, 184). It would not be surprising, then, that when this passage later cites teachings by a "Rabbi Yossi," it would be the same, tannaitic, Sage. 3. Within his fifteen teachings, Rabbi Yossi lists the names of his five sons. Two of them are *Tannaim* according to Albeck, *Mavo LeMishnah* (Jerusalem: Mosad Bialik, 1959, 1979): Rabbi Yishma'eil beRabbi Yossi and Rabbi Menaḥem beRabbi Yossi (Albeck, 233). Two of them are not identified by Albeck. That leaves one son, Rabbi Elazar/Eliezer beRabbi Yossi. There is an *Amora* named Rabbi Elazar/Eliezer (these names are often interchangeable in the various editions of the Talmud) who, when appearing without a patronymic "seems to be" the son of a Rabbi Yossi, according to Albeck. However, Rabbi Elazar/Eliezer also seems to appear only in the Palestinian Talmud (Albeck, *Mavo LeTalmudim*, 386), while these teachings of Rabbi Yossi appear here in the Babylonian Talmud.

Here is why I have come to that conclusion. This teaching of Rabbi Yossi's is part of a long passage in which fifteen of his sayings are grouped together (see all of them in my "Sources for Pesukei DeZimra" on Sefaria). His sayings reflect an interesting range of perspectives on piety. Some of them would resonate with moderns, such as, "Rabbi Yossi said: May my portion be among those who always pray with the reddening of the sun," i.e., so that the awe-inspiring sight of the reddening of the dawn and dusk sky may bring one into a prayerful mood. Other sayings of his might seem quirky or repellent to many moderns such as "Rabbi Yossi said: May I die from abdominal disease since (another) master said that most of the righteous die from abdominal disease," and "Rabbi Yossi said: May my portion be with one whom others suspect of sin and there is no basis for suspecting him" (perhaps reflecting a belief that it is better for one's ego not to be considered to be fully virtuous). The anonymous, editorial, voice of the Talmud—deriving from several hundred years after the time of Rabbi Yossi—comments on a number of his teachings, especially those that seem quirky or difficult to understand, pointing out the views of other Sages that contradict those of Rabbi Yossi, and then resolving those contradictions.

That is what happens to Rabbi Yossi's saying about our topic, *Pesukei DeZimra*, and it merits some study. Note that Rabbi Yossi himself did not express the desire to join those who recite a section of liturgy known as *Pesukei DeZimra*. Rather, he articulated his wish to join those who complete *Hallel* every day. Based on this, the later, editorial voice of the Talmud objects that another, anonymous Sage contradicted Rabbi Yossi's teaching. This other Sage taught that reciting *Hallel* every day—which Rabbi Yossi praises—is considered blasphemous, presumably because the daily recital of prayers reserved for the holy days to commemorate miracles (such as the Exodus from Egypt on *Pesaḥ*) might call into question the miraculous nature of those events. Then, the Talmud resolves its own objection by postulating that when Rabbi Yossi expressed his wish to be among those who complete the *Hallel* every day, he wasn't referring to the *Hallel* recited on holidays at all, but rather to *Pesukei DeZimra*, "Verses of Song."

In spite of what the editorial voice of the Talmud says, I believe it is quite likely that Rabbi Yossi was indeed referring to those Psalms usually recited

---

There is additional support within the larger passage here in Babylonian Talmud, Shabbat 118a-b, but this note has gone on long enough. While none of the various supports by themselves constitute a proof that this Rabbi Yossi is a *Tanna*, all of the supports together, along with Professor Langer's statement that "most presume that this was the fourth generation tanna, R. Yosi ben Halafta," carry enough weight to validate the presumption that this Rabbi Yossi is indeed a *Tanna*. I express my gratitude to Professor Judith Hauptman who, convinced that the Rabbi Yossi in our passage is indeed a *Tanna*, kindly guided me in researching and discovering the evidence adduced here.

only on holidays. This is because the expression "to complete *Hallel*" occurs in the Talmud in three other places (the earliest of which dates from the same general period as Rabbi Yossi), each time referring specifically and unambiguously to the Psalms recited on the pilgrimage festivals and which acknowledge miracles such as the Exodus from Egypt (Psalms 113-118). Furthermore, that is what the word *Hallel* by itself usually refers to throughout the Talmud.[20] This practice would reflect a piety that saw reason to praise God for miracles wrought not only on special occasions, but on each and every day and would be of a piece with the quirky nature of some of Rabbi Yossi's other statements.[21]

There is another source that might support the idea that Rabbi Yossi was aligning himself with those who chanted *Hallel* each day. In a defining passage that will be explored more closely in my discussion of *Hallel* itself, there is an early rabbinic teaching asserting that the recitation of *Hallel* is not to be confined only to the holidays:

> ...The Sages say that the prophets among them instituted that Israel should recite it (*Hallel*) at every event (that elicits it), and for every trouble, may it not come upon Israel. And when they are redeemed, they recite it over their redemption.[22]

[20] The three places are: *Tosefta Pesaḥim* 4:11, Lieberman edition (4:9 in printed editions), Babylonian Talmud, *Arakhin* 10a, and *Berakhot* 14a. The expression specifically refers to the practice to "complete" all six of Psalms 113-118 on some of the holy days as opposed to reciting *Ḥatzi Hallel*, "partial Hallel," on others. Occasionally, the term *Hallel* in the Talmud also refers to Psalm 136, but nowhere else does it refer to *Pesukei DeZimra*. Some may hold that he was suggesting a known group that chanted the entire Psalter, each day—a practice that has taken place at various times in Jewish and Christian history. On this practice, see James L. Kugel, "Topics in the History of the Spirituality of the Psalms," in Arthur Green, *Jewish Spirituality: From the Bible Through the Middle Ages* (New York: Crossroad, 1986), 113-144. In that case, his expression "who complete the *Hallel* every day" could be interpreted to mean, "who complete the Book of Psalms every day." While that is possible, the weakness in this argument is that there are no other examples of the word *Hallel* referring to the entire Book of Psalms elsewhere in rabbinic literature.

[21] After my research had convinced me that Rabbi Yossi was indeed referring to reciting *Hallel* on a daily basis, an article written by Louis Rabinowitz in 1944 came to my attention. Rabinowitz too had come to this conclusion, writing, "The obvious reference is to the 'Egyptian Hallel,' Psalms 113-119, and it clearly suggests that there was a group of choice spirits who used to read these unsurpassed Psalms of thanksgiving daily." However, he missed the importance of the phrase "to complete *Hallel*." See Louis I. Rabinowitz, "The Psalms in Jewish Liturgy," *Historia Judaica*, Vol. VI, No. 2, October, 1944, 112-113. See now as well, Abraham Jacob Berkovitz, "The Life of Psalms in Late Antiquity," (PhD diss., Princeton University, 2018), 254, cited in Ruth Langer, "The Early Medieval Emergence of Jewish Daily Morning Psalms Recitation, *Pesuqe de-Zimra*" in Claudia Bergmann, Tessa Rajak, Benedikt Kranemann, and Rebecca Sebbagh, eds., *The Psalms in Jewish Liturgy, Ritual and Community Formation from Antiquity to the Middle Ages: Biblical Texts in Dynamic, Pluralistic Contexts* (Brill, AJEC series, forthcoming), 6, n. 15.

[22] Babylonian Talmud, *Pesaḥim* 117a.

In other words, the recitation of *Hallel* was not originally confined to the holidays but was designed (by "the prophets"—meaning, probably, by some prior anonymous authorities) to be chanted whenever a need arises to pray for help and to express gratitude for that relief and release from harm. The fact that a teaching from mishnaic times provides a framework for the spontaneous recital of *Hallel* supports the possibility that there may have been individuals or groups who could have taken it a step further and recited *Hallel* every day. The theological psychology undergirding such a practice may have been an attunement to the need for, and experience of, divine support and deliverance in the face of daily ordeals, burdens, and suffering. In fact, the Book of Psalms itself is filled with examples of just such petitions for divine intervention in daily life's smaller and larger challenges, e.g., Psalms 2, 3, 4, 74, 121, and many others.

There is one additional, if tenuous, hint—contrary to my theory—that Psalms 145-150, which are part of every rite's version of *Pesukei DeZimra*, ought to be considered an appropriate introduction to daily prayer: The Mishnah famously says that "the early pious ones would pause for an hour (or "for a time") before praying (an early form of the *Amidah*)."[23] On this, the Talmud comments, citing early and later Sages, that an individual ought to pause for an hour (or "for a time") both before and after praying (the *Amidah*).[24] As a proof text for pausing before prayer, it cites Psalm 84:5, *Ashrei yoshvei veitekha*, interpreting it as "Happy are those who dwell (i.e., pause) in your house, they will (then) further praise you (in the *Amidah*)." This verse was prefaced to Psalm 145 in the later liturgical versions of this psalm in what would become *Pesukei DeZimra*, and Psalm 145 serves as the first of the last six psalms of the Book of Psalms. This, however, is certainly a tenuous hint at best since this text does not imply any knowledge of an already existing practice of reciting Psalm 145 as part of a preparation for reciting an *Amidah*. This source, however, may well have influenced the later development of *Pesukei DeZimra* to include this psalm.

In spite of the fact that Rabbi Yossi was probably not referring to *Pesukei DeZimra*, later deciders of Jewish law felt that they could not directly differ with an unopposed statement of the editorial voice of the Talmud, and so, even though the resolution of the editorial voice likely misconstrued Rabbi Yossi's teaching, it ultimately became authoritative. In this way, all later rabbinic authorities interpreted Rabbi Yossi to have said that he wished his

[23] *Mishnah Berakhot* 5:1.
[24] Babylonian Talmud 32b.

portion to be among those who completed a number of non-*Hallel* passages in an introductory liturgical section called *Pesukei DeZimra.*

But the story doesn't end there. Since the phrase *Pesukei DeZimra* does not occur elsewhere in the Talmud or in other documents of early Rabbinic Literature, what the editorial voice specifically meant by those two words was never clear. The editorial voice likely left the phrase undefined because it was assumed that the reader would easily be able to identify what was meant from then-contemporary practice, but all later commentators interpreted it based on the contents of their own eras' versions of a preliminary service which became known as *Pesukei DeZimra.*

In the post-talmudic era, the phrase *Pesukei DeZimra* occurs in a couple of *responsa* by Rav Natronai bar Hilai Gaon (mid-9th century). The questioner and Rav Natronai both understand *Pesukei DeZimra* to be a section of the prayer service recited before the major sections of the *Shema* and the *Amidah.*[25] The question regards what a latecomer to the service ought to do if they came to a service after the community had already recited *Pesukei DeZimra.* Rav Natronai, citing Rav Moshe Gaon (8th-9th century), suggests that the latecomer ought to recite "the first passage" (*parashah rishonah*), which he does not identify, presuming everyone knows what passage that is (although a later editor "helpfully" identifies it as Psalm 145) as well as "Praise God in his sanctuary" (Psalm 150:1).[26] This may be the earliest reliable hint at a version of *Pesukei DeZimra.*

The section of Tractate *Soferim* ("Scribes") which likely dates from the early Middle Ages also weighs in on what constitutes *Pesukei DeZimra.* Here, saying of Rabbi Yossi is cited but instead of the original version in the Talmud of "Let my portion be among those who complete the *Hallel* every day," here, he is quoted as saying, "Let my portion be among those who pray every day *those six psalms.*"[27] "Those six psalms" presumably refer to the last six psalms of the Book of Psalms (Psalms 145-150) which still form part of *Pesukei DeZimra* in all rites. It may be that Tractate *Soferim*—or the tradition it reflects here—was influenced by the festival *Hallel*—well known since early talmudic times, which consisted of six (other) psalms. Furthermore, the festival *Hallel* is introduced and followed by dedicated blessings, much the same as *Pesukei DeZimra* accrued by the time of our earliest *siddurim.*

[25] *Teshuvot Rav Natronai Gaon, Oraḥ Ḥayyim* 11. See Wilhelm Bacher, S. Mendelson, "Natronai II, ben Hilai," *Jewish Encyclopedia*, 1906. Accessed online, May 21, 2021, https://www.jewishencyclopedia.com/articles/11383-natronai-ii-b-hilai.

[26] Simḥa Assaf, Ed., "Gaon," *Encyclopedia Judaica* (Jerusalem: Keter Publishing House, 1972), 7:323.

[27] Tractate *Soferim* 17:1 (in some editions, 18:1).

Aside from the festival *Hallel*, there were individual psalms recited in the Second Temple according to Rabbinic Literature, especially the daily psalms, and these ultimately entered the daily liturgy.[28] None of these, however, correspond to the six psalms that conclude the Book of Psalms. Again, it is most likely that Tractate *Soferim* here is reading its own custom back several hundred years to Rabbi Yossi in the Talmud.

Beyond these opinions, there is wide-ranging variety in defining the contents of *Pesukei DeZimra*. During geonic times, there are definitions "ranging from the recitation of thirty-one psalms in their entirety (Pss. 120-150) to random collections of verses drawn from different psalms and strung together for the occasion. Amram (9th century) has our customary six selections, and Saadia (10th century), unaccountably includes five of the six, omitting Psalm 146."[29] Also unusual is Rashi's interpretation, appended to the Rabbi Yossi story, that *Pesukei DeZimra* consists of only two psalms, Pss. 148 and 150.[30] What all of these medieval models of *Pesukei DeZimra* have in common is the inclusion of Psalm 150, the last psalm in the Book of Psalms. This is probably the result of early (and likely incorrect) interpretations of Rabbi Yossi's desire to be among those who "complete" *Hallel* to mean that one ought to symbolically complete the Book of Psalms each day.

Thus, a teaching by Rabbi Yossi in the second century praising those who recited the festival *Hallel* not only on holidays, but every day, ultimately was interpreted as praising those who every day recite a different group of psalms—with much variation as to which ones over the centuries and between various Jewish communities—as well as much additional biblical material as an introductory service before the more official service of the *Shema* and its blessings plus the *Amidah*. The anonymous, editorial voice of the Talmud derives from about the seventh century. This was the stratum of the Talmud that (mis)identified Rabbi Yossi's saying as referring to *Pesukei DeZimra*—the very first time this phrase is found anywhere. Therefore, it is

---

[28] *Mishnah Tamid* 7:4, Babylonian Talmud *Rosh HaShanah* 31a. And see Amos Hakham, *Book of Psalms* [Hebrew] (Jerusalem: Mosad HaRav Kook, 1984) 1:1 (Hebrew pagination), n. 2 for a number of places in the biblical books of Chronicles and Ezra-Nehemiah where the expression *Hallel David* occurs referring to the singing of the Levites.

[29] Lawrence A. Hoffman, *The Canonization of the Synagogue Service* (Notre Dame, Indiana: University of Notre Dame Press, 1979), 128, citing Jacob Mann, "Genizah Fragments of the Palestinian Order of Service," 1925, reprinted in *Contributions to the Scientific Study of Jewish Liturgy*, edited by Jakob Petuchowski (New York: Ktav, 1970), 386; Daniel Goldschmidt, *Seder Rav Amram*, 11; and Israel Davidson, et. al., *Siddur Rav Saadia Gaon*, 43.

[30] Although a parallel source for the school of Rashi defines *Pesukei DeZimra* as the six psalms of Pss. 145-150. See *Siddur Rashi*, ed. Solomon Buber (Berlin, 1911), 6, cited in Lawrence A. Hoffman, *The Canonization*, 127. All of the teachings of Rashi were likely filtered through his students and for that reason, it is difficult to identify with confidence any one comment or interpretation authoritatively with Rashi himself.

likely that by the seventh century, a service existed that ultimately developed into something that came to be called by that same name, *Pesukei DeZimra*, in all Jewish communities. However, we know nothing about the original format of such a service.

The outline of the daily Ashkenazic *Pesukei DeZimra* in the contemporary Ashkenazic siddur consists of some twelve units; it can also be viewed as ten units with an opening and closing blessing.

## Outline of *Pesukei DeZimra*

1. Opening Blessing: *Barukh She'amar*, "Blessed is the One Who Spoke."
2. Prayer from when David brought the Ark to Jerusalem: I Chronicles 16:8-36 beginning with *Hodu L'YHVH kir'u vishmo.*[31]
3. An anthology of various verses from the Book of Psalms beginning with *Romemu YHVH Eloheinu* (Psalms 99:5).
4. A Psalm of Thanksgiving: Psalm 100 beginning with *Mizmor Le-Todah* (omitted on days when the Thanksgiving sacrifice was not offered at the Temple in Jerusalem).
5. Another anthology of various verses from the Book of Psalms beginning with *Yehi khevod YHVH l'olam* (Psalms 104:31).
6. The last six Psalms of the Book of Psalms: Psalms 145-150 beginning with *Ashrei.*

[31] Elbogen, 73, who may have relied upon Seligmann Baer, *Seder Avodat Yisrael*, 59, mentions that according to *Seder Olam* 14, this passage, with some variations, was chanted by the Levites in the Temple every morning after the morning sacrifice. (Baer may have been relying on similar reports from medieval sources; see the citation from Milikowsky below for sources). Reading that, one would think that the placement of this passage here in the early morning service of *Pesukei DeZimra* is preserving an ancient practice. However, a close reading of the passage in *Seder Olam* raises some issues. The first is that this source does not make any claims about Temple practice, but simply extends what the biblical passage itself in I Chronicles 16:4-7 records, namely that on the day that the Ark was brought up to the City of David and set up in the tent, "David first (*barosh*) commissioned Asaph and his kinsmen to give praise to YHVH" in the words of this prayer. *Seder Olam* then says that this prayer was recited every morning after the morning sacrifice <u>until the time that David's son, Solomon, built the Temple</u>, 43 years later. Chaim Milikowsky supposes that here, *Seder Olam* was perhaps relying on I Chronicles 16:6, *tamid*, "regularly." See Chaim Milikowsky, ed., *Seder Olam: Mahadurah Mada'it, Perush U'Mavo* (Jerusalem: Yad Yitsḥak Ben-Tzvi, 2013), 2:246, n. 3. I would add that *Seder Olam* seems also to be reacting to the word "first/*barosh*" in this verse, meaning, that this was the "first" time this passage was recited, and then adding how long this ritual lasted, namely, 43 years until the Temple was built. Therefore, *Seder Olam* makes no claim about the recital of this passage in the Temple at all. And even if it did connect to the Temple, it would be the <u>first</u> Temple, and precious little solid information about the liturgy of the first Temple has reached us. Secondly, the goal of *Seder Olam*, a work of midrash, is to fill in the missing links between dates provided in the Bible so that a fully accurate timeline could be traced, providing exact dates, from the creation of the world through all of biblical history, as well as through some post-biblical events. Its method is homiletical and not historical. Thus, Elbogen and others seem to put unwarranted weight on this source.

7. A series of three verses from the Book of Psalms that forms a chorus of concluding praises to God ending with "amen and amen" –
    a. Psalms 89:53—The conclusion of "Book Three" of the Book of Psalms.
    b. Psalms 135:21
    c. Psalms 72:18-19—The conclusion of "Book Two" of the Book of Psalms.
8. David's prayer as the work for Solomon's Temple began: I Chronicles 29:10-13 beginning with *Vayevareikh David.*[32]
9. Part of Nehemiah's prayer recounting God's goodness in Israelite history just up to the splitting of the Red Sea—Nehemiah 9:6-11 beginning with *Attah hu YHVH levadekha.*
10. The Song at The Sea—Exodus 14:30-15:19 beginning with *Vayosha YHVH.*
11. A series of three verses on the theme of God's kingship—
    d. Psalms 22:29
    e. Obadiah 1:21
    f. Zechariah 14:9
12. Closing Blessing: *Yishtabaḥ*, "May Your Name Be Praised."

On Shabbat and festivals, the units above are supplemented in between units 3 and 5 (unit 4 is omitted on Shabbat and festivals) with the following nine psalms:

4A. Psalm 19
4B. Psalm 34
4C. Psalm 90
4D. Psalm 91
4E. Psalm 135
4F. Psalm 136—Called *Hallel HaGadol* ("The Great *Hallel*") and recited here and as part of the Passover *Haggadah*, in contradistinction to the more typical *Hallel* recited on festivals (Psalms 113-118) and called *Hallel Mitzrayim* ("Egyptian *Hallel*").
4G. Psalm 33

[32] Compare this prayer to that in unit 2 of *Pesukei DeZimra*, above, I Chronicles 16:8-36—"This prayer is structurally and thematically similar to the Psalms anthology in ch. 16; together they form an inclusio of David's cultic activity." Adele Berlin and Marc Zvi Brettler, eds., *The Jewish Study Bible*, 2nd edition (New York: Oxford University Press, 2014), 1761.

4H. Psalm 92—"A Song for the Sabbath Day" (but also recited on festivals).
4I. Psalm 93

**Spiritual Commentary on *Pesukei DeZimra***

The traditional approach to *Pesukei DeZimra* is to recite all 10 units on weekdays and all 19 units on Shabbat and festivals. While the general theme of all the passages is praise of God, there are also requests, pleas, and other kinds of declarations mixed in. Given the amount of verbiage, it is difficult to expect the typical worshiper to be able to concentrate on the meaning of each phrase every single day, especially as only the introduction to the worship service proper. Ideally, though, the goal is that the overall effect of chanting these texts would bring a change in one's consciousness from a practical, workday viewpoint to a more elevated spiritual state. The use of various musical settings of the poems of this section can enhance that kind of state of mind. Those worshipers for whom chanting all of the passages in *Pesukei DeZimra* helps to serve as a transition to a more transcendent state should certainly continue to do so.

Those who find it difficult to wade through the large amount of text and/or who do not feel bound by the traditional approach might look to this section's history as a precedent to experiment with what they include in this portion of the service. They might, for example, keep in mind how varied the versions of *Pesukei DeZimra* were throughout its early history, and vary the texts recited on a given morning, concentrating more on smaller amounts of content at a time. It could even prove beneficial to double down on just one poem or a portion of a poem during the time one allots to this preliminary service.

Even from a traditional point of view, the relatively late development of *Pesukei DeZimra* as a defined portion of the service bequeathed a slightly lower status to this service in that there is no requirement for a *minyan* (a quorum of 10 individuals) to recite any of its units. That is not the case, for example, regarding the liturgical units of The *Shema* And Its Blessings or The *Amidah* that were canonized as essentials of the service very early on. Admittedly, *halakhah* nevertheless does not permit any flexibility in which passages to recite, but from a non-traditional point of view, the lower status of this section may support flexibility in its contents.

Whether or not we recite the full traditional panoply of texts, it is important to remember that the primary purpose of these words is not to study them. They aren't to be read as one reads for information. They are responses to God's world, to the universe beyond. That is the difference between reading and praying or chanting. I would suggest that the proper stance to take regarding any of these poems is to view them as offerings to God. That can help us in developing a meaningful approach to whatever version of *Pesukei DeZimra* we use, whether its full version or some abridgement thereof.

A radical approach to *Pesukei DeZimra* would be to view it as a completely independent and self-contained morning service in and of itself, without continuing on to The *Shema* And Its Blessings or The *Amidah*. The spiritual effect of reciting all or parts of the traditional texts of *Pesukei DeZimra* as an independent morning service would challenge the worshiper to limit their worship exclusively to presenting these poems as offerings to God. This adaptation would challenge the worshiper to take seriously Rabbi Yossi's original desire to attach himself to those who chanted *Hallel*—apparently as a separate and independent offering to God, and to see the miraculous in the everyday.

In keeping with the wide-ranging versions of *Pesukei DeZimra* early in its history, here is another non-traditional suggestion. Worshipers may choose to exit the framework of only the ten weekday (or 19 Shabbat/festival) units that have reached us through tradition and substitute other passages. There are many more texts in the psalms, in the rest of *Tanakh*, or elsewhere, that may well suit the role of offering praise to God as the day begins.

A final radical thought: Virtually all contemporary commentaries on *Pesukei DeZimra* describe this service as preparation for the more official, and older, sections of The *Shema* And Its Blessings and The *Amidah*. As we have seen however, it is quite likely that *Pesukei DeZimra* was not originally meant to serve in this role. Therefore, those commentaries have always seemed to me to be after-the-fact defenses of an inherited system; defenses presented without questioning whether *Pesukei DeZimra* actually serves the purpose of preparing the worshiper well. And so, I want to pose the question of whether it works to have 10 or 19 units (several of which comprise quite a few passages each) plus introductory and concluding paragraph-long blessings as preparation for the rest of the service. The answer to this question is necessarily subjective and there cannot be a simple "yes" or "no" response. Still, in the face of the ubiquitous commentaries defending this preparatory service, I would like to register at least a theoretical retort: The length of the traditional *Pesukei DeZimra* has the potential to inure and numb the worshiper through the sheer number of words even before reaching the more official sections of the morning service. Put another way, if one were to design a worship service with no pre-determined parameters, would one begin with this long an introductory section? I understand, of course, that this question is an unfair one because if every individual were asked to design any given Jewish prayer service or ritual with no preset assumptions, we'd have the situation that the Yiddish saying summarizes as "everyone making their own Shabbos," i.e., we'd have no communally shared rituals and no community. Furthermore, there is value and spiritual power to chanting words that have been chanted by generations and generations of our people for centuries. And so, I'm not advocating a systemic revamping of all of Jewish liturgy or of *Pesukei DeZimra*. I'm just posing a question about the efficacy of this service regarding whether it actually serves the preparatory function that it is supposed to perform. It seems to me that contemplating that question can only help individual Jews, prayer leaders, and praying communities. We all benefit when we try to attune ourselves to the simplest, most direct question to be asked of any prayer or prayer service: In what way does this, or could this, connect me to God, to the transcendent? And to the extent that it does not serve this goal, we can ask ourselves what we can do to improve our spiritual experience with this prayer or prayer service.

## Commentary on Select Units of *Pesukei DeZimra*

*The comments in the next section are keyed to the individual units that comprise Pesukei DeZimra delineated above. I will remark on several, but not all, of the individual units.*

### Unit 2: *Hodu L'YHVH Kir'u Vishmo*
### Prayer from when David brought the Ark to Jerusalem (I Chronicles 16:8-36)

According to I Chronicles, chapter 16, David commissioned the musician Asaph and his kinsmen to sing to God on the occasion of the installation of the Ark of God in the tent set up for it in the City of David, the city which eventually became Jerusalem. The poetry of this passage in *Pesukei DeZimra* was what Asaph and company chanted. A good portion of these lines are paralleled as well in Psalms 95 and 105. The midrashic work *Seder Olam* asserts that the first 15 of these verses were chanted not only on this occasion but accompanied the morning sacrifice (*Tamid shel Shaḥarit*) each day until David's son established the permanent Temple.[33] *Seder Olam* also declares that the final 14 verses accompanied the daily afternoon sacrifice (*Tamid shel*

[33] See Chaim Milikowsky, ed., *Seder Olam: Mahadurah Mada'it, Perush U'Mavo* (Jerusalem: Yad Yitsḥak Ben-Tzvi, 2013), 2:246, n. 3.

*Bein Ha'Arbayim*) as well throughout this period. Although this report of *Seder Olam* cannot be taken on face value as historical fact, it is a compelling tradition that can be of value for a contemporary worshiper.

### Spiritual Commentary on *Hodu L'YHVH Kir'u Vishmo*

Worshipers might chant this passage with the biblical context in mind: a dedication ceremony at a noteworthy crossroad in our history—the era just before the First Temple was built by King Solomon. This was the last phase in the biblical period before worship became completely centralized at Solomon's Temple in Jerusalem. So, there was a measure of malleability in the system of worshiping God, a pre-establishment phase, in a sense. Additionally, note how this prayer recited at such an early stage in our history itself looks back nostalgically to the period of Abraham, Isaac and Jacob. It is moving to consider, as we recite this prayer, that the Israelites at the time of David looked back to the Patriarchs for inspiration, just as Jews have done in all the generations up to and including ours. In this way, our text connects over time: It connects us to the period of the Patriarchs, to the period of King David, and to the countless generations of Jews who have hallowed these words by linking themselves to these same early stages of our history as they recited these same words.

## Unit 4: *Mizmor LeTodah*, A Psalm of Thanksgiving (Psalm 100)

A thanksgiving sacrifice, *korban todah*, could be offered by individuals in the ancient Temple in Jerusalem in gratitude to God for something that happened in their lives. In the midrash, Rabbi Pinḥas taught in the name of Rabbi Levi that, "In the world to come, all sacrifices will cease except the thanksgiving offering which will never cease."[34] According to that same midrash, the prayer of thanksgiving, namely, this psalm—Psalm 100—will also never cease. Although this midrashic passage does not say that the chanting of Psalm 100 accompanied the thanksgiving sacrifice in the Temple, later tradition made that assertion.[35] Because of that, the contemporary custom is to recite this psalm as part of *Pesukei DeZimra* only on those days when a thanksgiving sacrifice could have been offered in the ancient Temple, namely, on weekdays but not on Shabbat or festivals, because on those days only communal sacrifices were offered. While this practice holds true to this day

[34] *Midrash Tehillim* on Psalm 100, cited in Reuven Hammer, *Entering Jewish Prayer: A Guide to Personal Devotion and the Worship Service* (New York: Schocken Books, 1994), 115, n. 15.

[35] This assertion is found in myriad sources, for example, in Rashi's 11th-century commentary on Psalm 100:1.

in most communities, Rabbi Ya'akov ben Asher, the 14th-century authority who lived in both Ashkenazic and Sephardic lands, asserted with great faith in the future that there is no reason to omit Psalm 100 on Shabbat and festivals. His reasoning was that merely reciting this psalm on those days will not cause people to make the mistake of actually offering the thanksgiving sacrifice itself on those days when the Temple is rebuilt![36] The 16th-century *Shulḥan Arukh* expanded upon the midrashic text cited earlier by teaching that this psalm "ought to be said with a melody since in the future, all songs will cease except for The Psalm of Thanksgiving."[37]

Still, even if tradition connected this psalm with the thanksgiving sacrifice it is unclear why the Psalm of Thanksgiving ought to be recited every weekday during *Pesukei DeZimra*, since this does not parallel its supposed ancient use. After all, the thanksgiving sacrifice was only offered on those occasions when individuals desired to express their gratitude to God in a special way. The 19th-century scholar of Jewish liturgy, Rabbi Seligman Baer, addresses this issue by saying that miracles occur to all of us on each and every day, whether or not we are aware of them, and therefore we should express our gratitude to God daily for those miracles by reciting The Psalm of Thanksgiving.[38]

**Spiritual Commentary on *Mizmor LeTodah***

This 19th-century commentary by Rabbi Seligman Baer unknowingly brings us back full circle to the 2nd-century Rabbi Yossi. Rabbi Baer asserts that miracles occur every day and we, the recipients of these miracles, usually do not recognize the daily marvels that occur to us as miracles. For that reason, he says, we recite this Psalm of Thanksgiving every day in order to acknowledge daily miracles. My reading of Rabbi Yossi is that he had suggested the recitation of *Hallel* on a daily basis for the same reason. Now, the recital of any text on a daily basis can diminish its power but wise people of many traditions—and of no tradition—have observed that viewing the world with a sense of gratitude, viewing the many things we tend to take for granted, with a sense of appreciation, wonder, and marvel, can have a very positive influence on people. The recital of this psalm every weekday can serve as a challenge to us as worshipers to do just that. But for it to have the desired effect it would make sense, not to simply recite the words, but to bring to mind at least one thing for which we are grateful this day. As we

[36] *Arba'ah Turim, Oraḥ Ḥayyim* 51.
[37] *Shulḥan Arukh, Oraḥ Ḥayyim* 51:9, in the gloss by Rabbi Moshe Isserles.
[38] *Seder Avodat Yisrael*, 61.

do that, we can also have the satisfaction of joining Rabbi Yossi who wished his portion to be with those who express their gratitude for miracles large and small each day.

## Unit 6: *Ashrei* (Psalm 145)

The prayer known as *Ashrei*, "Happy"—based on its first word—is Psalm 145, preceded by two verses from elsewhere in the Book of Psalms (Ps. 84:5, Ps. 144:15), which together include the word *Ashrei* three times. The two verses were likely added to Psalm 145 to hint at the talmudic teaching that anyone who recites this psalm three times a day is assured of a place in the World to Come.[39] Psalm 145 also is followed by another verse from elsewhere in Psalms (Ps. 115:18) which concludes with the word *Halleluyah*, "Praise God." This final verse was likely added to align this Psalm with the next five, all of which end with the word *Halleluyah*. Together, these six psalms in *Pesukei DeZimra* conclude the Book of Psalms.

While there are several words in Psalm 145 which repeat quite a few times pointing to the psalm's central themes of "speaking" God's "praises" and "blessings," the word which recurs the most—fully 17 times!—is *kol*, "all, every." This striking literary device makes this text one of the most universal in the entire Hebrew Bible. It declares that "every" day, God's mercy extends to "all" of God's creations, that God sustains "all" life, and that God is close to "all," to "all" who call to God, to "all" who call to God in truth. According to this psalm, God's concern extends not just to a specific people or only to people at all, but rather to "all life" and beyond, to "all of God's creations." In fact, nowhere in Psalm 145 is the People of Israel mentioned; it is only hinted at in the second of the verses from one of the other psalms appended to the beginning of Psalm 145.

### Spiritual Commentary on *Ashrei*

The recital of *Ashrei* is an opportunity to concentrate on our connectedness with all people, all life—including animal life that joins us on the land, all marine life, all flying creatures, and all plant life. This kind of consciousness accords with the biblical account of God as the creator of all things.

[39] See Babylonian Talmud *Berakhot* 4b. Lawrence A. Hoffman correctly observes that the likely original reading of this talmudic teaching (based on manuscript evidence) omits the words "three times" and simply said that anyone who recites Psalm 145 each day (i.e., just once) is assured of a place in the World to Come. The words "three times" were likely added later to reflect the custom—which obtains today as well—of reciting this psalm three times each day: The first time here in *Pesukei DeZimra*; a second time as part of the conclusion to *Shaḥarit*, the Morning Service; and the third time as the opening to *Minḥah*, the Afternoon Service.

It also links with the modern scientific discovery that the Earth and all it encompasses—including people—are composed of the very same elements, atoms, subatomic particles, electrical and other energy found throughout the known universe. This poem can be a powerful meditation on the unity of all life. The many occurrences of the word *kol*, "all, every" in the psalm can be reminders of its universal implications. (Compare this comment with the Spiritual Commentary on the first line of the *Shema*, which is another opportunity to feel the oneness of all Creation.)

### Unit 6: Psalm 149

This psalm begins in a style typical to many psalms: It praises singing "a new song" to God with musical instruments and dance. But its last three verses are often ignored or interpreted out of existence because of the discomfort these lines cause many modern worshipers. In them, "the idea of a temple celebration of God with song and dance" transitions "to an image of warriors going out to battle joyfully praising God."[40] These verses call upon the faithful to celebrate

> With paeans to God in their throats, and two-edged swords in their hands, to impose retribution upon the nations, punishment upon the peoples, binding their kings with shackles, their nobles with chains of iron, executing the doom decreed against them. This is the glory of all his faithful. Halleluyah. (Psalm 149:6-9)

There is no avoiding the reveling in joyful battle here against the non-Israelite nations in the name of God, and yet a number of contemporary prayer books soften, mitigate, or justify the full-throated delight this psalm expresses in declaring it God's will to attack and enslave other peoples in chains. The most popular North American Hebrew-English Orthodox siddur seeks to justify the psalm by adding—without support from the psalm's wording—that, "Though Israel is forced to wage battle against its enemies, its primary goal is that they accept moral rebuke and mend their ways."[41] Similarly, the Conservative siddur attempts to mollify the message by imposing the assumption—also without textual support—that the psalm is not referring to the present, real-world, reality, but rather to a messianic "endtime"—

[40] Robert Alter, *The Book of Psalms: A Translation with Commentary* (New York: W.W. Norton & Company, 2007), 513.
[41] *The Complete Artscroll Siddur: Weekday, Sabbath, Festival*, 74.

"...the poet enunciates a vision of an endtime when justice is executed and corruption is repaid with the appropriate punishment. Israel, the symbol of the oppressed, will wage this war for justice."[42] And even if this were the intention of the psalm, I wonder how comfortable contemporary Jews really would be in praying daily for an "endtime" when the People of Israel would repay corruption with the appropriate punishment. Reuven Hammer also sought to soften the psalm's message by adding yet a different conjecture—perhaps partially based on the psalm's use of the word "vengeance" (*nekamah*)—namely, that the battle against the enemies is "presumably for their attacks upon Israel."[43] It seems to me, however, that the truth is that this psalm unequivocally rejoices in God's will for Israel to wage war against other nations and bring back their leaders in shackles, and it is better to acknowledge the truth than try to hide it. The current *siddurim* issued by the Reform and Reconstructing Judaism movements simply omit this psalm from *Pesukei DeZimra.*

**Spiritual Commentary on Psalm 149**

This psalm is an extreme example of the kind of self-righteous faith in one's own tradition and utter condemnation of the Other to the point of violence that is found at some point in nearly all religions. It may surprise some Jews to know that this is found in the Jewish tradition as well because we Jews view ourselves (with good historical reason) as an oppressed people. I view this type of anti-Other theme as unfortunate evidence of the all-too-human element that is part of almost all faiths. Thankfully, it is not a major theme in Jewish liturgy, but it does appear, and I have called it out in this commentary in a number of places (see, e.g., the commentaries on *Aleinu* and on *Birkat HaMinim* in the *Weekday Amidah*). This particular psalm is, as mentioned, an extreme example and that is because it actually celebrates violence against the non-Israelite Other. I confess that I cannot offer much guidance in reciting it in worship of God. But it can stand as humbling evidence that our religion is not altogether free of the kind of pernicious theology that stood behind persecutions our own people suffered at the hand of other, more powerful, peoples on more than one occasion in our history.

---

[42] *Siddur Lev Shalem for Shabbat and Festivals*, 140.

[43] Reuven Hammer, *Or Hadash: A Commentary on Siddur Sim Shalom for Weekdays* (New York: The Rabbinical Assembly and The United Synagogue of Conservative Judaism, 2008), 25.

## Unit 6: Psalm 150

Psalm 150 is the crowning conclusion of the Book of Psalms. True to this book's name in Hebrew, *Tehillim*, "Praises," the psalm abounds with the root *hallel*, "praise." There are ten occurrences of *hallelu*, "praise (God)" in a row, and the psalm begins and ends with the word *halleluyah*, "Praise God." It begins by charging its audience of listeners (worshipers at the ancient Temple?) to praise God because of God's greatness; it then shifts to directing praise by means of wind, string, and percussion instruments, dance, and finally, voice. The Talmud records a memory of this psalm being chanted, a verse at a time, as Israelites from villages throughout the land of Israel approached the Jerusalem Temple in stages with their first fruits on the holiday of *Shavuot*.[44] In a similar vein, it is possible that the verse that introduces each instrument was meant—in performance—as the entrance to each section of a Levitical orchestra into the song.

A final interesting interpretation is found in the two citations from this psalm in the weird and wonderful book known as *Perek Shirah*, "Chapter of Song." The oldest version of this short tract derives from about the 10th century, but there are possible connections in the text to the mystical *Hekhalot* literature from several centuries earlier. In it, the biblical David, lyre-player for King Saul, and traditional author of the Book of Psalms, is taught a lesson for growing smug and arrogant over his mastery of singing praises to God. In several chapters, creatures both animate and inanimate sing biblical verses to God, rivaling, and perhaps surpassing, the songs of David. In chapter four of *Perek Shirah*, a species of poisonous spider (*semamit*) is said to chant from our psalm: "Praise him with resounding cymbals" (Psalm 150:5). In chapter six, an animal variously understood in Rabbinic Literature as a mole, weasel or porcupine (*ḥuldah*)[45] is said to chant Psalm 150:6, "Let all that breathes praise God, Halleluyah." It isn't always possible to decipher the reason a specific animal is linked with the specific biblical verse it sings in *Perek Shirah*, but it may be possible in these cases. Regarding the spider, there may be a lexical link between its Hebrew name with the verse's word for "resounding"—both words begin with the same two letters, *shin, mem*. Regarding the *ḥuldah*, perhaps the idea is that this animal (whatever it actually is) is the last animal one might expect to utter divine praise, and its biblical verse comes to teach that all that breathes, even the *ḥuldah*, actually praises God.

---

[44] Palestinian Talmud *Bikkurim* 3:2, 65c. Cited in Amos Hakham, *Book of Psalms* [Hebrew], 2:611.
[45] Marcus Jastrow, *A Dictionary of the Targumim, The Talmud Babli and Yerushalmi, and the Midrashic Literature* (Originally published in 1903; reprinted many times), 433.

**Spiritual Commentary on Psalm 150**

In stark contrast to Psalm 149, Psalm 150 strikes a near-universalist message: No mention of Israel and just a possible hint of the sanctuary in Jerusalem (*bekodsho*, "in his sanctuary," Ps. 150:1), while it calls upon all life ("all that breathes"—Ps. 150:6) to praise God. The citations of its verses in *Perek Shirah* connect with this and may suggest that even animals in the wild know how to praise God in ways that surpass the greatest human attempts. The psalm's acclamation of the role of music in praising God has led to the creation of many melodious settings of this psalm in both Jewish and Christian traditions. I once organized a joyful interfaith Thanksgiving concert in which all the cantors and choirs from the synagogues and churches in town each offered a different musical version of this one psalm. If any passage in the siddur calls for musical interpretation, and not mere recitation, it is this one. If the opportunity for serious musical preparation presents itself, arranging for different instruments to join in as the various names of those instruments are mentioned in the text might fulfill the instrumentation actually hinted at in the psalm.[46] However, even an individual worshiper praying on their own can enter into the spirit of the psalm by chanting it in any melody they may know.

## Unit 4A: Psalm 91

Psalm 91 is one of the nine psalms added to *Pesukei DeZimra* on Shabbat and holidays. Its main theme is the sense of safety and security in God's protective embrace that the poet feels. "The Israeli scholar Yair Hoffman, noting its eloquent expression of God's unflagging providential protection, has interestingly characterized the poem as an 'amulet psalm' with the idea that its recitation might help a person attain or perhaps simply feel God's guarding power."[47] Hoffman's "amulet psalm" characterization links with a talmudic discussion of this psalm in which it is called both "The Song of Plagues" (*Shir shel Pega'im*) because it says "no plague shall touch your tent" (Ps. 91:10) or "The Song of Evil Spirits" (*Shir shel Nega'im*), interpreting its first nine verses as God's protection against evil spirits.[48] The Talmud identifies the beginning of this Psalm as one of three passages recited when either consecrating an addition to the ancient Temple or to the city of Jerusalem. Using part of this psalm in those contexts was probably meant as a plea for protection of that

[46] An ecstatic example of inviting various instruments to enter a song in stages was famously modelled by Sly and The Family Stone in their presentation of the song "Dance to the Music" at the Woodstock Festival in 1969. Video of that performance is widely available on the internet.
[47] Robert Alter, *The Book of Psalms*, 321.
[48] Babylonian Talmud *Shevuot* 15b.

additional construction. It then goes on to relate that Rabbi Yehoshua ben Levi would recite Psalm 91 as protection from evil spirits when he would go to sleep each night. The anonymous, editorial voice of the Talmud then argues with this seeming incantational use of the psalm, but ultimately finds a way to excuse Rabbi Yehoshua's usage of the psalm in this way. It is not hard to understand why people might recite this psalm to invoke a sense of security: The entire poem emphasizes God's caring support.

**Spiritual Commentary on Psalm 91**
The content of this psalm is indeed appropriate if one feels threatened by physical or emotional sickness. But that is not the context of its recital here in the *Pesukei DeZimra* supplement for Shabbat and holidays. Those are days when we are freed from workaday pressures and chanting this poem then can help evoke the sense of repose and inner security that we hope to achieve during a break from routine tensions. On Shabbat and holidays, the lines of this psalm may well be recited slowly and consciously to induce an enveloping feeling of comfort and wellbeing, a sense that comes from beyond our own selves that all is aright in the world.

## The *Shema* and Its Blessings

### Introduction
The *Shema* is one of the most famous prayers in Jewish tradition. Its recitation occurs in a number of places and circumstances, including the Torah Service on Shabbat and holidays and the ritual of going to sleep at night. However, according to the classic works of Jewish tradition its preeminent location is in the *Shaḥarit*, "morning," and *Ma'ariv*, "evening," services of every day: weekday, Shabbat, holidays. It is here that this prayer acquires its full designation, *Keri'at Shema U'Virkhoteha*, "The Recitation of The *Shema* and Its Blessings." In this role, it anchors the first half of both the morning and evening services, while the *Amidah* anchors the second half.

The Recitation of The *Shema* and Its Blessings consists of three biblical passages plus a cluster of blessings that precede and follow them. The three biblical passages are:

1. *Shema* + *V'Ahavta*, "Hear" + "You shall love," Deuteronomy 6:4-9.
2. *V'Haya Im Shamo'a*, "It shall come to pass if you hearken," Deuteronomy 11:13-21.

3. *Parashat Tzitzit*, "The section about wearing fringes," Numbers 15:37-41.

At the morning service, there are two blessings that precede the biblical passages and one that follows them. In the evening service, there are two blessings that precede the biblical passages; in the land of Israel, there are two blessings that follow them, while in the Diaspora, there are three blessings that follow them.[49] The blessings that the morning and evening services have in common share common themes but have different wording. We will deal with each in turn.

This *Shema* and its blessings, along with the *Amidah*, comprise the oldest sections in the liturgy. These two sections are dealt with extensively in Tannaitic literature, the oldest stratum of Rabbinic Literature. However, as usual in Rabbinic Literature, while the timing, structure, and themes of these sections are outlined and debated, the actual wording of these prayers is assumed and rarely mentioned. That is a bigger issue regarding the blessings than the biblical passages because the text of the Bible had been canonized much earlier in Jewish history than liturgical passages. The phrasing of the blessings is never fully spelled out in the Talmud or Midrash, and the first full texts of these passages are not extant from before the early Geonic period, the 9th-10th centuries. Though we have no definite knowledge about the exact wording of the blessings during the Rabbinic period, roughly the first eight centuries of the common era, there is evidence that it remained fluid and not entirely fixed, at least for the early stages of this period.

However, there are hints that reveal some possible variations in a very early period even regarding the composition of the three biblical passages. For example, in a Hebrew text from outside the rabbinic canon, a one-page sheet that may have been a Jewish prayer text, the Ten Commandments appear along with the first two verses of the *Shema*. I am referring to the Nash Papyrus, dated to about 150 BCE, from Fayyum, Egypt. The appearance of the Ten Commandments along with the first line of the *Shema* in the Nash Papyrus parallels a teaching in the Mishnah (edited ca. 225 CE).[50] This mishnah describes the daily worship in the ancient Temple in Jerusalem. Although animal and grain sacrifices as well as wine libations were the central forms of worship, some prayers were also recited. Just as the Nash Papyrus included the Ten Commandments along with a portion of the *Shema*, this mishnah

[49] *Nusaḥ Ari*, followed by most Ḥasidic groups, has two blessings following the biblical passages in the evening, even in the Diaspora.

[50] Mishnah *Tamid* 5:1.

describes a daily service in which the Ten Commandments as well as all three passages of the *Shema* were recited. Nevertheless, the Ten Commandments were eliminated from the section of the *Shema*, according to the Talmud, because of "the claims of the heretics."[51] Apparently, the reference is to early Jewish-Christians who emphasized the sanctity of the Ten Commandments while parts of the rest of the Torah were superseded by a "New" Testament.

The vast majority of rabbinic discussions of the biblical passages of this section already assume that the make-up of these passages is well known, and that they include the entire third passage as it is known to this day, Numbers 15:37-41. Even though the *Shema* is such a central prayer, the original reasons for the selection of these particular three passages is no longer known and was probably not known in even the earliest analyses in Rabbinic Literature. The discussions of these passages focus on their order and not on the initial rationale for their inclusion. And so, unfortunately, the initial motivation for choosing these three passages for this major prayer is not known for sure. Nevertheless, the basic topics of these texts are clear enough (and each text will be dealt with below):

- **First line of the *Shema***: God's oneness.
- **First paragraph, *V'Ahavta***: Love of God, meaning loyalty to God.
- **Second paragraph, *V'Haya Im Shamo'a***: Reward and punishment for observing/ignoring the commandments.
- **Third paragraph, *Parashat Tzitzit***: The commandment to wear blue fringes on one's garment as a symbol of all of the commandments.

The question of the order of the three paragraphs is a good one since the third passage precedes the first two in the Bible itself. Why would the liturgy cite the biblical passages out of order? The Mishnah includes an explanation: According to Rabbi Yehoshua ben Korḥah, the first biblical passage has the worshiper accept the authority of God ("the yoke of the kingdom of heaven") and on that basis, accepts God's commandments ("the yoke of the commandments") laid out in the second passage.[52] The second biblical passage precedes the third because the second concerns the commandments in general, which are in force always, during the day and night, while the third concerns one commandment—to wear fringes on one's garment—and

[51] Babylonian Talmud, *Berakhot* 12a.
[52] Mishnah *Berakhot* 2:2.

that decree was understood to apply only during the day. In any case, note that Rabbi Yehoshua ben Korḥah does not address why these three biblical passages were chosen in the first place. All of the treatments of that question (including mine!) derive from long after the selection was made and must be considered as "after the fact" theories.

It is often overlooked that the three biblical paragraphs of the *Shema* are unusual as forms of prayer. Many prayers address God quite directly, using the word "you" or "your," either praising God, thanking God, or beseeching God. All of these approaches are found in the *Amidah* for example. Some prayers address God indirectly, speaking about God but instead of saying "you" or "your," they will say "God is great," "God is our help," still addressing God. Good examples of these are found in the many psalms which are cited extensively in various sections of the liturgy. However, the passages of the *Shema* do neither of these things: they do not address God directly or indirectly. Rather, they address the worshiper. "Hear, oh Israel." "You shall love *YHVH* your God." "If you observe my commandments." In this sense, they are more like declarations that the worshiper offers in a prayerful context. It is as if the worshiper is playing a role in a drama—the role of Moses actually—and quotes God's words to... the worshiper! It is an unusual dynamic and its uniqueness ought to be kept in mind as we analyze the words of these declarations.

## The First Line of the *Shema*

Because of the importance of the first line of the *Shema* in Jewish tradition and current practice as well, I'm going to offer several different aspects and approaches to it.

### God is One: Two Interpretations

How to translate the first line of the *Shema* has been hotly contested for a long time. It is an important question because the way it is translated strongly affects the meaning of the words, and ultimately, the meaning we bring to the words in prayer. Although there are many small differences among the translations, there are two main ways that this line has been translated into English in the last hundred years or so. These two ways are epitomized in the two most important American Jewish translations of the last century, both published by The Jewish Publication Society. The first was part of its 1917 translation of the Bible and the second was its Bible translation which began in 1962. The main difference between the two major translations hinges on what to make of the last word in the sentence, *eḥad*, which can be rendered either as "one" or "alone."

> **Jewish Publication Society, 1917**
> *Hear O Israel, the Lord our God, the Lord is one.*
>
> **Jewish Publication Society, 1962**
> *Hear, O Israel! The Lord is our God, The Lord alone.*

According to the older translation, this verse is a declaration of monotheism: The Lord, who is Israel's God, is the one god in the universe. This translation, or variations thereof, was picked up by most of the siddur translations in the 20th century.

According to the newer translation, this verse is about loyalty: The Lord is Israel's God alone. The sentence is not weighing in on whether there are one or more gods in the universe, but about the nature of the relationship between Israel and this God. Israel is to serve this God alone. Bernard M. Levinson comments, "Many modern readers regard the Shema as an assertion of monotheism, a view that is anachronistic. In the context of ancient Israelite religion, it served as a public proclamation of exclusive loyalty to *YHVH* as the sole LORD of Israel... In this way, it assumes the same perspective as the first commandment of the Decalogue, which by prohibiting the worship of other gods, presupposes their existence."[53] His reference to the Ten Commandments is relevant because they are found just one chapter earlier than the *Shema* in the Book of Deuteronomy. Furthermore, as the newer translation records in a footnote, two Jewish commentators of the Middle Ages, Rabbi Shmuel ben Meir (Rashbam, 1085-1158, France) and Rabbi Abraham Ibn Ezra (1092-1167, Spain) interpreted this line as a statement about Israel's loyalty to this one God alone. There is no doubt that these traditional rabbis also believed that there was only one god in the world, and it was *YHVH*; they simply did not think that this verse was making that point.

Still, the older translation has by far been the more popular approach in most *siddurim*. It is found in the current *siddurim* of the Orthodox, Conservative, and Reform movements. The newer translation, or close variations of it, were found in the siddur translations of the Conservative Movement in the 1990s and early 2000s and currently, only in the siddur of the Re-

[53] In Marc Brettler and Adele Berlin, eds., *The Jewish Study Bible* (New York: Oxford University Press, 2014), 361.

constructing Judaism Movement. The more widespread acceptance of the older translation in the context of a prayer book is understandable. Modern study of the Bible has revealed that strict monotheism, denying the existence of other gods, is not found in most of the books of the Torah, and that is reflected in Levinson's comments. However, Levinson himself makes clear subsequently in the same commentary that true monotheism certainly became the approach of Judaism as it developed in post-biblical times. And the siddur is a product of post-biblical Judaism.

**The Name of God in the First Line of the *Shema***

The personal name of God in the first line of the *Shema*, *YHVH*, is translated as "The Lord" in both the newer and the older Jewish Publication Society translations. However, "The Lord" is not a translation of this Hebrew name. Rather, it is an approximate translation of the word *Adonai* that Jews have substituted for *YHVH* when reciting that name of God out loud.[54] There is evidence that during the First Temple Period, this name of God was routinely said out loud, and not only in worship contexts, but even as part of everyday greetings.[55] However, by sometime in the Second Temple Period, the oral pronunciation of this name of God was associated with supernal holiness and was only pronounced by the holiest person, the High Priest, on the holiest day, *Yom Kippur*, in the holiest place, the Holy of Holies in the ancient Temple. The word *Adonai* was substituted for this name for all other people, times, and places.

So, if "The Lord" is an approximate translation not of *YHVH* but of *Adonai*, what is the translation of *YHVH*? When Moses first meets God at the burning bush, he says to God:

> When I come to the Israelites and say to them, "The God of your fathers has sent me to you," and they ask me, "What is his name?" What shall I say to them? God said to Moses,

[54] It is an approximation only because a literal translation would be "my lords." Understandably, modern Jewish translations reflecting the strict monotheism of post-biblical Judaism want to avoid using the plural when referring to God. So, how did this word substituting for God's name acquire a plural form? The word itself is found in conjunction with *YHVH* in several places in the Bible, including Gen. 15:2, Deut. 3:24, 9:26. So the question becomes: Why did the Bible use a name in the plural form referring to God? One answer is that the plural form is simply a sign of authority or higher rank, like the royal "we" in English. Jeffrey Tigay presents this explanation. See "Excursus 4: 'The Lord,'" in Jeffrey Tigay, *The JPS Torah Commentary: Deuteronomy*, 431, n. 13. However, it seems to me that it may also be a linguistic vestige in Hebrew of the Bible of the pre-Israelite polytheistic view. This would be similar to the survival of the word *Elohim*, extremely common in the Bible, as the generic word for God even though the word is in the plural form, meaning literally, "gods."

[55] See, for example, Ruth 2:4.

> *"Ehyeh Asher Ehyeh."* He continued, "Thus shall you say to the Israelites, '*Ehyeh* sent me to you.'" (Exodus 3:13-14)

Both *Ehyeh* and *YHVH* share the root which means "to be." Therefore, *Ehyeh* is typically translated "I Am That I Am" and I would translate *YHVH* as "The One Who Is," or "The One Who Causes Existence."[56] The deeper meaning of this name is either that God is the ground of all existence, and so, "The One Who Is," or that God is the origin of all that exists in the world and so, "The One Who Causes Existence." It seems to me unfortunate that *YHVH* has long been rendered as "The Lord" since it is simply not related at all to the actual meaning of the Hebrew word *YHVH,* and that the authentic translation is much more spiritually resonant for a generation in which words like "Lord" or "my Lord" feel archaic and irrelevant. It is true that this name of God occurs throughout the liturgy, including in every blessing. So, why am I exploring the definition of *YHVH* here, in the discussion of the first line of the *Shema*? Because this one line of prayer occupies such a central place in Jewish liturgy and this name of God occurs twice within its six words. The first line of the *Shema* has long been viewed as the major declaration of faith in God by a Jew. The first line of the *Shema* has been, and should be, a focus of true contemplation about one's relationship with God. There is quite a difference between contemplating one's relationship to the clichéd term "The Lord" and one's relationship to "The One Who Is."

## The First Line of the *Shema* as Reenactment

There is another aspect to this line that is worth considering: Its original context in chapter 6 of Book of Deuteronomy. There, Moses, after all he has experienced as the adopted son of Pharaoh's daughter; after the transformative experience at the Burning Bush; after the Ten Plagues; the Ten Commandments; and the forty years of leading his people to the gateway of The Promised Land, is addressing the People of Israel, knowing he is near the end of his life. The words of the *Shema* are Moses' words, and he is exhorting Israel once more: Hear! Listen! *YHVH* is our God! We serve only *YHVH*, there is none other! Rabbi Elazar ben Yehudah, known, after the name of his major work, as The *Rokei'aḥ*, "The Perfumer," (13th century, Germany) called attention to this fact in his commentary on the siddur.[57]

---

[56] The second option is based on the possibility that *YHVH* may be in the grammatical form known as *hif'il,* the "causative" form, and thus, "The One Who Causes Existence."

[57] And he did it with an economy of words: "The interpretation is: Listen, People of Israel, thus said Moses!" See *Peirushei Siddur HaTefillah LaRokei'aḥ*, eds. Rabbi Moshe Hershler and Rabbi Yehudah

The point of knowing the original biblical context of this line of the *Shema* is to realize that reciting these words during worship is a reenactment. We are reenacting the scene from Deuteronomy. If there is a prayer leader at the service, then they are playing the role of Moses, calling out to the congregation whose role is that of Israel: Hear! Listen! *YHVH* is our God! We serve only *YHVH*, there is none other! If one is praying on one's own, then we are both Moses and Israel. This is the drama that takes place each time the *Shema* is recited.

**The First Line of the *Shema* as Testimony**

There is another commentary that is interested in the mindset of the worshiper more than the content of the words themselves. The first line of the *Shema* as written in Torah scrolls (and most printed Hebrew books of the Torah) appears with two of its letters enlarged or otherwise marked. The two letters are the *ayin*, the last letter of the word *Shema*, "Hear," and the *dalet*, the last letter of the word *eḥad*, "one." Clearly, this was meant to draw attention to these two letters, and there are varying explanations given over the centuries.[58] One explanation is found in the prayer book commentary of Rabbi David Abudraham (14th century, Spain). It holds that these letters are to be read backwards forming the word *eid*, "witness."

> It is a kind of testifying as if one says to his fellow, "Shema/ Listen! I believe that *YHVH* is our God and he is the only one in his world."[59]

It is doubtful that the biblical text meant for readers to find those two letters and to read them backwards. This is more of a later rumination on the text. Still, I cite it because it rings true to the unusual style of this prayer. As noted above, the *Shema* is not so much directed at God as it is a declaration of faith by the worshiper in a prayerful environment, in the presence of God. And that is what this commentary is asserting: When the worshiper recites this line of the *Shema*, they are testifying their religious faith to those around them. A similar characterization of the *Shema* is found in the work of Josephus, the 1st-century Jewish army officer who became a Roman.

Alter Hershler (Jerusalem: Makhon HaRav Hershler LeMeḥkar U'leHotza'ah shel Sifrut Toranit Ve-Hilkhatit, 1992, 1:283.

[58] See Jeffrey Tigay, "The Majuscule Letters in the Shema," *The JPS Torah Commentary: Deuteronomy*, 441.

[59] *Sefer Abudraham HaShaleim* (Jerusalem: Wertheimer, 1962), 80.

He called the recitation "bearing witness" (*martyrein* in Greek) to God's bounties.[60]

**"*YHVH* Is One"—**
**God as the Ground of Oneness and Coherence in the World**

Rabbi Alan Lew wrote movingly of an interpretation of the first line of the *Shema* in his memoir, *One God Clapping*. Lew had been born a Jew, but for a number of years studied and practiced Buddhism quite seriously, spending hours in the early morning sitting in meditation at Zen centers. In his middle age, he awoke to the possibility of finding spiritual depth in his Jewish heritage, and after years of full-time study, was ordained as a Conservative rabbi. The story of how he ultimately harmonized the power of meditation with observant Jewish life is told in his memoir, and it was not an easy path. In his book, he tells the story of a retreat he helped lead for serious practitioners of Buddhism who had been born Jewish. Crafting Jewish worship services at the retreat in a way that would speak to these people was challenging. These were spiritually sensitive people who had left Judaism years before, many of whom did not know Hebrew, and most of whom were angry at a tradition they were born into but which, for them, did not speak to their religious needs. They were at the retreat because they still felt something for their native religion and, deep down, they wanted to transcend their antagonism. But they were angry. Rabbi Lew's first attempts at running Jewish worship services did not work out very well. Finally, he stripped down the service to bare essentials and was able to reach the people on a deep level:

> ...(W)e went to the *Shem'a*, but only the first six words, which we said over and over until we were infused with them. The words spoke to us of the miracle of awareness and the mind-boggling idea that there is a oneness in all things, that despite appearances, we do live in a coherent world, and that God is precisely the ground of that oneness and that coherence.[61]

---

[60] Cited in Jeffrey Tigay, "The Majuscule Letters in the Shema," *The JPS Torah Commentary: Deuteronomy*, 441, n. 22.

[61] Alan Lew, *One God Clapping: The Spiritual Path of a Zen Rabbi* (New York: Kodansha International, 1999), 292-293. The religious world was bereft of a profound teacher and practitioner when Rabbi Lew suddenly died at the age of 65 in 2009. I had the privilege of getting to know him as a colleague when we both served in the same region of the country, and I had the further privilege of teaching at the same rabbinical retreat with Rabbi Lew. I still remember the meditation combined with light yoga that he led each morning before *Shaḥarit*. It beautifully intensified my *davening* experience each morning at *Shaḥarit*.

Here, Rabbi Lew has given eloquent expression to one of the ways that monotheism can have deep meaning for moderns. Saying that monotheism posits one god versus polytheism that imagines many gods is not the most evocative way to describe the difference between the two theological systems. It misses a profound idea that Rabbi Lew points to. That idea is monotheism's challenge to see the oneness in life and the unity of all people. We are all related, all brothers and sisters because we were all created by one heavenly Parent. The challenge is to view all that happens in this life as part of one divine plan. This is a deep and rewarding, but difficult, path. As Rabbi Lew writes, it requires going beyond appearances, because the events in an individual's life and in the life of nations often appear to be chaotic and amoral. And yet, our prophets apprehended "the oneness in all things" that we do indeed "live in a coherent world" with God as "precisely the ground of that oneness and that coherence."

### "*YHVH* Is One"—Nondualism: God Is All that There Is in the World

An insight from a different direction is found in Jay Michaelson's *Everything is God: The Radical Path of Nondual Judaism.* "Nondual Judaism" refers to that mystical stream in Jewish tradition, close to pantheism, in which everyone and everything is considered to be a manifestation of God. This path collapses the gap between God and nature, between God and humanity, and was most fully developed by Ḥasidism.

> ...(T)he nondual understanding is conveyed in these words attributed to the Baal Shem Tov: "When we say 'the Lord is One,' we mean that nothing other than God exists in all the universe. In the classic Ḥasidic commentary of the Sfat Emet (1847-1905), we are told, "the meaning of '*YHVH* is One' is not that He is the only God, negating other gods, but... there is no being other than Him, even though it seems otherwise to most people." That is to say, the Shema is not saying that there is only one God... It is not even saying that God is One in the philosophical sense.[62] Rather, it is saying that all is One, and thus that all is God. Thus the central truth of nondual Judaism is included in the central dictum of the Jewish people. And another level: *YHVH* is

[62] The philosophical sense is that saying God is one does not mean there aren't more gods than just one. It is not a mathematical statement. It means that God is unique; there is nothing else in the world as singular as God because nothing can compare with God.

> here called "our Elohim," our God. To say this is to subjugate the ego, which sees itself as separate, to the immanent and transcendent Is. It is not that I bow before someone or something else, but rather that the sense of "I" is no longer the ordering principle at all. If *YHVH* becomes my Elohim, I see clearly that this "self" is actually an illusion, a ripple on the pond of Is. There is nothing there to bow down at all.[63]

Michaelson's striking and daring explanation of the *Shema* in the nondual tradition dovetails with the meaning of the divine name *YHVH* as "Is" or "The One Who Is," but takes it a step further. Not only would the worshiper reciting the *Shema* try to bring into clear consciousness the reality of the ultimate "One Who Is," but they would also be challenged to accept that the worshiper's existence itself is no different than God's existence. When the *Shema* says "*YHVH* is one," it is saying that there is nothing but the One. And the nondual approach calls for the recitation of the *Shema* to bring that notion into focus, for the worshiper to dissolve their sense of separateness from God.

**Spiritual Commentary on the First Line of the *Shema***

I have observed that the amount of time it takes for many people to chant this line in the most common contemporary melody is nine seconds. This leads me to question whether that is enough time to concentrate on a line that has been so central in all periods of Jewish practice. If the reader takes nothing else from this discussion of this sentence, take this: It is very hard to concentrate on any weighty and deep thought while reciting six words in only nine seconds. This sentence is a statement about God and about what the worshiper feels about God. Most prayers address God, but few make statements about how this worshiper, at this moment, feels about God. So, take your time in saying the *Shema* and see what comes.

Now, several responses to the Analytical insights from above. I shared a number of perspectives in the Analytical Commentary. Each can elicit responses in a spiritual, practical, in-the-midst-of-davening, way. It can be helpful, and grant perspective, if, when reciting the *Shema*, we envision Moses calling out these words to the People of Israel assembled, soon to enter the Land of Israel. It can link us to our history, all the way back to the time of our teacher, Moses. If we allow ourselves, this scenario can also link us to

[63] Jay Michaelson, *Everything is God: The Radical Path of Nondual Judaism* (Boston & London: Trumpeter, 2009), 48-49.

the many, many generations of Jews who reenacted the panorama of Moses and Israel, on the small scale of their synagogue worship over the centuries. The sensitive worshiper can also easily adapt the other suggested readings of the *Shema* in the Analytical Commentary in their own ways.

Here, I want to share a practice I've used for a number of years that touches on what God's name, *YHVH*, actually means as well as the interpretations of Alan Lew and Jay Michaelson. This is by no means the only way or the best way to go. It is simply one with which I have long experience.

Instead of addressing God as "Lord," in the *Shema*, over the last few years, I have addressed God as "The One Who Is" or "The One Who Causes Existence." Noticing that "Lord" does not translate *YHVH* was a small revelation for me. Since then, when I recite the *Shema* as a participant in a service or on my own (but not when I serve as a prayer leader), I diverge from Jewish tradition and I do not pronounce *YHVH* as traditionally pronounced, *Adonai.* Rather, I pronounce it—but silently only—according to one of the theories as to how *YHVH* should be enunciated, namely, as *Yahvah*, and I dwell on the presence of "The One Who Is" for quite a while, dividing the word into its two syllables.[64]

I invoke God's presence by silently saying and repeating over and over *Yahvah*... and I dwell on that name as I contemplate the presence of the living God, the ultimate "is-ness," the vital force in the world, that animates all that is in it, across all generations. To help me get to the level of consciousness for which I am striving, I borrow a common technique from meditation, and focus on my breath. After that, I try to deepen my awareness by focusing on my heartbeat. I don't know if that is something that everyone can easily do—I've received some positive feedback on this in some of the teaching I've done—and I find that it isn't difficult to do, and that it has quite a positive effect. I employ these two techniques—centering on my breathing and on my heartbeat—to help me feel the presence of *YHVH*, the source of all that "is," within my own body, because I believe that God manifests within each person, in our physicality, along with all reality, and because God's presence within ourselves is the most accessible way to experience God. Getting to the point of being suffused with the presence of God within me can take a few minutes. Once I arrive there, I pause, exhale, and conclude my repetitions of the first time *YHVH* occurs in the first line of the *Shema.*

[64] See further, *The Anchor Bible Dictionary,* s.v., Yahweh, "A. Pronunciation" and "B. Meaning" (New York: Doubleday, 1992), 6 :1011.

Then, when I reach the second *YHVH* in the line, I again silently say and repeat over and over *Yahvah...* and I try to extend my consciousness of God outward, beyond my own body, and feel my connection—because of God's omnipresence—to all around me. I do that by first envisioning my family members and where they may be in the world, remaining with each for a few seconds at a time. Again, that is my way of beginning with the most accessible. Then, I stretch my awareness to my immediate surroundings. If that includes other people because I'm in a synagogue, I envision my connection to them. Whether I am in a synagogue or alone, I extend my perception as well to the non-living entities that surround me. I begin with the floor and feel my connection to it through my feet, and try to imagine the origin of the material of the floor: Is it wood and its origin a tree? Is it stone and its origin somewhere in the ground? Is it vinyl, and its origin as a by-product of oil or gas production, and originally, eons ago, in the organic matter of animal or marine life? I then attempt to trace the floor's connection to the framework of the building I'm in, and through that, to the soil beneath the building. Finally, I trace my connection—through *YHVH*, the origin of all that "is"—via the circumference of planet Earth to all the world. At that point, I exhale and pronounce *eḥad*, "one," at that point, usually feeling "at one" with all that the name *YHVH* connotes.

Sometimes I go through some, but not all the stages listed above, but I always begin by slowing down my recitation with concentration on the two appearances of God's name, *YHVH*, and do not pronounce the last word, *eḥad*, "one," until and unless I am satisfied that I have done all I can to envision myself "one" with God. Then... reciting the rest of the three paragraphs of the *Shema* slowly only deepens the union that I feel. This exercise, quite obviously, takes more than nine seconds. The truth is that when engaging in any attempt to deepen one's worship experience with the first line of the *Shema*, it is almost inevitable that it will put one out of sync with a conventional service in most contemporary synagogues. That can be challenging and so, I am herewith offering my encouragement and support to any of us who are willing to explore alternate ways to deepen their praying experience even if it sometimes disengages us with what the congregation around us is doing.

## First Paragraph of The *Shema*, *V'Ahavta* (Deuteronomy 6:5-9)

Earlier, I had noted that despite the voluminous commentaries on the three biblical passages of the *Shema* over the centuries, we actually do not know why these texts were originally chosen to occupy such a central role in the liturgy. There simply are no records that go back that far. Nevertheless, a close literary analysis will reveal much about these words which, traditionally, are recited twice a day, morning and evening, every day. I will review each of the three paragraphs separately.

The first paragraph of the *Shema*, known by its first word, *V'Ahavta*, "You shall love," continues in the Bible from where the line commencing with *Shema Yisrael*, left off. Our paragraph begins by commanding love of God: *V'ahavta*, "you shall love *YHVH* your God with all your heart, with all your soul, and with all your might." In the context of the Bible, the Hebrew root used here for "love," *aleph-heh-bet*, can yield several different connotations. It can refer to romantic or sexual love between human beings, love of qualities or things, love of neighbor or stranger, or love between God and human beings and between human beings and God. In the context of the Book of Deuteronomy, and of this particular passage, it is dealing with love between human beings and God.

> (This) has its conceptual roots... in the rhetoric of international relations in the (ancient near east) of the period, rather than from the sphere of conjugal intimacy. Rulers write to their equals with whom they are in treaty relationship concerning the importance of love; a ruler may command subject vassals to show love to the ruler as expression of their faithfulness to a treaty of protection provided by the ruler. Deuteronomy speaks of Israel's love for God in the context of the covenant established at Sinai, using terminology familiar from the political rhetoric of the culture.[65]

Thus, here, in the first paragraph of the *Shema*, "you shall love *YHVH* your God" probably connotes loyalty, faithfulness, and willing devotion to obey God's commandments.

A literary analysis of this paragraph reveals that the body is a major theme. There are three direct mentions of parts of the body:

> *Levavekha*, "your heart."
> *Yadkha*, "your arm."
> *Einekha*, "your eyes."

[65] *Anchor Bible Dictionary*, 4:376. See also Yochanan Muffs, *Love and Joy: Law, Language and Religion in Ancient Israel* (New York: The Jewish Theological Seminary of America, 1992).

There are six more indirect, implied, references to the body:

> *Me'odekha*, "your might" may refer to the body's might.[66]
> *U'keshartam*, "and bind them" implies the arm.
> *U'khetavtam*, "and write them" implies hand.
> *B'shokhbekha*, "when you lie down" and
> *U'vekumekha*, "and when you arise" imply the whole body.
> *Nafshekha*, "your life," or "your soul."

Integrating this theme into the larger message of the paragraph indicates: "You shall love *YHVH* your God"—meaning loyalty—"through the actions of your body."

Another theme that occurs four times in this passage adds to this message, the theme of daily routine time:

> *B'shivtekha beveitekha*, "when you sit in your house."
> *U'velekhtekha vaderekh*, "when you walk on the way."
> *U'veshokhbekha*, "when you lie down (to sleep)."
> *U'vekumekha*, "when you awake."

Together with the idea of the body, the theme of routine time augments the message to mean: "You shall love *YHVH* your God"—meaning loyalty—"through actions of your body and throughout your daily routine."

Finally, the singular form is used some 21 times in this short paragraph indicating that Moses here was directing himself to each individual further extending the message to: "Each individual among you shall love *YHVH* your God"—meaning loyalty—"through actions of your body and throughout your daily routine." This, ultimately, is the meaning of the *V'Ahavta* paragraph: A command to each individual to display loyalty to God through physical actions in each day's regular routine. A command to exhibit consciousness of God not only in a person's mind, but through the actions of a person's body, and on a daily, everyday, basis.

**Spiritual Commentary on *V'Ahavta***

Some people recite daily, or post in a prominent place, a credo that they hope will inspire them throughout the day. The *V'Ahavta* paragraph, which traditionally is recited each morning and evening, functions well as such a credo.

[66] Though it may also refer to "wealth, possessions."

It reminds each individual to cultivate consciousness of God throughout each day's routine. It further registers that such an awareness is not meant to be only intellectual but should affect our actions.

As I wrote in the introduction to this book, my wife and I once attended a day-long seminar with the eminent Vietnamese Buddhist teacher, Thich Nhat Hanh, at a Buddhist monastery in upstate New York. One of the lessons he taught was the value of not losing a sense of mindfulness throughout the day. He related that the nuns at the monastery program their phones to sound a gong on an hourly basis to bring their attention back to mindfulness from the inevitable mind-wandering that naturally occurs to all of us. It seems to me that perhaps the most basic and central goal of the many Jewish prayers and blessings traditionally recited each day is to bring our minds back to God-consciousness. That is why there are blessings for all sorts of mundane activities throughout the day including thrice-daily worship services, blessings before and after eating, and even a blessing of gratitude after each visit to the bathroom. The second-century talmudic Sage, Rabbi Meir, taught that one should strive to recite a hundred blessings each day.[67] The theology behind reciting so many blessings each day was labelled "Normal Mysticism" by Rabbi Max Kaddushin because these pauses brought a measure of mysticism to normal, that is routine, daily, activities.[68] That is exactly the challenge of the *V'Ahavta* paragraph: To bring an awareness a God's presence and perspective throughout our normal, daily activities.

## The Second Paragraph of the *Shema* *V'Haya Im Shamo'a* (Deuteronomy 11:13-21)

The end of this paragraph repeats the wording and message of the first paragraph and in much the same language: The charge to be conscious of loyalty to God in our daily, routine, activities. But the bulk of the paragraph is stated in an "if/then" format and states a clear theology of reward and punishment. **If** the Israelites remain loyal and observe God's commandments, **then** God will grant abundant rain so that their crops will grow and there will be ample herbage for their herds. **If** the Israelites are disloyal and serve other gods, **then** God will "shut" the heavens, drought and famine will follow, and the people will perish from the land. The wording, which contain no less than 17 references to agriculture, makes this stark message quite graphic.

---

67 Babylonian Talmud *Menaḥot* 43b.

68 See, for example, Max Kaddushin, *The Rabbinic Mind* (New York: The Jewish Theological Seminary of America, 1952), 252-253.

As was mentioned regarding the use of the word "love" in the first paragraph of the *Shema*, the rewards and punishments of the second paragraph too were likely based upon the language of treaties between rulers and vassals in the ancient Near East. The language was meant to warn allies or vassals not to break the agreement. Here, that language was adapted for the covenant between God and Israel. In other words, it may have been meant as a kind of standard warning clause not to abrogate the covenant and may not have been meant to be taken literally.

That political context is helpful because this explicit expression of reward and punishment does not accord with the reality experienced by most people. There are often droughts, as well as times of plenty, that seem unrelated to the general morality of communities. The graphic language makes it hard not to take it literally. Because of this, the Reform Movement's *siddurim* have, for many years, omitted this paragraph completely. The Reconstructing Judaism's siddur includes the traditional paragraph, but first offers an alternative paragraph, Deuteronomy 28:1-6; 30:15-19, which also comprises a similar theology of reward and punishment but emphasizes the reward.[69] The Orthodox Movement's siddur endorses a literal interpretation: This paragraph "specifies the duty to perform 'my commandments,' and teaches that when the nation is righteous, it will be rewarded with success and prosperity. When it sins, it must expect poverty and exile."[70] The Conservative siddur acknowledges the problem: "This description of reward and punishment has been a source of theological struggle for every Jewish generation..." But it advocates a non-literal, more general, approach: "What is expressed here in concrete terms may be understood more broadly: moral and immoral actions have consequences, both seen and unseen."[71]

**Spiritual Commentary on the Second Paragraph of the *Shema***

I would argue for a non-literal approach to praying this text, not in broad terms but in quite specific ones, the terms set out by the passage itself. Our agriculture, our domesticated herds, our land, and ultimately, we ourselves, will indeed suffer monumental consequences to the extent that we act as if we retain ultimate ownership over the land instead of God. It isn't hard to bring to mind the damage that modern society has caused to the environment by prioritizing short-term material wealth over long-term responsible stewardship. Many scientists have sounded the alarm that humanity is close

[69] *Kol Haneshamah: Daily*, 85-89.
[70] *The Complete Artscroll Siddur*, 92-93.
[71] *Siddur Lev Shalem For Shabbat & Festivals*, 42.

to having caused irreparable and irreversible harm to the climate, land, air, and waterways. This paragraph of the *Shema* can serve as a witness to us, each time we recite it, that the land is not ultimately ours, that we have been charged to act with the knowledge that "the earth is the Lord's and all it contains, the world and its inhabitants" (Psalms 24:1).

### The Third Paragraph of the *Shema* (Numbers 15:37-41)

The essence of this paragraph is: Wear fringes (*tzitzit*) of *tekhelet* ("blue" or "violet") on your garments as reminders of all of God's commandments. The paragraph concludes by connecting the obligation to observe the commandments with God's rescuing the people from Egyptian slavery. Originally, the idea was to wear these fringes on one's every-day, four-cornered, toga-like garment. When, over the centuries, fashions changed and people no longer wore togas, the custom developed to wear the fringes on a four-cornered undergarment as well as—during worship—on one's prayer shawl (*tallit*). It is often neglected that the text specifies that one thread in each fringe ought to be blue or violet (*tekhelet*) because the vast majority of *tzitzit* for many centuries has been only white. Already in talmudic times, the traditional dye for that color had been lost.[72] The future second Chief Rabbi of Palestine, Rabbi Isaac Herzog had, in 1914, written his doctoral dissertation on the topic of the source of the dye for this color.[73] He maintained that a certain mollusk, known as the murex, was the source, and, over time, as his conclusions became known, the manufacture of *tzitzit* with the thread of blue/violet has seen some modest success. An internet search of the words "*tekhelet tzitzit*" will yield several suppliers.

It may be wondered why the Sages chose this particular commandment to locate so centrally, as part of the recitation of the *Shema*. Why the command to wear fringes among all the commandments? In fact, there is a discussion in the Talmud about whether the third paragraph of the *Shema* should have been an excerpt from the prophecies of the non-Jewish prophet, Balaam (Numbers 22-25) instead of the passage about fringes.[74] It would have been quite interesting had a text from a non-Jewish prophet been included in this major prayer! However, since that discussion is in a relatively late literary stratum of the Talmud, it is hard to know whether it reflects an attitude from

[72] See Mishnah *Menaḥot* 4:1; *Bemidbar Rabba* 17:5.

[73] Much later, his dissertation was published in an updated edition as Ehud Spanier, ed., *The Royal Purple and the Biblical Blue* (Argaman *and* Tekhelet)*: The Study of Chief Rabbi Dr. Isaac Herzog on the Dye Industries in Ancient Israel and Recent Scientific Contributions* (Jerusalem: Keter, 1987).

[74] See Babylonian Talmud *Berakhot* 12b and Palestinian Talmud *Berakhot* 1:7, 3c.

the now lost original arguments about which biblical passages should be included with the *Shema*.

Still, the question of why tradition settled on a passage dealing with the specific commandment of *tzitzit* has not yet been answered. It must again be admitted that any explanation is an after-the-fact attempt since no clear accounting is extant in the early sources. Such an attempt at meaning is found in an interpretation by Jacob Milgrom. He explains how these fringes may symbolize the commandments as a whole as well as the holiness of the individual wearer. He demonstrates that in biblical times, the hem of a garment, and the fringe attached to it, could be an identification of nobility. Furthermore, the fringes and their color resemble the tassel and other garments of the High Priest. Thus, the *tzitzit* represent the holy authority of each Israelite; they hint at a kind of symbolic priestly status that derives from each individual's covenant with God and the commandments. In sum:

> The *tzitzit* are the epitome of the democratic thrust within Judaism, which equalizes not by leveling but by elevating. All of Israel is enjoined to become a nation of priests. In antiquity, the *tzitzit* (and the hem) were the insignia of authority, high breeding, and nobility. By adding the violet woolen cord to the *tzitzit*, the Torah qualified nobility with priesthood: Israel is not to rule man but to serve God. Furthermore, *tzitzit* are not restricted to Israel's leaders, be they kings, rabbis or scholars. It is the uniform of all Israel.[75]

The Reform Movement's *siddurim* have, for many years, presented a version of the third paragraph of the *Shema* as a shorter text than the inherited version. This text consists of the last two verses of the more traditional five-verse passage and omits all mention of the *tzitzit* itself:

> Thus you shall remember to observe all My commandments and to be holy to your God. I am Adonai, your God, who brought you out of the land of Egypt to be your God: I am Adonai your God.[76]

[75] Jacob Milgrom, *The JPS Torah Commentary: Numbers* (Philadelphia, New York: The Jewish Publication Society, 1990), 414.
[76] *Mishkan T'filah: A Reform Siddur*, 66.

Rabbi Isaac Mayer Wise (1819-1900), a major founder of the Reform Movement in North America, who sought to elevate inspirational ideas over ritual actions, denigrated the wearing of a *tallit* and omitted this paragraph entirely. Reform practice varied, even in the early years of the Movement, with many contemporary Reform Jews embracing the wearing of a *tallit*. Modern Reform liturgy, however, has retained the shorter text.

The traditional version of this paragraph links a life of *mitzvot*, "commandments," with both the symbol of the ritual fringes and with the Exodus from Egypt. The Reform version, citing just the last two verses of this passage, connects loyalty to the life of *mitzvot* not with ritual fringes, but only with the Exodus from Egypt. Among the many variations between the movements, this one is especially significant because of the historic centrality of the traditional biblical sections of the *Shema*. Reform's focus on the last two verses also raises the issue of the Exodus from Egypt in the liturgy. Israel leaving Egypt because of its attunement to God's liberating presence is a foundational moment in Jewish history. It is celebrated as such by innumerable references to the Exodus in the Bible, the liturgy, and among most other central documents of Jewish tradition. In the daily morning and evening service, the third paragraph of the *Shema* is immediately followed by a blessing extolling God for redeeming the Jewish People from Egypt. In this way, the blessing that follows the *Shema* is clearly connected with the final verse of the biblical sections of the *Shema*. The question of whether the other blessings that surround the *Shema* are similarly associated with the biblical sections is one we will take up in the commentary following the Spiritual Commentary on the *tzitzit* paragraph.

**Spiritual Commentary on the third paragraph in the *Shema***

Jacob Milgrom's stimulating explanation is that the *tzitzit* are meant to elevate the wearers to the status of a holy authority unto themselves. That is, the *tzitzit* worn by each individual marks them as a member of "kingdom of priests and a holy nation" (Exodus 19:6), without the need of another spiritual authority to mediate between them and God. Reciting this paragraph might re-awaken us to the meaning of wearing a *tallit*.

Building on the personal connection between each Jew and God in Milgrom's explanation of the *tzitzit*, I would suggest that inspiration can be derived from the relatively recent custom—found in traditional prayer books—of reciting several verses from the Psalms as one puts on the *tallit*. As we hold the *tallit*, just before enrobing ourselves, the custom is to recite Psalm 104:1-2 which declares:

> Bless the Lord, O my soul;
> O Lord, my God, you are very great;
> You are clothed in glory and majesty,
> Wrapped in a robe of light;
> You spread the heavens like a tent cloth.

Reciting these words as we hold our *tallit* in our hands, the verse implies in midrashic fashion that God, too, wears a *tallit*. God is "clothed" in a *tallit* of "glory and majesty," "wrapped in a" *tallit* "of light." "The heavens"—themselves envisioned as the cloth of a massive tent—form God's *tallit*. As we prepare to wear our *tallit*, we envision God as clothed in a glorious, majestic *tallit* made of heavenly light.

Then, once enrobed in our *tallit*, having recited the proper blessing, the custom is to recite the following verses from Psalm 36:8-11:

> How precious is your faithful care, O God!
> Humankind shelters in the shadow of your wings.
> They feast on the rich fare of your house;
> You let them drink at your refreshing stream.
> With you is the fountain of life;
> By your light do we see light.

With our *tallit* wrapped around our face, prior to settling it upon our shoulders, we imagine ourselves "sheltering in the shadow of your wings," that is, in the folds of cloth, which are re-imagined as God's "wings." Here, God is envisioned as a bird, protecting its young in its wings. A similar image is used elsewhere in the Torah to describe God protecting Israel in its desert journey, "Like an eagle who rouses his nestlings, gliding down to his young, so did he spread his wings and take him, bear him along on his pinions" (Deut. 32:11). Further, in the darkness of the creases of the cloth, shut out from the kind of light that our eyes can perceive, we declare, "by your light do we see light."

That is, in the safe and secure darkness within the folds of the *tallit* which are God's protecting "wings," we understand that there is another kind of light, "your light," an inner light, a "light" that "shines" within darkness, that is available to us. This inner light is hinted at by the ethereal light of the heavens, which forms God's own *tallit*.

With these Psalm-verses forming a *kavannah*, an "intention," the *tallit* can indeed become a true prayer shawl, a shawl that arouses prayer within us, because it helps us transition from routine, everyday, thought to an inner and meditative consciousness.

## The Blessings Surrounding the *Shema*

The *Shema* is one of the two major prayers (along with the *Amidah*) of the morning and evening services every day. Only *Minḥah*, the afternoon service, lacks the recitation of the *Shema*. On weekdays, there are three blessings that accompany the *Shema* in the morning service and four during the evening service.[77] These blessings are mentioned in the *Mishnah* but their wording is not recorded aside from a phrase or two in Rabbinic Literature.[78] Full, paragraph-long, texts of these blessings first appear in the Geonic Period, beginning in the ninth century. The themes of the three blessings that are shared by both the morning and evening service are the same, but the wording varies. We don't have hard evidence explaining the difference in wording between the same blessings in the morning and in the evening. However, it may be that these blessings have a parallel history to other prayers that have varying wording in different liturgical locations such as the *Kaddish* and the *Kedushah*. If that is the case, then the multiple wording of the same blessing may have originated in multiple geographical locations and then, at a later time, places within the siddur were found for the several different versions because by then, all of the versions had acquired legitimacy, authenticity, and "holiness." I will comment on each of the blessings in turn.

Some years ago, Reuven Kimelman published an article laden—as is his practice—with many, many fascinating sources in which he argued that each of the blessings surrounding the *Shema* is carefully connected in great detail to the content of the three biblical passages themselves.[79] I see some basic and relatively simple connections between the first and third biblical passages and the blessings, but despite Kimelman's impressive efforts, I am not convinced that there are many and varied links between them. Furthermore, I do not see any true links between the second biblical passage and any of the blessings. As mentioned above, there is no question that the last verse of the third biblical paragraph shares the theme of the Exodus from Egypt with the blessing that follows it. Similarly, the first biblical paragraph is in

[77] Only the first three blessings are recited at the evening service in Israel as well as in the Ḥasidic rite known as *Nusaḥ Ari* in the diaspora.
[78] *Mishnah Berakhot* 1:4; Babylonian Talmud *Berakhot* 11b.
[79] Reuven Kimelman, "The Shema' and Its Rhetoric: The Case for the Shema' Being More than Creation, Revelation, and Redemption" in *The Journal of Jewish Thought and Philosophy*, Vol. 2, 1992, 111-156. The full text is available on Kimelman's web page on academia.edu.

a kind of "dialogue" with the blessing that precedes it, as will be detailed below. But the second biblical passage, whose theme is divine reward and punishment, does not seem directly connected to any of the blessings that surround the *Shema.*

A thousand years ago or so, there was indeed a blessing that preceded the *Shema* that clearly and unambiguously was connected to the *Shema* itself. It is found among the thousands of pages in the Cairo Genizah, a treasure trove of texts that exemplified *Nusaḥ Eretz Yisrael HaKadum*, "The Ancient Palestinian Rite." This collection of liturgical prayers and customs was the norm for communities in the Land of Israel and Egypt from approximately the Arab conquest of the area in 640 CE until the armies of the First Crusade (1096 CE) destroyed this Jewish community. The words of the blessing are partly based on Chronicles 28:9 and read:

> Blessed are you, *YHVH* our God, king of the universe who has hallowed us through his commandments and commanded us about the recitation of the *Shema* and to crown him with a full heart and to unify him (i.e., declare that there is only one God) with a willing heart and to serve him with an eager soul.[80]

That blessing fell into disuse with the destruction of the Jewish community in 11th-century Israel by the Crusaders. Of the blessings that remain, the second blessing before the *Shema*—the one that immediately precedes the recitation of the *Shema* itself—is the only one connected so closely with the biblical passage that follows it to say that it may well have been composed specifically for that purpose (See the discussion of that blessing below). The other blessings, with either indirect or no real connection to the biblical passages of the *Shema,* may have developed independently from the paragraphs of the *Shema* and were then merged with biblical passages of the *Shema* sometime in the talmudic or geonic period. This is similar to my understanding of how the blessings of the *Amidah* came together which I've spelled out in a bit more detail on page 83.

## The First Blessing Before the *Shema*

The first blessing is prefaced by an invitation to formal prayer since the evening service begins here and, in the morning, the two previous sections of

[80] Jacob Mann, "Genizah Fragments of the Palestinian Order of Service," *Hebrew Union College Annual,* Vol. 2 (1925), 286.

the liturgy, *Birkhot Hashaḥar*, "Morning Blessings," and *Pesukei DeZimra*, "Verses of Song," are informal, not requiring a quorum. The invitation to formal prayer consists of two lines. The first, recited by the prayer leader, beginning with the word *Barkhu*, is "Bless is *YHVH* who blessed." The second is the congregational response, "May *YHVH* be blessed forever." This invitation was recorded already in the oldest stratum of Rabbinic Literature, but it is not known exactly where in the liturgy the invitation was recited in ancient times. There persists to this day a custom to recite it after the service concludes, and in some sources, it is associated with the *Kaddish*.[81] In any case, for over a thousand years, it has also been found here, introducing the section of liturgy called *Keri'at Shema U'Virkhoteha*, "The Recitation of the *Shema* And Its Blessings."

The theme of the first of the blessings is the daily rising of the sun at dawn, and in the evening, the daily setting of the sun and the emerging pinpoints of starlight. The changing light at dawn and dusk occasions poetry in this blessing—filtered through biblical creation imagery from Genesis, chapter 1—extolling God's creative power and celebrating the sun, moon, stars, and angels. Why the angels? As the commentary on *Eil Adon* in the Shabbat morning service makes clear, the stars were considered to be a class of angels; that is why a *Kedushah*, a prayer celebrating the angels' praise of God, is embedded in this the version of this blessing recited at the morning service.[82] This *Kedushah* is called *Kedushah DeYotser*, "The *Kedushah* of the Creator (Blessing)." The morning blessing refers to darkness several times and the evening blessing refers to light several times because they both reflect the arousal of human consciousness to the divine through changes in natural light. Feeling awestruck and pulled out of mundane consciousness can occur when we encounter fiery colors in the sky at dawn and dusk. This awareness may be behind the rule of the talmudic Sage, Rava, that each of

[81] It is alluded to in *Mishnah Berakhot* 7:3. It is specifically mentioned as a call and response in the Tannaitic midrash on The Book of Deuteronomy; see Louis Finkelstein, ed., *Sifrei on Deuteronomy* (Gezellschaft zur Forderung der Wissenschaft des Judentums, 1939, The Jewish Theological Seminary of America, 1969), Piska 306, p. 342. It is associated with the *Kaddish* in the post-talmudic *Massekhet Kallah* published by Nathan Coronel as part of *Ḥamisha Kunteresim*, Vienna, 1864, 4b-5a. See also Debra Reed Blank, "The Medieval French Practice of Repeating 'Qaddish' and 'Barekhu' for Latecomers to Synagogue," in Ruth Langer and Steven Fine, eds., *Liturgy in the Life of the Synagogue: Studies in the History of Jewish Prayer* (Winona Lake, Indiana: Eisenbrauns, 2005), 73-94.

[82] On the issue of why the *Kedushah* in every *Amidah* requires a *minyan* while this one and the *Kedushah DeSidra* at the conclusion of the morning service do not, see the following for sources and discussion: Ruth Langer, *To Worship God Properly: Tensions Between Liturgical Custom and Ḥalakhah in Judaism*, (Hebrew Union College Press, Cincinnati: 1998), Chapter 4, "Individual Recitation of the *Kedushah*: The Impact of Mysticism on Minhag and Halakhah," 188-244.

these two blessings must mention both light and darkness.[83] The context in which Rava is invoked is a discussion about why the opening words of this blessing amend a biblical text. Here is how the text occurs in the Book of Isaiah and how it is modified in the liturgy:

| **Isaiah 45:7** | **Liturgy** |
| --- | --- |
| I form light and create darkness;<br>I make peace and<br>create calamity—<br>*Oseh shalom u'vorei ra.* | I form light and create darkness;<br>I make peace and<br>create everything—<br>*Oseh shalom u'vorei et hakol.* |

The Talmud explains the liturgy's emendation of a biblical verse by positing the desire for *lishna ma'alya*, i.e., that the Sages preferred to use "lofty language," avoiding negative terms like *ra*, "calamity." An observation I haven't seen elsewhere is that a form of the word *kol*, "all," occurs at the end of the verse in Isaiah ("I, the Lord, do all—*hakol*—these things"), and therefore, likely affected the use of this term in the blessing. It is difficult to determine whether the talmudic discussion reflects any of the original reasoning for the emendation of the verse from Isaiah. The Sages who posit the language of the blessing in the talmudic discussion hail from a generation before Rava whose rule is then cited. And the "lofty language" idea is offered by the anonymous, editorial, voice of the Talmud from many generations later. It is possible that the later voice of the Talmud preserves earlier thinking, but it may also be an innovation conceived of many years after the fact. Similarly, there is a striking interpretation of this line of the liturgy from within a version of the famous, and lengthy, exposition on the greatness of peace. This discussion is linked to the last word of the Priestly Blessing, "and grant you peace" (Numbers 6:26). The Midrash comments: "Great is peace which is weighted equally with everything [*hakol*], [therefore] we say [in the blessing] *oseh shalom u'vorei et hakol*, "makes peace and creates everything."[84] And again, this interpretation may well reflect thoughts that antedate the origin of the blessing but may also preserve earlier thinking.

[83] Babylonian Talmud *Berakhot* 11b.

[84] *BeMidbar Rabba* 11:7. The commentary of Rabbi David Kimḥi (known as *Redak*, 1160-1235, Southern France), as well as of several 19th-20th-century commentators, on the verse from Isaiah reflects this understanding. See a fuller treatment of the entire blessing in Jeffrey Hoffman, *The Bible in the Prayer Book: A Study in Intertextuality*, D.H.L. Thesis, Jewish Theological Seminary of America, 1996, 25-43.

In any case, the verse from Isaiah itself reflects the themes and wording of the Creation story in Genesis with its use of "form" (*yotser*), "light" (*or*), "create" (*u'vorei*), "darkness" (*ḥoshekh*), "everything" (*khol*).

Wording from Genesis is invoked in the poetry throughout the many paragraphs of this blessing because it celebrates the rising and the setting of the sun as reenactments of the creation of the world. Reflecting this, the morning blessing twice declares God as "renewing creation every day, continuously, in his goodness." The morning blessing's text repeatedly strikes the creation theme in other ways. To graphically highlight just how central this theme is, I will cite a translation of this blessing in its entirety below; I have **bolded** those words that connect to the vocabulary of creation in Genesis as well as to angels:

> Blessed are you, *YHVH* our God, king of the universe, **former of light, creator of darkness, maker** of peace, **creator of all things.**
>
> He **illuminates** the earth for those who dwell on it, with compassion; and in his **goodness** renews every day, continually, the work of **creation**. How many are **your works** *YHVH*; you made them all with wisdom, **the earth** is full of your **possessions.** The king who alone is exalted from then, who is praised and glorified and uplifted, from the beginning of time. Eternal God, in your abundant mercy, have compassion on us, master, who is our strength, our rock, our stronghold shield of our deliverance, be a stronghold for us. The blessed almighty, great in knowledge, prepared and **made the rays of the sun**. The one who is all **good created** [the world] for the glory of his name: the **luminaries** he set around his stronghold [his throne]. **The leaders of his legions are holy beings (angels), the exalters of Shaddai** continually recount the glory of the almighty and his holiness. May you be blessed, *YHVH*, our God, for the praiseworthy **works of your hands, and for the light-giving luminaries which You formed**; they will glorify you forever.
>
> May you be blessed our **former**, our king, and our redeemer—**creator of holy beings.** Praised be your name forever, our king, who **forms ministering angels; and**

**whose ministering angels all stand at the height of the universe**, and proclaim with reverence, in unison aloud the words of the living God, king of the universe. **All of them are beloved, all of them are pure, all of them are mighty and all of them perform with awe and reverence the will of their creator. And they all open their mouths** in holiness and purity, with song and music, and they bless, and praise, and glorify, and revere, and sanctify, and proclaim the sovereignty of the name of the almighty, the king, the great, the mighty, the awesome one; holy is he. **And they all take upon themselves** the yoke of divine sovereignty **one from the other, and give leave to one another** to sanctify their **former** in a spirit of serenity with clear speech and pleasantness, all exclaim *Kedushah* in unison and reverently exclaim:

Holy, holy, holy is *YHVH* of hosts, the fullness of all the earth is His glory.

**The wheel-angels and the holy animal-faced angels, with a mighty sound rise toward the fiery angels. Facing each other,** they offer praise and say,

**Blessed is the glory of *YHVH* from his place.**

To the Blessed Almighty, they offer pleasant melodies; to the king, the almighty, living and enduring, they utter hymns and make praises heard. For he alone is **the performer of mighty deeds, maker of new things**; master of battles, **sower** of acts of righteousness, causer of deliverance **to sprout forth; creator** of cures. Awesome in praise, master of wonders, he renews in his **goodness, each day**, continuously, **the work of creation**, as it is said: "**Who makes the great luminaries**," for his kindness is everlasting (Psalms 136:7)." Shine a new light upon Zion and may we all soon merit its brightness. Blessed are You, *YHVH*, **former of the luminaries.**

The exaltation of the changing light as a sign of creation in this blessing is brought to a climax, toward the end of the blessing, with a midrash on Psalms 136:7. The larger context of the psalm makes it clear that the verb in this verse ought to be understood in the past tense:

> He **made** the great lights (i.e., the sun and the moon); his kindness is everlasting.

However, in the context of this blessing, the midrashic understanding takes the form of the verb, *l'oseh*, hyper-literally, yielding a transformation of the verb into the present tense, as if confirming that the daily rising and setting of the sun is a result of God's continuous and ongoing involvement in the creation of the world:

> He **makes** the great lights (i.e., the sun and the moon); his kindness is everlasting.

Immediately before its conclusion, the blessing offers a plea for messianic redemption:

> May you shine a new light upon Zion and may we all soon merit its light.

Rav Saadia Gaon, in one version of his 10th-century siddur, objects to this wording on the grounds that this blessing is not about the metaphorical light of redemption at the end of days, but rather about the daily renewal of the light of dawn.[85] While Rav Saadia is, of course, correct about the topic of this blessing, it bears mentioning that all three of the blessings surrounding the *Shema* in the morning service conclude with a plea for messianic redemption. This is not surprising in that the longing for messianic redemption permeates a great deal of Jewish liturgy and is mentioned in all kinds of prayers that otherwise are not related to redemption at all. In fact, if there is any surprise here, it is that none of the blessings surrounding the *Shema* in the evening service entreat God for messianic salvation.

The wording of the parallel blessing in the evening celebrates the oncoming night by poetically imagining that God "opens gates (of heaven)" into which the sun enters each evening, and from which the moon and stars emerge each night. Thus, God "rolls away light before darkness and darkness before light." The evening blessing specifies that God is called *Adonai Tzeva'ot.* This epithet is often translated as "Lord of hosts," meaning "Lord of multitudes," and refers to the clusters of stars. But that standard translation misses the military valence of the word *tzeva'ot*, and a better translation

[85] See I. Davidson, S. Assaf, B.I. Joel, eds., *Siddur R. Saadja Gaon* (Jerusalem: *Mekitzei Nirdamim*, 1941; 1985 reprint), 37 in commentary.

would be "Lord of legions," or even (less poetically), "Lord of battalions." The blessing is making the point that as the stars come out, we can better understand why one of God's names is "Lord of legions." The reason is that the orderly march of the constellations of stars across the sky reflects the marching orders, as it were, issued by their creator.

**Spiritual Commentary on the First Blessing Before the *Shema***

This blessing, whether the version recited in the morning or the evening, is the handiwork of one or more souls who experienced wonder at the changing hues and shades of the dusk and dawn sky, by the play of light and darkness, and by the glimmering light of the stars. To detach the recitation of this blessing from the arrival of dawn or dusk is to miss the point. Unfortunately, however, this point is often, if not routinely, missed by many devoted worshipers. One reason is probably that Jewish tradition has had a skeptical and suspicious, if not altogether negative, view of nature in the context of worship or study. This was likely in response to very strong biblical and rabbinic condemnations of enduring pagan worship of nature. A teaching from the *Mishnah* exemplifies this view:

> Rabbi Shimon says: He who is going along the way and repeating [his Torah study] but interrupts his repetition and says, "How beautiful is that tree! How beautiful is that ploughed field!"—Scripture reckons it to him as if he has become liable for his life.[86]

Specifically, about worship, the talmudic Sage Rav Kahana is recorded as saying:

> I consider irreverent one who prays in a field.[87]

Now, allow me to add that of course it is a generalization to declare that Jewish tradition has an essentially disparaging view of nature. There are many exceptions to this approach from all the eras of Jewish teaching. Nevertheless, it is my contention that the exceptions in this case do, indeed, prove the rule. Adherents of contemporary Jewish life may be surprised by this assertion because many Jewish teachers and leaders these days tend to espouse an overtly positive view of nature. The fact remains, though, that it would be

[86] *Mishnah Avot* 3:7.
[87] Babylonian Talmud *Berakhot* 34b.

difficult to locate many pre-modern Jewish teachings encouraging Jews to focus on features of nature, especially when praying. And yet, it is also my contention that the origin and purpose of this blessing would be missed if one recited it without paying attention—whether physically or inwardly—to the changing light of the morning or evening sky. In other words, this particular blessing is one of those precious exceptions to the generally suspicious Jewish view of nature. This blessing calls out for attention to nature as the sky transitions from darkness to light in the morning and from light to darkness at night. As the literary analysis above makes clear, the words of the blessing, whether for the morning or evening, are saturated with the feeling that there is something miraculous, something unmistakably divine, in the rising and setting of the sun.

I have found it helpful, while reciting this blessing, to visualize myself on the face of the earth, vis-à-vis the sun. This is one of those visualizations that is much easier to do now that we have seen innumerable photographs from space of the earth's alignment with the sun, moon, and planets within the solar system. In other words, I imagine in my mind's eye the earth rotating on its axis and try to locate—given the time of day or evening—where the line of the sun's light begins and ends in relation to where I am located. If it is early in the morning, the line of light begins quite close to where I am. If it is close to dusk, the line of light ends close to where I am. This kind of visualization can help us focus on something literally beyond ourselves and can enlarge our perspective, allowing us to transcend personal issues and focus instead on the day's new light and the evening's new darkness, the very cosmic events—as routine and familiar as they are—that this blessing celebrates.

Of course, reciting this blessing while outside, and with a view of the sky, is ideal. It is not, however, always practical. But it also raises the issue of whether, when praying indoors, we should try to situate ourselves near a window. The Talmud actually addresses this question:

> Rabbi Ḥiyya bar Abba said that Rabbi Yoḥanan said: One may only pray in a house with windows, as it is stated [with regard to Daniel's prayer]: "[In his attic] there were open windows facing Jerusalem." (Daniel 6:11)[88]

Rabbi Marc D. Angel, citing this source, writes thoughtfully about how windows may both inspire prayer and distract from prayer. On the one hand, he

[88] Babylonian Talmud *Berakhot* 34b.

considers the role of stained-glass windows "an attempt to keep the outside world outside... and (to) create an artificial world of inside spirituality." On the other hand, he references the synagogue of Rabbi Yosef Karo (16th c.) in Safed, Israel, where the clear windows open to the "wonderful mountainous scenery of the Galilee."[89] I'm sure that the effect of stained glass windows on the worshiper is a subjective matter: They may foster a sense of the spiritual for some people and they may detract from the spiritual for others. I found the deep reds and blues of the stained glass windows in a congregation I served for many years in Nyack, New York to be conducive to my own prayer experience simply because the rich colors filtering the sunlight struck a chord with my esthetic sensibility, and I have always felt that the esthetic/artistic sense and the spiritual sense are closely related. On the other hand, I have found that the naturally changing colors of the sky have more easily stirred me to pray. I have found myself praying *Minḥah*, the afternoon service, spontaneously, on my own, inspired by such diverse (and curious) settings as in the cavernous sanctuary the Cathedrale de Notre Dame in Paris—which possesses the most beautiful stained glass I've ever seen—and witnessing a rosy sunset in the mundane parking lot of a supermarket.

Simply put, the goal when we recite this blessing is to connect to the transcendent spirit that we can experience when we view an awe-inspiring sky.

## The Second Blessing Before the *Shema*

Just as there is a version of the first blessing before the *Shema* in the morning and another in the evening, so too are there two versions of the second blessing before the *Shema*. I will address the morning version first.

The morning version of the blessing is a complex and innovative literary creation in that it forms a kind of conversation with the first, biblical, paragraph of the *Shema*. In doing so, it celebrates Torah as a loving gift of God, and its language spans the past and present.

Firstly, let me address the dialogue between this blessing—known by its first two words, *Ahavah Rabbah*, "Great love," and the first paragraph of the *Shema*, *V'Ahavta*, "You Shall Love."[90] I posited in my commentary on the first paragraph of the *Shema* that the message of that paragraph is: "Each indi-

[89] "Prayer and Windows" in Rabbi Marc D. Angel, *The Rhythms of Jewish Living: A Sephardic Exploration of Jewish Spirituality* (Woodstock, Vermont: Jewish Lights, 2015), 21-23.

[90] Whether the title of the blessing should begin with the words *Ahavah Rabbah*, "Great Love," or *Ahavat Olam*," Eternal Love," is the subject of a dispute beginning in the Babylonian Talmud (*Berakhot* 11b) and leading to two different results. One is that in some rites (*Siddur Saadia Ga'on* and the Sephardic and Italian rites) *Ahavat Olam* was retained for both the morning and the evening. The other is based on a compromise worked out by the ancient academy of Pumbedita in Babylonia whereby *Ahavah Rabbah* is used in the morning and *Ahavat Olam* is used in the evening. See Elbogen, *Jewish Liturgy*, 19.

vidual among you shall love *YHVH* your God"—meaning loyalty—"through actions of your body and throughout your daily routine." The blessing too centers on the leitmotif of love as loyal action, meaning observance of the Torah. It co-opts the language of the biblical *V'Ahavta* paragraph by citing the root for "love" (*ahav*) no less than six times, and it is no coincidence that this root forms the first and last words of the blessing. This repeated usage of the root for "love" forms a strong literary link between the blessing and the biblical paragraph that follows it. The blessing's response to *V'Ahavta*'s command to love God is a request for the kind of love that God displayed toward the Patriarchs, namely that God teach to us *ḥukei ḥayyim*, "the laws of life"—which is to say, Torah—just as God taught our ancestors. There is a striking sentence in the blessing in which the blessing uses eight verbs in rapid, staccato, fashion, beseeching God to teach Torah to us as well. In it, we ask God to teach us...

| | |
|---|---|
| *Lehavin u'lehaskil,* | To understand, to comprehend, |
| *lishmo'a, lilmod u'lelameid,* | to listen, to learn, to teach, |
| *lishmor vela'asot u'lekayem.* | to observe, to do and to fulfill. |

In other words, the biblical *V'Ahavta* paragraph commands each individual to show loving loyalty to God bodily, in our daily routines, and this blessing responds, in effect, by saying: We will gladly show this kind of love to you, God, but in order to do that, we ask that you lovingly teach us Torah that we may understand it and observe it.

Part of the literary art of this part of this section is that while *V'Ahavta*, as a biblical passage, was composed many centuries before this blessing, the blessing appears immediately before *V'Ahavta* in the liturgy. Therefore, the worshiper, as it were, anticipates and "responds" to *V'Ahavta*'s command to lovingly observe Torah by first imploring God to lovingly teach us Torah. In these ways, the second blessing before the *Shema* in the morning service anticipates, and engages in a kind of dialogue, with the first paragraph of the *Shema*.

Secondly, the language in the blessing spans the past and the present. Put succinctly, the message is: God, just as you lovingly taught Torah to the Patriarchs in the past, so too, teach us now, in the present. This is based on many biblical examples in which a request to God is predicated on a kind of "motivating" phrase.[91] Here, the request is that God lovingly teach Torah

[91] On this, see Moshe Greenberg, *Biblical Prose Prayer: As a Window to the Popular Religion of Ancient Israel* (Berkeley and Los Angeles: University of California Press, 1983).

to us in the present, and the "motivation" is that we are the offspring of the Patriarchs to whom God had lovingly taught Torah in the past. Calling God "father" three times in the blessing is part of that "motivation," an attempt to elicit parental affection and devotion from God.[92] Toward the end of the blessing, the request to shower parental love on us—the distant descendants of the Patriarchs—is applied not only to teaching us Torah, but also to redeeming us from exile and restoring us to our land. The pattern in the blessing is:

> You, God, loved our ancestors in the past.
> Therefore, please extend that love to us as well in the present.
> Please remember your ancient connection with us in the past.

This outline may be traced graphically by following the tenses of the verbs in the blessing that are addressed to God:

| | |
|---|---|
| *Ahavtanu*, "you have loved us" | Past |
| *Ḥamalta*, "you have had compassion upon us" | Past |
| *VaTelemadeim*, "you taught them" (the Patriarchs) | Past |
| *Teḥoneinu*, "be gracious to us" | Present |
| *Raḥeim*, "deal mercifully with us" | Present |
| *VeTein*, "instill (in our hearts)" | Present |
| *VeHa'eir*, "enlighten (our eyes)" | Present |
| *VeDabeik*, "attach (our hearts)" | Present |
| *VeYaḥeid*, "unify (our hearts)" | Present |
| *VeHavi'einu*, "bring us" | Present |
| *VeTolikheinu*, "lead us" | Present |
| *Vaḥarta*, "you chose (us)" | Past |
| *VeKeiravtanu*, "you brought us near" | Past |

Thus, the version of this blessing in the morning service forms an impressive connection between present and past. This, along with its novel conversation with the first biblical paragraph of the *Shema*, marks it as a carefully crafted literary creation.

[92] *Avinu, avinu, ha'av*, "Our father, our father, father." For additional linguistic connections between the blessing and the biblical passage, see Jeffrey Hoffman, *The Bible in the Prayer Book: A Study in Intertextuality*, D.H.L. Thesis, Jewish Theological Seminary of America, 1996, 46-48.

The version of this blessing in the evening is a shorter and less complex composition and is called, from its first two words, *Ahavat Olam*, "Eternal Love." It, too, both begins and ends with the root for "love" (and mentions it one additional time as well), hence connecting with the first paragraph of the *Shema* which begins "You shall love." Its verbs too form a historical pattern:

> Because you, God, lovingly taught Torah to us in the past...
> We shall speak of, and rejoice in, your Torah in the present.
> Please never remove your love from us in the future:

| | |
|---|---|
| *Ahavta*, "you have loved" | Past |
| *Limadeta*, "you have taught" | Past |
| *Nasi'aḥ*, "we will speak" | Present |
| *VeNismaḥ*, "we will rejoice" | Present |
| *Nehgeh*, "we will meditate" | Present |
| *Tasir*, "remove" | Future |

Just as in the morning service, the evening service's text of this blessing too anticipates and is in dialogue with the first paragraph of the *Shema*. The biblical *V'Ahavta* paragraph commands each individual to show loving loyalty to God bodily, in our daily routines, and this blessing responds: We will indeed lovingly speak of, rejoice in, and meditate upon your Torah "day and night." Making the connection between the biblical and liturgical texts even clearer, the blessing's phrase *yomam valailah*, "day and night" echoes the biblical passage's *beshokhbekha u'vekumekha*, "when you lie down and when you wake up."

**Spiritual Commentary on the Second Blessing Before the *Shema***

I had a friend, Rabbi Pinḥas (Pinky) Saposh, who taught me an important lesson about the holiday of *Simḥat Torah*, which in turn, connects directly to this blessing. But first, a little about Pinky. We first met in June 1973, during the summer after we both graduated high school, in a counselor training program called *Mador* at Camp Ramah in the Berkshires, in New York State. We found that we had a lot in common, not least that we were both about to go to the same university, The State University of New York at Albany (where we decided to become suitemates), and that we were born on the same day in the same year. I discovered that Pinky was a great rock 'n roll dancer when we attended freshman dances ("mixers") hosted by the university's Jewish Students Coalition. His dancing involved amazing footwork, which I could never match. We went on to become roommates during our junior year in college, which we spent in Jerusalem, both of us attending Hebrew University as well as Brovender's Yeshivah. Pinky decided to remain in Israel at the end of the year, never to return to Albany or the U.S., and ultimately, became a Ḥaredi (ultra-Orthodox) rabbi.

The lesson I want to share is something Pinky taught me before he became Ḥaredi, and it is related to dancing. He pointed out that to dance with the Torah scroll on *Simḥat Torah*, we must hug the scroll close to our bodies as if we are performing a dance with a beloved partner. And so, every year on *Simḥat Torah*, Pinky attempted to arouse love, to feel his love, for Torah as he danced with it. Unfortunately, my friend passed away several years ago, but this teaching, among many others, will always stay with me. The dancing with the Torah on the holiday of *Simḥat Torah* is a once-a-year ecstatic expression of our love of Torah. The second blessing before the *Shema* is a twice-a-day meditative expression of our love of Torah. I understand "Torah" here in the largest sense: Not just the five books of Moses, nor the Bible as a whole, but the entirety of Jewish spiritual teachings over many, many centuries. This massive collection comprises the spiritual life of the Jewish People and this blessing is our love song to it. Just as Pinky would summon his love during his dance with the Torah scroll, so too might we, as we recite this blessing, stimulate and awaken our love and appreciation for the truly world-class spiritual legacy that is Torah. Reciting this blessing is the time to deeply feel how fortunate we are to be the heirs of one of the oldest sacred traditions in the world.

## The First Blessing After the *Shema*

In the morning service, this blessing is the only one that follows the *Shema*. In the evening service, this is the first of two or three blessings after the *Shema* depending upon which rite one uses; more about that when I discuss the third blessing after the *Shema* below. The blessing after the *Shema* in the morning is called, after its first two words, *Emet VeYatziv*, "True and Certain." The version in the evening is called, after its first two words, *Emet Ve'Emunah*, "True and Trustworthy."

There was a version of both the morning and evening text of this blessing already in talmudic times:

> Rabbah bar Ḥanina Saba said in the name of Rav: If one does not say "True and Certain" in the morning and "True and Trustworthy" at night, one has not fulfilled one's ob-

> ligation, for it is said, "To proclaim your steadfast love at daybreak, your faithfulness each night" (Psalms 92:3).[93]

However, as is the case for the vast majority of prayers mentioned in the Talmud, the full text is not given, and we cannot say how closely the talmudic texts resemble contemporary ones. In the contemporary Ashkenazic rite, the blessing recited in the morning consists of two parts. The first part of the blessing emphasizes the truth and eternity of the biblical passages of the *Shema* and mentions the word *emet*, "true," four times. The word *emet* is the first word of the blessing and commences a sixteen-word-long list of adjectives praising the truthfulness and perpetuity of the words of the *Shema*. This part of the blessing concludes with the words *ein Elohim zulatekha*, "There is no God but you." The second—and longer—part, which commences with the words *Ezrat avoteinu*, "The helper of our ancestors," emphasizes God's liberation of Israel from the Egyptians at the Red Sea but also includes wording celebrating God's saving power in every generation and concludes with a plea for God to rise up and save Israel in the present. This part of the blessing connects to the first part in that it, too, mentions *emet*, "truth," twice, but the bulk of the poetry concerns God's saving power at the Red Sea and includes two verses from *Shirat HaYam*, "The Song at the Sea," which Moses, Miriam, and the people sang in response to God's rescue at the Red Sea:

> Who is like you, O Lord, among the celestials;
> Who is like you, majestic in holiness.
> Awesome in splendor, working wonders. (Exodus 15:11)
> The Lord will reign for ever and ever. (Exodus 15:18)

Words relating to God's saving power occur some 14 times in this part of the blessing.[94] The *ḥatimah* ("seal") at the end of the blessing emphasizes the central theme of liberation in this blessing: "Blessed are you, who liberated Israel."

The version of this blessing recited in the evening is, like the previous two blessings, shorter than the version chanted in the morning. Its theme and its seal are identical to the version of this blessing recited in the morning, and it, too, includes the two verses from the Song at the Sea.

[93] Babylonian Talmud *Berakhot* 12a-b.

[94] *Ga'al*, "liberate"—6 times; *Azar*, "help"—3 times; *Padah*, "save"—3 times; *Yasha*, "deliver"—2 times.

Similarly, it emphasizes God's saving the people from Egyptian slavery but also acknowledges God's power to liberate not only in the past, but in the present as well.

### Spiritual Commentary on the First Blessing After the *Shema*

Not every people would want to recall that their origins were as slaves to a more powerful nation. One would think that just as an individual might want to forget and suppress traumatic and potentially embarrassing incidents of the past, a people too might want to at least de-emphasize negative experiences of the past. That is not the approach of the Jewish tradition, however. The Bible famously recalls explicitly that "you were slaves in Egypt" some 36 times. This blessing recited twice daily, keeps that painful past alive. Not only that, but it completely ignores any role that the people themselves played in their own salvation and ascribes their liberation entirely to God.

There are multiple effects of reciting this blessing consciously. One is that it cultivates an identity with oppressed individuals and peoples. The Jewish past as an oppressed people in Egypt, as well as its history of persecution at the hands of many majority cultures in the diaspora, creates sympathy with subjugated communities wherever they are. The Jewish People are the natural partners of the oppressed and this blessing instills that identity on a twice-daily basis.

Additionally, the ascription of our liberation to God, rather than to people, fosters the notion that liberation is essentially a spiritual process. It begins internally, when an individual or a community realizes that every human being is of infinite value, having been created in the image of God. Therefore, human beings are not subject to any ultimate authority except for God. Reciting this blessing elevates human freedom to the level of a foundational spiritual value.

## The Second Blessing After the *Shema* (evening)

In the morning service, the *Amidah* directly follows the conclusion of the blessing discussed immediately above. In the evening service, there are two more blessings before the *Amidah*. The first one is called, after its first word, *Hashkiveinu*, "Lay Us Down." A blessing beginning with this word is mentioned in the Talmud,[95] but only the first word, and so the ancient wording of the full blessing is not known.

[95] Babylonian Talmud, *Berakhot* 4b.

This blessing is clearly a plea for protection from fears of the night. That is obvious from its opening line which asks God to "Lay us down in peace and awaken us to life." In ancient times, the night was experienced as much darker than in the current era of abundant artificial light. While oil lamps were widely available in the talmudic era, oil was not cheap, and it was difficult to light more than a small area. The nighttime remained a time of insecurity. Thus, the blessing repeatedly requests that God "protect" us and envelop us in "peace"—the Hebrew roots for each of these, *shamar* and *shalom*, recur three times in this short paragraph.

The fears that the dark of night elicit are evoked, with six of them explicitly mentioned:

| | |
|---|---|
| *Oyev* | "Enemies" |
| *Dever* | "Pestilence" |
| *Ḥerev* | "Sword" (i.e., violence) |
| *Ra'av* | "Famine" |
| *Yagon* | "Sorrow" |
| *Sattan* | "Satan" |

Yes, "Satan" (*Sattan* in Hebrew) is specifically mentioned at the end of this list. In Jewish tradition, the notion of an evil angel with this name developed. While the characterization of the *Sattan* in Jewish tradition does not exactly match the image of Satan in either Christian, Muslim, or modern/secular thought, it doesn't completely differ either. The main aspect of the *Sattan* in Jewish tradition is that of a supernatural adversary, not unlike the character of the same name in the biblical Book of Job.

The wording in the first sentence of the blessing, "awaken us to life," reflects the talmudic belief that sleep is a kind of death:

> Fire is one-sixtieth of the fire of Gehennom (hell).
> Honey is one-sixtieth of manna.
> Shabbat is one-sixtieth of the World-to-Come.
> Sleep is one-sixtieth of death.
> A dream is one-sixtieth of prophecy.[96]

Rabbi Elliot Dorff points out that a blessing recited early in the morning reflects this same idea that sleep resembles death. Upon awakening, we recite,

[96] Babylonian Talmud, *Berakhot* 57b. This idea is found in the works of Shakespeare as well. See S. Viswanathan, "Sleep and Death: The Twins in Shakespeare," *Comparative Drama*, 13:1, Spring, 1979, 49-64.

in the section, *Birkhot HaShaḥar*, "Morning Blessings:" Blessed are you, Restorer of souls to dead bodies.[97]

In sum, this is a blessing invoking God's protection as we enter the uncertainty of night.

**Spiritual Commentary the Second Blessing After the *Shema* (Evening)**

Most moderns do not believe that sleep is akin to death, nor do most of us believe in a literal Satan. Nevertheless, there is something grounding about ending the day with a prayer for inner peace. Just as beginning one's day with meditative intention and prayer helps frame the day with a sense of the transcendent, so too ending the day with prayerful words bringing closure to the day's activities provides a calming bookend. The blessing's phrase *U'vetzeil kenafekha tastireinu*, "Shelter us in the shadow of your wings" is particularly evocative.

The "shadow" cast by God's "wings" may be the blessing's poetic recasting of the darkness of night into a warm and reassuring symbol. Reciting this blessing could be viewed as a path to a night of peaceful, restorative rest and sleep.

## The Third Blessing After the *Shema* (evening)

A third blessing following the *Shema* in the evening service is recited only by Ashkenazic Jews who live outside the Land of Israel. All of the primary sources agree that it was added as a substitute for the *Amidah*. According to the *Mishnah*, reciting an *Amidah* in the evening is not obligatory[98] and, the theory goes, some Jews felt a need to add an alternative to the evening service which already included the *Shema* and Its Blessings. However, there are two puzzles associated with this blessing. The first is that while the sources say that this blessing is an alternate to the *Amidah* because the blessing includes either 18 mentions of God's name, *YHVH*, or 18 biblical verses to symbolize the original 18 blessings of the *Amidah*, not one of the versions of this blessing in the various current or historical rites contains the 18 biblical verses or instances of God's name. Many, including the current Ashkenazic version, contain more than eighteen. The second puzzle is that while it became the nearly universal custom to add an actual *Amidah* to the evening service sometime soon after the close of the talmudic era, why was this "alternate" retained as well?

[97] Cited in Lawrence A. Hoffman, ed., *My People's Prayer Book: Traditional Prayers, Modern Commentaries*, 9:87.

[98] *Mishnah Berakhot* 4:1.

There have been any number of supposed solutions offered to the first puzzle of the non-existent 18 mentions, including ways to consider only *some* of the verses or only *some* mentions of *YHVH* as part of the 18 and the rest as part of supplementary material to the blessing, but all of the attempts seem artificial. My best guess is that the original version of this blessing did, indeed, contain biblical verses that contained 18 mentions of *YHVH*. Prayers that are mainly comprised of biblical verses tend to develop varying forms over the centuries, with some communities favoring certain verses, and other communities citing alternate verses. That is especially true of prayers that developed after the talmudic period such as *Pesukei DeZimra*, the first paragraph of *Havdalah*, and the service for taking out the Torah on Shabbat and Festivals. On the other hand, prayers comprising biblical verses that developed during the talmudic period, e.g., *Hallel* and the three biblical passages of the *Shema*, attained an aura of canonization and did not develop variations. Because this blessing developed after the era of the Talmud, several forms of the blessing developed over time, with different lists of verses and without regard to how many verses or examples of *YHVH* they contained, because the original purpose of the blessing was not always remembered. That is perhaps why we do not know of any examples of this blessing in which there are neither 18 mentions of God's name nor 18 biblical verses.

Elbogen offers a possible resolution to the second puzzle of why this blessing persisted even once an *Amidah* was added to the evening service and an alternate *Amidah* was no longer needed: It is possible that there were originally two customs, one corresponding to the Land of Israel and the other to Babylonia. "It may be that in one of the two lands, the *'Amida* was said, and in the other a substitute was said."[99] Thus, both practices acquired the kind of "sanctity" and authority that years of repetition can bestow; ultimately, both were retained even though this contradicts the original purpose of reciting an alternative to the *Amidah*.

Partially because of the somewhat unsatisfactory resolutions to these two puzzles, this blessing has not survived in all current rites. Sephardic practice omitted the blessing a thousand years ago. Ḥasidic practice is to omit it and the current practice in the Land of Israel—whether Ashkenazic or Sephardic—is to omit this blessing. The contemporary Reform siddur omits it, and the current siddur of the Reconstructing Judaism Movement offers an abridged version of the blessing.[100] Therefore, only Orthodox and

[99] See Elbogen, *Jewish Liturgy*, 88, who also sums up a number of the artificial attempts to count eighteen names of God in the various forms of this blessing.
[100] *Kol Haneshamah: Daily*, 289.

Conservative Ashkenazim outside the Land of Israel have retained a full version of this blessing.

In terms of content, the blessing defies a unified message. It does contain verses that request or mention God's protection during the day as well as during the night and the end of the blessing contains a petition for the messianic age to dawn. But not many of the lines refer to any of these ideas. Perhaps the content of the verses themselves are beyond the point. Perhaps the goal in this blessing is to mention God's name over and over, so that the overall effect of the verses is simply to invoke God's presence as night approaches more than anything else.

**Spiritual Commentary the Third Blessing After the *Shema* (Evening)**

As we saw, the original purpose of this blessing was as a symbolic stand-in for the 18-blessing *Amidah*, possibly by mentioning God's name 18 times. If so, the blessing evokes the entire *Amidah* by simply calling upon God's name over and over. In a way, this blessing teaches that the essential meaning of the *Amidah* is simply to call upon God's name; that is, to connect with the divine knowingly and intentionally. To become conscious of God's presence, without adding any of the content that the *Amidah* provides. This is both a very simple and a very profound idea. For all the supposed sophistication of this, and every other, commentary on the prayer book, the essence of all prayer is not so sophisticated: It is to be in conscious connection with God. If noticing and reciting God's name over and over in this blessing—not merely reading or pronouncing the words—brings us to that consciousness, then I would say we have achieved the most critical and important purpose of prayer. Viewed in this way, this blessing offers a precious opportunity to awaken us from semi-conscious recitation to true prayer.

Related to this blessing:

- See above, the discussion about the inner meaning of God's name, *YHVH*, in the commentary on the first line of the *Shema*, on page 32.
- See the commentary on a prayer that is also viewed as one long name of God, *Ana V'Kho'aḥ* in the *Kabbalat Shabbat* service, on see page 226.

## The Torah Service

The chanting of the entire Torah and selections from the Prophets is one of the oldest elements in Jewish liturgy. In fact, it appears that chanting from these parts of the Bible, accompanied by sermons and or study, constituted the main functions of early synagogues. This role of the early synagogue likely preceded communal worship. Synagogues emerged "as the central communal institution of Jewish communities throughout Judaea and the Diaspora" in the first century, CE—including while the Temple in Jerusalem still stood—and there is evidence that some synagogues or proto-synagogues may have existed as early as the third century BCE in Egypt.[101] Portions from the Torah (and on some of the following occasions, from the Prophets as well) are chanted each week as part of the morning service on Mondays, Thursdays and Shabbat; at the afternoon service on Shabbat; and at the morning service on every day of the Three Pilgrimage Festivals, *Rosh HaShanah, Yom Kippur, Ḥanukkah , Purim, Rosh Ḥodesh* (the beginning of each lunar month), and on fast days. In talmudic times, the entire Torah was read on a triennial basis (i.e., in three years) in the Land of Israel, and on an annual system (i.e., in one year) in Babylonia.[102] The service surrounding these readings is the topic at hand. The specific prayers in this service vary slightly depending upon the occasion, i.e., weekday, Shabbat, Festival; morning or afternoon service. Here, I will present some of the major elements of that service. An additional element in the Festival Torah Service, the chanting of the Thirteen Attributes of God, is addressed in the Festival Services section of this book.

According to Elbogen, "The most ancient sources do not know of any special prayers before, during, or after the reading of the Torah. The Torah was removed and replaced without any special ceremony, and the reading was not interrupted by prayers. This changed completely in the course of time... It is no longer only the words read from the Torah that are honored, but the Torah itself."[103] This observation will link with an innovation I will

[101] Lee I. Levine, *The Ancient Synagogue: The First Thousand Years* (New Haven: Yale University Press, 2000), 19-20. Levine's nearly 750-page *magnum opus* is a classic in the field. See also the insights as well as the primary and secondary sources listed in the following works: Most recently, Steven Fine, "The Emergence of the Synagogue," in Frederick E. Greenspahn, ed., *Early Judaism: New Insights and Scholarship* (New York: New York University Press, 2018), 123-146; Idem, *The Emergence of the Synagogue in the Ancient World* (New York: Oxford University Press/Yeshiva University Museum, 1996); and the papers from a conference held at The Jewish Theological Seminary of America and edited by Lee I. Levine, *The Synagogue in Late Antiquity* (New York: The Jewish Theological Seminary of America, 1987).

[102] Babylonian Talmud, *Megillah* 29b.

[103] See his *Jewish Liturgy: A Comprehensive History*, 158-159 where he cites *Mishnah Yoma* 7:1 and *Sotah* 7:7. For a comparative study of talmudic descriptions with the archeological evidence of The

describe in the Spiritual Commentary, below. The first source that offers details of prayers—mostly biblical verses—for the taking out of the Torah from the Ark, but not for returning it, derives from the early medieval period in Europe.[104] Probably on this basis, a brief prayer service thereafter developed for both taking out and returning the Torah to the Ark. However, as is true for many liturgies developed after the authoritative talmudic period, the actual wording varies greatly among the many rites of Jewish worship.

Here, then, is the analytical commentary on a few major elements of the Ashkenazic version of The Torah Service.

When the Ark is open for the Torah to be removed and read, Numbers 10:35 is recited:

> Advance, O Lord!
> May your enemies be scattered,
> And may your foes flee before you!

The very next verse from the Book of Numbers is chanted many pages later in the siddur—and many minutes later in the synagogue service—as the Torah is replaced in the Ark:

> Return, O Lord,
> You who are Israel's myriads of thousands.[105]

Because these two verses are chanted at such a distance from each other, the typical worshiper could not be blamed for missing the fact that in their original biblical context, one verse actually follows immediately on the other. However, in the Torah itself, the two verses describe recurring events distanced from each other in both time and space. They contain two lines of prayer that Moses would say invoking divine protection at the beginning and at the end of each portion of the march from Egypt to the Land of Israel. He would speak these lines as if the Ark contained God's presence. Thus,

---

Torah Service, see Jeffrey Hoffman, "The Ancient Torah Service in Light of the *Realia* of the Talmudic Era" *Conservative Judaism*, winter, 1989-90, 41-48. See more recently, Steven Fine and Aaron Koller, eds., *Talmuda de-Eretz Israel: Archaeology and the Rabbis in Late Antique Palestine* (Boston/Berlin: De Gruyter, 2014).

[104] Tractate *Soferim* 14:8-14.

[105] "Others 'Return, O Lord, unto the ten thousands of the families of Israel.'" So, NJPS. A third understanding is reflected in Joshua 10:12-13, Judges 5:20 and the ancient midrash, *Sifrei* Numbers 84 in which "Israel's myriads of thousands on earth are the counterpart of the Lord's hosts in heaven." Cited in Jacob Milgrom, *The JPS Torah Commentary: Numbers* (Philadelphia, New York: The Jewish Publication Society, 1990), 81, and n. 67.

the Ark itself was viewed as a powerful ritual object, protecting the people from hostility and even possessing the power to kill (see the story of Uzza in II Samuel 6:1-7 and I Chronicles 13:9-12).

In the Torah, the Ark moves, representing God's Presence, God's protecting power, scattering enemies, and the people move with it.[106] In the synagogue, on the other hand, the Torah scroll moves—is carried—around the circumference of the prayer space with the leaders of the congregation following it. In this way, a symbolic reenactment occurs. In the biblical desert, the Ark (which contained the stone tablets of the covenant) travels with the people on their march to protect them from adversaries; in the synagogue, the contents of the contemporary Ark, the Torah scroll, marches around the people. In both cases, the same lines of prayer are recited, which petition God for protection. In the case of the desert wanderings, the Ark itself provides that protection. In the synagogue, the Torah scroll performs that function. In both cases, the Ark or its contents are perceived as possessing divine power to protect. It is probably not a coincidence that calling on God to defend and guard the Jewish People is echoed in another prayer in the Torah Service that is recited just before reading from the Torah itself, *Av HaRaḥamim*, "Father of Mercy," which begins as follows: "Father of mercy, have mercy on the overburdened nation (i.e., Israel) and remember the covenant of the mighty and rescue us from difficult times..."

Following the first of Moses' prayers, and before the Torah scroll is removed from the Ark, another biblical verse is recited and it, too, evokes a reenactment... with a twist. Part of Isaiah 2:3 (bolded below) is chanted:

> And the many people shall go and say:
> "Come let us go up to the Mount of the Lord,
> To the House of the God of Jacob:
> That he may instruct us in his ways,
> And that we may walk in his paths."
> **For Torah shall come forth from Zion,**
> **The word of the Lord from Jerusalem.**

The New JPS translation clarifies that "Torah shall come forth" means that "oracles will be obtainable." So, the meaning of this verse in the context of

[106] In two passages (Num. 2:17; 10:21), the Ark travels in the midst of the people, with the Levites surrounding it. In another (Num. 10:33), it travels at the head of the people, in front of them. Regarding Num. 10:33, "The Ark of the Covenant of the Lord traveled in front of them,"—"The contradiction with verse 21 and 2:17 is self-evident...Some rabbis conjecture that there were two Arks, one in front and one in their midst." (Sif. Num. 82)—Jacob Milgrom, *The JPS Torah Commentary: Numbers*, 80 and n. 57.

the Book of Isaiah is that "in the days to come" (Isaiah 2:2), "many people," i.e., non-Israelite people, will join Israel in accessing God's word in "Zion," which is another word for Jerusalem. However, when the verse is chanted in the new context of the Torah Service its meaning is changed. Here, the Ark has just been opened, revealing scrolls of Torah as the words "Torah shall come forth from Zion, the word of the Lord from Jerusalem" are sung. The implication seems to be that the scrolls of Torah in the synagogue's Ark contain "the word of the Lord," and that the opening of the Ark has symbolically opened a passageway to Jerusalem, the source of God's teachings. This notion links with a famous theme in Jewish folklore that there is a hidden cave in the Diaspora that leads travelers directly, and almost instantly, to Jerusalem.[107] Chanting this part of the Isaiah verse in front of the open Ark serves to transform the Ark into a kind of mystical gateway to the presence of God in Jerusalem.

The blessings that precede and follow each *aliyah*, or section, of Torah that is chanted contain a theology of their own.[108] Both blessings conclude by praising God as *notein haTorah*, "The Giver of Torah." As Ruth Langer has pointed out, this phrase harks back to God's giving of the Torah at Mount Sinai described in Exodus 19-20 and Deuteronomy 5.[109] The connection to Sinai in these blessings was also commented upon by the 14th-century *Arba'ah Turim*, who noticed that they encompass 49 words (which is accurate for the contemporary version of these blessings as well), paralleling the 49 days that Moses remained on Mount Sinai.[110] The image of Sinai is also invoked in the chanting of Deuteronomy 4:44 during the Torah Service. This is the

[107] See S.Y. Agnon's version, *Ma'aseh Ha'Ez*, translated into English in *Commentary* Magazine, December 1966, as "The Cave to the Holy Land." See another version in Howard Schwartz, *Gabriel's Palace: Jewish Mystical Tales* (Oxford University Press, 1993), chapter 81, 164-166. Schwartz says in his commentary, 320: "This is a variant of one of the most famous oral tales in Jewish lore." The version in *Commentary* was accessed April 13, 2022, https://www.commentary.org/articles/s-agnon/three-stories-fable-of-the-goat

[108] While the text of the first blessing is found in the Talmud—*Berakhot* 11b—there, it is to be recited before daily Torah study, not as part of the public reading of the Torah. The text of the second blessing is post-talmudic.

[109] Ruth Langer has published two excellent analyses of the blessings, history, and meaning of The Torah Service in general. See her "From Study of Scripture to a Reenactment of Sinai: The Emergence of the Synagogue Torah Service" in *Worship*, 72.1, January 1998, 50. See also her "Sinai, Zion and God in the Synagogue: Celebrating Torah in Ashkenaz," in eds. Ruth Langer and Steven Fine, *Liturgy in the Life of the Synagogue: Studies in the Ḥistory of Jewish Prayer* (Winona Lake, Indiana: Eisenbrauns, 2005), 121-159. She summarized her research in her commentary in Lawrence A. Hoffman, ed., *My People's Prayer Book: Seder K'riat HaTorah*, vol. 4, 19-27. See also the interesting comments of Joseph H. Prouser, "Open Ye the Gates: Procedure for Returning the Torah to the Ark," in Robert A. Harris, Jonathan S. Milgram, eds., *Hakol Kol Yaakov: The Joel Roth Jubilee Volume* (Leiden, Boston: Brill, 2021), 409-417.

[110] R. Yaakov ben Asher, *Arba'ah Turim, Oraḥ Ḥayyim* 139. And see *Oraḥ Ḥayyim* 47 where the worshiper is to have the revelation at Mount Sinai in mind when reciting the first of the blessings each morning before the study of Torah. The latter passage is cited in Issachar Jacobson, *Netiv Binah*, 2:218.

verse chanted at the conclusion of the Torah reading when the scroll is lifted and displayed to the congregation (Sephardic custom has this done before the reading of the Torah): "This is the Torah which Moses presented to the Israelites." In the context of the Book of Deuteronomy, the word "Torah" in this verse refers to all of the teachings that Moses imparted to the Israelites just before they entered the Land of Israel. In the context of the Torah Service however, the word "Torah" refers to the scroll that is held aloft as this verse is chanted with the implication that this very scroll in this synagogue is the same Torah that Moses revealed to the Israelites back at Sinai. Originally, only Deuteronomy 4:44 was chanted; later the following words were added: "At the command of the Lord through Moses."[111] This addition seems to clarify that God, and not Moses, was the source of the Torah. The Zohar too interpreted this ritual as connecting to Sinai: "When the Torah scroll is lifted onto there (the pulpit), the whole people should arrange themselves in awe and fear, trembling and quaking, all below, intending in their hearts as if they were now standing at Mount Sinai to receive the Torah... Only one person is allowed to chant the Torah, and all should be silent and hear from his mouth, as if they were receiving it at that moment from Mount Sinai."[112]

Together, these several verbal cues to Sinai frame the reading of the Torah as a kind of mythic experience and as something more than the content of any given week's Torah portion. As Langer puts it, "The ritual reading of the Torah then, is not simply an act of study, but a reenactment of Sinai itself."[113]

The blessing before each portion of Torah reading sounds the theme of the Jewish People as the chosen people, as do a number of other blessings and prayers including the *Kiddush* for Shabbat and Festivals and all the *Amidot* for Festivals and the High Holidays. The Torah reading blessing says simply, "who has chosen us (*baḥar banu*) from among all the peoples and gave to us his Torah." The Conservative siddur retains the traditional blessing and accurately translates it. However, on the words "who has chosen us," it comments, "At the moment of approaching the Torah, one may feel especially chosen and may also experience the moment as being directly commanded."[114] Here, it removes the thorny issue of chosenness from the realm of nations to the realm of the individual. This allows retention of the conventional text

[111] This phrase occurs several times in the Torah including Numbers 4:37, 45; 9:23; 10:13.
[112] Zohar 2:206a. Translation by Daniel c. Matt, ed., *The Zohar: Pritzker Edition* (Stanford, California: Stanford University Press, 2011), 6:174-175.
[113] "From Study of Scripture to a Reenactment of Sinai: The Emergence of the Synagogue Torah Service," 52. For another view of The Torah Service as a kind of drama, see Michal Govrin, "Jewish Ritual as a Genre of Sacred Theater," *Conservative Judaism*, Vol. 36(3), Spring, 1983, 15-34.
[114] *Siddur Lev Shalem for Shabbat & Festivals*, 2016, 172.

without dealing directly with the questions of chosenness and superiority of the nation of Israel. (See the discussion of chosenness and the liturgy in the commentary on the *Amidah* for Festivals, beginning on page 323). The Reform siddur also retains the traditional wording and accurately translates "who has chosen us" but instead of "from among all the peoples," it translates "from among the peoples."[115] This is a subtle change from the original Hebrew, slightly softening the "us vs. them" impact. The Reform siddur also offers an alternative blessing, but only in English:

> HOLY ONE OF BLESSING, your Presence fills creation. You have enlightened this path with the wisdom of Torah, giving it to the Jewish people as their particular way. Blessed are You, Merciful One, who gives this Torah to the Jewish people.[116]

By emphasizing "their particular way" and "who gives this Torah," the alternative blessing carries the message that Torah is the way of the Jewish people with the implication that other peoples, too, may have their God-given "path."

The Reconstructing Judaism *siddurim* avert a direct comparison of the Jewish People to other nations by reformulating the Hebrew and the English of the first blessing as, "who has drawn us to your service" (*keravnu la'avodato*).[117] One approach among Renewal congregations is also to reject the traditional notion of Jewish chosenness of this blessing in both languages by substituting the words *im kol* ("with all [the peoples]) for the similar sounding *mikol* ("from among all [the peoples]).[118] Thus, the blessing reads "who has chosen us <u>with</u> all the peoples" instead of "who has chosen us <u>from</u> among all the peoples."

I cited the Zohar, the 13th-century Kabbalistic classic, above on the theme of reenacting the giving of the Torah at Mt. Sinai during the Torah Service. On that same page of the Zohar, it recommends a particular prayer to be recited during the Torah Service. That prayer in Aramaic—the language of the Zohar—was indeed later added to the Torah Service as a result of the influence of Rabbi Isaac Luria (16th c., Safed, Israel). It begins *Berikh shemeih*

115 *Mishkan T'filah: A Reform Siddur*, 2007, 106-107.
116 Ibid., 107.
117 The editions for Shabbat and the High Holidays reflect the language of the daily siddur, *Kol Haneshamah: Limot Ḥol/Daily Prayer Book*, 1996, 152-153.
118 See, for example, Rabbi David Zaslow, *Ivdu Et Hashem B'Simcha: A Siddur for Spiritual Renewal* (Ashland Oregon: We! The Wisdom Exchange, 1997, 2003), 117.

*demareih alma*, "Blessed be the name of the master of the world." It is recited in the Torah Service on Shabbat and, in some traditions, on weekdays as well, but not on holidays. Daniel Matt points out several interesting aspects of this prayer.[119] Firstly, the prayer contains the line, "Not in a human do I put my trust, nor in a son of God..." Matt notes that the phrase "son of God" (*bar elahin*) can mean angel (cf. Daniel 3:25, 28), but that here, "this wording probably represents a polemic against Christian belief." Secondly, this is the only prayer found in the Zohar that entered the liturgy. Thirdly, because of its prominent place in the liturgy, this prayer has become the most famous passage in the Zohar. That is ironic because, as Matt points out, the entire prayer, as well as the recommendation that it be recited in the Torah Service, are likely later additions to the Zoharic text and do not appear in the more reliable manuscripts of the Zohar!

On the Three Pilgrimage Festivals, two additional prayers are added to the Torah Service: The Thirteen Attributes of God and Psalm 19:15 (*Va'Ani tefillati*, "As for me, my prayer is")—each of which is chanted three times. For the commentary on these, see the section on liturgy of The Three Festivals, beginning on page 331

**Spiritual Commentary on the Torah Service**

The biblical verses and prayers of the Torah Service that surround the reading of the Torah connect the worshiper to two historically spiritual locations: Jerusalem and Sinai. Because of this, the worshiper who is sensitive to the wording of the blessings that precede and follow the actual Torah reading will understand that the Torah Service is more than the content of the Torah reading itself. It is the occasion of a community gathering to celebrate its historical roots in Jerusalem and at Mount Sinai. And when the Torah is actually read, the worshiper is meant to not only be reminded of Israel's origin stories and its wisdom, but to experience the Torah reading as a communal chanting linking us to the generation of Moses and to God. It is a mythic moment, a mythic retelling of story and law. It is for that reason that even the most liberal congregations preserve the Torah reading in the Hebrew language. The meaning of the Torah reading goes beyond its translation into the vernacular. It is meant to sound archaic. It is also for that reason that even the most liberal congregations chant from a Torah scroll made of animal skins. While the Torah is obviously widely available in both book form and digital format, the antiquated medium of the scroll evokes the

[119] Daniel C. Matt, *The Zohar: The Prizker Edition*, 6:175, n. 200.

mythic quality of the Torah Service. And so, whatever our level of Hebrew comprehension, it can be spiritually rewarding to occasionally listen to the Torah reading without the aid of a Hebrew or Hebrew-English book, and to just let the Hebrew words, chanted in a pre-modern melody, wash over us.

The idea that the Torah scroll contains mystical power to guard and defend the Jewish people would probably not resonate with most modern worshipers. Still, a slight tweak of that notion might be meaningful. The idea that the contents of the Torah—its teachings, laws, and stories—might metaphorically, if not literally, protect the Jewish People may well sound a deep and resonant chord for contemporary Jews. That approach might connect closely with the great honor that the Torah Service confers upon the Torah.

I'd also like to suggest a completely different, almost opposite, approach to the Torah Service. I cited Ismar Elbogen above to the effect that in talmudic times, there was no Torah Service per se. From all we can glean from the literary and archeological sources, the Torah scroll was simply brought in from another room, or taken down from a nave, and chanted. No biblical verses, no additional prayers. Only the Torah reading itself prefaced by a blessing and followed by a blessing. Several times, I witnessed a Torah Service led by Rabbi Sally Shore-Wittenberg, who reenacted the talmudic era and chanted no verses or prayers for taking out and replacing the Torah scroll; only the blessings before and after reading each Torah section. The wisdom of this approach was palpable to the participants in that service. It served to highlight and feature the Torah reading itself. The prayers and circling of the congregation with the scroll—both before and after the Torah reading—can take up quite a bit of time in the service, especially on Shabbat and holidays, and can obscure the Torah reading itself. As Elbogen wrote, "It is no longer only the words read from the Torah that are honored, but the Torah itself." Shore-Wittenberg's innovation in following the talmudic practice was to honor the Torah reading itself.

# Part Two:

# Weekday Services

## The Weekday *Amidah*

The *Amidah*, meaning "[Prayer recited while] Standing," is one of the two oldest and most important sections of any worship service, along with the *Shema* and its blessings. In one way, the *Amidah* may be viewed as even more important than the *Shema* in that the *Amidah* is recited at every worship service, three times a day, while the *Shema* is recited only twice a day, during the *Shaḥarit*, morning, service, and the *Ma'ariv*, evening, service. The *Amidah* is a set of 19 blessings with a discernable internal structure, although that structure is not quite as neatly arranged as many commentaries—ancient and modern—claim. More about that below. Here are the titles of the 19 blessings:

1. *Magein Avraham*—Shield of Abraham
2. *Meḥayei HaMeitim*—Reviver of the Dead
3. *Ha'Eil HaKadosh*—Holy God
4. *Ḥonein HaDa'at*—Gracious Giver of Knowledge
5. *HaRotzeh BiTeshuvah*—Desirer of Repentance
6. *Ḥanun HaMarbeh Lislo'aḥ*—God Who Graciously and Abundantly Forgives
7. *Go'Eil Yisrael*—Liberator of Israel
8. *Rofei Ḥolei Amo Yisrael*—Healer of the Sick of His People Israel
9. *Mevareikh HaShanim*—Blesser of the Years
10. *Mekabeitz Nidḥei Amo Yisrael*—Gatherer of the Dispersed of His People Israel
11. *Melekh Oheiv Tzedakah U'Mishpat*—King, Love of Righteousness and Justice
12. *Shoveir Oyvim U'Makhni'a Zeidim*—Breaker of Enemies and Humbler of the Arrogant
13. *Mish'an U'Mivtaḥ LaTzaddikim*—Support and Trust of the Righteous
14. *Boneh Yerushalayim*—Builder of Jerusalem
15. *Matzmi'aḥ Keren Yeshua*—Grower of the Horn of Salvation
16. *Shomei'a Tefillah*—Listener to Prayer
17. *HaMaḥazir Shekhinato LeTzion*—Restorer of His Presence to Zion
18. *HaTov Shimkha U'Lekha Na'eh LeHodot*—Your Name is "Goodness" And To You It Is Pleasant To Offer Thanksgiving

19. *HaMevareikh Et Amo BaShalom*—The Blesser of Peace to His People Israel

No modern scholar holds that the *Amidah* existed during biblical times. There is plenty of evidence of prayer in the biblical period, but there is no evidence that the *Amidah* existed in such early times. To this day, most traditional Jewish sources do not consider the obligation of daily prayer as biblical in origin.[120] The earliest references we have about the *Amidah* are in the oldest stratum of Rabbinic Literature, known as Tannaitic literature (from approximately 100-225 CE), which post-date the biblical period by a few hundred years.

While there are brief references to the *Amidah* in Tannaitic literature, in most of them, the *Amidah* is mentioned simply in passing. There is, however, one passage from the Mishnah (*Berakhot* 4:3-4) that seems to be speaking directly about the origin of this central prayer. It consists of notes from a debate on what form an "official" version of an *Amidah* ought to take, and, indeed, whether there even ought to be an "official" version:

> Rabban Gamaliel says: Every day, a person ought to pray 18 [blessings].
> Rabbi Yehoshua says: An abbreviated 18.
> Rabbi Akiva says: If he is fluent with it, let him pray 18; if not, an abbreviated 18.
> Rabbi Eliezer says: If he makes his prayer set, his prayer is not a true supplication [and therefore, is not acceptable to God].[121]

This mishnah records what may be just the barest outline of what may have been a long and contentious argument about consolidating and unifying Jewish worship. The expression "18 blessings," or simply "18," refers to the

[120] And even Rambam, the most famous authority who did consider the obligation biblical, held that the words of the *Amidah* were not composed until the very end of the biblical period. Before then, the obligation was to pray once a day, at any time of day, using any wording that one chose. See his *Mishneh Torah*, Laws of Prayer, 1:15.

[121] The interpretation that Rabbi Eliezer's opinion is that prescribed prayer is not acceptable to God is found in the commentary of Hanokh Albeck, *The Six Orders of the Mishnah*, [Hebrew] (Jerusalem/Tel Aviv, 1967), I: 21, 331. In traditional editions of the Mishnah, Rabbi Eliezer's opinion is not included in this discussion, but rather is included as part of the next unit. However, many modern and some traditional scholars (e.g., *Melekhet Shlomo* by Shlomo Adani, 16th c.) place his opinion as part of the discussion as I've transmitted it above. My thanks to Professor Robert Scheinberg for the reference to *Melekhet Shlomo*.

*Amidah* because it contained 18 blessings (on how the *Amidah* of today came to contain 19 blessings, see below).

The Rabban Gamaliel mentioned is Rabban Gamaliel II (late 1st century CE). He was the *Nasi*, or "Patriarch," a kind of Chief Rabbi of the Land of Israel. From the ensuing opinions, it appears that Rabban Gamaliel wanted to legislate that each Jew ought to recite, on a daily basis, an *Amidah* with 18 set and unchanging topics. Rabbis Yehoshua, Akiva, and Eliezer propose compromises between an *Amidah* with 18 set topics and what might have been the common practice of Jews at the time, of either reciting an abbreviated version or reciting a prayer of their own heart's choosing. Note that in this early period, it is likely that only the topics of the 18 blessings were set. It took another few generations before the actual wording of these blessings became set as well.

Rabban Gamaliel, Rabbi Yehoshua, and Rabbi Akiva all are considering an obligation to say specified topics as part of daily prayer. The sole dissenting voice is that of Rabbi Eliezer. Here, and elsewhere in the Talmud (e.g., *Berakhot* 30b), Rabbi Eliezer champions the view that only prayer which flows freely from the worshiper's heart is acceptable to God. Ultimately, the view of Rabbi Eliezer was rejected, and Jewish law ruled that a person is, indeed, obligated to recite specific wording that constitutes the *Amidah* daily—three times a day, in fact. Actually, the Talmud does not explicitly reject Rabbi Eliezer's view; it interprets it out of existence, so to speak. It does so by asserting that Rabbi Eliezer wasn't actually disagreeing with the other Sages in this mishnah. Instead, the Talmud asserts, while Rabbi Eliezer agreed with Rabban Gamaliel that a person must recite 18 specific blessings, he simply wanted to make clear that these must be recited as if it they weren't prescribed words, but rather as if they constituted a fresh and meaningful prayer each time.[122] Nevertheless, this talmudic interpretation likely derives from a time when the obligation to pray had already been defined for some time as the obligation to recite 18 specific blessings. Rabbi Eliezer's opinion in the context of the earlier, mishnaic, conversation almost certainly opposed any set wording for daily prayer.

The opinions of Rabbis Yehoshua and Akiva are also partially reflected in Jewish law in the rule that if one is so distracted by a dangerous or emergency circumstance at the obligatory time for the *Amidah*, one may recite an abbreviated version, known as *Havineinu* ("Give us understanding"), whose text is also set! The fact that Rabbi Eliezer's view did not win the argument

[122] See *Berakhot* 29b-30a.

has meant that the *Amidah* ultimately (after the talmudic period) became a prayer with a set wording and was not mainly an opportunity to pour out our heart in a free-form way. Nevertheless, countless commentaries have been penned over the centuries with the express purpose of helping worshipers to use the wording of the *Amidah* to connect with their own personal emotional and spiritual needs. And that is the purpose of the commentary you are reading now as well.

**How the 18-Blessing *Amidah* Became a 19-Blessing *Amidah***

The mishnah quoted above calls the *Amidah* the prayer of "18 (blessings)." And yet, the weekday *Amidah* (as opposed to the *Amidah* recited on Shabbat and holidays) as practiced in every rite that has reached modernity contains 19 blessings. In fact, the Babylonian Talmud itself asks why the mishnah refers to an *Amidah* of 18 blessings while it, apparently, only knows of an *Amidah* with 19 blessings.[123] In giving an answer, the Talmud here cites a Tannaitic tradition regarding the origin of one of the blessings of the *Amidah*: *Birkat HaMinim*, "The Blessing (Against) the Sectarians." This was a curse against the early Jewish-Christians cast into "blessing" form and inserted into the *Amidah* when the followers of Jesus proliferated in the second century CE. The Talmud argues that this tradition contains the key to resolve the "18 versus 19" controversy, namely, that the 18 blessings mentioned in the mishnah must reflect the original number of blessings, and that the addition of the Blessing (Against) the Sectarians must have brought the number to 19.

For nearly 20 centuries, this explanation of the mishnah's counting only 18 blessings in the *Amidah* was the accepted explanation until a discovery in the year 1896 led to a different conclusion. In that year, two Christian women visiting Egypt purchased some very old manuscript fragments in Cairo. Upon the conclusion of their trip, they showed these leaves to Solomon Schechter, who was then a professor of Rabbinics at Cambridge University. Studying those few old texts from Cairo, Schechter's formidable scholarly knowledge led him to realize that he was holding a part of an ancient book that was thought totally lost—it was the Hebrew original of an ancient Jewish holy book which had been known only from its Greek translation, *The Wisdom of Ben Sirah* (also called *Ecclesiasticus*). This find led Schechter to arrange a long-term stay in Cairo to investigate what has become known as The Cairo Genizah. *Genizah* denotes a storage place for Jewish holy books that have become too worn out for use. This *genizah* was in the attic of the

[123] Babylonian Talmud, *Berakhot* 28b, bottom.

medieval synagogue located in Old Cairo, or Fostat. Schechter—and, after him, other scholars—ultimately discovered over several hundred thousand texts and text-fragments, mostly from the 10th to the 13th centuries.

In the light of many "Genizah Studies," it has become clear just how revolutionary and eye-opening the discoveries of the Genizah are for Jewish liturgy. Scholars soon realized that the Genizah preserved not only early versions of prayers from the well-known *Nusaḥ Bavel*, "The Babylonian Rite," reflected, in part, in the Babylonian Talmud, but also a rite of Jewish prayer that had been lost for a thousand years. It is known as *Nusaḥ Eretz Yisrael* (*Ha'Atik*), or "The (Old) Palestinian Rite." This version of prayer was not based on the Babylonian Talmud, the more dominant of the two Talmuds, but upon the Palestinian Talmud, and formed the basic rite for Jews who lived in the land of Israel and its environs, including Cairo, for several centuries. When the Crusaders arrived in the land of Israel in the 11th-13th centuries, they wrested the land from the hands of the Muslims and slaughtered much of the Muslim and Jewish communities living there. In so doing, they also effectively destroyed the Palestinian Rite of Jewish worship. The Old Palestinian Rite was also on the wane because the Geonim, the *de facto* leaders of world Jewry in the early Middle Ages, ruled from Muslim lands, where the Babylonian Rite had held sway since the days of the Sages of the Babylonian Talmud (3rd-6th centuries).

In 1898, Schechter published a version of the *Amidah* that he had discovered among the documents at the *genizah*. The surprising thing about this *Amidah* was that although it contained *Birkat HaMinim*, "The Blessing (Against) the Sectarians," the supposed 19th blessing, it still contained only 18 blessings! In this version of the *Amidah*, a single blessing is made of what appears as two separate blessings in the conventionally known version. Blessings #15 (asking God to rebuild Jerusalem) and #16 (asking God to bring the Messiah) of the common version of the *Amidah* are fused together as one blessing in the Palestinian version.

The story of the 18 blessings versus the 19 blessings of the *Amidah*, then, is reconstructed by scholars as follows: In the Tannaitic era, there were two ways to pray in the *Amidah* for the rebuilding of Jerusalem and to bring the Messiah. One way was to pray for these in two separate blessings and the other was to combine the requests in one blessing.[124] Jews who lived in the land of Israel and Egypt followed the tradition of combining the two requests into one blessing. This approach is reflected in the mishnah—the "18" that

[124] See *Tosefta Berakhot* 3:25.

Rabban Gamaliel and the other Sages of the Mishnah mentioned. The Jews of Babylonia continued the tradition of separating the two requests into two blessings. Henceforth, the Babylonian version of the *Amidah* comprised 19 blessings. Part of the intriguing nature of this history is that the discovery and analysis of the Cairo Genizah has made it possible for modern scholars to determine that the anonymous editors of the Babylonian Talmud were simply mistaken when they resolved the "18 versus 19" blessings in the *Amidah* by saying that The Blessing (Against) the Heretics was the 19th! Apparently, by the time that answer was recorded in the Babylonian Talmud, knowledge of the tradition of combining both requests in one blessing was lost to the Sages of Babylonia.

**Analytical Commentary on the *Amidah* as a Literary Whole**

Most of the attention I will focus on the *Amidah* will be directed at the historical, literary and spiritual meaning of each of its 19 individual blessings. Here, however, I want to discuss the potential for meaning in viewing the *Amidah* as a literary whole. There is a school of thought that the *Amidah* as a whole contains a discernable pattern of ideas. There is a long history—and a large variety—of attempts to unveil such patterns in the *Amidah* when viewed in its entirety. I will survey a number of these theories and ask whether or not they seem reasonable.[125]

If one writer had written the entire *Amidah*, it would be easy to imagine that there is an internal logic to the flow of thought through the 19 blessings. After all, when almost any writer, in any period of history, creates one composition consisting of many paragraphs, there is usually some sort of discernable connection between the several parts of that literary creation. This kind of interconnectedness is usually a natural part of the act of writing. However, it may have been the case that the *Amidah* was not written by one writer. In fact, it is likely that of the total of 19 blessings that make up the weekday *Amidah*, several individual blessings or groups of blessings originally derived from distinct Jewish communities, and, at some point,

[125] There is a vast scholarly literature, in several languages, on the question of the origins of the *Amidah*. There is still no scholarly consensus. One would gain an idea of some of the approaches in the following two dated, but still helpful, articles in English: Ezra Fleischer, "On the Origins of the 'Amidah: Response to Ruth Langer," *Prooftexts* 20:3 (2000), 381-384; Ruth Langer, "Considerations of Method: A Response to Ezra Fleischer," *Prooftexts* 20:3 (2000), 384-387. See more recently, Ruth Langer and Richard Sarason, "Re-examining the Early Evidence for Rabbinic Liturgy: How Fixed Were Its Prayer Texts?" in Nuria Calduch-Benages, Michael W. Duggan and Dalia Marx, eds., *On Wings of Prayer Sources of Jewish Worship: Essays in Honor of Professor Stefan c. Reif on the Occasion of His Seventy-Fifth Birthday* (Berlin: de Gruyter, 2019), 203-232. See also Uri Ehrlich, *The Weekday Amidah in Geniza Prayer Books: Origins and Transmission* [Hebrew] (Jerusalem: Yad Izhak Ben-Zvi, 2013).

these were put together without an attempt to build a linear narrative. It is possible that the two different forms of Blessing #17 (*Modim* and *Modim De-Rabbanan*—see discussion of that blessing below) and of Blessing #18 (*Sim Shalom* and *Shalom Rav*—see discussion of that blessing below) which exist side by side to this day may be two such remnants of these blessings. Jewish liturgy tends to preserve popular variants of the same blessing or prayer by assigning them different roles or locations, e.g., the many versions of the *Kaddish* and the *Kedushah* in various parts of the prayer book.

In other words, before there was one "official" version of the *Amidah*, there may have been several different forms of shorter "unofficial" *Amidot*, from which the "official" version drew.[126] In this case, the "stitching together" of the several original groupings of blessings may or may not have led to an overarching literary aim. As will become clear, I am of the opinion that it did not lead to some sort of unified message. The main goal in editing together what may have been several shorter versions of "unofficial" *Amidot* may have been to simply preserve all of these various forms for one of several reasons. It could have been because each different community's set of blessings had acquired a measure of holiness through its many years of chanting, and, therefore, it may have become unthinkable and unacceptable to discontinue its recitation when an "official" *Amidah* was promulgated. Similarly, it may have been the result of a political motivation: Perhaps it was desired to unify the worship practices of the many different local communities that made up Israel following the destruction and chaos of the war with the Romans after 70 CE. If so, instead of replacing all of the shorter precursors to the *Amidah* that may have existed with an entirely new text, it may have been a stroke of political genius to preserve them all, and thereby unify all or many of the communities by incorporating all the blessings into one, longer, all-encompassing version of the *Amidah*. The point is that there may have been any number of likely scenarios in which the *Amidah* was composed without much attention paid to any "message" which resulted from viewing

[126] The English translation of Elbogen, *Jewish Liturgy*, 35-37, contains support and some evidence for this view added by the committee that updated this classic and translated it from German to Hebrew in 1972. The committee also points to passages resembling parts of the *Amidah* in a number of ancient sources, Jewish and Christian, which may testify to the independent existence of one or more of the *Amidah*'s blessings before they were amalgamated into the *Amidah* itself. See also Meir Bar-Ilan, "Major Trends in the Formation and Crystallization of the Kedushah," [Hebrew], *Da'at*, 25, 1990, 17-19. The theoretical original sources of the *Amidah* may not have been "unofficial *Amidot*" at all. One or more of the blessings may have served a very different function in their original context. For example, there is a theory that blessing #7, *Birkat Go'eil Yisrael*, "Liberator of Israel," functioned originally as blessing of thanksgiving by people who had been released from prison or some other form of servitude. See Reuven Kimelman, "The Daily Amidah and The Rhetoric of Redemption," *The Jewish Quarterly Review*, LXXIX, Nos. 2-3 (October, 1988-January, 1989), 170, n. 15.

the prayer in its entirety: It may simply have been a stringing together of parts which, ultimately, do not add up to anything more meaningful than the sum of its parts.

In dealing with these questions, it is important to make clear that we cannot expect airtight, unassailable proofs, confirming one side or the other in this theoretical debate. The reason is the somewhat startling fact that no clear statement about the original development of the *Amidah* has been preserved from the period in which this central Jewish prayer came into being. While there are some teachings about the creation of the *Amidah* from this early period, the period of the *Tannaim*, they contradict each other. When more than one rationale is offered for the source of a given prayer, that is often a sign that the original rationale has been lost. And while there are some unambiguous statements about the flow of ideas within the *Amidah* in Rabbinic Literature, these derive from the period after the creation of the *Amidah*, the period of the *Amoraim* (c. 225 CE - c. 550 CE) and seem to be after-the-fact theorizing.

I will summarize several of the theories of what the *Amidah* in its entirety may mean, but again, I am not convinced by any of them. The main reason is, as I will detail below, there simply isn't enough compelling evidence to confirm any of the theories. In spite of the fact that I am conscious of my own personal desire to find meaning in interpreting the *Amidah* in its entirety, I just do not find confirmation of any such message in the actual words of the prayer. It seems to me that an objective reading of the words of the *Amidah* does not conform to any of the theories of literary wholeness.

### 1. The *Amidah* as Based Upon Biblical Verses

The Talmud itself offers a theory of the order of the *Amidah*, namely that it is based on various biblical verses.[127] Perhaps this is an attempt to make up for a lack regarding a prayer as important as the *Amidah*: There is no biblical source for the *Amidah* as a whole! Numerous passages from Psalms, Isaiah, Ezekiel, Leviticus, and Numbers are invoked to explain the order of the blessings. No overall theme or message is discovered, but the impression is given that several of its sections reflect a logical order found in Scripture. For example, the first blessing of the *Amidah*, which centers around the Patriarchs is said to be based on Psalm 29:1, "Acclaim the LORD, O great ones," the "great ones" being identified as the Patriarchs. The second blessing, on God's *gevurot*, "mighty acts," is said to be based on the continuation

[127] Babylonian Talmud, *Megillah* 17b-18a.

of the verse in the Psalm, "Acclaim the LORD with glory and might," the "might" of the verse equating with God's "mighty acts" in the *Amidah*. The third blessing, which celebrates God's holiness, is connected to the end of the next verse in the Psalm, "bow down to the LORD, majestic in holiness." Thus, it is argued by the Talmud, the first three blessings follow the flow of ideas in the Psalm. However, the connections between the Psalm and the *Amidah*, as well as between the other biblical verses offered as connections to the various blessings of the *Amidah*, are indirect, midrashic, links. The attempt to connect the order of the blessings of the *Amidah* to biblical verses is not convincing as history, but rather as a homiletical attempt to ground a relatively new prayer in authoritative, biblical, legitimacy.

**2. The *Amidah* as Praise, Needs, Praise**

Another *Tannaitic* teaching, this one from the oldest collection of midrash on the Book of Deuteronomy, suggests another approach.[128] Interpreting The Blessing of Moses, just before Moses' death, at the end of the Torah (Deuteronomy, chapter 33), it characterizes the entire Blessing as adhering to a pattern: first, praise of God; then, praise of Israel; finally, praise of God again. Moses is compared to a lawyer, effectively using this pattern in arguing a case, and then David and Solomon are said to use the same pattern as Moses, and finally "the 18 blessings" of the *Amidah* are compared to this same pattern. In this way, the midrash finds an overarching framework in the *Amidah*. I will translate the source, then evaluate its schematic of the *Amidah*:

> The Torah says that when Moses began [his Blessing], he didn't open with the needs of Israel, but rather, opened with the praise of God. This is analogous to a lawyer who stood at the lectern [in court] and was hired to plead someone's case. He did not open with the needs of that man, but rather, opened with the praise of the King... So, too, Moses our teacher didn't open with the needs of Israel, but rather, opened with the praise of God...
>
> So too, King David opened with the praise of God as it says (Psalm 149:1), and [only] afterward he opened with

[128] *Sifrei Devarim* 343; *Sifre on Deuteronomy*, ed. Louis Finkelstein (New York: Jewish Theological Seminary of America, 1969), 394-395. This passage may be found in Reuven Hammer's English translation of this midrash: *Sifre: A Tannaitic Commentary on the Book of Deuteronomy* (New Haven: Yale Judaica Series, 1987), 351-356. See also The Palestinian Talmud *Berakhot* 2:4, 4d.

> the praise of Israel (Psalm 149:4), and "sealed" with the praise of God (Psalm 150:1).
>
> And so, too, Solomon, his son, opened with the praise of God (II Chronicles 6:14), and [only] afterward he opened with the needs of Israel (II Chronicles 6:25), and "sealed" with the praise of God (II Chronicles 6:41).
>
> And so, too, the 18 blessings that the early prophets ordained for Israel to pray daily—they didn't open with the needs of Israel, but rather, opened with the praise of God, "God, the great, powerful, the awesome" (the first blessing of the *Amidah*), "Holy are You and awesome is Your name" (the third blessing, according to the ancient Palestinian rite), and afterward, "Releaser of the Bound" (the 7th blessing?), and afterward, "Healer of the Sick" (the 8th blessing), and afterward "We acknowledge You" (the 18th blessing).

The overall framework of the *Amidah* that is put forth in this reading is:

1. Praise of God.
2. Needs of Israel.
3. Praise of God.

The midrash has in mind a general schematic equating the flow of blessings in the *Amidah* to that of the Blessing of Moses, as well as to prayers of David and of Solomon. This is one of the *midrashim* which seems to work better in its likely original setting as a sermon, making a general point about religious life based on the Bible, than as rigorous literary analysis of a section of the Bible. After all, there are other, more apt, ways to characterize Moses' Blessing in Deuteronomy, chapter 33. It seems to be general praise for the tribes of Israel—cast as a farewell blessing—much more than a plea for Israel's needs. The final section is described better as reassurance to Israel in the future because of its allegiance with God, rather than as pure praise of God. The general point of the midrash-as-sermon, though, is that it is preferable, when approaching God with a plea for the needs of the people, to use the politesse that one might use before an earthly ruler: introduce and follow your plea for help with praise. Make your submission to the powerful one clear so that your request does not seem audacious.

However, the last part of the midrash, dealing with the *Amidah*, is difficult. While in the previous three sections on the prayers of Moses, David, and Solomon, the passage specifically delineates which lines constitute the opening praise of God, the needs of Israel (or "praise" of Israel, in the case of David), and the final praise of God, the section on the *Amidah* does not identify which lines refer to which praise or need. Furthermore, we have some difficulty identifying exactly which blessings are being cited since there are five blessings that are cited and not just three. There are, apparently, two blessings referring to the beginning of the *Amidah*, the first and the third; two from the middle, the seventh and the eighth; and one from the end, the 18th. However, the words "Releaser of the Bound," *Matir Assurim*, are not found in most versions of the 7th blessing of the *Amidah*, while they are found in the first blessing, so it is not entirely clear to which blessing these words refer.[129] Finally, and most importantly, a close reading of the Amidah reveals that this final portion of the schematic doesn't conform with the actual wording of the *Amidah*: While the midrash cites "We Acknowledge You" (*Modim anaḥnu lakh*) as the final "praise of God," that is not the final blessing of the *Amidah* in all known versions. The final blessing of the *Amidah* is not praise, but, a request to fulfill a need: "*sim shalom...*," "grant peace..." It is true that the first three blessings of the *Amidah* do seem to constitute praise of God, and the next several are requests to fulfill needs. To that extent, this pattern is an accurate one. But since its characterization falls flat when it comes to the conclusion of the *Amidah*, it remains an unsatisfying overall approach.

### 3. The *Amidah* as Praise, Needs, Thanksgiving

One of the most popular approaches in explaining the pattern of the *Amidah* as a whole is stated, apparently for the first time, by Rambam in his *Mishneh Torah*:

> The first three (blessings)—praise to God. And the last three—thanksgiving. And the middle ones—they contain pleas for all things; they are like archetypes for all the needs of individuals and the needs of the community...[130]

[129] A glance at the listing of the manuscript variants in Finkelstein's edition of *Sifrei Devarim*, 395, reveals that there are several different readings of exactly which blessings of the *Amidah* are cited, and in what order. Kimelman makes much of a parallel of one of these variants, that of *Midrash HaGadol* as cited in *Midrash Tanna'im* which lists only the Blessing for Liberation (#7) as representing the entire middle section of the *Amidah*. This supports his thesis that the theme of redemption is the theme of the entire *Amidah*. However, this is just one version, among many, of this particular midrash. See Kimelman, "The Daily Amidah and the Rhetoric of Redemption," 179.

[130] *Hilkhot Tefillah* 1:4.

Many codes and commentaries, from the time of Rambam to modern times, cite Rambam's overarching explanation as an accurate description of the *Amidah*:

1. Praise of God: First three blessings.
2. Needs of Israel: Middle blessings.
3. Thanksgiving to God: Final three blessings.

The following is the main talmudic passage cited by commentators as the source for Rambam's statement:

> Rav Yehudah said: A person should never ask his needs in the beginning or final blessings, but rather in the middle ones because Rabbi Ḥanina said:
> In the first ones, [a person] resembles a servant who arranges praise before his master.
> In the middle ones, [a person] resembles a servant who requests payment from his master.
> In the final ones, [a person] resembles a servant who received a ration from his master and takes his leave and goes on his way.[131]

The descriptions of the first and middle groupings of blessings in the talmudic analogy match closely Rambam's characterization of these: Praise by the servant/worshiper of the master/God, followed by requests by the servant/worshiper of the master/God. If this talmudic teaching was indeed Rambam's source, his description of the final group of blessings as "thanksgiving" may have been his interpretation of Rabbi Ḥanina's saying that a person "resembles a servant who received payment from his master and takes his leave and goes on his way."

There are, nevertheless, two main problems with this portrayal of three main principles in the *Amidah*. The main issue is that while the descriptions of the first and middle groupings of blessings conform, more or less, with the wording of those blessings, the characterization of the last three blessings just does not. Two of the blessings in the final grouping match Rambam's characterization of the middle blessings more than they do to his description of the final blessings. I am referring to *Avodah*, "Worship," (the 17th

[131] Babylonian Talmud, *Berakhot* 34a.

blessing), and to *Sim Shalom*, "Grant Peace," (the 19th blessing). Even a casual reading of these two passages reveals many instances of the language of requesting, pleading, asking. *Avodah*, "Worship," asks that God restore the sacrificial system to its former glorious place in Jerusalem. *Sim Shalom*, "Grant Peace," asks that God bestow a series of benefits including peace, goodness, blessing, grace, loving-kindness, and mercy. Only the blessing sandwiched between these can accurately be called "Thanksgiving," namely, *Modim*, "We acknowledge/thank" (the 18th blessing).

### 4. *Amidah* as a Pattern of Personal and Communal Blessings

Another popular theory that attempts to trace a trend of thought throughout the entire *Amidah* sees a pattern of personal and communal blessings. According to this approach, one group of blessings of the *Amidah* reflects the needs of the individual, and another group represents the needs of the community or nation. These groupings are usually said to be found among the middle 13 blessings. The earliest mention of this schematic—if not fully developed—may be in a commentary of *Tosafot* (12th-13th c., France/Germany) on the Talmud,[132] and there are adherents of this way of looking at the *Amidah* up to the present day.[133] There is one basic flaw to this line of thinking about the *Amidah*. It is related to a well-known tendency within Jewish liturgy in general which favors communal expression of prayer over individual expression. Most Jewish prayers are articulated in the first-person plural as opposed to the first-person singular. While there are exceptions, the vast majority of the worship service is voiced in terms of "we," "us," "our," as opposed to "I, "me," "mine." This predilection is so strong within Jewish liturgy that often, even verses from holy Scripture, when cited within a prayer text, are pluralized. This style of presenting prayer in the communal plural is especially pronounced in the *Amidah*. In fact, the entire *Amidah* is written in

[132] Babylonian Talmud, *Berakhot* 34a, s.v. *Al*. Here, the focus is not the middle blessings, but the concluding blessings. The interpretation is brought in the names of *Rabbeinu Ḥananel* and *Rabbeinu Ḥai*. There are important divergences in the parallel comments in B. Lewin, *Otzar HaGeonim*, vol. 1 [Hebrew] (Haifa, 1928), Appendix: The Commentary of *Rabbeinu Ḥananel*, 42; *HaPeirushim*, 46-47, #140. See also R. Abraham ben Nathan of Lunel, *Sefer HaManhig*, vol. 1, Ed., Y. Raphael (Jerusalem: Mosad HaRav Kuk, 1978), 93-94.

[133] This approach is found in chart form in Eliezer Levy, *Torat HaTefillah* (Jerusalem: *Ḥorev*, 1993), 103. Interestingly, there are a number of modern commentaries on the *Siddur* which describe the flow of thought in the *Amidah* as reflecting both this approach—a pattern of personal, and then, national requests—as well the approach discussed above, "Praise, Needs, Thanksgiving." These include Joseph Hertz, *The Authorized Daily Prayer Book* (New York: Bloch Publishing Company, 1948, and reprinted many times), 130, 137; Elie Munk, *The World of Prayer*, vol. 1 (New York: Feldheim, 1961), 120, 128-129 (a translation of his *Die Welt Der Gebete*, 1933); Jules Harlow, *Pray Tell: A Hadassah Guide to Jewish Prayer* (Woodstock, Vermont: Jewish Lights Publishing, 2003), 82. See also Reuven Kimelman, "The Daily Amidah and The Rhetoric of Redemption," mentioned above.

this communal plural form, without any exceptions. This is exactly why it is so difficult, if not impossible, to claim that one can discern which blessings of the *Amidah* are truly meant as communal blessings, and which—even though they are written in the plural form—are, nevertheless, actually meant as prayers of the individual. The grounds on which "communal" versus "individual" blessings are made tend to be very subjective. Since they can't be based on the external, objective grammatical forms of singular or plural, they are based on whether a particular interpreter happens to define the content of a given blessing as "individual" or "communal." So, for example, Levy defines blessing #9 of the *Amidah* as from the point of view of an individual even though it asks God to bless the year with agricultural bounty—something which certainly seems to be at least as much the concern of the community as the domain of the individual.[134]

There may well be elements of an individual's perspective in some parts of the *Amidah*, but these are purposely subsumed in the pluralized form. The individual's praise and needs are intertwined with those of the community. In that sense, an individual can recite the blessings of the *Amidah* and identify with them as someone who is both part of the larger society, as well as a distinct personage within it. In the end, it is it futile to attempt to distinguish the exact passages within the *Amidah* which are meant for the individual and which are for the community. The search for the specific passages meant for the individual misses the point that the plural structure means that the rhetoric of the *Amidah* is the rhetoric of the group. The form of the *Amidah* makes it impossible to separate the individual from the communal.

### 5. The *Amidah* as a Unified Statement on Redemption

One of the most recent attempts to see a single line of thought reflected throughout the entire *Amidah* posits the idea that all the blessings of the prayer build sequentially and add up to a unified statement on redemption. The word "redemption" is the way many translate the Hebrew root *ga'al*, but it can also refer to *padah* and *yasha*. It connotes messianic deliverance. Among the adherents of this theory are Reuven Hammer, Lawrence A. Hoffman, and Reuven Kimelman.[135] According to this approach, each blessing of

[134] Eliezer Levy, *Torat HaTefillah*, 103.

[135] Reuven Hammer, *Entering Jewish Prayer: A Guide to Personal Devotion and the Worship Service* (New York: Schocken, 1994), 174-183; Lawrence A. Hoffman, ed., *My People's Prayer Book: The Amidah*, vol. 2 (Woodstock, Vermont: Jewish Lights, 1998), 33-36. Hoffman records this theory in the name of his teacher, Leon Liebreich; Reuven Kimelman, "The Daily Amidah and The Rhetoric of Redemption," 165-197. Kimelman's presentation was published in a format designed specifically for other scholars, and so it is the most detailed and scholarly of the three. As is true of Kimelman's work in general, this article, too, is brilliantly argued, abundantly referenced, and is fairly bristling with insights all along

the middle group of 13 blessings (#4 - #16) represents one step in the process of redemption. One of the most interesting aspects of tracing these phases of redemption, according to this approach, is that the arrival of the messiah comes only at the end of the process of redemption—reflected only toward the end of this grouping of blessings, in blessing #15. Based on this, the *Amidah* has been characterized as "a counter-messianic manifesto."[136] That is to say, that according to this theory, far from encouraging worshipers to expect the imminent coming of the messiah, the prayer cautions that the messiah will come only at the end of many other preliminary stages of redemption. Hammer and Hoffman explicitly connect this political agenda with historical events following the crushing defeat the Jews suffered—including the destruction of the Temple in Jerusalem—at the hands of the Romans in 66-70 CE. According to them, the rabbis in the 2nd century, post-destruction period who created the *Amidah* (especially Rabban Gamaliel) wanted to dissuade the nation from an apocalyptically-motivated rebellion against Rome. Their fear was that such extremism would lead to a repetition of the disaster of the rebellion of the first century or of the second century's Bar Kokhba Rebellion.

The strength of this theory is that it accounts well for the abundance of references to redemption in the *Amidah*. The weakness is the same one we have seen regarding all of the other schematics of the entire *Amidah*: Too many specifics of the actual wording of the *Amidah* which do not fit the overall pattern have to be reinterpreted or ignored in order for the theory as a whole to work. For example, Blessing #4 simply requests that God bless the worshiper with wisdom. There is no explicit connection to redemption whatsoever. To argue, as those who promote this theory do, that wisdom is necessary to reach the other stages of redemption may ring true, but it also rings true that wisdom is a necessary first step for the realization of anything. This theory requires many other examples of forced interpretations, in my opinion. I would suggest another way of accounting for the abundance of references to redemption in the *Amidah*. The idea of redemption is a major theme, if not the major theme, of Jewish liturgy in general. That is, the longing for national redemption is so pervasive in Jewish prayer texts across the board that there are pleas for God to rescue Israel in nearly every major prayer, as well as in many minor prayers. There are pleas to God for

---

the way. One of the challenges of reading Kimelman's scholarly work is that it tends to overwhelm the reader with the sheer number of references to primary sources, not to mention secondary literature. It is always beneficial for a student of Jewish liturgy to read Kimelman's writing. Nevertheless, when I read this particular article slowly and patiently, checking each reference, the sum of the parts does not add up to a convincing buttress for his thesis—that the *Amidah* represents a "rhetoric of redemption."

[136] Hoffman, *My People's Prayer Book: The Amidah*, 35.

redemption in the prayers for most life cycle events, including *brit milah* (circumcision) and weddings; they are found in the Blessing After Meals; in all the *Amidot*, not just in the weekday *Amidah*, as well as in the blessings which surround the *Shema*.

It is because of all of this that I put the theory of "The *Amidah* As A Unified Statement On Redemption" in the same category as the other four theories I've surveyed above: Interesting, but ultimately, unconvincing.[137] All of these attempts lend the impression that they were created by deeply thinking individuals who confronted a set prayer and tried to make some sense of it as a whole; an entirely natural enterprise. It is, of course, possible that Rabban Gamaliel—and/or whoever else had a hand in forming the *Amidah* as we know it—had in mind a certain rationale, and that rationale has so far eluded us. It is, conversely, also possible that the original editor(s) of the *Amidah* did not have a particular rationale in mind. They may simply have been preserving a number of different blessings and/or groups of blessings for the sake of unifying the worship practice of Israel, as I mentioned, with a bit more detail, at the beginning of this discussion. I tend to believe that this latter possibility represents the reality of the history of the *Amidah*.

**Spiritual Commentary on the Weekday *Amidah* as a Whole**

Phyllis Tickle, in her book, *Prayer is a Place*, captures the sense that the zone we enter, as we recite the words of a prayer, can transport us beyond the words themselves. This metaphysical experience can sometimes feel as real as the physical world around us. For this reason, she calls prayer "a place."

> ...(T)here a few things... almost descriptive principles, if you will... that I do know about prayer. The first is that prayer is a place. Prayer is a nonlocative, nongeographic space that one enters at one's peril, for it houses God during those few moments of one's presence there, and what is there will most surely change everything that comes into it. Prayer, its opal walls polished to transparency by the centuries of hands that have touched them, is the Tabernacle realized and the wayside chapel utilized... Prayer... is the entrance way to wholeness.[138]

[137] There are several other, less well known (but no more convincing) theories that attempt to demonstrate the ideational unity of the *Amidah*. For a number of them, see Kimelman, "The Daily Amidah and The Rhetoric of Redemption." Kimelman himself refers to a fuller list and analysis in Louis Ginzberg, *A Commentary on The Palestinian Talmud* [Hebrew] (New York, 1941), 1:333; 3:238-262.

[138] Phyllis Tickle, *Prayer Is A Place: America's Religious Landscape Observed* (New York, 2005), 68.

This portrayal of wholeness with the holy Other is available to a worshiper regardless of the content of the specific words of the prayer. This is an encounter "beyond the text."[139]

While that "descriptive principle" may be applied to any prayer that helps us enter that zone of wholeness with God, it is especially suggestive for the *Amidah*. In Rabbinic Literature, the Amidah is often called *HaTefillah*, "**The** Prayer." The *Amidah* is intended to be that "place" in the service in which we imagine ourselves directly in the presence of God. It is **The** Prayer that serves as the centerpiece and climax of each of the Jewish worship services. When one recites the *Amidah*, a sense of wholeness with God is available beyond the meaning of the words of the prayer.

Following this introduction to the *Amidah*, I will comment on each of the nineteen blessings which make up the *Amidah* in the weekday service, analyzing their words in detail. Understanding the literary import of the individual blessings within the *Amidah* can greatly help one sense the sacred as one recites the individual blessings. Nevertheless, one shouldn't lose sight of the forest for the trees. If one recites the *Amidah* with the consciousness that this prayer is the one designed to bring us in closest touch with the Divine Presence, then just reciting the words of the *Amidah*, without paying profound attention to their meaning, can also bring us to that same hallowed "place."

Following an academic conference in Israel, two seminal articles were published that tracked how the great importance placed by the Talmud on concentration and intention (*kavannah*) in reciting the *Amidah* was weakened over and over in the post-talmudic period (with the important exception of Rambam, 12th c., Egypt). These important articles opened my eyes to this disturbing trend in the attitude of Jewish law toward the importance of spiritual experience in prayer:

- Joseph Tabory, "Prayer and Halakhah."[140]
- Joseph Heinemann, "The Fixed and the Fluid in Jewish Prayer."[141]

In this Spiritual Commentary on the *Amidah* as a whole and in the Spiritual Commentaries on each of the individual blessings below, I am trying to

[139] Lawrence A. Hoffman has devoted an entire book to the academic study of this encounter. I have borrowed the phrase "beyond the text" from the title of his book: *Beyond The Text: A Holistic Approach to Liturgy* (Bloomington, Indiana, 1987). See my review of Hoffman's book in *Conservative Judaism*, Vol. XLVI, No. 3, Spring, 1994, 89-91.

[140] Published in Gabriel H. Cohn and Harold Fisch, eds., *Prayer in Judaism: Continuity and Change* (New Jersey: Jason Aaronson, 1996; Originally published in a Hebrew version in 1978), 53-68.

[141] *Prayer in Judaism: Continuity and Change*, 45-52.

counter this unfortunate trend away from the importance of inner intention in reciting the *Amidah.*

## Blessing #1
## *Magein Avraham*, Shield of Abraham

> Blessed are you, *YHVH* our God and God of our Patriarchs, the God of Abraham, the God of Isaac, and the God of Jacob. Great, mighty and awesome God. Supernal God. Bestowing kindnesses and Creator of all. Remembering kindnesses of the Patriarchs and bringing a redeemer to the children of their children, for the sake of His name, in love. King, Helper, Redeemer and Shield. Blessed are you *YHVH*, Shield of Abraham.

This blessing is already called *Avot*, that is, "Fathers," or "Patriarchs," in the earliest stratum of Rabbinic Literature.[142] Indeed, it is filled with references mainly to Abraham, but also to Abraham's son and grandson, Isaac and Jacob, and to *Avot*, "Patriarchs" in general.

God is praised in this blessing as *Elohei Avraham, Elohei Yitzḥak, V'Elohei Ya'akov*, "the God of Abraham, the God of Isaac, and the God of Jacob." The prayer book here is quoting the words that God uses to self-identify when Moses first encounters God, at the burning bush (Exodus 3:6). God first attracts Moses' attention through the appearance of a bush that is ablaze with fire, and yet, contrary to the rules of nature, does not burn up. When Moses approaches this marvelous sight, God speaks from the burning bush. God does not say, "I am the Creator of the world." Instead, God says, "I am the God of your father," and then continues, in the words cited in this blessing, "the God of Abraham, the God of Isaac, and the God of Jacob." In other words, instead of establishing the relationship with Moses as between the all-powerful Maker of the world and a fragile creature, God speaks of family connections. God asserts, in effect, that Moses is already connected to God through family. The sensitivity of God to human frailties is evidenced in many places in Scripture, and this conversation between God and Moses in chapter 3 of Exodus is a powerful example of it. As the conversation continues, God asks Moses to assume leadership of the Israelites, and, patiently, answers Moses' hesitations five times before Moses is convinced. God suspends the ability to overpower creatures out of respect for their fragility.

[142] For example, in *Mishnah Rosh HaShanah* 4:5.

It seems to me that the writer of this blessing takes his cue from the way that God self-identifies to Moses. He has the worshiper approach God, at the beginning of the *Amidah*, with the words God used in the very first divine conversation with Moses in order to remind the worshiper—and God—that they are already connected through family. When the Jewish worshiper begins the *Amidah* by mentioning, in this first blessing, that God is the God of "our" Patriarchs (*Avoteinu*), "the God of Abraham, the God of Isaac, the God of Jacob," "the Shield of Abraham," the worshiper is establishing a close, personal, relationship with God.

This phrase is immediately followed with the words that Moses himself uses, many years later, to describe God to the Israelites: *Ha'Eil, hagadol, hagibor, vehanora*, "the great, the mighty, and the awesome God" (Deuteronomy 10:17).[143]

God is then called *Eil Elyon*, "Supernal God." This description of God derives from the biblical story of Abraham and Melchizedek, where it is repeated some four times in Genesis 14:18-23. Melchizedek is called a priest of "Supernal God" and then both he and Abraham call God "Supernal God."[144] Apparently, Melchizedek—who was not part of Abraham's family or tribe—served as a priest to the same God that Abraham worshiped: Abraham links the name "Supernal God" with the name "*YHVH*," saying "I swear to *YHVH*, Supernal God, Creator of heaven and earth" (Genesis 14:22). This last expression, "Creator of heaven and earth," is alluded to in the very next phrase in our blessing, in the prayer book's phrase *koneih hakol*, "Creator of all." Abraham's "Creator of heaven and earth" was shortened in the blessing to "Creator of all," perhaps because "heaven and earth" equals "all" of reality.[145]

If the wording at the very beginning of the blessing connects to the God of the ancestors of the Jewish family, the wording here which connects to Melchizedek conjures the God of all the world. It is significant that God is invoked through the name "Supernal God" by which the non-Jewish priest knows God, making the point that the God worshiped in this prayer is not only the God of the Jews. This idea is emphasized in the blessing's use of the name "Creator of all." In other words, through the art of careful citation of the Bible here, the author of this blessing has the worshiper call upon the God of the worshiper's ancestors, but then asks the worshiper to realize that

[143] This phrase is also quoted in the Bible by Nehemiah, many centuries later, in a prayer to God when a portion of the people have returned to Israel from the Babylonian captivity (Nehemiah 9:32).
[144] The expression, "*Eil Elyon*," "Supernal God," occurs only one other time in the Bible, Psalms 78:35.
[145] In the ancient Palestinian version of the *Amidah*, the original biblical phrase is preserved in this blessing without being shortened. It also is cited in its original form in another place in all of the movements' contemporary prayer books, namely, in *Birkat Mei'ein Sheva*, which follows the *Amidah* on Friday nights.

this same God is also the God of all humanity, indeed, of all creatures and all of nature, as well.

The literary skill of this blessing's writer becomes similarly clear through his use of the word *magein*, "shield" to describe God twice at the conclusion of the blessing. The Bible uses forms of this word to portray God in relationship with Abraham twice within a few verses of the names of God we have just discussed (Genesis 14:20, 15:1). Therefore, again, Abraham is hinted at indirectly and poetically, simply through the prayer book's calling God a "shield."

This blessing not only celebrates God's special relationship with Abraham and the other two Patriarchs of the Jewish people. It also explicitly connects the unique association that God had with the Patriarchs to their distant descendants. In this way, the blessing links the contemporary worshiper with Abraham, Isaac, and Jacob, not merely as obscure historical figures, but as ancestors of the worshiper's own family: *V'Zokheir ḥasdei avot, u'meivi go'eil livnei veneihem*, "and (God) remembers the kindnesses of the Patriarchs and is bringing a redeemer to the children of their children."

The liberal movements in modern Judaism have added language to this blessing that acknowledges the Matriarchs along with the Patriarchs. This, too, helps to broaden the family connection between the worshiper and God, and to personalize it.

**Spiritual Commentary on *Magein Avraham***

The Jewish person who stands before God, conscious of the connection to the Patriarchs and Matriarchs who are invoked in this blessing, may experience this moment of prayer as one of reconnecting to God who has been associated with the family for generations. The fear and distance that a person initiating communication with God might feel are softened by the language describing the protective relationship God has had with the worshiper's family in the past. Therefore, a moment that might understandably be perceived with apprehension and remoteness is replaced with one of familiarity and ease. Just as God is introduced to Moses through a family connection, this blessing's theme is the connection between the worshiper and God through family. It is true, as we saw, that some cosmic and universal notes are sounded in this blessing as well: "Supernal God;" "Creator of all." This reminds us that Abraham's family is not the only group that calls upon this God. But most of the biblical allusions in this blessing connect to Abraham and his son, Isaac, and grandson, Jacob; the link with this clan is the central theme of the blessing.

Therefore, at the very beginning of the *Amidah*, the worshiper is invited to approach God by bringing one's ancestors to mind. Worshipers are reminded that their families have worshiped this God for hundreds of generations. The very words of this blessing, which assert the centuries-old bond between Abraham's children and God, have themselves been recited by Abraham's progeny for many centuries. There is a sanctity that accrues to words that have been repeated, over many generations, by one's family members. If we can be mindful of this while reciting this opening blessing of the *Amidah*, then we are creating a personal and direct connection with God at the very beginning of this central prayer.

## Blessing #2
## *Meḥayei HaMeitim*, Reviver of the Dead

> You are eternally mighty, *YHVH*, sustaining life in kindness, reviving the dead with great mercy, supporting those who fall, healing the sick, releasing the bound, keeping faith with those who sleep in the dust. Who is like you, Master of might, who compares to you, King who causes death and revives life, who causes redemption to flourish? You are faithful to revive the dead. Blessed are you *YHVH*, Reviver of the Dead.

The literary theme of this blessing is unmistakable: Within the few lines that make up this blessing, the phrase *meḥayei hameitim*, "restorer of life to the dead," occurs some five times in various linguistic forms. Added to that, a sixth occurrence of the same idea is expressed within the blessing in the following metaphorical terms, *u'mekayeim emunato lisheinei afar*, "and He keeps His faith with those who sleep in the dust." This blessing asserts, clearly and boldly, that God restores life to those who have died.

The blessing does not go into details as to when and how this is to take place. Does God restore life to us as soon as we die? Alternatively, does God revive us at some point in the future, perhaps when the *go'eil*, the "redeemer," mentioned in the previous blessing, will arrive? Will human beings be restored to life within our bodies, or in some incorporeal manner? Will the righteous enjoy a different quality of existence after death than the sinful? The text doesn't clarify these issues.[146] It simply includes restoration of life

[146] For a survey of Jewish views of the Afterlife, see: Rifat Sonsino and Daniel B. Syme, *What Happens After I Die: Jewish Views of Life After Death* (New York, 1990); Simcha Paull Raphael, *Jewish Views of*

as one of the *gevurot*,[147] "mighty acts" of God, among two others that it mentions: supporting those who have fallen and healing the sick.

**Spiritual Commentary on *Meḥayei HaMeitim***

When we recite this blessing, we are confronted with the assertion that there is more to reality than what one can perceive in this life and world. The words of this blessing praise God as the source of resurrection, just as God is the source, for example, of healing. These notions can be especially challenging to moderns because the contemporary world tends to denigrate claims that science cannot affirm. Life after death remains, of course, one of those notions which science has not been able to corroborate. Only those who totally embrace tradition, and have no trouble ignoring modern science, will be able to fully accept the message of this blessing with no hesitation.

Contemporary prayer books from the Reconstructing Judaism Movement have revised the Hebrew from *meḥayyei hameitim*, "restorer of life to the dead" to *meḥayei hakol*, "who gives and renews life," thus rejecting the notion of supernatural resurrection.[148] The current Reform prayer book displays an ambivalent approach to this blessing. It, too, uses the Hebrew wording *meḥayei hakol*, and translates "who gives life to all." But in parentheses, it includes the traditional phrase *meḥayei hameitim*, and translates "who revives the dead."[149] The Conservative Movement's *siddurim* of the past few decades had included the traditional phrase in Hebrew but obfuscated its challenging meaning by translating "Master of life and death." However, its current prayer book forthrightly translates that Hebrew phrase as "who gives life to the dead."[150]

The advantage to emending the Hebrew as the prayer books of Reconstructing Judaism and Reform Judaism have done is that the blessing more closely adheres to intellectual honesty: If we don't believe in an afterlife, we shouldn't pray as if we do. Its disadvantage is that it requires one to eschew a belief and expression that has been part of Jewish liturgy for at least 1,800 years.

---

*the Afterlife* (Lanham, Maryland: Rowman & Littlefield, 1994, 2009, 2019); Neil Gillman, *The Death of Death: Resurrection and Immortality in Jewish Thought* (Woodstock, Vermont, 1997).

[147] The Mishnah calls this blessing, simply, *Gevurot*, "Mighty Acts." See, e.g., *Mishnah Rosh HaShanah* 4:5. The root *g-v-r*, "mighty" occurs twice in this blessing.

[148] See, for example, *Kol Haneshamah: Daily* (Wyncote, Pennsylvania: The Reconstructionist Press, 1996), 102-103.

[149] See, for example, *Mishkan T'filah:A Reform Siddur* (Central Conference of American Rabbis, New York: 2007), 78.

[150] *Siddur Lev Shalem* (New York: The Rabbinical Assembly, 2016), 48.

A second way that people have viewed the original Hebrew blessing is as a symbolic, not a literal, statement. There is an occasion in which Jewish tradition itself applies the operative phrase of this passage outside of the *Amidah* in a symbolic way. When one encounters a close friend or family member after not having seen that person in at least a year, one praises God by saying *Barukh Attah... meḥayyei hameitim*, "Blessed are You... who restores life to the dead."[151] In this instance, the word *hameitim*, "the dead," is clearly meant metaphorically: meeting our friend after not having seen him or her for a year feels like our friend has been restored from the dead. Building on this non-literal reading of this concept, "restorer of the dead" can perhaps be taken to refer to God's power to restore hope and spirit to us when we are hopeless, that is, when we are emotionally or spiritually "dead." The meaning of this blessing then can be to praise God as the One Who can restore hope and a life-affirming frame of mind to one who is depressed and forlorn. Worshipers can recite this blessing with the intention of asking God to help them transcend depression and hopelessness.

A third way to view this blessing requires neither changing its wording nor its literal meaning, and yet does not require one to discount science. Science has discovered and documented the process of birth to an impressive degree. There are books that detail, in both words and illustrations, the development of new human life from the moment of conception to the moment of birth. Nevertheless, many moderns, no less than the ancients, are still filled with awe when we witness new life. The wonder involved in witnessing a human birth seems to transcend all the scientific explanations available to us. Birth still seems like a miraculous event, in spite of the impressive amount of knowledge modern civilization has gathered about it. It seems to point to a reality beyond that which we can explain even with the best efforts of science. We still are moved to ask, "Where did this new life come from?"

That same awe accompanies death. In spite of the ability of modern medicine to explain the causes of death, when we personally encounter the death of someone we knew, we are still moved to ask, "where did that person go?" The mystery that surrounds birth is the same mystery that accompanies death. Scientific details do not satisfy. When we learn of the death of someone close to us, we are still left feeling that we have experienced more than we can understand. Even for many moderns, when it comes to birth and to death, we often feel the presence of a reality beyond that which can be reduced to facts and figures.

---

[151] Babylonian Talmud, *Berakhot* 58b.

I do not mean to say that the awareness of such a reality inevitably leads to a belief in God restoring life to the dead. And yet, accepting the resurrecting power of God is not as big a leap of faith as it might seem, when it is put into the context of the sense of mystery that continues to characterize birth and death. This second blessing of the *Amidah* does not posit details about life after death. It is quite a bare statement. It simply praises God whose reality extends beyond life as we know it. And so, this blessing can be seen as a challenge to us. The challenge is to admit that science has not yet explained everything. Death remains a mystery, even in the modern age, and maybe, just maybe, this ancient Jewish tradition has intuited something true about the way God acts in the world. Seen in this way, when we recite the words of this blessing, we are challenged to praise God's involvement with us even after the death of those we love, as well as even after our own death.

## Blessing #3
## *Ha'Eil HaKadosh*, Holy God

**Individual's Version:**

You are holy, your name is holy, and holy ones every day praise you.
Blessed are you *YHVH*, the holy God.

**Communal Version (The *Kedushah*):**

We sanctify your name on earth as they sanctify it in heaven, as it is written by your prophet, "and one (angel) would call to another and say 'holy, holy, holy is *YHVH* of Constellations, his presence fills all the earth" (Isaiah 6:3).
Those facing them would say "Blessed"—"Blessed is the presence of *YHVH* in his place" (Ezekiel 3:12).
And in your holy writings it is written, "*YHVH* shall reign forever, your God, Zion, for all generations" (Psalms 146:10).
From generation to generation, we declare your greatness, we sanctify your holiness for all eternity.
Your praise will never leave our mouth forever, for you are a great and holy God and king,
Blessed are you, the holy God.

| Which *Kedushah* | Which verses | |
|---|---|---|
| ***Kedushah DeYotser*** | Is. 6:3 | Ez. 3:12 |
| ***Kedushah* in the Weekday *Amidah* —morning and afternoon and in the afternoon *Amidah* on Shabbat, Festivals, and *Rosh HaShanah*** | Is. 6:3 | Ez. 3:12 |
| ***Kedushah* in the morning *Amidah* on Shabbat and Festivals and *Rosh HaShanah*** | Is. 6:3 | Ez. 3:12 |
| ***Kedushah* in the *Musaf Amidah* on Shabbat** | Is. 6:3 | Ez. 3:12 |
| ***Kedushah* in the *Musaf Amidah* of Festivals and *Rosh HaShanahHaShanah*, and the morning, afternoon, and *Ne'ilah Amidah* on *Yom Kippur*** | Is. 6:3 | Ez. 3:12 |
| ***Kedushah DeSidra*** | Is. 6:3 + *Targum* (Aramaic Translation) | Ez. 3:12 + *Targum* (Aramaic Translation) |

There are two versions of this, third, blessing of the Amidah. The first, and simpler, version consists of just one sentence and the blessing formula; that is what is translated first above. The second, and more complex, version is known as "The *Kedushah*" ("Holiness") and is made up of several biblical verses, linked with connecting phrases, and concludes with the same blessing formula. When one recites the *Amidah* on one's own, the individual's version is utilized. When one recites the *Amidah* communally, the *Kedushah* version is recited. The literary theme of both versions is reflected in the recurring word *kadosh*, "holy." It is known in the most ancient rabbinic teachings as *Kedushat HaShem*, "Holiness of the Name (of God)."[152] In the Bible, one's name is considered an important portal to one's essence. This is why the divinely ordained changes in the names of Abraham, Sarah, and

[152] E.g., *Mishnah Rosh HaShanah* 4:5.

| | | | | |
|---|---|---|---|---|
| Ps. 146:10 | | | | |
| Ps. 146:10 | | | | |
| Ps. 146:10 | Dt. 6:4 | Nu. 15:41 | | |
| Ps. 146:10 | Dt. 6:4 | Nu. 15:41 | Ps. 8:2 | Zech. 14:9 |
| Ex. 15:11 + *Targum* (Aramaic Translation) | Is. 59:20-21 | Ps. 22:4 | | |

Jacob, among many others, signal changes in their destinies.[153] So, too, this blessing, "Holiness of the Name," deals with God's essence.

There are several versions of the *Kedushah* in Jewish liturgy both within any one rite (e.g., the Ashkenazic) and between the various contemporary rites that are still in use and the older rites for which we have only documentary evidence. There are six different versions of the *Kedushah* in the familiar form (Eastern European) of the Ashkenazic rite alone. Four of them occur within an *Amidah*; one occurs within the first blessing before the *Shema* in the morning (*Kedushah DeYotser*, "The *Kedushah* of the Creator Blessing"); and one occurs in the concluding service in the morning (*Kedushah DeSidra*, "The *Kedushah* of the Torah Lesson").

The six different versions of the *Kedushah*, along with the biblical verses included in each, are spelled out in the chart above.

[153] E.g., Abraham's name-change from Abram: Genesis 17:5; Sarah's name-change from Sarai: Genesis 17:15; Jacob's name-change to Yisrael (Israel): 32:28.

The Ashkenazic version of the *Kedushah* in the morning and afternoon weekday *Amidah* that I will deal with here in depth represent only two recensions of this prayer. Nevertheless, the basic themes found in this version apply to all the appearances of the *Kedushah*.

Central to our understanding of this blessing in all its versions is the famous verse (Isaiah 6:3):

> And (angel) one would call to the other,
> "Holy, holy, holy!
> The Lord of Hosts!
> His presence fills all the earth!"

The words "holy, holy, holy" in Hebrew are *kadosh, kadosh, kadosh*. The verse itself is quoted in its entirety in the *Kedushah*. It is hinted at in the shorter version of the blessing, because forms of the word *kadosh*, "holy," occur three times in the body of the blessing (although not three times in a row).

The background to this verse is a mystical vision conveyed to Isaiah before he served God and Israel as prophet. Isaiah beholds a likeness of God seated on a throne in a supernal Temple. He sees six-winged angels attending to God in this Temple. It is these angels who, referring to God, chant "one to another" the words "Holy, holy, holy..." Isaiah reports that when he heard these words, he felt the walls shaking and saw smoke fill the room. Overwhelmed, he cries out, "Woe is me; I am lost!" because he felt unworthy to have witnessed such a transcendant revelation: He saw a likeness of God and heard the chant of the angels. This vision turned out to be the experience that launched him on his path as a prophet.

The word *kadosh* in the Bible signifies "apartness, sacredness."[154] So, God's fundamental nature is identified as apart or other from reality as we usually know it. This blessing praises God as *Ha'Eil HaKadosh*, "The God who is *Kadosh*," that is, the God who is apart, separate, other, of a different reality.

When the *Kedushah*, the longer version of this blessing, is recited, a second biblical verse describing a prophetic vision of God's quintessence is added to the "holy, holy, holy" passage from Isaiah. That additional verse is Ezekiel 3:12:

[154] Francis Brown, S.R. Driver, Charles A Briggs, *A Hebrew and English Lexicon of the Old Testament* (Oxford, 1906), 871.

*Barukh kevod YHVH mimekomo—*
*"Blessed is the Presence of the Lord in His place."*

The background to this verse is not so different from Isaiah's vision: a visualization of God that becomes the commissioning of a prophet. The vision itself, however, is different, and is more detailed. Ezekiel sees an image in the midst of a storm that is slowly approaching. As the storm approaches, he sees four creatures in the swirling tempest. As their likenesses come closer, he can see that each had four faces: the faces of a human, a lion, an ox, and an eagle. Each creature also had four legs, and four wings. In other words, these creatures were thoroughly "other." As the tempest comes even closer, details become clearer. The fantastic nature of what he sees becomes even further realized. He sees that the creatures move by means of what he perceives to be "two wheels cutting through each other" underneath them, the rims of which "were covered all over with eyes."[155] They appeared to be carrying a platform, and upon that platform was a human-like form sitting on a throne. Ezekiel describes different parts of the appearance as shining like crystal, glowing like amber, gleaming like fire, radiating like a rainbow. Everything about what he saw seemed to be "apart" from normal reality. When he realized that he was peering at an image of God he flung himself down on his face. Then God spoke to him and commissioned him as a prophet.

Before this uniquely mystical encounter concludes, Ezekiel hears "a great roaring sound: 'Blessed is the Presence of the Lord in his place.'"[156] It is this line that is quoted in the *Kedushah* along with the "Holy, holy, holy" verse from Isaiah. Traditional Jewish exegesis interpreted this passage as Ezekiel hearing angels chant these words, "Blessed is the Presence of the Lord in his place."[157]

Although there are several more biblical verses that are quoted in the various versions of the *Kedushah*, there is one more, a third verse in addition to those from Isaiah and Ezekiel, that is found in most of the forms from an-

[155] Ezekiel 1:16, 18. See Syviu N. Bunta, "In Heaven or on Earth: A Misplaced Temple Question about Ezekiel's Vision" in Daphna Arbel and Andrei A. Orlov, eds., *With Letters of Light (Be-otiyot Shel Or): Studies in the Dead Sea Scrolls, Early Jewish Apocalypticism, Magic and Mysticism in Honor of Rachel Elior* (New York, Berlin: de Gruyter, 2011), 28-44.

[156] Ezekiel 3:12.

[157] Although modern scholars (beginning, perhaps, with Samuel David Luzzatto, 1800-1865, Italy), interpret the verse very differently. Based upon strong textual evidence, they emend one letter of the Hebrew and view this sentence not as a chant or a quote at all, but simply as a continuation of the narrative so that the whole verse would read: "Then a spirit carried me away, and from behind me I heard a great roaring sound as the Presence of the LORD rose from where it stood." So, the New JPS edition of the *Tanakh*. For further elucidation, see Moshe Greenberg, *The Anchor Bible: Ezekiel 1-20* (New York: Doubleday, 1983), 70-71.

cient and modern sources, and that is Psalm 146:10—"The Lord shall reign forever, your God, O Zion, for all generations. Halleluyah." There is much evidence that this line was understood to function as a kind of coronation ceremony of God in which both angels and humans participate. Note, for example, that a Sephardic version of the *Kedushah* commences with the words *keter yitnu lekha...* "A crown they give to you, *YHVH* our God, angels massed above, and your people Israel gathered below. All of them together three times proclaim your holiness..." The theme of "coronating" God is found explicitly, too, in an Ashkenazic version not recited as part of the *Amidah*, but as part of *Birkat Yotser Or*, the Blessing of Creating Light, that precedes the *Shema* in *Shaḥarit*: As the conclusion of six verbs, building dramatically in power, comes the final verb, *u'mamlikhim*—"(The angels) bless, praise, glorify, revere, sanctify, and coronate..."[158]

## The *Kedushah* and *Merkavah* Mysticism

Mystical contemplation of the two verses from Isaiah and Ezekiel played an important part in an ancient form of Jewish mysticism known as *Merkavah*, or "chariot," mysticism. The ancient texts that contain these teachings form the *Hekhalot* literature. The word *Hekhalot*, or "temples/sanctuaries" refers to the Temple that Isaiah saw in his vision. *Merkavah*, "chariot," refers to the vision of Ezekiel.[159] To Jewish mystics, Isaiah and Ezekiel had been granted the incredible opportunity to "listen in" on two lines of angelic prayer that resound, perhaps constantly, in heaven. The words that these two prophets heard were therefore considered very precious. After all, these were words of divine praise chanted by the angels themselves. The texts of this branch of Jewish mysticism describe heavenly journeys taken by adepts who sought to be vouchsafed the same visions as Isaiah and Ezekiel.

There have been some important studies in recent decades about the connections between ancient Jewish mystic literature and Jewish liturgy.[160]

[158] See a detailed analysis of this aspect of the *Kedushah* in Arthur Green, *Keter: The Crown of God in Early Jewish Mysticism* (Princeton: Princeton University Press, 1997), especially chapter two, "Coronation and *Kedushah*," 12-19. Joseph Heinemann considered this element to be central to the meaning of the *Kedushah*: He interpreted the *Kedushah* in general as a coronation of God. See his "*Kedushah* and Kingship in the *Shema* and in the *Kedushah* in the *Amidah*" [Hebrew], *Iyunei Tefillah* (Jerusalem: Magnes Press, 1981), 12-21.

[159] The word *merkavah*, "chariot," does not actually appear in the Ezekiel narrative. It is derived from another verse in the Bible, I Chronicles 28:18, and is the term that Jewish mystical tradition uses to describe the "vehicle" that the image of God seemed to be "riding," and which the four heavenly creatures seemed to be "leading."

[160] A fine summary of the pioneering scholarship is found in Vita Daphna Arbel, *Beholders of Divine Secrets: Mysticism and Myth in the Hekhalot and Merkavah Literature* (Albany: State University of New York Press, 2003). See additionally: Ezra Fleischer, *Liturgical Poetry in the Middle Ages* [Hebrew]

The picture is, as yet, still not completely understood. Scholarly opinion is divided on the chronology of this literature and on the circle that authored it. One school of thought places its origin at the early stages of Rabbinic Literature, in the Tannaitic period and continuing in the Amoraic period, with roots earlier in the Second Temple Period and with connections to the sect that wrote the Dead Sea Scrolls. Another school holds that the earliest stage may be in the late Amoraic period, extending into the early Geonic period. Some hold that its authors are the Sages of the Talmud, while others posit that its creators were outside of the circle of rabbinic Sages, whether deriving from circles of priests (whose power and prestige were lost with the destruction of the second Temple in 70 CE and who then symbolically "transferred" their expertise to heavenly sanctuaries), or professional scribes who drew on the ways and rites of magic, or other groups that were outside of the rabbinic elite. Scholars are also divided on the question of whether the mystical experiences described in it reflect actual experiences or are merely literary constructs. These writings include a number of descriptions of mystical ascent to chambers of the heavenly sanctuaries, *Hekhalot*, passing benevolent and malevolent angels, with the goal of beholding God sitting on the throne in the uppermost chamber. These descriptions utilize fantastical, sometimes unpronounceable, names of angels and of God. Throughout some of these documents, fragments of what we would recognize as unusual forms of the *Kedushah* abound, repeating dozens of times.

According to those scholars who see actual spiritual experience behind the writings, the various forms of the *Kedushah* may have been chanted to induce visions of the heavenly choir that chants these verses from Isaiah and Ezekiel. There is some evidence that they repeated the words over and over, in a kind of mantra, to help generate the vision they craved.

An unusual and strange passage from *Merkavah* mysticism regarding the *Kedushah* is cited in several medieval commentaries and codes of Jewish

(Jerusalem, 1975), 32-33, 49, 133, 179, 183, 280, 448f; Joseph Dan, "The Emergence of Mystical Prayer," in Joseph Dan and Frank Talmage, eds., *Studies in Jewish Mysticism* (Cambridge, 1982), 85-120; Meir Bar Ilan, *The Mysteries of Jewish Prayer and Hekhalot* [Hebrew] (Ramat Aviv, 1987); Idem, "Major Trends in the Formulation and Crystallization of the *Kedushah*," [Hebrew], *Daat*, 25, 1990, 5-20; Peter Schäfer, "Jewish Liturgy and Magic" in *Geschichte—Tradition—Reflexion: Festschrift fur Martin Hengel zum 70 Geburstag*. I Judentum. (Tubingen, 1996), 541-556; Ruth Langer, *To Worship God Properly: Tensions Between Liturgical Custom and Halakhah in Judaism* (Cincinnati, 1998), chapter 4, "Individual Recitation of the *Kedushah*: The Impact of Mysticism on Minhag and Halakhah," 188-244; Esther G. Chazon, "The *Qedushah* Liturgy and its History In Light of the Dead Sea Scrolls," in Joseph Tabory, ed., *From Qumran to Cairo: Studies in the History of Prayer* (Jerusalem, 1999), 7-17; Rachel Elior, *The Three Temples: On The Emergence of Jewish Mysticism* (Liverpool, 2004).

law.[161] In it, God addresses mystics who, through deep concentration, have achieved a vision of God on the heavenly throne. God says to them:

> ... Tell my children what I do during *Shaḥarit* and *Minḥah* prayers each day, each time Israel recites before me *Kadosh* ("holy," a reference to the *Kedushah* or a proto-*Kedushah*).
>
> Teach them and tell them: Raise your eyes to the firmament opposite your house of prayer at the moment that you recite before me *Kadosh*. For I have no enjoyment in all of my world which I created like that moment when your eyes are raised to my eyes and my eyes are raised to your eyes when you say before me *Kadosh*. For the sound which issues from your mouths at that moment quavers and rises before me like the sweet savor [of a sacrifice].
>
> And testify to them what you see me do to the sculpted image of the face of Jacob their Patriarch which is engraved for me on my throne of glory. For the moment that you say before me *Kadosh* I bow before it and caress it and embrace it and kiss it and my hands are upon his arms three times, parallel to the three times that you say before me *Kadosh* as it is said, *Kadosh, Kadosh, Kadosh.*

While it is hard to know the precise meaning of this fascinating teaching, it does say that the recitation of the *Kedushah* brings pleasure to God like no other pleasure.[162] Because of the power of the specific words recited—along with a mystical mutual gaze between the worshiper and God—a deep intimacy is effected. Each has lifted their eyes to meet the gaze of the other. This passionate description is reflected in the extraordinary language toward the end of the passage where the wording verges on the erotic and on the quasi-pagan. The description of God's reaction to Israel's chanting (bow, caress, embrace, kiss, placing hands) is reminiscent of the Mishnah's description of the pagan worship of idols.[163] The threefold usage of the root *nasa* "raise"

[161] It is cited in part, for example, in the 14th-century code by R. Yakov ben Asher, *Arba'ah Turim, Oraḥ Ḥayyim, Siman* 125. An echo of it—regarding lifting one's eyes—is found in the *Shulḥan Arukh, Oraḥ Ḥayyim*, 125:2, in the gloss. The entire passage, with manuscript variations, is found in the critical edition of *Hekhalot* literature edited by Peter Schäfer, *Synopse zur Hekhalot-Literatur* (Tubingen, 1981), 73, #163-164.

[162] For an analysis of this passage, see Moshe Idel, "On the *Kedushah* and the Vision of the Chariot" [Hebrew], in Joseph Tabory, ed., *From Qumran to Cairo: Studies in the History of Prayer* (Jerusalem, 1999), 7-17.

[163] *Sanhedrin* 7:6.

may carry a secondary valence of wedding language (*nisui'in*). It is hard to miss the implication that the recitation of the *Kedushah* is viewed as an opportunity for especially deep intimacy with God. Note that the *Kedushah*'s place in regular liturgy seems to be assumed by this text since it mentions the place of the *Kedushah* in the morning and afternoon services. While this mystical passage, therefore, did not precede the *Kedushah*'s liturgical role, scholars speculate that this ancient mystical passage, and the many mentions of the verses of the *Kedushah* within the *Hekhalot* literature may represent a kind of alternate liturgy to the mainstream worship developed by the talmudic rabbis. In this parallel liturgy, prayers and incantations abound in a kind of free-form structure with connections to magical and quasi-pagan practice. This literature removes the veil that separates the heavenly from the earthly, and visions of angels and, ultimately, God upon the throne, are close and palpable.

The *Kedushah* has stringencies in the halakhic literature because, apparently, of its elevated nature, reflecting its stature as a prayer of the angels. One is not to speak during the *Kedushah*. One is to bring one's feet together while standing for the duration of the prayer. One should be careful not to chant every line, but to preserve the antiphonal (i.e., dialogue; call and response) nature of the prayer in which the leader prompts the congregation to recite the biblical verses.[164] The uniquely sacred nature of the lines chanted, derived from its connection to angelic prayer, bestows a uniquely sacred quality to this blessing.

## Spiritual Commentary on *Ha'Eil HaKadosh*

The individual who is conscious of the literary history of this blessing understands that it may be an attempt to bring on the kind of mystical encounter with God that Isaiah experienced. In the expanded *Kedushah* version, the encounter Ezekiel also experienced is brought to bear, as well as the kind of mindset in which we are ready to accept God as our King, as an authority in the world above us. The instruction from the *Hekhalot* text about God and the worshiper locking eyes during this blessing recalls for me a passage by Arthur Green:

[164] *Shulḥan Arukh, Oraḥ Ḥayyim* 125:1-2. And see the parallel passage in *Arokh HaShulḥan*. The latter, as well as the *Mishneh Berurah* mention leniencies regarding preserving the dialogue between prayer leader and congregation, permitting the congregation to say the lines of both. However, both of these authorities acknowledge that the proper recitation, reflecting the literary structure of the prayer itself, is to chant it in an antiphonal way.

> "The eye with which I see God and the eye with which God sees me are the same eye," says the great Christian mystic Meister Eckhardt. The mirror turns both ways.[165]

It helps if a worshiper takes seriously the strictures against saying anything but the words that make up this passage, and against moving from one's place (swaying, or *shucklen*, is, of course, permitted). These rules can help in concentration. A participant in this prayer can take advantage of the mysticism of the moment that the words provide. If this is realized, a worshiper can be open to a truly spiritual encounter. Recalling the ancient name of this blessing, *Kedushat HaShem*, "Holiness of the Name," the words indicate an encounter with God's essence (God's name), to the extent that we can perceive it. The worshiper should keep in mind that we are repeating words that our prophets of 2,500 years ago felt overwhelmed to hear. It can deepen the moment if we also consider that the very words we are pronouncing have been the focus of Jewish mystics for countless generations, as they tried to sense God's essence. If one keeps these things in mind, and opens oneself up, chanting this blessing can become a peak moment of the service.

When one recites the shorter version of this blessing, one is celebrating and praising God as *kadosh*, as "apart, sacred." This is one of those times during prayer when it is most appropriate for the worshiper to slow down and concentrate on the experience behind the words. That experience involves an irony. On the one hand, the blessing describes God in words. On the other hand, the words refer to God as "apart" from our reality. How can we concentrate on something that is not part of our reality? One answer is that God's existence is not considered totally alien from the reality we know. Our tradition, like many religious practices, is filled with stories of ordinary people who feel that they have encountered the presence of God in the world, if even fleetingly. We may not be prophets, but as human beings, we are considered to have the capacity to apprehend hints of God's presence even in our mundane reality. In another context, the Talmud declares that even if prophets do not live in contemporary times, and so Israel "are not prophets, nevertheless, they are the descendants of prophets."[166] And so, we may yet be able to access the teachings and experiences of our ancestors, the prophets.

In order to engage this opportunity while reciting this blessing, we can call up those moments when we have perceived a hint of God's presence. We can

[165] Arthur Green, *Ehyeh: A Kabbalah for Tomorrow* (Woodstock, Vermont: Jewish Lights Publishing, 2003), 52.
[166] Babylonian Talmud, *Pesaḥim* 66a-b.

attempt to reconnect with the sensations we felt when we sensed God close to us. Reciting this blessing is an opportunity to induce the consciousness we had that God is right here, with us, right now in the most personal and intimate way. That is why this is one of those times to slow down in our recitation. One who is conscious of the significance of this blessing would want to linger in this sacred moment. We are challenged to make this a moment "apart" from our normal reality. One may not always succeed in focusing well enough to truly feel an intimation of God's presence, but that is the goal.

Another way to envision the experience of this blessing is to concentrate on God's presence within us. To say that God is "within us" does not mean that we are God. Rather, it means that the spirit of God animates us in some way. There are schools of Jewish mystical thought which have maintained that all existence is God; that one cannot divide between what is God and what is not God.[167] This mindset allows one, through concentration, to connect with that hint of God that resides within. Using this attitude, one would strive to unite with that part of oneself where God's presence is found while reciting the words of this blessing. In this way, the recitation of this blessing becomes an attempt to be at one with God's essence by being at one with the spark of God within.

A difficulty faced by many worshipers who endeavor to reach a spiritual high through the *Kedushah*, as in many parts of the service, is the pace at which the words are typically chanted in the synagogue service. Since the *Kedushah* is chanted twice a day, every weekday (and three times on Shabbat and festivals), the routinization of the ritual has led to the diminishing of the mystical moment as well. That is unfortunate. On Shabbat, when more time is often devoted to chanting the *Kedushah*, the central point of this blessing—to achieve a closeness with the Presence more than at most other places in the service—is, nevertheless, often lost. What remains from the original motivation for this blessing seems to be a sense that the congregation ought to be engaged in song more than in other areas of the service. And so, prayer leaders tend to weave multiple melodies into the various lines of the service. Song can, indeed, serve to bring worshipers a sense of the Presence. But a question in considering the purpose of the singing can be helpful here: Are the melodies chosen for the sake of achieving a spiritual high or they chosen simply to encourage participation, song for the sake of song?

[167] See the very thoughtful discussion of this non-dualistic understanding of God in Marcia Falk, *The Book of Blessings* (San Francisco, 1996), 419-421 and in Jay Michaelson, *Everything is God: The Radical Path of Nondual Judaism* (Boston, 2009).

## Blessing #4
## *Ḥonein HaDa'at*, Gracious Giver of Knowledge

> You grace humankind with knowledge and teach humanity wisdom.
> Grace us with knowledge, wisdom, and enlightenment.
> Blessed are you *YHVH*, Gracious Giver of Knowledge.

This is the first of a series of requests or pleas to God. Each of these blessings contains an appeal for something specific. The patterns of words that repeat in each benediction point to the unique request that is its theme.

This particular blessing consists of three parts: An opening sentence describing God, a plea, and a concluding *ḥatimah*, or "seal."

The opening sentence describes God as the granter of knowledge:

> You grace humankind with knowledge and teach humanity understanding.

Having described God as the source of knowledge, the blessing then continues with a short, direct plea for knowledge from God:

> Grace us with knowledge, wisdom, and enlightenment.

Finally, it concludes, as do all the blessings in the *Amidah*, with a *ḥatimah*, using the blessing formula, *Barukh Attah...*:

> Blessed are You, *YHVH*, Gracious Giver of knowledge.

Driving home the point that this blessing is concerned with knowledge are two literary devices. The first is the use of three synonyms for knowledge, *dei'ah* ("knowledge"), *binah* ("wisdom"), and *haskeil* ("understanding"). The second is that the root for "knowledge" (*dei'ah*) itself occurs three times.

Another word occurs three times in this brief entreaty, namely, the root for *ḥanan*, "to graciously give." It is significant that the text doesn't say that God simply "gives" knowledge, but that God "graciously gives" knowledge. *Ḥanan* is related to the word *ḥein*, "grace." "Grace" denotes a gift that is unmerited. Expressing that God grants knowledge as an unmerited gift implies that knowledge comes from God's domain and that we receive it as an unearned favor.

**Spiritual Commentary on *Ḥonein HaDa'at***

There are two kinds of inner intentions I would suggest when reciting this blessing requesting knowledge. The first relates to knowledge in general. The second is linked with specific knowledge.

When we approach God with the words of this passage, we are acknowledging that whatever wisdom we possess in general comes from the grace of God. In this manner, this blessing becomes a statement of humility. When we ask God to continue to grace us with understanding, we are acknowledging that the source of our knowledge is God.[168] This doesn't mean that human beings can't make efforts to increase our own knowledge. But it does mean that our capacity for wisdom and understanding is not completely the result of our efforts. We have been granted a certain facility for intelligence that we did not achieve through our own exertion. We were born with it. When we acknowledge the role of heaven in whatever intelligence we possess, we are humbly accepting that we don't deserve all the credit for whatever wisdom we've managed to acquire. We are crediting God. This is one kind of inner meaning available to a worshiper as we pray these words.

Another way we may direct our heart when reciting this text can relate to a specific issue or problem that we find challenging at the moment. The right way ahead may be unclear. In this situation, the words of this blessing can be used to ask God's help in pointing to the path we need to follow. When I have used this blessing in this manner, I recite the words up to, but not including, the *ḥatimah*, the seal (i.e., *Barukh Attah...*, "Blessed are You..."). I concentrate on the repeated assertion that knowledge comes from God. Then I stop and focus on the conundrum facing me. I try to bring the exact issue I'm facing to the very front of my consciousness. In so doing, I present the issue to God, the one who graciously grants wisdom. I try to quiet myself so that I can be open to guidance that may flow to me when I am centering on the presence of the Source of wisdom. I stand in this way for a minute or two instead of the usual five or ten seconds it takes to merely say the words themselves. Finally, I recite the concluding words, the *ḥatimah*. I often find that either immediately, or soon afterward, this sort of concentration leads to the beginning of a resolution to the challenge I was facing.

[168] Notice that the bulk of the English word "acknowledge" derives from the word "knowledge."

## Blessing #5
## *HaRotzeh BiTeshuvah*, Desirer of Repentance

Return us, our father, to your Torah,
Draw us close, our king, to your service,
And restore us, in complete repentance, before you.
Blessed are You *YHVH*, Desirer of Repentance.

Three brief pleas, followed by the *ḥatimah*, make up this blessing:

1. Return us, our Father, to Your Torah,
2. Draw us close, our King, to Your service,
3. And restore us, in complete repentance, before You.
Blessed are You, Desirer of Repentance.

Embedded within those words is the familiar phrase from the High Holidays, *Avinu Malkeinu*, "Our father... our king." This blessing contains a bit of the spirit of *Rosh HaShanah* and *Yom Kippur*, which is the call to repentance.

The blessing uses the same two literary devices as the previous blessing in order to make its theme obvious. The first is that it uses three synonyms for "return/repent:" *hashiveinu* ("return us"), *vekorveinu* ("draw us close"), *vehaḥazireinu* ("restore us"). The second is that the root of one of those verbs, *hashiveinu* ("return us") itself is repeated three times.

So: Three pleas plus the *ḥatimah*, "the seal," all on the same theme of repentance/return, add up to one extended request to God: Help us return to You![169]

### Spiritual Commentary on *HaRotzeh BiTeshuvah*

There is some irony in this entreaty. This blessing assumes that we feel guilt because we have strayed, in some way, from proper service to God and God's Torah. If so, the natural step would be to repent and then to ask God for

[169] Several of the prayer texts discovered in the Cairo Genizah attest to the version of the *Amidah* in medieval times in the Land of Israel, known as the Palestinian Rite. When the Crusaders attacked the Muslims in the Land of Israel, the mayhem and destruction they brought to the Jewish community there effectively destroyed this rite of Jewish liturgy. The version of this blessing in that rite is strikingly simple. It consists of one verse from the Bible plus the *ḥatimah*, the seal. The biblical citation is Lamentations 5:21: "Return us, *YHVH*, to You, and we shall return; renew our days as of old." This verse is the last verse of Lamentations chanted on the night of *Tisha B'Av*, the holiday dedicated to mourning the destruction of the ancient first and second Temples in Jerusalem. The destruction of those Temples is understood, in Jewish tradition, as coming as a result of our sinfulness. Interestingly, in this biblical verse, the root of the verb *hashiveinu* ("return us") occurs three times as well. See Elbogen, *Jewish Liturgy*, 42.

forgiveness. In fact, the theme of the blessing that follows this one is, indeed, forgiveness. However, this blessing appeals directly to God to cause us to repent. The irony is that in the words of this blessing, we concede that we cannot even begin to return to God without the help of God! Even though we admit that we have caused a breach in our relationship with God, we ask for God's help in effecting a change in heart. And when the blessing speaks of our need to return to God, it may be that the distance between ourselves and God is a result of our abusing something, or someone, in God's creation.

Although modern worshipers may feel that we are unnecessarily demeaning ourselves as we say these words, there is an insight that we can recognize within this blessing. We often do need help to even begin the process of repentance. This blessing accepts a psychological truth: We don't like to admit that we've done something wrong. We are masters of rationalization. Bob Dylan captured this in his song, "Man in the Long Black Coat" –

> Preacher was talking there's a sermon he gave
> He said every man's conscience is vile and depraved.
> You cannot depend on it to be your guide
> When it's you who must keep it satisfied.[170]

Without necessarily demeaning ourselves, we may find spiritual and ethical support in this blessing that has us ask for help from a reality greater than ourselves in admitting our own guilt.

## Blessing #6
## *Ḥanun HaMarbeh Lislo'aḥ*
## God Who Graciously and Abundantly Forgives

> Forgive us, our father, for we have sinned.
> Pardon us, our king, for we have transgressed.
> For you pardon and forgive.
> Blessed are you *YHVH*, who graciously and abundantly forgives.

[170] Recorded on his 1989 album, "Oh Mercy." Some have said that the title of the song relates to a Ḥasidic teacher of Dylan's. Dylan was known to study with teachers from the Chabad/Lubavitch sect, including with Rabbi Manis Friedman, who was active in the Twin Cities. Dylan contributed praise to one of Friedman's books which was published on the jacket cover. The book is: *Doesn't Anyone Blush Anymore?* (San Francisco: Harper Collins, 1990).

The theme of this blessing is connected to that of the previous one: Once we have recognized that we are guilty of some wrongdoing, we are moved to ask for forgiveness. This passage has us declare our guilt in unmistakable language in two synonymous ways: *ḥatanu*, "we have sinned," and *pashanu*, "we have transgressed."

What is stressed, however, is God's forgiving nature. Seven words, out of the twenty that make up this blessing, relate to God's pardoning characteristics: The root *salaḥ*, "forgive," occurs three times; the root *maḥal*, "pardon," twice; and the expression *ḥanun hamarbeh*, "graciously and abundantly," completes the picture.[171] There are many different images in the Bible of how God responds to sin. Among them, there are portrayals of God in a strict and punishing mode. The framers of this blessing could have emphasized the punishment that awaits the unrepentant sinner or the acceptance that awaits him or her. They chose, in this blessing, to stress tolerance and forbearance as the attributes of God that will greet one who admits sin.

Like the previous blessing, the words *Avinu* and *Malkeinu*, "our Father," "our King," familiar from the High Holidays, are found here, too. Asking for forgiveness is certainly related to the themes of the Days of Awe, but here, it is recited on a daily basis.

**Spiritual Commentary on *Ḥanun HaMarbeh Lislo'aḥ***

Why turn to God for forgiveness? If the wrong done is confined strictly to a ritual matter, then perhaps God is the only one who needs to be turned to for forgiveness. But if the wrong done by us was against another person, why turn to God? As was hinted at in the Spiritual Commentary to the previous blessing, there seems to be a sense that when we wrong another person, we wrong God as well. When a human being is hurt, God is hurt; therefore, we must not only ask forgiveness from the other person; we must also ask forgiveness from God. When we cause pain to another human being, we cause a tear in the spiritual fabric of the cosmos. That tear must be repaired.

It is well known that the High Holidays of *Rosh HaShanah* and *Yom Kippur* are times for introspection, especially regarding sinning against other people. Less well known is that this blessing of the *Amidah* gives Jews the opportunity to scan our relationships with others on a daily basis, three times

[171] *Hamarbeh lislo'aḥ*, "abundantly forgives" is based, almost exactly, on the last two words in Isaiah 55:7 (*yarbeh lislo'aḥ*), a verse that is recited on the High Holidays: "Let the wicked give up his ways, the sinful man his plans; let him turn back to *YHVH*, and he will pardon him; to our God, for he abundantly forgives."

a day, in fact. Viewed one way, this blessing's concern with daily sin may seem overly dark and kowtowing. But viewed another way, it can be a healthy moment of nurturing the relationships with people we care about. It can be a time to ask whether there are things that need repair in our connections to the people we love or with whom we work. A quiet time, a prayerful time, in the presence of God who is portrayed as welcoming of such thoughts, may lend itself very well for such *ḥeshbon hanefesh*, "accounting of the soul." If recited with true consciousness, this blessing can help us develop great sensitivity to the way our actions affect others. There is an ideal implied by this blessing. That ideal is a community in which each person reviews their relationship with those around them three times a day, in the presence of God. This ideal community puts great value in repairing the pain that we inflict on those close to us. The key is to allow the words to open our hearts.

## Blessing #7
## *Go'eil Yisrael*, Liberator of Israel

> Take note of our oppression,
> fight our fight and liberate us quickly for the sake of your name.
> For you are a powerful Liberator.
> Blessed are you *YHVH*, Liberator of Israel.

Liberation is the theme of this blessing. The Hebrew root *ga'al*, "liberate," stands out: it occurs some three times in the short passage: *u'ge'aleinu... ki go'eil ḥazak attah... Barukh attah Adonai, go'eil Yisra'eil*, "liberate us... You are a powerful Liberator. Blessed are You, Liberator of Israel." The root *ga'al* is usually translated as "redeem." The word "redeem," meaning "rescue," is an uncommon usage in modern American English. To translate the root *ga'al*, as "redeem," as many prayer books do, serves more to confuse than to clarify. The word "liberate" captures the sense of the Hebrew more closely in modern American usage. This blessing asks of God: "Liberate us... You are a powerful liberator. Blessed are You *YHVH*, Liberator of Israel."

This blessing is especially replete with biblical overtones. The opening phrase of the blessing is based upon Psalms 119:153-154. Psalm 119 is the longest chapter in the Book of Psalms, with 176 verses arranged in a multiple alphabetic acrostic. It is also one of the most easily accessible chapters of the Psalms for moderns. In it, the poet thanks God for God's presence in their life and asks for God to continue to teach them and to help them, using overtly emotional, as well as spiritual, expressions. Verses 153-154 function as the background to the opening of our blessing.[172]

In the psalm, the poet is talking about himself alone, and so, the wording is in the singular: "Take note of **my** oppression... Fight **my** fight and liberate **me**." In the blessing, as in most of Jewish liturgy, the language is pluralized: "Take note of **our** oppression... Fight **our** fight and liberate **us**."

As I mentioned, Psalm 119 is written in the form of an individual's prayer. The Psalms have long served as every person's prayer book. That is, Jews and Christians have traditionally recited the ancient words of the text, which were imagined to be written by King David, as their own heart's outpouring.[173] The tendency of the Jewish prayer book to pluralize language which, in the Bible, is in the singular form, is well known. In fact, we will see an example of an entire biblical verse cited *verbatim*, except that it is pluralized in the very next blessing of the *Amidah*, *Birkat Rofei Ḥolei Amo Yisrael*, "Healer of the Sick of His People, Israel." This literary style of adapting the words of an individual for group recitation has the effect of blurring the lines between the particular and the collective, between one person and the entire people.

The phrasing of the blessing's opening, *re'eih na v'onyeinu*, "take note of our oppression," is, as shown, based directly on Psalms 119:153. However, it bears mentioning that this same basic word pattern is used by individuals in many places in the Bible to ask for God's liberating help.[174] Similarly, this word pattern would also bring the communal rescue of our people from Egypt to mind. A striking parallel to the opening of our blessing is found in the Burning Bush story in Exodus 3:7:

| **The Blessing** | **The Burning Bush: Exodus 3:7** |
|---|---|
| Take note of our oppression... | I have taken note of the oppression of my people in Egypt... |

[172] Interestingly, a verse from Jeremiah with the theme of liberation—31:11—is recited every evening of the year, in its entirety, as part of the blessings surrounding the *Shema*. In it, the prophet reminds the people of God's care for them by referring to the liberation from Egypt with the root *ga'al*.

[173] On this traditional use of Psalms, see James L. Kugel, "Topics in the History of the Spirituality of Psalms," in *Jewish Spirituality, Vol. 1: From The Bible Through The Middle Ages*, ed., Arthur Green (New York: Crossroad, 1986), 113-144.

[174] This word pattern—*ra'ah...oni*, "see...oppression"—is used in the Bible by individuals ranging from the matriarch Leah in Genesis to anonymous Israelite worshipers in other Psalms to the prophet who witnessed the destruction of the First Temple in Lamentations to Job. See Gen. 29:32; Ps. 9:14; Ps. 25:18; Ps. 31:8; Job 10:15; Lam. 1:9. See also: 1S 1:11; Neh. 9:9.

And so, the phrasing in this blessing brings to mind both individual and communal pleas for God's help.

**Spiritual Commentary on *Go'eil Yisrael***

Spiritual grounding and determination are key factors supporting potential physical or military liberation. I use the word "spiritual" here in the sense of a consciousness of, and a commitment to, something beyond mere physical preservation of oneself, one's loved ones, or homeland. A person, or a people, who is convinced that it has a powerful ally in the spiritual realm will be positively disposed to take action toward liberating others or toward self-liberation.

Concentrating on the need to ask for support from God when confronting persecution of any kind can yield several benefits. It can reassure us that we are not alone in facing oppression, nor is any struggle for liberation hopeless. A core historical experience of the Jewish people, as reflected in its liturgy, is the liberation from Egypt.[175] The Exodus is paradigmatic of a seemingly hopeless struggle by a powerless, persecuted group against one of the great world powers of the ancient world. Over and over again, the Book of Exodus declares that the purpose of this liberation wasn't only to free the descendants of Abraham and Sarah, but to drive home the point that God's liberating power is superior to even the most ascendant human authority. That very point is hinted at in this blessing's description of God as *go'eil ḥazak*, "a powerful Liberator." Additionally, concentrating on the need to ask for God's help in facing a struggle can help us realize that the physical or military dimension is never enough. The combination of spiritual strength with physical strength is a much more potent force than brute force alone.[176]

The blessing from the *Amidah* under consideration here is certainly a natural one when we want to ask God's help in communal struggles or personal struggles.

A wise way to recite this blessing is to pause before actually reciting the words, and to ponder and identify the kind of oppression we wish to focus on when asking God's help. This passage gains much power and relevance when it is endowed with specific meaning by the worshiper. What can a plea for liberation mean when *u'ge'aleinu*, "and liberate us!" is intoned thought-

[175] Emil L. Fackenheim calls it a "root experience." See his *God's Presence In History: Jewish Affimations and Philosophical Reflections* (New York: Harper Torchbooks, 1972), 8-14.

[176] See the book-length study of the effect that the Book of Exodus has had on liberation movements of various peoples throughout history, Michael Walzer, *Exodus and Revolution* (New York: Basic Books, 1985).

lessly? We need to focus. Once we are holding in our mind the struggle for which we need God's help, we are ready to access the power of this blessing.

How does this blessing work?[177] Will the particular liberation we are requesting occur because we have demonstrated our faith in God, acknowledged that true liberation cannot occur without God, and so, God will reward us by granting our request? Does God answer the needs of only those who overtly recognize God's dominion? What of the morality of our request? In nearly every battle and war, there are people of faith on both sides who entreat God to help their side win. If God is good and God is all-powerful, then the moral side in any conflict ought to win without any request to God!

I believe that the blessing works in a different way than all of these approaches. I don't believe that it is an attempt to persuade God to reward us by answering our particular request among the myriad of prayers directed to God. I also don't believe that it is an attempt to ask God to act on our behalf, liberating us, by vanquishing some external or internal enemy.

Additionally, ethics play a role. Just as the Talmud declares invalid the use of a stolen ritual object in a ceremony,[178] so too, I would think that unethical applications of prayer are invalid. The Bible makes clear in many places that while God will never totally abandon the Jewish People, the right for the Jewish People to live in its land is subject to the nation's adherence to the Torah's laws. Therefore, a prayer for liberation by a Jewish community in Israel which brazenly flouted the Torah would, presumably, be an invalid prayer. I mention this to counter what seems to be a nearly universally held notion by religious people of all nations. That notion is that God supports us in every conflict. The Bible teaches that God's liberating allegiance is not absolute. No people can claim unequivocally that they are acting "with God on our side"[179] at all times and in all circumstances. One of the historical functions of religious leadership since ancient times has been to justify wars. This is a disturbing fact that ought to make us think deeply and clearly whenever we

[177] Here, I am influenced by the way Adin Steinsaltz speaks of the connections between the souls of human beings and God in his book *The Thirteen Petalled Rose* (New York: Basic Books, 1980; Reprint—Montvale, New Jersey: Jason Aaronson, 1992). See especially "Divine Manifestation," 35-47, and "The Soul of Man," 51-65.

[178] See, for example, chapter 3 of *Mishnah Sukkah* on the issue of a stolen *lulav*.

[179] As Bob Dylan famously phrased it in his song of the same name. The song appeared in 1964 on Dylan's album, *The Times They Are A-Changin'*. Less famously, Dylan recorded an anthem-like, eleven-verse song which staunchly defended the State of Israel, "Neighborhood Bully." It is cast in a sarcastic tone, quoting Israel's enemies who falsely and cynically call Israel the "Neighborhood Bully." It was recorded in 1983 on his album, *Infidels*.

ask God to liberate us by destroying others. God has been bombarded by such prayers since time immemorial.[180]

The act of prayer is, at its stripped-down, naked core, an act of uniting one's spirit with the spirit of God and that, to me, is the key to the way this blessing works. I believe in the efficacy of this blessing when a person consciously unites their spirit with that aspect of God which is a *go'eil ḥazak*, "a powerful Liberator." We can calibrate our spirit to be open to this particular attribute of the Spirit, and to therefore be strengthened and empowered to do more of what needs to be done to liberate ourselves, or others, from external or internal oppression. This blessing can affect not only an individual's struggle, but a community's or a nation's struggle to the extent that a group of individuals focus, in reciting this blessing, on a common experience of oppression as they unite their spirit with the liberating aspect of God's Spirit. In this way, a group—praying either together or separately—can strengthen themselves to work toward a specific liberation. Whether as an individual or as a group, the aim of those who would recite this blessing is to tap into the liberating power of the transcendent Presence.

The way to do it is to catch the threefold emphasis on the root *ga'al*, "liberate"—*u'ge'aleinu... ki go'eil ḥazak attah... Barukh attah Adonai, go'eil Yisra'eil*, "liberate us... You are a powerful Liberator. Blessed are You, Liberator of Israel."[181] As we do so, we should consciously try to feel the great liberating power that resides with the Spirit beyond us, and that can be experienced by human beings because we can connect with the Spirit. We should linger on those words, and then linger in the silence that follows our recitation of the words. As we pause, standing still or swaying, eyes closed, we can imagine ourselves connected—perhaps through a ray of light, unperceivable by eyes—to God's Presence. At that moment, we should attempt to feel in our very being, more than to merely be reminded of, or to know intellectually, God's great liberating power.

Ultimately, my approach doesn't take the words of the blessing literally, because the language employed by the blessing is the language that a powerless underling would use when addressing a plea to a more powerful superior:

[180] "The spreads of government and of religion have ... been linked to each other throughout recorded history, whether the spread has been peaceful... or by force. In the latter case it is often government that organizes the conquest, and religion that justifies it." Jared Diamond, *Guns, Germs, and Steel: The Fates of Human Societies* (New York: W.W. Norton & Company, 1997), 266. See, too, the many citations in the index under the heading "religion: conquest justified by."

[181] In spite of the phrase "Liberator of Israel," this may also be the place to ask God's help in struggles of other, non-Jewish, individuals, groups, or nations.

> Take note of our oppression,
> fight our fight and liberate us quickly for the sake of Your name.
> For You are a powerful Liberator.
> Blessed are You, Liberator of Israel.

Instead, I suggest reciting the words of this blessing as a preface and background to the core experience of the passage, which, if rendered into words, would read something like:

> I know you are aware of our oppression,
> Help my soul to merge with Your liberating power.
> For you are a powerful Liberator.
> Blessed are you, Liberator of Israel, who shares the power of liberation with his faithful.

## Blessing #8
## *Rofei Ḥolei Amo Yisrael,* Healer of the Sick of his People Israel

> Heal us, *YHVH,* and we shall be healed.
> Save us and we shall be saved.
> For you are (the object of) our praise.
> Bring a complete healing for all of our wounds
> For you, God, are a faithful and merciful king who heals.
> Blessed are you, Healer of the sick of his people Israel.

This blessing is a plea for healing. The root *rafa,* "heal," occurs some five times in this small paragraph. The blessing is intentionally ambiguous on the issue of whether this is a request for individual or communal healing. This is accomplished by opening with a direct quote from an entire biblical verse, Jeremiah 17:14—a prayer for healing by and for an individual—and then pluralizing it in typical rabbinic fashion.

The verse in the Bible reads:

> Heal **me** *YHVH* and **I** shall be healed, save **me** and **I** shall be saved, for you are **my** glory.

The verse in the siddur reads:

> Heal **us** *YHVH* and **we** shall be healed, save **us** and **we** shall be saved, for you are **our** glory.

Similarly, the question of whether physical healing alone is meant, as opposed to emotional or spiritual healing, is also blurred through the interplay between the context of the biblical verse in the Book of Jeremiah and the way the verse is cited in the larger paragraph of this blessing. The blessing adds words that call to mind sickness of the body: *makoteinu*, "our wounds, plagues;"[182] *ḥolei*, "the sick (among)." However, in the biblical origin of the verse itself, the particular type of healing that Jeremiah is requesting is both emotional and spiritual.

Jeremiah the prophet suffered because of the conflict between his love of his people and his love of God. He was called upon by God to deliver messages of chastisement and doom to Israel. He delivered the message: They had sinned, had spurned God, had violated the Covenant, and now God was going to deliver them into the hands of their enemies. Their only future, Jeremiah felt deeply, was through commitment to the one true God and Torah, not through homage to the many gods and their idols. The message did not fall upon willing ears. Jeremiah felt the pain of rejection; the shock of being called a traitor.

> It seems that Jeremiah was accused of feeling delight in anticipating the disaster which he had announced in the name of the Lord. He who loved his people, whose life was dedicated to saving his people, was regarded as an enemy. Over and above the agony of sensing the imminent disaster, his soul was bruised by calumny.[183]

Jeremiah's personality was in danger of unraveling; of splitting in two. And so, Jeremiah, in his isolation and alienation, prayed to God for healing. He prayed for emotional succor and spiritual wholeness. His prayer for emotional succor and spiritual wholeness is the verse upon which this blessing is built. Thus, the biblical context for this verse asks God for emotional healing while the blessing's phrasing adds physical recovery.

---

[182] In the Bible, the word means to be stricken, to be attacked physically. It is the word used to describe the plagues in Egypt (Ex. 3:20, 9:15). See Francis Brown, S.R. Driver, Charles A Briggs, *A Hebrew and English Lexicon of the Old Testament* (Oxford, 1906), 645-647. In the Talmud, *Makkot* is the name of an entire tractate of the *Mishnah* dealing with "lashes."

[183] Abraham Joshua Heschel, *The Prophets* (New York: Harper and Row, 1962), 123.

The *ḥatimah*, the seal, of the blessing calls for God to heal *ḥolei amo Yisrael*, "the sick among the People of Israel." This limited request of God's healing power to Israel alone has bothered liberal Jews throughout the modern period. The dean of historians of Jewish liturgy, Ismar Elbogen, an active Reform rabbi in Germany during the early decades of the 20th century, found ancient support for a more universal *ḥatimah* in the Palestinian Talmud: Simply *Rofei Ḥolim*, "Healer of the Sick." He proclaimed that the Reform Movement of his day "has restored the original version."[184]

**Spiritual Commentary on *Rofei Ḥolei Amo Yisrael***

The Analytical Commentary explained that the interplay between the biblical source of the blessing and the text of the blessing itself revealed ambiguities regarding the individual or communal nature of the request for healing, as well as whether the request is for physical or non-physical ailments. Given those sometimes-conflicting layers in the text, this blessing may be understood, in actual worship, to be a request for individual or communal healing. It may be used to ask for relief from physical symptoms or emotional and spiritual ailments. Although its language is clearly particularistic—it asks for healing just for Israel—the precedent of the more universalistic language of the Palestinian language might be invoked to apply it to the needs of non-Jews as well.

How does this prayer work? How does addressing the words of this blessing to God accomplish healing? I raised issues of morality in the Spiritual Commentary of the previous blessing, on Liberation. Here, too, one may ask: Does God need to be petitioned in order for human beings to be healed? If one "deserves" to be healed, but doesn't pray for it, is it ethical for God to permit that person to remain sick? These questions are based on the assumption that sickness and health depend upon righteousness. It is understandable that many hold that assumption. In the Bible, various forms of sickness are considered punishments by God for ethical or ritual violations.[185] The notion that sickness descends from a realm beyond the physical was more central in the pre-modern world, when the connection between spiritual/emotional health and physical health was recognized, but the physical bases for many sicknesses—including microscopic organisms—were not. At times, this blessing was understood as a kind of incantation—the power of

[184] Elbogen, *Jewish Liturgy*, 43. The labeling of this blessing in *Yerushalmi Berakhot* 2:4 as *Rofei Ḥolim*, "Healer of the Sick" is part of a listing of the blessings of the *Amidah* in general, parallel to Babylonian Talmud, *Megillah* 17b, in which the blessings are called by catch-phrases which summarize their content.
[185] See, for example, Leviticus 26: 16; Deuteronomy 28:22, 27.

the words deriving from a kind of numerology. This approach derives from 12th-13th century teachings of the circle of pietists in Germany known as Ḥasidei Ashkenaz who noticed that in the Ashkenazic version of the blessing, there are 27 words. This is said to parallel a number of texts in the Bible, each of whose theme is healing, and each of which contains 27 words or verses.[186] This approach assumes that if the proper words or letters or sounds are intoned just the right number of times, the hoped-for result will occur whether or not God wills it. And yet the seriousness with which the incantation approach takes the blessing for healing is not something that must, necessarily, be rejected in modern prayer.

Because the scientific revolution was so powerful, sweeping away many superstitions and ineffective, if not harmful, medical procedures, it is understandable that the whole approach of the pre-modern world was rejected. Understandable, but not necessarily warranted. The role of the emotions in physical ailments is currently receiving more attention than it once had. The role of the spiritual, too, has become more recognized as well. There have even been a number of scientific studies to determine whether prayer plays a role in healing. Specifically, the issue investigated has been the efficacy of prayer rendered on behalf of ill people who are not aware that they are the object of such prayer. The results of some of these studies have been characterized by the scientists who organized the experiments as guardedly positive, and they inevitably garner headlines. Nevertheless, every one of those studies has been questioned by other scientists who have pointed out methodological, or other, problems. None of these attempts to prove the efficacy of praying for the ill seems convincing to me strictly on scientific grounds. I don't believe that science has yet found a way to measure and quantify the elusive power of prayer to heal.[187]

I do, however, have a sense of how prayer, and specifically this blessing, can help in healing for oneself, or for a group that is praying for relief. I don't deny its power to help others, but I have no idea how that may work.[188] This is likely because I don't believe in the image of God, found prominently in many classic Jewish texts, that God has consciousness and power similar to

[186] Cited in *Arba'ah Turim, Oraḥ Ḥayyim*, 116. See, for example, Exodus 15:26 which contains 27 words and concludes with the words "for I the Lord am your healer." Also, the 27 verses in Genesis 17, in which Abraham circumcises himself and his household. Circumcision, here, is likely understood as a theurgic ritual, one that has almost a magical power to protect the body and keep it healthy. Other texts include Proverbs 4:22 and Psalms 103:3.

[187] For a summary of these studies, see Philip Zaleski and Carol Zaleski, *Prayer: A History* (Boston/New York: Houghton Mifflin Company, 2005), 338-346.

[188] Arthur Green has written of a similar approach. See his *Ehyeh: A Kabbalah for Tomorrow* (Woodstock, Vermont: Jewish Lights Publishing, 2003), 156-157.

those of humans, but just magnified infinitely in power. My belief is more closely aligned with those Jewish texts (like the Zohar and some other Kabbalistic sources) that do not attribute human-like consciousness to God, but rather imagine a series of energies, potencies, or forces that interact with each other, with the world, and with us. My feeling is that when one recites this blessing with deep intention, when one lingers in the words, and when one becomes adept at that interaction through repeated recitation, one accesses the healing power of God's Presence. We do that by uniting our body, our physical selves; our souls, our spiritual selves; and the real, potent, Source of our spiritual selves. This union has the power to strengthen a sense of holistic integrity. To partake in that aspect of God's Presence which heals, one must, as the language of the blessing does, ask for healing. The experience of many is that concentrating on the specific wound or pain, physical or emotional, as we pray for healing, can help one to focus on the ability of the Source of our spirit to heal.

I do not claim that reciting this blessing properly has the potential to cure all one's ills. I am saying that there is a healing power to praying this blessing. If it is integrated into a life marked by reasonable physical care, it can complement the work of medical professionals by tapping into the healing power of God's Presence.[189]

In point of fact, this kind of *kavannah*, "inner intention," is not entirely different from that of the numerological incantation described above. Both take seriously the possibility that praying for healing can be effective. My hope is that I have offered a way to chant this blessing in a modern, non-fundamentalist mode, which nevertheless keeps faith with its traditional understanding: That connecting with God for healing through this blessing can function as a spiritual practice that can have a physical effect.

[189] Rambam, in his *Guide For the Perplexed*, dealt with the problem of evil by referring to meditation on God's Presence and on uniting oneself with God. One of the greatest issues in a monotheistic faith is explaining how good people suffer in a world in which a good God's will is always done. Rambam held that the reason evil befell moral people is that morality itself isn't enough; one also needed to unite spiritually with God. As long as a good person stood in meditative connection with God, no evil would befall him. I've always considered this an ingenious way to resolve part of the problem of evil, but it also seems to be merely an intellectual key to a problem of logic, and not true to life. Still, there seems to be a connection between Rambam's idea, which I've known about for many years, and my perception about the way that the blessing for healing works. See Moses Maimonides, *The Guide for the Perplexed*, translated by M. Friedlander (New York: Dover Publications, 1956), 389 (originally published by Routledge & Kegan Paul Ltd. in 1904); *The Guide of the Perplexed* translated by Shlomo Pines (Chicago: University of Chicago, 1963), 624.

## Blessing #9
## *Mevareikh HaShanim*, Blesser of the Years

Bless for us, *YHVH* our God, this year and all its produce
for the good.
And grant
blessing [in the dry season in Israel]
dew and rain for blessing [in the rainy season in Israel]
upon the land and sate us with your goodness.
Bless this year like the good years.
Blessed are you, *YHVH*, Blesser of the Years.

In a prayer made of blessings, this blessing repeats the root for "blessing," *barekh*, four times (aside from the word *Barukh*, which is a formulaic part of the *ḥatimah*, "seal"). It asks God to bless this "year," *shanah*, a root also repeated four times in this blessing. The blessing appeals to God to bless the produce of this year "for the good," *letovah*; to give of God's "goodness," *mituvekha*, and to bless this year like the "good years," *hatovot*.

The kind of "blessing" sought is set in agricultural terms: *kol minei tevu'atah*, "all manner of produce;" *tal u'matar*, "dew and rain;" *al penei ha'adamah*, "upon the land."

To put all of that together, this is a request for God to bless this year with agricultural goodness. The language changes slightly by the season to reflect, by turns, the rainy season in Israel and the dry season: "grant rain and dew as a blessing" in the winter; "grant blessing," i.e., in whatever form, in the summer.

Already in the ancient and medieval periods, this blessing was interpreted to apply to the wider market, and not only to agriculture. One opinion in the Talmud claims that this blessing was "ordained to counteract those who undermine (through speculation) the market rates."[190] A number of medieval commentaries connect the number of words in this version of the blessing (30) with biblical verses whose letters add up to the same number.[191] That exercise is not unusual; we saw it regarding the previous blessing, on healing, and it is applied to other blessings of the *Amidah* as well. Those biblical

[190] Babylonian Talmud, *Megillah* 17b.

[191] Deuteronomy 28:12 (23 words) + Psalm 145:16 (7 words); Psalm 102:5 (30 letters). To reach the sum of 30 words in the blessing requires that one count the words recited during the winter season and during the summer season together, i.e., a text that no one ever says! Still, this approach understands that sometimes the actual words one says in prayer are less important than the underlying goal of the prayer. See *Arba'ah Turim*, *Oraḥ Ḥaim*, 117. For others who cite this tradition, see Baer, *Seder Avodat Yisrael*, 92.

passages address not only agricultural bounty, but more general commercial sustenance as well. So, this blessing was understood to be asking for general economic wellbeing, whether based on agricultural or the market.

**Spiritual Commentary on *Mevareikh HaShanim***

Like the previous blessing, this one too affects people not only communally, but also personally. For that reason, one can understand why, in the talmudic discussion about where an individual may add personal prayers in the *Amidah*, this blessing, along with the blessing on healing, are specifically cited as examples of where a person may want to add such requests.[192]

How shall modern Jews approach this blessing? We might recite the words while concentrating on that part of God's Presence which is connected to productivity, creativity, sustenance, and wealth. God is described not only as creator in the Bible, but also as the one who sustains human beings and animals and as the source of human prosperity. The verses referred to in the Analytical Commentary on this blessing contain all of those notions. From the perspective of this blessing, it is no sin to pray for a "good year" of productivity. Many moderns may have trouble praying for material success. I don't approach this blessing in terms of asking for a miracle, nor as asking for selfish riches. I view it as guiding us to align the creative and productive aspects of our own spirits with the parallel force in God's Spirit. We are seeking to unite with that part of God which is the source of fruitfulness, propagation, proliferation, richness, lushness, and abundance. When we do that, we may find these elements energized within ourselves. We can ask that God help us to meet the needs of this particular *shanah*, "year," varying our requests based on the season, as the blessing does.

## Blessing #10
## *Mekabeitz Nidḥei Amo Yisrael*
## Gatherer of the Dispersed of his People Israel

> Sound the great shofar of our freedom.
> Raise high the banner to gather our exiles.
> And gather us together from the four corners of the earth.
> Blessed are you, *YHVH,* Gatherer of the dispersed of his people Israel.

[192] See Babylonian Talmud, *Avodah Zarah* 8a. The Sages divided on whether to permit such prayers after each blessing of the *Amidah* or only after the 13 middle blessings.

Three times, in this blessing, we find language referring to the exiled of Israel, and three times referring to "gathering," all of which points to the theme of God as the Gatherer of the dispersed of God's people, Israel.

The three references to the exiled are:

> *Galuyoteinu*, "our exiles."
> *Arba kanfot ha'aretz*, "The four corners of the earth."
> *Nidḥei*, "dispersed of."

The three references to gathering are:

> *Lekabeitz*, "to gather."
> *VeKabtzeinu*, "and gather."
> *Mekabeitz*, "Gatherer."

This blessing combines wording from three verses in the Book of Isaiah, culminating in Isaiah 56:8 which parallels the language of the *ḥatimah*, the "seal" of this blessing, almost word for word: *mikabeitz nidḥei Yisrael*, "Gatherer of the dispersed of Israel."[193] Isaiah, like other classical prophets, combined harsh predictions of doom—mainly exile—with hopeful reminders of consolation—mainly national restoration. In the Book of Isaiah itself, these verses form part of several promises of the future national regeneration—the ingathering of the exiles—which will occur after the threatened doom has come about.

The siddur, in quoting from Isaiah's words of consolation here, is employing a literary technique found in several other places in the siddur (see, e.g., the 17th blessing of the *Amidah*). That technique involves quoting God's biblical promises back to God, with a combination of humility and a touch of *ḥutzpah*. It is as if the siddur is saying, "God, I am not asking much; I am merely reminding you of what you, yourself, promised to us: You promised to gather our dispersed back to the land of Israel!"

For nearly all of the many centuries that these words have been part of the *Amidah*, the "dispersed of his people Israel" have been the majority, usually the vast majority, of the Jewish people. As was demonstrated above, the blessing asks God to return the scattered exiles of the Jewish people to the land of Israel. Some of the political implications of such a request are referred to in the blessings which follow this one in the *Amidah*. Taken together, these

[193] The other two verses which form the backdrop to this blessing are Isaiah 27:13, 11:12.

blessings form a manifesto of sorts, toward the reconstitution of a Jewish state in the land of Israel. The early Reform Movement in Judaism was uncomfortable with such blatant nationalistic statements. Elbogen, writing in 1913 in Germany—the birthplace of Reform Judaism—noted about this blessing: "In the Reform prayer books this and the following national petitions have been radically altered to express a completely spiritual conception of the messianic redemption."[194] His statement serves to underline that the traditional version of this blessing puts before God a clear plea: Return the exiles who live outside the land of Israel back to their homeland in Israel.

**Spiritual Commentary on *Mekabeitz Nidḥei Amo Yisrael***

There is no doubt that the recitation of this and the following blessings about national renewal in the land of Israel had a powerful effect upon Jewish history. While nearly all of the pioneers in the actual rebuilding of a Jewish homeland in Israel during the 20th century were not religious and did not chant this blessing three times a day, their parents and grandparents almost certainly did. The pioneers inherited a nearly two millennia-long national consciousness that Jews living outside of Israel are exiles, and that returning to that land is a central Jewish concern. This blessing helped to keep alive the dream of a return to the land among the Jewish People for generations. The Bible, Talmud, and other important repositories of Jewish values certainly contain many teachings along these lines. But it is the siddur, and especially this section of the *Amidah*, which was actually recited by the Jews on a daily basis. That kind of active engagement with the text probably did the most to preserve the Jewish desire to return to its origins in the land of Israel.

When a person asks God to "gather our dispersed," and focuses on that request, repeating this plea regularly, that person is aligning their consciousness with that part of the Jewish experience of God which connects Jews with the land of Israel. That connection is surely related to physical and political realities. But it is linked as well with the spiritual bond that a people establishes with its homeland. When the modern Reform Movement finally embraced Zionism, it was recognizing the tremendous difficulty in separating Jewish religion from its ties to a specific land.

If this blessing is said with a kind of numbness to its content, then the entire drama contained within it of confronting God with God's own promise of restoring the Jewish People to the land of Israel is lost. To recite this blessing with inner intention, one must be aware that one is asking God to return

[194] Elbogen, *Jewish Liturgy*, 45.

me to the land of Israel, along with all other "exiled" Jews. If one lives in the land of Israel, then this blessing is a request to return all other Jews to Israel. We therefore ought to feel challenged, while reciting this request, to explore our connections to the land of Israel, our connections to the land that we are living in (if it isn't Israel), and our connections to land in a general sense.

As I wrote above, this blessing has certainly played an important role in the creation of the modern State of Israel. Another question is: What role will it play in the political/spiritual relationship between Jews in the contemporary world and the land of Israel?

For many ultra-Orthodox Jews, the meaning of this blessing hasn't changed at all in spite of the establishment of the State of Israel. They deny the spiritual significance of the secular State of Israel and continue to pray that God bring an entirely supernatural miracle that would end the exile of the Jewish People. They take very seriously the opening words of the blessing (based on Isaiah 27:13) *teka beshofar gadol*, "Blow the great shofar of our freedom." Jewish tradition has associated the "great shofar" with the Messiah. I do not take most of the language of miracles in our tradition literally; I ask what the underlying teaching might mean for moderns.

For modern Jews who live in the land of Israel, the ongoing conflict with another people for the same land poses an interesting challenge to reciting this blessing with consciousness. Does the Jewish connection automatically invalidate other nationalities' ties to the same land? The continued non-acceptance of Jewish ancestral ties to Israel by many, if not most, Palestinians makes an exclusionary reading of this blessing understandably tempting to Israelis. That kind of reading is akin to the first line of the famous musical theme to the movie "Exodus:" "This land is mine; God gave this land to me." Many peoples throughout history have felt that "the gods" sanctioned their nation's claim to its land. It is my sad conclusion that most pronouncements by the government-sanctioned rabbinate in Israel do not differ much from this sentiment. And yet, I doubt that this approach is the best that the Jewish tradition can offer. It seems to me that we can find a way to ask God to bring Jews back to their land without entirely denying the claims of others to parts of the land as well. Nevertheless, the ongoing political and military conflicts with the Palestinians and other Muslims in the Middle East creates an atmosphere of "us versus them" in the State of Israel. The more pressure and anxiety a society feels, the more it tends to find ways to assert that God supports only their side. The prophets of the Bible did not hesitate to condemn an Israelite king's policies, even in times of extreme peril for the country, if they felt that the policy violated God's will. That is why Jeremiah was thrown into prison by his own people (See Blessing #8, above). I hope that modern Jews who live in the State of Israel would feel that their political views are not only supported, but also challenged, by their invoking God's Presence in this blessing.

For non-fundamentalist Jews who live outside the land of Israel, it is no longer possible to continue to naively ask for God alone to render the miracle of the return to the land. That miracle has already begun as a partnership between God and the mostly non-religious Jews of the land of Israel. Rabbi Abraham Isaac Kook, first chief rabbi of (then) Palestine in the early 20th century was a most unusual representative of Orthodoxy. He was forthright in expressing the rarely heard view—then or today—that non-religious people can sometimes actualize the will of God in ways that religious people can't or won't. The fact is that there is a Jewish state in the land of Israel for the first time in 2,000 years. Jews who live outside the land and ask, in the words of this blessing, that God return the "exiles" to Israel are faced with a challenge that is pregnant with meaning. Such Jews, if they are to confront God with this blessing, are themselves confronted with several questions:

- ▷ Is the only valid option for Diaspora Jews who care about Jewish tradition to move to Israel?
- ▷ If we are asking God to restore Jews to the land of Israel, to what extent should we, ourselves, feel obligated to assist the State of Israel with money, with political support, with moral support?
- ▷ Is public criticism of the State of Israel permissible, or in order to earn the right to publicly criticize, must one either dwell in the land or be prepared to contend personally with the potential security and military results of such criticism?

In sum, the recitation of this blessing with inner intention attaches us to that part of the experience of God which links us to our ancestral land. A recitation of this blessing ought to challenge us to confront God on this issue with honesty.

## Blessing #11
## *Melekh Oheiv Tzedakah U'Mishpat*
## King, Lover of Righteousness and Justice

> Restore our judges as at first, and our counselors as at the beginning. And remove from us sorrow and anguish. And may you, alone, reign over us, *YHVH*, in lovingkindness and mercy, and may you find us righteous in [your] judgment. Blessed are you, *YHVH*, King, Lover of righteousness and justice.

This blessing asks God to restore just leaders who will judge Israel with righteousness. It also asks that God alone rule over Israel. These two ideas can be seen as conflicting with each other: Is the request for God to provide just leaders or for God to rule alone? Marc Brettler suggests that "Our benediction looks back nostalgically at the period of the judges as ideal, not because the judges are themselves so positively viewed, but because (following 1 Samuel 10:18-19) the subsequent election of earthly kings implied a rejection of God's kingship. Thus, the real focus is not the judges, but the absence of any king other than God..."[195] I think this is correct. This blessing is a plea for God to be the ruler over Israel and it is not by accident that we call God "King" at the conclusion of this blessing. Here, we are praying for God to be the ruler of that land as was the case at the time of the judges before there was an earthly king over Israel. In this way, the blessing connects to the previous one which longed for the return of Israel's exiles to the land of Israel. It is a plea to remove the corruption of human government and for it to be replaced by the righteousness of divine government.

The *ḥatimah* (the "seal") of our blessing builds upon the first half of Psalm 33:5, adding the word "King:"

| **Psalm 33:5** | **The Blessing** |
|---|---|
| <u>Lover of righteousness and mercy,</u> the earth is full of *YHVH*'s lovingkindness. | <u>King, Lover of righteousness and mercy.</u> |

[195] See Brettler's commentary in Lawrence A. Hoffman, *My People's Prayer Book: The Amidah*, volume 2—*The Amidah* (Woodstock, Vermont: Jewish Lights Publishing, 1998), 128.

The second half of Psalm 33:5, which speaks of God's lovingkindness, is echoed in the body of the blessing: "(rule over us in) lovingkindness." The blessing, echoing the psalm, asserts that God's way of ruling over us is in lovingkindness and mercy. We are praying for that kind of caring and benevolent authority over us. And the blessing implies that the current situation—when we are ruled by humans—is not characterized by lovingkindness and mercy, but by harshness and severity.

**Spiritual Commentary *Melekh Oheiv Tzedakah U'Mishpat***

I'm sure that many in previous generations recited this blessing with the intention of pleading with God to take action to replace unjust rulers who were persecuting innocent citizens, especially Jews. The language of the blessing certainly supports an approach that leaves the action entirely in God's hands. However, my theology is different. I take this blessing as a challenge to the worshiper. The blessing is a reminder to us of what ideal governmental authority should be, namely, informed by righteousness and justice, as well as lovingkindness and mercy. When I recite this blessing, I imagine God silently responding that it is up to me, and all who cherish these divine qualities of leadership, to never accept immorality in government, and to do what we can to challenge it.

I also interpret this blessing both on the communal and on the individual plane. This blessing dares us to acknowledge that the ultimate authority over us is the caring and loving power of God. If, when we pray, we take the time to internalize its words, we are challenged to know, to feel, that the only true authority we answer to is God. While others may hold temporal power over us—government officials, employers, anyone to whom we feel we must answer—this blessing reminds us that these are not supreme powers. The words of the blessing ask, "May you alone rule over us in lovingkindness and mercy," and the question is: What is preventing God from ruling over us in lovingkindness and mercy? As individuals, the only thing preventing God from ruling over us is... us! What a relief it can be to allow this blessing to sink in and remind us that we truly answer only to God. People involved in 12-step programs such as Alcoholics Anonymous and Narcotics Anonymous know the respite and release that comes with acknowledging God as the one who has power over us... and who judges us with tremendous love and mercy. This blessing is the daily mantra we need to do all we can to bring righteousness and mercy into our individual lives and into the world.

## Blessing #12
## *Shoveir Oyvim U'Makhni'a Zeidim*
## Breaker of enemies and Humbler of the arrogant

> And for the slanderers let there be no hope,
> and may all wickedness perish in an instant,
> and may all your enemies be cut down speedily.
> May you speedily uproot, smash, cast down, and humble
> the arrogant, speedily in our days.
> Blessed are You, *YHVH*,
> Crusher of enemies and Humbler of the arrogant.[196]

"No benediction has undergone as many textual variations as this one..."[197] Ismar Elbogen whets the reader's appetite for more information with this accurate observation on the history of the blessing we are considering. The reason for the proliferation of variations in the wording is that the text was the subject of centuries of censorship due to its content and self-censorship in the interest of self-preservation. This blessing is one of the central loci of anti-goyism in Jewish liturgy. It is one of those few places in Jewish liturgy (along with, for example, the prayer *Aleinu*) wherein hostility against the non-Jewish Other is given full expression. As I've mentioned elsewhere, most religions occasionally express distrust of other religions just as most political groups do of each other. It is a tendency that seems hardwired in human group psychology. It is of no use, in my opinion, to deny what is being expressed in this blessing. The only way to progress toward religious pluralism is to forthrightly identify those portions of our own tradition that express intolerance toward other religious outlooks. Only then can Jews request with integrity that other religions honestly come to grips with teachings in their own traditions that vilify Judaism.

The Talmud calls this blessing *Birkat HaMinim*, "The Blessing of the Sectarians," that is, the blessing whose subject is members of a separatist sect.[198] The sect in question was early Jewish-Christians, but later it was directed against Christians in general.[199] The Talmud itself was censored

---

[196] Cf. the JPS translation of *veshever poshim veḥataim yaḥdav* in Isaiah 1:28—"...But rebels and sinners shall all be crushed," the verse cited regarding this blessing in Babylonian Talmud, *Megillah* 17b.
[197] Elbogen, *Jewish Liturgy*, 45.
[198] E.g., Babylonian Talmud, *Berakhot*, 28b, *Megillah* 17b.
[199] For an excellent book-length (!) history of this blessing, see Ruth Langer, *Cursing the Christians?: A History of the Birkat Haminim* (New York: Oxford University Press, 2012).

and self-censored, so that even the title "The Blessing of the Sectarians" recorded there was changed to, among other things, "The Blessing of the Sadducees," in order to forestall charges of anti-Christian sentiment. Not only that, but Rashi's commentary to the Talmud's discussion of this blessing was also revised. An early, non-censored, edition of his comment makes clear that this blessing was directed against "the followers of Jesus of Nazareth," while later editions of the Talmud have Rashi saying it was directed against "those sinners (i.e., Jews) who don't believe in the canon of Moses which was from heaven."[200]

As mentioned earlier in the introduction to the weekday *Amidah* as a whole, the Talmud records a tradition of when this blessing was formulated:

> Our rabbis taught: Shimon HaPakuli (Shimon the flax maker) arranged the eighteen blessings in order before Rabban Gamaliel in Yavneh. Rabban Gamaliel said to the sages, "Can any among you frame a blessing regarding the sectarians?" Shmuel HaKatan (Shmuel the Younger) arose and framed it...[201]

The "Rabban Gamaliel" in this passage is Rabban Gamaliel II who served as the Patriarch, the spiritual and political leader of the Jewish community, in Israel toward the end of the first century CE. It was at this time that the followers of Jesus were still mostly Jews—and they viewed themselves as Jews—but because they believed that the messiah had come in the person of Jesus Christ ("Christ" being an English adaptation of the Greek word "Khristos," meaning "messiah"), the Jewish leadership viewed these Jews as members of a wayward sect. Their growing numbers were viewed as a threat to the Jewish community, hence a blessing directed against them was called for by Rabban Gamaliel.

I have occasionally presented the English translation of this blessing, above, (minus its last line, which contains the Hebrew name of God) to adult Jewish students and have asked the participants to guess which religion formulated these words of prayer. The answer most offered is, understandably, militant Islam. That is because this blessing directly and unequivocally calls on God to leave "no hope" for "slanderers, enemies, and the arrogant." It

[200] The early edition of Rashi's comment is found in the Steinsaltz edition of the Babylonian Talmud (Jerusalem: The Israel Institute for Talmudic Publicatons, 1989) *Megillah* 17b, s.v., *Kalu HaMinnim*. The common edition of the same page is the Vilna-Romm edition: s.v., *Kalu HaPoshim*.
[201] Babylonian Talmud, *Berakhot* 28b.

asks that God "cut (them) down speedily;" that God "speedily uproot, smash, cast down, and humble [them]." It concludes by calling God the "Crusher of enemies." And the version that I am quoting, one of the current Ashkenazic forms, has been tamed by centuries of revisions. So, for example, a phrase in this version, "and may all wickedness perish in an instant" is a modification of the earlier "and may all the wicked perish in an instant," replacing the word for actual people ("the wicked") with the more generic and philosophical term ("wickedness").

The earliest versions we have of this blessing come from the Cairo Genizah (approximately 10th-11th centuries). The wording leaves no doubt that this "blessing" was directed against Jewish "apostates" who were sympathetic to, or who had joined, the nascent Christian sect:

> May there be no hope for the apostates,
> and may the arrogant kingdom be speedily uprooted in our days,
> and may the Christians and sectarians instantly perish.
> "May they be wiped out from the book of the living and not written with the righteous" (Ps. 69:29).
> Blessed are you, *YHVH*, Humbler of the arrogant.[202]

There are, of course, many commentaries that have taken a defensive and rationalizing approach. That is to be expected since the language of this blessing has led to anti-Jewish sentiment and worse. Still, there have been sages even in medieval times who have described this blessing with little defensiveness and have even sharpened and intensified its anti-Other message. For example, the 14th-century *Arba'ah Turim* dispenses with calling it a blessing at all and instead labels it *Kilelat HaMinim*, "The Curse of the Sectarians."[203] In the 16th century, kabbalistic teachers in Safed, Israel interpreted this blessing as a kind of incantation against the forces of impurity—the *kelipot*, demonic "shells." And it was taught that those corrupting forces had gained in strength and power during the time of Rabban Gamliel through the rise of the sectarians, i.e., the early Jewish followers of Jesus. According to the teachings of two of the great kabbalists of that era, the Ari (Rabbi Yitzḥak Luria) and Rabbi Moshe Cordovero, Rabban Gamaliel called for the writing of this blessing to combat the rising contamination

[202] "The arrogant kingdom" in this recension was Rome. Elbogen, *Jewish Liturgy*, 46; Lawrence A. Hoffman, *My People's Prayer Book: Vol. 2, The Amidah*, 41.
[203] *Arba'ah Turim, Oraḥ Ḥayyim* 118.

that threatened the proper flow of spiritual energy within the divine which blocked the flow of blessing to the physical world. Because the forces of impurity were identified with non-Jews, this interpretation intensified the anti-Other dimension of the blessing.[204]

Ḥasidic interpretations viewed this blessing, as they did much of Jewish tradition, through the lens of Kabbalah. One Ḥasidic comment views this blessing as directed against the demonic shells that allow a "person's evil inclination to take control of him until his desires bring him to deny fundamental theological principles and to hate the sages..."[205]

Another Ḥasidic commentary asks, regarding the "enemies" specified in this blessing, "Whose enemies are these? God's or Israel's or the Torah's?" The answer given is that, "where not otherwise specified, these can only be God's enemies who act counter to God's will. To do so, though, is to be an enemy of Israel and of the Torah as, in Zoharic understanding, all three are one."[206]

This dilemma has occupied many commentators: Is this blessing directed against forces from within the Jewish people or from without—that is, whether its curses are aimed at Jews or non-Jews? Either way, however, the wording was understood by most commentators to curse God's enemies. And God's enemies were interpreted to be Israel's enemies. Not only that, but several versions of the blessing itself replaced "may all your [God's] enemies be cut down speedily" with "may Israel's enemies be cut down speedily."[207] Aligning Israel's enemies with God's enemies directly impugns the stature of non-Jewish nations because it assumes that out of all the nations in the world, God will specifically protect Israel. Of course, this not only a notion

[204] See, e.g., Rabbi Ḥayyim Vital, *Sefer Sha'ar Ḥakavanot*, Part I (B'nei Berak: Widbosky, 1986), 231-234; Rabbi Shabtai of Rashkov, *Siddur Ha'Ari Rav Shabtai, Shaḥarit LeḤol* (Koretz, 1794; reprint, Jerusalem, 2007) 365-366; Rabbi Moshe Cordevero, *Siddur Tefillah LeMoshe* (Przemylen, 1892; reprint, Jerusalem: 2004), 95b.

[205] The source of this interpretation is Rabbi Yitzḥak Isaac Yeḥiel Safrin of Komarno (1806-1874) and his son, Rabbi Eliezer Tzvi Safrin (d. 1898). See Langer, *Cursing the Christians?*, 154.

[206] The comment is by Avraham David Wahrmann of Buchach (c. 1770-1840), cited in Langer, *Cursing the Christians?*, 152.

[207] Among the prayer books that contain the phrase, "may Israel's enemies be cut down speedily" are Rabbi Shabtai of Rashkov, *Siddur Ha'Ari Rav Shabtai, Shaḥarit LeḤol*, 366 and *Siddur Tzelota D'Avraham* (Tel Aviv: Institute for Research of Jewish Liturgy, 1963), 1: 291. This siddur is based on the liturgical version established by the Ḥasidic rabbi Avraham Landau, 1789-1875, Ciechanow, Poland. This rabbi's grandson, Rabbi Menahem Mendel Hayyim Landau is the author of the main commentary in this siddur, and his interpretation of this blessing is a prime example of the deep interest in the question of whether the blessing curses external or internal enemies. Similar interest is evidenced in the commentary of Rabbi Aryeh Leib ben Shlomoh Gordon (1845-1912) in his commentary, *Tikkun Tefillah* in the compilation *Siddur Otzar HaTefillot*, 1: 336-337.

of some Jewish commentators; many nations and religions are guilty of believing that God is on "our" side.

Among contemporary American *siddurim*, the most recent Orthodox and Conservative *siddurim* faithfully translate the blessing without blunting its stark cursing of sectarians. The Orthodox siddur adds a commentary defending the blessing's message: "Despite the disappearance from within Israel of the particular sects against whom (this blessing) was directed, it is always relevant, because there are still non-believers and heretics who endanger the spiritual continuity of Israel."[208]

The Conservative siddur's commentary presents an ambivalent attitude toward this blessing in its commentaries. On the one hand, it identifies the origin and point of this blessing in the following way: "The reference is to members of the Jewish community or sectarians who reported on Jewish activities to governmental authorities, leading to adverse measures taken against the Jewish community as a whole." On the other hand, it labels this blessing "The End of Wickedness," as if this blessing were addressing wickedness in general and not wickedness directed against Jews. It also includes an interpretation that this curse against the wicked and arrogant be directed instead against the darker recesses of the worshiper's own soul: "The Ḥasidic master Mordechai of Lechovitz would teach: When we pray that evil be wiped out, we should meditate on what in our own behavior is sinful."[209]

The Reconstructionist and Reform *siddurim* emend the wording of the blessing itself, stripping it of any notion of cursing enemies of Israel, coming close to reinterpreting it as a request that God vanquish wickedness in general:

**The Reconstructionist Siddur**
Let all who speak and act unjustly
find no hope for ill intentions.
Let all wickedness be lost.
Blessed are you, JUST ONE,
who subdues the evildoers.[210]

**The Reform Siddur**
And for wickedness, let there be no hope,
and may all the errant return to You,

[208] *The Complete Artscroll Siddur*, 107.
[209] *Siddur Lev Shalem*, 275.
[210] *Siddur Kol Haneshamah: Daily*, 112.

> and may the realm of wickedness be shattered.
> Blessed are You, Adonai, whose will it is
> that the wicked vanish from the earth.[211]

**Spiritual Commentary *Shoveir Oyvim U'Makhni'a Zeidim***

I have written at length about the vindictive nature of this blessing because I believe it is essential for our religion, and all religions, to come to terms with the very human inclination to suspect, mistrust, and fear the Other. I have no doubt that the original meaning of this blessing was to ask God to curse Israel's enemies, especially early Jewish-Christians. I am equally sure that for many centuries, Jews used this blessing as a curse against contemporary Jewish informers as well as against non-Jews in general. Even though enemies of the Jewish People continue to exist in contemporary times, my own spiritual life doesn't resonate with a divine curse of my people's enemies. I am too aware of the role of religious leaders from ancient times through today blessing military campaigns against a given nation's enemies. The idea of calling upon God to "smash" and "crush" other human beings repels me.

I find real meaning in the Ḥasidic comment cited in the Conservative siddur. In this approach, one would recite the words of the blessing with the intention of asking God's help to eradicate whatever is arrogant and wicked within oneself. To seek God's aid in healing whatever tendency one harbors to slander others. I openly admit that praying this blessing in this way contradicts its traditional language and original meaning. But I also submit that I cannot, in good conscious, recommend the recitation of this blessing in any other way. Channeling the words of this blessing as a means to grapple with one's own very human proclivity to be wary of others who differ from us may be a step toward repairing and healing this blessing.

## Blessing #13
## *Mish'an U'Mivtaḥ LaTzadikim*
## Support and Trust of the Righteous

> Regarding the righteous, the pious, and the elders of your people, the house of Israel and their remaining sages, the righteous converts and us, may your mercy be aroused. Grant a goodly reward for all who truly trust in your name

[211] *Mishkan T'fillah: A Reform Siddur*, 88.

> and may our portion be with them forever. May we not be put to shame for we have trusted in you. Blessed are you, Support and Trust of the righteous.

In some ways, this blessing is the counterpoint to the preceding Blessing of the Sectarians. Instead of vilifying heretical sectarians, it asks God's mercy for faithful converts and instead of cursing enemies, it asks God's support for the righteous and pious. There are six groups enumerated in this blessing:

> The righteous
> The pious
> The elders of your people, the House of Israel
> Their remaining sages[212]
> Righteous converts
> Us

It is tempting to try to identify clearly who each of these clusters are, but it is hard to know whether these appellations actually connected to specific groups at some early stage because they also bear a sense of stock phrasing.[213] While one can discern that blessing #11 is mainly about restoring benevolent political leaders and blessing #13 is mainly about support for the righteous among us, the inclusion in #13 of "the elders" and the "sages"—both are categories of leaders—makes the distinction between the two blessings less clear. The vicissitudes of the texts of the *Amidah* may have blurred what was once more clear-cut central messages of each of these two blessings.

In one of the earliest versions of this blessing, from the Cairo Genizah, the six groups do not appear and only two groups are mentioned—righteous converts and "those who do your will," with righteous converts given pride of place:

> Regarding the righteous converts may your mercy be aroused

[212] Why their "remaining" sages? The phrase connotes the mournful expression of a people bereft of their leaders. The Roman rite as well as the manuscript versions of this blessing have, instead, "the remnant of your people, the house of Israel." That version seems more likely since both biblical and rabbinic texts contain that expression, and "their remaining sages," is quite rare. See Elbogen, *Jewish Liturgy*, 47.

[213] Lawrence A. Hoffman is of the opinion that these group names referred to collections of people that were recognizable: "Originally, this prayer must have referred to specific groups of identifiable classes, but over time, it has come to denote universal types deserving of divine reward." See *My People's Prayer Book: The Amidah*,137.

> And grant a goodly reward to those who do your will.
> Blessed are you, Support of the righteous.[214]

The focus on righteous converts in this ancient version strengthens the impression that this blessing ought to be viewed as part of a literary unit with the preceding blessing, in which #12 vilifies those who are seen as betrayers of the Jewish People by joining the non-Jewish Other, and in which #13 lauds those outsiders, members of the non-Jewish Other who, through a "righteous" spirit, join the Jewish People.

In any case, over the centuries, blessing #13 seems to have expanded, embracing additional sets of people for whom we are asking God's "mercy" and "goodly reward." The blessing then links the worshiper's community to these praiseworthy righteous groups by adding:

> ...and may our portion be with them forever. May we not
> be put to shame for we have trusted in you.

In other words, even though I, the worshiper, and my community, are not in the same praiseworthy category as the virtuous collectives mentioned in the first clause of the blessing, we are asking God to link and unite our fate with them. This request makes the inclusion of "us" in the original list of six groups seem superfluous and I suspect that the presence of both may be the result of a fusing of phrases from disparate sources.

**Spiritual Commentary *Mish'an U'Mivtaḥ LaTzadikim***
The recitation of this blessing is an opportunity to stop and to bring to mind righteous people. People who are personally known to the worshiper and people known because their righteous ways are publicly known. It is a time to unite our souls with those who are doing righteous work in the world. Often enough, acting righteously in the face of power involves risk and suffering. Connecting from afar with the acts of righteous people while we are engaged in prayer recognizes that righteous acts increase God's presence in the world. It also sustains and supports God's presence within ourselves. "The elders of your people... and their remaining sages" refers to leaders of the Jewish People and they deserve a place in our prayers. While it may not have been the original intent of this blessing, perhaps the first two groups mentioned, "the righteous and the pious," may spur us to consider virtuous individuals

[214] Elbogen, *Jewish Liturgy*, 37, n. 4.

and spiritual human beings in the non-Jewish world with whom we wish to connect from afar as we recite this blessing.

Another thought: "May we not be put to shame for we have trusted in you." This line probably means, "God, please honor the fact that we have trusted in you by not letting us come to shameful circumstances." In the modern era, it could also mean, "Let me not be ashamed to place my trust in a spiritual power greater than myself at a time when many only believe the physical and concrete."

## Blessing #14
## *Boneh Yerushalayim*, Builder of Jerusalem

> May you return to Jerusalem, your city. May you dwell in its midst as you promised. May you rebuild it soon, in our days, an eternal rebuilding and establish the throne of David quickly in its midst. Blessed are you, Builder of Jerusalem.[215]

There are two aspects to this blessing: A practical, this-worldly aspect and an idealized, other-worldly aspect. The practical piece is a plea that God see to it that the city of Jerusalem, the ancient capital of the Jewish People, be rebuilt physically, in the here and now, and re-establish the Davidic kingship to be based there. The idealized side is refracted through centuries of Jewish teachings that Jerusalem will be finally and eternally rebuilt only in the Messianic future. And so, from this perspective, this blessing is an entreaty that God bring the Messianic future as quickly as possible: Note that words for "quickly" occur three times in this short passage (*bekarov*, "soon," *beyameinu*, "in our days," *meheirah*, "quickly"). Both meanings of the blessing derive, of course, from the fact, and—as importantly—the Jewish memory of the fact, that Jerusalem was destroyed in ancient times and the city had not been considered a Jewish city for many centuries.

According to the Bible, David conquered Jerusalem from the Jebusites (2 Samuel 5:4-9). And by traditional Jewish interpretation, Jerusalem was the site that the Book of Deuteronomy mentions repeatedly as the one place where sacrifices may be made to God, even though the Bible identifies it only cryptically as "the place that I shall choose."[216] Jerusalem became the

[215] The last two words of this blessing call God "The Builder of Jerusalem," *Boneh Yerushalayim*, a phrase taken from Psalm 147:2, *Boneh Yerushalayim, YHVH*. Interestingly, JPS translates this phrase within the context of this psalm in the continuous present as, "The LORD rebuilds Jerusalem." (In traditional Jewish liturgy, this psalm in its entirety is recited daily as part of *Pesukei DeZimra*).

[216] See especially Deuteronomy, chapter 12, the first place this occurs.

site of the First Temple, constructed by David's son, Solomon, which was later destroyed by the Babylonians in 586 BCE. Some 70 years later, work began on rebuilding the Temple and this Second Temple lasted until the Romans destroyed it, and the city of Jerusalem, about 500 years later in 70 CE. Rabbinic literature—including liturgy—throughout its classic period is filled with despair and mourning over the destroyed Temple and city, with great longing for return and rebuilding. In the earlier centuries, there is some evidence that Jews still preserved the hope for rebuilding both the Temple and the city in a physical sense. The Roman emperor Julian (305-337 CE) apparently included support for a rebuilt Jewish Temple in Jerusalem as part of his program of re-paganizing the empire. A previous emperor, Constantine, had legalized Christianity throughout the Roman Empire via his Edict of Milan in 313 CE, and before the century was over, Christianity was made the official religion of the empire. However, Julian attempted to turn the clock back and establish Neoplatonic Hellenism in its place. It was during Julian's short reign (less than two years) that the last real efforts toward rebuilding a Jewish Temple in Jerusalem in the here-and-now were made. Slowly after that period, the idea of rebuilding the Temple and re-establishing Jerusalem as a Jewish city morphed into an ideal that God would bring about in the World to Come. So well-known and authoritative did this notion become that it took many years for traditional Jewish authorities to support modern, secular, Zionism, which championed rebuilding Jerusalem in the Messianic age but in this world. There is no doubt that this blessing helped keep alive the hope for a rebuilt Jerusalem, and filtered through a modern, secular approach, helped fuel Zionism.

And yet, in the contemporary reality in which Jerusalem has indeed been rebuilt as a Jewish city, in the here-and-now, as the capital of the State of Israel, what can this blessing mean? I will consider this question in the Spiritual Commentary, below. But first, I would like to examine what might be viewed as the dark, inverse, of this hopeful blessing, namely, *Naḥeim*, the blessing that, on the saddest day of the Jewish calendar, mostly replaces this blessing.

### *Naḥeim*, Remembering Jerusalem on *Tisha B'Av*

On the mournful day of *Tisha B'Av*, the blessing of The Builder of Jerusalem is mostly replaced by a version specially worded for this public fast day which commemorates the destruction of both ancient Temples and Jerusalem itself in 586 BCE by the Babylonians and in 70 CE by the Romans, among other calamities. This version of the blessing is known as *Naḥeim*, "Comfort," after its first word. The blessing asks God to comfort the mourners of Jerusalem and to rebuild the city. It employs dramatic language of destruction and dejection, and only includes a glimmer of hope at its conclusion, namely, that (following a midrashic interpretation of Zecharia 2:9) just as God destroyed the city with fire, so will God rebuild it with fire. The wording of this blessing is based on a shorter prayer in the Palestinian Talmud (although there, the first word is *Raḥeim*, "Have Mercy").[217] The Conservative Movement innovated a revised version, preserving the sense of loss but moderating it, asserting that Jerusalem "once was so desolate" but is currently "rebuilt from destruction and restored from desolation."[218] The *siddurim* of the Reform and Reconstructing Judaism movements have omitted this prayer entirely, presumably because of the diminished role of Jerusalem's ancient Temples and sacrifices in their theologies, and as well, perhaps, because of the less central place of the nationalistic aspects of Jewish tradition in those movements.

An unusual facet of this *Tisha B'Av* addition to the *Amidah* is that in the Ashkenazic rite, it is only added in the afternoon service of the fast day and not in the earlier evening or morning services. It is very unusual for the liturgy to mention a fast day or holiday in only one of its *Amidot* and not in all of them. The only other example of this is on minor fast days during which mention of the unique character of the day (in the prayer *Aneinu*, "Answer us") is made in the morning and afternoon services, but not in the previous evening's service. However, this can be explained by the fact that the fasting itself does not begin on those days until the morning, which is not the case for *Tisha B'Av*. Rabbi Asher ben Yehiel (known as "Rosh," c. 1250-1327, Germany, Spain) is quoted by his son, Rabbi Ya'akov, the author of *Arba'ah Turim*, as having expressed his surprise at the custom he inherited of reciting *Naḥeim* only at the afternoon service, and then Rabbi Ya'akov adds some additional intriguing information as well:

> All my days I've been astonished that we do not recite it except during the *Amidah* of *Minḥah*! Since we say [in the Palestinian Talmud] that "each individual must mention something of [the holiday]," the assumption is in <u>all</u> its *Ami-*

---

[217] Palestinian Talmud *Ta'anit* 65c, 2:2; *Berakhot* 8a, 4:3.

[218] *Siddur Sim Shalom for Weekdays*, 126. For several ways that the prayer has been revised—or defended in its traditional wording—in Israel in the wake of the 1967 Six-Day War during which Jerusalem was reunited as a Jewish city, see David Golinkin, "The Liturgical Dilemma of the Nahem Prayer on Tisha B'Av," https://schechter.edu/nahem-prayer-on-tisha-bav/. Accessed on July 28, 2020. See also Golinkin's "Nahem on Tisha B'Av: Is It Permissible to Change The Wording?" *Responsa in a Moment*, Vol. 16, No. 5, https://schechter.edu/nahem-on-tisha-bav-is-it-permissible-to-change-the-wording/. Accessed on August 4, 2022. See also Saul Wachs, "Birkat Nahem: The Politics of Liturgy in Modern Israel," in David Fine and Ruth Langer, eds., *Liturgy in the Life of the Synagogue*, 2005, 247-258.

> *dot* [as we do for] *Rosh Ḥodesh* and *Purim* in the evening, morning and afternoon services! And Rabbi Yehudah [ben Barzillai] Al-Bargeloni ["the Barcelonian," late 11th-early 12th c.] wrote that [his custom is to] mention something of the holiday in the evening, morning, and afternoon services... And there are places that have the custom to recite it as *Raḥeim* ["Have Mercy"] at the evening and morning services, and *Naḥeim* ["Comfort"] at the afternoon service. Behold, it all depends on custom even though there isn't any difference between "Comfort" and "Have Mercy" since throughout all of *Tisha B'Av*, we pray for [both] comfort and mercy.[219]

We learn from this that the question of whether to include the special blessing in all three of the day's services, or just in the afternoon service, as well as the question of the proper first word of the blessing, has a long history, marked by several different customs.

A common way of explaining a number of rituals on *Tisha B'Av* is that until the afternoon service, Jews are like people who have suffered the death of loved one but haven't yet buried the relative, and so, are not ready to receive "comfort;" in the afternoon, they are like people who have just buried the relative, and are open to comforting.[220] This notion has been marshalled to explain the custom of some communities who recite *Raḥeim* ("Have mercy") at the evening and morning services and *Naḥeim* ("Comfort") in the afternoon service. On the other hand, there is also a venerable diametrically opposed viewpoint explaining the custom of reciting "*Naḥeim*" in the afternoon. According to this opinion, "*Naḥeim*" is recited only in the afternoon because the mood of the day actually grows more severe and painful as the close of *Tisha B'Av* approaches because it was only then that our enemies

[219] *Arba'ah Turim Oraḥ Ḥayyim* 557. I added the clarifying comments in brackets as well as the punctuation and underlining. It is possible that the surprise expressed by Rosh was occasioned by the fact that he moved from Germany to Spain, and thus experienced the differing customs firsthand. I wish to thank my colleague, Professor Kenneth Berger, for pointing out this possibility to me as well as for help in clarifying a number of issues related to the *Tisha B'Av* addition to the *Amidah*. I also wish to thank my colleague, Professor Gordon Tucker, who reacted to a draft of this suggestion and suggested a number of sources and clarifications that have sharpened the writing about *Naḥeim*.

[220] Mentioned by R. Avraham ben Nathan HaYarḥi (1155-1215), Provence, in his *Sefer HaManhig, Ḥilkhot Tishah B'Av*, 24-26. This notion is also attributed to Ritva, Rabbi Yom Tov ben Avraham Ishvilli (ca. 1260-1320), Seville (as his surname indicates) by R. Yosef Karo in his *Bet Yosef* commentary to *Arba'ah Turim, Oraḥ Ḥayyim* 557, s.v., *Vekhatav*. See Rabbenu Yom Tov ben Avraham Ishvili, *She'eilot U'Teshuvot*, ed., Rabbi Yoseph Kapaḥ (Jerusalem, 1959) #63, p. 70.

introduced fire to the destruction of the Temples and Jerusalem.[221] This is an opinion that is usually ignored in modern discussions of the mood of *Tisha B'Av* as the day progresses from the evening to the morning to the afternoon even though this opinion is actually cited in the most important guide to contemporary Jewish law, the *Shulḥan Arukh*,[222] and the former opinion is not! I imagine that the reason for this is that the message of the latter explanation deprives the worshiper of the more optimistic and positive implication of hope as the day goes on, and moderns tend to gravitate to an optimistic view of life more than medievals did. But the more pessimistic view, that the mood of the day grows darker, is as authentic an approach as the more positive one.

Nevertheless, still unresolved is why some communities add a *Tisha B'Av* blessing to the *Amidah* at all services on that day, and why Ashkenazim do so only at the afternoon service. Similarly unexplained is why the first word of the prayer recorded in the Palestinian Talmud—*Raḥeim* ("Have mercy")—was changed in some rites to *Naḥeim* ("Comfort"). A reasonable theory was offered by Professor Yaakov Gartner in 1981.[223] On the basis of a study of the relevant sources, Prof. Gartner theorizes a few steps in the history of this prayer. Here is a summary:

---

[221] Rabbi Yosef Karo in his *Bet Yosef* commentary to *Arba'ah Turim, Oraḥ Ḥayyim* 557, s.v., *Vekhatav*. Rabbi Yosef Karo refers to Rabbi David Abudraham (14th c., Seville), who places the argument in the 9th-10th centuries, in which Rabbi Amram Gaon (9th c., Babylonia), championed saying *Naḥeim* at all three services, and Rabbi Sa'adia Gaon (10th c., Egypt and Babylonia), championed saying *Naḥeim* only at the afternoon service. Karo also cites this in his *Shulḥan Arukh, Oraḥ Arukh, Oraḥ Ḥayyim* 557:1. In the critical edition of *Seder Rav Amram*, indeed the instruction is to place the *Tisha B'Av* addition in all three services, although some manuscripts include *Raḥeim* and some *Naḥeim*. See *Seder Rav Amram*, 132. The critical edition of *Siddur Rav Sa'adia Gaon* does not designate only the afternoon service for the additional blessing—which begins with *Raḥeim*—but rather instructs that it be included in the blessing in the *Amidah* about Jerusalem without any limitation. Still, the critical edition of *Siddur Rav Sa'adia Gaon* does not rely on a large number of manuscripts. See *Siddur Rav Sa'adia Gaon*, 318. See also *Abudraham HaShalem*, 257. And note that the manuscript sources of *Maḥzor Vitry* (11th-12th c.), an important source for Ashkenazic practice, seem to support both practices! See *Maḥzor Vitry*, 3:611-612, end of n.12.

[222] *Shulḥan Arukh, Oraḥ Ḥayyim* 557. Although, interestingly, here it is not cited by R. Yosef Karo, who had innovated this thought in his commentary on *Arba'ah Turim* (see previous footnote), but rather in the gloss by R. Moshe Isserles. This can be explained by the fact that here, in the *Shulḥan Arukh*, it is the Ashkenazic Rabbi Isserles who rules that *Naḥeim* ought to be recited in *Minḥah* only—and therefore, a rationale for this unusual ruling is called for—while the Sephardic Rabbi Karo rules that *Naḥeim* ought to be recited in all three *Amidot* of the day—and therefore, no rationale is necessary to defend its inclusion only in the *Amidah* of *Minḥah*. Nevertheless, it is striking that Rabbi Isserles does not cite the alternative explanation that the mood of the day lightens by the afternoon to explain his ruling that it is only then, at *Minḥah*, that it is appropriate to plead for "comfort" from God, but rather chooses to support this unusual custom by referencing the notion that the mood of the day actually darkens as the afternoon and evening approach.

[223] Yaakov Gartner, "The Prayer *Naḥeim*: A Time of Comfort and the Karaites" [Hebrew], *Sinai* 89:3-4, *Sivan-Tammuz*, 1981, 157-164. My thanks to Professor David Golinkin for the reference to this important article.

1. Originally, communities were influenced by the teaching in the Palestinian Talmud by adding a prayer to each of the *Amidot* on that day, a prayer beginning with the word *Raḥeim* ("Have mercy").

2. In approximately the 10th-11th centuries, the Karaite community, which commemorated the destruction of the Temples on the tenth of Av (as opposed to the mainstream Jewish holiday on the ninth of Av) innovated reciting prayers of *Neḥamah* ("Comfort") on the afternoon of the fast day because they claimed that on this day God comforted the prophet Ezekiel who was mourning the loss of the Temple. The Karaites comprise a community which views itself as authentically Jewish even though it rejects talmudic tradition. Mainstream Jews are called "Rabbanite" Jews when contrasted with Karaites because they accept talmudic (= rabbinic, hence "Rabbanite") tradition. Mainstream Jews do not consider Karaites part of the Jewish community.

3. The Karaite custom of viewing the afternoon of the holiday as a transition from mourning to comforting and consoling influenced the Rabbanite Jewish community. Even though the Rabbanite community would never knowingly accept Karaite customs, the idea of the mood transition on the afternoon of the fast day began to be accepted in the Rabbanite community.

4. Some mainstream Jewish communities—who had heretofore recited the prayer *Raḥeim* ("Have mercy") in all three *Amidot* of the day—changed the first word of the prayer to *Naḥeim* ("Comfort") in the *Amidah* in the afternoon of the holiday, i.e., *Minḥah*. This most directly reflected the idea that the afternoon of *Tisha B'Av* is a time to shift from deep mourning to comfort and consolation. This approach prevailed initially in some French Jewish communities, especially in Provence.

5. Finally, over time, some of the French Jewish communities lost touch with the initial rationale of changing *Raḥeim* ("Have mercy") to *Naḥeim* ("Comfort") in the afternoon service—that is, they no longer recalled the idea of the change in the mood of *Tisha B'Av* in the afternoon. These communities were therefore hard pressed to explain why they recited *Raḥeim* in the evening and morning services but *Naḥeim* in the afternoon service. As a result, they eliminated the recitation of any addition to the *Amidah* at the evening and morning service and only retained the recitation of *Naḥeim* in the afternoon service. Eventually, this custom prevailed in French, German, and ultimately, Eastern European communities, which is to say that this became the Ashkenazic custom.

**Spiritual Commentary on *Boneh Yerushalayim***

What does it mean to ask God to rebuild Jerusalem when modern Jerusalem, the capital of the State of Israel, is rebuilt? And what can it mean these days to ask God "to return to your city"?

In the past, these requests have mainly been understood to mean that when the Temple in Jerusalem would be rebuilt, Jerusalem itself could be considered rebuilt and one could say that through the Temple's return, God, too, has returned to the city. However, the hope for the rebuilding of the Temple in this world—as opposed to in the messianic world to come—has been abandoned by most Jews for many centuries. Therefore, for many traditional Jews today, this blessing still is essentially a plea for God bring the messianic era and to rebuild the Temple in Jerusalem so that we may again offer within it animal and grain sacrifices as well as wine libations, as the Torah prescribes. But this is not a request that can honestly be made by many contemporary Jews including by some Modern Orthodox Jews. For these many contemporary Jews, the notion of worshiping God through sacrifices offered on a fiery altar is not an intellectually honest hope nor a spiritually satisfying wish.

Perhaps today we can understand this blessing's call for God's return to Jerusalem in a different way. For me, it is a call for true peace to reign in the city that Judaism, Christianity, and Islam all call holy. In the past, the holiness of this city has led not to peace, but to holy wars; Jerusalem has been conquered and reconquered many times in its history. In the past, religion plus military power has yielded religious war. This is because the three religions that view Jerusalem as holy have long played a zero-sum game which assumes that since there is only one chosen people, only one religion can lay claim to be God's truly chosen ones, and the other two must be shown to be unworthy pretenders. If, in modern times, these three faith communities could instead embrace the possibility that each of them is "chosen" to teach one aspect of God's truth—after all, who can claim to fully know God?—and to model that kind of mutual embrace in Jerusalem. For me, when that happens, it could be said that God has returned to Jerusalem.

I have felt the presence of God in Jerusalem many times over the three years I lived there as a student, as well as during frequent visits since my student years. Quite a few of those times have been amid my faith community in Jerusalem, the Jewish community. I have exulted over the rejuvenation of an incredibly vibrant Jewish spiritual life in Jerusalem, participating in inspiring worship in synagogues that reflect a broad spectrum of Jewish rites and customs, dancing for hours on the holiday of *Simḥat Torah* in a variety of *Yeshivot* and worship spaces, as well as studying with, and teaching, Jews from around the world. And I have experienced the presence of God in Jerusalem simply overhearing little children speaking fluent Hebrew as a living language, oblivious to the miracle that they, themselves, represent.

But I have also felt the presence of God when I have toured beautiful Christian and Muslim houses of worship—running the gamut from the most ornate to the most humble. And I have felt the presence of God when I have met Christian and Muslim religious leaders in the city and when I have witnessed Christian and Muslim worship there as well.

When I recite this blessing asking God to "return to your city" and to "rebuild" it, my inner intention is a request that God inspire the leaders of the three great monotheistic religions to occasion God's return by themselves returning to their better selves, transcending their own claim to a Jewish, Christian, or Muslim holy city, and attempting to view Jerusalem from a more inclusive point of view. When I recite this blessing, I transport myself in my mind's eye to Jerusalem and express my gratitude to God for both the Jewish spiritual rejuvenation of Jerusalem as well as for the Christian and Muslim contributions to Jerusalem's spiritual life. And I pray that that the religious leaders of these great religions will have the courage and wisdom not only to tolerate, but to embrace, each other's different spiritual paths as a model to political leaders. Finally, I ask for guidance from God as to how I can play my own part in paving the way for this kind of divine "return" to the holy city.

I also view one of the interpretations of the *Naḥeim* version of this blessing for *Tisha B'Av* mentioned above as a reinforcement of this interpretation of the blessing. I am referring to the teaching that the mood of *Tisha B'Av* grows darker and sadder as the day goes on. *Tisha B'Av* commemorates the destruction of the city of Jerusalem. The notion that the commemoration grows more intense as we remember the devastation and suffering that occurred on this day in ancient times takes very seriously the darkness that can find a home in the souls of people, including religious people. Almost by instinct, we can sometimes find ourselves very comfortable thinking about God strictly from the point of view of our own faith community, as if God can be contained only within a portion of the human family. When that kind of thinking is applied to specific pieces of geography viewed as "holy," dark things can happen. It is certainly true that the Jewish People were the victims in the events marked by *Tisha B'Av*. But sometimes, the Jewish community wraps itself too easily in the mantle of victimhood and convinces itself that because we were victims, we can never victimize. Yet all human beings carry both darkness and light within; all human beings have the capacity both to oppress and to liberate. It is certainly proper to mourn for Jerusalem destroyed on *Tisha B'Av,* but we must never permit our past victimhood to convince us that we are not capable of acts of darkness in our present and future. The prophets of Israel understood the status of the Chosen People to be something that must forever be earned and never be viewed as a guarantee of righteousness.

### Blessing #15
### *Matzmi'aḥ Keren Yeshua*, Grower of the Horn of Salvation

> Bring the flower of David your servant to blossom and raise up his horn through your salvation. For we hope for your salvation all day long. Blessed are you, Grower of the horn of salvation.

This blessing contains poetic imagery quite common in the Bible, but which can be quite challenging to modern worshipers. What is "the horn of salvation"? What is "salvation"? And "Bring the flower of David your servant to blossom"—what is that exactly? The conclusion of the blessing—which I have translated in admittedly clumsy English, "Grower of the Horn of Salvation"—what can that mean? The short answer to most of these questions is that the wording of this blessing constitutes a plea to God to send the Messiah.[224] "Salvation" and "redemption" commonly refer to the messianic age in Rabbinic Judaism. The blessing references "the flowering," i.e., the offspring, of King David because according to Jewish tradition, the Messiah will be a descendent of David.

Rambam (1135-1204, Spain, Egypt) provides a convenient summary of the role of the Messiah:

> King Messiah shall, in the future, return the kingship of David to its ancient glory, to its former governmental authority, and will build the Temple and gather the exiles of Israel. All the (biblical) laws will, in his days, return as in former times: We will offer sacrifices, hold sabbatical and

[224] A version of this blessing was found in the Cairo Genizah, dating from approximately the 10th-13th centuries. That version, which famously combines this blessing with the one before it, yields a total of 18 blessings instead of 19 in the weekday *Amidah.*

> Jubilee years, all according to the commandment stated in the Torah...[225]

It is worth unpacking further the imagery of the *ḥatimah*/seal of this blessing, "Grower of the Horn of Salvation." The term *keren*, "horn," is, as Robert Alter comments on its usage in Psalm 75:5-7, 11, "probably drawn from the image of the large curving horns that the ram uses to gore its natural enemies... a symbol of assertive power." The term *matzmi'aḥ*, "grower," is an agricultural term, referring to the flourishing or flowering of plants. Together (as in Psalm 132:17), although they seem a mixed metaphor, they refer to God in this blessing as the one who "grows the horn of salvation," i.e., who will powerfully bring salvation to fruition.[226]

The Jewish notion of the Messiah is a human being who will be sent by God to end mundane reality as we know it, restore the People of Israel to its land, and establish an idealized world of peace. This idea is a post-biblical notion. In the context of the Bible itself, the wording in this blessing along with many other biblical words and phrases that later were interpreted to refer to the messiah or to the world to come do not signify a messiah or the end of life as we know it, but rather a this-worldly rescue.[227]

A good example of the difference between the meaning of words such as "salvation" in the Bible and in later, Rabbinic Judaism, is our blessing's usage of the phrase *ki lishu'atkha kivinu kol hayom*, "for we hope for your salvation all day long." Here, in our blessing, this means that our constant hope is for God to bring the Messiah so that the daily drudgery of our routine lives and historic oppression of the Jewish People will be transformed into an ideal world in which the Jewish People will finally achieve its reward as God's loyal, chosen people in God's holy land, free from all oppression and pain. However, this phrase derives from the Bible and there it means something else entirely. It is based on the story in the Book of Genesis in which the Patriarch, Jacob, addresses his sons with deathbed blessings, curses, and prophecies of the future. In the middle of his speaking, just after addressing his son, Dan, and seemingly out of nowhere, he declares, *lishu'atkha*

---

225 Rambam, *Mishneh Torah*, Laws of Kings, 11:1.

226 See Robert Alter, *The Book of Psalms: A Translation and Commentary* (New York: W.W. Norton & Company, 2007), 262-264; 461.

227 A classic treatment of messianism in Judaism is Gershom Scholem, "Toward an Understanding of the Messianic Idea in Judaism," originally written in German in 1959; English translation in his collection of essays entitled *The Messianic Idea in Judaism And Other Essays On Jewish Spirituality* (New York: Schocken Books, 1971), 1-36. See also a series of essays based on three workshops that took place between 2009 and 2011: Michael L. Morgan, Steven Weitzman, eds., *Rethinking the Messianic Idea in Judaism* (Bloomington and Indianapolis: Indiana University Press, 2015).

*kiviti YHVH*, "I wait for your salvation, oh Lord" (Genesis 49:18). This is the biblical source for our blessing's phrase; the main difference is that the wording is in the singular when Jacob says it ("I wait for your salvation") and in the plural ("we wait for your salvation") in the blessing. One modern commentator on the biblical verse offers this insight:

> It might be a personal prayer for the strength to finish the Testament, at a moment of physical weakness. It might reflect the deep disappointment felt at the fate of Samson (Judg. 15) if the oracle about Dan really refers to him... The prayer could also be invoked by the discouraging experiences of the tribe of Dan in its struggle for a territorial foothold.[228]

What Jacob's prayer definitely does not refer to within the context of the Bible is messianic salvation. Nevertheless, as I indicated above, this phrase—and especially the word "salvation"—was later interpreted in the period of the Talmud and Midrash to indeed refer to otherworldly redemption precipitated by the advent of the Messiah, and that why this phrase is cited in our blessing.

The various translations of this blessing in modern American *siddurim* reflect the numerous approaches that the traditional notion of the Messiah elicits:

> ***Artscroll*** (Orthodox):
> The offspring of Your servant David may you speedily cause to flourish, and enhance his pride through Your salvation, for we hope for Your salvation all day long. Blessed are You, HASHEM, Who causes the pride of salvation to flourish.

Even aside from the curious translation of *keren* as "pride," this Orthodox translation offers phrasing that is difficult to decipher, though the Artscroll translation usually reliably offers a felicitous version of the Hebrew no matter how much it may clash with modern sensibilities. My guess is that the difficult English phraseology here is more a result of the highly symbolic language of the original Hebrew than discomfort with the literal notion of praying for the coming of the Messiah. A positive aspect of this translation is that it consistently translates the three times that the root *yod-shin-ayin*

---

[228] Nahum M. Sarna, *The JPS Torah Commentary: Genesis* (Philadelphia, New York, Jerusalem: The Jewish Publication Society, 1989), 341.

appears as "salvation," and so the modern worshiper would have at least a clue as to the meaning of the blessing.

> ***Lev Shalem*** (Conservative):
> Cause the shoot of Your servant David to flourish; may the honor of the house of David be raised up with the coming of Your deliverance, for we await Your triumph each day.
> *Barukh atah ADONAI*, who causes salvation to flourish.

In its effort to make this blessing understandable in idiomatic English, the Conservative translation uses three different words to translate the threefold repetition of the key root *yod-shin-ayin*, "deliverance," "triumph," and "salvation." Regarding the two instances of *keren*, "horn," it translates the first as "honor" and leaves the second (in the *ḥatimah*/seal of the blessing) untranslated.[229] The modern worshiper who may not be an expert in liturgical Hebrew would therefore likely get the impression that in this blessing we are petitioning God to "deliver" a this-worldly "triumph," i.e., rescue and respite from persecution, to "the house of David," which untrained laypeople might interpret as the Jewish People in general. That could be a meaningful understanding of this blessing for moderns. However, if this were the intention of the editors of this particular siddur, it would be more intellectually honest to either revise the Hebrew to actually reflect this translation or alternatively, to translate more accurately—reflecting the next-worldly intention of the blessing—and in an accompanying commentary to candidly share the problematics of this meaning and offer alternatives.

> ***Kol Haneshamah*** (Reconstructing Judaism):
> May you speedily redeem your people Israel, and raise their stronghold with your help, for we await with hope throughout our days the coming of your help.
> Blessed are you, THE GOD OF ISRAEL, who plants the stronghold of your hope.

[229] Even though I level this criticism at this particular translation, I also recognize the challenge of accurately translating this blessing. My own translation, offered above, translates the root *tzadi-mem-ḥet* in three different ways: "flower," "blossom," "Grower." Translating all three appearances of this root in the same, or very similar, way would result in a more literal, but also a much more awkward, rendering: "Bring the blossom of David your servant to blossom and raise up his horn through your salvation. For we hope for your salvation all day long. Blessed are you, Blossomer of the horn of salvation."

The Hebrew and English versions of this blessing in the siddur of the Reconstructing Judaism Movement deletes all references to David and, therefore, to a human messiah. It appeals directly to God to "redeem your people Israel," which most worshipers would surely take to mean rescue in this world.

> ***Mishkan T'filah*** (Reform):
> May truth spring up from the earth; May justice look down from the heavens (Psalm 85:12). May the strength of Your people flourish through Your deliverance for we continually hope for Your deliverance. Blessed are You, Adonai, who causes salvation to flourish.

The Reform adaptation of the Hebrew and English of this blessing is the most highly revised version. It not only also deletes "David" and any hint of a human messiah, but adds to the blessing a biblical verse on the theme of truth and justice that augments the sense of a petition to God for this-worldly "deliverance" so that "the strength (this version's translation of *keren*, "horn") of Your people flourish."

It is common to hear that Christianity is an otherworldly religion whereas Judaism is a more practical religion, concerned with this world. While there may be some limited validity to that generalization regarding the modern forms of these two faiths, the truth of the matter is that Judaism has placed great emphasis on messianic redemption and the world to come for over two thousand years, since the end of the biblical period to the dawn of the modern age. Support for this contention is the large number of (false) messiahs that emerged from the Jewish community throughout this period and beyond. I'll mention only four of the most famous examples: Jesus of Nazareth (1st c., Land of Israel); Shabbatai Tzvi (17th c., Ottoman Empire—who probably had a third of worldwide Jewry convinced that he was the Messiah);[230] Jacob Frank (18th c., Poland); and Rabbi Menachem Schneerson, the last Lubavitcher Rabbi (20th c., U.S.). And yet, this central teaching of classical Judaism is—as evidenced by the various translations of this blessing in contemporary American *siddurim*—quite challenging to many modern Jews.

[230] See Gershom Scholem's magisterial study, *Sabbatai Sevi: The Mystical Messiah*, translated from the 1957 original Hebrew edition by R. J. Zwi Werblosky (Princeton, NJ: Princeton University Press, 1973).

**Spiritual Commentary on *Matzmi'aḥ Keren Yeshua***

Almost 20 years ago, there was an article in *Moment Magazine* entitled "Ask The Rabbis: Are Jews Still Expecting A Messiah?" Orthodox Rabbi Yitz Greenberg offered an inspirational rationale for the traditional view: "As long as there is poverty, hunger, oppression and war, the world is still not perfected. We maintain [the hope for the Messiah] against the Christian claim that the Messiah has arrived and against secular messianic redemptive movements (Nazism, communism, socialism) that claim they have brought the true, final perfection." [231] Greenberg calls this a "continuing testimony of 'not yet.'" If a worshiper can go beyond this meaningful general approach of "not yet," of a not-yet-perfected world and truly believe in a personal messiah, a human being who will be sent by God to redeem the world, then the words of this blessing, without much of a stretch, can be supportive and helpful.

Each of the non-Orthodox rabbis represented in the article expressed their own version of interpreting this blessing to mean not waiting for a human messiah but rather a challenge each Jew should personally feel to bring about messianic change. In 2003, a book was published with a title that sums up this approach: "There is no Messiah and you're it."[232]

I must say that I find the thought behind that title to be quite meaningful. I find it hard to recite this blessing with the thought of imploring God to finally send the human messiah to save the world. Rather, during this blessing, I concentrate on one specific aspect of an ideal world when I am thinking communally, or one, specific, aspect of an ideal life when I am thinking personally. And then, as I recite the words of this blessing, I try to tap into whatever power God has given to me and challenge myself to work toward that ideal. In other words, I choose to consciously misinterpret, or reinterpret, "the offspring of David" not as the traditional notion of a human messiah, but rather as all of us, all Jews. And that all of us are tasked with bringing the messianic age without waiting for a human messiah sent by God. Sometimes social action, working to improve society at large, is a passion. At other times, working on self-improvement is the aim. I see no reason to have to choose between the two: they are both worthy goals.

The key, as I see it, is to engage with the words of this blessing in a way that feels honest, and if that means veering from what the traditional words

[231] "Ask The Rabbis: Are Jews Still Expecting A Messiah?" *Moment Magazine*, March/April 2002, https://momentmag.com/ask-the-rabbis-are-jews-still-expecting-a-messiah/ Accessed August 13, 2020.
[232] Robert N. Levine, *There Is No Messiah And You're It: The Stunning Transformation of Judaism's Most Provocative Idea* (Woodstock, Vermont: Jewish Lights Publishing, 2003).

plainly say, to be honest about it. When we do that, this blessing has the potential to be transformative.

One more thought, regarding the blessing's phrase *ki lishu'atkha kivinu kol hayom*, "for we hope for your salvation all day long." It is very human to lose hope, to become disillusioned and skeptical of one's ability to effect positive change. Society's ills do not easily heal even after years of effort by many people. Similarly, real problems within ourselves that we work on often seem to stubbornly remain unchanged for a long time. When we find ourselves concentrating on the hopelessness of the moment and our own powerlessness, it is good to shift our attention to this phrase within the blessing—*ki lishu'atkha kivinu kol hayom*, "for we hope for your salvation all day long," and to recall that the divine power within us for hope and for the power to effect positive change in ourselves and others is with us *kol hayom*, "all day long," every day.[233]

## Blessing #16
## *Shomei'a Tefillah*, Listener to Prayer

> Listen our voice, *YHVH* our God, have compassion on us, deal kindly with us. And accept our prayer with lovingkindness and favor. For you are a God who listens to prayers and supplications. Do not turn us away empty from you, our king, for you listen to the prayer of your people Israel in lovingkindness. Blessed are you, *YHVH*, Listener to prayer.

This is the thirteenth, and last, of the middle blessings of the weekday *Amidah.* As I wrote in the introduction to the *Amidah*, this is not the last of the blessings making a request of God in spite of what many commentaries assert: two of the last three blessings also are requests—Blessing #17, "Restorer of His Presence to Zion," and Blessing #19, "The Blesser of Peace to His People Israel." Nevertheless, it is clear that this blessing concludes a literary unit because it is the last of the middle 13 blessings that are recited as part of the weekday (as opposed to the Shabbat or holiday) version of the *Amidah.* Because of that, and because of the blessing's content which simply asks God to listen to the worshiper's prayer (more on that below), the codes of Jewish law attributed a special status to this blessing. They ruled that while one may add personal requests relating to the specific topic of each of the blessings in

[233] I wish to thank Laurie Hoffman for this insightful interpretation.

this middle section of the *Amidah*, after this particular blessing, in Blessing #16—"Listener to Prayer," one may add personal requests relating to the topics of any of the previous blessings. This blessing is viewed as kind of a general summation that "includes all of the (previous blessings of) requests."[234]

There is another aspect to the summing-up nature of this blessing as well: The root *shin-mem-ayin*, "listen," and the word *tefillah*, "prayer," both occur four times in this very short passage. Therefore, the core of this blessing's request is that God "listen" to the worshiper's "prayer." It is a plea that God hear the words of the worshiper and answer those prayers, as the blessing implores, "do not answer us empty-handed."

The Ashkenazic version of this blessing reminds God that "you listen to the prayer of Israel." In the classical Sephardic version of this blessing, however, there is no mention of Israel at all, and the line is more universalistic: "you listen to the prayer of every mouth." Based on this, the *siddurim* of the Reform Movement and of the Reconstructing Judaism Movement removed the particularistic reference to Israel in their adaptations of this blessing.[235]

**Spiritual Commentary on *Shomei'a Tefilla***

What does it mean to say that God "listens to" or "hears" prayer? If one's view conforms with a common image in traditional Jewish texts that God is a kind of superhuman being, that hears and has consciousness similar to the way human beings hear and have consciousness, then the answer to this question is relatively straightforward: God can listen and hear and respond similarly to the way we do the same things, except on a supercharged level. That is, God can literally listen to and respond to the prayers of innumerable people at the same time. Although that is one quite traditional Jewish image of God, it is not the one that many modern worshipers hold. An alternative view, based loosely on the image of God in the Zohar, is that God does not have a human-like consciousness. In this approach, it can be said that God listens to our prayers in a more metaphorical way. God "hears" our prayers to the extent that when we recite our prayers, we do so paying careful attention to the words we are saying and aligning our awareness with God's pervasive and permeating Presence. Using this approach during this blessing with its four-fold emphasis on God "listening," it would be an appropriate challenge to try to "listen" for the spirit of God. That is, as we recite the words of this blessing, or after having done so, to try to perceive, to sense, to intuit the Presence of God, and to linger in connection with the divine.

---

[234] *Arba'ah Turim, Oraḥ Ḥayyim* 119. Also see Babylonian Talmud *Berakhot* 31a and *Avodah Zarah* 7a-b.
[235] *Mishkan T'filah: A Reform Siddur*, 90; *Siddur Kol Haneshamah: Daily*, 117.

## Blessing #17
## *HaMaḥazir Shekhinato LeTzion*, Restorer of His Presence to Zion

> Be favorable, *YHVH* our God, to your people Israel and to their prayer, and restore worship to the Sanctuary of your Temple. Accept in favor the fire-offerings of Israel and their prayer in love. May the worship of your people Israel ever be favorable. May our eyes behold your return to Zion in lovingkindness. Blessed are you, Restorer of his presence to Zion.

In the Mishnah (3rd c.), an early version of this blessing is referred to by a one-word title, *Avodah*, "(Sacrificial) Worship," a good title for this blessing in its contemporary version as well.[236] Many modern Jews are turned off by the extensive language about the ancient animal sacrifices in the *Amidah* for the *Musaf* service of Shabbat and Festivals without realizing that every *Amidah* contains at least a reference to animal sacrifices because this blessing, which looks back longingly at that ancient mode of worship, is part of every *Amidah*. The presence of this blessing in every *Amidah* is testimony to the origin of the *Amidah* itself, which was founded by the early rabbis as a replacement of the twice daily sacrifices offered at dawn and dusk (the third daily *Amidah*, for the evening service, was a later innovation). Since only the sacrifices were ordained in the Torah, in great detail, as the way to worship God on a daily basis, daily oral prayer which replaced the sacrifices after the destruction of the Second Temple in 70 CE has been viewed, nearly unanimously in classical Jewish sources, as a poor, temporary, substitute. (And therefore, the synagogue was originally viewed as a temporary, barely adequate surrogate, for the ancient Temple, and only slowly, over centuries, came to be seen as possessing some measure of holiness.[237] Rambam (13th c., Spain, Egypt) stands as a significant, but nearly solitary, exception to this view. He famously argued that the elaborate sacrificial system commanded in the Torah was actually meant as a transition from the ancient world's universal use of sacrifices in worship of pagan gods to the ideal of worshiping the one God through oral prayer.[238] Nevertheless, the weight of Jewish thought over many centuries did not share Rambam's interpretation, and this

[236] See, e.g., *Mishnah Rosh HaShanah* 4:5.
[237] Steven Fine traces the slow development of the sacredness of the synagogue in his book, *This Holy Place: On the Sanctity of the Synagogue during the Greco-Roman Period* (Eugene Oregon: WIPF & Stock, 1997).
[238] See Rambam's *Guide for the Perplexed* 3:32.

blessing, itself, is part of the mainstream of Jewish thought, since it asks God to "Restore (sacrificial) worship (*avodah*) to the Sanctuary of the Temple."

Elsewhere in the Mishnah it is said that a blessing with this same title was actually recited by the priests in Jerusalem's Temple as part of the morning's sacrificial service.[239] The version that was recited in the Temple likely asked God to accept the sacrifices offered that day.

The earliest actual wording of the blessing, beyond the title, that has reached us is from about the 5th century in a midrashic work, and almost exactly matches the wording in the earliest liturgical setting we have of this blessing from the 10th-12th centuries. That liturgy is from the Cairo Genizah which reflects the rite of the Jewish community in Palestine just at the cusp of when the first prayer books were produced. The wording is a request, expressed in poetic hints, that God "dwell" again in in a rebuilt Temple in Jerusalem, so that we may again properly worship God by offering the biblically commanded sacrifices. Here is the wording from the Cairo Genizah:

> May you desire, *YHVH* our God, to dwell in Zion and may your servants worship you in Jerusalem. Blessed are you, *YHVH*, whom we worship in awe.[240]

Both appearances of the word "worship" in the Cairo Genizah's version are connected to the Hebrew root, *avodah*, and both refer to sacrificial worship.

The current, Ashkenazic, form of this blessing features that same basic request but expands the first sentence to ask as well that God accept the *Amidah* that is currently being offered:

> May you desire, *YHVH* our God, your people Israel and their prayer (= *Amidah*) and restore [sacrificial] worship (*avodah*) to the Sanctuary of the Temple...

This remains the version of mainstream Orthodoxy. The commentary in the contemporary Orthodox Artscoll siddur summarizes this blessing by saying, "We ask that the *true* service be restored to the Temple," connecting directly to the tradition of yearning for the return of the sacrificial system of worship.[241]

[239] *Mishnah Tamid* 5:1.

[240] The blessing from the Cairo Genizah is found in Elbogen, *Jewish Liturgy*, 37, n. 4. The ca. fifth-century source is *Vayikra Rabba* 7:2, cited in Elbogen, 50.

[241] *The Complete Artscroll Siddur*, 130. The italics are in the siddur's commentary. The siddur cites this interpretation in the name of the *Etz Yosef* commentary which was written by Hanokh Zundel ben Yosef (d. 1867) and published as part of *Siddur Otzar HaTefillot* in Vilna in 1915.

The *siddurim* of both the Reform and Reconstructing Judaism Movements completely delete the request to restore sacrificial worship from this blessing. Instead, they reword the blessing asking God to accept Israel's prayers alone.[242]

The siddur of the Conservative Movement deletes just two words from the current, Ashkenazic version: *V'ishei Yisrael*, "And the fire offerings of Israel." This small alteration yields the plea that God accept this prayer (= *Amidah*) and restore the Temple worship in Jerusalem with only oral prayers implies that the word *avodah* ("sacrificial worship") be understood to refer to oral worship and not sacrifices which were offered in fire.

It is noteworthy that the saintly first Chief Ashkenazic Rabbi of Palestine, Avraham Yitzḥak HaKohen Kook (1865-1935)—known universally as Rav Kook—wrote of his vision of a completely vegetarian system of sacrifices in a future-rebuilt Temple:

> Animals offered on the altar are transformed through their being elevated as an offering to God. Since they do not have (the capacity of) understanding, they cannot reach this elevated state except through the elevation to God of their blood and fat which constitute the essence of the site of the soul. But humankind, which in its understanding heart can apprehend the act of the sacrifice, can draw close to God through its understanding. However, in the future to come, the (divine) flow of understanding will expand and penetrate even animals: "In all of my sacred mount nothing evil or vile shall be done; for the land shall be filled with understanding of *YHVH*" (Isaiah 11:9). And the sacrificing then will be offering(s) of that which grows (i.e., plants). And that will be pleasing to *YHVH* "as in the days of yore and in the years of old" (Malakhi 3:4).[243]

**Spiritual Commentary on *HaMaḥazir Shekhinato LeTzion***

It seems false to declare the superiority of either animal sacrifice or prayer as a means of worship. An offering of a goat or of first fruits with a heart open to God's Presence can be just as genuine as a prayer recited mindfully. The

[242] *Mishkan T'filah: A Reform Siddur*, 92; *Kol Haneshamah: Daily*, 119.

[243] Avraham Yitzḥak HaKohen Kook, Tzvi Yehudah Kook, *Olat Re'iyah* (Jerusalem: Mosad HaRav Kook, 1962), 1:392. Rav Kook ate a vegetarian diet during the week and only indulged in eating meat on Shabbat and holidays.

key, of course, is the inner intention of the worshiper. Sacrifice or prayer offered mindlessly is equally bankrupt. Because of this blessing's link to Jewish worship of centuries ago, an appropriate inner intention might be to envision in our mind's eye the myriad generations of Jews who have worshiped God over hundreds of generations when we recite the blessing. We might imagine ancient Israelite farmers presenting God with a calf or sack of grain that they lovingly raised on their own land as a grateful gift for some perceived kindness or as a gesture of entreaty for some heartfelt need. We might picture an ancestor of ours, holding a siddur and praying to God reciting the same, or similar, words to those we ourselves are reciting in this very blessing. We might visualize ourselves praying to God in Zion, that is, in Jerusalem, the idealized center point of Jewish worship. This is a blessing celebrating the continuity of the worship of God by Jews through history. And its meaning can be enhanced when we direct our hearts to that holy history.

### Blessing #18
### *HaTov Shimkha U'Lekha Na'eh LeHodot*
### Your Name is "Goodness" and to You it is Pleasant to Offer Thanksgiving

> We are grateful to you because you are *YHVH* our God and the God of our ancestors throughout all time. Rock of our lives, shield of our redemption in every generation. We thank you and praise you for our lives which are in your hand, for our souls that are entrusted to you, for your miracles that are with us every day, for your wonders and acts of goodness in every season, morning, noon, and night. [You are] the Good One, your lovingkindness never ending. [You are] the Merciful One, your mercies never ceasing. Always we have placed our hope in you. For all of them, may your name be blessed and exalted always and forever. Blessed are you, Your Name is "Goodness" And To You It is Pleasant to Offer Thanksgiving.

(For the commentaries on *Al HaNissim,* "For the Miracles," the passage added to the end of this blessing on Ḥanukkah, Purim, and, in some contemporary *siddurim*, Yom Ha'Atzma'ut, see page 170.*)*

The idea of this blessing is gratitude to God—gratitude for God's connection to us and to our ancestors, for God's rock-like reliability and shield-like saving power. It expresses our utter reliance on a power outside of ourselves, "our souls are in entrusted into your hands," and reliance on God's "miracles that are with us every day... morning, noon, and night." It is a strikingly positive and hopeful blessing that has worshipers expressing thanks each time the *Amidah* is recited, namely, morning, noon and night.

The middle of this blessing is characterized by a five-fold list of things for which we are expressing our gratitude to God. Each item in the list is introduced by the word *al*, "for."

> **For** our lives which are in your hand
> **For** our souls that are entrusted to you
> **For** your miracles that are with us every day
> **For** your wonders and acts of goodness in every season, morning, noon, and night...
> **For** all of them, may your name be blessed and exalted always and forever.

Interestingly, there is an alternative version of this blessing which accompanies this blessing. Originally, each *Amidah* would be recited by those who had memorized it, and then it would be repeated by the prayer leader for the sake of those who had not memorized the prayer. There were very few copies of the prayer service; written material was quite expensive before the 15th-century invention of the printing press. During the repetition, those who hadn't memorized the *Amidah* were supposed to listen to each word and recite *amen* after each blessing. (Since the evening *Amidah* was not connected to either of the two biblically ordained daily sacrifices for the morning and afternoon, the level of the obligation to recite it is considered slightly lower, and so, the evening *Amidah* is never traditionally repeated). Already in the Amoraic period (3rd-6th c.), there arose the custom that when the prayer leader repeated the *Amidah* and reached the blessing in the repetition, the congregation would bow and recite an alternative version of the blessing in a whisper. (Although apparently not all of the sages were aware of this custom: The Palestinian Talmud tells of Rabbi Yasa who, upon visiting Israel from Babylonia observed this custom and asked, "What is this whispering?").[244] Both the Babylonian and the Palestinian Talmuds discuss this alternative version and each Talmud records brief phrases from several different Sages as the recommended wording. Ultimately, both Talmuds conclude that wor-

[244] The Palestinian Talmud *Berakhot* 3c; 1:4. In the continuation of this passage, the Palestinian Talmud records various Sages' suggestions for the wording of this alternative blessing.

shipers ought to recite a compilation of the suggestions of all of the sages. Because of this, this passage came to be known as *Modim DeRabbanan*, "The Thanksgiving (Blessing) of Our Rabbis." In the post-talmudic period, the Palestinian Talmud was considered authoritative for the Jews living in the vicinity of the lands of Israel Egypt and the Babylonian Talmud achieved authoritative status for Jews living in Babylonia and Europe. However, waves of Crusader attacks on the Jews of the land of Israel over the 11th-13th centuries more or less destroyed the Jewish community of the land of Israel; as a result, the authority of the Palestinian Talmud waned in most areas of Jewish life. Therefore, the version of *Modim DeRabbanan* of most modern rites consists of the compilation of the suggestions of the five Sages mentioned in the Babylonian Talmud.[245] The theme of all five of the Sages is gratitude to God for the very opportunity of... expressing gratitude. The first of the five, the Amoraic Sage known as Rav, put it most simply:

> *Modim anaḥnu lakh YHVH Eloheinu*
> *al she'anu modim lakh.*
>
> We thank you, YHVH our God,
> [for this: that] we thank you.

Because *Modim DeRabbanan* is a composite of the phrases suggested by the five Sages, the wording of Rav's modest and unpretentious, but very beautiful, prayer in contemporary *siddurim* is not as clear as it might otherwise be.[246]

**Spiritual Commentary on *HaTov Shimkha U'Lekha Na'eh LeHodot***

The spirit of this blessing is as clear as its wisdom is essential. It is the wisdom of expressing gratitude on a daily basis; more, on a thrice-daily basis! It is a challenge to regular worshipers to allow each blessing of the *Amidah* to touch them and to elicit a personal response because of over-familiarity with the liturgy. Extra care to slow down at this particular blessing and to permit the words to enter us is rewarded with a consciousness of thankfulness. The fact that each of several Sages of the Talmud had their own personal version of the gratitude to be said when the prayer leader reached this blessing can be taken as encouragement to each of us to add our own personal thanks

[245] *Sotah* 40a.
[246] It can be found if one connects the first three words of *Modim DeRabbanan*, namely, *Modim anaḥnu lakh*, "We thank you," with the last four words before the *ḥatimah*/seal, *al she'anaḥnu modim lakh*, "for (this: that we) thank you."

at this point in the *Amidah.* A very simple, but worthwhile and satisfying, exercise is to pause at this blessing and to summon from within just one thing for which we ought to express thanks. One recent event that made us smile, one person in our lives we love (but whose presence we may take for granted). While there is a separate blessing asking God for healing (Blessing #8), this blessing is a perfect time to recognize and acknowledge our routine health, if we are so fortunate. It is easy to complain, easy to feel entitled to more, easy to hold the grudge. And what a curse this ease to grumble is! But what a gift is the opportunity to thank! No wonder the talmudic Sage Rav said, "We thank you, *YHVH* our God, for this: that we thank you." I recently saw a documentary about comedians in which one comedian's mentor—his father—repeatedly challenged his son, as a boy, to find the humor in virtually any situation. The challenge of saying this blessing is to find a reason to be grateful in one's daily routine. Thank God for that nurturing challenge!

### Blessing #19
### *HaMevareikh Et Amo Yisrael BaShalom,*
### The Blesser of Peace to His People Israel

> ***Sim Shalom***:
> Grant peace, goodness, blessing, grace, mercy, and loving-kindness upon us and upon all of Israel your people. Bless us, our father, all of us, through the light of your face, for with the light of your face, you gave us, YHVH, our God: a Torah of life, and love of mercy, righteousness, blessing, loving-kindness, life, and peace. May it be good in your eyes to bless your people Israel at every season and in every moment with your peace. Blessed are you The Blesser of Peace to His People Israel.

> ***Shalom Rav:***
> Grant abundant peace upon Israel your people forever. For you are king, master of all peace. May it be good in your eyes to bless your people Israel at every season and in every moment with your peace. Blessed are you The Blesser of Peace to His People Israel.

According to the Mishnah (3rd c.), the sacrificial worship at the ancient Temple in Jerusalem each morning concluded with *Birkat Kohanim,* The Priestly

Blessing (Numbers 6:24-27).[247] Probably because of that, the morning *Amidah* concludes with a recitation of the Priestly Blessing (in the repetition of the *Amidah*) and a blessing—*Sim Shalom*, "Grant Peace"—whose wording is based on the Priestly Blessing. The *Amidot* of the afternoon and evening do not include *Sim Shalom*—perhaps because these *Amidot* do not include the recitation of the Priestly Blessing.[248] Instead, they conclude with a variant blessing for peace, *Shalom Rav*, "Abundant Peace." It is likely that *Sim Shalom* and *Shalom Rav* were two versions of the same blessing—perhaps among many others—that were in circulation during the period before the liturgy was canonized toward the end of the Geonic period. While examples of *Shalom Rav* were found in the Cairo Genizah (11th-13th centuries), it survived only in the Ashkenazic rite.[249]

The theme of this final blessing of the *Amidah*, in either of its two formulations, is a plea for peace. Forms of the word *shalom*, "peace," occur four times in both versions of the blessing. *Shalom Rav* is an expansion of the last few words of The Priestly Blessing ("and grant you peace") whereas *Sim Shalom* expands upon the entire Priestly Blessing:

| **Priestly Blessing** | ***Sim Shalom*** |
|---|---|
| May (*YHVH*) bless you | And blessing; bless us;<br>and blessing; to bless; the Blesser |
| May *YHVH* illumine his face | The light of your face |
| And be gracious to you | Grace |
| His face (twice) | Your face |
| May he grant | Grant |
| Peace | Peace; and peace;<br>with your peace; with peace |

[247] *Mishnah Tamid* 5:1.
[248] Although the afternoon *Amidah* for fast days does include the Priestly Blessing, and on those occasions, the afternoon *Amidah* does, indeed, conclude with *Sim Shalom*.
[249] Stefan Reif, "Peace in Early Jewish Prayer" in Stefan Reif, *Jews, Bible and Prayer: Essays on Jewish Biblical Exegesis and Liturgical Notions* (Berlin, Boston: Walter de Gruyter, 2017), 289-290.

When *Sim Shalom* expands upon the Priestly Blessing's "May *YHVH* illumine his face upon you," it makes the following request which has often been misunderstood:

> Bless us, our parent, all of us, through **the light of your face**, for **with the light of your face,** you gave us, *YHVH*, our God:
> a Torah of life
> and love of mercy
> righteousness
> blessing
> loving-kindness
> life
> and peace.

The message is that just as you, God, blessed Israel in so many ways through "the light of your face" when the Priestly Blessing was recited daily by the priests in the ancient Temple in Jerusalem, bless us, too, in these seven ways, through that same light, the light of your face, even though the Temple is gone.

Because *Shalom Rav* only expands upon the last few words of the Priestly Blessing, it is much shorter than *Sim Shalom*. The only wording that it does not share with *Sim Shalom* is the following:

> Grant abundant peace upon your people Israel forever, for you are king, master of all peace.

This beautiful name of God, *Adon HaShalom*, "master of all peace," is rabbinic; it doesn't appear in the Bible.[250] The notion that God is the "master of all peace," perhaps meaning that the source of peace is God, connects with the final line in both *Sim Shalom* and *Shalom Rav*, "May it be good in your eyes to bless your people Israel at every season and at every moment with **your peace**." Similarly, there are several examples of *Sim Shalom* found in the Cairo Genizah that begin *Sim Shelomkha*, "Grant **your** peace."[251] There

[250] A biblical phrase close to this is "*YHVH Shalom*," in Judges 6:24. A common Christian phrase for Jesus is "Prince of Peace." This is derived from different wording, *sar hashalom*, found in a verse in the Hebrew Bible that Christians interpret as a prophecy about Jesus, namely, Isaiah 9:5.
[251] Stefan Reif, "Three Genizah Peaces," *Genizah Fragments: The Newsletter of the Taylor-Schechter Genizah Research Unit*, Cambridge University Library, No. 61, April 2011.

is something about being at peace that moved the Sages to connect it directly to God.

Peace is, naturally, prized by all people, and so too was it prized by the Sages. There are many teachings by the Sages of the talmudic era that extol peace. These usually begin with the statement, *Gadol hashalom*, "Great is peace," which is then followed by numerous reasons for the preciousness of peace. One of the teachings, in the name of Rabbi Levi reads:

> Great is peace for all the blessings... that the holy blessed one gives to Israel are sealed with peace. The recitation of the *Shema* (in the evening is sealed with) "spreads the shelter of peace." The *Amidah* (concludes with) "he makes peace." The Priestly Blessing (concludes with) "and grant you peace."[252]

The *siddurim* of the Conservative and Reconstructing Judaism Movements add the word, *ba'olam*, "in the world," to the first sentence of *Sim Shalom* to universalize the plea for peace beyond only praying for peace for the Jewish People.[253] For the same reason, these two *siddurim* add the words *kol yoshvei teivel*, "all who dwell in the world" to universalize *Shalom Rav*.[254]

**Spiritual Commentary *HaMevareikh Et Amo Yisrael BaShalom***

Perhaps the talmudic Rabbi Levi pointed out that all the blessings that God gives to Israel are sealed with peace because no blessing can truly be enjoyed unless peace prevails. And yet, it is challenging that in our daily liturgy, God is also called *Ba'al Milḥamot*, "The Master of Wars (or Battles)" and "The Warrior."[255] And it is typical for congregations to offer a prayer for the State of Israel on Shabbat and holidays that invokes Israeli soldiers and asks of

---

[252] Palestinian Talmud 2:4, 5a; Leviticus *Rabba* 9:8. One could add that the contemporary, traditional, version of *Birkat HaMazon*, The Blessing After Meals, also concludes with the word "peace."

[253] *Siddur Lev Shalem*, 165. *Siddur Kol Haneshamah: Shabbat Vehagim*, 351. According to Rabbi Robert Gordis's Foreword to the 1946 Shabbat and Festival siddur of the Conservative Movement, it relied on a version of this blessing in the 10th-century siddur of Rav Saadia Gaon that added the word *ba'olam*, "in the world," at the end of the blessing. See *Siddur Rav Saadja Gaon*, 19 and Robert Gordis, ed., *Sabbath and Festival Prayer Book* (New York: The Rabbinical Assembly of America and The United Synagogue of America, 1946), xi. In an online discussion with me of this textual change in 2022, Professor Robert Scheinberg identified a *Genizah* fragment with the very same text as that of Rav Saadia: T-S 8H9.12.

[254] *Siddur Lev Shalom*, 51. *Siddur Kol* Haneshamah: *Shabbat Vehagim*, 105.

[255] God is called "Master of Wars" in the first blessing before *Keri'at Shema* in the daily *Shaharit* service, within the prayer *La'Eil Barukh Neimot Yiteinu*, "They Offer Melodies to Blessed God." God is called "The Warrior," *Ish milḥamah* (NJPS translation of Exodus 15:3) in the *Pesukei DeZimra* section of *Shaḥarit.*

God: *va'ateret nitzaḥon te'atreim*, "crown them with the crown of victory." Soldiers and religious leaders of nations throughout history have called upon the divine realm to give them victory in battle. They don't always consider the big picture that victory for one side in a battle means death to the human beings, God's creations, on the other.

There is a scene in the film *Patton* in which the famous American World War II general orders the chaplain to compose a prayer for clear weather so that the air force could bomb German positions. Whether or not the scene reflects historical reality, it contains a truth about the way we invoke God to help us in war. "Let's see if we can't get God working with us on this thing," General Patton says to the chaplain. The chaplain replies, "I don't know how this is going to be received, General. Praying for good weather so we can kill our fellow man." The chaplain's reply makes sense to me, but it didn't to Patton: the scene ends with the general saying, "I'll expect the prayer within an hour." The liturgies of nearly all people include prayers for victory in battle, which narrows God's purview to caring only about one side in a conflict.

Jewish tradition, like many other spiritual traditions, uses prayer in all the complicated ways that make us human. When we fear for our life, when we are threatened, we pray for God to destroy our enemy. When we feel secure, when our immediate needs are met and our hearts are open, we pray for peace for all. I don't know why it is that making war is as undeniably human as working for peace.[256] Somehow, I feel that when we turn to God in prayer, we must transcend that part of us, that naturally human part of us, that asks God to be on our side in a conflict and against our adversaries. We know that just as God created and cares for the people on our side, God just as surely created and cares for our enemies.

The blessing that concludes the *Amidah* is a plea for peace for the People of Israel. The innovations in the wording added by the Conservative and Reconstructing Judaism Movements broaden the plea to include all people.

---

[256] But Yuval Noah Harari has a theory. Harari is a professor of history at The Hebrew University of Jerusalem and the best-selling author of *Sapiens: A Brief History of Humankind*. His theory is that human beings leapt from the middle of the food chain to the top too quickly, in only a few hundred thousand years: "...humankind ascended to the top so quickly that the ecosystem was not given time to adjust. Moreover, humans themselves failed to adjust. Most top predators of the planet are majestic creatures. Millions of years of dominion filled them with self-confidence. Sapiens by contrast is more like a banana republic dictator. Having so recently been one of the underdogs of the savannah, we are full of fears and anxieties over our position, which makes us doubly cruel and dangerous." Yuval Noah Harari, *Sapiens: A Brief History of Mankind* (United Kingdom: Harver Secker First, 2014; first published in Hebrew in 2011), 11-12.

It is not enough to pray for peace. We ought to feel challenged, as we recite this blessing to act for peace, to seek out opportunities to bring peace. That is on the communal level.

On the individual level, the image of peace flowing from the light of God's face can help center us as we recite this blessing. It would be consistent with the wording of *Sim Shalom* to imagine being bathed in heavenly light, a beam that transmits a deep and abiding aura of peace to us from its divine source. As we recite the words *v'or panekha*, "with the light of your face," we might imagine being enveloped in a glow that brings with it a sense of calm, of harmony, and of quiet serenity.

An insight on *Sim Shalom* and inner peace is found in a commentary called, coincidentally, *Dover Shalom*, "Speaker of Peace," by Rabbi Yitzḥak Eliyahu Landau (1801-1876).[257] He points out that when the blessing asks God to grant peace "for us and for all Israel," it seems to only make sense if one is praying communally because in that case, one is praying for peace on behalf of one's local community ("for us") as well as for all of Israel. However, when one is reciting this blessing as an individual, what can it mean to ask for peace "for us," in the plural? His answer is that the individual is praying for internal harmony among any number of elements that are not in balance within, and thus, make a person feel less like an "I" and more like an "us." Therefore, the blessing asks God to bestow balance and peace between the individual and any other entities with which that person may be in conflict. These, according to Rabbi Landau, may include God, nature, other people, one's own body, and time itself. That commentary interprets this blessing as a profound guide for introspection with the goal of achieving inner peace.

## Additions for Ḥanukkah and Purim
## *Al HaNissim*, For The Miracles

Since medieval times, on the holidays of *Ḥanukkah* and *Purim*, a prayer known as *Al HaNissim*, "For The Miracles," is added to the *Amidah*, as part of *Birkat Hoda'ah*, The Blessing of Thanksgiving. In modern times, some *siddurim* have added a version of that prayer to the *Amidah* for *Yom Ha'Atzma'ut*, Israel Independence Day.

## *Al HaNissim* for Ḥanukkah

Since *Ḥanukkah* is an eight-day holiday, this prayer is added to the weekday *Amidah* throughout the holiday, and it is added as well to the *Amidot* of the Shabbat and of *Rosh Ḥodesh* that occur during *Ḥanukkah* as well. The text

[257] Yitzḥak Eliyahu Landau, *Dover Shalom* in *Otzar HaTefillot*, I: 362.

of the passage is relatively lengthy, longer than the version of *Al HaNissim* for *Purim* and *Yom Ha'Atzma'ut*, and longer as well than most of the blessings of the weekday *Amidah*.

*Birkat Hoda'ah*, "The Blessing of Thanksgiving," is an expression of daily gratitude divided into five general categories, each of which is introduced by *al* or *v'al*, "for." The *Ḥanukkah* passage is appended to the end of this blessing and is meant to be a seamless continuation of this blessing. For this reason, *Al HaNissim* begins its own list with the word *al*, "for," and adds five more examples of God's goodness related to the holiday, each of which elicits our gratitude:

**For** the miracles
**For** the redemption
**For** the mighty deeds
**For** the triumphs
**For** the battles you wrought for our ancestors during those days at this time [of year].

The passage then goes on to employ several more lists, overwhelming the worshiper with cluster after cluster of God's saving actions during the *Ḥanukkah* story. It sets the stage by commencing with two parallel expressions of the enemies' iniquitous plans:

To make them [Israel] forget Your Torah
To force them to transgress Your laws

Then, four expressions of God's support for Israel:

You stood by them
You fought their fight
You championed their cause
You avenged their wrong

This is followed by five celebrations of God's saving power, namely, that God delivered:

The strong into the hands of the weak
The many into the hands of the few

> The impure into the hands of the pure
> The wicked into the hands of the righteous
> The arrogant into the hands of those engaged in Torah

The passage concludes with four illustrations of what the Jews did in victory.

Your children:

> Entered your Sanctuary
> Cleansed your Temple
> Purified your holy place
> And established these eight days of *Ḥanukkah*

It all adds up to a dramatic interpretation of the complicated, and by no means clear-cut, events of the Maccabean revolt into a black and white, God-driven fight of good against evil.

The version from which these translated excerpts derive is the contemporary, traditional, Ashkenazic one. Versions of this prayer that derive from other eras and regions, as well as from contemporary liberal circles, contain alternatives to some of this wording. The variations likely originated because of alternative theological approaches to some of the content of the prayer and include variants to the phrases "during those days," "the battles," and "the impure into the hands of the pure." I will trace these developments in the course of a brief sketch of the textual history of *Al HaNissim*.

The oldest mention of a prayer for *Ḥanukkah* (and *Purim*) originates in about the 3rd century CE, and characteristically for that era, the actual wording of the prayer is left up to the worshiper:

> Any [holiday] on which there is no *Musaf* [sacrifice], for example *Ḥanukah* and *Purim*, in *Shaḥarit* and *Minḥah* one prays (the *Amidah* with) eighteen [blessings] and one mentions something about the occasion in [the blessing of] *Hoda'ah* [Thanksgiving]. And if one did not mention something about the occasion, one does not have to go back [to the beginning of the *Amidah*].[258]

[258] *Tosefta Berakhot* 3:14. The reason this source does not mention the *Amidah* of *Ma'ariv* (the evening) is likely that an *Amidah* of *Ma'ariv* was not yet customary. See also Babylonian Talmud, Shabbat 24a. For a detailed history of the text of *Al HaNissim* for *Ḥanukkah*, see Stefan Reif, "The Emergence and Textual Evolution of a Post-Talmudic Prayer: The Case of *'Al Ha-Nissim*," in Nicholas de Lange and Judith Olszowy-Schlanger, eds., *Manuscrits hebreux et arabes: Melanges en l'honneur de Collette Sirat* (Turnhout: Brepols, 2014), 369-385.

Not only is no specific text instituted, but in this very early stage, the tentative, almost optional, nature of the prayer is emphasized by the ruling that if one omitted any mention of the holiday in the *Amidah*, one does not have to repeat the *Amidah* and include it, as would have been necessary for other, more obligatory, prayers. The placement of the prayer within the *Amidah* in the blessing of *Hoda'ah* (Thanksgiving) contrasts with the placement of prayers in the *Amidah* for holidays mentioned in the Torah, holidays on which a *Musaf* sacrifice was ordained. For those holidays, namely, the three pilgrimage holidays of *Pesaḥ*, *Shavuot*, and *Sukkot*, mention is made in *Retzeh*, the *Amidah* blessing that asks for the restoration of the sacrificial system. Since the Torah does not ordain sacrifices for *Ḥanukkah* and *Purim*—holidays commemorating events that occurred after the time of the Torah—this source sets the blessing of *Hoda'ah*/Thanksgiving as the appropriate setting to express gratitude for the divine rescue that occurred on each of these occasions.

The first time the sources go beyond merely the obligation for a "mention... about the occasion," and suggest actual wording may be in Tractate *Soferim*:

> And we recite [in the blessing of] Thanksgiving: "May you perform for us [miracles and salvation] similar to the miracles and salvation of your Kohanim which you wrought during the days of the Hasmonean High Priest, Matityahu ben Yoḥanan and his sons, Adonai our God and God of our ancestors. [May you perform for us such] miracles and wonders, and we shall thank your name forever. Blessed are you, *YHVH*, the one [whose name] is Good... (this last phrase refers to the conclusion of the Blessing of Thanksgiving in the *Amidah*). [259]

This language, which connects an expression of gratitude for God's rescue of the Jewish People during the *Ḥanukkah* story with a plea that God similarly work wonders "for us," gained traction outside of Ashkenazic circles in the subsequent history of this prayer. An approximation of this plea is

[259] Michael Higger, ed., Tractate *Soferim* (New York: Devei Rabbanan, 1937), 20:6, p. 346; in printed editions of the Babylonian Talmud, 20:8. The printed edition seems to include corrupted wording. Furthermore, as Debra Reed Blank has pointed out, chapters 10-21 of *Soferim* were probably written in Europe in the early Middle Ages and appended to the Geonic early chapters. See her article, "It's Time to Take Another Look At 'Our Little Sister' Soferim: A Bibliographical Essay," *Jewish Quarterly Review*, Vol. 90, 1/2, Jul.-Oct. 1999, 4, n. 10.

mentioned at the end of a very different version of *Al HaNissim* in our two oldest *siddurim*, *Seder Rav Amram* (9th c.) and *Siddur Saadia Gaon* (10th c.), in Rambam's *Mishneh Torah* (12th c.), as well as in the later *siddurim* of the Sephardic rite. One likely reason that this plea is not found in the Ashkenazic version is that *Tosafot* (French-German authorities of the 12th-13th c.) and R. Meir of Rothenberg (13th c., Germany) objected to the inclusion of a plea in this part of the *Amidah*.[260]

*Seder Rav Amram* and *Siddur Rav Saadia Gaon* are the first to contain the text that, with some small (but occasionally significant) differences, became the standard version of this prayer up to and including modern times. Nevertheless, these two very early *siddurim* feature some interesting divergencies from the text found in the modern, traditional, Ashkenazic siddur. As mentioned above, the modern, traditional, Ashkenazic version begins with five examples of God's goodness related to the holiday, each introduced by *al* or *v'al*, "because of" or "and because of." The last of these concludes with the words *bazman hazeh*, "at this time:"

> [Because of the miracles, etc., you wrought for our ancestors
> during those days]
> at this time [of year].

In *Seder Rav Amram* and *Siddur Rav Saadia Gaon*, we find the addition of just one letter—a *vav* at the beginning of the first word—that just may change the meaning: Instead of *bazman hazeh*, "at this time," both read *u'vazman hazeh*, "and at this time."[261] In 1985, the Conservative Movement produced *Siddur Sim Shalom, A Prayerbook for Shabbat, Festivals, and Weekdays* and included this extra letter, and it has been included in all Conservative movement *siddurim* issued since then. In the introduction to *Siddur Sim Shalom*, the change in spelling was explained in this way:

> ...this Siddur follows the text of Rav Amram Gaon's *al ha-nissim*, amending the introductory formula which ex-

[260] *Tosafot*, for example, held that when we offer thanksgiving, it is for the sake of something that was done in the past. Hence, a plea for similar salvation in the future would be inappropriate in the context of the Blessing of Thanksgiving in the *Amidah*. See *Tosafot*, *Megillah*, 4a, s.v. *pesak*.

[261] E.D. Goldschmidt, ed., *Seder Rav Amram Gaon* (Jerusalem: Mossad HaRav Kuk, 1971), 97-98. I. Davidson, S. Assaf, B.I. Joel, eds., *Siddur R. Saadja Gaon* (Jerusalem: Mekitzei Nirdamim, 1985), 255. One manuscript of an important medieval source for Ashkenazic prayer also included the additional *vav*, although other manuscripts did not include it. See Aryeh Goldschmidt, ed., *Maḥzor Vitry* (Jerusalem: Mekhon Otzar HaPoskim, 2004), 2:335. See Reif, "The Emergence and Textual Evolution," 378-379, for a helpful discussion of the *vav*, although Reif seems to misquote *Siddur Rav Saadia Gaon* on this.

> presses gratitude for miracles "in other times, at this season," to read "in other times and in our day...[262]

That is, the change in spelling was interpreted to carry with it a change in theology: God not only delivered miracles for our people during the time of the Maccabees, but also delivers miracles during contemporary times. Interestingly, the commentary in the most recent Conservative prayer book, *Siddur Lev Shalem for Shabbat and Festivals* (2016) posits that the interpretation of the additional letter *vav* offered in the earlier Conservative siddur may actually have been a stretch:

> The prefixed letter *vav*, meaning "and," is found in the siddur of Amram Gaon (9th century), the earliest source of this prayer. Some see in the "and" a reference to our own time, though the phrase may simply be referring to the time of year.[263]

Thus, the most recent edition of the Conservative prayer book theorizes that the extra "and" may carry no theological message at all; it may simply mean that God wrought miracles for our ancestors "during those days," meaning in ancient times, "and at this time [of year]," meaning during the wintry month of *Kislev*. In truth, it is difficult to know whether that one letter meaning "and" really does carry the theological message that the miracles of *Ḥanukkah* occurred not only once, many centuries ago, but may also occur in contemporary times. In citing the precedents for the additional "and" therefore, one ought to use humble and cautious language in asserting an inspiring theological lesson.

Two other phrases from this prayer have been subject to revision over the centuries: *v'al hamilḥamot*, "because of the battles," and *temei'im beyad tehorim*, "[you delivered] the impure into the hands of the pure."

*V'al hamilḥamot*, "because of the battles," is indeed found in the major ancient and medieval prayer books, except for one genizah fragment (10th-11th century?) and the Spanish commentator, Rabbi David Abudraham (14th c.), who substitutes the word *neḥamot*, "consolations."[264] Following

[262] Jules Harlow, ed., *Siddur Sim Shalom, A Prayerbook for Shabbat, Festivals, and Weekdays* (New York: The Rabbinical Assembly and The United Synagogue of America, 1985), xxvii.

[263] Edward Feld, ed., *Siddur Lev Shalem for Shabbat and Festivals* (New York: The Rabbinical Assembly, 1985), 430.

[264] For the Genizah fragment, see Reif, "The Emergence and Textual Evolution," 376-377. The word may be familiar to worshipers in a liturgical context from its Aramaic form in the third paragraph of

Abudraham, the Sephardic Rite omits "battles" and includes "consolations." Among modern *siddurim*, the Reconstructionist *Kol Haneshamah* also substitutes "consolations" for "battles."[265] No doubt, "consolations" appealed more to this modern, liberal, movement more than "battles" in a prayer of thanks to God. Two other modern, liberal, movements, the Conservative Movement and the Reform Movement, dealt with this issue differently. In their several *siddurim*, issued in the 1970s, 80s, and 90s, they included the Hebrew for "battles," but simply refrained from translating the word, so those worshipers lacking Hebrew knowledge would have had no idea that the Hebrew text they were reciting expressed gratitude for God's military intervention in history.[266] Intriguingly, the current *siddurim* of both of these movements continue to include the traditional Hebrew phrasing of *milḥamot*, but this time, they translate directly and forthrightly (Reform: "for the wars;" Conservative: "for the battles You fought."[267]

The phrase, *temei'im beyad tehorim*, "[you delivered] the impure into the hands of the pure" is found in the major ancient and medieval prayer books.[268] The interesting story is how modern prayer books dealt with this idiom. Although this prayer contains several adverse, even hostile, descriptions of the Syrian-Hellenistic enemies of the *Ḥanukkah* saga, both "impure" and "pure" hint more at a state of being than a characterization of one's actions. Calling the enemy "impure" seemed to have struck some as inappropriate, implying an inherent malevolent, almost demonic, quality to the enemy. In addition, describing Israel as "pure," may have been understood to imply a wholesome, untainted perfection, which similarly felt like an unfitting, and perhaps, cringe-worthy, exaggeration. Regarding this wording, the Reconstructionist siddur chose to omit the phrases entirely in both the Hebrew original and the English translation. And again, the Conservative and Reform *siddurim* issued from the 1970s to the early 2000s included the Hebrew

---

the *Kaddish*: *neḥemata*, "consolations."

[265] David A. Teutsch, ed., *Kol Haneshamah, Daily* (Wyncote, Pennsylvania: The Reconstructionist Press, 1996), 120-121. Also see Eric Caplan, *From Ideology to Liturgy: Reconstructionist Worship and American Liberal Judaism* (Cincinatti: Hebrew Union College Press, 2002).

[266] Reform: Chaim Stern, ed., *Gates of Prayer: The New Union Prayerbook* (New York: Central Conference of American Rabbis, 1975), 45. Conservative: Jules Harlow, ed., *Siddur Sim Shalom, A Prayerbook for Shabbat, Festivals, and Weekdays* (New York: The Rabbinical Assembly and The United Synagogue of America, 1985), 116-117; Avram Reisner, ed., *Siddur Sim Shalom for Weekdays* (New York: The Rabbinical Assembly and the United Synagogue of Conservative Judaism, 2002), 42.

[267] Reform: Elyse D. Frishman, ed., *Mishkan T'filah: A Reform Siddur* (New York: Central Conference of American Rabbis, 2007), 556. Conservative: Edward Feld, ed., *Siddur Lev Shalem for Shabbat and Festivals* (New York: The Rabbinical Assembly, 2016), 430.

[268] While the generally less reliable *Seder Rav Amram* (9th century) does not include it, one of its manuscripts does include it. See Daniel Goldschmidt, ed., *Seder Rav Amram* (Mossad HaRav Kuk, 1971), 98.

phrasing but provided a less than honest translation. The Reform siddur simply ignored all five negative portrayals of the enemy in the body of this prayer. The Conservative *siddurim* of this period translated the phrase as "(You delivered...) the corrupt into hands of the pure of heart." But translating it in this way softens the effect—if even slightly—by transferring the image from the realm of intrinsic and essential states of being (impure/pure) to the realm of ethical values (corrupt/pure of heart). The enemy is still cast in a negative light: They are corrupt compared to Israel's purity of heart. However, they are not tainted with an inherent and innate negative quality compared to Israel's essential virtuousness. And yet again, both movements' current *siddurim* include the Hebrew phrase and translate it much more directly (Reform: "the unclean into the hands of the pure;" Conservative: "the impure into the hands of the pure").

**Spiritual Commentary on *Al HaNissim* for Ḥanukkah**

The variations in the older and newer versions of *Al HaNissim* for Ḥanukkah are quite suggestive. The changes to the phrases *al hamilḥamot*, "because of the battles," and *temei'im beyad tehorim*, "(You delivered) the impure into the hands of the pure" reflect theological unease over the way the prayer characterizes the enemy in this holiday's story. The modification of *bazman hazeh*, "at this time" to *u'vazman hazeh*, "and at this time" indicates a different theological desire: To assert that God's involvement in history, God's miracles, is not limited to the past, but may also be encountered today.

For me, though, the most thought-provoking aspect in the literary history of this prayer is the very first reference to it, from the third-century *Tosefta*. This early source simply instructs that "one mentions something about the occasion in [the blessing of] *Hoda'ah* (Thanksgiving)." I take that as a challenge to every worshiper: Whatever version of *Al HaNissim* you recite on Ḥanukkah, mention something about the occasion! That is, have some inner intention about the holiday. Don't recite the prayer—in Hebrew or English—mindlessly! Actually say something about the occasion as you are standing in the presence of God. And especially, add some words, some thoughts, of your own. Becoming familiar with the history of this prayer includes confronting the fact that the current wording was not always recited by Jews at Ḥanukkah . The changes made in the phrasing because of changes in theological sensitivity ought to goad us into expressing something true and honest to God about *Ḥanukkah* when this prayer is recited. The historical account I've traced here might encourage us to think about and add at least one thought or feeling we have on this day of *Ḥanukkah* . For what are we grateful? How does whatever we know about the holiday influence how we feel today about Jewish religious freedom or about others' religious freedom? About persecution of Jews? About persecution of others? About the spiritual hope embodied in lighting the candles?

This prayer challenges every worshiper to actually "mention something about the occasion" to God about this holiday, something genuine and real and true.

## *Al HaNissim* for *Purim*

The earliest history of *Al HaNissim* for *Purim* parallels that of *Al HaNissim* for Ḥanukkah : The first mention in the early third century of what would eventually become *Al HaNissim* for *Purim* contained no specific wording (see above for that history).[269] However, unlike *Al HaNissim* for *Ḥanukkah*, the text of this prayer for *Purim* was still entirely unformed even in the next stage of development. *Seder Rav Amram* (9th c.) and *Siddur Rav Saadia Gaon* (10th c.) are again the first documents that contain a specific text for *Purim*.[270] The wording in these, our first two *siddurim*, parallels almost exactly the traditional contemporary Ashkenazic text. One small difference is that both thank God for miracles that occurred at the time of the holiday "and at this time." Another difference is that in *Seder Rav Amram*, the prayer concludes by expressly asking God to cause similar miracles to occur "for us." The significance of these differences was discussed above, regarding *Ḥanukkah* .

As we saw regarding *Ḥanukkah* , *Al HaNissim* for *Purim* also contains language that has proven challenging for modern *siddurim*. The beginning of this version of the prayer—much shorter than the one for *Ḥanukkah* —emphasizes the viciousness of Haman's plan, echoing Esther 3:13:

> ...to destroy, massacre, and exterminate all the Jews, young and old, children and women, on a single day, on the thirteenth day of the twelfth month—that is, the month of Adar—and to plunder their possessions.

The end of the prayer describes the retribution dealt to Haman, echoing Esther 9:25:

[269] *Tosefta Berakhot* 3:14.

[270] Daniel Goldschmidt, ed., *Seder Rav Amram*, 100. Davidson, Assaf, Joel, eds., *Siddur Rav Saadia Gaon*, 257. *Massekhet Soferim*, from the early medieval period, still simply says. "and we mention the miracles of Mordecai and Esther" without including the text of the prayer. Michael Higger, ed., Tractate *Soferim* (New York: Devei Rabbanan, 1937), 20:6, p. 346; in printed editions of the Babylonian Talmud, 20:8.

> ...let the evil plot, which he devised against the Jews, recoil on his own head!' So they hanged him and his sons on the gallows.

Most contemporary liberal *siddurim* emended the wording of the brutal force of Haman's scheme and/or the payback he received either in the Hebrew, the English translation, or both.

While the 1985 and 2002 versions of the Conservative liturgy preserved the traditional wording in the Hebrew, in the English translation they softened the more literal description of Haman's plan "to destroy, massacre, and exterminate" to the more general "plotted their destruction."[271] Similarly, they couldn't bring themselves to say that Haman and his sons were "hung" even though they did reference "the gallows." Instead, Haman and his sons either "suffered death on the gallows" (1985, p. 182) or were "put to death on the gallows" (2002, p. 129). On the other hand, the 2016 edition of the Conservative prayer book restored a more literal translation to both phrases:

> ...to destroy, to kill and to annihilate the entire Jewish people... he and his sons were hanged on the gallows.[272]

The previous version of the Reform siddur includes the traditional wording of the beginning of *Al HaNissim*, but similarly modified the apparently too violent "to destroy, massacre, and exterminate" to the less extreme "planned to destroy them." This previous version also chose to omit entirely, in both the Hebrew and the English, the final phrase of the prayer, "he and his sons were hanged on the gallows."[273] The most recent version of the Reform siddur also includes the traditional phrasing of the beginning of the prayer in the Hebrew but softens the English translation in exactly the same way. However, regarding the end of the prayer, it restored the Hebrew for "he and his sons were hanged on the gallows," and yet decided to leave that phrase untranslated.[274]

The siddur of the Reconstructing Judaism Movement elected to preserve the traditional Hebrew for the beginning of *Al HaNissim* and faithfully trans-

[271] Avram Reisner, ed., *Siddur Sim Shalom for Weekdays* (New York: The Rabbinical Assembly and the United Synagogue of Conservative Judaism, 2002), 42. Jules Harlow, ed., *Siddur Sim Shalom, A Prayerbook for Shabbat, Festivals, and Weekdays* (New York: The Rabbinical Assembly and The United Synagogue of America, 1985), 118-119.

[272] Edward Feld, ed., *Siddur Lev Shalem for Shabbat and Festivals*, 2016, 431.

[273] Chaim Stern, ed., *Gates of Prayer: The New Union Prayerbook*, 46.

[274] Elyse D. Frishman, ed., *Mishkan T'filah: A Reform Siddur*, 2007, 557.

lated it as "seeking to destroy, to kill, and to eradicate all Jews." However, it uniquely decided to replace, "he and his sons were hanged on the gallows" in both the Hebrew and the English with a much more positive phrase from Esther 8:16, "And to the Jews came light and happiness, and joy and glory."[275]

It is, in fact, not surprising that fiercely negative anti-gentile language is employed in this prayer for *Purim*. It reflects the descriptions of violence in the Scroll of Esther itself—including the number of Persians killed by the Jews, and the hanging of Haman and his ten sons—and the bitter wording of the blessing recited at the conclusion of the reading of *Megillat Esther* which contains several synonyms for "vengeance" and "retribution:"

> Blessed are you, *YHVH*, our God, King of the universe, who fights our fight, judges our claim, avenges our wrong, who visits retribution upon all of our enemies, and avenges us from our adversaries. Blessed are you, *YHVH*, who takes vengeance for his people Israel, the rescuing God.[276]

Further on the issue of the image of the non-Jewish Other on the holiday of Purim, there is a remarkable history behind a song traditionally sung after the *Megillah* reading. I am referring to the song known as *Shoshanat Ya'akov* ("The Lily of Jacob"). This song opens with two lines which begin with the last two letters of the Hebrew alphabet (*shin*, *tav*), and—unbeknownst to many—these two lines comprise the end of a much longer alphabetic acrostic called *Asher Heini*.[277] The song in most contemporary prayer books has been sanitized from its original version and reads:

> Cursed be Haman who sought to destroy me.
> Blessed be Mordecai the Jew.
> Cursed be Zeresh, the wife of the one who terrorized me.
> Blessed be Esther for me.

As we shall see, what was likely the original wording contained a strong anti-gentile element. These lines are based on a teaching in Rabbinic Literature related to the chanting of the Scroll of Esther that took on an interesting literary afterlife in the commentaries and codes. This literary afterlife involves

[275] David A. Teutsch, ed., *Kol Haneshamah, Daily* (Wyncote, Pennsylvania: The Reconstructionist Press, 1996), 122-123.

[276] The wording for this blessing is fully spelled out already in the Babylonian Talmud, *Megillah* 21b.

[277] See Israel Davidson, *Thesaurus of Mediaeval Hebrew Poetry* [Hebrew] (New York: The Jewish Theological Seminary, 1924), v. 1, 343, #7559, #7560.

censorship—or more likely, self-censorship, because of the disparaging message about non-Jews.

The teaching to which I'm referring in Rabbinic Literature (and which I will cite below) connects to the contemporary practice regarding the chanting of the Scroll of Esther in which certain verses or individual words invite congregational responses. For example, each time the name of Haman is mentioned, it is met with the sounding of noisemakers in order to drown out the name of the villain of the story. Similarly, some entire verses are chanted first by the congregation and then repeated by the reader. A very old teaching related to these customs is found in the Palestinian Talmud in which a number of talmudic Sages either spontaneously responded or instructed that one should make it a practice to respond, to one or more specific verses in the book of Esther as they were chanted.[278] Within this discussion the Sage, Rav, is cited as saying that one should respond to the chanting of the names of the ten sons of Haman whose hanging is recorded toward the end of the Book of Esther (Esther 9: 7-9) by saying, "Cursed be Haman, cursed be his sons."

For some reason lost to history, in the citations of this teaching in post-talmudic literature, Rav's instruction was interpreted to mean that one must say that line, "Cursed be Haman, cursed be his sons" after the entire scroll has been recited, and not during the reading itself when the names of the ten sons of Haman are chanted. In any case, over the centuries, the wording that Rav suggested was expanded to include a curse against non-Jews in general and ultimately, an expanded version was incorporated into the song *Shoshanat Ya'akov*, a contemporary version of which is cited above. A non-sanitized version of the song appears in a recent edition (2007) of the medieval code, *Shulḥan Arukh*. In it, the line reads as follows:

> Cursed be Haman,
> blessed be Mordecai.
> Cursed be Zeresh,
> blessed be Esther.
> Cursed be all gentiles,
> blessed be all Israel.[279]

This version is, obviously, quite extreme, cursing not only Haman and Zeresh, but "all gentiles." A review of the history of this line, through many

[278] *Megillah* 3:7, 74b; 27a. See also *Bereshit Rabba* 49:1.

[279] *Shulḥan Arukh* with the commentary of the *Mishnah Berurah* (*Mifal Shoneh Halachoth*, Jerusalem: 2007), 690:16.

citations over many centuries, suggests that it was—quite understandably!—subject to either censorship or self-censorship. A few representative examples follow.

A version from the 11th century reads:

> Cursed be Haman,
> blessed be Mordecai.
> Cursed be Zeresh,
> blessed be Esther.
> Cursed be all the evil ones,
> blessed be all the Jews.[280]

In reading this version, one wonders whether self-censorship was at work, replacing "cursed be all gentiles" with "cursed be all the evil ones," since "all the evil ones" does not parallel "all the Jews" nearly as well as "cursed be all gentiles." In fact, a 16th-century version, perhaps "correcting" for the lack of parallelism between these phrases, contains the following wording: "Cursed be all the evil ones, blessed be all the righteous."[281]

Two different versions from the 14th century read as follows:

> Cursed be Haman,
> blessed be Mordecai.
> Cursed be Zeresh,
> blessed be Esther.
> Cursed be all the uncircumcised,
> blessed be all of Israel.[282]

> Cursed be Haman, blessed be Mordecai, cursed be Zeresh his wife, blessed be Esther, cursed be all idolaters, blessed be all of Israel.[283]

[280] *Tosafot* to Babylonian Talmud, *Megillah* 7b, s.v. *dela yada. Tosafot* attribute this wording to the Palestinian Talmud, i.e., to Rav's teaching cited above, but it is not found in our printed edition of the Palestinian Talmud nor in any manuscript version that has reached us.
[281] *Bet Yosef* commentary by R. Yosef Karo to *Arba'ah Turim, Oraḥ Ḥayyim* 690:16.
[282] *Rabbenu Yeruḥam, Sefer Adam*, 10:3.
[283] R. David Abudraham, *Sefer Abudraham HaShalem* (Jerusalem: Usha, 1962), 209. This source, too, ascribes the origin of this version of the wording of this line to the Palestinian Talmud, though again, it is not found in the contemporary printed version nor in any manuscript version that has reached us.

As we've seen, the negative image of the non-Jewish Other is intricately involved in this *Purim* song as well in the *Al HaNissim* prayer. It is also quite present in other liturgical compositions for the holiday of *Purim*.[284]

**Spiritual Commentary on *Al HaNissim* for Purim**

The world has in the past, and does today, contain hostile enemies of the Jewish people. It seems to me that there is nothing wrong with celebrating the rescue of our people from an implacable enemy—whether or not the *Purim* story represents historical fact. The Jewish people have been subject to many, many attacks over the centuries during our long historical experience as a minority culture hosted by majority cultures. I do, however, find myself identifying with the discomfort of contemporary, non-Orthodox, *siddurim* which have modified the harsh language of Haman's plans at the beginning of this prayer because it is so provocative. It is the kind of language that can, and I think has, perpetuated an unhealthy Jewish national obsession with our victimhood. Similarly, I understand the motivation to alter the language of retribution at the conclusion of *Al HaNissim*. Elliott Horowitz has traced the central role that retribution has played in Jewish religious poetry and commentary on the holiday of *Purim* as well as to Jewish anti-gentile violence that happened occasionally as a result.[285] I am comforted with *Al HaNissim* declaring that God "disrupted (Haman's) plans," but I am uncomfortable crowing that, "He and his sons were hanged on the gallows." Do we really want to promote such revenge in our prayers? And however common it might have been in ancient times to take vengeance on the otherwise innocent children of our enemies, I cringe at the image of the hanging of Haman's ten sons. The Scroll of Esther says nothing of their role in their father's murderous plot. For me, therefore, the modifications of *Al HaNissim* by the non-Orthodox prayer books ring true, especially when the changes are reflected not only in the translation, but in the Hebrew text itself.

I find it meaningful when engaged in prayer on this holiday, to meditate both on the real suffering of our people at the hands of more powerful neighbors, as well as on the equally real, and near-universal, human attribute of hostility to the minority, the individual or group on the margins of the larger society. To assertively call out contemporary versions of anti-Jewish prejudice as well as to allow our inheritance of affliction to inform the way we view

[284] For examples of violently anti-gentile language in *piyyutim* for *Purim* see Elliott Horowitz, *Reckless Rites: Purim and the Legacy of Jewish Violence* (Princeton and Oxford: Princeton University Press, 2006), 111-113.

[285] Elliott Horowitz, *Reckless Rites: Purim and the Legacy of Jewish Violence* (Princeton and Oxford: Princeton University Press, 2006).

intolerance against all minorities in modern times. If we would add some personal words on these themes to the traditional *Al HaNissim* for *Purim*, I think we would be fulfilling the third-century *Tosefta*'s charge to "mention something about the occasion."

## *Taḥanun*—Supplication

*Taḥanun*, "Supplication," is the name of a series of prayers offered after the weekday *Amidah* at *Shaḥarit* and *Minḥah*. These prayers are not recited on Shabbat or holidays. There are two forms of *Taḥanun*: A longer version and a shorter version. The longer version is recited on Mondays and Thursdays at *Shaḥarit*, while the shorter version is recited at *Shaḥarit* on the other weekdays as well as at *Minḥah* on all weekdays. The longer liturgy for Mondays and Thursdays was likely marked for those particular days because these were the market and court days in ancient times—which likely also accounts for the fact that the Torah is read on these same weekdays: Since more people congregated in the public domain on those days, the longer liturgies occurred then.[286] This section of the service includes two unique features: a distinctive form of prostration, and the fact that for part of this section, the prayer leader abandons the pulpit and sits with the congregation.

As we will see, the basic theme of this section is confessing the essential sinful nature of humanity and appealing for God's mercy.[287] Because of that, *Taḥanun* is omitted on days of joy including Shabbat or holidays (and at *Minḥah* on the afternoon before those days), on the day of a *Brit Milah* or baby naming, and the like. It is also omitted at worship in a house of mourning, perhaps out of sensitivity to the feelings of the mourner who may feel a profound absence of God's mercy, having just lost a loved one.

The historical development of this section is quite fascinating. It may have begun as an opportunity, following the scripted blessings of the *Ami-*

[286] There are numerous additional, and most likely apocryphal, reasons offered. See Elbogen, *Jewish Liturgy*, 68-69.

[287] Ruth Langer surveyed the early history of this liturgical section, witnessed by documents in the Cairo Genizah (approximately 10th-13th centuries) and the writings of the Geonim (7th-11th centuries). In these texts, a move took place from what may have originally been individual, personal requests to a quasi-communal venue expressing "human humility, penitence, and reliance on God's mercy, lovingkindness, and above all, willingness to forgive human weakness." In *Taḥanun*'s later, medieval, development, the original "penitential nature, especially (its) confessional elements can be obscured by the wash of words asking for God's forgiveness and salvation." See Ruth Langer, "'We Do Not Even Know What To Do!': A Foray into the Early History of Tahanun," in *Seeking the Favor of God, Vol. 3: The Impact of Penitential Prayer Beyond Second Temple Judaism*, eds. Mark Boda, Daniel Falk, and Rodney Werline (Society for Biblical Literature, 2008), 54-55.

*dah*, for the worshiper to express whatever prayers may arise in the heart in an unscripted way. The fact that, to this day, the prayer leader vacates the pulpit for part of this service may be mute testimony to the free-form basis for this section: that part of the service is not led by anyone—even though all of *Taḥanun*, including this seemingly leader-less part has been scripted for many centuries. The origin of *Taḥanun* may be related to two liturgical occurrences, one in the ancient Temple in Jerusalem, and one in the talmudic era. In the ancient Temple, the daily morning and afternoon sacrifices were followed by shofar blasts, the chanting of psalms by the Levites, and most importantly, prostration by the Israelite worshipers gathered in the courtyard of the Temple.[288] As we have seen, the *Amidah* was based upon, and replaced, the daily Temple sacrifice. Therefore, prostration in this section which immediately follows the daily morning and afternoon *Amidah* may have been modelled after the prostration that immediately followed the daily morning and afternoon Temple sacrifice. In the talmudic era, the Sages had a practice of adding their own impromptu prayers following their recitation of the *Amidah*. They taught that while "one may not add words (i.e., private prayer)" following the recitation of the *Shema* and its blessings, "one may add words after the *Amidah*, even (as long as) the confessional of *Yom Kippur*."[289] The Talmud records the texts of the private prayers of numerous Sages.[290] It is possible that the prostration in the Temple following the morning and afternoon sacrifices combined with the talmudic precedent of offering private prayers following the *Amidah* may together have formed the beginnings of what became *Taḥanun*.

The unique form of prostration that is commonly done today during part of *Taḥanun* is that one rests one's head on one's left forearm (during *Shaḥarit*, if one is wearing *tefillin* on one's left forearm, one rests one's head on the right forearm). This derives from the talmudic custom—that may be an early form of *Taḥanun*—in which the Sages would not engage in a full prostration, but merely "turn to the side" (*matzlei atzluyei*).[291]

[288] *Mishnah Tamid* 7:3—Following the sacrifice, "...the Levites sang the Psalm. When they came to a pause, they blew a shofar blast and the people bowed down. At every pause there was a shofar blast and at every shofar blast, a bowing down. This was the order of the regular daily sacrifice..."
[289] *Tosefta Berakhot* 3:6 (in some editions 3:10). See Ruth Langer's article, cited above, for additional discussion of this, and other, talmudic texts.
[290] Babylonian Talmud, *Berakhot* 16b-17a and Palestinian Talmud *Berakhot* 4:2; 7d. One of those private prayers—that of Mar, the son of Ravina—ultimately was appended to the conclusion of each *Amidah*. It begins, "My God, guard my tongue from evil and my lips from speaking deceitfully."
[291] Babylonian Talmud, *Megillah* 22b-23a, *Berakhot* 34b. The exact form of this symbolic prostration has varied from locale to locale.

The wording of *Taḥanun* was a matter of custom throughout the Middle Ages. Even as late as the 16th century's *Shulḥan Arukh*, the wording is barely mentioned, thus leaving it up to the individual worshiper.[292] Ultimately, though, as time went on, this section acquired more and more of a fixed text. In both Ashkenazic and Sephardic practice, the longer version is characterized by the prayer *VeHu Raḥum*, "(God) the Merciful," first mentioned in the 11th century, and the subject of a legend found in various medieval formulations.[293] The basic contours of the legend are that after the destruction of the Temple in 70 CE, the Roman ruler Vespasian sent a number of Jews on three ships with no rudders. The three ships arrived in Europe (either France or Spain, depending on the version of the story). At first, the travelers were treated well, but when the ruler who dealt kindly with them died, they were robbed and persecuted. They declared a fast and two brothers, Yosef and Binyamin, along with their uncle, Shmuel, supposedly composed *VeHu Raḥum* to ask for God's mercy and help with their plight. The prayer entreats God not to punish us according to our sins, but to deal mercifully with us. It also contains notes of persecution, e.g., "let not your heritage be the object of insult for other nations to rule."

In Ashkenaz, the shorter version includes Psalm 6, and in the 18th century, it was prefaced by II Samuel 24:14. It is for these two texts that one assumes the partial prostration form of resting one's head on one's forearm, and for which the prayer leaders sits with the rest of the congregation. Only beginning in the 19th century, Psalm 6 was followed by *Shomer Yisrael*, "Guardian of Israel," a prayer that in non-Ashkenazic rites is only recited on fast days and as part of the penitential prayers in the weeks leading up to the Days of Awe.[294]

## Psalm 6

This psalm is expressed entirely in the first-person singular, e.g., "*YHVH*, don't punish **me** in anger, don't chastise **me** in fury..." That conforms nicely with this section of the service that was likely meant to be recited by the individual. In keeping with the overall theme of *Taḥanun*, this psalm appeals to God for mercy, the psalmist guilt-ridden and fearful of persecutors. It includes three expressions for crying: "every night I drench my bed, I melt my couch in tears, my eyes are wasted by vexation" (Ps. 6:7-8). Twice the psalmist expresses inner terror ((Ps. 6:3-4) and concludes by wishing terror

[292] *Shulḥan Arukh, Oraḥ Ḥayyim* 131.
[293] For bibliography of the various versions of the legend, see Elbogen, *Jewish Liturgy*, 70, n. 17.
[294] Elbogen, *Jewish Liturgy*, 68.

upon his enemies (Ps. 6:11). This passage is a cry from a dark inner place and a call for relief and pity.

**II Samuel 24:14**

This brief biblical passage is recited as the introduction to Psalm 6. The background to this verse is King David's taking a census of the number of soldiers available to him. Upon the completion of the census, he reproached himself for taking the census, apparently because it exposed his lack of faith in God's protection of his kingdom. And indeed, the prophet Gad tells David that God will punish him and presents David with a choice of three kinds of punishment: an attack by enemies, a famine, or a plague. David's reply, picking anything but enemy attack, is the verse recited here in *Taḥanun*:

David said to Gad: "I am in great distress. Let us fall into the hands of the *YHVH*, for his compassion is great; and let me not fall into the hands of men."

This verse was presumably deemed appropriate for *Taḥanun* because it is the expression by a remorseful sinner of utter and complete reliance on the compassion of God. This, too, comports with the central theme of *Taḥanun*, that of wayward human beings pleading for God's compassion.

***Shomer Yisrael*, "Guardian of Israel"**

*Shomer Yisrael* is a short, three-verse, poem pleading for God to save the nation of Israel from its persecutors. It reminds God of the loyalty of the Jewish people who recite the central prayers of *Shema Yisrael* and the *Kedushah*. The tone here, too, is bleak, with a three-fold chorus of "do not let Israel be destroyed... do not let this unique nation be destroyed... do not let this holy nation be destroyed."

**Spiritual Commentary on *Taḥanun***

During one of the three years I spent studying Torah in Jerusalem, I was a student at a small yeshivah, Yeshivat HaMivtar, that was housed in the larger Yeshivah of Navahrudak. The larger yeshivah was originally founded in Navahrudak, Russia toward the end of the 19th century. It was a *Mussar* yeshivah, that is, a yeshivah that stressed the abnegation of the ego and the physical while emphasizing one's intellectual, moral, and spiritual development. I will never forget that during *Taḥanun*, the Rosh Yeshivah, an elderly man with a long grey beard, would cry, would actually shed tears, with complete abandon, on a daily basis. The central place of focusing on one's own unworthiness fit nicely within the philosophy of the Navahrudak Yeshivah.

However, Navahrudak's approach is not within the comfort zone of most modern Jews. My own inner intention when reciting *Taḥanun* is less mournful, less self-deprecating, and more introspective and reflective. During *Taḥanun*, I find that the posture of half-bowing, while remaining conscious of the presence of God, is conducive to self-examination. I tend to recite some of the traditional wording and take the opportunity to do some unscripted prayer. I usually review my day up to the time of this worship service and ask myself where I have veered from the Jewish and personal principles by which I strive to live. I ask myself where I have lacked the confidence to live up to those principles in my day so far. It can be a helpful break and I often emerge refreshed with renewed commitment to my true religious beliefs and ethical values.

# Concluding Prayers of the *Shaḥarit* (Morning Service)

The concluding prayers of the *Shaḥarit*, "Morning," Service, are just that: a collection of several prayers as opposed to a unified "service." Each entered the liturgy separately and there really aren't organic connections between them. The Ashkenazic collection is as follows:

- *Ashrei* (Psalm 145 with verses added from Psalms 84:5, 144:15, and 115:18).
- Psalm 20—A supplicatory psalm omitted on holidays and in a house of mourning.
- *Kedushah DeSidra*, "The *Kedushah* of the Torah Lesson."
- *Kaddish Shalem*, "Full *Kaddish*."
  *Aleinu*, "It Is Upon Us."

*Ashrei* in this location is the second of its three daily recitations (along with its place in *Pesukei DeZimra* and as the first prayer in *Minḥah*, The Afternoon Service) to fulfill the Talmud's suggestion that *Ashrei* recited three times daily assures one of a place in the World to Come. See the commentary on *Ashrei* in *Pesukei DeZimra*, page 22.

Psalm 20 was originally a passage in *Taḥanun*, the "Supplication" service that follows the weekday *Amidah*. Part of the evidence for this is that it is omitted on the same days that *Taḥanun* is omitted.

## *Kedushah DeSidra*

The title of this prayer, *Kedushah DeSidra*, "The *Kedushah* of the Torah Lesson," points to its origin. It was apparently recited after a teaching session that served as the conclusion of the *Shaḥarit*, "Morning," Service in ancient times. Although the custom to hold a teaching session at the conclusion of *Shaḥarit* eventually ceased, the tradition of reciting the prayer that apparently followed it continued.[295] (It is also recited toward the beginning of the

[295] For supporting sources, see Ismar Elbogen, *Jewish Liturgy*, 70, n. 23. On the issue of why the *Kedushah* in every *Amidah* requires a *minyan* but this one (and the *Kedushah DeYotser* earlier in the morning service) does not, see the following for sources and discussion: Ruth Langer, *To Worship God Properly: Tensions Between Liturgical Custom and Ḥalakhah in Judaism* (Cincinnati: Hebrew Union College Press, 1998), Chapter 4, "Individual Recitation of the *Kedushah*: The Impact of Mysticism on Minhag and Halakhah," 188-244.

*Minḥah*, Afternoon Service, on Shabbat and holidays because it originally followed a teaching session held on the afternoons of those days).

This prayer consists of biblical verses, a version of the *Kedushah*, and brief lines of rabbinic prayer. The themes of the biblical verses emphasize hope for the messianic age, praise of Torah, and praise of God's reliability. The rabbinic prayers similarly praise Torah and express the hope for the messianic era. A *Kedushah* appears to be an original component of this prayer since the word *Kedushah* has been part of the title of this prayer since talmudic times.[296] It may be that a *Kedushah*, literally, "a sanctification" of God by chanting the angels' praises of God was considered part and parcel of the messianic hope that traditionally concluded ancient Torah lessons. For extensive notes on a *Kedushah*, see the commentaries on the *Kedushah* in the Weekday *Amidah*, beginning on page 101.

**Spiritual Commentary on *Kedushah DeSidra***

*Kedushah DeSidra* connects Torah and messianism. One way I interpret the many messianic prayers in Jewish liturgy is as encouragement to work for a perfected world, a reminder of our ideals and inspiration toward actualizing them. I don't pray for a human messiah to bring the ideal world; I view prayers for the Messianic Age as challenges to us as individuals and as groups to advance our communities toward the goal of an Edenic, idyllic, age. For me, such prayers are calls to calibrate where we are in accordance with our highest ideals.

In this prayer, *Kedushah DeSidra*, the call is to align the study and application of Torah in accordance with our highest ideals. This implies that even Torah can be used and abused for less-than-ideal purposes, and prayers like this one ask us to consider our study and teaching of Torah. I connect to this challenge the Zohar's provocative interpretation of the sin of the Golden Calf. Typically, the sin is understood as the Israelites' reverting to the worship of a concrete idol instead of praying to the unseen presence of the true God. But the Zohar, ever stretching the envelope, has its own take on what that central biblical sin was about. The Zohar asserts that the sin was to separate the "lower," more concrete *sefirot*, or mystical embodiments, of God from their "higher," mystical source. Arthur Green boldly explains this as a dismissal of "much of Western religion as idolatry."[297] How so? By

[296] Babylonian Talmud, *Sotah* 49a.

[297] Arthur Green, *Radical Judaism: Rethinking God and Tradition* (New Haven: Yale University Press, 2010) 102, n. 45. I consider this a remarkable and insightful understanding of the Zoharic text. In Green's book, the citation to n. 45 is Zohar 1:3a, but the correct reference is Zohar 1:2a.

divorcing ritual from its meaning. Confusing means and ends. Acting as if the means, the rituals and the texts, are in and of themselves holy, even when removed from their ends, namely, connecting to, and revering, the divine presence. It happens when we end up worshiping the words on the page of the prayer book instead of using the words to worship God. It happens when we are punctilious about saying the correct prayers for the correct occasion, checking and rechecking page number, psalm chapter and verse number, but forgetting that these are merely the means to connect us to the ultimate end of raising awareness of God. It means giving the impression (if we are prayer leaders) or getting the impression (if we are participants in a worship service) that praying is synonymous with reading or singing the words on the printed prayer book page. The Zohar is challenging us to recognize that when we confuse the means and the ends in worship, we are committing a form of idolatry.[298]

### Kaddish

The *Kaddish*, "Holiness" or "Sanctification" (Aramaic), has a long and fascinating history. It is found in five different forms in the Ashkenazic rite and in numerous additional forms in other rites. An exploration of its history and literary forms will reveal a great deal about the evolution of its meanings.

In post-talmudic times, the *Kaddish* acquired two different functions which still obtain in contemporary liturgy: It signaled the conclusion of a worship service, or a portion of a service, and it is a prayer recited by mourners of their dead. The *Kaddish* attained the role of concluding a service already in our earliest *siddurim* of the 9th and 10th centuries. It may have been assigned this role because its wording, *birkhata veshirata tushbeḥata veneḥemata*, "(God is above all) blessings, songs, praises, and consolations" may have been interpreted to refer to the prayers just recited in the worship service.[299]

---

[298] Rabbi Abraham Joshua Heschel addressed this disconnect specifically regarding prayer in many of his published works and these writings have sustained and challenged me over many years. He expresses the problems with modern worship, and offers inspiration for renewing Jewish worship, in sparkling language that remains among the best of its kind. Here, I will only point to one of his essays which was originally given as a speech to Conservative rabbis at their annual convention, in 1953. His critique of then-contemporary Jewish worship was trenchant, to the point of veering into the acerbic at times, but many of the points he makes still ring true. I am referring to his "The Spirit of Jewish Prayer," in Susannah Heschel, ed., *Moral Grandeur and Spiritual Audacity* (New York: Farrar Straus and Giroux, 1996), 100-126.

[299] Elbogen, *Jewish Liturgy*, 81-82.

The five forms of the *Kaddish* are:

- *Ḥatzi Kaddish*, "Half *Kaddish*"
- *Kaddish Shalem*, "Full *Kaddish*"
- *Kaddish DeRabbanan*, "*Kaddish* of Our Rabbis"
- *Kaddish Yatom*, "Mourner's (literally, "Orphan's") *Kaddish*"
- *Kaddish De'Itḥadeta*, "*Kaddish* of Renewal"

*Ḥatzi Kaddish* concludes a portion of a worship service. *Kaddish Shalem* concludes an entire service and concludes with prayers for peace in Aramaic and Hebrew. *Kaddish DeRabbanan* adds a line praying for the welfare of scholars and is recited at the conclusion of Torah study. *Kaddish Yatom* is recited by mourners, the development of which is traced below. *Kaddish De'Itḥadeta* is recited at a burial and at a *Siyyum*, the ceremonial conclusion of study of a talmudic tractate; in this way, it functions a little like both *Kaddish Yatom* and *Kaddish DeRabbanan*.

To understand how forms of the *Kaddish* became the mourner's prayer, we need to first survey its earliest role, namely the way it operated in talmudic times and how a post-talmudic folktale merged with, and augmented, the theological power of this prayer.

In the Rabbinic Period, the early version of the *Kaddish* functioned as a messianic prayer recited mainly (but not only) at the end of lessons taught by the ancient Sages.[300] In Rabbinic Literature, the text of the *Kaddish* is referred to by the citation of just one sentence or one sentence fragment in about a dozen places. It was customary to conclude teachings with prayers for eternal peace and the coming of the Messiah and these proto-*Kaddish* prayers seemed to be among the prayers that fulfilled that role. In contemporary worship, the recital of *Kaddish DeRabbanan* after Torah study and *Kaddish De'Itḥadeta* at the conclusion of study of talmudic tractate reflect this ancient practice. In the Talmud and Midrash, the sentence that commonly appears is the line that functions as the congregational response in contemporary practice:

[300] See the sources in David De Sola Pool's study, still relevant after over a hundred years, *The Old Jewish-Aramaic Prayer The Kaddish* (New York: The Bloch Publishing Company, 1909), 8-10. See also, much more recently, the sources and analysis in the revised doctoral dissertation (in German) of Andreas Lehnardt, *Qaddish: Untersuchengen zur Entstehung und Rezeption eines rabbinschen Gebete* (Tubingen: Moer Siebeck, 2002). See also David Brodsky, "Mourner's Kaddish, The Prequel: The Sassanian Period Backstory That Gave Birth to the Medieval Prayer for the Dead," in Geoffrey Herman, Jeffrey L. Rubenstein, eds., *The Aggada of the Bavli and Its Cultural World* (Providence, Rhode Island: Brown Judaic Studies, 2018), 335-370.

> *Yehei shemeih rabbah mevorakh, l'alam u'lalmei almaya.*
> "May his name be blessed forever and ever."

The rest of the prayer, to which this line is the response, is not included in the ancient sources. It was assumed that the rest of the prayer was well known. For that reason, we cannot know for sure what the rest of the wording was in talmudic times. Nevertheless, all the forms of the *Kaddish* in all of the rites of the Jewish People begin with very similar language petitioning God to commence the messianic age now, during our lifetimes. In the Ashkenazic rite, four of the five forms of the *Kaddish* express that wish with the same wording (the exception is the *Kaddish De'Itḥadeta*, which expresses the same idea but with slightly different wording):

> *...veyamlikh malkhuteih beḥayyeikhon u'veyomeikhon u'veḥayyei dekhol beit Yisrael ba'gala u'vizman kariv.*
> ...May his (messianic) kingdom reign in your lifetimes and in your days and in the lifetimes of the whole House of Israel, swiftly and soon.

The wording above is in Aramaic, the spoken language in most of the rabbinic era. Although, this line—with no difference in meaning—sometimes appears in talmudic sources mostly in Hebrew.[301] Beyond the theme of messianism, many of the rabbinic sources describe the proto-*Kaddish* as a theurgic prayer. Theurgy refers to rituals or prayers that have a strong effect, even a forceful effect, on the divine. Below, I will cite five talmudic texts that depict this prayer as having this mystical, quasi-incantational, nature.[302]

> 1. Rabbi Yehoshua ben Levi said: All who respond, "Amen, *Yehei shemei rabba mevorakh*" with all their strength, the evil decree is torn up for them.[303]
>
> 2. Rava said: Each day is more accursed than the one before, as it says (Deut. 28:67) "In the morning you will say 'if it were only evening,' and in the evening you will say, 'if it only

[301] For example, in Babylonian Talmud *Berakhot* 21b: *Yehei shemo hagadol mevorakh*. Sometimes, the line is cited in a combination of Aramaic and Hebrew as in Babylonian Talmud, *Berakhot* 3a, cited below.
[302] I thank Professor Debra Reed Blank who first directed my attention to the theurgic nature of the rabbinic texts that cite the proto-*Kaddish*.
[303] Babylonian Talmud, *Shabbat* 119b.

were morning.'" ...That being the case, what sustains the world? It endures by virtue of the *Kedushah DeSidra* and the *Yehei shemeih rabba* of the study session.[304]

3. (If in a dream), one responds, *Yehei shemei rabba mevorakh*, one is assured of a place in the World to Come.[305]

4. The question was raised: Does one interrupt (their private recitation of the *Amidah* to respond) *Yehei shemo hagadol mevorakh*? When Rav Dimi came, he said that Rabbi Yehudah and Rabbi Shimon, students of Rabbi Yoḥanan, said: One does not on account of anything interrupt (their private recitation of the *Amidah*) except for *Yehei shemo hagadol mevorakh*; even if one is engaged in the (mystical contemplation of the beginning of the Book of Ezekiel known as) "The Enterprise of the Chariot," one interrupts that. Although the *halakhah* (the law) does not follow this opinion.[306]

5. It was taught—Rabbi Yossi says: I was once travelling on the road, and I entered one of the ruins of Jerusalem in order to pray (an *Amidah*). Elijah of blessed memory appeared and waited for me at the door till I finished my prayer. After I finished my prayer, he said to me: Peace be with you, my master! And I replied: Peace be with you, my master and teacher! And he said to me: My son, why did you go into this ruin? I replied: To pray. He said to me: You ought to have prayed on the road. I replied: I feared lest passers-by might interrupt me. He said to me: You ought to have said an abbreviated prayer. Thus, I learned from him three things: One must not go into a ruin; one may say the *Amidah* on the road; and if one does say one's *Amidah* on the road, one recites an abbreviated *Amidah*. He further said to me: My son, what sound did you hear in this ruin? I replied: I heard a divine voice, cooing like a dove, and saying: Woe to the children, on account of whose sins I

[304] Babylonian Talmud, *Sotah* 49a.
[305] Babylonian Talmud, *Berakhot* 57b.
[306] Babylonian Talmud, *Berakhot* 21b.

> destroyed my house and burnt my Temple and exiled them among the nations of the world! And he said to me: By your life and by your head! Not in this moment alone does it so exclaim, but thrice each day does it exclaim thus! And more than that, whenever Israel goes into the synagogues and study houses and responds: *Yehei shemeih hagadol mevorakh*, the Holy One, blessed be He, shakes his head and says: Happy is the king who is thus praised in this house! Woe to the father who had to banish his children, and woe to the children who had to be banished from the table of their father![307]

These texts demonstrate the theurgic power ascribed to the early *Kaddish*. In source #1, reciting it "with all their strength" causes an evil decree to be torn up. In other words, if one has sinned and has earned punishment ("an evil decree"), reciting the words of the *Kaddish* has the capability to cancel that punishment. Note that this source does not require repentance; the quasi-magical character of the prayer is sufficient.

In source #2, the world grows more accursed every day and it is only because of the potency of two prayers—one of which is the *Kaddish*—that the world does not descend into utter devastation.

In source #3, dreaming that one has recited this prayer will ensure one's eternal place of blessing in the World to Come; dreaming in ancient Israel was often viewed as potentially a source of divine messages.

Source #4 asserts that one may interrupt one of the holiest of prayers, the *Amidah*, as well as mystical contemplation, in order to recite the *Kaddish*. Even though the source goes on to say that this did become authoritative law, it is significant that a major Sage of the 4th century CE, Rabbi Yoḥanan, asserted the primacy of the *Kaddish*.

Finally, source #5 contains a dramatic story. Here, Elijah the prophet appears to the 2nd-century Sage, Rabbi Yossi ben Ḥalafta, and tells him that each time Israel recites the *Kaddish*, God nods and acknowledges how wonderful it is to be praised through such a prayer. In this way, the *Kaddish* is recognized as a prayer that is clearly heard by God and a prayer that has the power to especially move God. Additionally, there is the first hint of mourning in this source, because this prayer moves God to mourn punishing the Jewish People, God's children. The "table of their father" refers to the altar

[307] Babylonian Talmud, *Berakhot* 3a.

in the ancient Temple, which, in the rabbinic imagination, God allowed the Romans to destroy in 70 CE.

These sources, taken together, demonstrate the theurgic aspect of reciting the *Kaddish*: It has the power to cancel evil decrees, to sustain the accursed world, to assure one's place in the World to Come, to interrupt holy prayer and contemplation, and to arouse deep pathos in God.

One aspect of the literary format of the *Kaddish* may have added to its theurgic character. It has often been pointed out that the wording of this prayer never mentions death or the dead. It is less often noticed that instead of actually mentioning any of the numerous names of God, the *Kaddish* refers obliquely and mysteriously to "the name" of God:

In the first and second sentences: *shemeih rabba*, "the great name."

In the third sentence: *shemeih dekudsha berikh hu*, "the name of the blessed holy one."

The first two sentences bless and praise this "name," while the third sentence acclaims it with eight staccato adjectives in a row, *Yitbarakh, veyishtabaḥ, veyitpa'ar, veyitromam, veyitnasei veyithadar, veyitaleh, veyit'halal*, "(May the name) be blessed, praised, glorified, exalted, extolled, adorned, lauded, and adored."

These first three sentences of the prayer form the contemporary *Ḥatzi Kaddish* ("Partial *Kaddish*") which may have constituted the entirety of the prayer in the oldest stratum of its development, and it is this version of the *Kaddish* that invokes and lavishly praises "the name" of God without mentioning any divine names. The second sentence, which, as mentioned above, is the line most often cited in Rabbinic sources as a representative of the entire prayer (whose full ancient text is not known), closely resembles the blessing recited in the ancient Temple in Jerusalem: *Barukh shem kevod malkhuto l'olam va'ed*, "Blessed be the name of his majestic glory forever."[308] This was the response of the people congregated in the Temple upon hearing the divine name *YHVH* pronounced out loud. Perhaps it is *YHVH*, the name referring to "being," that is referred to as "the name" in the *Kaddish*. (See the discussion of this name on page 32 in the context of the recitation of the *Shema*; the *Barukh shem* line originally recited in the Temple is recited in contemporary times as a response to the first line of the *Shema*). The prominence of the unidentified but repeated divine "name" found in the first three sentences of the *Kaddish* is an example of the practice across time and cultures of reverence for the power of divine names. And the fact that the core

[308] Elbogen, *Jewish Liturgy*, 80-81, 83, who also cites biblical parallels to some of the wording of this prayer.

of the *Kaddish* repeatedly cites, but doesn't identify, the "name" of God, yet profusely praises it, supports the talmudic depictions of the theurgic weight and authority of this prayer. The 13th-century sage of the German mystical sect, *Ḥasidei Ashkenaz*, Rabbi Elazar of Worms, connects the name of God to the *Kaddish* in a striking way. He posits that "the *Kaddish* is recited after the reading of the Torah because every single word in the Torah conceals the Ineffable Name of God, and therefore each word merits the recital of the prayer which sanctifies that name."[309] In this reading, the title this prayer acquired in post-talmudic times, *Kaddish* ("Holiness" or "Sanctification"), refers to its role as sanctifying the unmentioned, powerful name of God, the praise of which was viewed as enough to exert theurgic influence.

We saw that the quasi-magical potency of this prayer that sanctifies the name of God is reflected in Rabbinic texts as well as in its wording. These are two crucial elements in the development of its place as a mourner's prayer. The other element is the role played by the folktale of Rabbi Akiva and the soul of the dead man. The story appears, or is cited, in many sources.[310] Here is the version found in the 12th-13th-century *Maḥzor Vitry*:

> A tale of Rabbi Akiva. He was walking in a cemetery by the side of the road and encountered there a naked man, black as coal, carrying a large burden of thorns on his head. Rabbi Akiva thought him to be alive and he was running under the load like a horse. Rabbi Akiva ordered him to stop. "How comes it that a man does such hard work?" he asked. "If you are a servant and your master is doing this to you, then I will redeem you from him. If you are poor and people are

[309] *Sefer HaRoke'aḥ*, 311, cited in Joshua Trachtenberg, *Jewish Magic and Superstition: A Study in Folk Religion* (Philadelphia: University of Pennsylvania Press, 1939, 2004 reprint), 314, n. 4. See also chapter 4, "In the Name of...," 78-103. Elbogen, *Jewish Liturgy*, 81, notes that "As a liturgical prayer we find Kaddish first in... Tractate *Soferim*... there it comes at the end of the Torah reading (21:6) in connection with 'Bless the Lord' (10:8), and at the conclusion of the service (19:1)." These chapters of *Soferim* likely date from the early medieval period in Europe.

[310] It apparently first appears in a post-talmudic collection of possibly earlier material, the Tractate *Kallah Rabbati* ("The Longer Bride Tractate") first published only in 1864 in Vienna as part of *Ḥamishah Kunterasim* by Nathan Coronel, 4b-5a. There is no scholarly consensus on the date of this collection, but it may have been edited at the same time as the other "minor tractates" of the Talmud, around the 7th-8th centuries. The *Kaddish* itself appears in the story only beginning with the versions in the 12th century in Central Europe. See Rabbi Isaac of Vienna (1180-1250), *Or Zaru'a*, II, 11b and Rabbi Simḥah of Vitry (France/Germany), *Maḥzor Vitry*, Aryeh Goldschmidt, ed. (Jerusalem: Mekhon Otzar HaPoskim, 2004), 1:223-224. See also in *Maḥzor Vitry*, 1:50, which records a connection between the *Kaddish* and the eternal battle with Amalek. See as well in *Maḥzor Vitry*, 1:56, a narrative in which an angel reveals terrible future persecutions of the Jewish People and the role the *Kaddish* plays in warding off only the very worst of them.

avoiding you, then I will give you money." "Please, sir," the man replied. "Do not detain me, because my superiors will be angry." "Who are you," Rabbi Akiva asked, "and what have you done?" The man said "The man whom you are addressing is a dead man. Every day they send me out to chop wood." "My son, what was your work in the world from which you came?" "I was a tax collector, and I would favor the rich and kill the poor." (In an earlier version, he adds: "There is no forbidden act in the world which I left undone"[311]). "Have your superiors told you nothing about how you might relieve your condition?" "Please, sir, do not detain me, for you will irritate my tormentors. For such a man [as I], there can be no relief. Though I did hear them say something—but no, it is impossible. They said that if this poor man had a son, and his son were to stand before the congregation and recite (the prayer) 'Bless the Lord who is blessed!' and the congregation were to answer amen, and the son were also to say, 'May the Great Name be blessed!' (the key, central, sentence of the *Kaddish*), they would release him from his punishment. But this man never had a son. He left his wife pregnant and he did not know whether the child was a boy. And if she gave birth to a boy, who would teach the boy Torah? For this man does not have a friend in the world." Immediately, Rabbi Akiva took upon himself the task of discovering whether this man had fathered a son, so that he might teach the son Torah and install him at the head of the congregation to lead the prayers. "What is your name?" he asked. "Akiva," the man answered. "And the name of your wife?" "Shoshniva." "And the name of your town?" "Lodkya." Rabbi Akiva was deeply troubled by all this and went to make his inquiries. When he came to that town, he asked about the man he had met, and the townspeople replied: "May his bones be ground to dust!" (In an earlier version, the townspeople add: "He robbed and preyed upon people and caused them suffering; what is more, he violated a betrothed girl on the

[311] J. Rabinowitz, translator, *Kallah Rabbathi* Abraham Cohen, ed., *The Minor Tractates of the Talmud* (University of California: 1965), 52a.

> Day of Atonement"[312]). He asked about the man's wife, and was told: "May her memory be erased from the world!" He asked about the man's son, and was told: "He is a heathen—we did not even bother to circumcise him!" Rabbi Akiva promptly circumcised him and sat him down before a book. But the boy refused to receive Torah. Rabbi Akiva fasted for forty days. A heavenly voice was heard to say: "For this you mortify yourself?" "But Lord of the Universe," Rabbi Akiva replied, "it is for You that I am preparing him." Suddenly the Holy One, Blessed Be He, opened the boy's heart. Rabbi Akiva taught him Torah and "Hear, O Israel" and the benediction after meals. He presented the boy to the congregation and the boy recited (the prayer) "Bless the Lord who is blessed!" At that very moment the man was released from his punishment. The man immediately came to Rabbi Akiva in a dream and said: "May it be the will of the Lord that your soul find delight in the Garden of Eden, for you have saved me from the sentence of Gehenna." Rabbi Akiva declared: "Your Name, O Lord, endures forever, and the memory of You through all the generations!" (Psalm 135:13). For this reason, it became customary that the evening prayers on the night after the Sabbath are led by a man who does not have a father or a mother, so that he can say, "Bless the Lord who is blessed!" or *Kaddish*.[313]

Here, the towering talmudic figure of Rabbi Akiva is invoked as a kind Sage concerned enough for his fellow human beings that he goes to great lengths to relieve the afterlife punishment of a thoroughly sinful Jew. The outcome of the tale is that a son's recitation of certain prayers—including *Kaddish*—can cancel even the seemingly justified punishment of a parent in the afterlife. In this way, this narrative partly echoes the teaching of the talmudic Source #1, cited above, that the full-throated recitation of *Yehei shemeih rabba* cancels the evil decree. The specific mention of the *Kaddish* as one of the prayers that has the power to cancel the dead man's punishment connects strongly with the theurgic role of this prayer found in the talmudic sources and with

[312] *Kallah Rabbati* 52a.

[313] Rabbi Simḥah of Vitry (France/Germany), *Maḥzor Vitry*, Aryeh Goldschmidt, ed., 1:223-224. This translation is mainly the excellent work of Leon Wieseltier, *Kaddish* (New York: Alfred A. Knopf, 1998), 42-43, which I've edited slightly based upon the most recent critical edition of *Maḥzor Vitry* edited by Goldschmidt.

the glorification of the unnamed name of God in the wording of *Kaddish*. The unique role of the story was to invest the theurgic role of the *Kaddish* with the power to relieve suffering in the afterlife.

The conclusion of the tale, that it is an origin story for the custom of an orphan leading the service and *Kaddish* on Saturday nights is based upon earlier teachings.[314] According to these sources, sinners in the afterlife exit Gehinnom, relieved of their torments, each Sabbath and return to Gehinnom as soon as the Sabbath concludes. Therefore, the recitation of *Kaddish* at the moment of their return to their abuse was meant to mitigate their suffering. The fact that the stature of Rabbi Akiva was featured in the story lent it great authority over the ages, and it is cited throughout medieval and early modern sources on the *Kaddish* and mourning practices. In the centuries following the appearance of this story, the custom developed and transformed from that of an individual mourner leading the service on Saturday night—including what was likely the routine *Kaddish Shalem* ("Full *Kaddish*")—to a specially designated additional *Kaddish Yatom*, "Mourner's (literally, "Orphan's") *Kaddish*," to be recited not just by a single mourner, but by all mourners present in the synagogue, not only on Saturday night, but on every day of the week, and not only at the evening service, but at all three daily services, and not only once at the end of the service but (especially at the morning service) at several junctures within the service.[315] In its initial stages of development, the *Kaddish* did not seem to require a *minyan* (a quorum of ten adults), but at a later stage, that requirement was added.[316] The custom of the congregation standing whenever any version of the *Kaddish* is recited was attributed to the 16th-century Kabbalist, Rabbi Isaac Luria. But there are other, authoritative, opinions that do not require standing.[317]

---

[314] See De Sola Pool (who follows Zunz), *The Kaddish*, for sources.

[315] For a fascinating ranked list of which individuals get priority to recite *Kaddish*—reflecting that in 16th-century Poland, only one individual at a time recited the prayer—and for which dead relatives, see the uncharacteristically long comment of *Rema* in *Shulḥan Arukh, Yoreh De'ah* 376:4. Among other details, *Rema* here rules that the children of a Jewish apostate who was murdered (by non-Jews?) may recite *Kaddish* over him. The commentary of *Siftei Kohen* (by Rabbi Shabtai Kohen, 17th century, Lithuania, Moravia, Poland), #15, rules that this applies only if the apostate were murdered, because that kind of death will bring the kind of atonement that death traditionally offers, "but if he died in his bed," they are not permitted to recite *Kaddish*.

[316] This development needs additional study. See *Arba'ah Turim, Shulhan Arukh—Oraḥ Ḥayyim* 55. See also Elbogen, 83; Hammer, *Entering Jewish Prayer*, 283, n. 12 who cites Max Kadushin, *Worship and Ethics: A Study In Rabbinic Judaism* (Evanston, Illinois: Northwestern University Press, 1964), 141-142.

[317] See David Golinkin, "Should We Stand or Sit for the Kaddish?" https://schechter.edu/should-we-stand-or-sit-for-the-kaddish/, accessed on December 21, 2021.

**Spiritual Commentary on the *Kaddish***

Let me first address the role of *Kaddish* as a mourner's prayer and then I'll offer thoughts on *Kaddish* in its other main role as a marker of divisions within a worship service. It seems to me that for most moderns in mourning, the theurgic ramifications of reciting *Kaddish* would not be meaningful. The idea that there is real power to any quasi-magical incantation probably does not resonate with most non-fundamentalist contemporary Jews. Nor, I think, would they find meaningful the notion that there is literal truth to traditional concepts of reward and punishment in the afterlife. And so, the thought that any individual has the capability, through the recitation of a prayer, to diminish the suffering of their loved one in the afterlife similarly would likely not be a helpful insight.

And yet, there may be meaning for moderns in the general notion that through prayer, one may be able to connect, in some mysterious way, with the souls of our departed loved ones. And that basic belief underlies all the traditional teachings about *Kaddish* as a prayer for mourners. Here is one way for a contemporary worshiper to tap into the general approach of so many of the traditional teachings about *Kaddish* without necessarily accepting all the pre-modern values that characterize those teachings: Even in these times when science has explained so much, the realm of death and the soul remains a mystery. Just as intellectual honesty compels us to wonder about and entertain skepticism about life after death, it also obliges us to admit that we don't know, that nobody knows, what happens after death.

In an address to an international conference in 1969, three years before his death, Rabbi Abraham Joshua Heschel delivered a talk called "Death As Homecoming." Typical of Rabbi Heschel's writings, it is more poetry than prose, more a gathering of disparate and wise insights than a well-argued essay. Nevertheless, one central message it contains has stayed with me ever since I first read it when it was reprinted a year after his death: The audacious, yet provocative and tantalizing, notion that our souls may survive death to the extent to which we nurture sensitivity to the spiritual dimension while we are alive.

> Eternity is not an automatic consequence of sheer being, and survival is not an unconditional epilogue of living. It must be achieved, earned... The life that follows must be earned while we are here. It does not come out of nothing; it is an ingathering, the harvest of eternal moments achieved while on earth. Unless we cultivate sensitivity to the glory

> while here, unless we learn how to experience a foretaste of heaven while on earth, what can there be in store for us in life to come? The seed of life eternal is planted within us here and now. But a seed is wasted when placed on stone into souls that die while the body is still alive.[318]

Thus, reciting the *Kaddish* ought to be viewed in the context of how we view this life, how we view prayer, how we view the possibility of the human soul. To the extent that we are conscious of a dimension of life beyond the immediate physical plane, the *Kaddish* may, even for moderns, serve as the gateway to connect with the souls of those who have died. Praying the *Kaddish* in this way can be both challenging and comforting.

Because of the personal and spiritual nature of this approach to the *Kaddish*, I discourage the practice of hiring others to recite *Kaddish* in memory of a loved one. There are numerous organizations that offer this service. Presumably, paying for others to perform this ritual brings comfort to people who know that they will not regularly recite the prayer in memory of their relative. Nevertheless, my feeling is that the quality of the ritual takes priority over the quantity of its performance. If one doesn't believe that this prayer literally reduces potential afterlife punishment, then it is far better for one to recite *Kaddish* oneself when one can—even if it is not as often as one might desire—than to hire someone else to recite. The question is: Do we believe that the mourner's *Kaddish* is primarily to save our loved one from potential punishment in the hereafter, or is it primarily to connect with our loved one as we deal with grief and loss? If its purpose for moderns is to connect in moments of prayer with our loved one, then it does not make sense to parcel it out for others to recite.

Now, let's consider the role of *Kaddish* outside of its role for mourners, as a frequent pause in between sections of a given worship service. This pause serves as a marker that one unit of the service, or the worship service as a whole, has concluded. Scholars call prayers that function in this way a "doxology," from the ancient Greek "doxa" meaning "glory," and "logia" meaning "saying." A doxology is usually a short hymn that glorifies or praises God. This definition fits this role of the *Kaddish* because its content is not connected to the themes of the sections of the service themselves, but rather stands by itself. Doxologies are often a kind of clearing of the palate with

---

[318] Susannah Heschel, ed., *Moral Grandeur and Spiritual Audacity: Essays—Abraham Joshua Heschel* (New York: Farrar, Straus and Giroux, 1996), 327, 373, 378. I had originally read it as "Reflections on Death" in a memorial edition of the journal *Conservative Judaism*, Vol. XXVII, Number 1, Fall, 1973, 3-9.

generic praise of God. In the case of the *Kaddish*, instead of generic praise of God, there is specific praise of God's name. If one concentrates on this central aspect of the *Kaddish*, it can be a corrective for the typical wordiness of Jewish worship services. One of the great challenges to inner devotion in traditional Jewish services is the sheer number of words involved. It can be difficult to connect to all of the passages, let alone find inspiration, when poem after poem after poem is recited. The *Kaddish* reminds us that one of the key goals of prayer, if not the key goal, is connecting with that mysterious presence that seems to lie within life, as well as to dwell beyond it. The names we associate with God evoke that mystery. Oftentimes, we say the word "God" or one of the names of God as if its connotation is as clearly defined as some concrete entity that we can see and feel and know. The truth is that the moment we settle upon a confidently fixed definition of God, we have immediately entered the realm of idolatry and have lost touch with the ineffable nature of something that we sense but cannot accurately label. The *Kaddish* can, in the midst of a worship service, serve to remind us that God's name and essence is ultimately *le'eila mikol birkhata veshirata tushbeḥata veneḥemata de'amiran be'alma*, "beyond all blessings, songs, praises, and consolations that are said in the world." And therefore, the number of words we say in a worship service matters less than making the words we say count. That is, merely increasing the number of words we say in prayer doesn't automatically increase our connection to God since God's name and essence lie "beyond all blessings..." The *Kaddish* reminds us that the quality of the spiritual connection we attempt to make in reciting our prayers trumps the quantity of the words we recite.

## Aleinu

For regular attendees at synagogue services, *Aleinu* is a familiar prayer because it is part of every worship service. Furthermore, since it is chanted near the end of each service, it has become familiar even to those who come late to services. The central questions about this prayer include: How, when, and why did it become part of the conclusion of every service and what are its major themes? In its initial historical stages, it was not recited morning, afternoon, and evening, nor was it chanted on a daily basis at all.

*Aleinu* first appeared in two separate kinds of literature: The liturgy for Rosh HaShanah and a work of ancient Jewish mysticism known as either the *Hekhalot* literature or *Merkavah* mysticism (ca. 6th-9th centuries; possibly earlier). Actual texts of either of these two sources in our hands go back no further than about the 10th century. It is of course possible, and perhaps even likely, that this prayer appeared in either or both locations prior to the 10th century but it is not mentioned in talmudic literature and we are not in possession of documentary evidence from any source deriving from an earlier period.[319] While *Aleinu* makes some sense in the context of both locations, it also doesn't fully fit the themes and style of either place. For this reason, it is uncertain whether *Aleinu* was originally composed for the Rosh HaShanah liturgy or for the *Hekhalot* literature or for a now-lost prior context and adapted for use in both the Rosh HaShanah literature and the *Hekhalot* literature.[320]

In the *Hekhalot* literature, *Aleinu* appeared as a prayer recited by the talmudic Sage, Rabbi Akiva, in gratitude for emerging safely from the potentially dangerous experience of ascending through the various levels of heaven and being granted heavenly visions. The goal in this literature was for the mystical adept to rise through the various heavenly sanctuaries (*Hekhalot*) to be vouchsafed a vision of God in the highest sanctuary. However, many obstacles block the path to that goal. The adept must be righteous and pious. Even if this condition is met, there are many dangerous heavenly creatures that block a mere mortal from ascending higher and higher through the sanctuaries and the very sight of these fiery and malevolent angels is enough to cause the adept to lose his way, if not his very life. In the passages under consideration,[321] Rabbi Akiva successfully ascended to the highest sanctuary. He is depicted as narrating the details of his ascent to Rabbi Yishmael. In his narration of the final stage of his visionary journey, he told Rabbi Yishmael, "I saw 6,400,000,000 angels of service before the throne of glory, and I saw the knot of Tefillin[322] of [here a multi-word, untranslatable, divine name is inserted], the God of Israel, and I gave praise for all of my limbs." Following this, the actual "praise" that Rabbi Akiva recited is recorded, namely, the prayer we now know as *Aleinu*. "Praise" (*shevaḥ*) is, of course, the root of the

---

[319] For historical and textual points that are not here specifically sourced, see the extensive citations in Jeffrey Hoffman, "The Image of the Other in Jewish Interpretations of *Aleinu*," *The Journal of Christian-Jewish Studies*, 10:1, February 2015, 1-41. That journal is now called *Studies in Christian-Jewish Relations* (the peer reviewed electronic journal of the Council of Centers for Jewish-Christian Relations). https://ejournals.bc.edu/index.php/scjr/article/view/5904 - Accessed 1/14/2022. A discredited theory held that the talmudic Sage, Rav, composed *Aleinu*. For the reasons this approach has been discredited, see "The Image of the Other," 9, n.19.

[320] This last possibility is suggested by Michael D. Swartz, "*Alay le-shabbeaḥ*: A Liturgical Prayer in *Ma'aseh Merkabah*," *Jewish Quarterly Review*, 77, nos. 2-3 (October 1986-January 1987), 190. For additional theories of its origin—not mentioned here because they are not considered credible by this author—see Jeffrey Hoffman, "The Image of the Other in Jewish Interpretations of *Aleinu*."

[321] The passages are found in Peter Schäfer, *Synopse zur Hekhalot-Literatur* (Tubingen, 1981), paras. 544-596. See also Michael D. Swartz, "*Alay le-shabbeaḥ*, A Liturgical Prayer in *Ma'aseh Merkabah*," *Jewish Quarterly Review*, LXXVII, Nos. 2-3 (October, 1986-January 1987), 179-190.

[322] God's *tefillin* are mentioned in Babylonian Talmud *Berakhot* 7a and *Menaḥot* 35b.

second word in *Aleinu—leshabe'aḥ*—"to praise." While the text of this prayer is quite close to the versions of *Aleinu* found in contemporary liturgy, there are some variations—most strikingly, the first word in the *Hekhalot* text is in the singular, *Alai*, "it is upon me" as opposed to the usual plural, *Aleinu*, "it is upon us." In this mystical passage, the prayer fits because it purports to be the very prayer that Rabbi Akiva recited when he was safely granted a vision of God on the throne in the highest heavenly sanctuary. On the other hand, its style and content do not match its immediate surroundings in this mystical passage. It "reads" as if the text of the prayer may have been imported from elsewhere and merely interpolated into the narrative of Rabbi Akiva.

As mentioned, its initial appearance in the liturgy is in the service for Rosh HaShanah. There, it is first found in texts of the *Musaf Amidah* from the 10th century in the second prayer book in our history, *Siddur Rav Saadia Gaon*, and in fragments from the Cairo Genizah.[323] In that *Amidah*, *Aleinu* functions as the introduction to a section of the service known as *Malkhuyot*, or "(Biblical) Kingship Verses." It fits that role well because the root for "king," *mem-lamed-khaf*, occurs four times in *Aleinu*'s first paragraph and seven times in its second paragraph (more about the two paragraphs and the literary style of the prayer below). On the other hand, the prayer's style and content do not coalesce with the surrounding prayers in this section of the liturgy, especially the passages that introduce the other two sections of the *Amidah* for *Musaf* on Rosh HaShanah, namely, *Zikhronot*, "(Biblical) Remembrance Verses" and *Shoferot*, "(Biblical) Shofar Verses." Nevertheless, from the Rosh HaShanah liturgy, *Aleinu* migrated also to the *Musaf Amidah* of Yom Kippur, even though that *Amidah* lacks the *Malkhuyot*/Kingship section (and therefore, *Aleinu*'s place in the Yom Kippur service is actually out of context!). By the 13th century—about 300 years since its first documented appearance in the Rosh HaShanah liturgy—it began to appear in daily services in the Ashkenazic rite. Not long thereafter, it is found in daily services in all rites. How did *Aleinu* move from recitation in one service once a year on Rosh HaShanah to recitation three times a day, every day?

The evidence points to the part played by a historical event: The Blois Massacre. In 1171 in the town of Blois, France, the Jews were accused of having crucified a Christian child during Passover and throwing the body into the river. As a consequence, a massacre of the Jews of that town took place. The exact number of those killed is not known; some sources suggest thirty, some say all the Jews of the town, without mentioning a number. In order to understand how the Blois Massacre played an important role in the

[323] *Siddur Rav Saadia Gaon*, eds., Davidson, Assaf, Joel, 221.

proliferation of the times that our prayer was recited, we need to first identify the key themes of the prayer.

Most Jewish worshipers, as a matter of course, assume the benign nature of the liturgy as a whole, since it is not often that contemporary rabbis, cantors, and Jewish educators point out negative or objectionable elements of the liturgy—or of Jewish religion in general. After all, one of the main roles that Jewish religious leaders play is to interpret Jewish tradition in as positive and relevant a way as possible in order to attract and maintain practitioners of Jewish religion. However, no religion—including Judaism—originated in all its details, from all eras, by God in a state of absolute perfection. And not even the most traditional Jew has ever claimed that the prayer texts of the liturgy are perfect because they were written by God. It is universally accepted that human beings wrote the liturgy.[324] Therefore, the liturgy is fallible and may, occasionally, include less than perfect ideas. That, in my view, is the case with *Aleinu*. To facilitate identifying the main message of this prayer, I will translate it in as accurate a way as I can. And I would ask those readers who recite *Aleinu* frequently to try and read this prayer as if it is new, and with an open mind:

> It is our duty to praise the master of all,
> to ascribe greatness to the former of creation,
> that he did not make us like the nations of the lands
> and did not place us like the families of the earth.
> That he did not make our lot like theirs,
> nor our fate like all their multitudes.
> (The oft-censored sentence:) For they bow to vanity and emptiness,
> and pray to a god who does not save.
> But we bow and prostrate and thank the king of kings,
> the holy one blessed is he.
> For he stretches out the heavens and establishes the earth.
> His seat of glory is in the heavens above,
> and his powerful presence is in the highest heights.

[324] The one near-exception to this is the short-lived German ascetic-pietistic movement known as Ḥasidei Ashkenaz (12th-13th century). While they did not attribute authorship of the liturgy to God, they did assume that the Sages who authored the prayers were heavenly-inspired and infallible. For this reason, they would apply to the liturgy some of the interpretative techniques used in Torah interpretation, such as *Gematria*—counting the number of letters or words in a phrase or paragraph—in order to "reveal" secret, encoded, meanings. They would also therefore decry any change, even of one letter, to the texts of the liturgy that their particular community inherited and considered authentic.

He is our God, there is no other.
He is our true king, there is no other.
As it says in his Torah:
"Know therefore this day and keep in mind that the Lord alone is God in heaven above and on earth below; there is no other." (Deuteronomy 4:39)
Therefore, we hope in you, Lord, our God,
to soon see your powerful splendor.
(And to see you) remove detestable things[325] from the earth,
cut down idols, and perfect the world in the kingdom of the Almighty.
All flesh would (then) call on your name,
all the wicked of the earth would turn to you.
All that dwell in the world would acknowledge and know
that to you every knee bends and every tongue swears.
Before you, Lord our God, they will bow and fall (upon their knees),
and they would ascribe honor to your glorious name.
All would accept the yoke of your kingship.
May you reign over them soon and forever.
For the kingdom is yours, may you reign forever in glory,
as it says in your Torah:
"The Lord will reign forever and ever." (Exodus 15:18)
And it is said:
"And the Lord shall be king over all the earth; in that day
there shall be one Lord with one name." (Zechariah 14:9)

The prayer is divided into two paragraphs. The style of the first paragraph is that of praise recited to God in the third person: "It is our duty to praise the Lord of all..." The second paragraph forms a request or petition directed to God in the second person: "Therefore, we hope in *you*, Lord our God..." The word "all" (*kol*) serves as a kind of *leitmotif* in the prayer, occurring some nine times. In the first paragraph we, Israel, declare our gratitude that we worship the God of "all;" "all" others worship nothingness. In the second paragraph, we ask that God cause "all" others to accept our God as the one God of "all." The two paragraphs form a complete message: We praise God because God chose us as the only ones who worship the true God and we

[325] *Gilulim*, a derogatory word for idols. See Deuteronomy 29:16.

hope and request that "all flesh," "all the wicked of the earth," will join with us and accept the one true God. It is a message that is likely difficult for contemporary Jews to accept since it equates all non-Jews as "the wicked of the earth" because they do not worship the true God, which the Jews do.

The prayer also contains one sentence—without doubt part of the original text of the prayer—that was subject to widespread censorship (including self-censorship) from the Middle Ages through modern times: "For they bow to vanity and emptiness and pray to a god who does not save."[326] Even without this line, however, the message of the prayer as a whole remains a triumphalist one that accords with a narrow, but prevalent, component of Jewish tradition: God chose Israel whose worship remains the only valid worship of God, and we hope that God will soon cause all others in the world to join us. Furthermore, the several mentions of "idols" in the prayer's text ought not to be taken as referring only to what we today would consider polytheistic religions. Ancient and medieval Jewish writing often viewed Christianity as fully or partially polytheistic because, among other things, of its understanding of God as a trinity and its usage of statues and icons representing God. And notwithstanding Islam's strictly monotheistic approach, several medieval Jewish commentators applied *Aleinu*'s condemnation of non-Jewish worship to Islam as well.[327] We will deal with the way in which modern movements of Judaism have dealt with this message and this prayer below. For now, however, it is important to keep *Aleinu*'s central message in mind in order to trace its path from a prayer recited only on Rosh HaShanah and Yom Kippur to a prayer recited every day, three or more times a day. That central meaning is that only the Jewish People worships God in the proper way (= the first paragraph) and that along with the hope that God will both sweep away the improper worship from the world, all peoples will join the Jewish People in the correct worship of God (= the second paragraph).

I can now connect the literary themes of *Aleinu* with the Blois massacre. Jewish Chronicles that were written several decades after the 12th-century massacre at Blois report that as the Jews were burned at the stake, they chanted the prayer *Aleinu*. The literature of the medieval Chronicles is best understood as subjective reports of events. The notion of writing history in as objective way as possible is a modern ideal that does not apply in the Middle Ages. There is some reason to doubt whether *Aleinu* was actually chanted since some of the Chronicles claim that Christian onlookers at Blois were

[326] The wording of this sentence is based upon Isaiah 30:7 and 45:20.

[327] See Jeffrey Hoffman, "The Image of the Other in Jewish Interpretations of *Aleinu*," 17-19, and especially n. 39.

impressed and commented on the Jews' spiritual strength reflected in their chanting the prayer as they were burned alive. Scholars have questioned whether it is reasonable for the Jewish authors of the Chronicles to have had knowledge of Christian reaction in real time since the Chronicles were written after the fact. Nevertheless, as these reports circulated in the Jewish communities of Ashkenaz, more and more locales began to integrate *Aleinu* into their daily services. The reason the Chronicles included the observation that the Jews at Blois chanted *Aleinu* and that Christian onlookers were impressed by it seems to be that *Aleinu* forms a strident statement of pride in the Jewish religion's correct understanding and worship of the true God and a condemnation of the nations' false theology and rituals. In other words, the claim of the Chronicles is that this prayer was recited at Blois as a way of expressing defiance and the faith that while the Christian attackers had won a temporary, physical battle, they had already lost the eternal battle for spiritual truth.

Jewish communities of the region appear to have taken the Chronicles quite seriously and literally. Whether *Aleinu* was actually chanted at Blois is immaterial. Its reported role, on the other hand, is crucial. It is likely that Jewish communities in the region, following the report about Blois, began to chant *Aleinu* on a daily basis in support of their faith that the martyrs of Blois went to their deaths singing of the superiority of Judaism over Christianity. The very fact that the Jews showed themselves willing to die for their faith indicated to medieval Jews the truth of Judaism, and the testimony of their chanting *Aleinu*—whose theme echoed this view—only emphasized the ultimate vindication of the martyrs and their religion.

The movement of *Aleinu* from the High Holidays to daily worship represents vicarious vengeance for the antisemitic attack at Blois.[328] The fact that *Aleinu* is not found in the daily services in Sephardic sources (e.g., Maimonides, Abudraham), until much later supports the impression that its movement to daily use began in Ashkenazic circles soon after Blois and proliferated in French-German locales within a couple of centuries.

The negative image of non-Jews in *Aleinu* resonated with Jewish communities through the Middle Ages and early Modern Periods. Religion was considered part and parcel of the essential identity of ethnic groups and

[328] For another example of this same phenomenon, in the same region, less than a century earlier, See Jeffrey Hoffman, "*Akdamut*: History, Folklore, and Meaning," *Jewish Quarterly Review*, 99:2, Spring 2009,161-183, especially 171f. In the case of *Akdamut*, it is doubtful, and ultimately irrelevant, whether the author meant his poem as a protest against Crusader violence. The poem, as a result of the Yiddish folktale that extolled the poet as an avenging hero, became a paean of Jewish triumph and a source of relief in the centuries following the Crusades.

competition—including commercial and military competition—and conflicts played out in religious teachings and prayers of Jews, Christians, and Muslims. So, for example, Rabbi Yosef Caro (16th century, Israel), one of the most important sages of the Middle Ages, wrote this about the inclusion of *Aleinu* in the Rosh HaShanah liturgy:

> *Aleinu LeShabbei'aḥ* was instituted only because we are (about to) recite the Kingship verses. (Therefore), we first praise God, may he be blessed, (through the words of *Aleinu*) for having separated us from the misguided ones (*ha'to'im*).[329]

For this source, the meaning of chanting *Aleinu* on Rosh HaShanah is to affirm the loyalty of the Jewish People to its king, the one true God, by invoking the misguided path of the non-Jewish Other, who is not loyal to the true king of the universe. There are numerous other pre-modern commentaries on this prayer that sound similar themes. There is even a version of the prayer itself with additional wording disparaging both Jesus and those who bow down to him.[330]

*Aleinu*'s central message of the distinction between the "correct" way of the Jewish religion versus the "misguided" way of other religions does not accord with the orientation of many modern Jews. For this reason, contemporary movements have dealt with the prayer in various ways. All of them, including the Orthodox Movement, have taken steps, in their editions of the siddur, to soften the adverse representation of non-Jews in *Aleinu*. These steps range from preserving the full Hebrew text (with or without the censored sentence) and translating it reliably but adding a moderating commentary, to preserving the Hebrew text but blunting the true meaning of the words in the translation, to altering the Hebrew text and offering a translation of the modified Hebrew text.

While most of the pre-modern commentaries accepted the unsympathetic view of other religions, there were some in earlier ages that also tried to modify the harshness of the message. An interpretation that dates from the 13th century, from soon after *Aleinu* entered the daily liturgy, proved to be a model for the way some contemporary *siddurim* have presented this prayer. That interpretation reads as follows:

---

329 *Bet Yosef* on *Arba'ah Turim, Oraḥ Ḥayyim* 591, s.v., *V'omer Aleinu leshabei'aḥ*.
330 See Jeffrey Hoffman, The Image of the Other in Jewish Interpretations of *Aleinu*," 14-16.

> Joshua Bin Nun instituted it (*Aleinu*) when he besieged Jericho and conquered it. He saw there the people's idols that were emptiness and products of their delusions, and he (therefore) began to recite, "It is our duty to praise the Lord of all, to ascribe greatness to the former of creation" (i.e., the beginning of *Aleinu*).[331]

Ascribing the authorship of the prayer to the biblical personage Joshua is certainly an ahistorical assertion. There is no support anywhere in the Bible for such an idea and no liturgical works from the biblical period—outside of those already included in the Bible itself—have reached us. Nevertheless, the connection to Joshua may have been drawn because in medieval Jewish folklore, Joshua the biblical warrior was viewed as an anti-Jesus figure[332] and the Talmud had already—also ahistorically—ascribed part of another prayer to Joshua: the second blessing of *Birkat HaMazon* (The Blessing After Meals).[333] Placing the prayer's origins long before the advent of Christianity was a way of denying that the prayer was anti-Christian, since Christianity didn't exist in Joshua's time. Put another way, attributing the authorship of *Aleinu* to Joshua is asserting that the prayer was aimed at the idolatrous religions of ancient Canaan.[334] Similar assertions, that *Aleinu* derived from a period before the advent of Christianity, were made in contemporary times by a scholar of Conservative liturgy and a scholar of Reform liturgy in their attempt to deny that *Aleinu* was directed against any other monotheistic religion.[335] As I observed at the beginning of this commentary on *Aleinu*, the earliest version of this prayer in the liturgy dates from the 10th century but it also appeared in the ancient mystical *Hekhalot* literature. Scholars are divided as to the exact period of the *Hekhalot* literature, but nearly all agree that it post-dates the origin of Christianity by several centuries.[336] It seems to

---

[331] *The Siddur of R. Solomon ben Samson of Worms*, ed. Moshe Hershler (Jerusalem: Ḥemed, 1971), 124.
[332] See Yisrael Rosenson, *Aleinu LeShabei'aḥ*—The Legends About the Ancient Author" [Hebrew], *Meḥkerei Ḥag* 12 (2001), 74-86.
[333] Babylonian Talmud *Berakhot* 48b. The connection was likely made to Joshua because Joshua was the conqueror of the Land of Israel in the Bible, and this blessing thanks God for the gift of the Land of Israel.
[334] Ascribing the prayer to such an important biblical figure also may have been meant to support the relatively new practice of chanting it on a daily basis. See Ruth Langer, "The Censorship of *Aleinu*," in *The Experience of Jewish Liturgy: Studies Dedicated to Menahem Schmelzer*, ed. Debra Reed Blank (Leiden: Brill, 2011), 149, n. 8.
[335] Reuven Hammer, *Entering Jewish Prayer: A Guide to Personal Devotion and the Worship Service* (New York: Schocken Books, 1994), 207-208, and Jakob J. Petuchowski, *Prayerbook Reform in Europe: The Liturgy of European Liberal and Reform Judaism* (New York: The World Union for Progressive Judaism, 1968), 299-300.
[336] See Jeffrey Hoffman, The Image of the Other in Jewish Interpretations of *Aleinu*," 10, n. 21.

me that these modern scholars who dated *Aleinu* to pre-Christian times have allowed their discomfort with the fact that *Aleinu* disparages all religions other than Judaism to affect their better historical judgment.

It is always interesting to consult the translation and commentary (if there is one) for *Aleinu* in any given prayer book to gauge how that particular siddur dealt with the troubling wording of this prayer. As I suggested above, all modern prayer books try, in one way or another, to mollify the negative image of non-Jews in *Aleinu* and to modify its central meaning as pride in the Jewish tradition without the hope that people of other religions will abandon their faiths and accept Judaism.

Perhaps the most interesting approach—certainly the most radical—was suggested by Rabbi Zalman Schachter-Shalomi, one of the founders of Renewal Judaism.

Jewish Renewal is a small, liberal approach within contemporary Judaism whose origins are related to the formation of *ḥavurot*, small Jewish worship and study fellowships, in the late 1960s in the United States. Schachter-Shalomi was born in Poland, raised in Vienna, and ultimately, fleeing Nazi Europe, arrived in the United States in the early 1940s. Although ordained as an Orthodox rabbi by the Chabad-Lubavitch Movement of Ḥasidism, he went through a series of life-changing transformations that led him to help found this decidedly non-Orthodox approach. Jewish Renewal maintains a loose connection to Jewish law and combines Jewish mysticism and ritual with spiritual teachings and modes from other traditions including Buddhist meditation and Hindu chant. Schachter-Shalomi's approach to *Aleinu* crystallized during the summer of 1974 at Naropa University in Boulder, Colorado, where he was on the faculty along with the poet Allen Ginsberg. Schachter-Shalomi's father died that summer, and he gathered a group of Jewish-Buddhists—including Ginsberg—to form a *minyan*, that is, a quorum, so that he could hold a worship service in his father's memory.

> I said the kaddish and then we said *aleinu*… In the middle of *aleinu* it was like lightning hit me. There's a line that goes, "For they bow down to emptiness and void and we bow down to the king of kings, the holy one blessed be he." Now usually it means, they bow down to *gornisht mit gornisht* (Yiddish: nothing with nothing), emptiness, void, stupid… But *there*, I read it: They bow down to Emptiness… and Void… and we bow down to the King of kings… and both of these are legitimate ways. You can imagine how that hit me.

> That's a story I tell people who are involved in Buddhism. If you do meditation and you see deep in meditation what this is all about, you see that emptiness and void is just one look and king of kings is the other look.[337]

Schachter-Shalomi eventually embodied his insight into a new translation of *Aleinu*, a translation that completely transformed the negative image of the Others into the admiring and accepting approach that he first experienced at Naropa. That translation has influenced many Renewal worship groups. Jewish Renewal is the only non-Orthodox American group I know of that retained a version—albeit a completely transformed version—of the often-censored line, reading now, "Some of us like to worship You as emptiness and void; Some of us want to worship You as King of Kings." For Schachter-Shalomi, "emptiness and void" is a positive way of referring to God. Here, he is channeling the Kabbalistic identification of God as the great *Ayin*, "Nothingness." Not that God is "nothing" of course, but rather that since God's essence is ultimately unknowable and defies any real description, the best way to capture the sense that God is both absolutely real and absolutely ineffable is to call God *Ayin*, "Nothingness." (This Kabbalistic notion, in turn, is influenced by Rambam's earlier suggestion of "negative theology," that is, that while we can identify many things that God is not, God's utter intangibility means that there is nothing positive we can say to define God).

Schachter-Shalomi made another noteworthy revision to the passage in the prayer that reads: *shelo asanu kegoyei ha'aratsot*, "That he did not make us like the nations of the lands." First, he changed the spelling of *shelo* from שלא to שלו, thus emending the first half of the line from "That he did not make" to "That he made us his," while preserving the same pronunciation. In the second half of the line, he substituted the word *im* ("with") for the prefix *ke-* ("like") in the word *kegoyei*, thus changing the meaning from "like the nations of the lands" to "with the nations of the lands." This he then translated, not as "That he did not make us like the nations of the lands," but as "You made us one with all of Life." Thus, the entire Hebrew sentence was transformed from "That he did not make us like the nations of the lands" to "That he made us his; You made us one with all of Life."

[337] Cited in Rodger Kamenetz, *The Jew in the Lotus: A Poet's Rediscovery of Jewish Identity in Buddhist India* (San Francisco: HarperSanFrancisco, 1994), 238.

**Spiritual Commentary on *Aleinu***

I am aware that I have presented a very challenging and deprecating interpretation of *Aleinu* in the Analytical Commentary, above. I do so out of a sense of honesty and scholarly integrity. I am especially attuned to negative portrayals of the Other in Jewish tradition, such as we see here in *Aleinu*, exactly because we Jews ourselves have so often been the victims of prejudice, persecution, and worse simply because we were considered Other to majority cultures. We, who have suffered as a result of such bias and chauvinism, ought to be especially sensitive to instances in which we—even unintentionally—disparage others. We cannot, in good conscience, ask other religions to acknowledge and revise negative images of Jews that appear in their liturgy—as we did in conversations surrounding The Second Vatican Council (known colloquially as "Vatican II") in the 1960s—and pay no attention to *Aleinu* as an example of what I call "anti-goyism." I take some inspiration from others who love their people and culture, and precisely because of that love, critique their culture when necessary. One exemplar of such a person is Ashley M. Jones, a Black American who is the Poet Laureate of the State of Alabama. She often is unflinching in her criticism of inequalities in American life:

> "The biggest thing that I learned moving away is that love is a complete word," she said. "It's not just, 'I like this thing, it's always good to me.' Love means also understanding what's wrong and committing to pointing that out and trying to change those things that are wrong. And that's how I feel about the South." Her love of family and of Alabama and its people is what makes it possible for Ms. Jones to praise it and criticize it, and why she is able to, in the same beat, say that Alabama is beautiful and in desperate need of repair.[338]

For some of us, it would be difficult, if not impossible, to recite the traditional text of *Aleinu* if fully intending what the words say because we don't actually believe that our way of serving God is superior to others'. And therefore, some of us may recite the traditional wording, and express pride in our Jewish tradition, but ignore or reject the language that disparages others' traditions. For some of us, the revised Hebrew and/or English versions offered

[338] *The New York Times*, Sunday, November 24, 2021: "Alabama's Next Poet Laureate Writes Searingly About Race." https://www.nytimes.com/2021/10/21/us/ashley-jones-poet-laureate-alabama.html?-searchResultPosition=1 Accessed March 3, 2022.

by some contemporary *siddurim* may offer a more honestly inspirational experience.

I will share one interpretation of the traditional text of *Aleinu* that, while it ignores the central anti-Other message, presents a refreshing take on this challenging prayer. It derives from Rabbi Avraham Mordecai of Ger (Poland, 20th century), the son of Rabbi Yehudah Aryeh Leib Alter, the author of the popular commentary, *Sefat Emet* ("The Language of Truth").[339] Rabbi Avraham Mordecai noticed that each of the two paragraphs of *Aleinu* begins with the letter *ayin* and concludes with the letter *dalet*. Putting this together, both paragraphs spell out the Hebrew word *eid*, which means "witness." He asks the worshiper to imagine that the two appearances of the word *eid*, "witness," represent the two witnesses who are traditionally needed to offer testimony in Jewish jurisprudence. The worshiper is to further imagine at the end of each service—for *Aleinu* comes toward the end of every service—that these two paragraphs of *Aleinu* will function as "witnesses," and will offer testimony as to the sincerity of the prayers we've just recited. In this way, *Aleinu* serves a kind of challenge to us at the end of each worship service, reminding us that the ultimate worth of any given set of prayers is the extent to which we have been sincere in reciting the words of that service.

### Adon Olam

*Adon Olam*, "Eternal Lord," concludes the weekday morning service. Its earliest recorded place in the liturgy in the 15th century, however, is at the very beginning of the morning service, where it "appears in manuscripts shortly before the invention of printing, and then passes with the printed books into all the rites, usually opening the weekday morning service."[340] Many prayer books include *Adon Olam* at both the very beginning and the end of the morning service. Its author is not known; its attribution to the 11th-century poet-philosopher, Solomon Ibn Gabirol, first suggested by the 19th-century scholar Leopold Zunz, amounts to no more than an educated guess. It has proven to be a very popular prayer, appearing not only at the beginning and at the end of the weekday morning service, but also at the same places in the liturgy for Sabbaths and festivals, as well as part of the Moroccan wedding ceremony, the bedtime *Shema* liturgy, and by those present at a deathbed. The last two of these locations are likely due to the poem's penultimate line:

[339] The interpretation is cited in Arthur Green, *The Heart of the Matter: Studies in Jewish Mysticism and Theology* (Philadephia: The Jewish Publication Society, 2015), 333-334. Published originally in Green's essay, "Abraham Joshua Heschel: Recasting Ḥasidism for Moderns," *Modern Judaism* 29, no. 1 (2009), 62-79.

[340] Elbogen, *Jewish Liturgy*, 77.

> Into (God's) hand I commit my spirit
> When I go to sleep and when I awake.

The first six of its ten lines[341] comprise a philosophical statement: There is only one God, and that God is eternal. God had no beginning, and will have no end; God existed before creation and will continue to exist after creation's end. Because God's timelessness is such a major motif, its first two words, *Adon Olam*, ought to be translated as "Eternal Lord," and not "Lord of the Universe" as some *siddurim* have it. The word *olam* can carry a geographical valence, "world, universe," or a temporal valence, "eternal, forever." The context here supports the temporal meaning.

The *piyyut*'s last four lines complement the theme of God's eternality with a personal statement: The eternal God is my God. The first strophe of each of these four lines each contains the suffix *i*, "my" (twice in three of the strophes), emphasizing the relationship to "my" God.

Therefore, the meaning of the prayer as a whole is: The one God who exists beyond time is also my personal God.[342]

**Spiritual Commentary on *Adon Olam***

*Adon Olam* poses a worthy challenge for prayer in general: The challenge of personalizing whatever theological statement is made in the words. A prayer is not fully explicated by summarizing its historical and literary context, because a prayer is not simply read as an intellectual pursuit; it is prayed, which is a spiritual pursuit. So, too, the act of worship does not occur when we simply recite the words of a prayer text; a personal connection must be made for worship to occur. As one of the first and one of the last prayers in the morning service, this challenge of *Adon Olam* ought to remain with worshipers throughout that, and every, service.

---

[341] Sephardic versions of *Adon Olam* contain extra verses which seem to be later additions.

[342] For additional sources and analysis see Reuven Kimelman, "The Poetics and Theology of Adon Olam," in Nuria Calduch-Benages, Michael W. Duggan and Dalia Marx, eds., *On Wings of Prayer Sources of Jewish Worship: Essays in Honor of Professor Stefan C. Reif on the Occasion of His Seventy-Fifth Birthday* (Berlin: de Gruyter, 2019), 187-202.

# Part Three:

# Shabbat Services

## Kabbalat Shabbat

The parts of *Kabbalat Shabbat* that were innovated by the Kabbalists of Safed in the 16th century consist of six psalms, Psalms 95-99 and 29, as well as the prayers *Ana VeKhoʹaḥ* and *Lekhah Dodi.* These psalms and prayers were added to the already existing Psalms 92-93. But the *Kabbalat Shabbat* service did not necessarily emerge fully formed. In fact, there is a fascinating description, in the name of the Ari, of what might be called a "proto" *Kabbalat Shabbat* service. The *de facto* scribe of the Ari, Rabbi Ḥayyim Vital, in his *Sha'ar HaKavannot*, "The Gate of Intentions," recorded the following description:

> This is the order of (self) elevation, an abridged order of *Kabbalat Shabbat*:
>
> You should go out to the field and say *Bo'u veneitzei likrat Shabbat malketa, leḥakal tapuḥin kaddishin* ("come let us go to welcome the Shabbat Queen, to the holy apple orchard" in Hebrew and Aramaic)...
>
> Assume a standing position in one spot in the field, and if on a high hill, so much the better. That place should be clean in front and back of you, to the extent that you can see, for four *amot* (four "cubits," about two yards). Face west where the sun is setting. At the exact moment of the setting of the sun, close your eyes and put your left hand on your chest and your right hand upon your left hand. Concentrate in fear and trembling as one who stands before a king in order to receive the additional holiness of Shabbat.
>
> Begin by saying the psalm of *Havu L'Adonai benei elim* ("Render to God, you sons of the powerful," i.e., Psalm 29) in its entirety with a melody.
>
> Afterward, say three times *Bo'i kallah, bo'i, kallah, bo'i kallah, Shabbat Malketa* ("Come, oh bride; come, oh bride; come, oh bride, Shabbat Queen;" the last word is in Aramaic).
>
> After that, say Psalms 92 and 93 and then open your eyes and return home.[343]

[343] Ḥayyim Vital, *Sha'ar HaKavvanot* (Rabbi Tzvi Mikhel Widovsky, Israel: 1986), Vol. 2, 48-49. Many of the sources adduced here were first gathered in Reuven Kimelman, *The Mystical Meaning of Lekhah Dodi and Kabbalat Shabbat* [Hebrew] (Los Angeles: Cherub, 2003), chapter 1, 1-32.

This passage contains much Kabbalistic imagery. The field represents *Shekhinah*, a feminine *sefirah*. The field as symbolizing the feminine aspect of divinity parallels many cultures calling the ground "Mother Earth" or the equivalent of that phrase in different languages. A key aim of the Kabbalistic system is to unify the masculine divine aspect with the feminine divine aspect, and so the male worshiper here (rabbinic authors in the 16th century would only have had male worshipers in mind) placing himself in a field means he is consciously connecting with *Shekhinah*. For the Kabbalah, a mortal man connecting with the divine feminine, using the proper awareness can effectively induce the divine masculine (the *sefirah* of *Tiferet*) to link with the divine feminine. The recitation of "come let us go to welcome the Shabbat Queen" makes this plain since one of the ways *Shekhinah* is imaged is as Shabbat. Even clearer is Vital's identifying the field "the holy apple orchard," because that expression, too, constitutes yet another quite potent epithet for *Shekhinah*. The idea is that if pious male Jews in the material sphere practice the proper symbolic rituals, with the appropriate consciousness, they gain access to the divine feminine, with the hope that that will induce a parallel unification between the divine male and the divine female in the spiritual sphere.

Similarly, placing one's right hand over one's left hand—both over one's chest—is also a sympathetic ritual: It is meant to stimulate the divine "right hand," the *sefirah* of *Ḥesed* (= love, compassion) to "cover up," or override, the divine "left hand," the *sefirah* of *Gevurah* (= strict judgment, anger).

Doing all of this "at the exact moment of the setting of the sun" means that one is attempting to unify divine masculine and feminine, arousing love between them, as well as mercy upon the worshiper, all at the very moment most propitious for unification—at the arrival of Shabbat. We will see that the attempt to unify the divine masculine and feminine forms as the main theme of *Lekhah Dodi*, the *piyyut* that ultimately became a centerpiece of *Kabbalat Shabbat*. In the Spiritual Commentary on *Lekhah Dodi*, I will address how a modern worshiper might incorporate the attempt to unify the divine masculine and feminine. Here in this introduction, I will present some very early interpretations of the service of *Kabbalat Shabbat*.

Over time, the rudimentary service reflected in the teaching above was elongated to include six psalms. There are three mini-services in Jewish liturgy that, in their elemental forms, consist of six psalms each: *Kabbalat Shabbat*, *Hallel* (Psalms 113-118), and the daily *Pesukei Dezimra* (Psalms 145-150). *Hallel*, recited on the Three Pilgrimage Festivals plus *Ḥanukkah* and *Rosh Ḥodesh*, is the oldest of these, and is mentioned as a unit already in Tannaitic sources.[344] It may well be that the fact that *Hallel* contains six psalms influenced the framers of the other two mini-services to choose the six-psalm structure—*Pesukei DeZimra* sometime in the Geonic period, probably in Babylonia, and *Kabbalat Shabbat* in 16th-century Safed, in the Galilee.

Modern prayer books often say that these psalms were chosen because they celebrate God as the Creator of Nature. While images of nature do figure in these psalms, the Kabbalists left no indication that that is why they chose these particular six psalms. Rather, the Kabbalists of that era left two kinds of commentary regarding the choice of these psalms. The first refers to the letters and words in these psalms using *Gematria*—mystical math—while the second points to the preponderance of the theme of God's kingship, interpreted in the specific way of the Kabbalah.

There are various editions of a book called *Tikkunei Shabbat*, "Arrangements (of prayers) for Shabbat." These are collections of the Shabbat customs of the most influential Kabbalist in 16th-century Safed, Rabbi Isaac Luria, known as the Ari, "The Lion," from the acronym of the Hebrew words for "The Ashkenazi Rabbi Isaac"). The customs listed in the various editions are not always consistent with one another. Above, I cited a custom attributed to the Ari in which worshipers go outside and recite three psalms to welcome Shabbat. In a 1648 version of *Tikkunei Shabbat*, the custom of reciting six psalms is attributed to the Ari and the following interpretations of reciting those psalms are offered:

> First of all, we begin by saying these six psalms. Each psalm corresponds to a day of the week. One should have the intention (to connect) each psalm to each day and (thereby) to cut away and disperse the shells (*kelipot*) that ruled and intensified on each day through the secret of "the words of our lips" (cf. Hosea 14:3)...

Here, the Ari teaches that an inner meaning for reciting these six psalms that is that the very act of our lips reciting the words of these psalms can—with the correct intention—"disperse the shells that ruled and intensified on each day..." The recitation of each psalm can counteract the power of the demonic and evil shells that accrued to each day of the week.

*Tikkunei Shabbat* goes on to explain the power of these specific six psalms:

[344] See, for example, *Mishnah Pesaḥim* 5:5, 7; 10: 6,7; *Tosefta Sukkah* 3:2.

> Behold, the sum of the first letters of (all) six psalms add up to the sum of [the word] *nefesh*, "souls"... In these six psalms you will find 65 verses corresponding to the sum [of the letters of] *Adonai* (a name of God)... [Through] these 65 verses [said] in truth and wholeness... all of the shells of the Other Side will be cut off. No strength or authority will be left for them to become a mask and a divider to the brilliant, abundant, splendor [of the] additional soul (*neshamah yeterah*) which emerged from the sanctuary of the king of the world to every one of Israel, each according to his own source and light...[345]

In this passage, the Ari teaches that the sum of the numerical equivalent of the first letters of all six psalms adds up to the same number (430) as the numerical equivalent of the word *nefesh*, or "soul."[346] Further, the total number of verses[347] in the six psalms, 65, corresponds to the numerical equivalent of the name of God, *Adonai*.[348] The idea is that when one recites these verses concentrating on the fact that the first letter of each psalm adds up to *nefesh*, "soul," the additional soul given to us on Shabbat according to Jewish tradition is strengthened. Our inner spiritual essence is strengthened. And when one concentrates on the fact that there are a total of 65 verses in all of the psalms combined, one is actually reciting, and connecting to, one very long name of God.

Another commentary from the foundational period of *Kabbalat Shabbat*—the 16th century—views the content of the psalms as central, as opposed to the external structure of the psalms reflected in the mystical math. R. Moshe ben Maimon Elbaz, in his *Heikhal HaKodesh* ("The Holy Sanctuary"), says the following:

> There are those who have the custom to chant *Lekhu Neranenah* ("Come let us sing," the first verse of Ps. 95)—Psalms 95 and 96 and 97 and 98 and recite *Mizmor havu l'Adonai benei elim* ("Render glory to God, you sons of the powerful," i.e., Psalm 29) because all these psalms refer to accept-

345 *Tikkunei Shabbat*, Venice, 1648, 54, 58-59.

346 Ps. 95—*Lamed* = 30; Ps. 96—*Shin* = 300; Ps. 97—*Yod* = 10; Ps. 98—*Mem* = 40; Ps. 99—*Yod* = 10; Ps. 29—*Mem* = 40. Total: 430.

*Nefesh*: *Nun* = 50; *Peh* = 80; *Shin* = 300. Total: 430

347 Ps. 95 = 11; Ps. 96 = 13; Ps. 97 = 12; Ps. 98 = 9; Ps. 99 = 9; Ps. 29 = 11; Total: 65

348 *Aleph* = 1; *Dalet* = 4; *Nun* = 50; *Yod* = 10; Total: 65

> ing Shabbat and the kingdom of heaven—which manifests on Friday night throughout the world. All the shells are concealed and suppressed and are fearful and tremble and quake before Her. So, it is clear in Psalm 98[349]—"The Lord reigns, the peoples tremble." For in all of these psalms, we aid the side of holiness to cause the *Shekhinah* to reign over the whole world.[350]

Although Elbaz only directly mentions five psalms, and not six, he most likely was referring to a custom of six psalms. The sixth is Psalm 99, which he actually quotes, but the text ascribes the citation to Psalm 98. Whether this was the error of a copyist or of the author is not clear.

Elbaz identifies "the kingdom of heaven" as a dominant image in the psalms of *Kabbalat Shabbat*, citing an example from the first verse of Psalm 99, "The Lord reigns..." In fact, the root *malakh* ("reign, king, kingdom") referring to God as king occurs at least once in each of the psalms of *Kabbalat Shabbat*.[351]

Not only did Elbaz correctly pinpoint a running theme in these psalms, but he also astutely noticed that many of the references to God as king in these psalms explicitly present God in opposition to the non-Israelite nations (or their gods). There are at least five examples of this juxtaposition within the six psalms:

> Ps. 95:3—"For the Lord is a great God,
> the great king over all gods."
> Ps. 96:10—"Declare among the nations,
> 'The Lord is king!' the world stands firm;
> it cannot be shaken;
> He judges the peoples with equity."
> Ps. 97:1—"The Lord is king!
> Let the earth exult,
> the many islands rejoice!"
> Ps. 98:6—"With trumpets and the blast of the horn
> raise a shout before the Lord, the King."

349 The text here should read "Psalm 99," referring to Ps. 99:1.

350 Moshe ben Maimon Elbaz, *Heikhal HaKodesh*, chapter 50, 166. First published sometime between 1575 and 1599.

351 Ps. 95:3; Ps. 96:10; Ps. 97:1; Ps. 98:6; Ps. 99:1, 4; Ps. 29:10.

The subject of that sentence, those who are called upon to "raise a shout" with trumpet and horns, is not entirely clear but slightly earlier, the psalm celebrates God's saving power "in the sight of the nations" (v. 2); "all the ends of the earth beheld the victory of our God" (v. 3).

Ps. 99:1 is the verse that Elbaz singled out: "The Lord reigns, the peoples tremble." Verse 2 specifically says that the Lord is not only "great in Zion" (= Jerusalem), but also that he is "exalted above all peoples."

In noticing the theme of God's kingship, Elbaz is, indeed, identifying an important image in these psalms. In Kabbalah, God's kingship is a major feature among the many aspects attributed to the tenth, and most approachable, of the *Sefirot*. In fact, one of its two most common names is *Malkhut*, "Kingship" (another is *Shekhinah*, "Presence"). And among the many symbols associated with *Malkhut* is *Shabbat*. Therefore, Elbaz's claim is that when these particular psalms celebrate God's kingship, they are, at the same time, also invoking Shabbat. Of course, it is an historical anachronism for the Psalms, or any of the passages of the Bible, to relate to the ideational system of *Kabbalah*. That symbolic system developed almost 2,000 years later, in the Middle Ages. Nevertheless, it is a typical move by the Kabbalists to read their new and innovative system back into the literary and theological creations of previous generations.

It is not God's kingship alone that Elbaz is referring to, but the battle, and ultimate victory—at least on Shabbat—of God's kingship, the "side of holiness"—against "the shells." Elbaz expressly connects the shells, tokens of the demonic dimension of life, with "the peoples," i.e., the non-Israelite peoples.

While the Kabbalistic system contains many spiritual treasures, it must be admitted that, as a medieval work, it also contains some ideas that are offensive to moderns. Among those are the general way non-Jews and women are portrayed (although, while Kabbalistic literature devalued human females, it did, ironically, vaunt the divine feminine). The masterpiece of Kabbalah is the 13th-century work known as The Zohar.[352] For the Zohar, the source of the souls of non-Jews is "the other side," (*sitra aḥra*), i.e., the demonic realm, and non-Jews are commonly considered sub-human. A typical passage is:

> [O]n the other side, side of impurity: the spirit spreading through the other nations emerges from the side of impu-

[352] For general background, see Gershom G. Scholem, *Major Trends in Jewish Mysticism* (Jerusalem: Schocken Publishing House, 1941), 156-243; Isaiah Tishby, *The Wisdom of the Zohar*, tr. By David Goldstein (Oxford: Oxford University Press, 1989), 3 vols.; Arthur Green, *A Guide to the Zohar* (Stanford, California: Stanford University Press, 2004).

> rity. It is not human (*Adam*), and so does not attain this name. The name of that spirit is Impure, not attaining the name human, having no share in it."[353]

While some have attempted to explain Kabbalistic negativity toward other religions as responses to antisemitism, the fact is that demonizing the members of other faith communities is, unfortunately, a typical feature of pre-modern religions, regardless of historical circumstances.[354]

In sum, Elbaz's claim is that these psalms are recited at the beginning of Shabbat because it is on Shabbat that God's kingship is most freely manifested, uninhibited by the interference of the demonic realm.

**Spiritual Commentary on *Kabbalat Shabbat* As A Whole**

The first of the two teachings, the Ari's teaching in *Tikkunei Shabbat*, relates three ideas:

1. As one recites each of the six psalms, one should have the intention to connect each psalm to each day of the week that is just ending and thereby, to purify the days of the past week.

2. Based upon mystical math, there is a connection to a concealed message in the six psalms: *nefesh*, "soul," is numerically spelled out. The additional Shabbat soul is strengthened through the conscious act of reciting the letters of the words of these psalms. The soul is protected from the *kelipot*, the demonic "shells" through the chanting of these words. When we compare this teaching to Elbaz's *Heikhal HaKodesh*, we find a similar teaching, but in *Heikhal HaKodesh* it seems to be more cosmically directed: "For in all of these psalms, we aid the side of holiness to cause the *Shekhinah* to reign over the whole world." There, the *Shekhinah* itself is strengthened whereas here, it is the worshiper's additional Sabbath soul that is strengthened.

3. Additionally, the Ari taught that the number of verses in all the psalms (65) is equivalent to the number hinted at in the letters of God's name, *Adonai*.

---

[353] Zohar 1:20b. Translation from Daniel C. Matt, *The Zohar: Pritzker Edition* (Stanford, California: Stanford University Press, 2004), 1:157. As Matt noted in n. 386, "For parallel medieval Christian views of the demonic nature of the Jews, see Trachtenberg, *The Devil and the Jews*."

[354] For the view that Kabbalistic negativity toward other faith communities was a response to antisemitism, see Hartley Lachter, *Kabbalistic Revolution: Reimagining Judaism in Medieval Spain* (New Brunswick, NJ: Rutgers University Press, 2014) and Ellen D. Haskell, *Mystical Resistance: Uncovering the Zohar's Conversations with Christianity* (Oxford: Oxford University Press, 2016). I thank Rabbi Daniel M. Horwitz for the references to these volumes.

**What are we to make of these teachings?**

Viewing the liturgical texts as containing meaning and potency beyond the content of the words is common to all of these teachings. Moderns don't usually approach texts in this way. We read for content. We may pay attention to style and skill in the writing, but we tend to consider all of the external features of writing as supporting the content. And yet, the enterprise of prayer is not the same as the enterprise of reading. Attention to some of the external features of a prayer passage may actually free us to wrest new and inspiring meaning, especially in texts that we pray over and over again. After all, what new content do we expect to gain from the hundredth time we read a prayer text? On the other hand, the Kabbalistic teachings are telling us that the essential element in these texts is not in the content but in the external structure. That if we concentrate on each of the six days of the past week as we recite the six psalms, we can purify them. That the first letter of each word adds up to *nefesh*, "soul." That the total number of verses, 65, hints at God's name, *Adonai*. And that God's kingship is mentioned in each of the psalms.

Praying the psalms with this kind of consciousness would mean pronouncing the words without paying much attention to their meaning as individual words and sentences, but rather remaining conscious of an overarching theme.

This kind of praying allows us to reflect on each of the days of the past week, to review what "impurities" occurred, that is, what difficulties we experienced on each day. We are challenged in this interpretation to briefly face the difficulties of each day and with the power of each psalm, to let go of them.

Praying the psalms this way would mean remaining conscious that as we recite the words, we are spelling out the word *nefesh*, "soul," and thereby adding power to our relaxed, sustaining, Sabbath soul. We would be given the opportunity to relax into the Sabbath.

Praying the psalms with this "meta" kind of intention would mean reciting the words of the six psalms as one very long name of God. That chanting each psalm is acknowledging the presence of the spiritual center of the universe.

While it would probably prove difficult to keep in mind all three of these themes as one recites the six psalms, one might engage one of the themes during a given Friday night service.

Viewed this way, the psalms of *Kabbalat Shabbat* comprise one long invocation designed to strengthen the spiritual within us and beyond us, in the world. That's not a bad way to welcome the Sabbath! For this kind of praying to work for us, we would need to let go of our usual way of reading and truly embrace that praying is a very different activity. It is an activity that uses reading not to yield information but to induce a state of spiritual union with the divine.

### *Ana V'Kho'aḥ*

The prayer *Ana V'Kho'aḥ* parallels the spirit of the Ari's teaching that the total number of verses in the six psalms of *Kabbalat Shabbat* (65) equals the symbolic number in the letters of God's name, *Adonai*. The idea behind *Ana V'Kho'aḥ* is also that a name of God is spelled out through mystical math.[355] The Talmud asserts that among the mystical names of God is a forty-two-letter name. This prayer hints at one version of that forty-two-letter name.[356] The prayer consists of seven lines plus an eighth line that forms a response to the first seven lines. The first seven lines contain six words each. Seven times six equals forty-two. The first letter of each of these forty-two words combine to spell out a concealed name of God. The eighth line resembles a verse from the Psalms (72:19). More importantly, the Mishnah (*Yoma* 3:8) teaches that this line was recited by the people gathered in the ancient Temple as a response to hearing the High Priest pronounce the four letter (*YHVH*) name of God.

### Spiritual Commentary on *Ana V'Kho'aḥ*

Again, the idea here is to recite this short prayer, barely paying attention to the meaning of the individual words and sentences, while concentrating on invoking a mystical name of God. The placement of this prayer after the six psalms, but just before *Lekhah Dodi* and the psalm for the Sabbath day itself adds drama to the moment just before we embrace the beginning of the Sabbath. With the recitation of *Ana V'Kho'aḥ*, we spend a couple of moments meditating on a name of God, which is another way of saying that we spend a couple of moments meditating on God, trying to become aware of God's presence. Then, in *Lekhah Dodi*, we will concentrate on exoteric and esoteric ideas about God just before we welcome the Sabbath day itself by reciting Psalm 92, the Psalm for the Sabbath day.

[355] See Joshua Trachtenberg, *Jewish Magic and Superstition: A Study in Folk Religion* (Philadelphia: University of Pennsylvania Press, 2004; Originally published by Behrman's Jewish Book House in 1939), 93-95.
[356] Babylonian Talmud, *Kiddushin* 71a.

## *Lekhah Dodi*

*Lekhah Dodi*, composed by Rabbi Shlomo Alkabetz in 16th-century Safed,[357] is—along with the prayer *Ana V'Kho'aḥ*—the poetic bridge between the six psalms representing the six days of the week and Psalm 92, which already in the Bible is called "The Psalm for the Sabbath Day." It serves to focus the worshiper's attention on consciously welcoming Shabbat in two ways. On the one hand, *Lekhah Dodi* can be read as a typical, non-mystical, *piyyut*, weaving biblical verses and rabbinic commentary together as it expresses its themes in relatively accessible, non-Kabbalistic, terms. On the other hand, it can also be read as a deeply mystical prayer, immersed in Kabbalistic imagery. Because it uses intricately constructed lyricism and symbolism on both the exoteric level as well as on the esoteric level, it is a masterpiece of liturgical art. I will explore its meaning first on the non-mystical plane and then on the mystical plane.

### Analytical Commentary on the Non-Mystical Meaning of *Lekhah Dodi*

*Lekhah Dodi* is a poem that comprises nine stanzas and a repeating refrain or chorus. Like a *piyyut*, its language is largely constructed from biblical verses—with a large representation of love imagery from the Song of Songs and messianic imagery from the book of Isaiah[358]—as well as hints to teachings from Rabbinic Literature.

The biblical citations tie the notions of love and messianic expectation into the weekly advent of Shabbat. The implications are that divine love is more easily felt on Shabbat than on other days and that the overall experience of Shabbat evokes and hints at the experience of the messianic era.

### The Refrain of *Lekhah Dodi* in the Non-Mystical Interpretation

The poem begins with the refrain, which repeats after each verse. Therefore, let's begin by examining the imagery and meaning of the refrain: "Come, my companion, to greet the bride, let us welcome Shabbat."

---

[357] R. Alkabetz's name "Shlomo HaLevy" is spelled out in the first letter of each of the first eight stanzas.

[358] *Lekhah Dodi* cites wording from the Bible in the following order:

Chorus: Song of Songs 7:12, 4:8-11, 5:1.
Verse 1: Deuteronomy 5:12, Exodus 20:8, Deuteronomy 26:19.
Verse 2: Proverbs 8:23.
Verse 3: Amos 7:13, Genesis 19:29, Psalms 84:7, II Samuel 5:22-23.
Verse 4: Isaiah 52:2, 52:1, Psalms 69:19.
Verse 5: Isaiah 51:17, 52:1, 60:1, 40:5.
Verse 6: Isaiah 54:4, 45:17, Psalms 42:12, Isaiah 14:32, 49:19.
Verse 7: Jeremiah 30:16, Isaiah 62:5.
Verse 8: Isaiah 54:3, 25:9.
Verse 9: Proverbs 12:4, Deuteronomy 7:6.

The first half of the refrain invites us to greet "the bride." The second half of the refrain identifies the bride as a representation of Shabbat. The wording here alludes to a passage in the Talmud:

> Rabbi Ḥanina would robe himself and stand on the eve of Shabbat (and) would say, "Come, let us go to welcome the Shabbat Queen."
>
> Rabbi Yannai would dress in his robe on the eve of Shabbat and would say, "Come, oh bride; come, oh bride."[359]

The talmudic passage occurs in the midst of a collection of practices of various Sages in honor of Shabbat. This particular passage apparently describes a weekly practice of two Sages who lived a little over a thousand years before *Lekhah Dodi* was written. The two Sages would consciously welcome Shabbat by dressing up and calling Shabbat a bride or a queen. The refrain of *Lekhah Dodi*, cites Rabbi Yannai's image of Shabbat as a bride and his words are also quoted verbatim in the 9th and last verse as the conclusion of *Lekhah Dodi*, "Come, oh bride; come, oh bride."[360] The poem therefore both begins and ends with allusions to the weekly custom of the two talmudic sages. One might say that the entire poem was created in order to make a communal ritual, centuries later, out of the private rite of Rabbi Ḥanina and Rabbi Yannai. The purpose of the ritual is to help worshipers usher in Shabbat with awareness.

It is worth noting that the Talmud does not frame the two Sages' ritual as part of a worship service. It is difficult to pin down exactly what might have been the worship experience of Jews on a Friday night during Amoraic times because we don't have a clear picture about evening services in general during that era. Regular evening worship service (including, especially, the *Amidah*) was not accepted as a universal custom during Tannaitic times and apparently only gradually caught on during Amoraic times. So it is not even certain that these two sages would have felt obligated to attend any worship service at the onset of Shabbat on Friday evening. If this was the case, then their welcoming Shabbat by dressing up and saying just one brief sentence

[359] Babylonian Talmud, Shabbat 119a. Another version of this same teaching, elsewhere in the Talmud (*Bava Kamma* 32a-32b), reads as follows:

Rabbi Ḥanina would say: 'Come, let us go forth to meet the bride, the queen!' Some say: 'to meet Shabbat, the bride, the queen.'

Rabbi Yannai would dress in his Shabbat attire and stand and say: 'Come, oh bride, come, oh bride.'

[360] The figure of Shabbat as bride also recurs in the 7th verse, using wording based upon Isaiah 62:5: "May your God rejoice over you as a groom rejoices over a bride." The image of Shabbat as queen is hinted at, if not fully expressed, in the 9th verse as well in the words *ateret ba'alah*, "crown of her husband."

may have been a stand-alone ceremony, performed simply, as the talmudic passage tells us, on "the eve of Shabbat." If a formal worship service did exist in these Sages' communities, it could have been a brief rite done before or after that service, or perhaps at home as a ceremony preceding Shabbat dinner.

The imagery used by the Sages is interesting: Shabbat as "bride" or as "queen." If one considers this talmudic passage in the context of other related depictions of Shabbat in Rabbinic Literature, the identification of Shabbat as a bride or a queen here probably means more than simply: Let us welcome Shabbat with the joy that we would feel if we were in the presence of an actual human bride or queen.[361] Rather, it expresses the joy of the worshiper welcoming Shabbat as if Shabbat itself were Israel's angelic bride. (Or, in Rabbi Ḥanina's formulation—which is not as prominent in *Lekhah Dodi*, as God's angelic bride; after all, if Shabbat is queen, who but God is king?). In another rabbinic teaching that uses marital imagery to depict the love between Israel and Shabbat, each day of the week pairs with another as male/female couples. Only Shabbat is left without a mate until God declares that the Community of Israel will be Shabbat's mate. The midrash supports its teaching by citing the biblical verse, "Remember the Sabbath day *le-kadsho*" (Ex. 20:8). *Le-kadsho* is usually understood as "to sanctify it [the Sabbath]." However, the midrash plays on another meaning of the word, namely, "to betroth it," yielding the interpretation, "Remember the Sabbath day in order to betroth yourself to it."[362] Here, we encounter the theme of sacred, or divine, marriage. This idea has a long history in world religion as well as in Jewish tradition.[363] The non-mystical meaning of "companion" in the refrain ("Come, let us go to welcome the Shabbat Queen"), may be fellow worshipers. In sum, then, the non-mystical meaning of the refrain of *Lekhah Dodi* seems to be:

---

[361] The relevant imaging about Shabbat in rabbinic literature as well as in Kabbalistic literature is analyzed in Elliot K. Ginsburg, *The Sabbath in the Classical Kabbalah* (Portland, Oregon: The Littman Library of Jewish Civilization, 1989, 2008), 101-120; and in Elliot Wolfson, "Coronation of the Sabbath Bride: Kabbalistic Myth and the Ritual of Androgynisation," *The Journal of Jewish Thought and Philosophy*, 6:2, 1997, 301-343.

[362] Genesis Rabba 11:8, Theodor-Albeck edition (Jerusalem, 1965), 1:95-96. Quite interesting is the fact, noted by Ginsburg, 103, n. 179, that in various manuscript editions of this midrash, Shabbat is sometimes represented as female and Israel as male, and sometimes the opposite. I will return to this ambiguity in the discussion of the mystical meaning of *Lekhah Dodi* below.

[363] Scholars of religion call this notion *Heiros Gamos* or Hierogamy. See the scholarship cited by Ginsburg, *The Sabbath in the Classical Kabbalah*, 101, n. 175 which includes Mircea Eliade, *Myths, Dreams and Mysteries* (New York: Harper & Row, 1967), 158; 171-183 and *The Myth of the Eternal Return* (Princeton, New Jersey: Princeton University Press, 1965), 23-27; 57-58.

> Let all Jews at this moment of dusk on Friday evening welcome Shabbat with the proper intent because at this moment, we, Israel, fulfill our role as the loving partner of Shabbat.

**The Verses of *Lekhah Dodi* in the Non-Mystical Interpretation**

The verses of *Lekhah Dodi* sound two main themes, Shabbat and Jerusalem, with a messianic undertone throughout. The first two verses and last verse speak of Shabbat, while the middle six verses focus on Jerusalem. Part of the artistry of the *piyyut* style is the fact that of the three verses that speak of Shabbat, only the second actually includes the word "Shabbat." The other two verses use imagery that hint at the Shabbat theme.

The first verse clues the worshiper in to its theme by alluding to a teaching about Shabbat in Rabbinic Literature. The verse begins "'Observe' and 'remember' spoken at once." This hints at a passage in the Talmud about the Ten Commandments.[364] The command to observe Shabbat appears in both versions of the Ten Commandments in similar, but not in identical wording. In the version in the book of Exodus (20:8), the commandment begins with the word *zakhor*, "remember," while the version in the book of Deuteronomy (5:12) begins with the word *shamor*, "observe." To resolve the difference, the Talmud explains that God said both words at one and the same time. When the verse uses the word *eḥad*, "at once" referring to God having said "remember" and observe" at one and the same time, it also displays its poetic skill by hinting at a second theme, the theme of "oneness." That theme registers four times in this brief verse. The other three times refer to God: In three different ways, God is declared to be a unity. Oneness, we will see, is central to the mystical meaning of this prayer, but it is also found in the non-mystical meaning as well.

The second verse begins by explicitly referring to Shabbat: "Let us go to welcome Shabbat." The end of the verse, "last in creation, first in thought," points to the idea that while Shabbat occurred last in the Creation story, it was the first thought, the primary thought, when God conceived of Creation. It was the aim and pinnacle of Creation. That premise will recur in the blessing about Shabbat in the *Amidah*, later in the Shabbat evening service.

Like the first verse, the ninth verse only hints at its theme and never uses the word "Shabbat." Rather, it mentions "the crown of her husband," and twice says "bride."

---

364 Babylonian Talmud, *Shevuot* 20b.

The topic of the six middle verses of *Lekhah Dodi* (verses 3-8) is the future messianic rebuilding of Jerusalem. In each of these verses, the poem addresses the destroyed Jerusalem directly, in the second person. Using phrases drawn mainly from the latter chapters of the Book of Isaiah—after the destruction of Jerusalem by the Babylonians in 586 BCE—the poem delivers message after message of renewal, rebuilding, and hope. It is this message of the future rebuilding of Jerusalem that lends the strong undertone of messianism to *Lekhah Dodi.* Two mentions of code names for the Messiah are included in these verses: In verse 4—*Ben Yishai,* "the son of Jesse," (Jesse's son was David, from whose line the Messiah will be born, according to Jewish tradition), and in verse 8, *Ben Partzi,* "the son of the Perizite" (referring to Peretz, another ancestor of David, see Ruth 4:12, 18).

The combination of the theme of Shabbat with the theme of the future messianic rebuilding of Jerusalem was likely meant to call to the worshiper's mind the rabbinic teaching that Shabbat is *mei'ein olam haba,* "a foretaste of the world to come."[365] As worshipers recite this prayer just as Shabbat begins, they are reminded that the cessation of work and the sense of peace and wholeness that characterize Shabbat will last forever in the messianic future, and not just for one day a week. And the rebuilding of Jerusalem will, in the physical realm, accompany the sense of peace and wholeness that will occur in the spiritual realm.

**Spiritual Commentary on the Non-Mystical Meaning of *Lekhah Dodi***

The import of reciting *Lekhah Dodi* infused with its non-mystical meaning is characterized by a sense of awareness or consciousness of welcoming a singular and sacred day.

The recitation of the refrain over and over—"Come, my companion, to greet the bride, let us welcome Shabbat"—is meant to bring a worshiper out of their immediate environment and instill in them a joyful, upbeat, bright, and buoyant mindset of expectancy. The emotion suggested in *Lekhah Dodi*'s refrain is that of a human lover (the worshiper) about to be united with one's precious, spiritual, mate (Shabbat). The emotion would certainly have something in common with that of a person anticipating reunion with one's lover. But the difference is that here, the worshiper is connecting not with another person, but with a moment, with an evening, with an entire day, that somehow "belongs" to me, that is especially coupled to me, "belongs" to my

[365] The notion that Shabbat is "a taste of the world to come" is found in *Mekhilta DeRabbi Yishma'Eil, Ki Tissa* 1, Horovitz-Rabin, ed. (Jerusalem, 1970), p. 341, and is cited in many later layers of rabbinic literature. See Wolfson, "Coronation of the Sabbath Bride," 301, n. 19 for a listing.

people; generations of my ancestors called it their special time; my people perceived that the divine "gave" this day to them, and tonight I am not alone in embracing this day as a badly needed, intensely welcomed, time to restore myself. I am joining numberless Jews for a thousand generations who have understood that this is our time to renew the link between our souls and the timeless, formless, but real divine presence in the world.

This mood dovetails with the cumulative meaning of the verses. The verses imply that there is a sense of incompleteness and existential brokenness prevailing during the six weekdays that corresponds to the sense of exile experienced by the Jewish People while the Land of Israel and, especially, Jerusalem, is not yet rebuilt in peace. That feeling of unfulfilled promise, of never achieving a sense of perfect completion (in other words, real life as it is experienced by nearly all people!) lifts, temporarily at least, with the arrival of Shabbat. Shabbat as messianic ideal in this poem represents the hoped-for-but-never-quite-attained reward of complete and total rest and relaxation at the end of an arduous period of toil. Tasting this delicious sense of joyful relief and respite—in its messianic context—makes clear how different the authentic significance of Shabbat is from a mere "day off," and how different it can be from the typical weekend experience in the modern, Western, secular world. The weekend days so often turn into days of running errands so that one ends up just as busy and feeling just as scattered as on a weekday. Weekday or weekend, we are *doing*, we are engaged in tasks. It's just that on the weekend, the doing and the tasks are different than during the week. But the essential mindset is the same. The great challenge is to take the words of *Lekhah Dodi* seriously enough to induce the wonderful and optimistic feeling of arriving at the very beginning of a truly restorative break from the protean reality. A worshiper sensitive to the full meaning of this poem would chant it or listen to it as if it were one long, cleansing, restoring, healing, exhaled breath that leaves them feeling whole because they are reunited with their soul's spiritual partner, the soul's "bride," Shabbat. People can feel intensely connected to other people. That's the deep and loving link to lover, or spouse and family. People can feel intensely connected to a place; that's the powerful and passionate link to homeland, to ancestral land. Instead of having us connect to another beloved person or place, *Lekhah Dodi* attempts to ignite a parallel intense bond to a moment in time.[366]

[366] This interpretation owes much to Abraham Joshua Heschel, *The Sabbath*, (Farrar, Straus, and Giroux, New York: 1951).

**Analytical Commentary on the Mystical Meaning of *Lekhah Dodi***

The mystical meaning of *Lekhah Dodi* is based upon teachings of Kabbalah that may seem strange and even "un-Jewish" to many modern Jews. If readers who are new to *Kabbalah* have trouble following the mystical meaning of this prayer, it is understandable. If there is one principle of Judaism that most modern Jews are aware of it is the principle of strict monotheism. That there is one, all-powerful, God. Kabbalah did not violate that principle, but let's say it "stretched" it. The *raza demehemnuta*, "the secret of faith," in medieval Jewish mysticism is that God is made up of ten *sefirot* (*sefirot* = potencies or energies). Kabbalists hasten to add that of course God is one. They would never openly contradict that predominant tenet of Jewish tradition. But they say that if human beings could apprehend true divine reality, they would understand that indeed God is absolutely one, and at the same time, God also manifests as ten separate entities that sometimes need human help in order to be fully connected. As noted above, in the discussion of the non-mystical meaning of *Lekhah Dodi*, the poem is made up of a repeating refrain plus nine verses. That sum of ten unmistakably points to one of the central principles of Kabbalah, the claim that God comprises ten *sefirot*. The poem's external structure of nine verses plus a refrain adding up to ten is one of many connections to the Kabbalistic system.[367]

**The Refrain of *Lekhah Dodi* in the Mystical Interpretation**

The non-Kabbalistic analysis above discussed divine marriage, and that is a key idea in Kabbalah as well, but the mystical approach adds some new elements. Here, the worshiper gets even more actively involved in the drama of divine marriage. If in the non-mystical interpretation of the refrain the invitation to "my companion" (*dodi*) to greet the "bride" (*kallah*) refers to fellow worshipers, in the mystical interpretation, it means both fellow worshipers and the masculine *sefirah* of *Tiferet*. One hint of this identity of the "companion" is the fact that the word *dodi* can be read backwards to indicate the tetragrammaton, the familiar divine name *YHVH*,[368] and in the sefirotic

[367] I am indebted here to Reuven Kimelman who deciphered the Kabbalistic meaning of *Lekhah Dodi* in *The Mystical Meaning of Lekhah Dodi and Kabbalat Shabbat*, though he only fully explained the chorus, and three of the nine verses (verses 1, 5, and 8). Kimelman published a very short synopsis of his interpretation in Lawrence E. Hoffman, *My People's Prayer Book*, V. 8 (Woodstock, Vermont: Jewish Lights, 2005), 118, 128-132. Another accessible summary of Kimelman's work is found in Daniel M. Horwitz, *A Kabbalah and Jewish Mysticism Reader* (The Jewish Publication Society, The University of Nebraska Press, 2016), 335-342. See also Arthur Green, "Some Aspects of Qabbalat Shabbat" in *Sabbath: Idea, History, Reality*, ed. Gerald Blidstein (Beer Sheva: Ben Gurion University of the Negev Press, 2004), 95-118.

[368] It is not unusual for the Hebrew letter *dalet* to stand in for the more common *heh* in representing God's name.

system, that name is associated with *Tiferet*. The *sefirah* of *Shekhinah* (also commonly called *Malkhut*), as the primary feminine *sefirah*, would easily be recognized by the initiated as the "bride." Therefore, the added meaning is that in each refrain, the worshiper is calling upon the "companion," i.e., a masculine manifestation of God, *Tiferet*, to "welcome," and to unite with, *Shekhinah*, a feminine manifestation of God.

Additionally, the refrain's first strophe ("Come, my companion, to greet the bride") comprises 15 letters and its second strophe ("let us welcome Shabbat") adds up to 11 letters. Now, in the medieval Jewish take on "geometry" known as *Gematria*, each letter of the Hebrew alphabet also represents a number. The 15 letters of the first strophe symbolize the sum of 15 when the first two letters of the tetragrammaton, *yud—heh* are added together using *Gematria*. The 11 letters of the second strophe represent the numerical sum of the last two letters of God's name, *vav—heh*. The fact that the refrain only fully makes sense when all 24 letters are read together as a unified statement hints at the concealed message that each time the refrain is chanted, the worshiper is urging—and, in fact, in a mysterious way—is aiding, the divine union of the *Shekhinah*, a feminine *sefirah* and *Tiferet*, a masculine *sefirah*.

The mystical meaning of the refrain is the celebration of the union of the disparate parts of God on Shabbat. In Kabbalah, the six days of the week symbolize exile when the masculine and feminine aspects of God are separated from one another and Shabbat represents redemption—if only for one day—when the divine presence is fully united.[369] This helps explain why life often feels so chaotic: According to Kabbalah, just as Israel is in exile, so too is God, and that allows demonic forces to exert power. On Shabbat, the divine flow is fully integrated just as God will be permanently in the messianic era. The chanting of the liturgy on Friday night, including *Lekhah Dodi*, is viewed as aiding God's union, paralleling the singing and celebration of an earthly marriage.

A suggestion of eroticism is hard to miss here, and that is no accident. Kabbalah posits that what is experienced on the physical, creaturely level as sexuality is found in the divine world as well. Indeed, the mystics may say that the reason the erotic pull is experienced in the physical world is exactly because deep attraction occurs between divine elements in the supernal world. As Jewish (and many non-Jewish) mystical works often point out, "as above, so below."

[369] See Wolfson, "Coronation of the Sabbath Bride," 308.

A suggestion of paganism is also hard to miss here. As much as Kabbalists would cringe from such an interpretation, their system nevertheless has much in common with ancient polytheistic religion. In Kabbalah, God is not unequivocally one, but rather ten that is one. For pagan religion too, unity among the gods was a desideratum: the more peaceful the life above, the more peaceful will life be below. Paganism also valued the godly in the body and in nature. The battle that the biblical prophets waged against Israelite belief in multiple gods was not won by the time the Bible closed. It seemed to have been concluded in the rabbinic period. The truth seems to be, however, that the quasi-pagan allure of sensing the divine in nature, in sensuality, and in other multivalent ways, only went underground. It was always there in various ways in Jewish thought and practice even if it wasn't mainstream from the end of the biblical period until the emergence of Kabbalah in the Middle Ages. (A similar claim could be made about Christian theology in which God is three that is one). The deeply intimate, colorful, earthy, and sensual tones that infuse the *Kabbalat Shabbat* service in general, and *Lekhah Dodi* specifically, may well "feel" a little strange for modern mainstream Jews. It is a bit strange and unfamiliar, and that is because it preserves some elements of the pre-history of Jewish religion. But it does so in a way that marries some of the great insights of our pagan roots with our monotheistic mainstream, namely, the possibility of encountering the divine everywhere, not just in heaven; a frank recognition of how often God's presence is encountered in a fragmented way, and the active role human beings can play in bringing integration and oneness to the world. All of this is reflected in *Kabbalat Shabbat* and in *Lekha Dodi.*

**A Sample Verse of *Lekhah Dodi* in the Mystical Interpretation**

Just as the chorus of *Lekhah Dodi* involves esoteric symbolism reflected in a number of code words, so too, the nine verses hint at numerous technical terms and abstruse concepts. A full interpretation of all the verses would require the mastery of Kabbalistic terminology of an advanced student of Jewish mysticism. Therefore, I will present a full explanation of the first verse only and that will serve as an example, in microcosm, of the full poem. Even this one verse contains quite a complicated amalgam of mystical images.

The first verse:

> *Shamor* ("observe") and *zakhor* ("remember") in a single utterance,

The unified God announced to us;
*YHVH* is one and his name is one,
For renown, for beauty and for praise.

**Line 1:** As explained above, in the non-mystical commentary, "'Observe' and 'remember' in one utterance" refers to the fact that in the two versions of the Ten Commandments, the commandment about Shabbat begins with two different words, "observe" and "remember." The midrash resolved the apparent contradiction by asserting that God caused Israel to hear both words at once. In the Kabbalistic system, the two biblical words are taken to mean to Shabbat has both a male and a female aspect. How so? Because the word *zakhor* ("remember") is akin to the word *zakhar*, meaning "male." Therefore, *shamor* ("observe") symbolizes the female aspect. In the system of the *sefirot*, *shamor* corresponds to the tenth *sefirah*, *Shekhinah*—one of two feminine *sefirot*—and *zakhor* represents the sixth *sefirah*, *Tiferet* ("beauty"), a masculine *sefirah*. *Shamor* also refers to Friday night and *zakhor* to Shabbat day. The midrashic teaching that God said both words at once intimates that throughout all of Shabbat, both Friday night and Shabbat day, the male and female aspects of God—*Shekhinah* and *Tiferet*—are in complete unity so that the flow of divine energy is unimpeded.

**Line 2:** "The unified God"—When God announced the commandment of Shabbat to Israel at Mount Sinai using both words—*shamor* and *zakhor*—upon giving the Ten Commandments, God appeared at that moment as God-united-in-all-the-*sefirot*.

**Line 3:** The divine name, *YHVH*, is a code word for *Tiferet*, a masculine *sefirah*. The word renown (*shem*) is a code word for *Shekhinah*, a feminine *sefirah*. The phrase "*YHVH* is one and his name is one" means that on Shabbat, these two *sefirot* become one as they unite together.

**Line 4:** "Renown" (*shem*) as we've seen twice already in this verse, refers to the tenth feminine *sefirah*, *Shekhinah*. We have also already seen that "beauty" (*Tiferet*) is a code-word for the sixth, masculine, *sefirah*. "Praise" (*Tehilah*) refers to yet another *sefirah*, *Binah* ("understanding"), the third *sefirah*, and the one other feminine *sefirah* in the Kabbalistic system. The dynamic symbolized in this line is that the unity and the smooth flow of divine energy between the divine masculine and feminine represented by *Tiferet* and *Shekhinah* continues as well between *Tiferet* and *Binah*. *Shekhinah* is the lower feminine, or "daughter" and *Binah* is the upper feminine, or "mother."

While it would be too simplistic to say that all eight other verses connote the same thing as the first verse, it would also not be entirely off base to assert that the import of the other eight verses is at least related to that of the first verse.

Putting together the chorus and the first verse of *Lekhah Dodi*, the meaning is that on Shabbat, the disparate parts of God—especially the masculine and feminine aspects—come together so that the cosmos is ruled on Shabbat by a fully integrated and empowered divine energy. The power of evil, of semi-divine demonic forces—active during the "exilic" six weekdays—dissipates on Shabbat precisely because the *sefirot* are integrated and united. Just as the non-mystical interpretation of this prayer connects to the older notion in Rabbinic Literature that Shabbat is a taste of the messianic era, so too does the mystical interpretation. The difference is that in Rabbinic Literature and in the non-mystical view of this prayer, the prime beneficiary of Shabbat's hint of the messianic era is human, the worshiper; while in the mystical view of this prayer, the prime beneficiary is God. This is one of the concepts that can be difficult for modern Jews—the notion that the all-powerful God seems less than all-powerful. It may be easier to understand if one keeps in mind that this is one of the ways that Kabbalah tries to resolve the most problematic tenet of Jewish monotheism: If there is only one God, and that God is both good and all-powerful—meaning that God's will is always fulfilled—why does evil exist in the world? Why is there undeserved suffering in a world fully ruled by a good, omnipotent God? The Kabbalistic answer is that the sins of the Jewish people empower demonic forces during the six weekdays and they can disrupt the divine flow within the *sefirot*. But on Shabbat, with the help of the prayers of the Jewish people, the demonic forces flee, the *sefirot* unite, and the divine flow of blessing streams unrestrained. The role of the Jewish people is to recite Shabbat prayers—like *Lekhah Dodi*—to stimulate the unification of the *sefirot*. The Kabbalists describe this role as akin to a lover singing to their beloved in order to induce romance. They hasten to add that this is an inadequate comparison, and yet, the sense of the romantic and the erotic permeates Kabbalistic commentaries.

**Spiritual Commentary on the Mystical Meaning of *Lekhah Dodi***

The spiritual experience of reciting *Lekhah Dodi* in its non-mystical meaning centers on the worshiper. The spiritual experience of reciting *Lekhah Dodi* in its mystical meaning, on the other hand, centers on God. It requires the worshiper to intensely enter the life of God as the Kabbalists imagined it. As we recite the words of the refrain, *Lekhah dodi, likrat kallah*, "come, my companion, to greet the bride," we are addressing both our fellow worshipers, and encouraging them to greet "the bride," the Shabbat, but we are also—and primarily—addressing the *sefirah* of *Tiferet*, the "groom," and encouraging it to greet its "bride"—the *sefirah* of *Shekhinah*. Beyond that, in all the verses, we are prompting all of God's energies, all the *sefirot*, to bond. We are singing our prayer as an inducement to the divine "pleroma," or "fullness" to completely unite and integrate. This mindset requires that as we sing the words of this poem, we imagine that we are singing to the divine presence. We imagine that as dusk approaches and with it, Shabbat, the divine presence is beginning to come together and to gain in power. And our singing, our praying—and the singing and praying of others with us in the synagogue, and the chanting of Jews in synagogues everywhere, grants additional force and potency to God's gathering strength. As we sing the words of *Lekhah Dodi*, words encouraging integration and unification, we imagine God's presence in the cosmos slowly coming together in harmony. We feel our partnership with God in very intimate terms as we sing. We feel God's closeness. With God's unification and strength come peace, wholeness, and increased divine blessing to our, physical, world. In the Kabbalistic system, individual Jews are viewed as partnering with God in more intimate terms than in any other Jewish philosophy. Above, it was suggested that in the non-mystical understanding of *Lekhah Dodi*, chanting or listening to this prayer is akin to one long cleansing breath, leaving the worshiper feeling whole because they are reunited with the soul's "bride," Shabbat. In the mystical interpretation, a worshiper who took the symbolism seriously would feel a deep sense of wholeness and fulfillment because on the day of symbolic redemption, on Shabbat—and with the worshiper's help—the "bride" and the "groom" within God unite, all the *sefirot* link together, the strength of evil diminishes, God's power is enhanced, and all is right with the world.

As mentioned above, authentic Kabbalistic theology may feel unusual and even alien to modern Jews. Nevertheless, I encourage us to "try on" this approach in worship. As foreign as this approach may feel to us, Kabbalistic philosophy was the dominant, mainstream, Jewish philosophy in many areas of the Jewish world for several centuries. It continues to be the dominant approach in many Ḥasidic groups and has experienced a kind of revival in Renewal and other Jewish communities. And this type of philosophy, especially when attached to the act of prayer, can be very moving because of the intimate and palpable connection between worshiper and God. The attraction of Kabbalistic worship is probably at its most accessible on Friday night through the recital of *Lekhah Dodi*.

## Psalms 92 and 93

These two psalms formed an introduction to the evening service for Friday night already in Geonic times, preceding the Kabbalists by several centuries. They celebrate the arrival of Shabbat (Psalm 92) and God's kingship over the world (Psalm 93). It is to prepare us for this moment—the actual arrival of Shabbat—that the psalms of *Kabbalat Shabbat*, and especially *Lekhah Dodi*, were arrayed.

Psalm 92 posits a world in which the wicked are punished and justice prevails. When "a righteous person will flourish like a palm tree and grow as tall as a cedar in Lebanon" (Psalm 92:13). Psalm 93 describes God as a fully enthroned king of the world, recalling a primordial rebellion of the world and especially its rivers and seas against God's power. This psalm preserves a memory of ancient pagan Middle Eastern legends of the earth and the seas—gods themselves—rebelling against the power of creator gods. In the psalm, the pagan elements are mostly expunged, and the rebellion of the earth and its waters is against the power of Israelite creator God, *YHVH*.[370]

Since mourners do not observe external forms of mourning during Shabbat of the week of *shivah*, and Shabbat is fully welcomed at this point, with the recital of these two psalms, it is immediately before these psalms that mourners first enter the synagogue and are greeted with traditional words of comfort: "May the one who is always present comfort you among the other mourners of Zion and Jerusalem." The theology of this line is that all Israel are mourners of our homeland until it is rebuilt and dwells in peace. Thus, when we ask that God comfort and console the mourners whose loss is so fresh in their minds, we declare all of our people to be national mourners as well. And that line is recited here and mourners enter the synagogue at this point specifically because Shabbat fully arrives with the recitation of these psalms.

### Spiritual Commentary on Psalms 92 and 93

Psalm 92 envisions a world in which justice finally and completely triumphs. Rashi comments that this is a vision of the world to come; an image of Shabbat in which justice flourishes and the world is in harmony. Psalm 93 views God as fully king, fully ruling the world. A worshiper reciting these psalms would relax into Shabbat, experiencing this one day of the week as if things

[370] See the commentaries on this psalm in Hermann Gunkel, *An Introduction to the Psalms: The Genres of the Religious Lyric of Israel*, trans. James D. Nogalsgy (Macon, Georgia: Mercer University Press, 1968) (originally published in German in 1926); Sigmund Mowinckel, *The Psalms in Israel's Worship*, trans. by D.R. Ap-Thomas (Oxford: Basel Blackwell, 1962) (originally published in Norwegian in 1921-24).

were as they should be in the world. Experiencing this one day out of seven as a symbol of the perfected messianic era.

## Shabbat *Ma'ariv* (Evening Service)

The basic structure of the Evening Service for Shabbat resembles closely the structure of the Evening Service for weekdays. Like the Evening Service for weekdays, it consists mainly of two major prayer clusters: The *Shema* and Its Blessings and the *Amidah*. There are no differences in the first section of the service, the *Shema* and Its Blessings.[371] The differences occur in the *Amidah* and in a passage unique to Friday night following the *Amidah* called *Birkat Mei'ein Sheva*, "A Blessing Comprising Seven [Blessings]," sometimes referred to as *Berakhah Aḥat Mei'ein Sheva*, "One Blessing Consisting of Seven [Blessings]."

Let's begin by examining the differences within the *Amidah* itself. The middle section of the weekday *Amidah* contains 13 blessings of petition—requests from God—and that entire section is replaced on Shabbat and all holidays with one blessing celebrating the essence of the holy day. That middle blessing is known as *Birkat Kedushat HaYom*, "The Blessing of the Holiness of the Day." Contrary to what is often taught, it is not true that the *Amidah* of Shabbat and holy days do not contain petitions. In fact, the added blessing on Shabbat and holidays contains a number of petitions. However, these petitions are mainly of a spiritual character as opposed to the petitions recited on weekdays, which are mainly of a material character.

### Shabbat Evening *Amidah*, Part 1

The first three and last three blessings of each Shabbat *Amidah* are identical to those recited on weekdays and Festivals. On Shabbat, in between those bookends, *Birkat Kedushat HaYom*, "The Blessing of the Holiness of the Day" consists of three paragraphs, the first two of which are connected to each other and the third of which stands on its own. Those first two paragraphs read as follows:

> You dedicated the seventh day to your essence (literally, "to your name"). It is the end-goal of the creation of the heavens

[371] Although the 10th-century Siddur of Rav Saadia Gaon does contain very different—and quite beautiful—poetic wording for Shabbat in the blessings surrounding the *Shema*. These additions, however, did not find their way into the Ashkenazic service. See *Siddur R. Saadja Gaon*, eds. I. Davidson, S. Assaf, B.I. Joel (Jerusalem: Mekitzei Nirdamim, 1951, 1985), 110-111.

> and the earth. You blessed it above all days and sanctified it over all times, and so (i.e., and because of this) it is written in your Torah:
>
> The heaven and the earth were finished, and all their array. On the seventh day God finished the work that he had been doing, and he ceased on the seventh day from all the work that he had done. And God blessed the seventh day and declared it holy, because on it God ceased from all the work of creation that he had done. (Genesis 2:1-3)

What we have in the first paragraph is a creative re-reading of the second paragraph, a biblical passage; in other words, this is a classic midrash. Rabbinic literature abounds with such re-readings, but the siddur, too, contains many, many examples.[372] The midrash addresses a difficulty in the biblical text quoted here that has bothered commentators for centuries. How can the Bible say that "On the seventh day God finished the work that he had been doing" since that seems to imply that God did some work on Shabbat itself! Yet the Hebrew plainly says that God completed his work *bayom hashevi'i,* "on the seventh day." Many interpretations have been offered for this seeming conundrum over the centuries. Before explaining how the midrash embedded in the Shabbat eve *Amidah* resolves the problem, it is instructive to explore a few of these interpretations.

An early commentary is found in the Talmud:

> King Ptolemy gathered 72 [Jewish] elders and ensconced them in 72 [separate] houses and said to each one of them, "Write for me the Torah of Moses your teacher." The Blessed Holy One intervened[373] and they wrote, "On the <u>sixth</u> day God completed all his work and rested on the seventh day."[374]

This is one of several legendary descriptions in Rabbinic Literature of how the Septuagint came to be written. The Septuagint is a translation of the

[372] See Mayer I. Gruber, "*Attah Kiddashta:* A Poetic Midrash on Genesis 2:1-3," *Conservative Judaism,* September/October, 1980, 37-39. For midrash in the liturgy in general, see Jeffrey Hoffman, *The Bible in the Prayer Book,* doctoral thesis in Liturgy for The Jewish Theological Seminary, 1981; Richard Sarason, "Midrash in Liturgy," in *Encyclopedia of Midrash: Biblical Interpretation in Formative Judaism,* ed. Jacob Neusner and Alan J. Avery-Peck; 2 vols. (Leiden: Brill, 2004), 1:463-492; Elie Gershon Kaunfer, *Interpreting Jewish Liturgy: The Literary Intertext Method,* doctoral thesis in Jewish Liturgy for The Jewish Theological Seminary, 2014.

[373] Literally, "granted counsel to each one of them."

[374] Babylonian Talmud, *Megillah* 9a.

Bible into Greek composed so that Jews in 3rd-century BCE Alexandria, Egypt could understand it. Here, God was concerned that the pagan king Ptolemy II of Egypt (implying, perhaps, non-Jews in general) would misunderstand this passage to mean that God was still actively creating the world on the Sabbath day if it were literally translated as "on the seventh day God finished the work." In point of fact, it is doubtful that any non-Jewish king commissioned the Septuagint. It was much more likely composed by Jews for Jews and the concern was over whether Jews would misunderstand this verse. Nevertheless, assuming that the ancient translators of the Septuagint had the same Hebrew original version of this passage that we do, the fact that they did, indeed, translate this verse as "on the sixth day God finished his work," shows the extraordinary lengths they were willing to take—consciously mistranslating a biblical passage—in order to avoid a theologically unacceptable outcome.

A few centuries later, the *Peshitta*, the ancient translation of the Bible into Syriac (Syria, ca. 2nd century CE) also translated this verse as "on the sixth day God finished the work." Among more modern translations of the Bible, the most famous English translation—the King James version from 1611—rendered "on the seventh day" as did the two most recent Jewish sponsored translations into English, that of the 1917 and the 1962 Jewish Publication Society versions. Still, the mistranslation of "the sixth day" persisted into the 20th century in at least one standard Christian translation into English, that of The New English Bible (1961).

The midrash embedded in the *Amidah* for Friday night deals with the problem in a different way. Let's look at it again. In the first paragraph, I will emphasize the word "end-goal" in bold because of its importance in interpreting the second paragraph:

> You dedicated the seventh day to your essence (literally, "to your name"). It is the **end-goal** of the creation of the heavens and the earth. You blessed it above all days and sanctified it over all times, and so (i.e., and because of this) it is written in your Torah...

The second paragraph, with the problematic phrase **bolded** reads:

> The heaven and the earth were finished, and all their array. **On the seventh day God finished** the work that he had been doing, and he ceased on the seventh day from all the

> work that he had done. And God blessed the seventh day and declared it holy, because on it God ceased from all the work of creation that he had done. (Genesis 2:1-3)

By using the word *takhlit*, "end-goal" in the first paragraph, the liturgy is implicitly connecting with the problematic word *vayekhal*, **"finished,"** in the second paragraph since they seem to share the same Hebrew root. The first paragraph is implying that the word *vayekhal* in the second paragraph doesn't carry its usual meaning of "finished," but rather interprets it as related to the word *takhlit*, "end-goal" or "purpose."[375] The liturgy's interpretation reads the verse not as "On the seventh day, God finished the work that he had been doing," but as "God designated the seventh day as the end-goal of the work that he had been doing," with the paragraph now reading:

> The heaven and the earth were finished, and all their array. **God designated the seventh day as the end-goal of the work that he had been doing,** and he ceased on the seventh day from all the work that he had done. And God blessed the seventh day and declared it holy, because on it God ceased from all the work of creation that he had done. (Genesis 2:1-3)

This interpretation avoids the problem entirely of whether God "finished," i.e., actually performed, some of the work of creation on the seventh day because it interprets "finished" as "designated as the end-goal." Beyond avoiding the difficulty of whether God actively did some of the work of Creation on Shabbat, it offers the view that Shabbat, the day of rest and repose, was the purpose of creation. That is quite an evocative claim that will be explored in the Spiritual Commentary. And see an alternate midrashic interpretation of this same word in the *Musaf Amidah* for Shabbat on page 305.

**Spiritual Commentary on the Shabbat Evening *Amidah*, Part 1**

The midrash embedded here in the Shabbat evening *Amidah* challenges the priorities many of us set in life. Typically, we prioritize the work we do in the world and the accumulation of material possessions. That is a natural consequence of the human condition: Most of us need to spend most of our time making enough money to guarantee our physical security. It is

[375] Both *veyehal* and *takhlit* derive from the same Hebrew root, *kaf-lamed-heh*.

quite understandable that many civilizations have held the accumulation of wealth as a basic goal in life. And yet, this part of the Shabbat evening *Amidah* asserts that the goal woven into the very fabric of creation is to step back from the activities that consume most of the week in order to spend one day in seven enjoying the fruits of our work and enjoying Creation itself, the fruits of God's work. When we recite the words of this prayer text we are challenged to relax into a weekly interlude of appreciating and valuing what we already have in our world, appreciating what we have created for ourselves, and appreciating what God has created. This includes our material possessions, but also the presence in our lives of people we love and the beauty of the natural world. Concentrating on the words of this passage can bring a feeling of gratitude that we have a full day's pause in accumulating things and an opportunity to be fully satisfied with what we have, because it asserts that this very mind-frame, the mind-frame of Shabbat, was actually God's purpose in creating the world in the first place.

### Shabbat Evening *Amidah*, Part 2

The third, and final, paragraph of The Blessing of the Holiness of the Day in the Shabbat evening *Amidah* reads as follows:

> Our God and God of our fathers, accept our rest. Sanctify us through your commandments and grant our portion in your Torah. Satisfy us through your goodness and gladden us through your redemption. Purify our hearts to serve you in truth. Allow us to inherit, *YHVH* our God, in love, willingly, your holy Shabbat. May Israel, the sanctifiers of your name, rest on it. Blessed are you, *YHVH*, Sanctifier of Shabbat.

While each *Amidah* of Shabbat contains wording unique to itself, this clause is found in every Shabbat *Amidah* in this same place—as the final paragraph of The Blessing of the Holiness of the Day. Elbogen asserts that the fact that it is found in every Shabbat *Amidah* is a hint that at some early period this clause, by itself, comprised the entire Blessing of the Holiness of the Day in every one of the four *Amidot* of Shabbat (*Ma'ariv*, *Shaḥarit*, *Musaf*, *Minḥah*). He points out that to this day the parallel blessing in the Festival *Amidah* is, indeed, identical in three of the four *Amidot* of Festivals (the exception being *Musaf*). The fact that the four *Amidot* of Shabbat ultimately did develop unique wording (in addition to this final paragraph) "has a natural explanation," according to Elbogen, "in the fact that the Sabbath recurs far more frequently than the festivals, so that repeating the same text four times every Sabbath would have been too monotonous."[376]

Aside from the first request, "Accept our rest," and the last phrase asking that we inherit Shabbat, there are several brief pleas in a row unrelated to Shabbat that may have been part of stock phrases of blessing.

A close look at some of the phraseology of this paragraph reveals meaning not obvious in a quick read.

**"Accept our rest" (*retzeh vimenuḥateinu*)**

Why are we asking God to "accept" our rest? It is likely that this phrase is a response to the many places in the Bible in which God commands Israel to observe Shabbat by resting from our daily work.[377] It must have struck some ancient poet as appropriate to request validation from God—during worship on Shabbat itself—that the worshiper's act of resting is indeed proper fulfillment of these commands. The word "accept" (*retzeh*) parallels the very same word which opens the next blessing of the *Amidah*. While we do not know whether this word began the next blessing in talmudic times, we do know that this next blessing (known as *Avodah*, "Worship," a request for the return of the sacrificial worship system) is quite ancient. It was mentioned—among just a few of the blessings of the *Amidah*—in the earliest stratum of talmudic literature, namely, Tannaitic literature.[378] All of this strengthens Marc Brettler's creative interpretation that "Accept our rest" (*retzeh vimenuḥateinu*) here in our passage, is an alliterative play on the similar-sounding *retzeh viminḥateinu*, "accept our sacrificial offering," the subject of the next blessing. In this way, "Shabbat replaces the defunct sacrificial system."[379]

Another phrase from this paragraph is quite familiar—probably over-familiar—to regular worshipers, and yet is difficult to define. I am referring to **"Grant our portion in your Torah" (*VeTen ḥelkenu beToratekha*)**. It may feel over-familiar to regular worshipers because it occurs in a number of other prayers in the siddur. Versions of the phrase, "grant my/our portion"

[376] Elbogen, *Jewish Liturgy*, 97; see also 93. Ezra Fleischer also held that initially the text of all the *Amidot* on Shabbat were the same, and he published a text that he felt may have been that original text. See his "Toward The Early Text of The Blessing of the Holiness of the Day in the Amidot of Shabbat," [Hebrew], *Yearbook of Bar-Ilan University: Jewish Studies and Humanities*, vol. 26-27, 1995, 249-258.

[377] Among the many examples: Ex. 20:8-11, Ex. 31:12-17, Lev. 23:3, Deut. 5:12-15.

[378] *Sifrei* on Deuteronomy, 343, Finkelstein edition, p. 395, lines 3-4.

[379] Brettler contributed one of the commentaries in Lawrence A. Hoffman, ed., *My People's Prayer Book: Shabbat Morning*, vol. 10, 109. And see Arthur Green, "Sabbath as Temple: Some Thoughts on Space and Time in Judaism," in S. Fishman and R. Jospe, eds., *Go and Study: Essays and Studies in Honor of A. Jospe* (New York: Ktav, 1980), 287-305. Reprinted in *Arthur Green, Heart of the Matter: Studies in Jewish Mysticism and Theology* (Philadelphia: Jewish Publication Society, 2015), chapter 2.

occur several times not only in the siddur but also in Rabbinic Literature.[380] Comparing its use in other contexts may be helpful in defining its meaning. Each time, it seems to refer to one's path, destiny, fate, future. It may best be understood in the context of a talmudic prayer that uses the similar phrase "you set my portion" (*samta ḥelki*). According to the Mishnah, R. Neḥunia ben HaKaneh used to say a prayer upon entering and exiting the House of Study. The Talmud then offers a possibility for what his prayers were on those occasions. The prayer suggested for his exiting the *Bet HaMidrash* begins:

> I thank you, *YHVH* my God, that you have **set my portion** among those who sit in the House of Study and you did not **set my portion** among those who sit at street corners. For I rise early and they rise early. I rise early for words of Torah and they rise early for worthless words...[381]

Ignoring the judgmental attitude in this text, the meaning of granting or setting one's portion seems to refer to God's setting one's role or position or place in life. Therefore, "Grant our portion in your Torah" here in the Friday night *Amidah* would mean that we are asking of God that our path in life be a path of Torah: involved with study and observance of Torah.

**"Satisfy us through your goodness" (*Sabenu mituvekha*)**

Some have understood this expression as a request for "satisfaction" through God's goodness in the world to come.[382] The very next saying is

[380] In the siddur:
- In the weekday *Amidah*, in *Birkat Mish'an u'mivtaḥ latzaddikim*: *vesim ḥelkeinu imahem*, "and put our lot with them."
- In *Aleinu*: *shelo sam ḥelkeinu kahem vegoraleinu kekhol hamonam*, "who has not made our lot like theirs, nor our fate like all of their masses." (Note that here, *ḥelkeinu*, "out lot" is in poetic parallelism with *goraleinu*, "our fate").
- In *Birkhot HaShaḥar*: *Ashreinu mah tov ḥelkeinu*, "Happy are we, how good is our lot."
- In the *Amidah* of *Musaf* on *Shabbat*: *Yismaḥ Moshe bematnat ḥelko*, "May Moses rejoice in the gift of his lot."

Some examples in Rabbinic literature:
- Mishnah *Avot* 5:20, Yehudah ben Teima includes this phrase in a prayer of his.
- Palestinian Talmud, *Berakhot* 33a, this phrase occurs in a blessing that, according to Rabbi Yannai, one is supposed to say upon awakening from sleep.
- Babylonian Talmud, *Berakhot* 60b, the same phrase but in the singular, "grant my portion in your Torah" occurs in a prayer to be said upon retiring to sleep.
- Babylonian Talmud, *Shabbat* 118a—The phrase is use in the singular, *ḥelki*, "my lot," in ten different sayings attributed to a tanna, by Rabbi Yossi. In each instance, Rabbi Yossi says, "May my lot be among those (who do/say X)."

[381] Babylonian Talmud, *Berakhot* 28b.

[382] Based on somewhat similar language in Jeremiah 31:14, Marc Brettler takes the phrase, "satisfy us through your goodness" in the blessing here in the *Amidah* for Friday night to refer to the world to

"and gladden us through your redemption" and in Rabbinic Literature, the term "redemption" very often refers to the world to come. However, it is quite possible that "Satisfy us through your goodness" is meant to be a stand-alone expression, unconnected to the "redemption" in the one that follows it. It seems to me, in fact, that the meaning here is indeed this-worldly. An expression with wording very similar to this is found just before this very paragraph in the *Amidot* of *Shaḥarit* and *Musaf* on Shabbat: *Kulam yisbe'u veyitangu mituvekha*, "may all of them (= those who observe Shabbat) be satisfied and delighted through your goodness."[383] I understand that expression in a similar vein—a request that all who observe Shabbat be satisfied and delighted from God's goodness in this world.[384] The second to last blessing in every *Amidah* declares that *HaTov*, "the Good one," or "Goodness" is a name of God. The connotation of that blessing also does not appear to be other-worldly.

***VeTaher libeinu l'ovdekha be'emet***
**"Purify our heart to serve you in truth."**

The following biblical verse may well stand behind this phrase from our prayer:

> 1 Samuel 12:24—*V'avadetem oto be'emet bekhol levavkhem*,
> "serve him in truth with all your heart."

The context of this verse is part of the ambivalent response of the prophet Samuel to the people's request for a king. Samuel takes the people's request as a surrender to lower ideals. They want a king like the other nations, when they could have served God directly. Samuel reports, in God's name, that the people may have a king, however, he warns them here to continue to serve God—not the king—"in truth, with all your heart."

come. See his commentary in Lawrence A. Hoffman, *My People's Prayer Book, Shabbat Morning*, vol. 10, 109. However, the verse from Jeremiah isn't the only biblical verse that may be relevant. Nehemiah 9:25, suggested by the 14th-century siddur commentator, Rabbi David Abudraham, also contains the words "satisfy" and "goodness." See *Abudraham HaShalem*, ed., S.A. and A.J. Wertheimer (Jerusalem, 1959, 1963), 146. There are also numerous citations of God's goodness, especially in the Psalms, that are not related to eschatology (though these verses do not contain a reference to "satisfy"). See, e.g., Pss. 34:9; 54:8; 100:5; 106:1; 107:1; 118:1, 29; 136:1; 135:3.

[383] It occurs as well in the weekday *Amidah* in *Birkat Mevareikh HaShanim*.

[384] The word *veyitangu*, "delighted" in this phrase shares the same root that occurs twice in Isaiah's exhortation to make Shabbat "a delight" in Isaiah 58:13-14. And see the interpretation of this passage in the Babylonian Talmud, Shabbat 118a.

Therefore, this line is a plea that God help us achieve a pure heart, serving God, not others, in truth. That our state of mind remain focused on ultimate goals and undistracted by our tendencies to take the easy way.

Before turning to the spiritual commentary on these passages, it should be mentioned that in place of the first two paragraphs of this blessing in the Friday night *Amidah* (what I've termed "Part I" above), our two oldest *siddurim* contain a completely different prayer text.[385] Instead of the passage beginning, "You dedicated the seventh day to your essence...," *Seder Rav Amram* (9th century) and *Siddur Rav Saadia Gaon* (10th century) offer wording that has not survived in any modern rite. The wording in each of these two ancient prayer books varies slightly from the other, but they basically reflect the same text. It reads as follows:

> Out of your love, the love you have for Israel your people, and out of your compassion, our king, the compassion you have for members of your covenant, you have given to us, *YHVH* our God, this great and holy seventh day for love, for rest, for service, for gratitude, giving—from you to us—life and loving kindness.[386]

One can't help but notice the abundance of words relating to love in this prayer: "love" is mentioned three times; "compassion" twice; and lovingkindness once. This very short prayer is an eloquent description of Shabbat as a loving gift to the people Israel.

## Spiritual Commentary on the Shabbat Evening *Amidah*, Part 2

### *Retzeh vimenuḥateinu*, "Accept our rest."

Above, I posited that the literary meaning of this phrase may be asking God to accept our abstinence from labor on Shabbat as fulfilling the biblical commands. I think that is what the text, in the milieu out of which it sprang, probably meant. Taken at face value, this text doesn't speak to me, and I would imagine that it wouldn't speak to most modern Jews because it imagines God as a beneficent but powerful king or legislator or parent whose way is to issue commands. It is therefore humanity's way to observe and uphold those commands. And thus, in abject obeisance, the worshiper

[385] And these, in turn, seem to be based on a much earlier fragment of a prayer text found in *Tosefta Berakhot* 3:7.

[386] *Siddur Rav Saadia Gaon*, 111-112. See the parallel version in *Seder Rav Amram*, 63.

stands before God several times on Shabbat and expresses the wish that their observance of this Shabbat fulfills what the almighty lawgiver meant with the biblical Sabbath commands. What may not work for a modern is the sense of answering to a cosmic parent who issues orders. It just isn't the way many of us imagine the divine.

The Reconstructing Judaism siddur addresses this concern, I think, when it translates *Retzeh vimenuḥateinu* not as a plea to this almighty ruler to "accept our rest," but as "take pleasure in our rest."[387] The same discomfort motivates the Reform siddur to translate "be pleased with our rest."[388] These soften the harshness of the servant-to-master language, but still assume that the worshiper answers to a commander of sorts.

While one might be tempted to throw out this expression altogether, I don't think that is necessary. For this expression to work for me, I need to slightly adjust the image of God here away from a commanding authority. When saying *Retzeh vimenuḥuateinu*, "Accept our rest," I change the direction in which I address these words from "up there" to "in here." "Up there" means up in the heavens where the proverbial old man with a beard sits and judges the world. "In here" means that place within us where the *nitzotz haKadosh*, "the holy spark," resides.[389] In this way, when we say, "Accept our rest," we are speaking to that deep space within us where a spark of God lives, in our deep consciousness, the well of wisdom within, that we can access in moments of calm and clarity. With this change of direction in the conversation, the phrase is enlivened, and it asks us in this moment of prayer: Can we, in fact, accept the kind of rest that in which we are engaged on this Shabbat as true Shabbat rest? It asks that deep part of us to judge whether we are just going through the motions. Have we ceased from our workaday labor in an outward way only—in that we are not in our physical place of work—but are continuing to engage in workaday labor, nevertheless? Are we engaged in the kind of thinking, conversation, and activity that promote the material and physical goals of our weekdays (e.g., are we "networking"?) or do our outlook and actions liberate us from material goals? In this way, the phrase *Retzeh vimenuḥuateinu*, "Accept our rest," may be a meaningful touchstone in each of the *Amidot* of Shabbat.

---

387 *Kol Haneshamah Shabbat Veḥagim*, 96.

388 *Mishkan Tefillah*, 172. Interestingly enough, this is very close to the rendering of the Orthodox *Complete Artscroll Siddur*'s "may You be pleased with our rest," 340.

389 The phrase *nitzotz haKadosh*, "the holy spark," is found very frequently in the teachings of Rabbi Yehudah Leib Alter of Ger. The five volumes of his collected teachings are called *Sefat Emet*, "The Language of Truth." For an abridged, one-volume, Hebrew-English version, see Arthur Green, ed., *The Language of Truth: The Torah Commentary of the Sefat Emet* (Philadelphia: The Jewish Publication Society, 1998).

> *VeTen ḥelkeinu beToratekha*, "Grant our portion in your Torah."
> *Sabeinu mituvekha*, "Satisfy us with your goodness."
> *VeTaher libeinu l'ovdekha be'emet*, "Purify our heart to serve you in truth."

We are making three more requests here, and again, they mean one thing if addressed to the all-powerful ruler-God "up there," and they mean quite another thing if addressed "in here." When addressed "up there," we are asking for help from completely outside of ourselves. When directed "in here," we are asking for help from that part of ourselves that is intimately connected to the mystery of life, to the divine within.

***VeTen ḥelkeinu beToratekha*, "Grant our portion in your Torah."**

With these words, we are asking about our path in life. As we saw, this general concern appears in several contexts in the siddur and in Rabbinic Literature and may not be directly connected with Shabbat. One way to interpret this phrase is simply, "that we occupy ourselves with Torah and mitzvot," as the late 19th-century Rabbi Yitzḥak Eliyahu Landau put it.[390] Another interpretation comes from the medieval (14th c., Spain) commentator, Rabbi David Abudraham: "Let the Torah be as close to you as [your] betrothed fiancée."[391] This last comment may contain within it a kernel of inspiration for moderns if one penetrates a bit underneath the archetypal gender language. It is asking that the Torah be with us as closely as we would hold the object of new love, of young love, of passionate love. Almost: Let us lust for Torah. A key for moderns is to go beyond defining Torah so clearly as "Torah and mitzvot." Perhaps we need to apply Bob Dylan's words to what "Torah" means when, regarding "good and bad," he sang sarcastically, "I define these terms quite clear, no doubt, somehow. Ah, but I was so much older then, I'm younger than that now."[392] If Torah only means observing mitzvot in exactly the way a previous generation defined it, the way a book defines it, then it is "quite clear, no doubt," and narrowly defined. But it may also be thought of as a way of looking at life. Let a God's-eye view of life be as close to you as the love of your life. Let the big picture be as close to you as the love of your life. Let the spiritual side of life be as close to you as the love of your life. If so, then this plea, "Grant our portion in your Torah," is

[390] Yitzḥak Eliyahu Landau, in the commentary *Dover Shalom*, in *Siddur Otzar HaTefillot*, I:604.
[391] *Sefer Abudraham HaShaleim*, 146. Based on Ecclesiastes 9:9.
[392] Bob Dylan, *My Back Pages*. Released on Dylan's 1964 album, *Another Side of Bob Dylan*.

an appeal to transcend our narrowness, our self-centeredness, our personal troubles and issues. "Grant our portion in your Torah" could then mean: Grant that we view all from the point of view of Torah. And since "Torah" defies easy definitions, it requires one to transcend the immediate, the material, and the physical.

***Sabeinu mituvekha*, "Satisfy us with your goodness."**

Shabbat is a day on which our lack of productive activity makes us—at least symbolically—more reliant on God's goodness in this material world than on weekdays. I therefore understand "Satisfy us through your goodness" to be a request that on this day on which we take a break from trying to increase our material well-being, we find ourselves to be satisfied with the goodness that already exists in the world, that already exists in our lives. This request comprises just two words and is easily "speed-davenned" and missed. But it is worthy of long and deep contemplation.

***VeTaher libeinu l'ovdekha be'emet***
**"Purify our hearts to serve you in truth."**

Rabbi Landau, quoted above, interprets the phrase in the following way: "Purify our hearts so that we do not have the intention to delight in Shabbat only for the sake of bodily enjoyment, but rather only for the sake of serving you in truth."[393] But perhaps it may be interpreted more expansively as a turn to the divine to stay on the path of truth, with a pure heart. The wording of this line recalls history in the time of Samuel the prophet. In the idealized view of the Bible, the Israelite people at that time squandered a relationship with the ultimate ruler in their desire to appoint a human king. This is akin to the natural human tendency to concretize the spiritual, esthetic, idealistic aspects of life. On some level, that can't be helped because life is lived both in the mystical dimension that defies easy definition—the ways in which we are inspired, enlivened, made to feel whole, to feel in touch with the universe—and on the physical level, here and now, engaged in the world. The mystical dimension is that which motivates us to rise above the routine and mundane. This can happen when we plan it—as in going to a worship service—and it can happen spontaneously in the midst of routine.

And so, this line of prayer, "Purify our hearts to serve you in truth," is challenging us not to ignore the spiritual side of life, and not to settle for less true expressions, or expressions mitigated by others. To not set up a "king"

[393] Yitzḥak Eliyahu Landau, in the commentary "Dover Shalom," in *Siddur Otzar HaTefillot,* I:604.

that will act as the arbiter of the spiritual life for us. It is a call to be active and assertive in seeking the spiritual dimension, the hints and appearances and manifestations of the divine in the world.

Finally, the alternate blessing found in the ancient prayer books:

> Out of your love, the love you have for Israel your people, and out of your compassion, our king, the compassion you have for members of your covenant, you have given to us, *YHVH* our God, this great and holy seventh day for love, for rest, for service, for gratitude, giving—from you to us—life and loving kindness.

This is a paean to a spiritual day off, "this great and holy seventh day." The Sabbath as a gift from God is hinted at twice here ("given to us," "giving—from you to us"). The poet who wrote this felt the "love" and "compassion" behind this gift. This text can be a simple and refreshing change from the inherited passages. A natural response to the emotions of its words can be a deep breath of gratitude.

### *Birkat Mei'ein Sheva*

At the conclusion of the *Amidah*, another blessing is added in the traditional Friday night service that presents a number of interesting problems. This prayer is known *Birkat Mei'ein Sheva*, "The Blessing Summarizing Seven," or as *Berakhah Aḥat Mei'ein Sheva*, "One Blessing Summarizing Seven." The "Seven" in its title refers to the seven blessings of the *Amidah* that had just been recited silently. It appears to be a kind of repetition of the *Amidah* as is common for morning and afternoon services. Yet there is no other example of a repetition of the *Amidah* in an evening service. Repetitions of the *Amidah* originated at a time before the printing press permitted large numbers of people to own their prayer books, and thus read the words of the silent *Amidah*. The audible repetition allowed those worshipers who had not memorized the *Amidah* to fulfill their obligation. The reason there is no other example of such a repetition for an evening service is that the evening *Amidah* is not considered obligatory on the same level as the morning and afternoon *Amidot*. The morning and afternoon *Amidot* more directly parallel the biblically ordained dawn and dusk sacrifices while the evening *Amidah* is recited "merely" by custom... a custom approximately 1,500 years old! While such a longstanding custom may seem quite authoritative, it still doesn't reach the level of a practice parallel to a biblical commandment.

Even if this blessing does represent some kind of repetition of an *Amidah*, it deviates in form from the repetitions that have developed for the morning and afternoon *Amidah*. Those *Amidot* are repeated in almost the exact same wording as the silently recited text whereas the repetition on Friday night is a summary, in much briefer form, of the Shabbat evening *Amidah*. Further, although the *Birkat Mei'ein Sheva* summarizes in very short phrases all seven blessings of the Shabbat evening *Amidah*, it also includes paragraph-long versions of parts of the first and fourth blessings. If those two blessings were already summarized by short phrases, why add these longer versions of the same two blessings? The story gets even more interesting because the part of the first blessing doesn't match the wording of the first blessing in the full, silent, version of the Friday night *Amidah*. Rather, it corresponds to wording found in a thousand-year-old version from the long defunct "Ancient Palestinian Rite" known to us mainly from the Cairo Genizah!

In 1966, Prof. Joseph Heinemann published an article that attempted to resolve all of these conundrums.[394] While he did not, I think, completely settle all of the problems in this fascinating blessing, he did succeed in presenting some compelling theories. What follows is my take on the development of *Birkat Mei'ein Sheva*, using Heinemann's insights, but veering from his approach where I feel it is necessary to comport with the historical and literary evidence.

In fact, *Birkat Mei'ein Sheva* is not a repetition of the silent *Amidah*. Its true origin and role involve unraveling the many relevant sources spanning about a thousand years from the 2nd century CE to about the 12th century CE.

This blessing's history begins with the observation that in the earliest talmudic period, the Tannaitic period, rabbis and those Jews who followed them likely did not recite an *Amidah* in the evening as they did in the morning and in the afternoon. This was for the same reason that—once an evening *Amidah* did develop later in history—there are no repetitions of an evening *Amidah*: An evening *Amidah* does not parallel a biblically-ordained sacrifice as the morning and afternoon *Amidot* do.

There is evidence however, that at least one influential rabbi, Rabbi Tsadok who lived in the land of Israel in this early period, recited an *Amidah* one evening each week—Friday night—in honor of Shabbat.[395] Perhaps he felt

[394] Joseph Heinemann, "One Benediction Comprising Seven," *Revue Des Etudes Juives*, #125 (1966), 101-111.
[395] *Tosefta Berakhot* 3:7, end.

the desire to recite an *Amidah* on this night because of the special holiness of Shabbat.

Now, in a puzzling talmudic passage from a later period, it was reported that in Babylonia, there was a practice to recite a "*Berakhah Aḥat Mei'ein Sheva*," "One Blessing Summarizing Seven," not in place of an *Amidah*, but rather, in place of the Friday night *Kiddush* when wine was not available.[396] It is known from several talmudic sources that wine was scarce in the Babylonian Jewish community at different times. Apparently, a text of a Friday night *Amidah*, one that appeared so brief as to "summarize" a lengthier version, was being recited in Babylonia to replace the *Kiddush* when wine was not obtainable. That practice did not develop in ancient Palestine because wine was not rare there. And this summary of a Friday night *Amidah* was adapted as a kind of substitute *Kiddush* because it emphasized Shabbat, just as the text of the *Kiddush* does. The theory is that this substitute for the *Kiddush* was akin to the text that Rabbi Tsadok had earlier innovated as a proto-*Amidah* for Friday night in the Land of Israel before it became customary for everyone to recite a full *Amidah* on Friday nights. There probably were a number of such unofficial prayers that circulated among Jewish communities in the Land of Israel and one of those proto-*Amidot* reached and was recited in Babylonia even after reciting a full *Amidah* became customary. Therefore, synagogue services on Friday nights during the later talmudic period in Babylonia contained both a full *Amidah* as well as a shorter, proto-*Amidah* that seemed to summarize that full *Amidah*.

All of that might explain how an early version of a Friday night *Amidah* that first appeared in ancient Palestine was used in Babylonia as an alternative *Kiddush* when wine was not available. But once an expanded text of the Friday night *Amidah* was established, and the availability of wine was no longer an issue in Babylonia and elsewhere in the Jewish world as the centuries progressed, why was this mini-*Amidah* retained in the Friday night liturgy, directly after the full silent *Amidah*? The answer appears to be that, as is often the case in liturgical history, once a text has become part of the liturgy, it tends to stay in the liturgy even when its original purpose (here: to replace the *Kiddush* when wine was scarce) may have been lost. The very presence of this blessing in the liturgy over a period of many years bequeathed a kind of holiness to the blessing. Add to this the fact that once its original purpose was forgotten over time, another, different, purpose

[396] Palestinian Talmud *Berakhot* 11d, *Pesaḥim* 37c.

was assigned to it, and the survival of this blessing over nearly 2,000 years becomes clearer.

Prior to Prof. Heinemann's research, tradition assigned a rationale to this blessing. This explanation probably should be abandoned in the face of Prof. Heinemann's conclusions, however, it is quite intriguing in its own right. This explanation connects *Birkat Mei'ein Sheva* with demonology.

The new rationale for this blessing began when medieval scholars resolved a puzzling passage in the Babylonian Talmud by tying it to *Birkat Mei'ein Sheva*. The passage asserts that there would be no worship service on the eve of a Festival unless it coincided with Shabbat.[397] This assertion is immediately contradicted by the claim that even on Shabbat there would be no worship service except that the Sages instituted one "because of danger" (*mishum sakanah*). Perhaps this teaching reaches back to a time when a regular evening service had not yet been established for the eve of a Festival. However, this text was confusing to medieval commentators because by their time, a worship service always occurred on the eve of a Festival whether or not it coincided with Shabbat. Therefore, Rashi (died 1105) interpreted that this passage was not actually referring to an entire worship service, but rather just to the blessing we are discussing, *Birkat Mei'ein Sheva*. The strength of this argument is that it accorded with the medieval practice known to Rashi and his contemporaries: they did not recite the *Birkat Mei'ein Sheva* on Friday nights that coincided with a Festival. The weakness is that the talmudic text does not actually mention *Birkat Mei'ein Sheva*! Nevertheless, Rashi's authority was very great, and his interpretation became accepted.

At this point, what needed explaining was exactly what the Talmud meant when it said the evening worship service (now understood to refer only to *Birkat Mei'ein Sheva*) was instituted only "because of danger." What danger was addressed by reciting this blessing?

The danger was linked to another text in the Babylonian Talmud in which Rabbi Yossi ben Rabbi Yehudah instructed Rabbi Yehudah HaNasi not to go out alone at night.[398] This warning is further limited to avoid going out alone at night on Tuesday nights and Friday nights because of a female demon named Igrat bat Maḥalat. A Tannaitic teaching is quoted as follows:

> A person should not go out on Tuesday nights or Friday nights because of Igrat bat Maḥalat. She and 18,000 angels

---

[397] Babylonian Talmud, *Shabbat* 24b.
[398] Babylonian Talmud, *Pesaḥim* 112b.

> of destruction go out (at that time), and each one of its own has the authority to destroy.[399]

This is then commented on by a later stratum on the same page of the Talmud as follows:

> At first, they were found every day (i.e., the angels of destruction were found not just on Tuesday and Friday nights). Then one time, she (Igrat bat Maḥalat) encountered Rabbi Ḥanina ben Dosa (who had a reputation of possessing miraculous powers). She said to him, "If it weren't that they say about you in heaven: beware of Ḥanina and his Torah, I would have attacked[400] you." He (Rabbi Ḥanina ben Dosa) said to her, "If I am thought of so highly in heaven, I decree that you never pass through areas inhabited by people!" She said to him, "Please, give me a little space." So, he permitted her Friday nights and Tuesday nights.
>
> And also (an alternative version of the story is told): One time, she encountered Abayyei (another talmudic sage). She said to him, "If it weren't that they say about you in heaven: beware of Naḥamani (another name for Abayyei) and his Torah, I would have attacked you." He said to her, "If I am thought of so highly in heaven, I decree that you never pass through areas inhabited by people!" But (objects the anonymous voice of the Talmud), we see that she does pass through (areas inhabited by people)! They explained: That is only when their horses bolt and veer from their paths and bring them (the demons) along (to areas inhabited by people).

Quite a pair of stories! Rashi connected this talmudic passage about the danger of encountering the evil spirit Igrat bat Maḥalat and her minions with the previous passage which asserted that *Birkat Mei'ein Sheva* was instituted

[399] She is mentioned as well on the page before this one in the BabylonianTalmud, *Pesaḥim* 111a, as part of an incantation. The name *Igrat* may refer to one who is "armed." The name *Maḥalat* is related to the root for "disease" and, according to Genesis 28:9, was the name of a daughter of Ishmael whom Esau took as a wife. In Jewish tradition, both Ishmael and Esau were negative figures and so, it is not entirely surprising to find the name of Ishmael's daughter associated with a demon.

[400] The Aramaic word for "attacked" here, *sakintikh*, shares the same root as the Hebrew word for "danger," which, along with the mention of Friday nights, connects with the previous passage about *Birkat Mei'ein Sheva*.

only "because of danger." Rashi explained that the danger was encountering demons after services on Friday night, and, in fact, because there were always some latecomers to the Friday night service, *Birkat Mei'ein Sheva* was instituted to lengthen the service. This would allow latecomers to catch up to the rest of the congregation and then everyone would leave together. This blessing was established in order that individuals who came late to the service would not have to walk home individually when they might encounter demons. Recall that the "danger" mentioned in the talmudic text was only when one went out on Tuesday nights and Friday nights "alone."

Another medieval liturgical compendium that also preserves traditions from the school of Rashi, *Maḥzor Vitry* (ca. 12th century), has a slightly different explanation.[401] It, too, begins by saying that *Birkat Mei'ein Sheva* was instituted "because of danger," that is, Igrat bat Maḥalat and her 18,000 demons. But it continues by saying that even according to the version in which Abayyei forbade these evil spirits to ever enter inhabited areas, there is still "danger" from the spirits of the dead who dwell in the synagogue for 12 months after death. The danger was that these spirits would attack any latecomer who was left praying alone in the synagogue after the rest of the congregation had left. Again, according to this explanation, *Birkat Mei'ein Sheva* was added so that everyone would leave together and no individual would be susceptible to demonic attack. According to the 16th-century *Shulḥan Arukh*, which is still the authoritative guide to practice for traditional Judaism, *Birkat Mei'ein Sheva* is not recited on a Friday night when a service is held in a private house of a groom or in a house of mourning because people do not come late to those services.[402] Similarly, *Birkat Mei'ein Sheva* is not recited when the first night of *Pesaḥ* coincides with a Friday night because the first night of *Pesaḥ* is traditionally known as *leil shimurim*, "a night of protection"—just as the Israelites were protected on that night from the angel of death who slayed the first-born Egyptians, contemporary Jews find protection on that night from demonic forces.[403]

## Spiritual Commentary on *Birkat Mei'ein Sheva*

If one approached this prayer from a traditional perspective and wished to find reasons to recite *Birkat Mei'ein Sheva* with meaning, one could cite a

[401] Aryeh Goldschmidt, ed., *Maḥzor Vitry* by Rabbi Simḥah bar Shmuel (Jerusalem: Mekhon Otsar Ha-Poskim, 2004), I:172-173.
[402] *Shulḥan Arukh, Oraḥ Ḥayyim* 268:10.
[403] *Shulḥan Arukh, Oraḥ Ḥayyim* 487:1 and see commentary of *Mishneh Berurah*, #9.

few possibilities. Chanting this blessing to keep in mind its colorful history, for example.

The Conservative siddur simply comments, "The Amidah is never repeated aloud in any evening service, but on Shabbat we celebrate the day by including each of the themes of the Amidah in a single *b'rakhah*, which we chant or sing aloud after the conclusion of the silent Amidah."[404] The value of preserving this blessing is assumed and not addressed here; the comment is merely descriptive of what is done. However, the Reconstructionist siddur offers that the blessing "provides a joyous communal reprise of the themes first invoked in the privacy of the *Amidah*."[405] In other words, it can be "joyous" to sing together the themes that were just recited silently by the congregation as individuals.

Approaching this prayer from a non-traditional perspective, that is, without an a priori commitment to retaining it just because it has been part of the liturgy, it is harder to advance a defense that is true to spiritual experience. Chanting a prayer in order to invoke its history could be an inspirational act if that history actually resonated with modern sensibilities. In the case of this blessing, however, it would be difficult to argue that moderns would connect spiritually with the history of the blessing, as interesting as it is. The fact that it originally served as an alternative *Kiddush* in ancient Babylonia when wine was scarce, while interesting on an intellectual level, would probably not spiritually move moderns. Similarly, while it might be alluring to learn of the connection between this blessing and demonology, it is hard to imagine moderns welcoming a blessing whose function it was to lengthen the service so worshipers would not have to walk home without the protection of a group, vulnerable to attack by demons.

Perhaps, however, liberal Jews might appreciate the freshness of occasionally substituting *Birkat Mei'ein Sheva* for the traditional Friday night *Amidah*. Both feature the very same themes, but *Birkat Mei'ein Sheva* does so in a briefer manner, using some different wording that harks back to the ancient Palestinian rite.

---

[404] *Siddur Lev Shalem*, (New York: The Rabbinical Assembly, 2016), 53.
[405] *Kol Haneshamah: Shabbat Veḥagim*, (Elkins Park, Pennsylvania: The Reconstructionist Press, 2004), 110.

# Shabbat *Shaḥarit* (Morning Service)

## *Nishmat Kol Ḥai*

The first major difference between the weekday and the Shabbat *Shaḥarit* service is found at the conclusion of *Pesukei DeZimra*. On weekdays, *Yishtabaḥ* is the blessing that forms the concluding bookend paralleling the opening bookend of *Barukh She'Amar*. On Shabbat and festivals, *Yishtabaḥ* itself constitutes the concluding paragraph of a much longer poem called (after its first three words) *Nishmat Kol Ḥai*, "The Breath of All." I will briefly survey some of the history of its text and then analyze its very interesting literary structure.

When the Mishnah discusses the Passover *Seder*, it says that the chanting of *Hallel* (Psalms 114-118) is followed by *Birkat HaShir*, "The Blessing of Song."[406] Two sages of the Talmud differed in their identification of the source of this blessing.[407] One held that this blessing is *Yehallelukha*, "May They Bless You." The blessing concluding *Hallel* in post-talmudic prayer collections begins with the word *Yehallelukha*. The other held that it was *Nishmat Kol Ḥai*. As is typical of the Talmud, the full versions of these prayers are not recorded, assuming, perhaps, that its readers were quite familiar with the wording. We cannot, therefore, be confident that extant versions completely match the Talmudic wording.[408] Since the Talmud does not come to a conclusion as to which one of these is *Birkat HaShir*, many *Haggadot* include both. Nevertheless, only *Nishmat Kol Ḥai* concludes *Pesukei DeZimra* on Shabbat and festivals.

A series of verses found in *Nishmat Kol Ḥai* is also cited as one talmudic sage's version of a blessing to be recited upon the appearance of rain after a drought.[409] The series of verses begins "Were our mouths as full as song as the sea and our mouths [full of] song as the roar of the sea..., we

[406] *Mishnah Pesaḥim* 10:7.

[407] Babylonian Talmud *Pesaḥim* 118a.

[408] An interesting connection between current versions of *Yehallukha* and *Nishmat Kol Ḥai* is that they both share the exact wording of one sentence: *yodu vivarkhu vishabḥu vifa'aru viromemu vaya'aritzu veyakdishu veyamlikhu et shimkha malkeinu*, "let them thank and bless and praise and exalt and glorify and exalt and sanctify and accept the sovereignty of your name, our king." Whether one blessing borrowed this wording from the other is not clear. An amazing cantorial rendition of this line, emphasizing, in staccato fashion, the repetition of the eight synonymic verbs in a row, was recorded by Yossele Rosenblatt. This famous version is found, among other places, on *The Complete Cantorial Collection*, Israel Music, Tel-Aviv, 2006, and in various places on the Internet.

[409] *Mishnah Berakhot* 9:2; Babylonian Talmud *Berakhot* 59b. The citation in the Talmud is *Ilu finu malei shirah kayam*, etc., *ein anu maspikim lehodot lekha Adonai Eloheinu ad 'tishtaḥaveh,'* "Were our mouth as full of song as the sea, etc., we still would not adequately thank you, Adonai, our God, until 'bow.'" This parallels over one hundred words in the modern version of *Nishmat*, but again, it is not clear what the version was in the talmudic period.

still would not adequately thank you." Perhaps the two allusions to water comprise the connection to the rain that the blessing celebrates. It may be that one blessing borrowed the phrase from the other or it could have been a stock expression of praise.[410]

A remarkable comment found in the 12th-century *Maḥzor Vitry* and other contemporaneous sources denies that the author of *Nishmat Kol Ḥai* was Simon (also called Peter), the apostle of Jesus! If this suggestion had to be denied, it is evident that at least some people were asserting that this was, indeed, the author:

> There are those who say that that scoundrel Simon Peter the ass[411] is the author of this, and other, prayers, when he was on the rock. This is an error [worthy of] hell. God forbid that such a thing should occur among Israel. Anyone who makes this claim will have to bring a big, fat, sin offering when the Temple is rebuilt.[412]

This tradition can be traced back to a short medieval Jewish text sometimes called *Aggadeta deShimon Kefa*, "The *Aggadah* of Simon Kefa (*Kefa*

[410] When the Talmud discusses at what point, early in the rainy season, one should recite the blessing over rain (i.e., when the first droplets appear or when the rain is steady), it replies, "From the time the groom goes out to meet the bride," that is, when drops of rain ricochet from puddles back up toward the rain that is falling. Barry Freundel suggests that because marriage imagery is associated in rabbinic literature with Shabbat, *Nishmat Kol Ḥai* was transferred from the *Haggadah* to the conclusion of *Pesukei DeZimra* on Shabbat (and from there, to the pilgrimage festivals). See Barry Freundel, *Why We Pray What We Pray: The Remarkable History of Jewish Prayer* (Jerusalem, New York: Urim Publications, 2010), 83-91. While that is possible, marriage imagery is found in many settings in rabbinic literature, and even granting the major connection between marriage imagery and Shabbat, there are literally dozens of other images in this long prayer, and the groom/bride image to which he refers isn't even mentioned in the prayer itself; it is mentioned in the context of another setting (the onset of rain) for one passage from this prayer. More evidence than this is needed before one can account for the transference of *Nishmat* from *Pesaḥ* to Shabbat. Below, I suggest a connection between the very beginning of *Nishmat* and the wording of the service on Shabbat morning just before and just after its location in the service.

[411] A play on Exodus 34:20, *u'feter ḥamor*, "the firstling of an ass." Reading the Hebrew word *feter*, "firstling" as a transliteration, the phrase may be read as "Peter, the ass."

[412] Aryeh Goldschmidt, ed., *Maḥzor Vitry* by Rabbi Simḥah bar Shmuel (Jerusalem: Mekhon Otsar Ha-Poskim, 2004), II: 412. And see the notes there regarding the other prayers attributed to Simon the apostle. The editor, in n. 20, observes that the previous critical edition of *Maḥzor Vitry* (the 1860 edition edited by Simeon Hurwitz and Heinrich Brody) emended this passage to read *ta'ut shel Roma* ("error of Rome") by changing the *dalet* of *Duma* ("Hell") to a *resh* ("Roma"). The editor criticizes this emendation since there is, he claims, support for understanding the image of *Duma* itself as a symbol of Rome, and then marshals as evidence the Palestinian Talmud *Avodah Zarah* 3:6 and *Bereishit Rabba* 39. However, I find no support for this claim in those two passages, though there is support in another place in the Palestinian Talmud, namely, *Ta'anit* 1:1, 64a, in which it is said that in Rabbi Meir's copy of The Book of Isaiah, the prophecy of doom pronounced against the locale called "Duma" is identified in a note as Rome.

is Aramaic for "Peter," i.e., "rock," a reference to Matthew 16:13-19).[413] The identification of the author of *Nishmat Kol Ḥai* with the apostle Peter must be regarded as in the realm of myth since there is no historical evidence to support it. However, the attribution of this prayer to Simon/Peter the Apostle is part of a larger, extraordinary, legend found in these texts. According to these teachings, Simon/Peter, an elder among the Jews at the time of Jesus, volunteered to "go undercover," as it were, and infiltrate the newly emerging Christian religion in order to protect Jews and Judaism. Christian tradition teaches that Simon/Peter was made the first bishop of Rome (and so, the first Pope). These medieval Jewish traditions claim that this appointment was all part of the Jewish Simon/Peter's plan. In Rome, he had a tower built for himself wherein he could live alone and conduct a secret Jewish life, while at the same time, he could issue laws that both separated Christianity from Jewish practice and also denigrated Christian religion, thus protecting Judaism. He also issued instructions not to harm Jewish communities and individuals. These legends go on to say that during his years in Rome, he composed numerous liturgical poems.[414]

One theory proposes that *Nishmat Kol Ḥai* was identified as one of the hymns composed by Simon/Peter because this prayer contains wording clearly asserting that there is no other god or savior other than the one God:[415]

> And other than you, we have no king who redeems, saves (*moshi'a*, same root as *Yeshu*, Jesus), rescues, sustains and deals mercifully at every instance of difficulty and distress. We have no king but you...

[413] Three versions of this tradition were published by Adolph Jellinek: *Bet ha-Midrasch: Sammlung kleiner Midraschim und vermischter Abhandlungen aus der alteren judischen Literatur* (Wien, 1873; Jerusalem, 1938), Vol. V, 60-62; (Wien, 1878; Jerusalem, 1938), Vol. VI, 9-11; 155-156. English translations and analysis may be found in Wout Van Bekkum, "The Rock on Which the Church is Founded: Simon Peter in Jewish Folktale," in Marcel Poorthuis, Joshua Schwartz, eds., *Saints and Role Models in Judaism and Christianity* (Leiden: Brill, 2004), 289-310. See also *Idem*, "The Poetical Qualities of the Apostle Peter in Jewish Folktale," *Zutot* (Leiden: Brill, 2004), 16-25.

[414] Samuel David Luzzatto (1800-1865), in the introduction to the Italian Prayer Book, mentions him as the author of a hymn for *Yom Kippur* and cites a *responsum* by Rabbenu Tam (1100-1171) establishing Simon/Peter as the author of another *piyyut* for *Yom Kippur*. See the citations in van Wout, "The Rock on Which the Church is Founded," 307, and notes 69-71.

[415] See Freundel, *Why We Pray What We Pray*, 103-106. He writes "...support was found for the claim that Simon Peter composed *Nishmat* while he was Pope from the text of the liturgy itself" without identifying who actually found such support. Allow me to add that I am aware that Rabbi Freundel was convicted of a crime and was imprisoned because of it. My citation of his scholarly work does not, of course, imply any endorsement of his criminal activity, but rather a recognition that since no individual may be reduced to just one facet of their lives; his scholarship does not deserve to be ignored.

While this is reasonable, it must also be admitted that this passage from *Nishmat Kol Ḥai* constitutes a very small segment of this long prayer.

More deserving of support is Freundel's proposal for the reason the *Sheli'aḥ Tzibbur* leading *Shaḥarit* in Ashkenazic custom begins chanting from the words *shokhen ad* within *Nishmat Kol Ḥai* instead of from *Barkhu*, which would make much more sense because that actually is the beginning of *Shaḥarit*. The suggestion is that the letter *shin* (the first letter of Shimon, "Simon" in Hebrew) with which *shokhen ad* begins is, according to a folk tradition, meant to invoke the name Shimon, which itself is encoded and spelled backwards over various intervals in *Nishmat Kol Ḥai*.[416] While I would wish for more substantiation of this theory (and at the same time understanding that the lack of documentation may have been a result of perceived self-protection), it is certainly suggestive.

In any case, the wording of this lengthy blessing is nearly identical in all rites which may attest to its ancient pedigree.[417]

The location of this prayer at the conclusion of *Pesukei DeZimra* may be related to the fact that its first words parallel those of the last verse of Psalm 150 which was recited in *Pesukei DeZimra*. Thus, this prayer begins by invoking the last words of that psalm:

**Psalm 150:** *Kol ha-neshamah...* ("all that breathes...").

**The prayer:** *Nishmat kol ḥai* ("The breath of all").

This literary link may continue toward the beginning of the next section of the service, in *Shaḥarit* itself. There, the prayer *Eil Adon* contains wording that adds another echo to the end of Psalm 150 and the beginning of *Nishmat Kol Ḥai*:

**Psalm 150:** *Kol ha-neshamah...* ("all that breathes...").

***Eil Adon:*** *Kol neshamah* ("everyone that breathes").

These three exemplars of nearly identical wording may constitute an aural thread connecting *Pesukei DeZimra* with *Shaḥarit*.

An important key to the literary structure of the *Nishmat Kol Ḥai* in general is that its author was very fond of lists; there are several individual lists, or litanies, of praises within it. The lists are not merely individual thought-units within a longer piece; rather, they connect to form an extended and complete thought. That thought is: Even though the gratitude to God that

[416] The folk tradition is mentioned by J.D. Eisenstein, *A Digest of Jewish Laws and Customs* [Hebrew] (New York: Hebrew Publishing Company, 1938), 279. My thanks to my colleague, Prof. David Golinkin, for this citation.

[417] Elbogen, *Jewish Liturgy*, 96.

our puny bodies are capable of expressing is wholly inadequate, all we have is our bodies, and therefore it falls to us to use all the parts and powers of our bodies to do our inadequate best in expressing our thankfulness to God. This message is climaxed by two midrashic interpretations of Scripture with the individual units within the prayer (some of them containing their own midrashic citations of, or expansions on, biblical verses) building toward them. Because of that, the whole prayer may, in a sense, be viewed as one long poetic midrash.[418]

The first midrashic interpretation is of "All of my bones shall say who is like You" (Psalms 35:10), taking this phrase to mean that our limbs themselves ought to be the vehicles of praise to God, and that we should not only use verbal praise. The second is extracted from Psalms 103:1, "[Let] my soul bless the Lord and [let] all my innards [bless] his holy name." "Soul" and "innards," taken together, add up to one's entire physical body. The idea of using one's physical body in praise of God is rare in Jewish liturgy, where oral expression is the default mode; this prayer stands out in its call for whole-body worship.

The art of this prayer is how the individual lists are woven together, creating the larger call for worship through the physicality of the human body. The following is a chart of the essence of this long liturgical composition that tracks how the lists form the larger message. **The bolded words** serve as key phrases in the narrative arc of the poem:

**The breath of all blesses your name...**
Beside you, we have no
King
Redeemer
Savior
Liberator
Rescuer
Sustainer
And merciful one
At every time of trouble and distress.
Aside from you, we have no king... (Note how this last phrase parallels the phrase at the beginning of this list).

[418] I thank Professor Avraham Holtz, one of my first teachers of Jewish liturgy, for this insight.

*YHVH* "does not sleep nor slumber" (Psalms 121:4)
He wakes the sleeping
Arouses the slumbering
Gives speech to the dumb
Supports the fallen
Raises the bowed low

**IF ONLY:**

| PARTS OF THE BODY | DESCRIPTION | ALLEGORY |
|---|---|---|
| Our mouths (were) | Full of song | As the sea |
| Our tongues | (Full of) exultation | As the roar of its waves |
| Our lips | (Full of) praise | As the breadth of the sky |
| Our eyes | Shining | As the sun and moon |
| Our hands | Outstretched | As the eagles of the heavens |
| Our feet | Swift | As deer |

**WE WOULD STILL NOT MANAGE TO THANK YOU (BECAUSE):**

| OUR SITUATION | GOD'S SALVATION OF US |
|---|---|
| From Egypt | You redeemed us |
| From the House of Bondage | You saved us |
| In famine | You fed us |
| In plenty | You sustained us |
| From the sword | You rescued us |
| From plague | You sheltered us |
| From severe enduring sickness | You released us |

**THEREFORE...**

| PARTS OF OUR BODY | WHICH YOU PUT IN US |
|---|---|

| | |
|---|---|
| Limbs | Which you placed within us |
| Spirit and Breath | Which you blew into our nostrils |
| Tongue | Which you put into our mouths |

**THEY THEMSELVES (SHALL)...**

Thank
Bless
Praise
Extol
Exalt
Glorify
Sanctify
Crown

**BECAUSE EVERY...**

| BODY PART | WILL EXTOL GOD IN THESE WAYS |
|---|---|
| Mouth (shall) | Acknowledge you |
| Tongue (shall) | Swear allegiance to you |
| Knee | Shall bend to you |
| Back | Shall bow to you |
| Heart (shall) | Stand in awe of you |
| Innard and Entrail | Shall sing to your name |

**AS IT IS WRITTEN, "ALL MY BONES SHALL SAY WHO IS LIKE YOU..." (PSALMS 35:10).**[419]

Who compares to you?
Who is equal to you?
Who matches you?

"God great, mighty and awesome" (Deut. 10:17).
"Supernal God, creator of heaven and earth" (Gen. 14:19).

---

[419] Elsewhere, this verse is also cited as a possible text for the congregation's response in an undertone to the prayer leader's chanting of *Modim*, "we acknowledge" in the midst of the *Amidah* and this, too, is a moment of physicality, namely bowing. See Palestinian Talmud, *Berakhot* 1:8, 3d.

We shall sing to you
We shall praise you
We shall extol you
We shall bless your holy name

**AS IT SAYS, "OF DAVID: LET MY SOUL BLESS GOD, LET ALL MY INNARDS (BLESS) YOUR HOLY NAME" (PSALMS 103:1).**

(Now expanding on each word of Deut. 10:17, quoted above):

GOD in the power of your strength
GREAT through the glory of your name
MIGHTY forever
AWESOME in your awesomeness

Thus, the separate components of the poem—many of which comprise lists and encompass biblical verses accompanied by midrashic interpolations—add up to a greater whole: An artful appeal for the worshiper to use the entire body in expressing praise and gratitude to God.

### Spiritual Commentary on *Nishmat Kol Ḥai*

If any prayer called out for expression in movement, it is *Nishmat Kol Ḥai.* To merely recite the words of the prayer seems to miss its very point: All parts of our body must be marshalled to express the gratitude that is due to God for sustaining us in every way. That is both the least we can do and the most we can do. And the prayer makes the case that we ought to convey our thanks for God's steadfastness in good times and in bad. The recitation of this prayer calls for swaying in one's seat. It also calls for dance. It calls for creative souls to compose melodies for parts or all of the poem so that it may be sung and danced to at joyous occasions, and not just at *Shaḥarit* of Shabbat and holidays.[420] It also lends itself to guided meditation of bringing various parts of the body into service of the divine.

Given the religious polemic involved in attributing the prayer to Simon/Peter, recitation of this prayer also calls for some thought about the division and conflict that religion has wrought, along with all of the beauty that re-

[420] As we've seen, this prayer migrated from one place in the liturgy—the *Haggadah shel Pesaḥ*—to another, the conclusion of *Pesukei DeZimra* on Shabbat and Festivals. Both of these became permanent locations for it. I encourage us to consider other places that the prayer, as a whole or in part, may contribute to the spirit of an occasion on a temporary or one-time basis. It conjures, for me, the Dixie Chicks' 1999 song "Some Days You Gotta Dance."

ligion brings. In opposition to the Jewish-Christian clash embedded in the prayer's history, the opening words of the prayer strike a note of universality:

> The breath of **all that lives** shall bless your name, and the spirit of **all flesh** shall glorify and exalt you forever.

The substantial fruits rewarding close reading of this prayer leads one to lament the fact that this richness is usually missed not only by the many worshipers who tend to arrive at the service after *Nishmat Kol Ḥai* is recited, but also by those who might speed-daven through it.

## *Eil Adon*

*Eil Adon*, "God, the Master" is one of several *piyyutim* (liturgical poems) or *piyyut* fragments embedded in the first blessing before *Keri'at Shema* (the recitation of the *Shema*) in *Shaḥarit shel Shabbat* (the morning service on the Sabbath) in the Ashkenazic rite. It is encountered soon after the opening of this blessing which is known as *Birkat Yotser Or*, "The Blessing of the Creator of Light."

The placement of this *piyyut* within this particular blessing is not by accident. The theme of the blessing is the daily rising of the sun at dawn and the various *piyyutim* and *piyyut* fragments contain poetic outpourings in response to the daily renewal of sunlight. In the version of this blessing recited on Shabbat morning, dawn occasions poetry—filtered through biblical creation imagery from Genesis, chapter 1—extolling God's creative power and celebrating the sun, moon, stars, and angels. One would, therefore, expect *Eil Adon*—a poem embedded in *Birkat Yotser Or*, a blessing celebrating dawn—to contain references to the newly visible light, and indeed it does. We will find that this is a major theme of *Eil Adon*, though it is refracted not only through the language of the Bible's creation story, but also through Ezekiel's vision of God on the "chariot." These two scriptural passages are, not coincidentally, the two most famous biblical foci of early Jewish mystical contemplation and are known as *Ma'aseh Bereshit* ("The Enterprise of Creation") and *Ma'aseh Merkavah* ("The Chariot Enterprise").

We will see that the main message of *Eil Adon* is that the luminaries in the sky—the sun, moon, and stars—are considered angel-like entities. And just as other angels praise God through singing in the prayer that soon follows this one, the *Kedushah DeYotser*, the angelic heavenly lights praise God by means of shining their light. It is because of this that *Eil Adon* is filled with praise to God for the return of sunlight at dawn. There is no Shabbat symbolism at all in this prayer and, indeed, Sepharadim recite *Eil Adon* on Festivals as well as on Shabbat.[421]

Ezra Fleischer, one of the most important modern scholars of Jewish liturgy—especially regarding the role of texts found in the Cairo Genizah—commented that *Eil Adon* properly comes before *Kedushah DeYotser* and is meant to thematically prepare the worshiper for it.[422] The form of the *Kedushah* that appears in *Birkat Yotser Or* contains a number of images related to creation that other forms of the *Kedushah* lack.[423] The specific connection that Fleischer noted was, that at the very least, both *Eil Adon* and *Kedushah DeYotser* prominently mention several classes of angels. Beyond that, however, it is likely that the author of *Eil Adon* viewed the sun, moon, and stars themselves as angelic beings. As will be demonstrated below, these beings are portrayed in *Eil Adon* as conscious entities who participate in the cosmic praise of God. Therefore, just as the angels that Isaiah and Ezekiel saw and heard glorify God through chant, so too do the sun, moon, and stars glorify God—but in their own way—fulfilling the verse from Psalm 19:2, *Ha-shamayim mesaprim kevod Eil, u'ma'aseh yadav magid ha-raki'a*, "The heavens declare the glory of God, the sky proclaims His handiwork."

Ismar Elbogen says little about the history of *Eil Adon* except that it is found in all the rites.[424] That usually means that this poem entered the prayer book at a very early stage. However, it cannot reliably be said that it is found in the earliest prayer books in our possession.[425] Perhaps the first prayer

---

[421] Macy Nulman, *The Encyclopedia of Jewish Prayer: Ashkenazic and Sephardic Rites* (Northvale, New Jersey: Jason Aaronson, Inc., 1993), 61.

[422] *LeTefutsatan shel Kedushot HaAmidah VeHaYotser BeMinhagot HaTefillah shel Benei Erets Yisrael* ("On the Spread of the *Kedushot* of the *Amidah* and of (*Birkat*) *Yotser* Among the Inhabitants of the Land of Israel"), *Tarbitz* 38 (1969), 270-271.

[423] ***Borei*** *kedoshim* ("**Creator** of holy ones <= angels>"), ***Yotser*** *meshortim* ("**Maker** of those who serve <angels>"), *Retson* ***Konam*** ("the will of their <i.e., of the angels'> **Originator**"), ***LeYotsram*** ("their <the angels'> **Maker**").

[424] Ismar Elbogen, *Jewish Liturgy*, 96.

[425] It appears in only one of the several extant manuscripts of what is functionally the earliest prayer book (actually a long *teshuvah*, or *responsum*), *Seder Rav Amram* from the 9th century CE. Nevertheless, the manuscript tradition for *Seder Rav Amram* is irreparably compromised. Since it carries such great authority, later generations inserted—knowingly or not—prayers that were not found in the original version of *Seder Rav Amram*. See Daniel Goldschmidt, ed., *Seder Rav Amram* (Jerusalem: Mossad Ha-rav Kook, 1971), 71. It does not appear at all in the 10th-century *Siddur Rabbi Sa'adia Gaon*, I. Davidson, S. Assaf, B. I. Joel, eds. (Reuven Mass, Jerusalem: Mekitse Nirdamim, 1951). The location in this edition of *Siddur Rav Sa'adia* that would parallel the location in which *Eil Adon* is found in later *siddurim* would be 120-121, but *Eil Adon* does not appear there. See Israel Davidson, *Otsar ha-shirah veha-piyyut* ("Thesaurus of Mediaeval Hebrew Poetry") (New York: Jewish Theological Seminary, 1924), I:155, #3320. Nor is *Eil Adon* found in the 11th-12th c. *Maḥzor Vitry*. See Rabbi Simḥah of Vitry, *Maḥzor Vitry* (Jerusalem: Makhon Otsar Ha-Poskim, 2004), 181. Davidson lists Landshuth's theory—recorded also by Elbogen, *Jewish Liturgy*, 96, and by Lawrence A. Hoffman in *My People's Prayer Book, Volume 10, Shabbat Morning*

book that can be said to have definitely included *Eil Adon* is *Siddur Ḥasidei Ashkenaz* (ca. 13th c.).[426]

Meir Bar-Ilan connects this prayer to one of the ancient strands of Jewish mysticism.[427] This literature likely dates from sometime during, or toward the end, of the talmudic era, before the appearance of the first prayer book in the 9th century CE (*Seder Rav Amram*).[428] The particular text in which *Eil Adon* appears within this literature is known today as *Ma'aseh Merkavah*.[429]

That passage closely parallels the second half of *Eil Adon*. The prayer as we know it from the prayer book is an alphabetic acrostic, with consecutive letters of the alphabet beginning each strophe. The passage from *Ma'aseh Merkavah* is not in alphabetical order, and so, Bar-Ilan logically theorizes that the version in the prayer book is later and depended upon the text from *Ma'aseh Merkavah* since alphabetizing can be considered a more developed form of the same passage.

*Eil Adon* is not mentioned in any of the mainstream (i.e., non-mystical) texts of the talmudic era. Therefore, Bar-Ilan's discovery of the text in *Ma'aseh Merkavah*, which seems to be an earlier version of the second half of *Eil Adon*, is quite significant. Bar-Ilan has long championed *Hekhalot* literature

(Woodstock, Vermont: Jewish Lights Publishing, 2007), 81—that *Eil Adon* is an expansion of a *piyyut* in a similar location in *Birkat Yotser Or* in *Shaḥarit shel Ḥol* (weekday morning service) known as *Eil barukh gedol de'ah*. That *piyyut* is an alphabetic acrostic in which each word begins with a letter of the alphabet. *Eil Adon* is an alphabetic acrostic in which each strophe begins with a letter of the alphabet. The fact is, as Fleischer points out (*LeTefutsatan*, 270, n. 53), that only the first four strophes of the two *piyyutim* begin with the same word, and therefore this theory is not very securely grounded.

426 Moshe Hershler, ed., *Siddur Rabbenu Shlomoh, Siddur Ḥasidei Ashkenaz* (Jerusalem: Ḥemed, 1971). 159f.

427 Bar-Ilan, *Sitrei Tefillah V'Hekhalot*, 118.

428 "Any dating of *Ma'aseh Merkavah* is necessarily approximate. The text provides no historical allusions, accurate attributions, or citations in early Rabbinic literature to ground it in history. Therefore, the criteria for dating the text are necessarily literary and stylistic." Michael D. Swartz, *Mystical Prayer in Ancient Judaism: An Analysis of Ma'aseh Merkavah* (Tubingen: J. C. B. Mohr, 1992), 216. Swartz, 218, ultimately says that the text was probably "composed in Palestine between the fourth and seventh centuries." See Ithamar Gruenwald, *From Apocalypticism to Gnosticism: Studies in Apocalypticism, Merkavah Mysticism and Gnosticism* (Frankfurt am Main: Verlag Peter Lang, 1988), 53: "Jewish Apocalypticism and *Merkavah* mysticism are the two kinds of esoteric literature in the time of the Mishnah and the Talmud (ca. 180 BCE to 600 CE)." Rachel Elior, in *The Three Temples: On the Emergence of Jewish Mysticism* (Portland, Oregon: Oxford University Press, 2004), 232, holds that it was created "around the time of the Mishnah and the Talmud." See further in Elior, 232, n. 3, in which she cites other opinions from the earliest views (Tannaitic period—Gershom Scholem and Arthur Green) to the latest period (Peter Schäfer, who places Hekhalot literature in a range from the late talmudic period to well into the Geonic era).

429 *Ma'aseh Merkavah* was published by Alexander Altmann in 1946 in "Shirei Kedushah BeSifrut HaHekhalot HaKedumah," *Melilah*, 2, 1-24. Gershom Scholem published the entire text in 1960 in his *Jewish Gnosticism, Merkavah Mysticism, and Talmudic Tradition* (New York, 1960; rev. ed. 1965), 103-117, although Scholem did not acknowledge Altmann's prior publication. It is also included in Peter Schäfer's critical edition of *Hekhalot* literature, *Synopse zur Hekhalot-Literatur* (Tubingen: J. C. B. Mohr, 1981). The specific parallel passage containing the passage which parallels the second half of *Eil Adon* is found in Schafer, *Synopse*, 230.

as the origin of a great deal of Jewish liturgy, while many talmudic scholars of his generation have been skeptical. In the case of *Eil Adon*, Bar-Ilan seems to be on solid ground.[430]

The poem is in the form of an alphabetic acrostic consisting of twenty-two strophes.[431] The subject of the first eight strophes is God. They describe what seem to be God's supernal attributes filling the world and surrounding God. They furthermore describe the setting of the poem: It is a vision of God seated upon "his throne" (*khis'o*) which, in turn, sits upon the "the chariot" (*Merkavah*). The chariot, in turn, is held aloft by the heavenly creatures (*ḥayot hakodesh*). The scene of God upon a throne supported by celestial creatures—*ḥayot hakodesh*—mentioned in the *heh* line and at the end of the poem, in the *tav* line—as well as the chariot is reminiscent of Ezekiel, with some changes of nomenclature:

The word for throne, *kisei*, is consistent between the poem and Ezekiel (Ez. 1:26, 27). The word *Merkavah*, "chariot," is never used in Ezekiel. Rather, in the Book of Ezekiel, the "vehicle" upon which the throne rests is called a *demut*, "form," and *raki'a*, "expanse" (Ez. 1:22, 23, 25, 26). The term *Merkavah* was conceived by later mystics as the biblical story became the focus of contemplation known as *Ma'aseh Merkavah*, "The Chariot Enterprise." The creatures in Ezekiel are called *ḥayot*, simply "creatures" (Ez. 1:5, and many times in the chapter as well as in 3:13). They are not called *ḥayot hakodesh*, "holy creatures" as in the poem.

In the poem, what may be understood as God's attributes are portrayed as follows: God's "greatness" (*godlo*) and "goodness" (*tuvo*) fill the world, while "knowledge" (*da'at*) and "insight" (*tevunah*) surround God. "Merit" (*zekhut*) and "straightforwardness" (*mishor*), as well as "lovingkindness" (*ḥesed*) and "mercy" (*raḥamim*), are "before" God.

If the subject of the first eight strophes is God, the subjects of the final eighteen strophes are the heavenly luminaries, that is, the sun, moon and stars. Every noun or pronoun in these lines (from the line beginning with the letter *tet* to the end of the acrostic) refers directly to the sources of light in the sky.

These sources of light are either mentioned directly, or are referred to, some eleven times as follows:

---

[430] Ezra Fleischer dated *Eil Adon* to a period earlier than that of the *payyetanim* whose names we know, and on this basis of this, Bar-Ilan dated it to the 3rd or 4th centuries CE. See Fleischer, *LeTefutsatan*, 270 and Bar-Ilan, *Sitrei Tefillah VeHekhalot*, 120.

[431] The letter *sin* appears in *Eil Adon* where one would expect the letter *samekh*. In Medieval Hebrew literature, this is not unusual: the two letters are often used interchangeably.

*Me'orot*—luminaries
*Or*—light
*Shemesh*—sun
*Halevanah*—the moon
*Ziv* (twice)—radiance, light
*Nogah*—brightness
*VaYizraḥ*—and shined
*Tseitam*—their rising
*V'vo'am*—their setting
*Kol tseva marom*—all the supernal host (= the constellations or the stars).

Eleven references to the same image is significant in a passage of this short length.[432] The repeated use of this kind of wording makes it clear that the sun, moon, and stars form the major theme of this poem. This theme connects to that of the blessing in which the poem finds itself, namely, *Birkat Yotser Or*, the blessing of the Creator of Light. The appearance of the sun is celebrated by reciting *Eil Adon* at this place in the liturgy as a symbol of all the luminaries in the sky.

Furthermore, this theme of the sun, moon and stars connects with the other focus of mystical contemplation, *Ma'aseh Beresheet*, "The Enterprise of Creation." Light is prominently mentioned in the biblical Creation story (Gen. 1:3-5; 1:14-16) as are the sun and moon and stars (Gen. 1:16). The connection between *Eil Adon* and *Ma'aseh Beresheet* is strengthened through the poem's use of wording parallel to that of the Creation story. The four times that the word *kol*, "all," is used in the poem corresponds to the 20 or more times that word is used in Genesis 1 and 2 referring to creation.[433] The poem's use of *bara*, "created," *yetsaram*, "formed them," *or*, "light," and *me'orot*, "luminaries," parallels those terms use in Genesis 1 and 2.[434]

Earlier, I mentioned that the first eight strophes of the poem portray God's attributes: God's "greatness" (*godlo*), and "goodness" (*tuvo*), knowledge" (*da'at*), "insight" (*tevunah*), 'merit" (*zekhut*), "straightforwardness"

[432] That excludes the two additional references to these same images as pronouns or in possessive suffix: *yetsaram*, *bahem*, and the one additional reference to them in a verb: *notnim*.
[433] These also parallel the six times the word *kol*, "all," is mentioned at the very beginning of *Birkat Yotser Or*, the blessing in which *Eil Adon* is embedded.
[434] It is also worth noting that the difficult word used in Ezekiel to refer to the vehicle, *raki'a*, "expanse" (Ez. 1:22), also is featured in the Creation story where it refers to the division between the waters of heaven and the waters of earth (Gen. 1:6-8; 15-17). This may be a commentary of one part of the Bible (Ezekiel) on another (Genesis). The implied interpretation found in the Book of Ezekiel may be that the vehicle upon which God's throne rested was not, as *Eil Adon* posits, a chariot, but rather the expanse of sky that divides the heavenly waters from the earthly waters.

(*mishor*), "lovingkindness" (*ḥesed*) and "mercy" (*raḥamim*). However, there is evidence for interpreting these items not as characteristics of God but as independent angelic entities. Not only that, but the sun, moon and stars in this poem also may be meant to be understood as angelic beings themselves. All of this is implied in the context of the ancient mystical text, *Ma'aseh Merkavah*, in which we find the non-alphabetic verses that parallel the alphabetic acrostic of *Eil Adon*.[435]

The following is the context in *Ma'aseh Merkavah*: Rabbi Ishmael asks Rabbi Akiva, "How can one gaze above the *Seraphim* who stand over the head of *Rozi'i Adonai*, God of Israel?"[436] Rabbi Akiva's answer is that when he reached the first (of seven) palaces/sanctuaries (= *Hekhalot*), he prayed a specific prayer, as well as practiced several other rituals, and this permitted him to gaze upon God. It is in Rabbi Akiva's prayer itself that we find language paralleling *Eil Adon*. In this long prayer (59 lines), the passage of interest is found in an extended section depicting the angels. The passage is as follows:

> Full of splendor they give forth shining light.
> Their splendor glistens throughout the world.
> Joyful at their going forth, and happy at their coming in.
> Their glow is pleasant before the throne of your glory.
> In awe and fear they do your desires.
> They bring to your name, great, mighty and awesome adornment and glory.
> And they recite for the recitation of your kingdom shouting and gladness,
> because there is none like you...[437]

Those same words, with some minor variations, are found in *Eil Adon*, and, as mentioned, they comprise that part of Rabbi Akiva's prayer that describes the angels. In our prayer, they describe the sun, moon, and stars. Most likely, the poet who composed our prayer consciously applied Rabbi Akiva's descriptions of the angels to the heavenly luminaries because to our poet, the

[435] A translation of the entire book of *Ma'aseh Merkavah* is found in Naomi Janowitz, *The Poetics of Ascent: Theories of Language in a Rabbinic Text* (Albany, New York: State University of New York Press, 1989), 29-81. Her translation of the prayer which contains the parallel to *Eil Adon* is found on 65.
[436] Janowitz, *The Poetics of Ascent*, 64. *Rozi'i*, part of this name of God, derives from the root *raz*, "secret."
[437] Translation mainly that of Janowitz, *The Poetics of Ascent*, 65. I modified her translation when necessary since she used, as the basis of her translation, Schaefer's ms. New York 8128 while Bar-Ilan identified Schaefer's ms. Munich 22 as the most reliable text.

two are one and the same: the sun, moon, and stars are angels or angelic entities. Similarly, the "attributes" of God mentioned in our prayer are also angelic entities. The composer of *Eil Adon*, therefore, did not simply list several metaphoric praises of God as surrounding God's throne. "Knowledge, wisdom," etc., which surround God, do so not metaphorically, but actually: the angels known as *da'at, tevunah, zekhut, mishor, ḥesed* and *raḥamim* actually surround God upon the throne.

These words, and others like them, are found in *Merkavah* literature, and their meaning is not always certain, but they often seem mixed in with other terms for angelic beings. Reuven Hammer commented that, "These and other descriptions refer to the *s'firot*, or Godly emanations described in kabbalistic mystical speculation."[438] Indeed, one could point to six terms in the poem which are connected to the *sefirot*: *Da'at, Ḥesed, Binah, Gevurah, Tiferet*, and *Malkhut*. The question of the presence in this early mystical poem of so many terms which, much later, became central to *Kabbalah*, is an important one. No doubt later *Kabbalah* drew upon some of these terms from earlier mysticism and adapted and transformed their meaning from angelic presences to the actual emanations, actual parts, of God. However, what we find in the poem itself derives not from the ideational world of *Kabbalah*, but rather from that of *Merkavah* mysticism.[439] In that world a transformation of terms and ideas occurred: The sun, moon, and stars transformed from the status of gods in the pagan world into angelic entities in this poem.[440] As Jewish mysticism continued to develop, these symbols

---

[438] Reuven Hammer, *Or Ḥadash*, 108.

[439] There was apparently a long process by which various divine attributes became the 10 *sefirot*. One element in this process is certainly related to angels. But the attributes were also likely hypostatized in various other ways, and only gradually become the full-blown kabbalistic scheme. See Yehudah Liebes, "*Middotav shel ha-Elohim*," ("The Attributes of God"), *Tarbitz* 70:1, 2001, 51-74; Moshe Idel, *Absorbing Perfections: Kabbalah and Interpretation* (New Haven, Connecticut: Yale University Press, 2002), 226-230. I am grateful to Professor Daniel C. Matt for pointing out to me the additional complexities in this issue and for drawing my attention to the passages in Liebes' article and in Idel's book.

[440] Rachel Elior records that "... Angelological traditions comprise the major part of the *Hekhalot* literature and are presented in hundreds of paragraphs in the Synopsis; so many that it would be impossible to list them in detail..." Rachel Elior, "Mysticism, Magic and Angelology: The Perception of Angels in Hekhalot Literature," *Jewish Studies Quarterly* 1, 1 (1993-1994), 4, n. 8. She further says, 8-9: the worship of God by the angels "in the celestial shrines is a liturgical model which is imitated by those who descend to the Merkabah: the ceremony which the angels celebrate before the Throne of Glory, which includes immersion, the recitation of praises, the singing of hymns, the recital of prayers, the attachment of crowns, and the uttering of the Name, is taken as a basic ritual pattern which those who descend to the Merkabah seek to learn and imitate... (T)he focus upon the figure of the angels and the deep concern with the details of the celestial ritual derive from the fact that the world of the angels is conceived as a source of authority for religious innovation, and its ceremonies serve as a paradigm determined at the time of ascent to heaven, as a cosmological framework and also as a background for the mystic and ritual conception of the worship of those who descend to the Merkabah."

slowly morphed—by the Kabbalistic period several centuries later—into emanations of the divine presence itself.

As we have seen, *Eil Adon* also makes sense in this particular place in the liturgy not only because it paves the thematic way for this *Kedushah DeYotser*, but also because it relates directly to the main theme of the blessing in which it is embedded: the theme of the renewed sunlight in *Birkat Yotser Or*. In this way, the poem is both a paean to God elicited by the reappearance of the sun, but it is also grand praise to God who created the sun-angel, the moon-angel, and the star-angels who, together, praise God through emitting light, night and day.

Given this background, I want to suggest a new understanding of the last two strophes of the poem. The usual understanding of these lines is reflected in the following translation—iterations of which may be found in virtually all *siddurim* with translations:

> *Shin*—The host of heaven (= sun, moon, stars) give praise to him,
> *Tav*—Splendor and greatness—the *seraphim*, and the *ofanim* and celestial creatures (*ḥayot hakodesh*).

In this typical translation, the heavenly bodies (sun, moon, stars) and the angels (*seraphim, ofanim*, celestial creatures) utter praise to God, and that praise celebrates God's "splendor and greatness."

However, if *Eil Adon* consists, to large degree, of angels praising God—angels in the form of *ofanim* and celestial creatures, in the form of "knowledge," "wisdom," etc., and in the form of the sun, moon, and stars—then perhaps it concludes with another listing of some of these angels. That is, perhaps all the words in the final strophe refer to angels. This would clear up the syntax as well: In the *tav* line, understanding the first two words (*tiferet u'gedulah*) as descriptions of the praise that "the host of heaven" offers interrupts the flow of thought. If, rather, these two words are also names of angels, then there is consistency in the entire *tav* line—all the words refer to angelic entities. This understanding is reflected in the following translation:

> *Shin*—The host of heaven (= sun, moon, stars) give praise to him,

> *Tav—Tiferet* (the name of an angel), *Gedulah* (the name of an angel), the *seraphim*, the *ofanim* and celestial creatures.[441]

The praise of God by non-human beings continues in the passage which follows *Eil Adon*, namely, *La'Eil Asher Shavat*, "God Who Rested." I will comment on that shortly. Here, though, I want to point out that between that passage and *Kedushah DeYotser* some transitional wording is found which is very suggestive. It is contained in the first of two sentences beginning with the word *titbarakh*, "may you be blessed"—

> May you be blessed, our savior, through the praise of the work of your hands, and through the luminaries of light which you have made; may they glorify you, *selah*.

This sentence sums up *Eil Adon* and leads into the *Kedushah*: May the beacons of light in the sky—the work of God's hands—which constitute one category of angels, continue to praise you through the streaming of their light (the subject of *Eil Adon*), and may the other category of angels (the subject of *Kedushah DeYotser*) praise you through their song.

All of this, as mentioned above, may be seen as a long *midrash* on the verse from Psalm 19:2, *Ha-shamayim mesaprim kevod Eil, u' ma'aseh yadav magid ha-raki'a*, "The heavens declare the glory of God, the sky proclaims His handiwork."

**Spiritual Commentary on *Eil Adon***

The knowledge that angels play a central role in the theology of this prayer may be interesting to the modern worshiper, but most moderns would probably not be moved by a literal approach to angels. And yet, we might respond to viewing the astronomical bodies as carrying messages for us, as the original Hebrew word for angel, *malakh*, means "messenger." The message of the

[441] The fact that *Eil Adon* refers, in its depiction of the sun and the moon, to an image also found in the Babylonian Talmud *Ḥullin* 60b is well known and cited by many commentators as far back as Abudraham (Spain, 14th c.). The image is of the moon complaining that there can't be two master-lights in the sky. This is based on Gen. 1:16a that records two "great lights" in the heavens, understood by the Talmud here referring to a time when the moon was as large as the sun. God "rewards" this observation by causing the moon to reduce in size. This accords with Gen. 1:16b which speaks of a "greater light" and a "lesser light." As the story goes on, the moon, like a recalcitrant but beloved child, is not consoled until God "atones" by offering a "sin-offering" to the moon on the occasion of every *Rosh Ḥodesh*. This conclusion of the story construes the sin-offering ordained for Israel to bring uniquely on this holiday (Num. 28:15) as if it were brought by God to the moon. *Eil Adon* hints at all of this—in style typical to *piyyut*—in the *resh* strophe, "(God) saw and ordained the size of the moon."

luminaries is that we, in contemporary times, can expand our search for, and connection to, cosmic beginnings. It is only in the last several decades that human beings have been able to travel and to see beyond the limits of earthly skies. Our modern era can, with pride, contribute new visions to the Jewish treasury of symbols that speak to us in this prayer. Those images are the beautiful photos of planets, stars, suns, red giants, white dwarfs, solar systems, galaxies, and nebulae. Perhaps most inspiring are the photographs of our home planet, planet Earth, that graphically demonstrate the illusory nature of all that separates people, that separates all living and non-living things in our shared world. All of this may be added to the panoply of thoughts and forms that this prayer may genuinely elicit.

It will be eye-opening to many simply to point out that the natural occurrence of the sunrise elicited the poetry of *Birkat Yotser Or* and *Eil Adon* within it. That the several pages in a typical prayer book surrounding this blessing may be viewed as a collection of writing by sensitive souls who recorded their awe and wonder at the seemingly miraculous reappearance of the sun at dawn, the stars and moon at dusk. In fact, chanting this poetry in the synagogue service without being aware of the natural events that sparked it misses the very point of why these lines are chanted in the worship service connected to the morning.

The ancient poet of *Eil Adon* responded to dawn by imagining praise offered to God by the angelic heavenly luminaries. Modern astronomic discoveries only add to the appreciation of this part of the liturgy. The basic facts of our solar system are known by all moderns—that the earth rotates on its axis and that it revolves around the sun, that the moon circles the earth, and that the much smaller points of light in the night sky represent relatively nearby planets and much more distant stars. It would make sense to prepare worshipers for chanting *Eil Adon* by invoking these facts to enhance the sense of wonder. Possession of modern astronomical knowledge has not caused visual artists to abandon painting sunsets and sunrises, nor has it dampened contemporary poets from composing verse celebrating the beauty of the stars. *Eil Adon* and the other poetry in *Birkat Yotser Or*—all of them ancient Jewish artistic responses to the grandeur of the light of dawn and dusk and moon and stars—may be viewed as prompts for modern worshipers to also respond spiritually and emotionally to our physical place in the cosmos. Reciting this prayer, and the others around it, is an opportunity to disengage from our immediate reality and to contemplate our larger reality, as living beings residing on a planet within our solar system, itself nestled in the Milky Way Galaxy, which in turn, is located in one tiny corner of the universe.[442]

It may make sense to experiment with reciting these prayers outside, or at least near a window through which worshipers could see the sky. Or, worshipers might be asked to close their eyes and imagine exactly where they are on the surface of the earth vis-à-vis the arc of the sun's light as it traverses the face of the planet. That arc is constantly in motion as the earth both orbits the sun and rotates on its axis. Locating ourselves in reference to the earth and sun may help us enter into the mindset of our poem. I have found it meaningful to prepare for this prayer by taking a few minutes locating myself in my mind's eye in just this manner, viewing myself as situated wherever I am on the surface of the earth, and imagining the "ride" the earth is providing to me as it rotates, with the sunlight and shadows slowly changing around me.

Keeping in mind the thrall inspired by the reappearance of the sun which stands behind *Eil Adon* may have implications for the appropriateness of melodies applied to it. Here, we enter an area of great subjectivity, but it seems to me that slow, meditational tunes may be more apt than fast anthems.[443]

### *La'Eil Asher Shavat*

This short *piyyut* (not recorded before the 9th century)[444] in *Birkat Yotser Or* follows *Eil Adon,* which features praise of God from a non-human source (the sun, moon, and stars) and precedes *Kedushah DeYotser* (see commentary on this prayer on page 49), which also includes non-human praise of God (the angels). This prayer too presents praise of God that originates from a non-human source. It declares:

> This is the praise of the Sabbath day on which God rested from all of God's work. And the Sabbath day [itself] praises [God] saying "A song by the Sabbath day, it is good to thank *YHVH...*" (Psalm 92:1)

---

[442] See *Nehalel beShabbat,* a modern, Orthodox siddur that complements most pages of the Shabbat liturgy with modern photographs. The photos that surround *Eil Adon* include views of a "sun pillar over the Arctic plain," the *aurora borealis,* a comet, a sunset over Mars from NASA's rover Spirit, and a sunrise over Jerusalem. Michael Haruni, Ed., *Nehalel beShabbat (Ashkenaz)* (Jerusalem: Nevarech, 2013), 264-273; 640-641.

[443] And perhaps it is not entirely off the mark to suggest that if a worshiper desires to study *Eil Adon,* outside of a Shabbat worship setting, with appropriate music playing in the background, they could do worse than to play recordings of the following pieces: *The Planets, Opus* 32 by Gustav Holst, *Nocturnes* by Claude Debussy or Frederic Chopin or *Dark Star* by The Grateful Dead.

[444] Elbogen cites the 9th-century Rabbi Natronai Gaon, *Jewish Liturgy,* 96. It is found also mentioned in the 9th-century *Seder Rav Amram,* but it is likely a later addition. See Daniel Goldschmidt, ed., *Seder Rav Amram* (Jerusalem: Mossad HaRav Kook, 1971), 71.

If one proceeds too quickly through this brief paragraph-length passage, one may easily miss its unusual and beautiful message: the Sabbath day itself is imagined as offering a song to God. It is the only remaining example in the current liturgy of a cycle of prayers in which each day of the week utters its own, unique, praise to God. The way in which this prayer expresses the idea that Shabbat itself sings a Sabbath song to God is through a very creative, midrashic, reading of the first verse of Psalm 92. That verse functions as the title of the psalm itself. Instead of reading it in the conventional way (and as it most likely was meant to be read) as "A song *for* (i.e., in honor of) the Sabbath day," it reads it playfully as "A song *by* (i.e., composed by) the Sabbath day"!

**Spiritual Commentary on *La'Eil Asher Shavat***

The notion of a day of the week chanting to God is an evocative poetic metaphor. It is an expansive and artistic way of thinking about time and creation. Just as the planets and stars are visualized as able to express praise to God through emitting light in the previous prayer, and just as angels are thought of as expressing praise through song in the next prayer, time itself—or more exactly, the Sabbath day—is thought of as capable and desirous of expressing itself through song. It is possible that the prayer considers Psalm 92 itself as the song that the Sabbath day sings. In that case, it is a song about the righteous receiving justice, since that it is the theme of this particular psalm. On the other hand, if the prayer is merely citing the first verse of that Psalm as evidence that the Sabbath day sings a song to God, then it leaves the content of that song to the worshiper's imagination. Perhaps the implication is that the song changes each Shabbat. The day itself praises God on Shabbat by uttering a song and the planets, moon, and stars also praise God by shining their light. What a view of nature and time! The poets who composed these prayers felt that the cosmos and time itself stand constantly in awe of God! This view is a needed corrective to modern utilitarian views of nature and time.

This prayer about Shabbat alone remains in the liturgy while the poems in which the other six days of the week celebrate God have all disappeared. Perhaps that is a testament to how difficult it is to maintain a spiritually sensitive notion of time during the six days when we work and shop and create and do and make and try to get as much done on our task lists as we can. The fact that only the poem in which Shabbat praises God remains in the liturgy dovetails nicely with the essence of Shabbat as a break from scheduling time, using time, monetizing time. If we experience Shabbat as a day that itself lauds God in some mystical way, then our response can be to appreciate the hours and minutes of this day, to not take them for granted, to be as aware as we can of the incredible worth of all the time contained in just one day.

The rest of the poetry surrounding the three paragraphs of the *Shema* on Shabbat does not differ from that of the weekday liturgy; therefore, I won't comment further on it here. The next place that the liturgy of Shabbat morning offers unique wording is in the *Amidah shel Shaḥarit.*

## The *Amidah* for Shabbat Morning

As was pointed out in the discussion of the Friday night liturgy, the first three and last three blessings of the Shabbat *Amidah* are identical to those recited on weekdays and Festivals. The distinction is that the middle 13 blessings recited on weekdays don't appear. On Shabbat, as on Festivals, there is but one blessing, the fourth, that occupies the middle slot. The first three paragraphs of this blessing are unique to this *Amidah*, recited on Shabbat morning. The fourth paragraph, asking God to accept our Shabbat rest, is found in all four Shabbat *Amidot* and I offered comments on it in the discussion of the Friday night *Amidah*. I will now turn to the three paragraphs which are unique to this *Amidah*. A key question is how these three paragraphs connect to each other. There has been a longstanding scholarly controversy on this issue, and the contributions to this learned discussion in the modern period, involving the discovery of long-lost manuscripts, are quite remarkable.

The three paragraphs are:

1. A section about Moses receiving the commandment to observe Shabbat as part of the Ten Commandments:

> Moses rejoiced in the gift of his portion,
> for you called him a trusted servant.
> You placed a crown of beauty upon his head
> as he stood in your presence upon Mount Sinai.
> He brought down two stone tablets in his hand
> upon which is written the observance of Shabbat,
> as it is written...

2. A biblical citation, Exodus 31:16-17, beginning with the word *VeShamru*, "(The people of Israel) shall observe":

> The people of Israel shall keep the sabbath,
> Observing the sabbath throughout the ages as a covenant for all time.
> It shall be a sign for all time between me and the people of Israel.
> For in six days the Lord made heaven and earth, and on the seventh day he ceased from work and was refreshed.

3. A segment about the Sabbath as the sole possession of Israel:

> You did not, *YHVH* our God, give it to the nations of the lands,
> nor did you bequeath it, our king, to the worshippers of idols,
> and as well, in its rest the uncircumcised shall not dwell.
> For to Israel, your people, you gave it in love,
> to the seed of Jacob whom you have chosen.
> A nation of sanctifiers of the seventh,
> they shall all be satisfied and delight in your goodness.
> You were pleased with the seventh
> "The choicest of days" you called it,
> a remembrance of the act of creation.

There is no question that the first two paragraphs are connected. The last line of the first paragraph itself makes the connection to the second paragraph by concluding, "as it is written..." The function of that phrasing is well known in Rabbinic Literature: it introduces a proof text from the Bible that establishes the point that was just made and the second paragraph supplies that biblical proof text. The first paragraph makes the point that Moses rejoiced because of his special relationship with God through which he received the Ten Commandments, including the fourth commandment, to observe Shabbat. Therefore, if there were to be a biblical proof text for this idea, one would expect an appropriate citation from either Exodus, chapters 19-20 or Deuteronomy, chapter 5, since those two chapters contain the story and content of the Ten Commandments. Instead, the citation is from Exodus 31:16-17 (*VeShamru*) which—while it is about the Sabbath—does not relate at all to the Ten Commandments. In fact, no less a figure than Rashi (Rabbi Shlomo ben Yitzḥak, France/Germany, 11th c.) is reported to have made it a point not to recite this wording for this very reason![445] Still, commentators over the generations struggled mightily to justify the placement of Exodus 31:16-17 here. For example, Rabbi Tzedekiah ben Avraham Anav, author of *Shibbolei HaLeket* ("The Gleaned Ears," 13th-century Italy) compiled a list of several supposed connections between the biblical proof text in the second paragraph and the paragraph that precedes it:

- ▷ The Torah was given on Shabbat and since it was given through Moses, the prayer grants honor to Moses here in a prayer recited on Shabbat.
- ▷ Since Moses died on Shabbat and it is the custom to speak praises of a sage on the day he died, we offer praise of Moses on here in the Shabbat *Amidah*. And even for those who say that Moses didn't actually die on Shabbat, but rather on the eve of Shabbat, still, the timing "is not far off" (*eino raḥok*).
- ▷ The midrash says that Moses successfully argued with Pharaoh to give the Israelite slaves one day off a week so that they would be more productive; when Pharaoh agreed and allowed Moses to choose the day, Moses chose Shabbat. In the negotiation, Pharaoh called this "a gift," which is the word our prayer uses. Once the Ten Commandments were given, Moses rejoiced when he saw that God chose this same day as the day off for all time. (Of course, the word "gift" in our prayer does not refer to the Sabbath, but rather to the fact that God called Moses a faithful servant).[446]

When several alternative reasons are offered for a custom, it often testifies to the fact that no one reason truly resolves the issue and, in fact, the resolution is not clear at all. There is no getting around the fact that the biblical proof text here does not seem to link directly to the paragraph that precedes

[445] Reported by Rabbi Avraham ben Natan HaYarḥi (Germany, 13th c.), author of *Sefer HaManhig*. Cited in Naphtali Wieder, "*Yismaḥ Moshe—Hitnagdut VeSenigoriyah*" in *The Formation of Jewish Liturgy in the East and the West* [Hebrew] (Jerusalem: Mekhon Ben Tzvi and The Hebrew University, 1998), vol. 1, 298. Originally published in Ezra Fleischer, Jakob Josef Petuchowski, *Meḥkarim Ba'Aggadah, Targumim, U'Tefillot Yisrael LeZekher Y. Heinemann* (Jerusalem: Magnes Press, 1981), 75-99.

[446] Rabbi Tzedekiah ben Avraham Anav, *Shibbolei HaLeket HaShalem*, Solomon Buber, ed. (Jerusalem: Alef Publishing Company, 1962; reprint of the 1891 edition), #76, 28a-b. The midrash referred to is found in *Shemot Rabba* 1:28.

it and that an explicit reference to The Ten Commandments would be much stronger and much more direct.

In 1965, Aharon Mirsky published an article that presented a thoroughly fresh approach to the problem. Mirsky built on the prior discovery by Menahem Zulai, who had discovered in the Cairo Genizah a version of the first paragraph of our prayer with one word missing, and that opened up for him an entirely new path.[447] The version Zulai found lacks the word *shenei*, "two" in the line "He brought down two stone tablets in his hand." When Zulai paid close attention to that minute change he noticed an engaging pattern: Three strophes of this poetic passage form a mini-alphabetic acrostic—in the middle of the alphabet—

*Yod—Yismaḥ*—(Moses) rejoiced
*Kaf—Kelil*—Crown
*Lamed—Luḥot*—Tablets

On this basis, Zulai wondered if this brief set of verses might be part of a longer poem structured on the entire alphabet. Mirsky then sketched a theoretical outline of such a poem using the model of many such liturgical poems known from the medieval period. In his outline, the 22 lines of the imagined poem—each line representing one letter of the Hebrew alphabet—are interspersed among the standard seven blessings of the Shabbat *Amidah*, with three verses per blessing plus four in the last blessing to round out the twenty-two letters of the alphabet. The Ten Commandments would have been cited. These kinds of expanded, poetic, versions of the *Amidah* were often composed for a specific Shabbat or holiday with its unique Torah reading. Mirsky's theory is that this poem was composed for one of the Shabbatot on which the Torah reading included the Ten Commandments.

The reconstruction of this theorized version of the *Amidah* supposes that the Ten Commandments would have been cited in this way: The first four in the first four blessings; the last six distributed two to each of the last three blessings. In this way, the fourth blessing—the blessing we are dealing with—is appropriately designated with the fourth Commandment, the Sabbath Commandment.

An outline of the reconstructed *Amidah* would look something like this:

[447] Aharon Mirsky, "*Yesod Kerovah*," *Sinai*, 57, 1965, 127-132.

**Blessing #1:**

Blessed are you, *YHVH*, our God and God of our ancestors...
*Aleph* (Each letter of the alphabet listed in this outline would be the first letter of a poetic line beginning with that letter).
*Bet*
*Gimmel*
As it is written in your Torah:
(Citation of the first of the Ten Commandments).
Blessed are you, Shield of Abraham.

**Blessing #2**

*Dalet*
*Heh*
*Vav*
As it is written in your Torah:
(Citation of the second of the Ten Commandments).
Blessed are you, Reviver of the Dead.

**Blessing #3**

*Zayin*
*Ḥet*
*Tet*
As it is written in your Torah:
(Citation of the third of the Ten Commandments).
Blessed are you, Holy God.

**Blessing #4**

*Yod—Yismaḥ Moshe bematnat ḥelko...*
(Moses rejoiced in the gift of his portion)...
*Kaf—Kelil tiferet berosho natata...*
(You adorned his head with a crown of splendor)...
*Lamed—Luḥot avanim horid beyado...*
(He carried down stone tablets)...
As it is written in your Torah:
(Citation of the fourth of the Ten Commandments about the Sabbath).
*VeShamru venei Yisrael et haShabbat...*
(The people of Israel shall observe Shabbat)...

*Eloheinu v'Elohei Avoteinu...* (Our God and God of our ancestors)...
Blessed are you, Sanctifier of Shabbat.

**Blessing #5**
*Mem*
*Nun*
*Samekh*
As it is written in your Torah:
(Citation of the fifth and sixth of the Ten Commandments).
Blessed are you, Restorer of His Presence to Zion.

**Blessing #6**
*Ayin*
*Peh*
*Tzadi*
As it is written in your Torah:
(Citation of the seventh and eighth of the Ten Commandments).
Blessed are you, Your Name is "Goodness" And to You It Is Pleasant to Offer Thanksgiving.

**Blessing #7**
*Kof*
*Resh*
*Shin*
*Tav*
As it is written in your Torah:
(Citation of the ninth and tenth of the Ten Commandments).
Blessed are you, The Blesser of Peace to His People Israel.

This theory has its weaknesses which I will spell out below. But here, let me say that the strength of this very creative reconstruction is that it does not have to search for far-fetched explanations as to why the Ten Commandments are not cited here; it proposes that the Ten Commandments were indeed cited here. This theory, however, must account for why the theoretical version that did include the Ten Commandments was replaced by the current version which cites instead Exodus 31: 16-17 (*VeShamru*). The explanation is that in the early medieval period, the text of the *Amidah* was much more fluid than it is today. As indicated above, the *Amidah* could take very different forms from week to week, mirroring the different Torah readings. However, the *Amidah* for Shabbat morning was not totally different each week. The wording for the first three and last three blessings was mostly consistent. Beyond that, another consistent element was that Exodus 31:16-17 (*VeShamru*)—or parts of it—seemed to be a standard feature of the fourth blessing—the blessing we are considering here. That biblical passage was included presumably because its theme of the eternal command for Israel to observe the Sabbath relates nicely to the *Amidah* recited on each Sabbath. As time passed, the custom of creating alternate poetic versions eventually diminished and ultimately came to an end, and by about the 11th-12th centuries, the *Amidah* for Shabbat took on a uniform and stable shape with only minor variations between communities.

According to Mirsky, what happened then was that, in the process toward canonization, for some unknown reason, the *Amidah* for Shabbat morning preserved one building block from one version of a former poetic form of the *Amidah*—a version composed for a week when the Ten Commandments was read, namely the first paragraph describing Moses receiving the Sabbath command of The Ten Commandments—followed by one building block that was a standard element of the *Amidah* recited on every Shabbat, Exodus 31:16-17 (*VeShamru*). However, the building block from the poetic *Amidah* was not preserved intact; its proof text—which was part of the Ten Commandments—was dropped; as a result, Exodus 31:16-17, the biblical citation that was never connected to this one Sabbath's poem but was part of the *Amidah* framework that recurred every Sabbath, appeared as if it were the proof text.

Recall that this whole theory is based upon the discovery of a manuscript of the same text of the *Amidah* in use today (with minor variations), but with the word *shenei*, "two," missing. The fact that a full text of the theorized poetic *Amidah* with a citation to the Ten Commandments has never been found is the greatest weakness of this approach. When Mirsky first wrote, only one manuscript with the missing word had been discovered. Since his research was published, two other scholars have found a total of six more such manuscripts in the Genizah material, and it has gained more scholarly acceptance.[448] Nevertheless, the problem of how the first two paragraphs of this blessing of the Shabbat morning *Amidah* are connected cannot be considered solved in a final way and future discoveries from liturgical history

[448] Although many more examples of this blessing in the Genizah did contain *shenei*, "two" is missing in these seven manuscripts. See Ezra Fleischer, *Eretz-Israel Prayer and Prayer Rituals: As Portrayed in the Geniza Documents* [Hebrew] (Jerusalem: The Magnes Press, 1988), 52, n. 86. Fleischer located three of the examples and Naphtali Wieder had earlier located three others. See Naphtali Wieder, "*Yismaḥ Moshe*," I: 299, n. 18.

may shed light on this. Toward that end, I would like to record a tantalizing observation of mine which, if corroborated by future discoveries, would clear things up in a different way: The very next biblical verse after Exodus 31:16-17 (*V'Shamru*) contains language that explicitly mentions the "two tablets" of "stone."

> When he [God] finished speaking with him on Mount Sinai, he gave Moses the two tablets of the Pact, stone tablets inscribed with the finger of God. (Exodus 31:18)

If this verse were cited in the Siddur along with the two previous verses of the *VeShamru* passage, it would tie together the two paragraphs of this blessing very nicely because it refers to the giving of the Ten Commandments to Moses on Mount Sinai. Is it possible that this verse is "implied" by this prayer's citation of the two previous verses? That is, can we assume that the very act of quoting Exodus 3:16-17 was meant to evoke Exodus 31:18 as well, presuming that worshipers knew the Torah by heart and would mentally continue the quotation to the next verse? I think probably not, but perhaps future research will support a more solid explanation to the puzzle of why Exodus 31:16-17 is found in this blessing.[449]

Beyond the question of the narrative flow between the first two paragraphs of this blessing, there are two expressions within the first paragraph that deserve attention. They are highlighted in the quote below:

> Moses rejoiced in the gift of his portion,
> for you called him **a trusted servant.**
> You placed **a crown of beauty** upon his head
> as he stood in your presence upon Mount Sinai.

"A trusted servant," *eved ne'eman*, is a subtle allusion to a brief story in chapter 12 of the Book of Numbers. There, Moses' sister and brother, Miriam and Aaron, exchanged gossip about their illustrious brother "because of

[449] The title of a recent article centers exactly upon our question, however it ignores the research of Zulai, Mirsky, Wieder, and Fleischer: Ian Silverman, "*Yismach Moshe*: What Is the Reason for *V'shamru* in the Shabbat *Shacharit Amidah*?," *CCAR Journal: The Reform Jewish Quarterly*, Summer, 2018, 97-108. Silverman's conclusion is that the Ten Commandments were not cited in the blessing because the rabbinic sages endeavored to de-emphasize the importance of the Ten Commandments in the face of early Jewish-Christians who claimed that only the Ten Commandments (and some other, few, biblical passages) were divinely given. It is an interesting theory, but the timing seems off—the origin of our blessing likely derives from much later than the original Jewish-Christian schism—and there is no documentary evidence that links this concern with our blessing.

the Cushite woman that he had married." Apparently, the objection was about the ethnicity of this woman.[450] Their gossip then turns to jealousy at the supreme leadership position Moses occupies: "They said, 'Has the Lord spoken only through Moses? Has he not spoken through us as well?'" (Numbers 12:2). At this point, the Torah defends Moses, calling him the humblest man on earth, and then God intervenes. God talks directly to Miriam and Aaron, saying that Moses' connection to God is, indeed, superior to theirs. It is this statement of God's that forms the basis for "the trusted servant" wording in our prayer:

> ...my **servant** Moses is **trusted** throughout my household (Numbers 12:7).
> Our prayer asserts:
> Moses rejoiced in the gift of his portion,
> for you called him **a trusted servant.**

The siddur here is a midrashic expansion on the story in the Torah. The Torah does not record how Moses reacts to God's defense of him. But the siddur does. It declares that "Moses rejoiced!" This very brief expression in the midst of the Shabbat morning *Amidah* is meant to bring this story in the Book of Numbers to the worshiper's mind and to praise, as well as to humanize, Moses; Moses rejoiced at the spiritual closeness he achieved with God.

This brings us to the second clever hint to a story in the Torah in this prayer:

> You placed **a crown of beauty** upon his head
> as he stood in your presence upon Mount Sinai.

These two lines likely hark back to a charming little anecdote in which Moses descends from his encounter with God on Mt. Sinai unaware that his face is radiating light (Exodus 34: 29-35). Moses apparently realizes that something is different about himself when he notices that "Aaron and all the Israelites saw that the skin of Moses' face was radiant; and they shrank from coming near him" (Exodus 34:30). Moses reassures them, and they draw near. Nevertheless, from then on, according to the account in the Torah, Moses would put a veil on when speaking with his fellow Israelites and remove it when speaking with God. Our prayer appears to creatively react to this passage

[450] See Jacob Milgrom, *The JPS Torah Commentary: Numbers* (Philadelphia, New York: The Jewish Publication Society, 1990), 93.

by calling the radiance emanating from his face "a crown of beauty." This line in the midst of the Shabbat morning *Amidah* too is meant to bring to the worshiper's mind a story in the Torah and to offer an artful image as a visual interpretation of the story: the radiance emanating from Moses was "a crown of beauty." Certainly, this image too is in praise of Moses.[451]

The final passage of the *Amidah* that is unique to Shabbat morning is the third paragraph of this blessing:

> You did not, *YHVH* our God, give it to the nations of the lands,
> nor did you bequeath it, our king, to the worshipers of idols,
> and as well, in its rest the uncircumcised shall not dwell.
> For to Israel, your people, you gave it in love,
> to the seed of Jacob whom you have chosen.
> A nation of sanctifiers of the seventh,
> they shall all be satisfied and delight in your goodness.
> You were pleased with the seventh
> "The choicest of days" you called it,
> a remembrance of the act of creation.

As mentioned above, the point of this section of the blessing is that God gave the Sabbath as the sole possession of Israel. The blessing expresses this idea three different ways in the negative and then four different ways in the positive:

You, God, did not give the Sabbath...

> ...to the nations of the land
> ...to the worshipers of idols
> ....to the uncircumcised

[You gave it in love] to...

> ...Israel
> ...your people
> ...the seed of Jacob
> ...whom you have loved

[451] Michelangelo's famous sculpture of Moses in the church of San Pietro in Rome also seems to be based on this passage from Exodus. However, the statue portrays Moses as having horns, which was apparently based on the Latin translation of the Bible (The Vulgate) of this verse taking *karan*, "radiance," as "horn," which, in very different contexts, could theoretically be a proper translation.

The notion that the Sabbath is the inheritance of the people of Israel alone is found not only in this blessing, but in several places in ancient and medieval Jewish literature. An early example (approximately 1st century CE) that includes this notion, as well as the view that God blessed the Sabbath more than the other days, is found in the Book of Jubilees (2:31-33):

> 31: The Creator of all blessed it, but he did not sanctify any people or nations to keep the Sabbath thereon with the sole exception of Israel. He granted to them alone that they might eat and drink and keep the Sabbath thereon upon the earth.
> 32: And the Creator of all, who created this day for a blessing and sanctification and glory, blessed it more than all days.
> 33: This law and testimony was given to the children of Israel as an eternal law for their generations."[452]

That the Sabbath was given by God only to Israel is also found in a 3rd-century CE midrash:

> It (the Sabbath) shall be a sign for all time between me and the people of Israel" (Exodus 31:17), but not between me and the nations of the world.[453]

Finally, a 13th-century compendium of laws and customs records another version of the same idea:

> A parable: To what does the matter resemble? To someone who had a son and he had a choice garment and didn't want to bequeath it except to his son. So too, the holy one, blessed be he, did not wish to bequeath the day of blessing and holiness and rest that he had except to Israel. And know that it is so for when Israel left Egypt, he gave them the Sabbath before he gave them the Torah.[454]

[452] Elbogen, *Jewish Liturgy*, 97, n. 13 cites Jubilees 2:31, but the two verses which follow are relevant as well because verse 32 connects with the idea in our passage that God called the Sabbath the "choicest" of days. Verse 33 sounds the same theme as Exodus 31:16-17 (*VeShamru*), that the Sabbath is an eternal institution for Israel. The translation is from the Ethiopic version of Jubilees in James H. Charlesworth, *The Old Testament Pseudepigrapha* (Garden City, New York: Doubleday & Company, Inc., 1985), 2:58.
[453] Jacob Z. Lauterbach, ed., *Mekilta de-Rabbi Ishmael* (Philadelphia: The Jewish Publication Society of America, 1935, 1961, 1976), v. 3, 204 (Massekhta DeShabbta, 1).
[454] Rabbi Tzedekiah ben Avraham Anav, *Shibbolei HaLeket HaShalem*, #76, 28b.

As I pointed out above, this passage expresses the idea that the Sabbath is exclusively Israel's in both positive and negative terms. The negative terms are:

You, God, did not give the Sabbath...

...to the nations of the lands
...to the worshipers of idols
...to the uncircumcised

Modern liberal *siddurim* have dealt with these negative expressions in various ways. The editor of an early Reform siddur articulated his particular discomfort with identifying non-Jews as *arelim* ("the uncircumcised") in these lines, finding it offensive to classify an entire group of people by the condition of their reproductive organ. Rabbi Isak Noa Mannheimer (1793-1865) therefore substituted the word *reshai'm* ("evildoers") in Hebrew and *Suender* ("sinners") in German.[455] Other early Reform *siddurim* omitted the entire third paragraph of this blessing, considering the statement of Israel's sole possession of the Sabbath problematic. The contemporary Reform siddur, *Mishkan Tefillah*, and the contemporary Reconstructionist siddur, *Kol Haneshamah*, both follow suit and delete the entire paragraph. The Conservative movement has taken several different paths with its *siddurim* over the last 70 years or so. Its first Shabbat prayer book (1946) included the entire paragraph but followed Rabbi Mannheimer's precedent by substituting *resha'im* ("the wicked"). Its 1985 version restored the word *arelim* ("the uncircumcised") but did not translate it. The 1998 edition again contained *arelim* but drained the word of its offensiveness by (mis)translating it as "others." The current Conservative prayer book, *Siddur Lev Shalem* (2016), casts the three negative phrases in a smaller font with the instruction: "Some omit." The accompanying comment explains that the passage does not appear in early Ashkenazic liturgy and was "probably added in the High Middle Ages, due to the competition between Judaism and Christianity..."[456] I'm not sure which texts in "early Ashkenazic liturgy" the comment is referencing. The classic early work of Ashkenazic liturgy, the 11th-12th century *Maḥzor Vitry* characteristically refers to our blessing by its first two words, *yismaḥ Moshe* ("Moses rejoiced") without listing all the wording. Thus, the most one can say is that it is not certain what the version of this blessing was in this source.[457]

[455] Cited by David Ellenson in Lawrence A. Hoffman, ed., *My People's Prayer Book: Traditional Prayers, Modern Commentaries* (Woodstock, Vermont: Jewish Lights Publishing, 2007), 10:112.
[456] *Siddur Lev Shalem*, 163.
[457] See Aryeh Goldschmidt, ed., *Maḥzor Vitry LeRabbeinu Simḥah MiVitry* (Mekhon Otzar HaPoskim, Jerusalem: 2004), 1:181.

The slightly later *siddurim* of *Ḥasidei Ashkenaz* ("German Pietists") of the 12th-13th centuries do specifically mention our passage.[458] Be that as it may, discomfort with these negative images is clearly behind the contemporary Conservative siddur's smaller font for this passage, the instruction "some omit," and the accompanying comment.

Finally, it is worth pointing out that the last few lines of this paragraph occur both here, in the Shabbat *Amidah* of *Shaḥarit* and also in the Shabbat *Amidah* of *Musaf*:

> A nation of sanctifiers of the seventh,
> they shall all be satisfied and delight in your goodness.
> You were pleased with the seventh
> "The choicest of days" you called it,
> a remembrance of the act of creation.

For the commentary on these lines, see the discussion of the Shabbat *Amidah* of *Musaf*, page 294.

**Spiritual Commentary on The *Amidah* for Shabbat Morning**

The probable role of a variant text of the *Amidah* for Shabbat morning as part of the explanation for why Exodus 31:16-17 (*VeShamru*) is cited reminds us of the fluidity of the liturgy, including for the central prayer, the *Amidah*, in the talmudic and early medieval periods. It really wasn't until the 11th-12th centuries that the liturgy became nearly as fixed as it is today. And so, for the first thousand years or so of Rabbinic Judaism (Judaism since the destruction of the Second Temple in 70 CE), the text of this Shabbat *Amidah* was relatively flexible, with various communities praying alternate wording (even within the same community), the text sometimes changing from week to week depending on the theme of that week's Torah reading. That knowledge might alter the way we view the fixed text in our prayer book as we recite this *Amidah*. The awareness that the words we are reciting represent only one of probably dozens of versions of the text might make us realize that the wording we find in today's printed prayer books is not quite as absolute as it may seem. Add to that the appreciation that each version was meant to heighten the spiritual connection between the worshiper and God with the consciousness of the restfulness of Shabbat. At the least, this knowledge

[458] See Moshe Hershler, ed., *Siddur of Rabbi Solomon ben Samson of Garmaise including the Siddur of the Ḥaside Ashkenaz* (Jerusalem: Hemed Publishing, 1971), 165; Moshe Hershler and Yehudah A. Hershler, eds., *Pirushey Siddur Hatefillah Larokeach* (Jerusalem: Machon Harav Hershler, 1992), vol. 2:531-532.

could empower us to pause occasionally and to add our own thoughts in the midst of the *Amidah* for Shabbat morning.

I have been a student of the Chinese discipline called Chi Gong (sometimes spelled XiGong) for many years. Related to Tai Chi, it is a very slow, meditative, series of movements meant to facilitate what the ancient Chinese viewed as the flow of *chi*, ("energy," "spirit") within our physical bodies. Sometimes, the leader of our Chi Gong classes encourages us to pause briefly after each movement to allow us to more fully feel the effect of whatever physical movement we have just done. I would similarly encourage us to pause at the conclusion of any given passage of the *Amidah* to see what feelings come to us. Again and again, it is crucial to recall that praying is not the same as reading. We're not following the words of the *Amidah* to glean information as we do when we are engaged in reading most other kinds of written material. We are following the words in order to effect a spiritual connection. The fact that the text of our *Amidah* is ultimately just one version of what our ancestors prayed might help us to view it for what it actually is: A vehicle, a tool, to connect ourselves with the divine spirit that is within us and beyond us. If we approach the recitation of the Shabbat *Amidah* with that mindset—as opposed to viewing it as simply the words we're "supposed" to read at this point of the service—we increase the chances that our recitation of the *Amidah* will, indeed, be a transcendent experience.

The hints in the two stories about Moses contain a different kind of potential for our worship experience. One of the stories hints at God calling Moses a servant trusted throughout God's "household." The other references the glow that radiated from Moses as a result of his closeness to God. The persona of Moses in these narratives is one of a holy man, an individual who has become enlightened with an intimate sense of the divine in his everyday experience. As we recite the words in the *Amidah* that contain these hints, we might try to consciously bring to mind an image of Moses as a wise, enlightened, spiritual seeker and leader, very much in touch with the divine spirit. We might linger with that image for a short while, just dwell with it, and see where it takes us.

Finally: the text about Shabbat as the sole possession of Israel. It is true that the traditional Jewish rules and experience of Shabbat are exclusive to the Jewish People. But there are scholarly theories that the Bible borrowed and adapted a quasi-Sabbath (Shabbatu or Shappatu) from the Babylonians and Assyrians. It is also true that Judaism's daughter religions, Christianity and Islam, have developed their own approaches to the idea of a Sabbath day. I must confess that it doesn't help my own worship experience to assert that the "uncircumcised" and the non-Jewish nations of the world (*goyyei ha'aratzot*) do not share in the Jewish Sabbath. I am aware that in ancient and medieval times, religion was understood as a zero-sum game in which there was only one true religion, and if mine is true, then yours isn't. I choose to de-emphasize these negative expressions and to linger with the positive ones:

> (You gave it in love) to...
> ...Israel
> ...your people
> ...the seed of Jacob
> ...whom you have loved.

I leave it to each modern worshiper to determine whether, and how, these passages affect the practice of their worship.

# Shabbat *Musaf*

## The *Musaf Amidah* for Shabbat

There is a second *Amidah* added on Shabbat mornings called *Musaf*, literally, an "Additional" Amidah. The reason it is added is because during Temple times, there was a second, "additional," sacrifice offered on Shabbat mornings (as well as on all holiday mornings). It was "additional" to the *Shaḥar*, or "morning" sacrifice, which was offered every day of the year. In contemporary times, the *Musaf Amidah* is particularly associated with its origin as a sacrifice because the wording of this prayer very centrally features a description of the lambs, cakes, and wine that were offered on the altar as the ancient *Musaf* sacrifice. What is usually overlooked is the fact every morning (*Shaḥar*) and afternoon (*Minḥah*) *Amidah* is based on lambs, cakes, and wine offered on the altar in the ancient Temple in exactly the same way that the *Musaf Amidah* is based on those same ancient sacrifices (See Exodus 29:38-42 and Numbers 28:1-8).[459] The reason this is often overlooked is because the wording of the morning and afternoon *Amidot* do not dwell on the details of their origins as Temple offerings the way that the *Amidah* of *Musaf* does. The morning and afternoon *Amidot* do hint at their sacrificial origins in the *Avodah* ("Worship") blessing, in which God is beseeched to restore "worship to the sanctuary of your Temple, the fire-offerings of Israel." However, even though that petition comprises an entire blessing in those *Amidot*, it is relatively brief and doesn't mention the actual ingredients of the daily morning or afternoon Temple sacrifices upon which those *Amidot* are based. On the other hand, the *Amidah* of *Musaf* goes into intricate detail about those ingredients, quoting the Torah's instruction:

> On the Sabbath day: two yearling lambs without blemish, together with two-tenths of a measure of choice flour with oil mixed in as a meal offering for every Sabbath, in addition to the regular burnt offering and its wine libation. (Numbers 28:9-10).

When these verses specify "in addition to the regular burnt offering and its libation," that means that these items are to be offered "in addition" to the "regular," i.e., daily morning and afternoon, sacrifices which include the same

[459] The *Amidah* of the evening, *Ma'ariv*, was not based on sacrifices—there were no sacrifices offered at night. This *Amidah* was apparently innovated as a popular, folk-based, ritual.

ingredients. Beyond the details of the sacrifice itself, the *Amidah* of *Musaf* also acquired another couple paragraphs that mourn the loss of this Temple ritual and appeal to God for its return, and in this way firmly cemented the view that the *Amidah* of *Musaf* is especially connected to the sacrificial rites of the ancient Temple.

The question naturally arises, therefore, that if the morning and afternoon *Amidot* are based on the very same sacrifices in the very same way as the *Amidah* of *Musaf*, how is it that only the wording of the *Amidah* of *Musaf* dwells so centrally on the sacrifices while the *Amidot* for the morning and afternoon do not?

The beginning of the answer is found in a teaching in the Palestinian Talmud, dating from a time before the texts of the *Amidot* were set. This teaching addresses the question of how long a person must wait in between praying the *Amidah* of *Shaḥarit* ("morning") and the *Amidah* of *Musaf*:

> A person prays [the *Amidah* of *Shaḥarit*] and then walks four handbreadths and prays [the *Amidah*] of *Musaf*.
>
> Rabbi Abba said: In the end [this will be interpreted to mean] that a person [must actually] walk four handbreadths. Rather [it means] that even if a person waits the [very brief] amount of time it takes to walk four handbreadths [then one may pray the *Amidah* of *Musaf* right after the *Amidah* of *Shaḥarit*].
>
> Rav said: One must say something new in it (in the *Amidah* of *Musaf*).
>
> Shmuel said: One does not have to say anything new in it.
>
> Rabbi Zeira asked of Rabbi Yossi whether one must say something new in it. He replied: "Even if one said, 'And may we [again in the future] offer our obligatory daily and additional [*Musaf*] sacrifices,' one has fulfilled one's obligation."[460]

The discussion began with the question of how long one has to wait between the *Amidah* of *Shaḥarit* and the *Amidah* of *Musaf* (answer: the time it takes to take four steps) and continued with the issue of whether the second *Amidah* may be identical to the first or not, that is, whether one

[460] Palestinian Talmud, *Berakhot* 7:1; 8c.

must add something new to the *Amidah* of *Musaf* that one did not say in the *Amidah* of *Shaḥarit.* The way Rabbi Yossi's answer to that question was later interpreted proved to be crucial to the development of the text of the *Amidah* of *Musaf.*

There are at least two ways to interpret his answer. The first is that, yes, one does need to add something new to the *Amidah* of *Musaf,* but that the new element ought to be the very brief petition, "And may we [again in the future] offer our obligatory daily and additional [*Musaf*] sacrifices." The second possible way to read his answer is, yes, one does need to add something new to the *Amidah* of *Musaf* but that the new element may be as short as just one brief sentence, any brief sentence, and then Rabbi Yossi gave an example of such a terse prayer: "And may we [again in the future] offer our obligatory daily and additional [*Musaf*] sacrifices." The key point in both interpretations is that one need only add something brief in order to differentiate the *Amidah* of *Musaf* from the *Amidah* of *Shaḥarit.* That is why Rabbi Yossi says, "Even if one said...," meaning "even if one said something as brief as the following short sentence." Let's keep in mind that this interchange occurred during a time when the texts of all the *Amidot* were in flux, in a period of formation. And that these prayers were mainly memorized and not set down in writing. Therefore, it just may be that Rabbi Yossi was saying one must add some brief prayer of one's own heart to the second *Amidah* to distinguish it from the first one. And while the loss of the sacrificial system was very dear to the ancient Sages in ways that may be difficult for moderns to appreciate, his conditioning of his reply, "Even if one said...," may apply not only to the brevity of the required additional prayer, but to the flexibility of the wording as well. While it is difficult to know whether Rabbi Yossi meant to establish the exact wording or just to model how very brief that wording would need to be, the *Amidot* of *Shaḥarit, Minḥah,* and *Musaf* are all equally based on the sacrifices that were offered in the ancient Temple.

Nevertheless, most religions typically revere the teachings of their ancient sages. And when the actual wording of personal prayers of revered holy people is preserved, it tends to become even more precious. And thus, the generations that followed this talmudic conversation required the use of Rabbi Yossi's actual words in the *Amidah* of *Musaf* instead of requiring the worshiper to add some brief new thought of one's own heart. Ultimately, the middle blessing of the *Amidah* of *Musaf* was built around an expansion of Rabbi Yossi's words. And that is how this prayer, the *Amidah* of *Musaf,* became saturated with imagery and poetry longing for the return of the ancient sacrificial worship, even though the other two major *Amidot—Shaḥarit* and *Minḥah*—are based no less upon the very same sacrificial system.

There are two additional talmudic sources which suggest possible inner meaning to the *Amidah* of *Musaf*. In the first, the Talmud informs us that in the ancient Temple, when the *Musaf* sacrifice was offered on Shabbat, the Levites would chant the long, poetic, first section of *Parashat Ha'Azinu* (Deuteronomy 32:1-43).[461] The topic of that hymnic unit is Moses' prediction that in the future, the Israelites will stray from the Torah and God will punish them. The second source connects the timing of the *Musaf* service to noon.[462] For the possible implications of these teachings, see the Spiritual Commentary on The *Musaf Amidah* for Shabbat, below.

While the *Musaf Amidah* for Shabbat is, as I've mentioned multiple times, certainly based upon the additional sacrifice that was offered on Shabbat in the ancient Temple, nevertheless, there is evidence of *Musaf Amidot*—for occasions other than on Shabbat—that have no connection to sacrifices. I am referring to a statement in the following *mishnah*:

> On three occasions in the year priests raise up their hands (in the priestly benediction) four times a day:
> - In the (*Amidah* of) *Shaḥarit*
> - In the (*Amidah* of) *Musaf*
> - In the (*Amidah* of) *Minḥah*
> - And in the (*Amidah* of) the Closing of the Gates (in the evening)
>
> [Those three occasions are]: During public fasts, during [the prayers of the] delegations [*Ma'amadot*], and on *Yom Kippur*.[463]

According to this *mishnah* there is an *Amidah* of *Musaf* on three occasions of the year, two of which (the two aside from *Yom Kippur*) are not based on biblically commanded sacrifices. Those two are public fasts and the prayers of the delegations (*Ma'amadot*).

The public fasts referred to here do not include Yom Kippur since Yom Kippur is specifically mentioned on its own afterward; nor do they include Tisha B'Av or the four minor fast days, but rather the spontaneous fasts that

[461] Babylonian Talmud, *Rosh HaShanah* 31a.
[462] *Tosefta Ta'anit* 3:1. Compare to *Mishnah Ta'anit* 4:1.
[463] *Mishnah Ta'anit* 4:1.

are called by community leaders as a sign of contrition and repentance in times of drought. The theological assumption was that God causes droughts as punishment for communal sin and therefore, the appropriate response is to call communal fast days.

*Ma'amadot* ("delegations") refer to worship services that were held by laypeople in the home communities of priests whose turn it was to serve in the Temple. Neither of these events—the communal fasts nor the worship of the delegations—is based on a biblically commanded sacrifice. Sacrifices, including those of *Musaf*, were only offered if the Bible instituted them; the *Amidot* were meant as replacements of the biblically ordained sacrifices. And yet, this *mishnah* stipulates *Amidot* for these occasions. Therefore, there was a phenomenon of an "independent" *Amidah* of *Musaf*, that is, *Amidot* called *Musaf* (so called because it was "additional" to the *Amidah* of *Shaḥarit*) for occasions independent of any sacrifice.[464]

Now I will turn to the poetry that is unique to the *Amidah* of *Musaf* for Shabbat. One could chart the units of the fourth blessing of the *Amidah* of *Musaf* this way:

1. An introduction to Rabbi Yossi's words, most of which is cast in a reverse alphabetic acrostic, i.e., each word beginning with a letter from the Hebrew alphabet in reverse order:

> You established Shabbat and desired its sacrifices. You commanded its details with the order of its wine libations. Those that delight in it will forever inherit honor. Those who savor it have merited life. And as well, those who love its particulars have chosen greatness. From Sinai they were commanded about it, and you have commanded us, *YHVH* our God, to properly offer on it (the Sabbath day) the additional Shabbat sacrifice.

[464] In my original study of the *Musaf Amidah*, published almost 35 years ago, I posited that the *Musaf Amidah* of Shabbat might have been an example of an independent *Musaf Amidah*. However, I no longer feel the evidence warrants that conclusion. See Jeffrey Hoffman, "The Surprising History of the *Musaf 'Amidah*," in *Conservative Judaism* XLII:1, Fall, 1989, 41-45. For additional sources and discussion related to the history of the *Amidah* of *Musaf*, see Stefan C. Reif, "Approaches to Sacrifice in Early Jewish Prayer," in Robert Hayward and Brad Embry, eds., *Studies in Jewish Prayer*, (Oxford: Oxford University Press, 2005), 135-150; David Golinkin, "The Restoration of Sacrifices in Modern Jewish Liturgy," in Alberdina Houtman, Marcel Poorthuis, Joshua Schwartz, Yossi Turner, eds., *The Actuality of Sacrifice: Past and Present* (Leiden: Brill, 2014), 275-283.

2. Rabbi Yossi's words in an expanded version:

> May it be your will, *YHVH* our God and God of our fathers, that you bring us in joy to our land, and plant us within our borders. And there, may we offer to you our obligatory daily and additional (*Musaf*) sacrifices according to their laws. And may we, in love, offer the additional (*Musaf*) sacrifice of this Sabbath day according to your own commandment, as you wrote for us in your Torah, through Moses your servant, from your very mouth, as it says...

3. A citation of the biblical description of the additional Shabbat sacrifice, from Numbers 28: 9-10:

> On the Sabbath day: two yearling lambs without blemish, together with two-tenths of a measure of choice flour with oil mixed in as a meal offering for every Sabbath, in addition to the regular burnt offering and its wine libation.

4. A prayer extolling those who observe the Sabbath with wording that nearly matches that of the parallel blessing in the *Amidah* of *Shaḥarit*. Here, in the *Amidah* of *Musaf*, the prayer appears with a preface of six additional words in the Hebrew:

> (The preface):
>
> May those who observe the Sabbath and call it a delight rejoice in your kingdom.
>
> A nation of sanctifiers of the seventh, they shall all be satisfied and delight in your goodness. You were pleased with the seventh and sanctified it. "The choicest of days" you called it, a remembrance of the act of creation.

5. A final prayer that is included in all of the *Amidot* of Shabbat (and which I analyzed in my commentary on the Friday night *Amidah*):

> Our God and God of our fathers, accept our rest. Sanctify us through your commandments and grant our portion in your Torah. Satisfy us through your goodness and glad-

> den us through your redemption. Purify our heart to serve you in truth. Allow us to inherit, *YHVH* our God, in love, willingly, your holy Shabbat. May Israel, the sanctifiers of your name, rest on it. Blessed are you, *YHVH*, Sanctifier of Shabbat.

Charted in this way, the centrality of the theme of the sacrifices is obvious, with the first three, of a total of five parts, devoted to this theme.

The very first words the worshiper utters that are unique to this *Amidah*, namely, paragraph 1, immediately and lovingly invoke the close connection between Shabbat and its ancient sacrifices. Paragraph 2 is where Rabbi Yossi's words are cited, but here they are expanded and set in a context of longing to return to the land of Israel so that we may rebuild the Temple and again offer these very sacrifices. Below is paragraph 2 once more, with the original, talmudic, version of Rabbi Yossi's words bolded:

> May it be your will, *YHVH* our God and God of our fathers, that you bring us in joy to our land, and plant us within our borders. **And** there, **may we offer to you our obligatory daily and additional [*Musaf*] sacrifices** according to their laws. And may we, in love, offer the additional [*Musaf*] sacrifice of this Sabbath day according to your own commandment, as you wrote for us in your Torah, through Moses your servant, from your very mouth, as it says...

Paragraph 3 continues the thought by quoting the passage in the Torah where the lambs, cakes and wine ingredients for this additional Sabbath sacrifice are commanded.

Paragraph 4 is the first place in this blessing where we find a new idea, an idea unconnected with the Sabbath sacrifices, namely, the joy of the Sabbath for both humans and God. The bulk of this passage is also found in the Shabbat *Amidah* of *Shaḥarit*, minus the first sentence that is found only in the version here in the *Amidah* of *Musaf*:

> **Only in the *Amidah* of *Musaf*:**
> May those who observe the Sabbath and call it a delight rejoice in your kingdom.

**In Both the *Amidah* of *Musaf* and of *Shaḥarit*:**
A nation of sanctifiers of the seventh, they shall all be satisfied and delight in your goodness. You were pleased with the seventh and sanctified it. "The choicest of days" you called it, a remembrance of the act of creation.

The reason for the discrepancy is not clear. Elbogen assumes that the fuller version, found here in *Musaf*, is the original version and that the shortened form appears in *Shaḥarit* because of "the expansion" of the poetry that immediately precedes it.[465] He also mentions that the Sephardic rite on Shabbat includes the full version in both *Shaḥarit* and *Musaf*. Given the lack of documentary evidence available, there really is no way to know for sure whether the original version was the longer one and it was shortened for some reason in *Shaḥarit*, or whether it originally was shorter and only later was a beginning sentence added to it in *Musaf*. In any case, I will deal with the fuller version here in the discussion of *Musaf*.

There are several literary devices occurring in the short passage contained in paragraph 4. To begin with, the first half describes people in three ways, while the second half focuses on God in three ways. The form of the verbs regarding the people are participles which function at one and the same time as present-tense verbs and as nouns. The people of Israel are:

*Shomrei Shabbat*, "those who observe the Sabbath/Sabbath observers."
*Korei oneg*, "Those who call it (the Sabbath) a delight/Sabbath 'delighters.'"
*Am mekadshei shevi'i*, "A nation that sanctifies the seventh (day)/A nation of seventh-day sanctifiers."

All the verbs regarding God are in the perfect form, indicating past actions:

*Ratzita bo*, "you were pleased with it."
*Vekidashto*, "and you sanctified it."
*Ḥemdat yamim oto karata*, "you called it 'the choicest of days.'"

[465] Elbogen, *Jewish Liturgy*, 97.

If this brief passage were a piece of music, it would add up to a kind of dialogue in contrapuntal form: The first melody, in higher notes perhaps, would depict the people of Israel who loyally and continually observe, delight in, and sanctify the Sabbath. The second, in lower notes, would represent the source of the people's actions way back in the past, in the first week of Creation when God was pleased with, and sanctified, the Sabbath, and when God called it "the choicest of days."

Another literary tool at work in paragraph 4 is a reference to a biblical passage, Isaiah 58:13-14. The bolded words in the biblical verse parallel those same bolded words in this liturgical poem:

| Isaiah 58: 13-14[466] | *Amidah* of *Musaf* |
|---|---|
| If you refrain from trampling the sabbath,<br>from pursuing your affairs on my **sanctified day**; if **you call the sabbath "delight,"**<br>the Lord's **sanctified day** "honored";<br>and if you honor it and not go your ways<br>nor look to your affairs, nor strike bargains—<br>then you will truly **delight in the Lord...**[467] | May those who observe the Sabbath and **call it a delight** rejoice in your kingdom.<br>A nation of **sanctifiers of the seventh (day),** they shall all be satisfied and **delight** in your goodness. You were pleased with the seventh and **sanctified** it. "The choicest of days" you called it, a remembrance of the act of creation. |

The genius of the liturgy's reworking of Isaiah is that it took the prophet's negative description of what should be "refrained" from on the Sabbath and turned it into a positive portrayal of an ideal experience of the Sabbath. And so, when the worshiper recites these words, it becomes an inspirational reading meant to motivate the worshiper to aspire to this ideal view of

[466] In fact, these two verses from Isaiah are also referenced above in part of paragraph 1:
...Those that **delight** in it will forever inherit **honor.**
It is possible as well that Paragraph 1's use of *To'ameha* "Those who savor it" (literally, "taste it") may parallel the phrase in Isaiah 58:14, *veha'akhaltikha*, "and I shall feed you..."

[467] This passage may be familiar because it forms part of the *Haftarah* for the morning of *Yom Kippur*. It was chosen for that holiday because earlier in the chapter, the prophet eloquently compares a true fast to a false one.

Sabbath observance: to achieve a sense of "delight" in the "sanctity" of this seventh day.[468]

Finally, the last line in this passage contains an interesting idea. It reads:

> "The choicest of days" you called it, a remembrance of the act of creation.

Whenever the liturgy has God "calling" or "saying" something, it usually means that God "called" or "said" that same something in the Bible. The writer of the prayer presumed that the educated worshiper would catch the reference and call to mind the biblical verse alluded to. Almost always, the connection between the biblical verse and the prayer text is a midrashic one, a connection that moderns would usually regard as "a stretch," and that seems to be the case here as well. There is a long chain of medieval commentators who identify the active verse in our case as Genesis 2:2.[469]

The verse in the context of the beginning of chapter 2 of Genesis is:

> On the seventh day God finished the work that he had been doing, and he ceased on the seventh day from all the work that he had done.

The midrashic approach to this verse interprets the first Hebrew word of the verse (*vayekhal*) not as "(On the seventh day God) **finished**," but rather as "(God) **yearned for** (the seventh day)."[470] In this sense, our prayer has God declaring—at the beginning of the very first Sabbath in the Creation story—that God "yearned" for the seventh day. Therefore, according to our prayer, God indeed "called" the seventh day the "choicest of days."

Modern Orthodox *siddurim* accept the abundant language about sacrifices in the *Amidah* of *Musaf* on Shabbat as doing nothing other than asking

[468] It is also possible in this liturgical passage that the word *yisbe'u*, "satisfied," may be meant as a play on the two times that the central word *shevi'i*, "seventh" is cited, since they both share the same three root letters in Hebrew, *shin-bet-ayin*.

[469] The earliest reference appears to be in a (now lost) interpretation in the Aramaic translation known as *Targum Yerushalmi* of this verse (final editing of this translation: probably 7th century, Israel). For a list of the medieval commentators who cite this, see Simhah ben Shmuel, *Maḥzor Vitry*, ed., Aryeh Goldschmidt, 1:170-171, notes 2-4. It is clear from several early Ashkenazic commentaries that during the formative period of Ashkenazic liturgy this line occurred both in the Shabbat *Amidah* of Friday night as well as that of *Shaharit* and *Musaf*, as is the Sephardic custom to this day.

[470] Based on an ancient Aramaic translation of *vayekhal*, "finished," as "yearned" using the same Hebrew root, *ḥet-mem-dalet*, as our prayer uses in the phrase *ḥemdat yamim*, "choicest of days" (the day most "yearned" for). See an alternate midrashic interpretation of this same word in the *Amidah* for Friday night, on page 243.

God to allow us to offer loyal service by worshiping God in the way we were asked to in the Torah. This is a cogent and logical approach to this *Amidah*, though not in keeping with modern negative views of animal sacrifice. The modern liberal movements in American Judaism do not envision a rebuilding of a Jerusalem Temple with animal and meal sacrifices and wine libations. Therefore, they evolved several paths in dealing with these passages that so directly reference the sacrifices and express a desire for their return. The first Reform prayer books in the early 19th century in Germany, from 1819 to 1860 or so, did not immediately excise these statements.

> There was, above all, one very practical reason. The *Shaḥarith* Service in the average German synagogue was not too well attended. It was only when the Torah was taken from the Ark that the majority of the worshippers assembled, and that the chief cantor and the choir made their appearance... (The) "main service" consisted of Torah and *Haftarah* readings, the sermon, some German prayers and—*Musaph*. Even Seligmann, who in 1910, edited a prayerbook reflecting a pronounced Reform point of view, was aware of the realities of the situation, and wishing to avoid meaningless repetition, he sacrificed the Seven Benedictions of the *Shaḥarith* Service (for which he substituted a brief German prayer for silent devotion) to the retention of the Seven Benedictions of *Musaph*.[471]

However, over several decades, they slowly reduced the wording in Hebrew and/or in the German translation, until finally deleting the entire *Amidah*.

The contemporary Reform siddur, *Mishkan Tefillah* (2007), and the contemporary Reconstructionist siddur, *Kol Haneshamah* (2004), delete the entire Shabbat *Amidah* of *Musaf*. The first Conservative Movement prayer book for Shabbat (1946) included the traditional Hebrew phrasing but with two innovations in the text. Instead of praying for a future restoration of the sacrificial service, it changed the verbs from the future to the past tense. In this way, it paid tribute to sacrificial worship as a relic of the past and did not pray for its return in the future. And in doing so, this siddur was following the precedent set by the Hamburg Prayerbook of 1819.[472] The second

[471] Jakob J. Petuchowski, *Prayerbook Reform in Europe: The Liturgy of European and Reform Judaism* (New York: The World Union for Progressive Judaism, 1968), 241-242.
[472] See Petuchowski, *Prayerbook Reform*, 242.

change was that where the traditional text of this *Amidah* actually spelled out the details of the sacrificial animals, cakes, and wine (paragraph 3), this siddur only preserved that wording in the Hebrew, but in the translation merely wrote "The Sabbath Offering: (Numbers 28:9-10)," as if the typical worshiper would know these biblical verses by heart. Clearly, the editors of this prayer book had decided to prioritize what they considered the spiritual and esthetic predilections of their movement's worshipers over honest translation.[473] The current Conservative prayer book, *Siddur Lev Shalem* (2016), both built on and revised the innovations of its 1946 predecessor, as well as building on the two other Shabbat prayer books the movement produced in the interim. *Siddur Lev Shalem* restored an English translation of Numbers 28:9-10, making it clear to worshipers that in this prayer, they were referring to flesh and blood sacrifices. It also offers, as an option, an alternative to nearly the entire middle blessing of the *Amidah* of *Musaf*, replacing the language yearning for a return of the sacrifices with language yearning for a return of the Jewish People to the Land of Israel.

**Spiritual Commentary on The *Musaf Amidah* for Shabbat**

It seems to me that in reciting the Shabbat *Amidah* of *Musaf*, we have a perfect opportunity to restore Rabbi Yossi's interpretation of its possible original intent: as a goad to express something spontaneous and different from what we've said in the presence of God up to now in the Shabbat morning service. That holds true whether we replace the written text with our own words or we recite the written text but add our own thoughts to it. If we actually yearn for the return of the sacrificial service, well then, here is a good place to express that. My guess, though, is that most modern worshipers—including many, if not most, modern Orthodox worshipers—do not sincerely hope for such a return. Therefore, the middle of the Shabbat *Amidah* of *Musaf* is an excellent place for us to take a breath and articulate what needs to be said before God on this particular Shabbat. This day. Here. Now. When we find ourselves in worship on a Shabbat morning, we would do well to notice where we are: We are not at work, not out shopping, not acquiring anything, not under pressure or stress to accomplish anything or to prove anything or to succeed. We don't need to "do our best," or worry about how others perceive us. Whether we believe God has consciousness, is simply a spiritual "presence," or something else entirely, it would serve us well to notice the opportunity we have to actually feel what we're feeling at

[473] Morris Silverman, ed., *Sabbath and Festival Prayer Book* (The Rabbinical Assembly of America and The United Synagogue of America, 1946), 141.

this particular moment as we stand in the *Amidah*, which is to say, as we stand in consciousness of the presence of the divine on this day of rest.

It must be admitted that one of the ironies of the typical contemporary synagogue experience is that worshipers could be forgiven if they actually do feel pressure, even in the midst of worship. Pressure to conform to what appears to be the "expected" way of worship, namely, to competently read or sing the words on the page in proper Hebrew and with the proper melodies along with what appears to be the majority of the congregation. But reading is not worshiping, and singing, by itself, is not worshiping. Reading and singing may lead to worship but reading and singing—in and of themselves—do not constitute worship. For worship to occur, there needs to be *kavannah*, "consciousness." Consciousness that one is in the presence of the divine. That one is outside of ordinary time. We need to notice where we are and the sublime opportunity we have to enter into worship with consciousness and intention. That is the first step toward fulfilling what Rabbi Yossi suggested.

Perhaps we ought to consider the advice of Isaiah as we engage in prayer in the late morning on Shabbat. Isaiah exhorted his community to notice the "delight" of this day and to sense its "holiness." Once we express whatever it is that we are truly feeling at the moment, we might allow ourselves to be challenged, across more than two millennia, by that great voice of justice and spirit, Isaiah the prophet. In doing so, we may well feel "delight" at having arrived at a "holy" moment. As Rabbi Heschel formulated it, the gift of the Sabbath is that it is an opportunity to simply be, and not to do.[474] For me, one of the truest definitions of "delight" is the chance to escape the pressures to produce, to perform, to achieve. The opportunity simply... to be. Late morning on Shabbat, in synagogue, given the break to actually pray in one's own words is indeed a delight. And that, I believe, is what the middle of the *Amidah* of *Musaf* offers us.

Beyond that, I cited the Talmud earlier to the effect that when the Shabbat *Musaf* sacrifice was offered in the ancient Temple, the Levites would chant Moses' prediction in *Parashat Ha'Azinu* that in the future, the Israelites would stray from the Torah and suffer as a result. Perhaps an implication of that teaching is that an inner meaning of one's Shabbat *Musaf Amidah* ought to be *teshuvah*: thoughts about, and commitment to, repentance.

The other talmudic teaching cited above connected the timing of the *Musaf Amidah* with noon. Typically, the timing of the *Musaf Amidah* in congregations that offer it, is indeed approximately noon. This association

[474] See his slim book (just over 100 pages): Abraham Joshua Heschel, *The Sabbath* (New York: Farrar, Straus, and Giroux, 1951).

can be an opportunity to connect to God, through a phenomenon of nature, namely, to when the sun is highest during the day. People in pre-modern societies lived much more in sync with the changing light of the sky than we do for a simple reason: It was expensive to illuminate interiors with oil at night. They naturally went to sleep not long after the sun set and awoke with the dawn. They were much more attuned to the changing colors of the sky because they relied on the sun's light far more than we moderns do. Nevertheless, we moderns are also moved and awed by the reds and purples of dawn and sunset and by the glimmer of starlight at night. The awe-inspiring changes in the light during those liminal times of the day tend to awaken in us a sense of a reality greater than us. It is likely for this reason that the sacrifices in the ancient Temple—which are the bases for the *Amidot* in general—were offered at dawn and at dusk, and that a need was felt to add an additional *Amidah* in the evening. The *Amidah* recited at the *Ma'ariv*/ evening service can connect us spiritually through the arrival of darkness, and the emergence of the moon and stars. The *Amidah* of *Shaḥarit*/morning can connect us through the new light of dawn. The *Amidah* of *Minḥah*/ afternoon can connect us through the arrival of dusk. The links between those *Amidot* and the times of the day are well known in our tradition. But the teaching that links the *Musaf Amidah* with noon is much less cited. The nexus between *Musaf* and high noon offers the possibility of trying to recite this prayer outdoors in pleasant weather, to bask in the warmth of the sunlight, or if indoors, to contemplate where we are on the planet as the earth perfectly aligns our location with the sun directly overhead, and to become aware of a cosmic reality much greater than ourselves. This awareness can serve as the content of our *Musaf Amidah*.

# Shabbat *Minḥah* (Afternoon Service)

## *Kedushah DeSidra* (*U'Va LeTzion*)

*Kedushah DeSidra*, "The *Kedushah* of the Torah Passage," is the title of a prayer mentioned in Rabbinic Literature and found in several places in traditional *siddurim* (with some textual differences) in all the eras.[475] In modern *siddurim*, it is mainly recited as part of the concluding prayers of weekday *Shaḥarit*, toward the beginning of Shabbat and festival *Minḥah*, and toward the end of *Ma'ariv* at the conclusion of Shabbat.[476] As with all prayer texts mentioned in Rabbinic Literature, it is not clear how closely the text of the prayer as it reached even the earliest *siddurim* (9th-11th centuries) corresponds to the text(s) of the prayer referred to in the Talmud (6th-7th century).[477] This prayer is also sometimes referred as *U'Va LeTzion*, "A Redeemer Will Come to Zion," based on its first two words. However, the prayer also appears, even in contemporary prayer books, in a version lacking these words as well as its first couple of sentences, (e.g., in the evening service at the conclusion of Shabbat). The title, *Kedushah DeSidra*, "The *Kedushah* of the Torah Passage," hints that it was originally connected to Torah reading or Torah study. A number of talmudic, geonic, and early medieval sources seem to support an original link between this prayer and Torah study, or more accurately, between this prayer and *derashot*, the shared experience—on Shabbat afternoons in Geonic times (8th-11th centuries)—of listening to rabbinic interpretations of biblical passages, especially from the latter two sections of the Bible, namely, the Prophets and the Writings.[478] Therefore, although this prayer appears in various places in contemporary *siddurim*, it may be that its original location was here, on Shabbat afternoon.

The contemporary Ashkenazic version of *Kedushah DeSidra* consists mostly of biblical verses from the Prophets and Writings with a few non-biblical lines woven in. The non-biblical wording is found in two places within

[475] For example, in the Babylonian Talmud, *Sotah* 49a.

[476] For a listing of all the places this prayer is recited, as well as a summary of various reasons offered for its recitation at various liturgical locations—though many of the reasons offered are quite fanciful and belie an "after the fact" character—see Macy Nulman, *The Encyclopedia of Jewish Prayer* (Northvale, NJ: Jason Aaronson, 1993), 333-335.

[477] Although the reference to this prayer in the Talmud opens with a statement by Rava, a Sage who flourished in the first half of the 4th century, the specific mention of "*Kedushah DeSidra*" appears to be an anonymous statement deriving from the later *Stam*, or "anonymous," literary layer. Scholars date this layer to approximately the 6th-7th centuries.

[478] See Elbogen, *Jewish Liturgy*, 99 and n. 2 for sources. Rabbi Yehudah bar Barzilai al-Bargeloni (Spain, 12th c. "al-Bargeloni" = The Barcelonian"), the author of *Sefer Ha'Ittim* (Cracow: Mekitzei Nirdamim, 1903), 289, cites specific Geonim and sketches two different customs of how the biblical study and the recital of this prayer had been practiced in Geonic times.

the patchwork of biblical language. The first integrates rabbinic phrases with the ancient Aramaic translation of the three most typical verses found in the various recensions of the *Kedushah.* Together, this quilt of rabbinic and biblical lines within the larger prayer forms one of the many versions of the *Kedushah*, called by the same name as this prayer as a whole, *Kedushah DeSidra.* The other network of rabbinic and biblical wording, toward the end of the prayer, consists of a few lines praising Torah.

These two instances of integrated rabbinic and biblical wording, the *Kedushah* and the praise of Torah, demand a bit more attention. The *Kedushah* because it begs the question of why a *Kedushah* is found in the middle of this prayer, and the lines praising Torah because they include strident denigration of the non-Jewish nations that do not possess Torah.

Versions of the *Kedushah* occur in three places in the traditional Ashkenazic siddur: Each time an *Amidah* is repeated, as part of the cluster of prayers surrounding the recitation of the *Shema* in every *Shaḥarit* service, and here in the *Kedushah DeSidra.* I deal with each in its place, and each time, one of the questions that arises is: What is a mystical prayer doing here? It is generally accepted that the *Kedushah* originated in circles of mystics; when it originated is still debated. It appears to me to have occurred approximately in the late talmudic period to the early Geonic era. Any discussion of the place of mystical prayers must take into account the tension between the reticence of the mainstream rabbinic community to openly teach mystical tenets and practices on the one hand, and the oft-expressed openness in the mystical literature itself to share their teachings with the general community.[479] The reticence comes from the same kinds of fears that mainstream religionists in any tradition harbor vis-à-vis mystics. Mystics tend to emphasize the immanent and immediate experience of God over traditional rules, rituals and interpretations and thus, mystics can be threatening to established religious systems and communities. Mystics themselves also sometimes like to preserve their insights and innovations for their select and elite circle of adepts who are willing to separate themselves from the accepted, conventional ways of religion.

However, specifically regarding the *Kedushah*, there are texts that encourage mystics to invite others into their experience (such a text is translated and discussed in my commentary on the *Kedushah* of the *Amidah*, page 108).

[479] Ruth Langer expresses these tensions regarding the circle that produced the origins of the various forms of the *Kedushah*, i.e., the *Merkavah* mystics of the *Hekhalot* Literature in *To Worship God Properly: Tensions Between Liturgical Custom and Halakhah in Judaism* (Cincinnati: Hebrew Union College Press, 1998), 199-200; 203. And see the entire chapter of this book, "Individual Recitation of the *Kedushah*: The Impact of Mystics on Minhag and Halakhah" for important sources and context.

So, why is this mystical prayer embedded in a larger prayer recited after the study of the Bible? There are no extant sources which directly address the question, and so answering it is a matter of speculation. My surmise is that for some in the ancient Jewish community, Shabbat afternoon was a time of mystical study and mystical practice. All of the versions of the *Kedushah* bring one into the heavenly realms because they quote the angelic praises that Isaiah and Ezekiel heard in their transcendent visions. Study of what appear to be the actual praises the angels constantly sing to God in heaven may have been accompanied by attempts to replicate the prophets' visions and to hear and see the angelic worship directly. It may be that the inclusion of the *Kedushah* in a mainstream prayer represents an attempt by the established religious leadership to co-opt a practice that was viewed as threatening. Or it may have been an innovation of the mystics themselves who wished to expand their community of ecstatic worshipers. Until definitive evidence is discovered it is difficult to know whether either of these options, or a third, unknown motivation is behind the inclusion of a *Kedushah* in this prayer.

The prayer as a whole sounds notes of comfort and consolation with messianic overtones—including its first sentence:

> A redeemer shall come to Zion, to those in Jacob who turn
> back from sin, declares *YHVH*.[480]

If the prayer's original purpose was to provide a kind of hopeful conclusion to the experience of Torah exposition, its tone is quite appropriate. However, the comfort and support expressed here includes an example of what I call Anti-Goyism, kind of a reverse Antisemitism. Note the following line which occurs in the second collage of biblical and rabbinic wording, toward the end of the prayer. It is very much within the binary view of us versus them; the zero-sum game, which holds that only one religion may be true and that therefore, all others are false. The line specifically ties Torah to Israel's claim of true religion:

> Blessed is our God who
> created us for his glory
> separated us from those who err,[481]

[480] Isaiah 59:20.

[481] "Err," *to'eh*, has overtones in the Bible of erring physically, ethically, mentally, or as a result of intoxication. See Francis Brown, S.R. Driver, Charles A. Briggs, *A Hebrew and English Lexicon of the Old Testament* (Oxford: Clarendon Press, 1906, 1951), 1073.

gave us true Torah,
and planted everlasting life within us.

This is just one line in a long prayer, but it is not the only expression of Anti-Goyism in Jewish liturgy and I have pointed it out in several places.

**Spiritual Commentary on *Kedushah DeSidra* (*U'Va LeTzion*)**
This prayer is, in essence, a prayer designed to follow the study of Torah, especially the kind of Torah study whose aim it is to reveal ethical and spiritual teachings. That kind of study tends to be open-ended, expansive, inclusive, and creative. For many of us who have engaged in that kind of spiritual exercise—analyzing biblical passages for their deeper meanings—it is a truly delightful, even sublime, experience. It is for that reason that such Torah study is, traditionally, forbidden on the fast day of *Tisha B'Av*, specifically because it brings joy to those engaged in it. When reciting this prayer, it is quite appropriate to be aware of, and awake to, the sheer pleasure and enjoyment that Torah study can bring, and to express gratitude to God for that joy through the words of this prayer. This kind of study can, in fact, be a mystical experience—depending on the kinds of deeper meanings discovered through such inquiry—and therefore, the presence of a mystical prayer embedded within the larger prayer can also help us express thanksgiving for the experience of religious study.

As for the presence of the sentence that I have labelled an example of Anti-Goyism, it is important for all peoples, including persecuted peoples, to come to terms with the fact that we, too, succumb to that human tendency of vaunting our own merits, even claiming godly support for the truth of our spiritual path, while denying truth to the Other. I do not believe in the typically medieval zero-sum game of assuming that there is only one true spiritual path. Therefore, when I recite this sentence, I consciously do not take its point seriously, that those whose spiritual path does not include Torah may be labelled as "those who err." I am supremely grateful for our tradition's spiritual teachings, and I embrace whatever I may also learn from other peoples' spiritual traditions as well.

## Shabbat *Amidah* of *Minḥah*
The Shabbat *Amidah* of *Minḥah*, like the other three *Amidot* of Shabbat, contains wording in its fourth blessing specific to this blessing followed by the paragraph that is shared by all the *Amidot* of Shabbat, i.e., "Our God and God of our fathers, find favor in our rest..." The wording specific to this

*Amidah* comes just before this passage and begins with the theme of the distinctiveness of God and Israel but then quickly centers upon Sabbath rest:

> You are one, and your name is one, and who is like Israel, your people, unique (lit., "one") on earth. The glory of greatness and the crown of redemption [is Shabbat]; you gave a day of rest and holiness to your people. Abraham rejoices, Isaac revels, Jacob and his sons rest thereon. A rest of love and devotion, a rest of truth and faith, a rest of peace and calm, quiet and refuge, a complete rest that you favor. May your children notice and know that their rest comes from you, and through their rest may they sanctify your name.

Sabbath rest, *menuḥah*, is mentioned some seven times; the same root, *nun-vav-nun*, within the verb *yanuḥu*, with the same meaning, occurs an additional time. The eight times that this theme is sounded here connect with a ninth time in the first line of the next paragraph, the paragraph shared by all of the Shabbat *Amidot*, "Our God and God of our fathers, find favor in our **rest**..."

It is worth mentioning that our two oldest *siddurim*, *Seder Rav Amram* (9th century)[482] and *Siddur Rav Saadia Ga'on* (10th century)[483] record this passage—the passage recited by virtually all contemporary Jewish rites—but they identify it as merely a variant that some people recite, and present the following paragraph as the standard passage. That passage begins very differently, but ends with the same wording as the contemporary text for the Shabbat *Amidah* of *Minḥah*:

> Give us rest, *YHVH* our God, for you are our father. Reign over us soon for you are our king. Because of your name—the great, the heroic, the awesome—through which Israel and the seventh day is called, we shall cease (work) upon it as is your command. May there not be pain or grief or anguish on the day of our rest. And may our rest be a rest of love and devotion, a rest of truth and faith, a rest of peace

[482] Ed., Daniel Goldschmidt, *Seder Rav Amram*, 79.

[483] I. Davidson, S. Assaf, B.I. Joel, eds., *Siddur Rav Saadia Ga'on*, 113. The passage these two texts present as the primary one for the Shabbat *Amidah* of *Minḥah* is also found in several Genizah fragments. See Elbogen, *Jewish Liturgy*, 100.

> and calm, quiet and refuge, a complete rest that you favor. May your children notice and know that their rest comes from you, and through their rest may they sanctify your name.

We do not know how the text considered by our first two *siddurim* to be merely a variant of their preferred text ultimately became the primary text, but the fact is that after the 10th century or so, it is consistently recorded as the main text to be recited in this *Amidah*.[484] This is one of those interesting issues in the history of Jewish liturgy that cannot yet be explained and which calls out for further research or perhaps a chance discovery of a long lost crucial document that closes the gap in our understanding. Also interesting is that when these very early liturgical sources cite what is for them the variant text—and for the rest of Jewish liturgical history the primary text—they cite it with an additional line missing in the version that has become canonized in the centuries since. I will reproduce their version with the additional line bolded:

> You are one, and your name is one, and who is like Israel, your people, unique (lit., "one") on earth. The glory of greatness and the crown of redemption, you gave a day of rest and holiness to your people. Abraham rejoices, Isaac revels, Jacob and his sons rest thereon. **You said to Moses your servant on Mount Sinai, "I will go in the lead and give you rest" (Exodus 33:14): complete rest**. A rest of love and devotion, a rest of truth and faith, a rest of peace and calm, quiet and refuge, a complete rest that you favor. May your children notice and know that their rest comes from you, and through their rest may they sanctify your name.

Regarding this additional line, Elbogen comments, "This last at least partially explains the rather surprising words 'Abraham rejoices, Isaac sings, Jacob and his sons rest thereon.'"[485] Elbogen noticed that this addition is clearly a midrashic, i.e., creative, interpretation of the cited verse. Exodus 33:14 in the

[484] The 12th-century *Seder Ḥibbur Berakhot* says to recite *Attah eḥad*, "You are one," in the silent version of the *Amidah* and *Hanaḥ lanu*, "Give us rest," in the communal repetition of the *Amidah*. (*Siddur Rav Sa'adia*, 113, notes).
[485] Elbogen, *Jewish Liturgy*, 100.

context of the Book of Exodus is translated as the new JPS edition renders, "I will go in the lead and will lighten your burden," because it represents God's reassurance to Moses, following the sin of the Golden Calf, that God will not abandon him and the people. However, I translated as I did in the context of the prayer, "I will go in the lead and give you rest," understanding the word *vehaniḥoti*, not as "lighten your burden" but hyper-literally as "give you rest." This interpretation is confirmed by the fact that the prayer adds the words, "complete rest." The point of the prayer is that here, God is granting Moses and the People of Israel the gift of Shabbat, and God had done the same for Abraham, Isaac, and Jacob. Of course, there is no mention in the Bible of Shabbat regarding the Patriarchs, and that is what Elbogen originally found "surprising" about these words. But adding Moses to these founding fathers—Moses, to whom the Bible connects Shabbat on several occasions—seems to make the point that just as Shabbat was observed by Moses and his generation of Israelites, so too was it observed by the families of Abraham, Isaac, and Jacob. In fact, this passage hints, Shabbat has always been a part of the Jewish family.

There are other minor variants of this paragraph as well (mainly toward the end of the passage, adding that Shabbat is not only "a rest of love and devotion," etc., but also a rest of x, y, and z) and there are many interpretations that have been penned over the centuries. I will just cite one of them here. The 13th-century Italian work *Shibbolei HaLekket* offers an explanation for why the threefold repetition of the word *eḥad*, "one, unique" is found in the first sentence, basing himself on teachings of Rashi:

> It is pleasant for the one God to unite with the one, unique people on the one, unique day, namely, Shabbat.[486]

An interesting thought, and it may capture what is behind this line of poetry because it rings true to the wording. Note that this comment only explains why this language might be used on Shabbat and not why it is especially appropriate for the afternoon service of Shabbat. Nevertheless, this poetry may have been composed for Shabbat in general and as I've emphasized in several places, there was no consistent "editor" nor even an "editorial committee" for our siddur. Therefore, it is quite possible that a prayer text penned for Shabbat in general might have found a place within any Shabbat

---

[486] See Tzedekiah ben Avraham, *Shibbolei HaLekket*, Solomon Buber, ed. (Jerusalem: Alef Publishing Company, 1962, reprint of 1891 version), 96-97. And indeed, the essence of this teaching is found in *Maḥzor Vitry*, from the school of Rashi, though the author of *Shibbolei HaLekket* sums it up in a pithier way. See Simḥah ben Shmuel, *Maḥzor Vitry*, ed., Aryeh Goldschmidt, ed., 1:213.

service whether it had any tangible connection to a specific service. For this reason, I view with a touch of skepticism some of the appealing and inspiring comments about why certain words or themes occur in specific prayers of Shabbat. These types of interpretations often betray a sense of after-the-fact guesswork. They do have value for the inspiration they offer, but they usually do not reflect historical truth. In this category I include a commentary found in many sources that traces a kind of narrative arc in the changes to one word in the paragraph that is shared by all the *Amidot* of Shabbat. In the evening service that initiates Shabbat, that paragraph expresses the hope that "Israel may rest on it (Shabbat)," and the word for "it," *vah*, is in the feminine form. The morning service has that same word in the masculine form, *vo*, while the Shabbat afternoon service has "them," *vam*. The interpretation relates to (and perhaps adds to) a Kabbalistic view that Friday night is connected to the feminine side of God, Shabbat morning to the masculine side, and Shabbat afternoon to both sides. The main reason I detect an after-the-fact element here is that there are numerous versions of these *Amidot* that do not contain those three words; some versions simply have the same word for all three *Amidot* and some contain some of these words but in a different order.

**Spiritual Commentary on The Shabbat *Amidah* of *Minḥah***

I find some of the literary and historical elements of this blessing quite inspiring: The fact that it repeats the word "rest" over and over, with knowing appreciation for the tremendous benefits that flow from reserving a spiritual day off each week. The fact that the line about Abraham, Isaac, and Jacob observing Shabbat becomes less surprising when a "lost" line about Moses' rest on Shabbat is considered. The occasional capriciousness of the historical paths certain words take in the development of our liturgy has a stirring side to it: As we've seen over and over again, holiness resides in both the long textual continuity in our prayers as well as in its occasional discontinuity. How wonderful to rediscover a line of text that disappeared from the prayer centuries ago to dispel confusion about another line that it used to accompany and clarify! And finally, the fact that the Jewish Sabbath, while sharing some aspects with Sabbaths of other traditions, does indeed contain much unique, charming, intimate, and soul-refreshing poetry and practice. When we recite the words specific to this Shabbat afternoon *Amidah*, we are entering a consciousness of gratitude for a very special brand of spiritual rest. Therefore, as we recite these words, let's allow a general feeling of gratefulness wash over us; gratefulness for the respite and repose of Shabbat rest that we are experiencing at this very moment of prayer.

## Conclusion of Shabbat (*Havdalah*)

The conclusion of Shabbat is marked by a prayer known as *Havdalah*, "Distinction," i.e., the distinction between holy time, i.e., Shabbat, and non-holy, or profane, time, i.e., the weekdays. *Havdalah* is found in two forms. One is a prayer inserted into the fourth blessing of the *Amidah* of *Ma'ariv* at the conclusion of the Sabbath. The other is a brief ceremony unto itself following the *Ma'ariv* service. The ceremony encompasses biblical verses and three blessings praising God for creating wine, spices and fire. Both versions of *Havdalah* are expressly discussed in the Talmud which attributes the origin of *Havdalah* to "The Men of the Great Assembly."[487] This is likely the Talmud's way of ascribing archaic roots to this prayer (modern scholars are skeptical as to whether this "Great Assembly" ever actually existed), and indeed Tannaim, Sages of the earliest rabbinic period, are cited as discussing the wording and guidelines of *Havdalah.* The current Ashkenazic versions of this prayer, whether in the *Amidah* or recited as a ceremony unto itself, praise God for making *havdalot*, "distinctions" between four pairs:

1. Holy and profane
2. Light and darkness
3. Israel and other nations
4. The seventh day and the six days of work

The Talmud records a different version of the prayer containing four additional distinctions:

1. The unclean from the clean
2. The sea from dry land
3. Upper waters from lower waters
4. Priests from Levites, from (other) Israelites

Lawrence Hoffman summarizes the basic message of this prayer as follows:

> The basic diad is the dichotomy between holy and profane which itself may be reflected in the structuring of time, or of society (Sabbath/weekdays; Israel/other people); it may

[487] Babylonian Talmud, *Berakhot* 33b and *Pesaḥim* 103b-104a.

> be combined with a secondary symbol of late Roman times (light/dark); or it may be stated baldly (holy/profane)... That message is the essential cultural distinction of holy/profane: it is the categorization of reality into two disparate realms that I take to be the rabbis' ultimate *a priori* characterization of human experience; and it is *havdalah*'s function to ritualize that *a priori* experiential grid.[488]

I think this is basically correct: *Havdalah* as a ritual concretizes a fundamental way that Jewish tradition characterizes life, namely as a drama between the holy and profane. Another way of saying this is that Jewish ritual and tradition challenge us to see holiness, to invite the presence of God, in as much of our reality as possible. That includes, in this case, motivating us to see, to recognize, the departure of the holy time of Shabbat just as *Havdalah*'s parallel ritual, the Friday night *Kiddush* invites us to see, to recognize, the arrival of Shabbat as holy time.

At the same time, because this prayer is all about making distinctions between the holy and profane, it invokes a classic comparison between "Israel" (holy) and "the other nations" (profane). This juxtaposition parallels the statement made in the Friday night *Kiddush* that God "chose us from among all the nations." This particular distinction can be both benign and malignant. It can be benign in the sense that it is so common, nearly universal: Almost every human group makes the distinction between members of the in-group and members of the out-group. It can also be destructive in the ways in which groups of people vilify each other. Unfortunately, it is a very human perspective and may derive from the need of our caveman origins to distinguish between the (friendly) members of our own clan and the (dangerous) members of other clans. This tendency occurs in the way people often compare their country to others, their city to others, their political party to others, and their religion to others. It is such a widespread human tendency that it extends, sometimes in extremely intense and powerful ways even to what may be viewed as artificial and unimportant ways, for example, in how we cheer on "our" sports teams and denigrate, boo, and hiss rival sports teams.

Obviously, however, distinguishing between the holiness of our nation and the profaneness of the other nations can lead to conflict and violence. The Jewish nation has, of course, suffered greatly over its long history at

[488] Lawrence A. Hoffman, *Beyond the Text: A Holistic Approach To Liturgy* (Bloomington and Indianapolis: Indiana University Press, 1987), 37.

the hands of more powerful nations which condemned the Jews as unholy nonbelievers and infidels. That fact, though, has not prevented Jewish liturgy from containing the same kinds of anti-Other statements such as are found in *Havdalah* simply because this kind of in-group/out-group characterization is so naturally human. The best we can do, perhaps, is to name it, to be aware of it, and to resist its malignant tendencies. That is exactly why I point out its occurrence here in *Havdalah*.

From the earliest *siddurim*, the ceremony of *Havdalah* has been introduced by biblical verses. Which particular verses are cited, and how many, has varied over the centuries and between the various liturgical rites. But common to all of them is the theme of reassurance that God will be with us as we leave the day of rest and enter the insecurities of the work week. We ought not forget that a two-day weekend break from work is only a few decades old. For centuries on Saturday nights, Jews fortified themselves emotionally for the work week that was about to start. As we exit the holy time of Shabbat when God's closeness could more easily be felt, and contemplate the rigors and stresses of making a living the next morning, biblical verses such as the following, from among those chanted in the current Ashkenazic liturgy, are meant to be comforting:

> Behold God is my salvation, I shall trust and not be afraid, for God is my strength and my might and he has been my salvation. You can draw water with joy from the fountains of salvation. (Isaiah 12:2-3)
>
> Salvation is God's; your blessing be upon your people! (Psalm 3:9)
>
> The Jews enjoyed light and gladness, happiness and honor (Esther 8:16)

In addition to the biblical verses and the blessing of distinctions, there are also three ritual objects that play roles in the ceremony of *Havdalah*: wine, a lit candle, and aromatic spices. The presence of the wine, candle and spices probably originally had relatively straightforward practical or symbolic meaning, but over time, acquired very interesting, folkloric, even magical, interpretations. First let me list what was, in all probability, their original meaning, and then I will discuss some of the remarkable later connotations ascribed to them.

The drinking of wine at the conclusion of Shabbat parallels the drinking of wine at its beginning, in the Friday night *Kiddush*. Wine plays the role of initiating and concluding not only Shabbat, but all holidays commanded in the Torah (except the fast day of *Yom Kippur* which is only concluded with wine). Wine commands this central position probably because the chemical reaction it causes in our brains has the capacity to change our consciousness as we enter or exit holy time.

The candle likely originally symbolized all the uses we will make of fire during the work week—for light, for heat, and for cooking. At the conclusion of the Sabbath day on which it is forbidden to kindle or extinguish fire, we recite a blessing over the flame of a candle to express gratitude for all the uses we will make of it during the week.

Elbogen posits that just as the Sabbath commonly began with a communal meal, it also concluded with one in ancient times. At the conclusion of the ancient meal, incense on coals was brought to the table to cleanse and refresh the air from the smells of the food.[489] The spices inhaled at the *Havdalah* ceremony may be the remnant of this early custom.

The folkloric meanings ascribed to the wine, candle, and spices are all quite colorful, and some verge on the incantational.

Regarding the wine, our earliest siddur records the custom of rinsing the wine cup with water after drinking the wine and then drinking some of the water from the cup as well as rubbing some of the water onto one's face. "And we have heard from our rabbis that it is a commandment to do this because the remnants (i.e., the secondary elements) of a commandment prevent calamity."[490] That is, there is quasi-magical power to the water associated with this cup of wine, and placing the water on oneself may have the power to prevent mishaps during the ensuing week. There are many variations to this custom, including placing some of the wine itself on one's eyes for the same reason, and in one's pockets, probably to prevent financial misfortune.

A charming association attached to the candle is a tradition that fire was first revealed to humans on the very first Saturday night in history, and we light a candle each Saturday night to commemorate its anniversary:

> Rabbi Levi said that on Saturday night (at the end of the first week of Creation), the blessed holy one summoned two flints to appear to Adam and he knocked them together

[489] Ismar Elbogen, *Jewish Liturgy*, 101, citing *Mishnah Berakhot* 6:6.

[490] *Seder Rav Amram*, Daniel Goldschmidt, ed., 83-84. The phrase about the power of the secondary elements of a commandment is found in the Babylonian Talmud, *Sukkah* 38a, where it is applied to the waving of the *lulav*—which is a "remnant" of a the ritual in the sense that it is not part of the ritual object itself—and it is stated that the waving of a *lulav* prevents harmful winds and harmful dews (i.e., dews that might rot crops).

> and [a spark of] light issued from them, whereupon Adam recited the blessing '...who creates the light of fire.' Shmuel said that therefore we recite this blessing at the conclusion of [each] Sabbath, because that is the origin of its creation.[491]

There is also a custom of looking at the palm of one's hand or one's fingernails by the light of the candle kindled during *Havdalah.* The 14th-century *Arba'ah Turim* says that it was the custom in older times to use the candle to distinguish between the lines of the palms of one's hand, "and we have heard from the elders that within the lines of the hand there is an omen of blessing. And another custom of ours is to look at the fingernails because they [are a sign of being] 'fruitful and multiply' in the world." Here we have a custom that associates personal blessings associated with palm reading and another that connects looking at one's fingernails which constantly grow ("are fruitful and multiply") and the wish that the worshiper might also be fruitful and multiply in offspring or wealth.[492]

Finally, an interesting practice is recorded in case the conclusion of Shabbat finds one outside. In that case, one ought to:

> Open one's hand to the light of the stars, since they are [made of] fire and recite "...who creates the light of fire." And if the sky is darkened by clouds, one ought to pluck a stone from the earth and recite "... who distinguishes between the holy and the profane.[493]

The idea of reciting the blessing acknowledging God as the creator of the light of fire over starlight is a lovely idea that, I think, is rarely practiced today, and ought to be revived. And if it is too cloudy to see the stars, then one ought to at least do some action that uses even the diffuse starlight to distinguish between two things, the stone and the earth.

There are two similar rationales that connect the use of the spices at *Havdalah* with the healing of the soul. The first is that the spices revive the soul "which suffers pain from the conclusion of Shabbat."[494] The second is that at the end of Shabbat the "additional soul" which is given to people at the onset of Shabbat leaves, and it is because of this loss that a person needs

[491] *Seder Rav Amram*, Daniel Goldschmidt, ed., 85 citing Palestinian Talmud *Berakhot* 8:6, 12b. See also *Bereshit Rabba* 12: 6 and Babylonian Talmud, *Pesaḥim* 54a.
[492] Yakov ben Asher, *Arba'ah Turim, Oraḥ Ḥayyim*, 298.
[493] Yakov ben Asher, *Arba'ah Turim, Oraḥ Ḥayyim*, 296.
[494] Yakov ben Asher, *Arba'ah Turim, Oraḥ Ḥayyim*, 297.

to be revived with the spices.[495] Both of these are related to the talmudic understanding that the soul enjoys the aroma of scents and that the World to Come abounds with fragrant plants.[496]

**Spiritual Commentary on The Conclusion of Shabbat (*Havdalah*)**

The end of Shabbat is a liminal time, a vulnerable time, because it is the boundary between the one day of rest and relaxation and the six days of work and toil. A theme connecting nearly all the interpretations of *Havdalah*'s biblical verses, blessings, and rituals is the challenge to be conscious of the transition between the holy, restful, time of Shabbat as it concludes, and the beginning of busier, secular time as a new week begins. The few moments it takes to participate in the *Havdalah* ceremony present an opportunity to align ourselves with this important transition.

For too many of us who recite *Havdalah* each week, it can become just another ritual, and we miss the opening to pray for a successful week. Yet, this weekly ceremony truly offers a wonderful spiritual practice: To take a moment at the conclusion of physical rest and spiritual expansiveness, as we recite *Havdalah*'s words and participate in its rituals, to spiritually prepare for a new week, and to pray for a successful week ahead. A "successful" week can include material success, as some of the interpretations shared above suggest. It can also include physical security and health. It can include carrying the benefits of the physical rest and spiritual expansiveness we experienced on Shabbat to the rest of the week. *Havdalah* can offer a centering and grounding axis for our week if we take advantage of its inner meaning. The ritual itself comprises a kind of *kavannah*, or prayerful "intention," for the coming week. We moderns, who live such busy lives—including on Sundays—could truly benefit from consciously using the colorful rituals of *Havdalah* as a weekly opportunity to focus on living the coming week more closely in harmony with how we really would define "success." Each week, *Havdalah* may be experienced as a "check-in" with ourselves to ask: How closely did we achieve the kind of physical, material, emotional, and spiritual success that we truly believe in this past week? And: How can we come love closer to our truest values this coming week?

---

[495] *Tosafot* to Talmud, *Pesaḥim* 102b, v. *Rav* This is cited in the name of Rashbam.
[496] This is explored by Abraham Ofir Shemesh in his "Scents, the World of Souls and Paradise," [Hebrew], *Daat: A Journal of Jewish Philosophy and Kabbalah* v. 47, July, 2001, 53-68.

# Part Four:

# The Three Pilgrimage Festivals, *Shalosh Regalim*

## The Festival *Amidah*

Unlike the *Amidot* recited four times a day on Shabbat, the *Amidot* of The Three Festivals all contain the same language—with the exception of the *Musaf* ("Additional") *Amidah*, which will be treated separately below. The key unit in all of the Festival *Amidot* is the fourth blessing, *Birkat Kedushat HaYom*, "The Blessing of the Holiness of the Day," which embraces all the passages unique to these *Amidot*. The units that make up this blessing are already present in the earliest post-talmudic sources, although their exact wording and their order varied. It is impossible to date each unit accurately beyond saying that they are at least as old as these sources, that is, the 9th-11th centuries. A number of individual phrases in this blessing are found even earlier, in talmudic sources, but because they appear without a fuller text—and in some cases, not even related to Festival prayers—it cannot be determined whether those phrases attest to the existence of these units in the talmudic period.[497]

This blessing may be divided into four literary units:

1. *Attah Veḥartanu*, "You have chosen us"... *VaTitein Lanu*, "And you gave to us." A declaration of Israel's chosenness and uniqueness of the relationship between God and Israel. Because of that unique relationship, God gifted the People of Israel with The Three Festivals.
2. *Ya'aleh VeYavo*, "May we be remembered." A holiday plea to be remembered positively by God on this holiday.
3. *VeHasi'einu*, "Grant to us." A plea for a special holiday blessing.

[497] For further detail, see Elbogen, *Jewish Liturgy*, 111-116.

4. *Kadsheinu BeMitzvotekha*, "Sanctify us through your commandments." A plea for God to accept our observance of the holiday. This passage contains much the same language as the final passage in the parallel blessing in the Shabbat *Amidot.*

Let us consider each of the first three of these units in turn. Since the fourth unit mainly comports with its parallel in the Shabbat Amidot, there is little of significance to add here and the reader is referred to the commentary on the parallel passage in the Shabbat Amidot on page 244.

## Unit 1: *Attah Veḥartanu,* "You have chosen us" ...*VaTitein Lanu,* "And you gave to us."

This unit begins with a declaration of Israel's chosenness and the uniqueness of the relationship between God and Israel. The passage is dominated by seven verbs that define the chosenness of the People of Israel, declaring that God **chose** Israel from among all the peoples, **loved**, **desired**, and **elevated** Israel above all tongues, **hallowed** Israel through the commandments, **drew** Israel close and **proclaimed** God's name upon Israel, and gifted Israel with The Three Festivals.

I want to express as clearly as I can the way this brief liturgical passage articulates The Chosen People doctrine. The blessing not only emphasizes God's active role in choosing Israel by repeating over and over the sounds *ta/nu* ("you/us"), but it also twice compares Israel's role with the non-Jewish nations: "You chose us from among all the peoples"; "You elevated us from among all the tongues." All of this makes it clear that according to this blessing, God selected Israel out of all of the nations of the world to serve God through God's commandments, and thereby elevated Israel above all other nations. Voicing it this way clashes with the way many modern Jews (including me) would like to conceive The Chosen People idea. Scholarly integrity, however, requires that I express what the blessing actually says as opposed to what we might wish it to say. In the Spiritual Commentary below, I'll offer some thoughts on how modern Jews might nevertheless recite these words in worship. But here, it is important that I clearly and honestly spell out the import of the blessing's words themselves. The blessing does not embrace the modern, liberal, idea that God has "chosen" every nation in to play an equal role in God's plan. Rather, as the Orthodox Artscroll siddur comments on the words "You have chosen us"—"God has chosen Israel to be the bearers of His mission on earth."[498] The 13th-century commentator, Rabbi Elazar ben Yehudah (known by the name of his most famous book as "The *Rokei'aḥ*"), similarly understood the blessing's phrase "And elevated us above all tongues" in his comment:

> [God] gave us the language that the angels speak... and through which the world was created, and which was spoken [by everyone] until the generation of the dispersion (i.e., the Tower of Babel, Genesis 11:1-9) when the languages multiplied into 70 languages, and the holy language (i.e., Hebrew) remained for Israel, God's people."[499]

In sum, the message of the first unit of this blessing is that God chose Israel above all the other nations and as a token of God's loving selection of Israel, gave the gift of The Pilgrimage Festivals.

The contemporary Conservative siddur presents the traditional Hebrew text and accurately translates it. Its commentary, however, does not engage the supremacist language of the wording even though many members of the Conservative movement would certainly find it disturbing.[500] The Reform and Reconstructing Judaism editions of the prayer book have sought, in various ways, to mollify the supremacist message of this unit. The Reconstructing Judaism's version omits in both the Hebrew and the translation "you have chosen us... you have elevated us," as well as all comparisons to other nations. Thus, some of the harshest aspects of chosenness were excised.[501] The Reform siddur preserves all of the traditional Hebrew wording but does not accurately translate it. The translation omits the comparisons to the other nations as well as the phrase "you have elevated us," even though all of these are still present in the Hebrew this prayer book contains. In this way, the Reform worshiper who does not know Hebrew would not realize the extent to which the Hebrew text of the Reform prayer book preserves the stark differential between the chosen Jews and the unchosen non-Jews.[502]

Finally, a comment on the phrase surrounding the last of the seven verbs declaring Israel's special relationship with God: "You have **proclaimed** your great and holy name upon us." This phrase is based upon Jeremiah 14:9. The

[498] Rabbi Nosson Scherman, Rabbi Meir Zlotowitz, eds., *The Complete Artscroll Siddur*, 662.
[499] Rabbi Eleazar of Worms, Rokeach, *Pirushey Siddur HaTefilah LaRokeach*, eds., Rabbi Moshe Hershler, Rabbi Yehudah A. Hershler (Jerusalem: Machon HaRav Hershler, 1992), 2:632.
[500] *Siddur Lev Shalem*, 309.
[501] *Kol Haneshamah: Shabbat Veḥagim*, 605.
[502] *Mishkan T'filah: A Reform Siddur*, 478.

wording is the same in the siddur except for two additional words which do not change the meaning in a substantial way. The two words are: *hagadol vehaKadosh*, "the great and holy."

| **Jeremiah 14:9** | ***Siddur*** |
|---|---|
| ***VeShimkha aleinu karata.*** | ***VeShimkha*** *HaGadol vehaKadosh* ***aleinu karata.*** |
| **And you proclaimed your name upon us.** | **And you proclaimed your** great and holy **name upon us.** |

In the Book of Jeremiah, the prophet is praying for God's help because of a drought and because of military attacks by surrounding peoples. Jeremiah calls upon God to come to Israel's aid because God's name is proclaimed upon us (14:9). The connotation seems to be: Come to our aid because "Your name is attached to us," as the new JPS edition translates. This is an example of synecdoche, in which part of a thing symbolizes the entire thing. Here, the attachment of God's name to Israel symbolizes the attachment and closeness of God in general to Israel.

Another interpretation of the language in the siddur sometimes offered is that God's name is proclaimed upon Israel because the final syllable of *Yisrael*, is *Eil*, "God."[503] However, the closeness of the siddur's wording to the biblical verse confirms for me, at least, that Jeremiah is the referent, and its meaning there—that God's name upon Israel connotes God's closeness to Israel—is its meaning in the siddur as well, with the additional idea that the gift of the holidays to Israel is a token of that closeness.

## Unit 2. *Ya'aleh VeYavo*, "May we be remembered." A holiday plea to be remembered positively by God on this holiday.

The author of this passage was fond of lists. It asks that on this holiday, remembrance of six entities (ourselves—mentioned twice, our ancestors, the Messiah, Jerusalem, all of Israel) come before God in eight different ways (arise, come, reach, be seen, be accepted, be heard, be recalled, be remembered) for seven positive outcomes (for deliverance, for the good, for grace, for loving kindness, for compassion, for life, for peace). Then, repeating itself,

[503] Mentioned among other less likely interpretations by Rabbi David Abudraham (14th c., Spain), in addition to the reference to Jeremiah 14:9. See *Abudraham HaShalem*, 211. And compare Isaiah 4:1.

it asks that on this holiday, all of those entities be remembered in five different ways (for good, for blessing, for life, for deliverance, in compassion). As part of these lists, synonyms for "remembering" recur nine times—the root *zakhar* occurs some six times and the root *pakad*, three times. It all adds up to a plea for God on this holiday to remember the worshiper and the Jewish People for all good things in this world and for messianic deliverance. Because of the preponderance of the theme of "remembrance" in this prayer, some scholars surmise that its original place may have been in the liturgy of the Days of Awe—where "remembrance" is such a major theme—and from there, it was also transferred to the liturgy of the Pilgrimage Festivals.[504]

### Unit 3: *VeHasi'einu*, "Grant to us." A plea for a special holiday blessing.

This unit is just one sentence long, but it is quite pregnant with meaning:

> Grant, *YHVH* our God, the blessing of your festivals for life and peace, for joy and gladness, as you desired and as you said you would bless us.

Again, we have a plea for God's blessing on this holiday, as we had in the previous unit, but with a hidden meaning. In the liturgy, when a phrase addressed to God such as "as you said" is found, the reference is almost always to a passage in the Bible. I agree with Rabbi David Abudraham (14th c., Spain) who identified the passage as Deuteronomy 16:17. However, Abudraham (and the many commentators over the century who followed him—often without attribution), do not make clear that the liturgy here is referencing this verse in a midrashic way, that is, twisting its original, biblical, meaning. The verse says that each male should not appear before God on the Three Pilgrimage Festivals empty-handed, "but each with his own gift, according to the blessing that *YHVH* your God has bestowed upon you." In the Bible, the point of the verse is that on these holidays, the pilgrims ought to bring a "gift," that is, a symbolic token, reflecting the yield of the harvest, which is "the blessing" that "God has bestowed upon you." But the liturgy has the worshiper saying to God that "you said you would bless us." The Orthodox siddur translates here, with some justification, that God "promised to bless us."[505] This is the midrashic twist on the biblical verse:

[504] See Elbogen, *Jewish Liturgy*, 121, 123; Daniel Goldschmidt, ed., *Maḥzor for the Days of Awe* [Hebrew] (Jerusalem: Koren, 1970), I:19.
[505] *The Complete Artscroll Siddur*, 666.

While the verse only commands that pilgrims bring a token of the harvest "according to the blessing" that God has bestowed, the liturgy audaciously interprets the verse as if God, in this verse, promised to bless us by granting a bountiful harvest in all three of the growing seasons that precede each of the Festivals. And having interpreted the verse this way, the liturgy turns to God and says, in effect, "We are reminding you that you promised to bless our harvest, so please, God, follow through and bless us!"

The *Musaf* ("Additional") *Amidah* for Festivals contains units 1, 3, and 4 but instead of Unit 2, *Ya'aleh Veyavo*, it presents a text expressing longing for a return to the Festival service in the ancient Temple in Jerusalem which centered on animal sacrifices. While it may be tempting to try to find explanations for why the *Musaf Amidah* lacks *Ya'aleh Veyavo*, the reason may well just be communal custom with no deep theological implication. The support for this possibility is that the Festival *Musaf Amidah* in the ancient Palestinian rite (reflected in the materials in the Cairo Genizah up to about the 11th century) did contain *Ya'aleh Veyavo*.[506] The pleas here for a return to animal sacrifice parallel the same pleas in the *Musaf Amidah* of Shabbat. The history of those prayers was traced in the commentary on the *Musaf Amidah* of Shabbat and the reader is referred to page 294. Since the talmudic discussion about the content of the *Musaf Amidah* in the Talmud centers on Shabbat liturgy, it is likely that the prayers for a return of sacrificial worship originated on Shabbat and from there, similar prayers were added to the Festival liturgy.

While the sentiments expressed in *Musaf Amidah* for Shabbat and Festivals are similar, the pleading, longing, and sense of loss for animal sacrifices are even more acute in the Festival liturgy. This section of the *Musaf Amidah* for Festivals commences with the plaintive confession that the exile of the Jewish People was caused by our own transgressions:

> Because of our sins, we were exiled from our land, distanced from our land, and we cannot ascend to appear to bow before you and to offer our obligations in your chosen house, in the great and holy house called by your name... Draw near our scattered ones from among the peoples and our dispersions from the ends of the earth.

[506] See Daniel Goldschmidt, Jonah Fraenkel, eds., *Maḥzor Sukkot, Shemini Atzeret* and *Simḥat Torah* [Hebrew] (Jerusalem: Koren, 1981), 11.

After listing the specific animal sacrifices that cannot be offered any more, the sense of loss of the ancient Temple in Jerusalem continues to be expressed:

> Merciful king, have mercy on us, the one who is good and does good, answer us, return to us in your great mercy because of the patriarchs who did your will. Rebuild your house as at the beginning...

The contemporary *siddurim* treat these pleas for the return of the animal sacrifices similarly to the ways they treat the parallel pleas in the *Musaf Amidah* for Shabbat. See page 303 for that discussion.

**Spiritual Commentary**

As mentioned in the commentary above about Unit 1, *Attah V'ḥartanu*, "You have chosen us," it is important to be honest about what the prayer actually says, and in this case, what it says will likely make many modern Jews uncomfortable. Its message is that God gifted the Jewish People with the Festivals because God chose Israel out of all of the nations of the world and thereby elevated Israel above all other nations. It seems to me that *siddurim* that include the traditional language ought to translate it honestly and if a commentary is included, ought to forthrightly deal with the implications of this theology. I am disappointed that not all contemporary *siddurim* have done so.

For those who recite this passage using a traditional siddur and are, like me, uncomfortable with its message, I suggest the following: Acknowledge what the words are actually saying; acknowledge that our beloved Jewish tradition here has succumbed to the very human tendency to promote the in-group and denigrate the Other. It is important not to deny the truth. But then recite the words of the siddur, admittedly attaching a different meaning to them: Offer heartfelt thanks to God for the gift of the holiday, with pride for the specifically Jewish ways that the holiday is celebrated. However, divest the prayer of the supremacist message that the words contain if we don't believe in them; if we don't believe that God prefers the Jewish People over other peoples. When we recite this blessing of the Festival *Amidah*, we can express our gratitude for the inspirational meanings of the particular Festival, and for our ability to participate in their celebration, without comparing our celebration to the rituals and worship of others.[507]

[507] For an eloquent and cogent counterargument to my interpretation, an argument for the inseparability of the Chosen People idea from the essence of Jewish religion, see Joel S. Kaminsky, *Yet I Loved Jacob:*

The astute reader may ask: Why not suggest to the worshiper who is uncomfortable with the triumphalist message of this unit to simply use the version in the siddur of the Reconstructing Judaism Movement, cited above, which deleted that message from the Hebrew and the translation? I would respond in two mutually exclusive ways which, for me, are held in creative tension with each other. Firstly, that is indeed an option for the worshiper; changes in the liturgy have occurred in all eras of Jewish liturgy. Secondly, the option of consciously reciting Hebrew words while attributing new meaning to them is also attested time and again in all eras of Jewish liturgy. If each individual opted to omit every passage in the siddur that they do not fully believe, then every individual would end up with their own customized prayer book, unlike any other individual's prayer book, and that would spell the end of communal prayer.

Regarding Unit 2 - *Ya'aleh VeYavo*, "May we be remembered," and Unit 3 - *VeHasi'einu*, "Grant to us": Both of these passages ask for God's blessing on this holiday. While the traditional wording has the worshiper ask God directly for a holiday blessing—similar to the way one might, in ancient times, petition a king to grant a specific request, many moderns, myself included, do not view God in such an anthropomorphic way. Another approach when reciting these parts of the *Amidah* is first to try to connect to the presence of God. Then, while feeling the divine connection, to embody and feel the blessing of the essential historical and agricultural elements of the holiday. On *Pesaḥ*, for example, to appreciate the freedoms we enjoy and to resolve to act on behalf of those who lack freedom. On *Shavuot*, to appreciate the depth and breadth of the Torah and all the commentaries and rituals it has spawned over the centuries. On *Sukkot*, to sense the wisdom of living in a fragile hut, that real security doesn't come from strong walls but from justice in the community. Those are the blessings that connect to the historical sides of the holidays. From the agricultural connections of the holidays, the challenge is to be grateful for the blessings that are already ours in the bountiful harvest available to us. Beyond that, *Sukkot*, as we shall see, is especially concerned with adequate rainfall. So when we recite these passages in the Festival *Amidah* on *Sukkot*, the challenge, as God's partner, is also to ask whether we are facilitating the blessing of adequate, but not harmful, rainfall; in other words, what are we doing to either support or undermine ecological balance?

---

*Reclaiming the Biblical Concept of Election* (Nashville: Abingdon Press, 2007).

## The Festival Torah Service

On the Three Pilgrimage Festivals (as well as on the Days of Awe), another prayer was added to the Torah Service under the influence of the Kabbalistic master, Rabbi Isaac Luria (16th c., Safed, Israel), based on earlier, talmudic, teachings. I am referring to the Thirteen Attributes of God which are chanted three times during The Torah Service. According to the Torah, these attributes were originally revealed by God to Moses in Exodus 34:6-7 as a response to Moses' request to see God's essence (*kavod*). God tells Moses that a human being cannot view God's face and live. Instead, God's "back" is revealed to Moses as God chants the Thirteen Attributes. Later in the Torah, Moses recites these attributes to appeal to God's mercy when the people respond to the negative majority report of the spies' reconnaissance of the Land of Israel by rebelling and refusing to enter Israel. God threatens to destroy the rebellious Israelites but is assuaged by Moses' recital of the attributes (Numbers 14:11-20). Probably on this basis, the Talmud suggests that these verses ought to be chanted whenever the People of Israel need God's mercy. The verses entered the liturgy as a "selective" citation of Exodus 34:6-7; "selective" because while the siddur cites God's attributes of mercy, it omits God's attribute of punishment found toward the end of these verses.

| **Exodus 34:6-7 in the Bible** | **Exodus 34:6-7 in the siddur** |
|---|---|
| (6) The Lord passed before him and proclaimed: "The Lord! the Lord! a God compassionate and gracious, slow to anger, abounding in kindness and faithfulness, (7) extending kindness to the thousandth generation, forgiving iniquity, transgression, and sin; **yet He does not remit all punishment, but visits the iniquity of parents upon children and children's children, upon the third and fourth generations."** | (6) The Lord passed before him and proclaimed: "The Lord! the Lord! a God compassionate and gracious, slow to anger, abounding in kindness and faithfulness, (7) extending kindness to the thousandth generation, forgiving iniquity, transgression, and sin... |

The extraction of God's thirteen merciful attributes from the wording of Exodus 34:6-7 is not obvious. As may be imagined, there are numerous commentaries that attempt to connect God's attributes of mercy to the wording in these two biblical verses. In the Midrash on Psalms, the Sages count <u>ten</u>

while the talmudic sage Rav counts eleven, and in the Dead Sea Scroll of Thanksgiving (16:16), the count is also ten.[508] The following enumeration of thirteen attributes is based on the list in the Conservative movement's *Maḥzor Lev Shalem*:[509]

1. *Adonai*: I am God before you sin.
2. *Adonai*: I am God after you sin.
3. *Eil* (God): Merciful to all, Gentile and Jew.
4. *Raḥum* (Compassionate): To those with merit.
5. *Veḥanun* (Gracious): To those without merit.
6. *Erekh apayim* (Patient): With the wicked, who may repent.
7. *Verav ḥesed* (Abounding in kindness): With those in need of kindness.
8. *Ve'emet* (And Faithfulness): Rewarding those who do My will.
9. *Notzer ḥesed la'alafim* (Assuring love for a thousand generations): When you do good deeds.
10. *Nosei avon* (Forgiving iniquity): When you sin deliberately.
11. *Vafesha* (And transgression): When you rebel maliciously.
12. *Veḥata'ah* (And sin): When you sin unintentionally.
13. *Venakeih* (And "clearing," i.e., granting pardon): When you repent.

The Talmud is quite explicit in recommending recitation of the Thirteen Attributes in prayer:

> ...The verse states: "And the Lord passed by before him and proclaimed..." (Exodus 34:6). Rabbi Yoḥanan said: Were it not explicitly written in the verse, it would be impossible to say this: The verse teaches that the Holy One, Blessed be He, wrapped himself in a *tallit* (prayer shawl) and showed Moses the structure of the order of the prayer. He said to him: Whenever the Jewish people sin, let them act before me in accordance with this order. Let the prayer leader wrap

[508] *Midrash Tehillim*, Solomon Buber edition, Vilna, 1891, 416, and the Dead Sea Scroll of Thanksgiving are cited in Hayyim Herman Kieval, *The High Holy Days: A Commentary on the Prayerbook of Rosh Hashanah and Yom Kippur*, David Golinkin and Monique Susskind Goldberg, eds. (Jerusalem: The Institute of Applied Halakhah, The Schechter Institute of Jewish Studies, 2004), Yom Kippur section of the book, 416, n. 19.

[509] Edward Feld, ed. (New York: The Rabbinical Assembly, 2010), 336. The following sources are cited there:

Rabbeinu Tam, France (1100-1171 France, in *Tosafot, Rosh HaShanah*, 17b, s.v. *Shelosh Esreih Middot*); *Sefer Abudraham HaShalem* (14th-century Spain, 1963 edition), 251-252; *Sefer HaBakashah* by Moshe HaKohen Niral (Metz, France, 1788). For a slightly different enumeration of the thirteen attributes, see *The Complete Artscroll Siddur*, 817.

> himself in a *tallit* and recite the thirteen attributes of mercy, and I will forgive them...[510]

While the Thirteen Attributes of God are quite appropriate for the worship services on the Days of Awe when the Jewish People pray for God's mercy, their recitation on the Three Pilgrimage Festivals—which are joyous celebrations—seems out of place. The Thirteen Attributes are chanted numerous times on the Days of Awe: They are not only chanted as part of the Torah Service on the mornings of *Rosh HaShanah* and *Yom Kippur*, but on *Yom Kippur*, they are traditionally chanted several times elsewhere in the services, culminating in their recitation eight times during the final, *Ne'ilah*, service. Each time, their recitation is meant as a plea for mercy to God for forgiveness of sin. For this reason, the Thirteen Attributes are commonly associated with a plea for God's mercy. However, the reason the Thirteen Attributes are chanted on the Three Festivals is not related to a plea for mercy. Not long ago, Itzhak Brand published a theory to explain their recitation on the Pilgrimage Festivals.[511] Here, I've adapted and expanded upon his theory.

God's revelation of the Thirteen Attributes in the Torah was in response to Moses' request to see God's essence. The Thirteen Attributes that God shares are therefore understood to be a substitute for seeing God's essence. Furthermore, the Three Pilgrimage Festivals were viewed as opportunities for "experiencing" God's essence. This understanding is based on a literal interpretation of Exodus 34:20, 23 found in the Talmud.[512] Those verses say that on the Three Pilgrimage Festivals, Israelites should "appear before God." But taken hyper-literally, the wording could be interpreted to mean that on these holidays, God's "face shall be seen" (***yeira'u fanai; yeira'eh** et **penei** ha'adon YHVH*). That was symbolically accomplished by opening the curtain of the Holy of Holies in the ancient Temple so the pilgrims could view the cherubs on top of the Ark of the Covenant:

> Rabbi Ketina said: When the Jewish people would ascend for (one of the pilgrimage) Festivals, (the priests would) roll up the curtain for them and show them the cherubs, which were clinging to one another, and say to them: "See how you are beloved before God, like the love of a male and female."[513]

[510] Babylonian Talmud, *Rosh HaShanah* 17b.
[511] Itzhak Brand, "The Attributes of Mercy and Beholding the Divine Presence on the Pilgrimage Festivals" [Hebrew], *Da'at: A Journal of Jewish Philosophy & Kabbalah*, No. 87, 2019, 239-260.
[512] Palestinian Talmud *Ḥagigah* 1:1; 76a in the name of Rabbi Yehoshua ben Levi.
[513] Babylonian Talmud *Yoma* 54a.

The opening of the Ark in the synagogue during The Torah Service on the Three Festivals was seen as a parallel to the opening of the Ark on those same festivals in the ancient Temple. But since the cherubs are missing in synagogues, the chanting of the Thirteen Attributes at that moment was understood as a substitute for beholding God's essence, just as it functioned for Moses. Thus, the chanting of the Thirteen Attributes during the Torah Service on the Festivals is not related to a plea for mercy, which would indeed be out of sync with the joy of those occasions. Rather, the chanting of the Thirteen Attributes is meant to parallel the experiencing of God's essence or presence on the festivals that occurred in the ancient Temple.

As mentioned above, the earliest suggestion we know of to recite the Thirteen Attributes on the Festivals comes from Rabbi Yitzḥak Luria (also known as the Ari). What is not fully satisfying in the theory I've laid out here is that while Rabbi Luria's suggestion is in line with earlier, talmudic, teachings, he uncharacteristically does not give them a Kabbalistic twist. That is, he does not explicitly tie the prior sources to the mystical inner life of God. More typically, he would reinterpret previous teachings to reflect his complicated expansion of the Zohar's description of the ten *Sefirot* that comprise God's quintessence. This weakness in the theory expressed here is worth keeping in mind. At the same time, this approach is the most convincing explanation of the recitation of the Thirteen Attributes on the Festivals that I have seen.

Rabbi Luria's 16th-century recommendation to recite the Thirteen Attributes was not communally accepted in the form he suggested (and apparently, even he expressed second thoughts about it, given the Attributes' long association with the Days of Awe). His suggestion was to recite them during the Three Festivals as follows: Once at the Torah service, a second time at the *Musaf* service, and a third time during the first blessing before the *Shema* on the second day of each holiday.[514] About a hundred years later, an

[514] Ḥayyim Vital, *Peri Eitz Ḥayyim* (Benei Berak, Israel: Tzvi Mikhel Widbosky, 1986), II:485. I am grateful to Rabbi Jordan Hersh who brought the following problem to my attention: Since both the Ari and Vital were located in Safed, Israel (though they had both previously lived outside the Land of Israel), and since in Israel, there is only one day of each festival—there is no "second day" of the festival—why would they recommend any ritual for the second day of the festival? It is always good to keep in mind that Rabbi Luria left few, if any, written works. Therefore, we are dependent upon the varying traditions left by his disciples. There was competition among those disciples for the role of spokesman, and Rabbi Ḥayyim Vital worked mightily—among others—for that role. It is ironic that one modern version of Vital's record comprises a 15-volume set entitled *Kitvei Ha'Ari*, "The Writings of the Ari," since it is likely that Rabbi Luria actually wrote none of it. The record of the Ari's teaching about the Thirteen Attributes on the Three Festivals is found within this set. I am grateful to Professor Morris Faierstein who, in personal correspondence, pointed out that the several editors and printers of Vital's work over the centuries took various liberties. According to Professor Faierstein, it is likely that the editor or printer of the current edition of *Kitvei Ha'Ari* lived in Europe and thought like a European Jew. In other words, since the editor or printer celebrated two days of Festival observance, he inserted his own

Eastern European Kabbalist, Rabbi Nathan Nata Hannover, prescribed the recitation of the Thirteen Attributes both for the Three Pilgrimage Festivals as well as on the Days of Awe three times at the Torah Service, and to follow that by reciting Psalm 19:15 (*Va'Ani tefillati*, "As for me, my prayer is...") three times as well.[515] It was Rabbi Hannover's prescription that achieved broad communal acceptance including in the contemporary Orthodox, Conservative, and Reconstructing Judaism prayer books (the Reform prayer book omits these passages).

**Spiritual Commentary on the Festival Torah Service**

As mentioned above, the chanting of the Thirteen Attributes of God is broadly known from the Days of Awe, where it functions as a plea for mercy. The Kabbalistic interpretation of reciting the Attributes on the Pilgrimage Festivals is not related to asking for God's mercy, but rather constitutes an experience of God's presence. It seems to me that this interpretation can resonate with modern worshipers. Each Pilgrimage Festival confers agricultural and historical symbolism unique to each of these three dates. In this way, we come before God with thanksgiving on each holiday for the harvest and for the foundational historical events of our people. When we do so, we reenact two moments. One moment is the intimate encounter with God that occurred on these festivals in the ancient Temple when the curtain before the Holy of Holies was opened. But the Ark in synagogues does not contain the Holy of Holies. Therefore, when the synagogue Ark is opened during the Festival Torah Service, we reenact the other moment: Moses at Mount Sinai hearing these Attributes as God's essence. More important than the words describing God's merciful nature in these Attributes is the experience the chanting offers. When we chant the Attributes, we are meant to feel God's essence. We are meant to experience the mysterious presence of the One who miraculously freed us from Egypt on Passover, revealed the Torah to us on

---

"Lurianic" ritual of chanting the Thirteen Attributes on the second day of Festivals into the instructions from the Ari himself. I subsequently received a personal communication from Professor Itzhak Brand, referenced above, suggesting much the same theory as that of Professor Faierstein. For two book-length English translations of (nevertheless) small parts of *Kitvei Ha'Ari*, see "Book of Visions" in Morris M. Faierstein, *Jewish Mystical Autobiographies: Book of Visions and Book of Secrets* (Mahwah, New Jersey: Paulist Press, 1999), 41-263; and Eliahu Klein, *Kabbalah of Creation: The Mysticism of Isaac Luria, Founder of Modern Kabbalah* (Berkeley, California: North Atlantic Books, 2000). On the competition among Rabbi Luria's disciples, see Lawrence Fine, *Physician of the Soul, Healer of the Cosmos: Isaac Luria and His Kabbalistic Fellowship* (Stanford, California: Stanford University Press, 2003), 2-5 and the copious sources cited in the notes.

[515] Nathan Nata Hannover, *Sha'arei Tzion*, Prague: 1692, *Sha'ar Gimmel.* HebrewBooks.org, accessed April 25, 2022. Apparently, at some later date, the three-fold repetition of Psalm 19:15 was added to the Torah Service on the Days of Awe as well.

*Shavuot*, sheltered us in booths on *Sukkot* and—just as miraculously—causes the harvest to occur at each of these turns of the year. When we chant the Attributes on the Festivals, it is as if we are warmly greeting the spiritual presence behind all that the Festivals celebrate, and—at the same time—are warmly greeted by the Spirit as well.

In corresponding on this issue with Cantor Sandy Horowitz of New York City, both of us felt that since chanting the Thirteen Attributes on the Festivals reflects a different meaning from the chanting of the same words on the Days of Awe, the melody used on the Festivals ought to mirror that as well. At the least, if the same melody is used (which seems to be the near-universal current practice), it ought to be tweaked somehow—in tone, or in mode (switch to the major key?), or in some other way.[516] Perhaps the Thirteen Attributes deserve to be chanted on the Festivals in either a brand-new tune for the Festivals in general, or in new tunes created in the spirit of each of the Three Festivals themselves.

## Hallel

Immediately after the *Amidah* of *Shaḥarit* on every Festival day—and at the Passover *Seder*—*Hallel* is chanted. *Hallel* consists of Psalms 113-118 and is known as "Egyptian *Hallel*" because the Exodus from Egypt is featured in Psalm 114. (The other form of *Hallel* is "The Great *Hallel*," which is comprised of Psalm 36 and is chanted as part of *Pesukei DeZimra* on Shabbat and holidays and as part of the Passover *Seder*.) These six psalms are introduced by a blessing and concluded with a blessing. The ancient sources attest that *Hallel* was chanted in the ancient Temple in Jerusalem on each day of Ḥanukkah, Shavuot, Sukkot, and on the first night and day of Passover.[517] No

[516] The suggestion of switching to the major key was suggested to me by classical music Professor Andrew Rosenfeld.

[517] See, for example, *Mishnah Pesaḥim* 5:7; *Mishnah Succah* 3:9, 4:1, 8; *Tosefta Succah* 3:2. When looking for interpretations of the psalms of *Hallel* from the talmudic era, the following is important to keep in mind. The classic work of midrash on the Book of Psalms, Midrash *Tehillim* (also known as Midrash *Shokher Tov*)—apparently edited soon after the close of the talmudic era but containing some material from much earlier—contains few commentaries on the psalms included in Hallel. According to Adolph Jellinek, it was for that reason that a separate, short composition, Midrash *Hallel* (sometimes also called *Sefer HaMa'asim*, "The Book of Deeds") was created soon afterward, containing extensive interpretations of the six psalms that make up Hallel. See Adolph Jellinek, *Bet Hamidrasch* (Vienna: Winter Brothers, 1873), 5:97. Of course, the fascinating question is why so few commentaries on the psalms of Hallel were included in the larger work of midrash on the Book of Psalms. However, the compilation of that larger work was likely done by several editors at several different times. Because of that, it is possible, and perhaps likely, that the lack of extensive interpretation of Hallel's psalms did not reflect an intentional choice.

later than the 3rd century CE, the Jewish community in Babylonia—probably sensitive to the lack of *Hallel* on the other days of Passover, as well as the semi-holiday of *Rosh Ḥodesh*—added a slightly abbreviated *Hallel* to those days as well.[518]

Why these particular psalms were chosen to be chanted on these holidays is not clear; even the earliest sources we have take the existence of *Hallel* for granted and don't convincingly reveal its origin.[519] There are talmudic discussions on its origin as well as about why these particular holidays include *Hallel*, and not, for example, Purim, Rosh HaShanah and Yom Kippur, but these discussions are more homiletical and less historical in nature.[520] Nevertheless, the Sages of the Talmud did portray the content of *Hallel* quite accurately. The word *Hallel* means "praise" and because of that, many prayer books and commentaries characterize this service as entirely joyful and exultant, but this does not fully reflect the themes of these psalms. This was already noticed by the Sages of the Talmud as part of their discussion of the origin of *Hallel*. Here is how they portrayed *Hallel*'s content:

> The Prophets among them instituted that the Jewish People should recite it at every incident and for every trouble, may it not come upon the Jewish People. And when they are redeemed, they recite it over their redemption...[521]

Put this way, it sounds as if *Hallel* contains both pleas for divine help as well as gratitude and praise for when that help arrives, and indeed, this depiction

[518] For additional sources and a theory on why *Hallel* was not originally chanted on Passover except for the first day, see Reuven Hammer, "On the Origin of the Partial Hallel," *Conservative Judaism*, 23:4, Summer 1969, 60-63. In n. 9, Professor Hammer cited *Mishnah Pesaḥim* 5:6 by mistake when he clearly meant 5:7. See also Josiah Derby, "Purim and Hallel," *Dor le Dor, Our Biblical Heritage* 11:2 (1982-1983), 104-110. Additionally, there was an interesting custom among some Ḥasidim to sing *Hallel* during the baking of the matzah specifically for use at the Seder. See Gedalia ben Yehiel Oberlander, "The Custom to Sing Hallel During the Baking of the Mitzvah-Matzah on Eve of Passover" [Hebrew], *Heikhal HaBesht: Me'asef LeMishnat HaḤassidut, Toldotehah U'Genazehah*, 1, 2 (2003), 72-82.

[519] Reuven Hammer argues that the six psalms as a whole celebrate the Exodus from Egypt, but aside from Psalm 114, I am not convinced that this is so. See his "Hallel: A Liturgical Composition Celebrating the Exodus," *The Experience of Jewish Liturgy: Studies Dedicated to Menahem Schmelzer*, Debra Reed Blank, ed. (Leiden, Boston: Brill, 2011), 101-113. Erich Zenger presents a cogent case for the textual unity of the six psalms but does not argue that their content is unified around the Exodus. See his *Psalms 3: A Commentary on Psalms 101-150*, English translation from the German by Linda M. Maloney (Minneapolis, Minnesota: Fortress Press, 2011), 178-179.

[520] For example, Babylonian Talmud *Pesaḥim* 117a; *Arakhin* 10a. Louis Finkelstein published an essay that attempted to locate the origin of *Hallel*, pointing especially to the period of the Hasmoneans and the holiday of *Ḥanukkah*. While the sources marshalled by Finkelstein are important in themselves, his conclusions are not supported by those sources. See Louis Finkelstein, "The Origin of the Hallel," *Hebrew Union College Annual* (Vol. 23, 1950/51), 319-337.

[521] Babylonian Talmud *Pesaḥim* 117a.

of *Hallel* is truer to its content than the typical description of *Hallel* as all joyful praise.[522] The main themes of the six psalms of *Hallel* indeed may be characterized as a combination of praise and pleas in the following way (note that I am characterizing these psalms as whole psalms, the way they appear in the Bible. That is not the same way they are presented in the siddur, where some of them are subdivided into smaller units):

**Psalm 113**: Praise: Praise of God who resides on high and raises up the lowly to the heights.

**Psalm 114**: Praise: Nature itself celebrates the Exodus of Israel from Egypt.

**Psalm 115**: Plea: A plea to God to save and bless Israel; a plea to Israel to remain faithful to God because the pagan gods are nothing, as are those who trust in them.

**Psalm 116**: Plea and Praise: I prayed to God when I faced death; God saved me, and I praise God. (The entire psalm is expressed in the first-person singular).

**Psalm 117**: Praise: Let all the nations praise God because God's love for us is great. (This two-verse Psalm is the shortest among the book's 150 Psalms, and indeed, the shortest chapter in the entire Bible).

**Psalm 118**: Praise for the fulfillment of a Plea: I praise God who granted me victory after I was attacked by the nations (Again: all in the first-person singular).

This mixture of praise and pleas in *Hallel* rings true to the historical events that stand behind the holidays on which these psalms are chanted. While each holiday contains historical high points for which praise of God would be appropriate, each also includes hardships and challenges for which pleas to God would also be appropriate.

The *Ben Yehoyada* commentary (Rabbi Yosef Ḥayyim, 1834-1909, Baghdad) on the talmudic excerpt cited above took the pleading nature of *Hallel* quite seriously. The talmudic excerpt said: "The Prophets among them instituted that the Jewish People should recite it (*Hallel*) at every incident and for every trouble, may it not come upon the Jewish People." According to this commentary:

> It further seems to me that [the Talmud] used such language to say that they [the prophets] ordained to recite it

[522] That the psalms of *Hallel* present a more complicated set of themes than merely praise was also noted by Jeremy Schonfield in his article "Psalms 113-118: Qualified Praise?" *European Judaism: A Journal for the New Europe*, Vol. 50, No. 2 (Autumn 2017), 147-157.

> [*Hallel*] over every event, and they intended through this that there is also a benefit through its recital regarding each misfortune that may be decreed to come upon the world: That they will be rescued from it because of the *Hallel*. The merit of reciting the *Hallel* prevents the misfortune from [coming] upon them. And also, if it must come upon them, [the recital of *Hallel* will bring about that] they will be rescued from it quickly.

According to this interpretation, when the Talmud instructed that *Hallel* ought to be recited "for every trouble, may it not come upon the Jewish People," it meant that the very recitation of *Hallel* could prevent, or at least diminish, imminent troubles and misfortunes from materializing. In this way, the commentary understands *Hallel* as a kind of reenactment of the Jewish People's pleading for redemption during the original historical events that the holidays celebrate, for example, praying for redemption from Egyptian slavery. And according to Rabbi Yosef Ḥayyim's explanation, chanting the ancient pleas for redemption contained in *Hallel* will be effective in cancelling, or at least moderating, imminent misfortunes in contemporary times as well.

**Spiritual Commentary on *Hallel***

When reciting *Hallel* on the holidays, our inner intention ought not be guided by the title of the service alone, "praise," but also by its content, praise and pleading. Thus, during the recitation of *Hallel* on any given holiday, when we chant the appeals to God for help, we might bring to mind the challenges our ancestors faced on that particular holiday. For example, on Passover, we could imagine the pain of slavery; on Shavuot, the challenge of truly believing that God reveals law and ethics to human beings; on Sukkot, the difficulties of wandering in the desert for years; and on Ḥanukkah, the lack of freedom to openly practice one's religion. During those *Hallel* passages in which we chant joyful praise, we could recall the exultation of our ancestors on that particular holiday. For example: on Passover, the release from slavery; on Shavuot, the sense that God has indeed lovingly revealed the principles of righteous living to human beings; on Sukkot, the sense of God's presence on a trek in the wilderness; and on Ḥanukkah, the righteous triumph of the few and the weak over the many and the powerful.

It is always helpful for prayer melodies to relate to the content of the prayer text. Melodies for *Hallel* are often chosen only to convey a sense of praise and joy. We would do well to choose (and to compose) melodies that conform to either joy or to longing, depending on the meaning of the passages sung.

There is a tradition to recite psalms when an individual or a community is in need of God's help. The psalms of *Hallel* are not always included in this kind of recitation... but they ought to be.

Finally, I want to share an adaptation of one small passage from *Hallel* as it was once led by Rabbi Zalman Schachter-Shalomi, one of the founders of Renewal Judaism. In the early 1980s, Reb Zalman came to visit Vancouver, British Columbia, where I was serving as the rabbi of a congregation. I invited him to lead a pre-Passover workshop for us, which he graciously agreed to do. At the workshop, he asked participants to stand, form a circle, and to join hands. Then he instructed us to chant—over and over, meditatively—a plea found toward the end of *Hallel* (Psalm 118:25):

| | |
|---|---|
| *Ana YHVH hoshi'a na* | Please God, save |
| *Ana YHVH hatzliḥa na* | Please God, grant success |

As we chanted these words, Reb Zalman challenged us to ask God for whatever we needed to truly and meaningfully celebrate the holiday of Passover which was about to begin. He encouraged us to try to silently articulate to God specifically what we would need to celebrate the holiday in the most fulfilling way, whether that would mean physical, financial, emotional, or spiritual help. I have often repeated this *kavannah*, this inner intention, for myself on the Three Pilgrimage Festivals themselves when the congregation reaches this verse in *Hallel*, asking for whatever it is that I need to truly celebrate the current holiday. This inner approach to this line of *Hallel* can imbue more meaning to a line that might otherwise be chanted with less intention.

## Yizkor

Jews include prayers memorializing their dead relatives as well as martyrs on the last day of each of the Three Pilgrimage Festivals and on Yom Kippur. This brief service is known as *Yizkor*, "May God Remember," based on the first word of one of its prayers, and takes place during the Torah service, in between the *Haftarah* and the *Amidah* of *Musaf*. While various psalms and other readings are often included in this service, only two prayers form the core of this service: The prayer that begins with the word *Yizkor* and *Eil Malei Raḥamim*, "God Full of Mercy." I will comment on each of these in turn.

The *Yizkor* prayer derives from about the 13th century and memorializes relatives of worshipers. The traditional text of this prayer is as follows:

> May God remember the soul of my [father my teacher; mother my teacher; etc.] who has gone to his/her world because, without formally vowing, I pledge to give charity on his/her behalf so that his/her soul will be bound up in the bundle of life with the souls of Abraham, Isaac, and Jacob, Sarah, Rebecca, Rachel and Leah, and all the other righteous in the Garden of Eden, and let us say Amen.

For many years, it was assumed that this prayer began as a tribute to Jews killed by Crusaders on their way to fight Muslims in the Holy Land. That was the conclusion of a seminal article by Solomon Freehof.[523] Freehof traced several prayers that were indeed chanted in memory of martyrs of the Crusades beginning in the 11th century, and later, as a result of Christian persecution blaming Jews for the Bubonic Plague—known as the Black Death—in the 14th century. He theorized that, over time, it became customary to add prayers to honor the deceased relatives of congregants who died natural deaths in addition to the prayers memorializing martyrs. The problem with this theory is that the medieval Jewish books of customs and law that deal with the *Yizkor* prayer recited for relatives do not make any reference to martyrs. The theory has no hard evidence to support it.

Recent scholarship—especially by Elisheva Baumgarten and Judah Galinsky—has established a more likely origin of this practice.[524] It relates to an interesting back and forth influence between Judaism and Christianity. In talmudic times the biblical verse "Charity saves from death" (Proverbs 10:2) was understood to mean that giving charity could redeem donors from death, that is, could assure them a place in the afterlife.[525] This teaching in-

[523] "Hazkarath Neshamoth," *Hebrew Union College Annual* 36 (1965), 179-189.

[524] See Elisheva Baumgarten, *Practicing Piety in Medieval Ashkenaz: Men, Women, and Everyday Religious Experience* (Philadelphia: University of Pennsylvania Press, 2014), 104-115. Among several articles by Galinsky, see "Charity and Prayer in the Ashkenazic Synagogue: *Yizkor* in the Middle Ages" [Hebrew], in *Ve-hineh Rivkah Yotzet: Essays in Jewish Studies in Honor of Rivka Dagan* (Jerusalem: Tzur-Ot, 2017), 163-174. See also Judah D. Galinsky, "Commemoration and *Heqdesh* in the Jewish Communities of Germany and Spain During the 13th Century," in Michael Borgolte, ed., *Stiftungen in Christentum, Judentum und Islam vor der Moderne* (Berlin: Akademie Verlog, 2005), 191-203.

[525] For sources, see Alyssa Gray, *Charity in Rabbinic Judaism: Atonement, Rewards, and Righteousness* (London: Routledge, 2019), 183-184. Cited in Baumgarten, *Practicing Piety in Medieval Ashkenaz*, 107.

fluenced early Christianity, which accepted it as well. But in this early period, neither religion instituted formal prayers that connected the giving of charity to a place in heaven. By the Middle Ages, Christians did introduce prayers acknowledging charitable gifts with the reward of a place in the afterlife. Beginning in the 13th century when the practice of *Yizkor* seems to have begun, Jews seem to have been influenced by the growing importance of these Christian prayers that mentioned the giving of charity *pro anima*, "for the soul," meaning that the donation to charity would assure a place in heaven for the contributors or for their relatives. This was part of a heightened theological concern for the afterlife in 12th-13th century European Christianity. The general religious milieu influenced the Jewish community as well, which also evinced great interest in assuring a place in the afterlife. The older talmudic teaching that charity could "save from death" along with the contemporary Christian practice of actually mentioning such contributions in their liturgy influenced Jews to also compose such prayers. Of course, Jews did not simply copy Christian prayers. Rather, "...Jews adopted rituals from their cultural surroundings and situated them in the framework of ancient Jewish beliefs and practices while also revising their parameters to fit Jewish thought and to justify the Christian custom being incorporated."[526] Jews adopted the general idea of the Christian prayers (which, as mentioned above, were themselves was based on earlier talmudic teachings), and composed the prayer that begins with the word *Yizkor*, "May God Remember." These memorial prayers were assigned to the last day of each of the Three Pilgrimage Festivals because the Torah reading for those days concludes with Deuteronomy 16:17, which contains the command for each pilgrim to bring *kematnat yad*, "his own gift" to offer to God. These words were later interpreted to mean a gift of charity. To this day, the traditional formulation of this prayer includes an explicit mention of a pledge of charity (*tzedakah*) on behalf of the deceased relative—which the contemporary Orthodox and Conservative prayer books preserve.[527] The prayer books of the Reconstructing Judaism and Reform movements omit the pledge of charity, thus severing this prayer from its probable original theology.[528] (The non-Orthodox versions of the prayer also omit the mention of the patriarchs, matriarchs "and all the righteous in the Garden of Eden").

The prayer itself is quite short. It mainly calls upon God "to remember" the soul of the worshiper's relative. It includes a striking image: "May his/her

[526] Elisheva Baumgarten, *Practicing Piety in Medieval Ashkenaz*, 114.
[527] See *The Complete Artscroll Siddur*, 810f.; *Siddur Lev Shalem for Shabbat and Festivals*, 335.
[528] See *Kol Haneshamah Shabbat Veḥagim*, 638; *Mishkan T'filah A Reform Siddur*, 580.

soul be bound up in the bundle of life." The phrase comes from the Bible—I Samuel 25:29. The word for "bundle" is *tzeror* which means "bundle, parcel, pouch."[529] In its biblical context, it was part of a blessing upon David uttered by Abigail, the wife of Nabal. The biblical phrase reads:

> And if anyone sets out to pursue you and seek your life, the life of my lord (i.e., David) will be bound up in the bundle of life with *YHVH* your God.

The blessing expressed Abigail's wish that God would protect David by binding him to God's "bundle of life," that is, to God's vessel or repository of life. An early talmudic tradition interpreted the expression to apply not to the life of David, and not to this life at all, but to "the souls of all righteous people" who would be guarded in the afterlife. Because the verse says, "bound up in the bundle of life with *YHVH* your God," the Talmud understood this to mean "with *YHVH* your God," in heaven.[530] It is because of the talmudic expansion of the meaning of the verse that this wording appears in our prayer asking that the soul of our loved one who died be "bound up in the bundle of life," that is, with God, in heaven.

The second prayer at the core of the *Yizkor* service is *Eil Malei Raḥamim*, "God Full of Mercy," known to us from the 17th century. Its traditional text is as follows:

> God full of mercy who dwells on high, grant fitting rest on the wings of God's Presence [*Shekhinah*] among the holy and pure who shine like the glow of heaven, to the soul of [name of the relative] who has gone to his/her world. Because without formally vowing, I pledge to give charity for the remembrance of his/her soul, may his/her resting place be in the Garden of Eden. Therefore, master of mercy, shelter him/her in the shadow of your wings forever and bind his/her soul in the bundle of life forever. *YHVH* is his/her inheritance, may he/she rest in peace and let us say Amen.

---

529 Francis Brown, S.R. Driver, Charles A. Briggs, eds., *A Hebrew and English Lexicon of the Old Testament* (Oxford: Clarendon Press, 1906, 1951), 865.

530 See Babylonian Talmud Shabbat 152b and *Ḥagigah* 12b (among other parallels in Rabbinic Literature).

This prayer is first mentioned in a book by Rabbi Nathan Nata Hannover—a 17th-century East European spiritual leader I mentioned earlier in reference to the chanting of the Thirteen Attributes of God in the Torah Service on the festivals. In addition to the book in which Rabbi Nathan Nata mentioned the Thirteen Attributes, he also composed a chronicle of the 1648 attacks of Bogdan Chmielnicki and his Cossacks upon the Jewish communities of Ukraine and the surrounding areas. The chronicle mentions that *Eil Malei Raḥamim* was chanted in memory of the Jews killed by Chmielnicki but does not claim that the prayer was composed for this purpose.[531]

Aside from its history, the content of *Eil Malei Raḥamim* is quite similar to that of the *Yizkor* prayer treated above. *Eil Malei Raḥamim* also asks that the deceased's soul be with God in heaven ("on the wings of God's Presence," "in the shadow of your wings," "in the Garden of Eden"), that the soul be "bound up in the bundle of life," and it also has the worshiper pledge charity (although all the non-Orthodox versions of this prayer omit the pledge of charity). When Rabbi Nathan Nata records that *Eil Malei Raḥamim* was recited in memory of the martyrs, he may well have meant that a version of the prayer was adapted to honor the martyrs of 1648. All of this makes one wonder whether *Eil Malei Raḥamim* was originally simply another version of the *Yizkor* prayer itself. If this is the case, then what would make the most sense is for the memorial service to contain either the *Yizkor* prayer or *Eil Malei Raḥamim*, but not both. However, the liturgy doesn't always develop in a linear, rational, way. It is likely that the link between *Eil Malei Raḥamim* and the commemoration of the Chmielnicki massacres granted the prayer special status, and as a result, it has taken a place along with the *Yizkor* prayer to this day.

In contemporary worship, *Eil Malei Raḥamim* is usually chanted two separate times during the *Yizkor* service: Once to honor the memories of relatives and the second time to memorialize Jews killed *al kiddush hashem*, "for the sanctification of Gods' name," i.e., as martyrs—of the Holocaust, for example. This prayer also forms part of the funeral and burial service liturgy.

**Spiritual Commentary on *Yizkor***

While the desire to memorialize departed loved ones on the Three Pilgrimage Festivals first inspired formal prayers in about the 13th century, that

[531] The prayer is mentioned in Rabbi Nathan Nata's *Yeven Metzulah*, "Abyss of Despair." The 1653 edition I checked on June 21, 2022 was posted on Hebrewbooks.org. It is an unpaginated edition. The reference to *Eil Malei Raḥamim* is on page 8 of the PDF version of the book. I first saw the allusion to Rabbi Nathan Nata in connection to this prayer in Lawrence A. Hoffman, *May God Remember: Memory and Memorializing in Judaism*, (Woodstock, Vermont: Jewish Lights Publishing, 2013), 13.

kind of yearning has not diminished in the centuries since. The ancient and medieval idea that giving charity is the key to securing a place in the afterlife probably is less resonant for many in the modern era. It may be difficult for many contemporary Jews to believe that there is any ritual we may do, no matter how well-intentioned, that can guarantee a place in the World to Come. That is, no doubt, the reason that some of the non-Orthodox prayer books do not mention the giving of charity in the *Yizkor* prayer and that all of the non-Orthodox prayer books omit it from *Eil Malei Raḥamim*. Nevertheless, the opportunity to spiritually link ourselves with loved ones who have died remains meaningful. Both prayers express the wish that the souls of the deceased be with God in heaven. For moderns, that may be understood as saying that the location of the souls of our loved ones who have died is as much of a mystery—and yet is just as palpable—as the presence of God. Both prayers are opportunities to bind ourselves with the souls of loved ones who have died. They are opportunities to invoke, if only for a few moments, the presence of our loved ones. They are opportunities to allow ourselves to express our deeply held emotions of loss and love for our parents, or siblings, or a spouse, or others who have died. Tears often accompany this service and for good reason. We never fully heal from the loss of close family members and yet, we could not live a normal life if we constantly mourned. The *Yizkor* service, several times a year (in addition to the *Yahrtzeit*, the annual anniversary of the death) is a chance to give voice to the grief and the joy of intensely reconnecting with our loved ones who have died.

Any time we come into contact with death, it is also natural to contemplate our own mortality. It may be comforting to consider that after we depart this world, there will hopefully be family members who will connect spiritually with us during the *Yizkor* service on the Three Pilgrimage Festivals.

For some of us, the conventional notion of the soul continuing to have independent existence after death may be challenging. Another option comes from the Jewish mystical and Ḥasidic tradition, the approach of a non-dualistic view of God and the universe. According to this view, everything is part of God; the perception of separate existence is just that—a perception. In this approach, after death, we slough off all appearance of independent existence and seamlessly rejoin the divine whole.[532]

[532] For more on this theology see Jay Michaelson, *Everything is God: The Radical Path of Nondual Judaism* (Boston: Trumpeter Books, 2009).

## *Hoshanot*

*Hoshanot*, "Please God Save," is the name given to a group of *piyyutim* recited on each day of Sukkot. They are chanted after the *Amidah* of *Musaf* (a lesser-known custom is to chant them after *Hallel*) in a slow circle dance (*hakafah*) with *lulav* and *etrog* in hand. In this ritual, the synagogue has adapted and expanded a service that was enacted in the ancient Temple in Jerusalem on this holiday. The *Mishnah* records that on each day of Sukkot, the altar would be circled once as participants held willow branches and it would be circled seven times on the seventh day of the holiday which ultimately came to be known as *Hoshana Rabba* ("The Great *Hoshana*"):

> There was a place below Jerusalem called Motzah. They would descend to there and gather from there large willow branches... Every day [of Sukkot] they would circle the altar one time and say, "Please *YHVH* save, Please *YHVH* grant success" (Ps. 118:25). Rabbi Yehudah says [they would say] "*Ani VaHo*, save." And on that particular day (the seventh day of the holiday), they would circle the altar seven times.[533]

After the Temple was destroyed, this practice was continued in the synagogue with many *piyyutim* composed to accompany the circle dance. The circling is done around someone holding a Torah scroll as an alternative to the ancient Temple's altar. From the medieval period, the custom has been to carry the *lulav* and *etrog* during the circling instead of the more ancient custom, seen in the Mishnah cited above, of carrying just willow branches. Sukkot was considered the season when the year was judged for rain, and thus, the time of year that was judged for the quality of that year's harvests.[534] This was likely the reason for the Temple's ritualized chant (from the end of *Hallel*): "Please *YHVH* save, Please *YHVH* grant success." This, in fact, seems to be the point of the *Hoshanot* service—praying for rain and the success of the harvest over the coming year. It can be challenging to find these themes in some of the *Hoshanot*; their main theme seems to simply be petitions for salvation. However, a careful read of the many *Hoshanot* composed for

[533] *Mishnah Sukkah* 4:5.
[534] See *Mishnah Rosh HaShanah* 1:2, end.

Sukkot reveals that the content of that salvation is, indeed, from drought and famine.[535] Here are excerpts from several of the *Hoshanot* on those themes:

> Cause an abundance of crops, of trees, of vegetation—save. Do not condemn the ground, but sweeten the luscious fruits—save. Let the wind bring the soaring clouds, let the stormy rains be emplaced, let the clouds not be withheld...[536]
>
> Renew the face of the earth—planting trees in desolate lands, winepresses and stands of grain, vineyards and sycamores. To the demarcated land—to heal with powerful rains, to give life to forsaken wastes, to sustain with vegetation...[537]
>
> [Protect the] Ground from accursedness... grain from scorch... flocks from leanness.[538]
>
> Please open the treasure troves of your rains for us as you water the parched earth from them—and bring salvation now.[539]
>
> Where milk and honey flow please make not arid. With watering clouds clothe her produce—and save us, God of our salvation.[540]

The point of chanting the *Hoshanot* on Sukkot was to plead for ample rain to sustain the land's crops.

I want to return to a cryptic teaching in the *Mishnah* cited earlier:

---

535 "The *Hoshanot* on *Hoshana Rabba* are characterized by their mention of the *aravah* ("willow branch")... or with an explicit and overt petition for rain... **The *Hoshanot* for the rest of the days correspond in general to those for *Hoshana Rabba*, and according to all the manuscripts, those for *Hoshana Rabba* are also recited on the previous days.**" Emphasis added. Daniel Goldschmidt and Jonah Fraenkel, eds., *Maḥzor Sukkot, Shemini Atzeret, V'Simḥat Torah* [Hebrew] (New York: Leo Baeck Institute Inc., 1981), 40 in the Hebrew pagination.

536 *The Complete Artscroll Siddur*, "Lord Who Saves," 731.

537 *The Complete Artscroll Siddur*, "Man and Beast," 731.

538 *The Complete Artscroll Siddur*, "Ground from Accursedness," 731.

539 *The Complete Artscroll Siddur*, "Please Bring Salvation Now," 743.

540 *The Complete Artscroll Siddur*," "Be Merciful, please, with the congregation of Jeshurun's flock; forgive and pardon their iniquities; and save us, God of our salvation," 753. See also two entire *piyyutim* on the theme of rain: "Please God, please! Save now and bring salvation now, for you are our father," 744-748; "Save now, please God, please bring salvation now, Save now, forgive now, bring success now, and save us, God, our Fortress," 750.

> Every day [of Sukkot) they would circle the altar one time and say,
> "Please *YHVH* save, Please *YHVH* grant success" (Ps. 118:25).
> Rabbi Yehudah says they would say] "*Ani VaHo*, save."

The phrase *Ani VaHo* seems to be an alternate name of God: Just as in the *Mishnah*'s first sentence we read, "Please *YHVH* save," the parallel in the second sentence is, "*Ani VaHo* please save." The first of this two-word name, *Ani* means "I" in Hebrew. However, the second word, *VaHo*, is a word that defies easy translation. It <u>sounds</u> like the Hebrew word *hu*, "he/him," but it isn't clear.

The 11th-century commentator, Rashi, posits that, in fact, *Ani VaHo* is a name of God hidden within three verses in the Torah (Exodus 14:19-21).[541] This accords with a mystical tradition that there is a seventy-two-letter name of God hidden in these three verses.[542] According to Rashi, the following is the method to decipher the name of God within these 72 letters: Take the first letter of the first verse, add the last letter of the middle verse, and add the first letter of the last verse and you have one three-letter name of God. Then take the second letter of the first verse, the second to last letter of the middle verse, and the second letter of the last verse for another three-letter name of God. Continue the pattern and you'll end up with 24 three-letter names of God. Following this technique, one of the names is *Ani* and another is *VaHo*. Thus, the *Mishnah*'s *Ani VaHo* is indeed an alternate name for *YHVH* according to Rashi.

The commentary known as *Tosafot*, written by Rashi's students and descendants, then points out that it isn't enough to identify *Ani VaHo* as names of God.[543] The question is: Why did Rabbi Yehudah in this *mishnah* specifically use <u>these</u> two names of God among all the divine names found within the 72 biblical letters? They supply a startling answer, citing an interpretation from the Midrash on the Book of Lamentations. They comment that the

[541] Rashi's commentary to Babylonian Talmud, *Sukkah* 45a, s.v., *Ani VaHo*. This is Rashi's second interpretation. His first interpretation observes that via *Gematria*, the numerical value of the letters of *Ani VaHo* equals the numerical value of *Ana YHVH*, and thus, the phrases would mean the same thing. Probably unsatisfied with this interpretation (since if the two phrases are equivalent, why did Rabbi Yehudah have to add his comment?), Rashi supplies his second interpretation.

[542] On the 72-letter name of God, see, for example, Joshua Trachtenberg, *Jewish Magic and Superstition: A Study in Folk Religion* (Philadelphia: University of Pennsylvania, 2004 reprint of the 1939 original edition), 90, 95-97.

[543] *Tosafot* on Babylonian Talmud *Sukkah* 45a, s.v. *Ani VaHo*. And see the interpretations of this *mishnah* in the Palestinian Talmud *Sukkah* 54b; by Rambam (12th c., Egypt); and by Hanokh Albeck, *The Six Orders of the Mishnah* [Hebrew] (Jerusalem: Mosad Bialik, 1959, 1973), II:271-272; 476.

word *Ani* ("I") refers to the prophet Ezekiel in the biblical verse, "I (Ezekiel) am in the midst of the exile" (Ezekiel 1:1). They then identify the word *VaHo* with the word *Vehu* ("And he") in Jeremiah 40:1, "And he (Jeremiah) is in chains."[544] Finally, they assert that, contrary to the *peshat*, the meaning of these words in context refers not to the prophets, but to God! In other words, it is God who said, "I am in chains in the midst of the exile," meaning that God so identified with Israel's exile that God too felt exiled. (Rambam, 12th c., Egypt, in his commentary on this *mishnah*, cites Psalm 91:15, "I [God] will be with him [Israel] in distress"). The astounding conclusion of *Tosafot* is not simply that during the *Hoshanot* in the ancient Temple they would use this divine name, *Ani VaHo*, to appeal to God to save Israel by granting rain. Rather, says *Tosafot*, they would chant "*Ani VaHo* save," meaning, "God, save yourself!"

Recent research based on a careful analysis of many relevant sources by Moshe Ben Eliezer Zippor suggests a different interpretation of our *mishnah*.[545] According to him, the crux of the argument in the *mishnah* is on the proper way to pronounce God's name in the ancient Temple during the proto-*Hoshanot* service. The first opinion may be read to either mean that they would avoid pronouncing God's four-letter holy name (*YHVH*) and literally say *HaShem* ("the name") or that they would actually say God's four-letter holy name. The second opinion, that of Rabbi Yehudah, disagrees; Rabbi Yehudah held that they said *Ani VaHo*. Zippor argues that the meaning of *Ani* is not "I," but rather a misspelling of *Ana*, "please," and that *VaHo* is a nickname for God, spelled in Hebrew almost like God's holy name, *YHVH*. Thus, while the first opinion in the *mishnah* meant that they would either say *Ana HaShem* or *Ana YHVH*, Rabbi Yehudah differed and claimed that they would say *Ana VaHo*.[546] If this is correct, then the approach of Rashi and *Tosafot*, above, that *Ani VaHo* represent two of God's mystical names is more of a midrashic interpretation of the *mishnah*. If Zippor is correct, then the *mishnah* is revealing a heretofore unidentified name of God: Along with *YHVH*, there was also *VaHo*.

The *siddurim* of the Orthodox, Conservative, and Reconstructing Judaism movements include the *Hoshanot* service while that of the Reform movement omits it.

[544] In seeming support of this, the version of this *mishnah* in the Kaufman manuscript reads *VeHu*, "and he," not *VeHo*.

[545] Moshe Ben Eliezer Zippor, "Further on the Issue of *Ani VaHo Hoshi'a Na*," [Hebrew], *Moreshet Yisrael, Ketav-Eit LeYahadut LeTzionut VeLeEretz Yisrael* 10, 2014, 72-78. Zippor's suggestion is that this nickname ought to be pronounced *VaHu*—like the biblical names Yishayahu, Eliahu, etc.

[546] Here, I diverge slightly from Zippor's conclusion on the last page of his study.

**Spiritual Commentary on *Hoshanot***

As we saw, the *Hoshanot* service is mainly comprised of prayers for rain and agricultural security. Even though most Jews in the modern period no longer work on farms, the issues of climate change and food security are central for our world. Typically, contemporary worship service leaders are challenged by how to present this service. Asking for God's help to strengthen us in working to reverse climate change and for justice in food cultivation and distribution ought to enliven this service in the modern age. The *Hoshanot* could be introduced with a reminder of the biblical teaching that "The earth is the Lord's and all it contains" (Psalm 24:1) and reimagined as a possibility to bring a spiritual approach to this crucial challenge. Nicole Goluboff suggests an interesting perspective through which to view both the *Hoshanot* service offered each day of Sukkot as well as *Tefillat Geshem*, "The Prayer for Rain" on Shemini Atzeret. She points out that on Rosh HaShanah, many congregations initiate a food drive for those in need—whether connected to the fast of Yom Kippur or not. Goluboff proposes depicting Rosh HaShanah and Sukkot/Shemini Atzeret as two symbolic "bookends" in the Jewish season of the Days of Awe—each of which connects to justice in food cultivation: "We begin the season by trying to increase access to food and end it by praying for the ability to do so again next year; We begin by remembering those in need and end by remembering the true Provider."[547]

Beyond the content of these prayers, the *Hoshanot* service is that rare opportunity in Jewish liturgy that involves movement because the prayers are chanted while participants circle someone holding a Torah scroll. The possibility of physicality during a service ought to be embraced. The very act of movement can invigorate and brighten the ambience of a worship service. In many synagogues, the circling is done very slowly. I would encourage the inclusion of some fast circling as well, anticipating the ecstatic dancing of the final day of the holiday, Simḥat Torah. Just as a spiritual atmosphere may be created through slow chant and slow circling, so too, a more euphoric kind of spirituality may be reached through lively chant and fast circling. When the weather cooperates, communities may consider holding the *Hoshanot* service outdoors, on the synagogue grounds. Changing the worship mode in this way can help make the service that much more stimulating.

The traditional sequence of *Hoshanot* is after *Musaf*, toward the end of the morning service. However, to add *Hoshanot* just at the point, after the

[547] Goluboff, at the time of this writing, is a rabbinical student at The Academy for Jewish Religion, but will, *b'ezrat HaShem*, will be a rabbinical colleague within a short time after this book's publication. She shared this idea in a personal note to the author.

*Amidah* of *Musaf*, when on a typical Shabbat, congregants anticipate the final prayers of the service, can make the service feel unduly long. To avoid this effect, those congregations that include *Musaf* may want to opt for the lesser-known custom of adding *Hoshanot* immediately after *Hallel*.

Now, regarding the phrase "*Ani VaHo* save"—if the interpretation of Professor Emeritus (Bar-Ilan University) Moshe Zippor is correct, then we have a formerly unidentified name for God, *VaHo*, which is quite interesting. On the other hand, if we take the interpretations of Rashi and *Tosafot* seriously, it would mean that God may be found with those "in chains, in exile," in other words, with the oppressed. An important Jewish teaching.

But what can we make of the idea that God needs saving? After all, a mainstream teaching of Jewish tradition has been that God is omnipotent. Here, I take inspiration from an unlikely source: The lyrics of the song, "My God," written by Ian Anderson and recorded by his band, Jethro Tull, on their album *Aqualung* in 1971, which read, in part:

> People what have you done?
> Locked Him in His golden cage; golden cage.
> Made Him bend to your religion...
> He is the God of nothing
> If that's all that you can see.
> You are the God of everything
> He's inside you and me.

If God needs saving, in other words, it could be from the "golden cage" into which we sometimes confine God. I learned an explanation of idolatry early in my career from my colleague, Rabbi Jay Rosenbaum: Any time we feel we have defined God, that we fully know God, that we can explain the way God works, it is idolatry. God is beyond our comprehension. Those of us engaged in religious leadership need to keep this in mind; it ought to keep us honest and humble. Any time I hear or read of a religious leader speaking very confidently about what God wants, I think: God needs saving from being placed in that cage, in that box. Human beings have been given hints of God's presence but a full perception of the divine always eludes our reach. Thus, another meaning of chanting the *Hoshanot* is to be humble when we speak of God, lest we be guilty of causing God to need saving... from the golden cage into which we sometimes place God.

## Akdamut

*Akdamut*, "The Introduction (of Words)," is an Ashkenazic *piyyut* in the Aramaic language composed as an introduction (*reshut*) to the *Targum*—the Aramaic translation of the Torah reading—for the first day of Shavuot. The *Targum* was in use during the talmudic era when most Jews no longer understood Hebrew. Each verse that was read in Hebrew was then translated into Aramaic, the *lingua franca* of the Middle East for centuries until Arabic replaced it after the Muslim conquest of the 7th century CE. In the Middle Ages, although Jewish communities in Europe did not understand Aramaic (except for scholars), the Aramaic translation was still used in those areas for certain special Torah readings for several more centuries. Those special readings included the Ten Commandments read on the first day of *Shavuot*. For this reason, Rabbi Meir ben Isaac Nehorai (late 11th century, Germany) composed *Akdamut*, a 90-line Aramaic poem as an introduction to the *Targum* for the reading of the Ten Commandments on that holiday. There were other Aramaic introductions in circulation for the *Targum* to the Ten Commandments, but only this one, *Akdamut*, continues to be chanted in traditional synagogues to this day. Thus, *Akdamut* has not only outlived all other Aramaic introductions to the *Targum* for this Torah reading, it has also outlived—by many centuries—its original purpose, since the *Targum* fully disappeared from European synagogues not long after this poem was written (only the Yemenite Jewish community continues to use the *Targum*). Since the *Targum* is no longer chanted in Ashkenazic contemporary congregations, this poem is now chanted just before the usual Hebrew reading of the Ten Commandments on the first day of Shavuot.

The question is: Why has this particular *piyyut* continue to play a role in the liturgy for Shavuot when its original *raison d'etre* as an introduction to the *Targum* disappeared centuries ago? The answer is that this *piyyut* acquired a life of its own independent of the *Targum* and of the holiday of Shavuot. Its theme is the great merit, and eventual reward, of the People of Israel in resisting temptations and persecutions meant to cause them to convert. It was written just before the First Crusade (in the year 1096) by a rabbi who resided in Worms, one of the Jewish communities in the Rhenish towns attacked by the Crusaders on their way to fight the Muslims in the Holy Land. The poem's message of encouragement proved popular in the wake of the crusader attacks. However, what provided for its thousand-year longevity is the central role played by a medieval Yiddish tale which portrayed the author of *Adkamut* as a hero, and the poem itself as an expression of triumph over a demonic monk who had threatened thousands of Jews. The tale lent to the poem a sense of vicarious vengeance for Ashkenazic Jewry which suffered centuries-long trauma from the Crusaders' attacks. Those attacks constitute the first instance of Christian mass-murder of Jews in history.[548] After a brief scan of the content of the poem itself, I'll share a summary of the tale.

In terms of content, after a short introduction and standard praise of God's glory, the poem establishes God's preference for the People of Israel over the angels. The longest section of the poem, the last 50 lines, emphasizes that the People of Israel will be rewarded in the world to come for their loyalty to God in the face of the non-Jewish nations' manipulative and violent attempts to convert them. In the poem, Israel is taunted, with the poet, following the midrash, ironically putting the words of the Song of Songs (5:9) in the mouths of the non-Jewish nations.[549] They mock the fact that while Jews are attacked, their "love"—God—does not seem to help them:

> From where and just who is your love, (you) who are beautiful to behold,
> For whose sake you die in the lion's den?
> Honored and beautiful will you be if you intermingle with the realms,
> Your will we will do everywhere.

While *Akdamut* is often explained as an introduction to the reading of the Ten Commandments, that is mainly true only in an external way (i.e., it was written as an introduction to that reading), but since its content barely links with the Ten Commandments, it is misleading to portray it in this way. *Akdamut* is an anthem meant to strengthen the will of a minority people who were subject to enticements and threats for conversion. It sings the praises of a people loyal to its God including the next worldly reward that God has in store for this people.

The *piyyut* itself displays great literary craft. Nearly every line alludes to a biblical or talmudic teaching. Among these, it notes the midrashic depiction of two mythical creatures in gladiatorial combat at the end of days:

---

[548] I published a detailed academic study and annotated translation of *Akdamut* a number of years ago, "*Akdamut*: History, Folklore, and Meaning," *Jewish Quarterly Review*, Vol. 99, no. 2, spring, 2009, 161-183. Here, I summarize that study. The article provides additional details and sources. See also Eliezer Yehuda Brandt, "The Recital of '*Akdamut*' and '*Yetziv Pitgam*' on the Holiday of *Shavuot* [Hebrew], *Yerushateinu: Sefer Shanah LeToratam shel Ḥakhmei Askenaz, Orḥoteihem U'Minhagam*, 10 (2019), 514-534; Aton M. Holzer, "*Akdamut*: An Alphabet of Tenth-Century Ashkenaz," *Tradition* 53:2, 2021, 68-93.

[549] *Mekhilta DeRabbi Yishmael, Mesekhta DeShirata*, 3. Jacob Z. Lauterbach, *Mekilta de-Rabbi Ishmael* (Philadelphia: Jewish Publication Society, 1935, 1961), 2:26-27.

Leviathan, a huge sea-creature, and a giant ox (*Shor HaBar*) who fight to the death, and the feast for the righteous that is served of their flesh. The poem celebrates a talmudic teaching that "wine preserved in its very grapes" from the time of Creation will be served at that banquet. Every line ends with the same sound—*ta*—not such an easy feat to accomplish over 90 lines! The poet also showed great skill in weaving quite a bit into the first letter of each line when those letters are read in sequence: It begins with a double alphabetic acrostic, continues with spelling of the poet's name, and concludes with a prayer that the poet grow in Torah and good deeds.

But as I mentioned above, the poem mainly owes its endurance to the Yiddish tale that was and, in traditional Jewish circles, still is widely known. The tale raised Rabbi Meir to the status of a glorious hero and advanced *Akdamut* above the standing of just one more prayer to an anthem that celebrates a miracle. In the Yiddish story, the 11th-century Rabbi Meir is selected to represent the Jewish community of Worms against the threats of a practitioner of black magic who pretended to be a monk. Rabbi Meir is told in a dream that help will be forthcoming from the Ten Lost Tribes of Israel, so he travels far and wide to find these lost Jews. After nearly a year of travel, he arrives at the border of the land of these Jews, sometimes called "the red Jews" in folk tales.[550] The border is the river Sambatyon, a legendary river whose turbulence makes it impossible to navigate except on the Sabbath, when the waters become calm and placid; but it is forbidden to cross a river by boat on the Sabbath. For the sake of saving lives, Rabbi Meir violates the Sabbath and crosses the river in a boat. Upon hearing the plight of the Jews of Worms, an old, short, lame member of the Ten Lost Tribes, named Dan, is sent to fight the black monk (as he is called in the tale). Rabbi Meir must then remain forever among the Ten Tribes; he could not justify violating the Sabbath again since Dan will now take the fight to the black monk. Dan, the anti-hero (based on his outer appearance), makes his way back to Worms and, wielding mystical names of God in round after colorful round of battle, counters the magic of the black monk, kills him, and saves the Jews. At the conclusion of the contest, Dan relates that Rabbi Meir had composed the poem *Akdamut*, recited it to Dan, and requested that it be chanted each Shavuot "for the sake of his name," since his name is signed in the alphabetic acrostic.

[550] On the Red Jews of the Ten Lost Tribes who live beyond the Sambatyon river, see Rebekka Voss, "Entangled Stories: The Red Jews in Premodern Yiddish and German Apocalyptic Lore," *Association for Jewish Studies Review*, 36:1 (April 2012), 1-41 and Idem, "Connecting Stories? A Yiddish Folktale and Its Unpopular Hebrew Versions," in Francesca Bergoli, David B. Ruderman, eds., *Connecting Histories: Jews and Their Others in Early Modern Europe* (Philadelphia: University of Pennsylvania Press, 2019), 23-35.

The tale linked together Rabbi Meir, his *piyyut*, and the black monk—who was understood as a symbol of the Crusader soldiers who, to the Jews, only pretended to be good Christians—in such a way as to provide comfort to the Jewish communities who suffered great trauma in the wake of the First Crusade.

> Jews in successive generations of medieval Europe took hope and courage from the poem. In this way, the tale and the memory of the Crusader violence bolstered and augmented the power of the main theme of *Akdamut* to offer consolation, faith, hope, and strength to Jewish communities over the centuries. All of this was encompassed in the annual recitation of *Akdamut* on the holiday of *Shavuot*. *Akdamut* would likely have fallen into desuetude not long after the *Targum*, which it was meant to introduce was itself discontinued in Europe. However, the original theme of the poem, as seen through the lens of the Yiddish tale and as filtered through the memory of the losses of the First Crusade, has preserved this 90-line Aramaic poem in the liturgy for nearly a thousand years since its composition.[551]

While *Akdamut* is a staple of Orthodox Shavuot liturgy, it has long been omitted from the liturgy of the Reform and Reconstructing Judaism movements. And while the Conservative Movement's *siddurim* have always included the full text of *Akdamut* (although its 1985 edition of *Siddur Sim Shalom* contained no translation!), a full chanting of the poem has been disappearing from worship in the movement's synagogues. Most Conservative congregations suffice with the recital of a brief excerpt.

**Spiritual Commentary on *Akdamut***

In the poem, the taunts of the non-Jewish nations that God did not care about Israel's suffering were answered by the Jews in a similarly supremacist way:

> With wisdom she answers them; the (messianic) End (she) describes:
> If you only knew him in wisdom, in intimate knowledge.

[551] Jeffrey Hoffman, "*Akdamut*: History, Folklore, and Meaning," 173. A fuller summary of the tale is found in my article.

> What significance has the "greatness" (that you promise) compared to that great praise,
> Of what he will do for me when the Redemption shall come!
> When he shall bring light to me, but you will be covered in shame…

The *piyyut* offers a vision of ultimate vindication when in the messianic period God "shall bring light to me, but you (non-Jews) will be covered in shame."

I find it difficult to recommend a spiritual experience for this *piyyut* beyond appreciating it as part of the historical record of a grim period in the life of the Jewish People. While *Akdamut* is a document from the interaction between medieval Jews and Christians, it stems from a time when all three of the Abrahamic religions believed that only their religion was true, and the other faiths were false. Of course, politics and economics also played roles in the power struggles within European Christendom and between Christians and Jews as well. But the conflict was often expressed in religious terms.

It cannot be denied that antisemitism still exists, and its most dangerous forms are barely concealed under the surface of modern society. Jews around the world, including in North America, would be foolish to ignore the threats that exist from both the political left and right. And there may be worshipers who would consider this *piyyut* a relevant prayer to counsel Jews to remain vigilant, to shun complacence, against the ongoing threat of antisemitism. However, I cannot honestly encourage contemporary worshipers to recite this poem with that kind of personal inner meaning. The reason is that *Akdamut* is part of the *us versus them* mindset. Its main point is that God will, in the messianic end, reward Jews for their loyalty and bring shame on our oppressors, the non-Jewish nations. It lacks any nuance of contemporary interfaith relations simply because it is a product of its time. As a religious poem of the late 11th century, it is an outstanding piece of literary art. As a theological statement, its worth to me is only as a gateway to experience a tragic epoch in our history.

As a kind of footnote to this discussion, I will share the following true-life incident. When I was researching the study I previously published on *Akdamut*, I visited an ultra-Orthodox bookstore in Monsey, New York a few weeks before Shavuot. Sure enough, among the books set out on a display for the upcoming holiday were several booklets, specially printed for the holiday, that contained a Hebrew version of the Yiddish tale. I approached the bookseller and told him that I was writing a commentary on *Akdamut* and asked if he was familiar with the tale. He replied that of course he was, he had known it since it was told to him as a child. While I was dressed respectfully, it was obvious from my dress that I was not a member of his community, but rather a more modern Jew. Presumably noticing this, he asked me a captivating question: With all the scientific advances that have been made, has anyone yet discovered the actual location of the Sambatyon river? It took me a moment to realize that he was asking whether in my research, I, as a member of contemporary society, had come across any record of explorers having discovered the location of the Sambatyon river. It was a poignant moment: A very traditional Jew, who took the tale and the existence of the Sambatyon river literally, asking a modern Jew, who took the tale symbolically, whether any modern explorers had yet discovered the famous river. With deference to the bookseller, I simply answered that no, I hadn't come across any such discovery.

## *Tefillat Tal* and *Tefillat Geshem* The Prayer for Dew and The Prayer for Rain

On the first day of Passover, a prayer is added to the *Amidah* of *Musaf* known as *Tefillat Tal*, "The Prayer for Dew," petitioning God to send dew during the dry season in the land of Israel to support agriculture. Similarly, on Shemini Atzeret, a prayer is added to the *Amidah* of *Musaf* known as *Tefillat Geshem*, "The Prayer for Rain" petitioning God to send rain during the rainy season in Israel to ensure a proper harvest. The timing of these two prayers is related to a teaching in the *Mishnah*:

> ...On Passover judgment is passed concerning grain...
> On the festival (of Sukkot) they are judged concerning water (i.e., the rainfall of the coming year).[552]

Although the *Mishnah* does not specifically mention dew regarding Passover, this teaching was interpreted to mean that on Passover, judgment is passed on the extent to which dew will fall, nurturing the late spring grain harvest.

Various forms of these two prayers were created over the centuries. The Ashkenazic rite has, for many centuries, utilized *piyyutim* ascribed to Eleazar Kallir (6th-7th c., Israel). Originally, these two prayers were much longer than they appear in even the most traditional contemporary *siddurim*.

[552] *Mishnah Rosh HaShanah* 1:2.

Initially, they were composed in the *piyyut* form known as a *Shivata*. This term is Aramaic for "seven," referring to the seven blessings of the festival *Amidah*. As such, these *piyyutim* included additional poems for each one of the seven blessings in that *Amidah*. Already centuries ago, various regional rites abridged these extended literary masterpieces with the result that I know of no contemporary Jewish rite that chants The Prayer for Dew or The Prayer for Rain in its original, lengthy, format.[553] Rather, one-seventh (if that much!) of these *piyyutim* are part of the contemporary liturgy—only the passage composed for the second blessing of the *Amidah* of *Musaf* is chanted. This blessing is known as *Gevurot*, "[God's] Heroic Acts," which—appropriately—include natural phenomena such as the appearance of rain and dew. Because of the element of being "judged" as to whether the land has merited dew or rain, the custom has developed that when these (mini) *piyyutim* are chanted, the prayer leader dons a white robe, or *kittel*, and recites them in the musical mode of the Days of Awe, the holidays of judgment.

*Tefillat Tal*, "The Prayer for Dew," recited on the first day of Passover, is mainly comprised of six verses beseeching God to provide dew. Each verse begins and ends with the word *tal*, "dew," and each strophe begins with a letter that forms part of a reverse alphabetic acrostic. Interestingly, both literal and metaphorical meanings of "dew" are intertwined in each verse. The literal meaning is invoked as each verse petitions God for actual dew while the metaphorical meaning is contained in the entreaties to end the exile and rebuild Jerusalem, thus vivifying a people whose soul is "dried out" by the harshness of the exile.

*Tefillat Geshem*, "The Prayer for Rain," is recited on Shemini Atzeret, at the end of Sukkot. While the ancient Temple in Jerusalem stood, the ceremony of pouring water at the altar took place at the beginning of the holiday, which was meant to stimulate rain from above. However, after the Temple's destruction in the year 70 CE when the water ceremony was discontinued, The Prayer for Rain was instituted. The recitation of The Prayer for Rain was put off until Shemini Atzeret so as not to ask for rain when the commandment to dwell outdoors in the sukkah was still in effect. This *piyyut* also mainly comprises six verses, asking God to provide rain. Each verse begins with the word *Zekhor*, "Remember," and ends with the word *mayim*, "water." In subsequent verses, it appeals to God to provide "water," i.e., rain, in "remembrance" of the merit of the three Patriarchs, as well as Moses,

[553] For more on the prayers for dew and rain as forms of the *Shivata*, their variations and history, see the discussion in Ezra Fleischer's classic work, *Hebrew Liturgical Poetry in the Middle Ages* [Hebrew] (Jerusalem: Keter Publishing House, 1975), 196-198.

Aaron, and the twelve tribes of Israel. Each strophe begins with a letter that forms part of a regular alphabetic acrostic. Here, the repeated word *mayim*, "water," refers literally to rain throughout except for the last verse in which God is asked to remember the merit of the twelve tribes, that is, the merit of the Jewish People as a whole. In this verse, the twice-mentioned "water" is meant metaphorically, asking God to deliver rain because of the merit of the Jewish People "whose blood was been spilled for your sake like water" and whose persecutions have nearly "surrounded their souls like water" (echoing Jonah 2:6).

The siddur of the Reconstructing Judaism Movement substituted even shorter excerpts from Sephardic *piyyutim* for both The Prayer for Dew and The Prayer for Rain, but these are included in the *Amidah* of *Shaḥarit* since that siddur does not include an *Amidah* for *Musaf*.[554] The Conservative Movement's siddur contains most of the traditional versions of both The Prayer for Dew and the Prayer for Rain, but it also offers an alternative version for each. The alternative for the Prayer for Dew is a Sephardic form of the prayer that had previously been included in the siddur of the Reconstructing Judaism Movement. The alternative for The Prayer for Rain replaces several of the verses with newly written stanzas that feature the Matriarchs.[555] The Reform Movement's siddur omits both *piyyutim*. However, in place of The Prayer for Dew, it includes a short English prayer for all three Pilgrimage Festivals that praises God for "dewdrops of light and blessing." In place of The Prayer for Rain, it includes a short English prayer that integrates some of the wording of the traditional Prayer for Rain, though the Matriarchs are added as well. These English prayers are both followed by the Hebrew and English conclusion of the traditional versions of both The Prayer for Dew and the Prayer for Rain:

> For blessing and not for curse.
> For life and not death.
> For abundance, not want.[556]

**Spiritual Commentary on *Tefillat Tal and Tefillat Geshem***

It seems to me that most contemporary Jews do not believe that they can affect the amount of dew or rain in each season by praying to God, by attempting to persuade God to provide these forms of moisture that are es-

[554] *Kol Haneshamah: Shabbat Veḥagim*, 330, 332.
[555] *Siddur Lev Shalem*, 376, 379-380.
[556] *Mishkan T'filah: A Reform Siddur*, 473.

sential for successful harvests. We live in the age of science and we cannot pretend that we still believe that adequate dew and rain depend directly on God's judging us, and that therefore, we ought to beseech God for a favorable judgment. And yet, both the literal and metaphorical meanings of these two prayers can still be significant in the modern age.

There are multiple dimensions in a spiritual view of life. Two of them were exemplified in the life of Rachel Carson.[557] One is a feeling of awe before the beauty of nature. A deep appreciation for the esthetics of the natural world: The green of the trees, the blue of the sky and the sea, the artistry of cloud formations. This, to me, parallels the many times that the first chapter of Genesis has God observing that each stage of Creation was good. The other dimension is a corollary of the first: A sense of stewardship, of responsibility for preserving nature. This parallels the teaching in chapter two of Genesis that God placed Adam in the Garden "to till it and to preserve it" (Gen. 2:15). Rachel Carson published four books. The first three derive from the first dimension of a spiritual life: a feeling of awe before the beauty of nature. Those books are: *Under the Sea-Wind* (1941), *The Sea Around Us* (1951), and *The Edge of the Sea* (1955). These books were widely praised for their poetic and transcendent writing. Her final book, *Silent Spring* (1962), derived from the second dimension, a sense of responsibility to preserve the planet. This book was a stark wakeup call that unless America stopped polluting the air and water, the country would one day encounter "a silent spring," without the calls of birds and animals. The book became the catalyst for the environmental movement.

Jewish liturgy contains an intricate system of blessings over beauty in nature, including blessings celebrating the splendor of dawn and dusk (the first blessing before the *Shema* in *Shaḥarit* and *Ma'ariv*) as well as blessings over the first blossoms of spring, shooting stars, the first gaze of the ocean, etc. This aspect of Jewish liturgy reflects the first dimension of a spiritual view of life described above. The Prayers for Dew and Rain may be understood as reflecting the second dimension, that of stewardship and preservation of nature.

Reciting prayers about dew, rain, and the harvest in the synagogue raises the question of how the creator of heaven and earth would judge the way we as individual worshipers and as members of a faith community are responding to the crises of climate change and of the lack of food security for too many people. Extreme weather events—severe drought, unprecedented

[557] See the excellent biography by William Souder, *On A Farther Shore: The Life and Legacy of Rachel Carson* (New York: Crown Publishers, 2012).

flooding, the melting of the glaciers, increasing forest fires—are occurring more and more routinely. For me, the final three lines of both The Prayer for Dew and The Prayer for Rain raise these extreme events in my consciousness:

> For blessing and not for curse.
> For life and not death.
> For abundance, not want.

The main difference between the way our ancestors viewed these two prayers and the way we moderns might view them is this: Our ancestors believed that only God had the power over benevolent weather including nurturing dew and rain while we, in our generation, know that we human beings have a great deal of that power. When I recite these prayers on Passover and Shemini Atzeret, I feel the presence of God demanding that we accept responsibility for the way our actions affect the environment. That we take responsibility for the ways that our use of the earth's resources increases pollution, soil degradation, global warming, unprecedented flooding, natural resource depletion, deforestation, and generates unsustainable waste.

In this way, I interpret The Prayers for Dew and Rain in their literal meanings—referring to these physical forms of moisture—as great challenges to us, similar to the way I interpret the *Hoshanot* Service on Sukkot (see page 350). These two prayers can have great meaning and power when presented in this way to contemporary congregations.

Over 20 years ago, I wrote a *kavannah*, an "inner intention," for The Prayer for Dew, which—like the original prayer—interprets dew both literally and metaphorically. An excerpt follows:

> Bless the people of the Land, our people, B'nei Yisrael. They have learned from your presence in nature to nurture their harvest. They do not only water their crops with the artificial rain born of the *mamterah*, the sprinkler. They have learned from the way you grace the land with dew to provide the sprouting growth with droplets. These they tenderly cradle in plastic cocoons lest the liquid evaporate. Grant *B'nei Yisrael* the wisdom to conserve and protect the Garden.
>
> Turn your gaze to the Land and bless it with *Tal*.Bless the peoples of the land: Our people, *B'nei Yisrael* and their

neighbors, *B'nei Yishmael.* Let the moisture of the cool evenings trickle down and chill the heat of conflict. May the hard clay of hatred soften into the loose soil of openness. Hard rain will not penetrate, we need the gentleness of dew.

Turn your gaze to the Land and bless it with *Tal.*

Bless us, as well, who worship you this day. On *Pesaḥ*, we stand exactly half a year away from *Rosh HaShanah.* And we are aware that our souls have already begun to harden. They need to be tilled and loosened before we can present ourselves to you on the New Year. On this *Rosh Hodashim*, this "first of the months" (Exodus 12:2), may we open ourselves to feel the divine misting which the loam of our souls longs to receive.

Turn your gaze to the Land within and bless it with *Tal.*

# Afterword

## A Medieval Kabbalist on the Upper West Side

*As I wrote in the Introduction, I have written a short story to convey the concept of God that is evident in the "Spiritual Commentaries" in this book. Fiction, like poetry and the arts in general, can more felicitously allude to thoughts and feelings that defy clear and concise definition. My concept of God connects to contemporary scientific theories of cosmology, that is, the origin of the universe, and that is explored in this short story.*

I got the call one afternoon in the late summer from Sergeant Kanerek. I knew Kanerek from the 20-plus years I had served as a congregational rabbi in Manhattan before I entered the academic world full-time. I guess he kept my phone number even though I no longer had a congregation.

"Hey, Rabbi! Howya doin'? Jim Kanerek here. Been a while! I hope it's OK I called you; we got someone here down at the precinct who may be Jewish. This guy needs help. You're the first one I thought of."

Kanerek told me the story. The police were called about a guy wandering around the Upper West Side who seemed… different. New Yorkers are used to "different," but this man was unique even for New York. While he seemed disoriented and meandering, he also had an air of dignity about him. He wasn't threatening at all, and the shopkeeper who phoned was genuinely concerned about the person. Like he could have been a local's grandfather who maybe had a temporary memory loss or something.

And there was the way the man was dressed. He wore a flowing, green silk robe and on his head was a dark, turban-like head covering. In short, he seemed to be wearing a costume from some sort of theatrical production.

"Yeah," Kanerek continued, "so some of the cops in the precinct picked him up and brought him to the station on 100th Street. He seemed to be kind of lost, and he was talking in a foreign language. One of our guys, Hispanic fella, says to me that he thinks the man is speaking some sort of Spanish, but not the way it's spoken by Latinos. He said it's as if the man's talking out of a script from some old play. Our guy thinks this older gentleman may be saying something about Jews or synagogues or something. Maybe he's in a play at a nearby temple, had a little dementia and wandered out onto the street. So, I figured I'd give you a call. I know you don't have the congregation anymore, but you were here so long, I thought you might know something about it. Or you'd at least know someone else in the community who could get to the bottom of this and help the man out."

My first thought was to pawn this off onto one of my nearby colleagues who was still in the pulpit. But then I thought, congregational rabbis—like congregational clergy of all religions—are always incredibly busy. Much busier than the average congregant thinks. I wasn't teaching that day, it was a nice afternoon weather-wise, and I could use a nice walk. It would only take me about 15 minutes to walk from our place on 120th and Broadway to the police station. I didn't speak Spanish, but I figured if I could get the name of the synagogue he goes to out of him, I could connect him to the right colleague who would then help the guy out. I had been on a Jewish heritage tour of Spain earlier this year, and it occurred to me that maybe the man spoke Catalan, the language of Catalonia, that district of Spain that, like the Basque region, is always trying to break away and establish its own country. Their dialect is different from Castilian, spoken in most of the rest of Spain, and might sound very foreign to a Hispanic cop.

"Yeah, I'll be there, Sergeant. Give me a few minutes. I'll walk over to you."

The truth is, almost anytime I go out, I have an ulterior motive: Maybe I can pick up something fun to eat. It's a little embarrassing how much I think about food, but there it is. Although I'm a liberal rabbi, I only eat kosher food, and to someone like me, given the number of kosher restaurants and take-out places in New York City, I often think of my hometown as one big kosher marketplace. And a favorite take-out place of mine is the kosher deli on 90th and Broadway. So, while I'm hoping to help a fellow human being out by going down to the police station, I have to admit that I'm also thinking about picking up some pastrami for dinner afterward.

When I get to the precinct, Sergeant Kanarek is waiting for me.

"I gotta thank you, Rabbi. You came through for me again. Here, this way."

Kanarek guided me down the hall and there's the fellow, pacing alone in a room. Kanarek leaves the two of us alone. Sure enough, the man looks as if he walked off the set of a play, flowing robe, turban, and all. Like me, he's also got grey hair and a grey beard, but unlike me, his beard is quite long. I don't speak Spanish, but since he apparently said something about a synagogue, I decide to address him with the traditional Hebrew greeting, hoping that he'd know it and maybe view me as a friend.

"Shalom Aleikhem!"

He turns to me, his features tightened in puzzlement, but then, slightly more relaxed, he responds, "Aleikhem Shalom."

And then... he adds a few words of what I assume is Spanish to which I reply, "No hablo Espanol."

Then I try some Hebrew; the beginning of a well-known prayer.

"*Shema Yisrael*" ("Hear O Israel").

His eyes light up and he completes the prayer.

"*Adonai Eloheinu Adonai Eḥad*," ("Adonai is our God, Adonai alone").

"Are you a member of a shul nearby?"

Nothing.

"Do you speak English?"

"Anglia?"

Now that's an interesting response. Anglia. That's "England" in a number of old and contemporary languages. With that one word, I realize he is neither a member of a local synagogue, nor is he American. He must be saying he doesn't speak English. And I'm thinking that if he's dressed up for a performance, it's not for some neighborhood repertory because this guy's not local. But Lincoln Center isn't that far. Maybe instead of some confused old-timer from the neighborhood, he's actually an accomplished actor or singer who just doesn't know English. If he speaks Spanish, perhaps he knows French; aside from Jewish languages, I can hold my own in French.

"Vous parlez Francais?"

Nothing. Given his age (and mine), I try Yiddish.

"*Vos makhstu, a Yid*?" ("How are you, fellow Jew?").

Again nothing. Then, he raises a finger as if to say something. He pauses, rethinking. Finally...

"*Hayiti na vanad ba'aretz*."

So he does know Hebrew! And he has a sense of humor, quoting Cain's complaint to God, "I have become a restless wanderer on earth." And he pronounces Hebrew in the Sefardic way, as in Israel.

I can play along, and I quote the next verse.

"*Kol horeig Kayin shivatayim yukam*" ("If anyone kills Cain, sevenfold will be the vengeance taken upon him."

A smile. Now, I speak to him in Hebrew without resorting to the scholarly game of citing biblical verses.

"Where are you from? Somewhere in Israel? Are you here for some sort of performance? Can I help you in any way?"

"*Ayeih anokhi*?"

Now he's returned to biblical Hebrew, or at least pre-modern Hebrew. He asks, "Where am I?" I've met people who aren't familiar with modern, Israeli, spoken Hebrew, but can make simple conversation based on classical

Hebrew. Very elderly, scholarly Jews, mostly. And they'd pronounce Hebrew in the Ashkenazic way, not the way Hebrew is spoken in Israel. But given the longevity of the State of Israel—it's been around three quarters of a century now—even the most isolated Ḥasidim I've met have spent significant time in Israel and speak fluent, modern Hebrew. And this guy isn't so ancient; he's more or less my age, mid-60s. So, what's going on?

Now I try to speak to him in pre-Modern Hebrew, which I'm used to reading and teaching, but not speaking. So, this isn't easy. Slowly and a little haltingly, I reply.

"You're in New York."

"York? Anglia?"

"What? No. Not York, England. NEW York, in the United States. America."

Silence. But then…

"What are the carriages I see outside? I was taken to here in one of them. No horse. Do they move because of a spell cast upon them? Is Ashmodai the Demon King enslaved to do our will?"

Now he's really gotten my attention. "Ashmodai" is the name the Talmud uses for the king of the demons. And he called him by the name the Talmud actually uses; if he merely knew something about it, if he had, for example, read about it in English, he would have used the more Anglicized version of the name, "Asmodeus." So, the gentleman before me can not only cite the Bible in Hebrew, but he likely also knows Talmud! But beyond that, he is being playful again in a scholarly way: Are the cars outside moving without horses because the Demon King put a spell on them?! I'm beginning to like this man. I still don't know why he's dressed the way he is, but I'm sure he doesn't belong in the police station. Meanwhile, I play along with his question about the cars on the street.

"Ashmodai? No, he has got nothing to do with it. How do you call yourself?"

"Rabbi Yosef son of Avraham."

So, he's still playing a role, giving me his Hebrew name without telling me his last name. Either that, or maybe he actually is a little touched in the head. I'm not a hundred percent sure, though he seems pretty together to me. I decide to follow his lead and share my Hebrew name, but then I up the ante a bit.

"Rabbi Yosef. I am called Rabbi Yonatan son of Yosef. Shall we set a meal? There's a good market close by. Kosher."

I realize that as I've been trying to learn about him through this conversation, he too has been trying to learn about me at the same time. I guess that my answers have convinced him to trust me, because he agrees to come with me.

I arrange it with Kanerek, and the two of us walk over the few blocks to the deli on Broadway and we grab a table. I love this place. It's one of the few surviving old-school kosher delis in the city. It's made a few cursory attempts to cater to modern palates, like adding a few paninis and what the menu calls "lighter fare." But it remains the place to go for traditional, home-style, East European Jewish dishes. How many places still serve stuffed breast of lamb or Roumanian Hangar Steak that is so long it literally hangs over the side of the plate? Chicken soup not only with kneidlakh—matzah balls—but also with kreplakh—meat-stuffed dumplings. And this place serves a truly memorable version of the king of deli sandwiches, an over-stuffed sandwich with hot, juicy, tender, thick-sliced, pastrami. Since my guest seems unfamiliar with the place, and doesn't seem able to read the menu, I order us two pastrami sandwiches. The waiter brings over the complimentary cole slaw along with the dish of sour pickles, half-sours, and pickled green tomatoes, and soon enough, the sandwiches. We each take a bite. His eyes widen a bit and he manages a slight smile. Now, because he looks like a longer-bearded version of me, meaning a professorial grandfather-type with Eastern European roots, I decide to try out Yiddish again.

"*Geshmak*!" ("Delicious!").

To this, he responds with a querulous look on his face.

"Ashkenaz?"

Somehow, I get the impression that he is using the word in the Medieval sense of "German language" or the general area in which German is spoken, and it's my turn to look confused.

He continues by pointing down, meaning—I assume—"here" or "this place," and asks a one-word question.

"*Malkhut*?"

Malkhut means "kingdom," and I understand that for some reason, he's asking what country, or "kingdom" we're in. So, again, I say, "The United States. America." But once more, I get a blank stare.

Now the puzzled look on his face is replaced by one of determination and I catch a glimmer of what might be the slightest devilish grin as he says, "*Malkhut, Yesod...*" and his voice trails off.

And I immediately get it. He's continuing with the playful, scholarly, back and forth. He's using another meaning of the word Malkhut, "kingdom," its mystical meaning as the lowest of the ten Kabbalistic Sefirot, or "divine energies." And his voice trails off because he's inviting me—testing me—to see if I can continue the list after his mention of the tenth and the ninth Sefirot (Yesod, "Foundation" being the ninth). I am not a Kabbalist nor is Kabbalah my primary academic field. But I am a professor of Jewish Liturgy, and because of the major role that mysticism has played in the history of the liturgy, I have made the study of Kabbalah a secondary field that I also happen to teach. And so, I respond by listing the eighth through the second Sefirot, hoping that I've understood his intent correctly. I stop at the second Sefirah to see if he'll complete the list.

"*Hod, Netzaḥ, Tiferet, Gevurah, Ḥesed, Binah, Ḥokhmah...*"

And with a real smile, he does indeed conclude the list by mentioning the first Sefirah.

"*Keter*!"

We both laugh, and it feels like we've communicated something. We both know Kabbalah. We both enjoy scholarly wordplay. We both speak Hebrew, although he speaks an antiquated version of the language. With the tension eased a bit, we both sit back and take a few more bites of our food.

I'm a bit more relaxed, but I still don't know who this impressive, scholarly Jew is. The more we talk, the less he seems to have any kind of dementia. What I know is that he is dressed in unusual clothes, doesn't know English, might know some form of Spanish, and has a scholar's knowledge of Bible, Talmud and Kabbalah. Emboldened with our minor, but perhaps significant, breakthrough in understanding each other, I decide to try to circle back to his asking about where he is. Struggling to speak pre-modern Hebrew, I try something.

"What is your kingdom, your land?"

He seems happy to be asked this and immediately responds.

"Castilla."

Castilla? That's Castile, Spain. So, I was wrong about his possibly hailing from Catalonia. But I'm sure that someone who speaks Hispanic Spanish would understand someone speaking Castilian. Castilian is really just another word for the kind of Spanish that most Spaniards speak. So, why didn't the Hispanic cop understand him? Does he speak some kind of older form of Castilian for some reason, the way he speaks pre-modern Hebrew? And another strange thing: Anyone from Castile would say he's from Spain, not Castile. It would be like an American from, say, Minnesota, visiting Spain saying that he hails from the Midwest instead of saying from the States. Something's not right. So I ask him...

"How did you get here?"

Now, he looks a little guarded, like he's not sure he should tell me. Then he seems to make up his mind.

"*Temurah*. Rabbi Avraham son of Shmuel."

Now, we've really taken a turn to the surreal. The term *temurah*, which, in Hebrew means "exchange" is the name of a tractate of Talmud that deals with exchanging one sacrificial animal to the ancient Temple in Jerusalem with some other animal or gift. But in 13th-century Spain, Rabbi Avraham son of Shmuel Abulafia reinterpreted the word to mean exchanging the order of the letters of holy words to yield mystical meanings. Abulafia taught that one could reveal all kinds of mysteries, and even perform miracles, through combining and recombining words from the Torah. Abulafia was accused of impersonating a prophet or even a messiah and was eventually shunned by the mainstream Jewish communities in Spain.

So, is this guy actually saying that he travelled from Spain to New York by manipulating words from the Torah? I turn to my mysterious guest with one word.

"Abulafia!"

Now, he really looks animated.

"Yes, Abulafia!"

"Wait a minute. What is your name? Your full name? Mine is Rabbi Yonatan son of Yosef Kaufman, or just Yonatan Kaufman."

He straightens a bit in his chair and nods.

"Rabbi Yosef ben Avraham Chicatilla. Yosef Chicatilla."

Yosef Chicatilla? He must mean Rabbi Yosef Gikatilla. But Yosef Gikatilla died toward the beginning of the 14th century. Yes, he lived in Castile and yes, he was a disciple of Avraham Abulafia before he supposedly abandoned Abulafia's brand of "Prophetic Kabbalah" and then, with Rabbi Moshe de Leon, helped to usher in "Theosophical Kabbalah." This latter brand of mysticism was less interested in effecting miracles and more interested in contemplating the inner essence of God, the ten Sefirot. While de Leon seems to have written most of the classic Kabbalistic work, The Zohar, Gikatilla wrote a number of other books including the classic, Sha'arei Orah, "Gates of Light," in which he dedicated a full chapter to describing each of the ten Sefirot. In other words, Gikatilla was a major Kabbalist from the generation that produced the definitive works of that variety of Jewish mysticism.

So is this guy touched in the head? Does he think he is someone who died seven hundred years ago? That's probably what's going on. But in the back of my mind, almost against my will, I begin to entertain an outlandish thought. *If* this person were Rabbi Yosef Gikatilla, that would explain a few things. In fact, it would explain everything. (And then I think: Can I really even be considering this? But the thought process continues.) If Gikatilla manipulated the letters of the Torah to time-travel, that would explain why he is dressed the way he is, why he doesn't seem to recognize the existence of The United States of America, why he identifies his homeland as Castile and not Spain, why he speaks an antiquated version of Hebrew, and why the Hispanic cop didn't understand him; he must also speak an antiquated version of Spanish! When I finish thinking these wild thoughts, I look at my companion, and, as if the expression on my face reveals that I almost believe that he is Rabbi Yosef Gikatilla from 14th century Castile, he nods in a knowing way. He turns to me and speaks just a few words in Hebrew from the liturgy.

"True and certain and established... is this thing."

Incredulous, I say, "You are Rabbi Yosef Gikatilla from Castile, the author of The Gates of Light, and you traveled through many years, going behind the heavenly curtain. You entered through Rabbi Abulafia's 'exchange' of holy letters."

"True and certain and established... is this thing! What year is this?"

Still not really believing that this is real, I find myself telling him that we are in the Hebrew year 5783 (which corresponds to the Gregorian year 2023).

"And we are where?"

"We are in the city of New York in the land called America."

"And America is where?"

In that moment, I realize that knowledge of the western hemisphere wasn't widespread in Europe until after Columbus's voyage in 1492, almost a hundred years after Gikatilla's time.

"It is above and before. Let us have some... parched grain (the Talmud's way of saying "snack" or "dessert") and coffee before we enter above and before."

"Coffee?"

Oh, right. Recent scholarship has placed coffee's widespread arrival in the Middle East in the 16th century and in Europe in the 17th century as one of the reasons that the all-night study on the first night of Shavuot developed. It was an innovation of the Kabbalists in Safed, Israel. It is true that Spaniards in the 14th century would not likely have known of the bitter brew.

"Let's drink tea."

I look around for the waiter, who has successfully hidden somewhere in the restaurant, but I do spot the manager, my friend, Oscar. Oscar grew up in a Puerto Rican family in Queens, not too far from where I grew up. We got to know each other at the restaurant a couple of years ago. He noticed that I ate there often and when he found out that I was a rabbi-professor, and that my school was in catering distance, he took a real interest in me. And I was only too happy to be given special attention in one of my favorite places. Turns out that Oscar had cut his teeth in the Jewish deli business at Deli Masters which, until it closed in 2009, was on the service road, right next to the Long Island Expressway in Fresh Meadows, Queens. He knows more about kosher food than most Jews. He and I probably saw each other at Deli Masters years ago, before he moved up the ladder and before I would have been interesting from a catering perspective. When Oscar discovered that we knew the same neighborhoods and that I had a near obsessive fascination with Eastern European Jewish food, he gave me a tour of the sandwich and hotdog prep station (which also held the chicken soup and fixings) as well as the refrigerated vats downstairs where a dozen or more corned beefs were being pickled and a similar number of pastramis were aging in their thick coats of peppercorns and spices.

Our tea arrives along with the typically huge slabs of the two iconic kosher deli desserts — seven-layer cake, with its light brown chocolate cream between the layers of white cake and its darker, shiny, chocolate icing, and apple strudel, with its abundance of apple slices and golden raisins.

Once we finish, and the waiter makes an appearance, having wrapped up our copious leftovers, we emerge onto Broadway. My guest, who for now, I decide to call "Gikatilla," again asks about the vehicles which are not drawn by animals.

"They run by *haḥashmal* and *habazak*," I reply. These words refer to the lightning-like flashes that seem to transport the heavenly chariot in Ezekiel's vision. And by some sort of holy serendipity, these words became the focus of both mystics—quite understandably—and speakers of modern Hebrew, who designated the first word to convey "electricity" and the second as the name of an important Israeli telecommunications firm. Gikatilla takes this in with equanimity. Either he's playing his role or it makes sense to a 14th-century Kabbalist that 700 years in the future, people will have learned how to harness the power of Ezekiel's chariot.

As we walk the few blocks to my apartment, Gikatilla observes intently the people; the fruit and vegetable stands in front of the several markets; the books, CDs, and posters laid out by the street hawkers; the taxis, buses, cars, and stoplights.

"The women are walking as confidently as the men," he notices. "And it seems that there are women in the stores in a superior position over the men."

A moment later:

"The men, the women, even the children, are dressed so immodestly. But so beautifully. The colors shine like the rainbow, as colorful as the garments of Africa."

On the other hand, no one on the street bats an eye at the man with the long grey beard, turban, and green robe. The residents of the neighborhood of all ages, joined by Columbia and Barnard students, go about their business as they pass us on the sidewalk. The New York mindset reminds me of the music professor, Louis Thomas Hardin, who was known professionally as Moondog. In his latter years, he used to sit in a medieval cloak and horned helmet in downtown Manhattan and was known as the Viking of Sixth Avenue. Tourists used to stare at him, but New Yorkers weren't fazed. As a teenager, I took a photo of him while he sat there undaunted and developed it in the darkroom I set up in our basement. I didn't know anything about Moondog's professional life, nor the fact that he had been blind since his teen years, until I was shocked to read his obituary in the *Times* in 1999.

Gikatilla grows animated and points to a passerby seemingly talking to no one in particular. "That man is talking to a ghost!"

"No... Do you see the little white things in his ears? Those allow him to talk to people who might be many Roman miles away."

"And the people looking at those little writing tablets," he asks, indicating the many passersby whose eyes are on their mobile phones.

"Similar. But those tablets can also transmit whole books and many images."

"*Haḥashmal* and *habazak*?"

"Yes, they run on Ezekiel's lightning."

"They remind me of me," says my companion, "walking down the street staring at a parchment."

As we continue on toward my place, Gikatilla hears the faint whirl of helicopter rotors approaching. He cranes his head upward as the noise grows stronger, and finally, the copter appears overhead. Gikatilla stops in his tracks, stares, covers his ears with his hands, and cowers slightly. At nearly the same time, he notices an airplane much higher in the sky and uncovers one ear to point to the plane.

"Yes," I say. "We have learned how to fly like birds. But faster, much faster than birds. Like Ezekiel's chariot but much bigger. And yes, also powered by *haḥashmal* and *habazak*."

Gikatilla looks at me, trying to absorb what I've said. All he can do is shake his head as he contemplates these innovations and say, "May the Merciful One protect us."

Finally, we arrive at my apartment, and immediately upon entering the living room, Gikatilla delights to see my extensive library of Jewish holy books. But before we go into what my daughter—who is a cantor—calls, with mock disdain, "the rabbi's cave" (the holy equivalent, I suppose, of the rabbit hole), I offer to lend him some of my clothes. He may not have flustered the passersby outside, but he doesn't have a change of clothes with him for the next day. And it appears that he may be with me for another day.

"I'd be happy to lend you some clothes for tomorrow. You and I seem to be close in size."

"Well, I am 'Chicatilla,'" which he pronounces "cheeka-teeya." We non-Hispanic scholars all pronounce Gikatilla as "Jeeka-tilla," as if it isn't Spanish! Not very scholarly of us. "My name means little, small one. You could be called chicatilla too!"

He's right. I used to be almost five and a half feet tall. I've shrunk a bit as I edge toward old age.

I let him choose some items of clothing from a few choices I've laid out and set him up in the spare bedroom. My wife, who runs one of the divisions of Jewish engagement at the JCC-Y of Manhattan is out of town at a conference. The truth is that she would probably do better at handling the situation than me; she's certainly the more welcoming of the two of us. But for now, I'm happy to have the rabbi's cave to duck into with my guest.

Gikatilla emerges to examine the books and admires the abundance of volumes he recognizes on the Bible, Talmud, and Jewish law and lore. He settles in among the comfortable chairs and coffee table that face the bookcases, selecting a book or two at a time, perusing each for a couple of minutes, then replacing them with one or two more. He does this for quite a while.

Noticing that I have three different editions of Rambam's 12th-century masterpiece, Mishneh Torah, and apparently not surprised, he merely says, "Rabbeinu Moshe ben Maimon HaSefaradi," accentuating the last word, "the Spaniard."

Finally, he arrives at the Kabbalistic collection and spends more time examining them. Then he pulls out my copy of his book, Gates of Light. Just one book this time.

"It is new?"

Yes, the Gates of Light have been brought to light many, many times since you wrote it," I answer, emphasizing the Hebrew phrase for "having been published."

He takes the book and sits back on the red, upholstered chair that I favor when I do close reading of a holy book. Shaking his head in disbelief at the new edition of his work, he pages through, it stopping at my post-its and penciled notes in the margins. Finally, he looks up at me, his face filled with emotion. Then he looks back at the empty spot in the bookshelf where his book had been and narrows his eyes. Getting up, he reaches for the book next to the empty space and sits back down. He's found the 1994 English translation next to it.

"Anglia?"

"Yes, Anglia."

"And what is this illustration on the cover?"

He is referring to the woodcut of the Sefirot with a turbaned, enrobed, and bearded man grasping the central channel of the Sefirot. I explain that it is from the 1516 Latin translation of his book. His eyes widen.

"Latin? Non-Jews read my book?"

"Yes, there have been many non-Jews interested in Kabbalah over the generations."

He shakes his head in amazement. But by now, he looks exhausted, and seemingly relieved, to find his book still in print after all these centuries.

He says he'd like to say the evening prayers and then retire for the night. He asks again what land we are in and which direction he should face in order to fulfill the custom of facing Jerusalem in our prayers. Finally, I explain.

"About two hundred years after your time, an Italian mariner, Christopher Columbus, sailing for Spain, ventured west, across the great ocean, seeking a western sea route to the East Indies. Instead, he discovered lands unknown to the peoples of Europe. He claimed these lands for Spain, but the European powers fought over control of these lands for many generations, ignoring the fact that many thousands of people were already living here, people who never knew of the kingdoms of Europe or the holy land. Eventually, Anglia came to rule this land for over a hundred years until its very own settlers fought for independence. The kingdom they established about two hundred and fifty years ago is called The United States of America, and it is now the most powerful kingdom on earth."

Gikatilla tries to absorb the summary of events that are new and mystifying. And then, as if abandoning the effort to fully comprehend this history, he says, "And Jerusalem is which direction?"

"East," I say, and point out the living room window facing the east side of Broadway.

He begins to pray the evening service and I withdraw to my bedroom and contemplate what I've experienced this day. I'm finding myself thinking of him more and more as Rabbi Yosef Gikatilla, and not as some holy imposter. I know I can't fully process it yet. Yet it all feels too new and shocking to share with any of the people I would normally turn to when something so stunning knocks me off kilter. I decide to put it out there, to God, and in my own brief, non-traditional prayer, I ask for help in understanding this man I've invited to my home. And I go to bed.

The next day, he asks to borrow my tallit and tefillin, my prayer shawl and phylacteries, for the morning prayers. Feeling a little guilty because it's been a while since I donned these ritual items myself for morning prayers, I bring them out of my bedroom for him. After he prays, we share a brief breakfast of leftover apple strudel and tea and I get ready to leave for my classes. Gikatilla is dressed in my clothes, and he doesn't look bad. I tell him I'll be back in the afternoon after teaching a couple of classes and I show him where to find lunch in the kitchen—bagels and various cheeses—as well as the proper dishes to use. Once I leave and have gotten on the subway, I realize that I haven't given him a key to my place in case he wants to go out. I also realize that I'm assuming he'll still be there when I return, even though I have no reason to make that assumption.

I'm a bit relieved that my two classes today at the liberal rabbinical school where I teach are Festival Liturgy and Talmud, and that I'm not teaching Kabbalah this semester. I don't know how I would have kept it together teaching Kabbalah without mentioning that one of the masters of Kabbalah from the generation that created The Zohar might be ensconced in my apartment. If I were to let that slip, I wouldn't blame my students if they were either to lodge a complaint with the dean that I was mocking them, or worse, that they would tell the dean I've lost my marbles. As it is, I find it hard to keep it together enough to teach my two classes. But gaining a little distance from my visitor makes me realize that if it really is the Yosef Gikatilla in my apartment, I must find out what he is seeking, why he has traveled through time and space to the Upper West Side and to me.

I return in the early afternoon to find Gikatilla still in the apartment. He has not left. And he has clearly made himself at home because I find small piles of various books carefully stacked on the living room coffee table and on various chairs. He has gone through quite a few volumes.

"*Shalom aleikhem.*"

"*Aleikhem shalom.*"

Before I have a chance to act on my determination to find out why he is here, he has a question for me.

"You taught *tzurvaya mirabbanan*?"

He is asking if I taught those who, in the talmudic phrase, have "caught fire" by studying the teachings of the rabbis, in other words, did I just teach rabbinical students?

"Yes, and there are men and women among my students."

"Women?!"

He thinks silently for a moment. He looks quite shocked. But then, his features calm, as if taking in this startling change along with some of the other tokens of modernity he has witnessed.

"*Shekhinah* must be rejoicing" he says, referring to the feminine side of God. Quite remarkable that he can integrate such a radical change into his worldview. It brings to mind recent scholarship demonstrating that the Kabbalists of Spain may not have been community leaders, but rather independent scholars, not dependent upon the synagogues to earn a living. If this were true, they not only didn't have much invested in the established status quo of ritual but were frequently quite critical of their more mainstream rabbinical colleagues. If this were the case, I wonder if this outsider standing made it easier for Gikatilla to accept change.

"Now, this man," he says, pointing to an open volume. It is the one volume I have of the Hebrew writings of Gershom Scholem, the groundbreaking professor of Kabbalah. "This man is quite a prodigy. He has correctly deduced that Rabbi Moshe de Leon has himself penned most of what I see has come to be called "The Zohar" despite putting his teachings into the mouths of our talmudic sages. Of course, our circle also contributed teachings as well. But Rabbi Moshe could indeed be called the author. On the other hand, Rabbi Scholem speaks of the influence of the Christians in Calabria on the Torah we innovated. That is wrong. We never heard of them."

So, confirmation of one of Scholem's greatest scholarly insights, that Rabbi Moshe De Leon was the main author of The Zohar. And that Scholem's theory of the influence of the Christians of Calabria may have been completely wrong. I decide not to get into the fact that Scholem was neither a rabbi nor, except for a few years as a young man, observant of Jewish tradition.

"And this man," now pointing to the 15-volume set of Rabbi Yitzhak Luria's teachings. Rabbi Luria is also known as "the Ari," a loose acronym of his name meaning "the lion." The Ari—who, in the 16th century, lived most of his short life in the town of Safed in the Galilee—was the most influential creative mind in Kabbalah since Gikatilla's generation in 13th-century Spain.

"This man," says Gikatilla, "is clearly insane."

I had to laugh at that comment. While the Ari clearly built his theological system on the Zohar, he innovated so much and complicated Kabbalah so much that his spiritual machinations do seem to sometimes veer toward absurdity, and perhaps even toward psychosis. Nevertheless, those teachings have been viewed as holy insights by generations of Jewish mystics.

Then his face turns solemn.

"I found the prayer book for the black fast of Tisha B'Av brought to light by you," he says, pointing to me. I had edited an edition of the Siddur L'Tisha B'Av for the Rabbinical Assembly a number of years ago.

"May I ask you to give me the commentary on three *kinot* I don't recognize," he says, referring to the dirges chanted on that dark holiday that memorializes many tragedies of Jewish history. He opened the volume to a prayer commemorating the expulsion of the Jews from Spain, another remembering the millions lost in the Holocaust, and finally, the Naomi Shemer song, "Jerusalem of Gold," marking the Israeli victory in 1967, in which the Old City of Jerusalem was captured by Israeli forces.

"Yes. The first two ask God who is full of mercy to remember the martyrs of two very painful times, and third is not a *kinah* at all, even though it cites the words of The Book of Lamentations."

"Do I interpret correctly that the first one recalls the exile of our people from the kingdoms of Castila, Leon, and Aragon?

"Yes, and Andalusia and the other kingdoms as well. Very painful."

"All of the lands of Sepharad?" he asks with real hurt in his voice, sitting back further into his chair.

"Yes, and Portugal exiled us not long afterward."

Gikatilla adds, "We were close to many lords and kings. King Alfonso honored so many of us in translating Greek and Islamic science into Castilian. And yet, there was always murmuring. We did not accept their Christian savior. We knew that exile had been decreed against our people in Anglia and in the land of the Franks. We hoped it would never reach us. So, this exile too occurred and now, in your time, it is a holy memory on Tisha B'Av."

"It is very sad," I reply. "The evil opened in Sevilla, about a hundred years after your time, and spread throughout the country. Thousands of Jews were killed, their property stolen. Many of our people exchanged their faith. But the church never trusted us. As in Anglia and in the Frankish lands, those of our people who exchanged their faith were in double agony: They could not openly worship the God of Israel, nor were they trusted to escape persecution by accepting the Christian savior. In Sepharad, a horrible Inquisition was established that entered where it was not welcome, into the homes and workplace and families of the conversos. Like Pharaoh who said, 'let us be wily with them,' the Inquisition dealt with them 'ruthlessly,' *befarekh*. As the midrash interprets: *befeh rakh*, with a 'soft mouth,' enticing them deviously, pitting former neighbors and even family members against each other. Many of our people were tried in their false courts and burned in the town squares. It was two hundred years after your time that all the Jews of Sepharad were exiled."

Gikatilla sat up and in one quick move, tore his shirt in mourning. Upon realizing what he'd done, he immediately apologized, for it was my shirt. My reply was to rip my shirt as well. We both sat there for a time in sadness. Finally, I spoke.

"As for the second *kinah*, I'm so sorry to tell you that many centuries later, during the time of my parents, the worst tragedy occurred to our people since the Destruction of the Temple 2,000 years ago. An evil king arose in Ashkenaz 'who did not know Joseph.' He conquered nearly all of Europe and massacred most of our people in those lands. Sixty myriads of our people were killed, including my grandfather, who lived in the Slavic lands."

"And yet our Messiah has not come? Why did I come here? Why now? Right after this terrible destruction."

"You mean you couldn't control when and where you were sent?"

"It is in the hands of God. I entrust myself into God's spirit and the permutations of the letters carry me where I should go."

"But why did you 'travel' in this way to begin with?"

"I will tell you after you interpret the last... *piyyut*. Gikatilla uses the term for religious poetry in general since I told him Naomi Shemer's song is not a dirge.

"Three years after the massacre of Europe's Jews, we returned to the land of Israel and established a Jewish kingdom. It was not without struggle. There have been five wars and numerous battles with the neighboring kingdoms, the Ishmaelites. The Jews won each of the wars, but there has been much bloodshed on both sides. This piyyut was written just before the fourth war. In that war, the Jews won and conquered the old city of Jerusalem, and so, the poet rewrote the song to reflect the return to Zion. To my ongoing amazement, the Jewish kingdom, called Medinat Yisrael, is the strongest nation in the region. They have made peace with some of the Ishmaelite kingdoms, but not with all. And they rule over many myriads of Ishmaelites within their territory who are restless to raise up their own nation."

"We have returned to Zion! But not bloodless. And so, in your Siddur L'Tisha B'Av, you both mourn the losses and celebrate the return."

Gikatilla's face then brightens.

"Has the Temple been rebuilt? Do we sacrifice bullocks and lambs, meal-cakes and wine, on the altar as the Torah commands?"

"No, my friend. The Temple has not been rebuilt. We still pray, 'Next year in Jerusalem.' I understand your question: We have Jerusalem. Why not rebuild the Temple as Torah commands? All I can say is... *Devarim b'go.*"

Instead of entering into what feels like an impossibly complicated explanation, I instead rely on this talmudic expression which means, more or less, "It contains multitudes." No one simple answer. Then I realize that the expression came to mind because it is the title of a collection of essays by Gershom Scholem. And I add a thought.

"I want you to know that my wife and I and our three children have spent a lot of time in Jerusalem and in Medinat Yisrael in general. My wife and I were students there for several years, as our children after us have been, and we all visit often. Like many of our people, we have relatives who live there. Most were refugees from the terrible massacres in Europe. Having been born during the era of a rebuilt Medinat Yisrael has been one of the great joys of my life. Simply walking the streets there and hearing the holy language spoken returns life to the soul, as the Psalm says. The holy tongue spoken by children and elders, by peddlers and store owners, by bridegrooms and by brides. It is thrilling. And Torah is studied there in abundance. World-wide, Torah is now studied by more Jews than at any time in our history. Part of the reason is that we have our own kingdom again. The very existence of our own homeland bestows pride and honor upon us and upon the Torah. And the science pioneered in our land is famous and admired around the world."

Gikatilla begins to raise a finger in anticipation of responding, but then thinks better of it and lets it rest. Somehow, I sense that he was going to ask why I still live outside the land. I don't address the unasked question and instead suggest we continue the conversation over dinner out. My companion agrees and we depart again onto Broadway.

I decide to take him to The Kasbah, a kosher steakhouse dedicated to the cuisine of North Africa. That kind of Jewish cuisine may be the closest thing to medieval Jewish Spanish cooking outside of the few kosher places in Madrid. I've been to The Kasbah many times. On one visit, I went with a dean at my school. She is one of the few people who matches me in loving food, and especially red meat. My Spanish companion and I arrive and occupy a table for two. With a little help from me in deciphering the menu, we decide to order a couple of Argentinian chimichuri steaks. I go for the steak fries and he orders rice.

It doesn't take long for the food to arrive and once it does, we enjoy our meals without speaking much, although it isn't quiet in the restaurant. Most of the tables are occupied and there are noisy conversations all around us. Gikatilla observes the scene around us. Plenty of young and middle-aged men and women, businesspeople mostly. Many of the men with kippot and dressed in sport coats with or without ties, the women in business attire. A few older folks like us as well.

After a while, Gikatilla looks at me.

"I will tell you why I traveled. It is true that the ancient sages have said, 'One who contemplates four things, it would have been better had that person not come into the world: What is above, what is beneath, what came before, and what came after.' Nevertheless, masters of Torah in the generation before mine, especially in Sepharad, occupied themselves with these very questions. And it was permitted to do so if one were a master of Torah. Rabbi Moshe ben Nachman of Gerona, may peace be upon him, was the most famous of that generation to teach these mysteries, but of course, always with great discretion and only to the purest of souls. He taught my teachers. And we Jews also learned scientific knowledge from the peoples around us. The Ishmaelites had preserved the science of the Greeks and progressed beyond the Greeks in all areas of knowledge including medicine, mathematics, and astronomy. The Christians in our kingdom also valued the science that the Ishmaelites had advanced. The circle of scholars that I have the merit to study with considers all of those sciences part of Torah in our pursuit of the ways of God.

"All in my circle believe in the principle of 'as above, so below.' The planes of existence in the heavens are reflected in the planes of being below, in the material world. And all in my circle believe that each stage of existence contains within it all of the energy of every subsequent stage of existence, from the divine Sefirot, the heavens, and the angels, down to the grossest and most dense materiality in our world.

"But as I aged, I realized that the level of knowledge attained by the sciences in my time had not satisfied my quest to understand what is above and what came before. How did our world come to be? And so, I determined that before God ends my earthly existence, I would use the permutations of the holy letters to travel to the future to learn what future science has discovered about these ultimate questions. God has guided my travels to your time and to your place, Rabbi Yonatan. And so, this is why I have come. You are a student of the masters of Torah in your days. I hope that your teachers too understand that whatever science has learned, even from among the other peoples of the world, is also Torah. It appears to be God's will that I have come to your circle to ask you to share with me what has been discovered about the origin of our world."

We sit for a moment in silence. It is now my turn to be stunned and amazed. I was calling my guest "Gikatilla" and suspending disbelief all day to try and take seriously the possibility—as crazy as I really believed it was—that he actually was a visitor from seven hundred years ago. Now, I found myself hanging on to my hard-earned academic skepticism by a thread.

I suggest to Gikatilla that we bring dessert home with us and continue the conversation at my place. With his agreement, I pick up some baklava and baked apple empanadas to go from the cashier as I pay our bill, and out we go into the evening.

It happens to be a clear night in New York City. As we walk, some stars are visible in spite of some of the brightest artificial light on the planet. I gesture toward the heavenly points of light and I tell my companion that we'll talk of these worlds when we return to my apartment.

Upon arrival, I put up some water for tea, and I bring my laptop to the dining room table where we're seated.

"I am not an expert in all of the sciences, but I, too, am interested in what came before, in the origin of our world. I will share with you what I know.

"I told you that the little tablets that were distracting the people walking outside contain whole books and many images. That is true for this larger tablet too. I want to show you some images. The images were captured by some of those bird-like vehicles flying in the sky that we saw earlier today. But the vehicles that captured these pictures traveled much faster and much farther into the night than the ones we saw. They traveled for many months to faraway worlds and although I cannot explain to you how, they are able to acquire likenesses exactly as they appear, without drawing or painting. It is these likenesses of faraway worlds that I want to show you."

As I open the laptop, Gikatilla moves his chair closer to me to see what I'm talking about. As I've done before because of my own interest in cosmology, I visit several websites that display photographs of distant stars, galaxies, and nebulae. He views spectacular photographs in glowing colors with captions like "double lobe nebula," horse-head nebula," "quasar-driven super bubbles in luminous red quasars," "nuclear luminous transient events," "a supernova event," "red dwarf star," and so on, and so on. After a moment or two, I show him how to click on the next image, and he explores with enthusiasm. For the next half hour or so we view these fantastic depictions.

At some point, I get up and take out teacups and dessert plates. The tea kettle had already whistled quite a while ago, so I reheat it. I open the packages of baklava and the apple empanadas and place them in the center of the table. I pour us each a cup of tea.

"Rabbi Yosef, let's move from the images for now, eat a bit, and talk."

He looks up from the laptop, takes a breath, and looks around the dining room a bit, as if coming back to consciousness of his surroundings. We help ourselves to some of the sweets and look at each other. Before I have a chance to ask him what he is feeling, what thoughts are coming to him in response to the photographs of far-off space, he opens with a question.

"How old is... all the worlds?"

I turn back to the laptop and a few clicks brings me to the answer. But how do I convey 13.8 billion years using pre-modern Hebrew? The largest number I know in medieval Hebrew is "myriad" which represents 10,000.

"The age of the world... the worlds... is almost 140 myriads of myriads."

As if unfazed by this incredibly large number, he immediately asks a follow-up question.

"How did it begin? The Torah says that it all began with God calling it all into being. 'God said, Let there be light, Let there be a firmament in the heavens,' and so on. But our ancient sages already said that the Torah speaks in the language of human beings. In other words, when the Torah expresses things that people cannot grasp, it moves into parable. So, what has the science of your time said about how it began?"

I take a breath. I realize I have to describe The Big Bang in pre-modern Hebrew. I do my best to get the point across and then another thought enters my head. I recently read a book summarizing the science around The Big Bang for non-scientists, and there is something in that book that really caught my attention. I had written it down and shared it with Professor Emanuel Daat. Daat is one of the world experts on The Zohar as well as on the generation of Kabbalists in 13th- 14th-century Spain. I had sent the passage from the cosmology book to Manny because of the striking parallel between one element of The Big Bang and the way The Zohar depicts the emergence or "emanation" of the divine at the beginning of time. I began to grow very excited as I realized that here is my chance to see how one of the key Kabbalists of that Spanish generation of Kabbalists reacts to this aspect of The Big Bang.

"How did it begin? I want to share with you, Rabbi Yosef, a short passage from a recent book of science. It was written by an Italian scientist, a Christian most likely, and I wonder how you will interpret it. Let me translate this short text for you.

"The Great Thunderbolt (the best I could do in translating 'The Big Bang') has just occurred. What has come into being already has everything it will need to progress and expand during the next 140 myriads of myriads of years. Yet only the tiniest part of a second has elapsed. The very smallest object you can imagine has been born, the size of a fraction of a grain of sand. In the blink of an eye, however, it expands enough to become visible. After emerging from this violent phase, it is the size of a child's toy ball, and already contains all the matter and energy that it will need to expand over the course of centuries upon centuries to create all of the worlds. It expands at a speed faster than the speed of light... that is, the speed of lightning. The limits imposed by science—that nothing may move faster than the speed of lightning—hold true for whatever moves within space. For space itself, which expands in the *tohu vavohu*, the emptiness and void, or to be more precise, transforms the emptiness and void into space, these limitations do not apply.'"

Gikatilla stands up with a great smile. I stand up too and he grasps me in a warm embrace.

"Yes! This is what we saw! This is what we meant when we said that each stage of existence contains within it all of the energy and properties of every subsequent stage!

"From Keter, the crown of God, closest to the never-ending realm about which nothing can be said, down to the human and animal realms in our world, somehow, somehow, we knew. It is all part of God. But where does God end and the world begin? *Kola ḥada*, all is one. All is linked. Your wise men of science... and... women of science?"—(yes, I nod)—"have seen the evidence of all of this in the worlds before, beyond, this one. This is why I came. This is why the letters brought me to you. I thank you! All honor is due to you, for one must shower honor upon someone who has even taught us one letter, and here, you have connected my Torah to your Torah! You have fulfilled an aged man's hopes."

I am quite moved and respond, "Blessed is God who is good and who does good! This is miraculous! And you have been my teacher through your books for many years, so all honor to you! But let's sit down, my teacher, my friend."

I sit down but Gikatilla can barely calm himself enough to sit. Finally, he is sitting, still smiling, and I open up to him.

"Rabbi Yosef, what comes before the Great Thunderbolt? When I am brave enough to dispense with the parables and face *alma dekushta*, the world of truth, naked and unadorned, I concentrate on the moment of the Great Thunderbolt. It satisfies for a moment: This one tiny moment and tiny ball of energy and matter is as we said, *kola ḥada*, it is all one with all that is and with all that will ever be.

"But then, a burning question forces itself upon me: What came before? It isn't that I literally want to know the physics of the events that led to the Great Thunderbolt. That's not what I'm after. It's that the metaphysics of it all comes crashing down on me: Where do the events themselves even come from, the events that lead to the Thunderbolt?! Not factually and physically where, but—and this is what makes my head spin... If we admit that we barely can describe the beginning of the worlds in the Great Thunderbolt, it means that we know almost nothing about the Thunderbolt's origins. Which is to say, our origins. The origins of everything around us.

"I suspend all of the commentaries, all of the structures upon which my reality is dependent, and then I shiver with this great question for which we have no answer. The feeling is *nora*, awful and awesome, fearsome and thrilling, so scary and yet so delicious. The words we offer up, even—with great respect to you—the 300 names of God you explicate in your 'Gates of Light,' only serve to shore up the shaky structure of our conception of reality. The words don't get at it. It is the contemplation of the state of being just before the Thunderbolt, and the realization that you and I, and all the books ever written, all of our knowledge, and all physicality, all the worlds—came from... somewhere, some force, some something that remains almost totally veiled. I am drawn to envision that monumental burst of energy at the beginning... and the tantalizing void just before the beginning. It makes my head spin... and this spinning, this spiraling, feels like tremendously important... Torah."

"Yes, Rabbi Yonatan, my teacher and my friend. That is why we never settle upon one way, one word, to describe the One. Rabbi Moshe de Leon was aflame with the passion that draws you. In what you call The Zohar, he expands the vocabulary of divinity with colors: White, green, red, black; with music, calling the Sefirot 'the movements of melody'; describes the sages as constantly in motion, moving from one location to another, never settling long in any one place to create new-ancient words. Always in movement. Sometimes I regret writing my 'Gates of Light,' for as much as I intended it as a key to the gates of divinity and the gates of reality which never end, it can read like definitions, but when you stop the movement and define the spirit that draws you in, you kill it."

We nod to each other. We understand each other. Maybe we understand why Gikatilla came. Although, I can easily think of several other scholars who would have served the moment better than me. And that's when I realize that I must connect Gikatilla to them.

Gikatilla and I have exhausted each other and we bid each other good night. Before I retire, however, I sit down at my laptop to compose an email to Manny Daat and two other experts in Kabbalah. I invite them to a video session with my guest. How to describe what I have in mind without convincing them that I've lost my mind is challenging. But I find a way to write something enticing without giving it all away. I suggest a few dates and times over the next week.

I realize that my wife will be returning the next afternoon from her conference. She's going to find an unusual guest at our place. I'm too weary to think of some way to prepare her by writing or calling. I tell myself that she does best meeting life spontaneously anyway—much better than I do—but I know that facing her is facing my own scattered feelings, and I'm just not up to it. I call it a day.

In the morning, I dress and get ready for breakfast and prepare to go out. I've got my usual two classes to teach in the morning and afternoon. The door to the spare bedroom is closed. I want to at least share my schedule with Gikatilla before I leave. I assume he's awake, perhaps he's praying. I knock lightly on the door. Nothing. I call him softly.

"Rabbi Yosef? I just want to let you know when I'll be back..."

I gently open the door. The bed is made. The clothes I've lent him are neatly folded on the bed. His green robe and his trousers are gone. My copy of one of Abulafia's books is open on the bed. He's gone. He used Abulafia's text to travel back, or... travel somewhere, and knew that leaving the book open would be a signal to me that he's traveled on. I pick up the book. There's a short note sticking out of it: "Rabbi Yonatan—May God bless you and keep you."

So, he's gone. I think to myself that he must have gotten what he came for. I immediately feel embarrassed for having written to Manny and the two others who are experts in Kabbalah. But I know I'll think of something to say about having to cancel the Zoom invitation. I realize that this little embarrassment is nothing compared to the experience I just had. It was a total of only two days, but what an experience! I'll probably be processing it for the rest of my life.

I puzzle again over why Gikatilla didn't travel to Manny or to one of the other experts in Kabbalah. Then, a thought occurs to me. Kind of a wild thought. I had one of those genetic tests done a few months ago. The sort of test that tells you what ethnicities are present in your genetic material. Mine came back, unsurprisingly, 80% Ashkenazic Jewish. But then it said 17% Sephardic, and 3% "other." I'd been wondering about that 17% Sephardic background, and now, my crazy thought was: Is it possible that Gikatilla was brought to me because he's in my family tree? That I am a descendant of his? Then I think: My clothes fit him because we're the same size. And whenever my father, my older brother, or I get ten minutes of sun, our skin tans so deeply that in the winter, the three of us often are asked if we've vacationed somewhere warm. Not unlike the olive color of Gikatilla's face. I don't know if it's an inheritable trait, but he seemed to enjoy the fleishig food as much as I did. I realize I'll never know if I'm a descendant specifically of Gikatilla's, although one last thing I notice as I get my breakfast together makes me wonder. The last piece of leftover seven-layer cake is gone.[558]

[558] The idea that medieval Kabbalists viewed their theological system as a science, that is, as consistent with then-current scholarly opinions on nature, astronomy, etc., is made by J. H. Chajes, *The Kabbalistic Tree* (University Park, Pennsylvania: The Pennsylvania State University Press, 2022), especially 5, 7, 9. Chajes has devoted this massive volume to documenting the history and meaning of the Sefirotic *ilan*, "tree," i.e., the charts of the *Sefirot* that portray the divine system as a kind of tree with various branches. His contention is that the medium of these charts conveys part of the message: By co-opting the schematics of similar medieval scientific charts, the Kabbalists were asserting that their version of metaphysics is a legitimate part of contemporary science.

# Index

Abayyei, 256–57
Abigail, the wife of Nabal, 343
Abraham, 95–98, 102–3, 315
Abraham Ibn Ezra, Rabbi, 31
Abudraham, Rabbi David, 34, 147n221, 175–76, 250, 327
"Accept our rest," *retzeh vimenuḥateinu,* 245–46, 248–50
*Adon HaShalom,* "master of all peace," 167
*Adon Olam,* "Eternal Lord," 215–16
afterlife, 199–202, 341–45
*Aggadeta deShimon Kefa,* "The *Aggadah* of Simon Kefa," 260–61
agriculture, 127–28, 357–62
Aḥa bar Ya'akov, Rav, 3–4
*Ahavah Rabbah,* "Great love," 57–58, 57n90
*Ahavat Olam,* "Eternal Love," 57n90, 60
*Akdamut,* "The Introduction (of Words)," 209n328, 352–57
Akiva, Rabbi, 79–80, 197–200, 204–5, 272–73
*Aleinu,* 203–15
*Al HaNissim,* "For The Miracles," 170–84; for *Ḥanukkah,* 170–78; for *Purim,* 178–84
Alkabetz, Rabbi Shlomo, 227
alphabetic acrostic, 269–72, 269n425, 282, 298, 354, 358–59
Alter, Rabbi Yehudah Aryeh Leib, 215
Alter, Robert, 152
*Amidah,* 79n120, 114n169; *Ma'ariv,* "Evening" service, 63, 240–58, 316; *Minḥah,* "Afternoon," Service, 294–97, 311–15; *Musaf,* 205, 291, 294–307, 328–29, 346, 350–51, 357–58; *Pesukei DeZimra,* 12–14, 17–18; *Shaḥarit,* "Morning," Service, 63, 279–93, 295–307, 359; *Shema,* 27–30, 65–67
Amoraic period, 107, 163–64, 228
*Amoraim,* 85
amulet psalm. *See* Psalm 91
Anav, Rabbi Tzedekiah ben Avraham, 281
*Ana V'Kho'aḥ,* 226
ancient Temple in Jerusalem, 149, 159–62, 167, 185, 196, 328–29, 333–34, 336, 346
Angel, Rabbi Marc D., 56–57
angels, 50–53, 104–9, 190, 204, 255–56, 267–78, 273nn439–40, 310, 353
animal sacrifices, 159–62, 328–29
anti-goyism, 135, 180, 183, 214, 310–11
anti-Other message, 137–40, 214–15, 318, 329
antisemitism, 224, 356
apostates, 137, 200n315
Aramaic language, 352–57
*Arba'ah Turim* (Yakov ben Asher), 5–6, 71, 137, 320
Ark of the Covenant, 69–71, 70n106, 333–34
Asaph, 15n31, 19–20
Asher ben Yehiel, Rabbi, 145
*Asher Heini,* 180
Ashkenazic rite: *Aleinu,* 205, 209; *Al HaNissim,* "For The Miracles," 172–74, 178; concluding prayers of the *Shaḥarit,* "Morning," Service, 189; *Eil Adon,* "God, the Master," 267; first blessing after the *Shema,* 62; *HaMaḥazir Shekhinato LeTzion,* "Restorer of His Presence to Zion," 160–61; *HaMevareikh Et Amo Yisrael BaShalom,* "The Blesser of Peace to His People Israel," 166; *Havdalah,* "Distinction," 316–18; *Kaddish,* "Holiness" or "Sanctification," 191, 193; *Kedushah,* "Holiness," 103–4, 106; *Kedushah DeSidra (U'Va LeTzion),* 308; *Naḥeim,* "Remembering Jerusalem on Tisha B'Av," 145–48; *Nishmat Kol Ḥai* "The Breath of All," 262; *Pesukei DeZimra,* 15; *piyyutim,* 357; *Rofei Ḥolei Amo Yisrael,* "Healer of the Sick of his People Israel," 125; *Shomei'a Tefillah,* "Listener to Prayer," 158; *Shoveir Oyvim U'Makhni'a Zeidim,* "Breaker of enemies and Humbler of the arrogant," 137; *Taḥanun,* "Supplication," 186; third blessing after the *Shema* (evening), 65–67

Ashkenazic version of The Torah Service, 68–75
Ashkenazism outside the Land of Israel, 65–67
*Ashrei* (Psalm 145), 12, 22–23, 189
*Attah Veḥartanu,* "You have chosen us," 324–26, 329
*Av HaRaḥamim,* "Father of Mercy," 70
*Avodah* ("Worship") blessing, 89–90, 159–61, 294

*Ba'al Milḥamot,* "The Master of Wars (or Battles)," 168, 168n255
Babylonia, 254, 258
Babylonian Talmud, 9–10n19, 81–83, 163–64, 255, 275n441
Balaam, 44–45
Bar-Ilan, Meir, 269–70, 270n430
Bar Kokhba Rebellion, 92
*Barukh She'amar,* "Blessed Is The One Who Spoke," 8, 15, 259
Baumgarten, Elisheva, 341–42
*Ben Yehoyada* commentary on *Hallel,* 338–39
Berger, Kenneth xix, 146n219
biblical proof text, 280–82
*Birkat HaMazon,* "The Blessing After Meals," 211
*Birkat HaMinim,* "The Blessing (Against) the Sectarians," 81–82, 135–40
*Birkat HaShir,* "The Blessing of Song," 259
*Birkat Hoda'ah,* "The Blessing of Thanksgiving," 170–84
*Birkat Kedushat HaYom,* "The Blessing of the Holiness of the Day," 240–45, 323
*Birkat Kohanim,* "The Priestly Blessing," 165–66
*Birkat Mei'ein Sheva,* "The Blessing Summarizing Seven," 96n145, 252–58
*Birkat Yotser Or,* "The Blessing of the Creator of Light," 267–77, 271n433
*Birkhot HaShaḥar,* "Morning Blessings," 2–8, 65
Blessing of Moses, 86–88
Blois Massacre, 205–9
*Boneh Yerushalayim,* "Builder of Jerusalem," 143–51, 143n215
Book of Jubilees, 289
Book of Numbers, 69, 286–87
Brand, Itzhak, 333
Brettler, Marc, 133, 245, 246n382
Bubonic Plague, 341
Burning Bush story, 32–33, 95, 118

Cairo Genizah, 6–7, 49, 81–83, 114n169, 137, 141, 151n224, 160, 166, 184n287, 205, 253, 268, 282
candle, 319–20
Caro, Rabbi Yosef, 210
Carson, Rachel, 360
censorship, 6, 135–36, 181–82, 208
Chajes, J. H., 386n558
charity, 341–45
Chi Gong, 292
Chmielnicki, Bogdan, 344
chosenness, 72–73, 324–26, 329
Christianity, 144, 155, 261, 292–93, 341–42, 356
communal blessings, 90–91
communal fast days, 298
concluding prayers of the *Shaḥarit,* "Morning," Service, 189–216; *Adon Olam,* "Eternal Lord," 215–16; *Aleinu,* 203–15; *Kaddish,* "Holiness" or "Sanctification," 191–203; *Kedushah DeSidra,* "The *Kedushah* of the Torah Lesson," 189–91
Conservative movement, 7, 23–24, 31, 43, 67, 72, 99, 139–40, 145, 161, 168, 169, 174–75, 176–77, 179, 258, 290–91, 304–5, 325, 332, 342, 349, 355, 359
Cordovero, Rabbi Moshe, 137–38
Creation, 50–55, 230, 271, 303
Crusades, 49, 82, 114n169, 209n328, 341, 352–55

Days of Awe, 116, 331–36, 350, 358
Dead Sea Scrolls, 107
"Death As Homecoming" (Heschel), 201–2
demonology/demonic forces, 234, 237, 255–58
Deuteronomy, 31, 33, 40, 71–72, 86–88, 143, 230
Diaspora, 28, 71

Dimi, Rav, 194
divine marriage, 229–34
Dorff, Rabbi Elliot, 64–65
*Dover Shalom,* "Speaker of Peace," 170
doxologies, 202–3

early Jewish-Christians, 135–40, 286n449
18 mentions of God's name, 65–66
*Eil Adon,* "God, the Master," 267–69n425, 270nn430–31, 271n433, 275n441, 277nn442–43
*Eil Elyon,* "Supernal God," 96–97, 96n144
*Eil Malei Raḥamim,* "God Full of Mercy," 343–45, 344n531
Elazar ben Yehudah, Rabbi, 33–34, 325
Elbaz, R. Moshe ben Maimon, 221–24
Elbogen, Ismar, 9, 15n31, 66, 68–69, 75, 124, 130, 135, 244–45, 268, 301, 313–14, 319
Eliezer, Rabbi, 79–81, 79n121
Elior, Rachel, 273n440
*Emet VeYatziv,* "True and Certain," 61–63
eroticism, 234
Esther, 178–83
*Everything is God* (Michaelson), 36–37
evil, 5–6, 26–27, 126n189, 138–39, 172, 182, 193–96, 199, 237–38
exile, 43, 59, 128–34, 153, 232–34, 328, 349, 351, 358
Exodus, Book of, 118–19, 279–80, 281, 284–89, 291, 313–14, 331–33
Exodus from Egypt, 11, 46, 48, 336, 337n519
Ezekiel, 104–9, 106n159, 148, 271n434, 310

Festival *Amidah,* 323–30
Festival Torah Service, 68, 331–36
Finkelstein, Louis, 88n129, 337n520
first blessing after the *Shema,* 61–63
first blessing before the *Shema,* 49–55, 103, 334
Fleischer, Ezra, 268, 269n426, 270n430
forgiveness, 115–17
Frank, Jacob, 155
Freehof, Solomon, 341
Freundel, Rabbi Barry, 260n410, 261n415, 262
Friday night *Kiddush,* 254, 258, 317–19
fringes *(tzitzit),* 44–48

Gabirol, Solomon Ibn, 215
*Gadol hashalom,* "Great is peace," 168
Galinsky, Judah, 341
Gamaliel, Rabban, 79–80, 83, 92–93
Gaon, Rabbi Amram, 14, 147n221
Gaon, Rav Moshe, 13
Gaon, Rav Natronai bar Hilai, 13
Gartner, Yaakov, 147–48
Geiger, Rabbi Abraham, 6
*Gematria,* 206n324, 220, 234, 348n541
Genesis, 50–55, 152–53, 267, 271, 303, 360
*genizah,* 81–82
Geonic era, 48, 107, 166, 220, 239, 308–9, 308n478
Geonim, 82, 184n287
*gevurot,* "mighty acts," 85–86, 99, 358
God as the ground of oneness and coherence, 35–36
God's essence *(kavod),* 331–36
God's kingship, 16, 133, 220, 223–24, 225, 239
God's Presence, 110–11, 117, 126, 126n189, 128, 132, 142, 150, 158, 161, 235, 335, 361
*Go'eil Yisrael,* "Liberator of Israel," 84n126, 117–22
Golinkin, David xix, 145n218, 147n223, 200n317, 262n416, 298n464, 332n508
Goluboff, Nicole, 350
Gordis, Rabbi Robert, 168n253
"Grant our portion in your Torah," *VeTen ḥelkeinu beToratekha,* 245–46, 250–51
Green, Arthur, 109–10, 190–91
Greenberg, Rabbi Yitz, 156
*Guide For the Perplexed* (Rambam), 126n189

*Ha'Eil HaKadosh,* "Holy God," 101–11
Ḥalafta, Rabbi Yossi ben, 8–14, 18, 21–22
*halakhah,* 17
*Hallel,* 8–14, 11n20, 11n21, 18, 21, 219–20, 259, 336–40, 336n517, 337n518, 337n520, 351
*HaMaḥazir Shekhinato LeTzion,* "Restorer of His Presence to Zion," 159–62
Haman, 178–83
Hamburg Prayerbook of 1819, 304–5
*HaMevareikh Et Amo Yisrael BaShalom,* "The Blesser of Peace to His People Israel," 165–70

Hammer, Reuven, 24, 91–92, 273, 337n519
Ḥanina, Rabbi, 89, 228–29
Hannover, Rabbi Nathan Nata, 335, 344
*Ḥanukkah,* 170–78, 219, 339
*Ḥanun HaMarbeh Lislo'aḥ,* "God Who Graciously and Abundantly Forgives," 115–17
Harari, Yuval Noah, 169n256
*HaRotzeh BiTeshuvah,* "Desirer of Repentance," 114–15
*Hashkiveinu,* "Lay Us Down," 63–65
*Ḥasidei Ashkenaz* ("German Pietists"), 125, 206n324, 291
*ḥatimah,* "seal," 62, 112–13, 114, 114n169, 124, 127, 129, 133, 152, 154
*HaTov Shimkha U'Lekha Na'eh LeHodot,* "Your Name is "Goodness," 162–65
*Ḥatzi Kaddish,*"Partial *Kaddish*", 192–93, 196
Hauptman, Judith xix, 10n19
P
*Havdalah,* "Distinction," 316–21
*Havineinu,* "Give us understanding," 80–81
*ḥavurot,* 212
Ḥayyim, Rabbi Yosef, 339
healing, 122–26, 140
Hebrew text, 74–75, 153–55, 179–80, 210, 325
*Heikhal HaKodesh,* "The Holy Sanctuary," 221–22, 224
Heinemann, Joseph, 253, 255
*Hekhalot* literature, 25, 106–9, 203–13, 269–70, 273n440
Herzog, Rabbi Isaac, 44
Heschel, Rabbi Abraham Joshua, 191n298, 201–2, 306
Ḥiyya bar Abba, Rabbi, 56
*Hodu L'YHVH Kir'u Vishmo,*"Prayer from when David brought the Ark to Jerusalem," 19–20
Hoffman, Lawrence A., 22n39, 91–92, 91n135, 316–17
Hoffman, Yair, 26
holy and profane, 316–17
Holy of Holies, 335
*Ḥonein HaDa'at,* "Gracious Giver of Knowledge," 112–13
Horowitz, Elliott, 183
Horowitz, Sandy, 336
*Hoshana Rabba* ("The Great *Hoshana*"), 346–51, 347n535
*Hoshanot,* "Please God Save," 346–51, 347n535

idolatry, 190–91, 351
Igrat bat Maḥalat, 256
individual and communal pleas for God's help, 119
inner peace, 65, 170
invitation to formal prayer, 49–50
Isaac, 97, 315
Isaiah, 51–52, 70–71, 104–7, 109, 129, 231, 302–3, 302n466, 306, 310
Ishmael, Rabbi, 272
Islam, 136, 208, 292–93
Israel, 176–77, 324–26, 329
Isserles, R. Moshe, 147n222

Jacob, 97, 103, 152–53, 315
Jellinek, Adolph, 336n517
Jeremiah, 118n172, 122–23, 131–32
Jeremiah 14:9, 325–26
Jerusalem, 74–75, 143–51, 162, 230–32
Jesus of Nazareth, 155
Jewish mysticism, 106–11, 203, 269, 273–74
Jewish Renewal, 73, 212–13
Jones, Ashley M., 214
Josephus, 34–35
Joshua, 211
Julian, 144

Kabbalah, 138, 223, 233–35, 237, 273–74, 368–86
*Kabbalat Shabbat,* 218–40; *Ana V'Kho'aḥ,* 226; *Lekhah Dodi,* 227–37; Psalms 92 and 93, 239–40
Kabbalists, 218, 220, 223, 233, 235, 237, 239, 370, 382–83, 386n558
*Kaddish,* "Holiness" or "Sanctification," 191–203, 197n310, 200n315
*Kaddish De'Itḥadeta,* "*Kaddish* of Renewal," 192–93
*Kaddish DeRabbanan,* "*Kaddish* of Our Rabbis," 192

*Kaddish Shalem,* "Full *Kaddish*," 192, 200
*Kaddish Yatom,* "Mourner's *Kaddish*," 192, 200
Kaddushin, Rabbi Max, 42
Kahana, Rav, 55
Kallir, Eleazar, 357
Karaite community, 148
Karo, Rabbi Yosef, 57, 147n221, 147n222
*kavannah* (inner intention), 94–95, 126, 132, 162, 177, 306, 321, 339–40, 361–62
*Kedushah,* "Holiness," 50–54, 101–11, 309n479
*Kedushah DeSidra (U'Va LeTzion),* 308–11, 308n477
*Kedushah DeSidra,* "The *Kedushah* of the Torah Lesson," 103, 189–91
*Kedushah DeYotser,* "The *Kedushah* of the Creator (Blessing)," 50–55, 103, 267–68, 274–75, 277
*Kedushat HaShem,* "Holiness of the Name," 102–3, 110
*kelipot,* demonic "shells," 137–38, 220, 224
*keren,* "horn," 151–57
*Keri'at Shema U'Virkhoteha,* "The Recitation of the *Shema* And Its Blessings," 27, 50, 267
*Kilelat HaMinim,* "The Curse of the Sectarians," 137
Kimelman, Reuven, 48, 88n129, 91–92n135
King James Bible, 242
*Kitvei Ha'Ari,* "The Writings of the Ari," 334n514
knowledge, 112–13
*kol,* "all, every," 22–23, 271n433
*Kol Haneshamah,* 176, 290, 304
Kook, Avraham Yitzḥak HaKohen, 161, 161n243
Kook, Rabbi Abraham Isaac, 132
*korban todah* (thanksgiving sacrifice), 20–21

*La'Eil Asher Shavat,* "God Who Rested," 275, 277–79
Landau, Rabbi Yitzḥak Eliyahu, 170, 250, 251
land of Israel, 129–32
Langer, Ruth, 9–10n19, 71–72, 71n109, 184n287, 309n479
*Lekhah Dodi,* 218–19, 226, 227–37
Levi, Rabbi, 20, 168, 319–20
Levinson, Bernard M., 31–32
Levy, E., 90–91
Lew, Rabbi Alan, 35–36, 35n61
liberation, 62–63, 117–22, 118n172
life after death, 99–101
listening, 158–59
literary wholeness, 83–85
lovingkindness and mercy, 133–34
loyalty, 31, 42
Luria, Rabbi Isaac, 73, 200, 220–21, 224, 226, 331, 334n514
Luria, Rabbi Yitzḥak, 137–38, 334
Luzzatto, Samuel David, 261n414

*Ma'amadot,* "prayers of the delegation," 2n6, 297–98
*Ma'ariv,* "Evening" service, 27–28, 78, 228, 230, 240–58, 294n459, 307, 316; *Birkat Mei'ein Sheva,* "The Blessing Summarizing Seven," 252–58; blessings surrounding the *Shema,* 48; first blessing after the *Shema,* 61–63; *Naḥeim,* "Remembering Jerusalem on T*isha B'Av*," 145–48; second blessing before the *Shema,* 60; Shabbat Evening *Amidah,* Part 1, 240–44; Shabbat Evening *Amidah,* Part 2, 244–52
*Ma'aseh Bereshit* ("The Enterprise of Creation"), 267, 271
*Ma'aseh Merkavah,* "The Chariot Enterprise," 267–72, 269n428
*Magein Avraham,* "Shield of Abraham," 95–98
*Maḥzor Lev Shalem,* 332
*Maḥzor Vitry,* 197–99, 257, 260, 290
*Malkhuyot,* or "(Biblical) Kingship Verses," 205
Mannheimer, Rabbi Isak Noa, 290
martyrs, 340–45
*Matir Assurim,* "Releaser of the Bound," 88
Matriarchs, 97
Matt, Daniel, 74
*Matzmi'aḥ Keren Yeshua,* "Grower of the Horn of Salvation," 151–57
*Megillat Esther,* 180
*Meḥayei Hameitim,* "Reviver of the Dead," 98–101
Meir, Rabbi, 42, 354–55

Meir ben Isaac Nehorai, Rabbi, 352
Meir of Rothenberg, R., 174
*Mekabeitz Nidḥei Amo Yisrael,* "Gatherer of the Dispersed of his People Israel," 128–32
Melchizedek, 96–97
*Melekh Oheiv Tzedakah U'Mishpat* King, "Lover of Righteousness and Justice," 133–34
*Merkavah* mysticism, 106–11, 203, 273
Messiah, 131, 151–57, 192, 231
messianic era, 144, 149, 190, 227, 234, 237, 240
Messianic future, 143
messianic redemption, 54, 130, 155–56
*Mevareikh HaShanim,* "Blesser of the Years," 127–28
Michaelson, Jay, 36–37
Midrash, 28, 51, 153, 192, 236, 241–44, 331–32
Midrash *Hallel,* 336n517
midrashic interpretations of Scripture, 263–66
Midrash *Tehillim,* 336n517
Milgrom, Jacob, 45–46
*Minḥah,* "Afternoon," Service, 308–15; *Amidah,* 252–53, 294–97, 311–15; blessings surrounding the *Shema,* 48; *Kedushah,* "Holiness," 109; *Kedushah DeSidra (U'Va LeTzion),* 308–11; *Naḥeim,* "Remembering Jerusalem on T*isha B'Av,*" 145–48, 147n222; *Taḥanun,* "Supplication," 184
*minyan,* 2, 200, 212
miracles, 21–22, 131, 170–78
Mirsky, Aharon, 282, 285
*Mish'an U'Mivtaḥ LaTzadikim,* "Support and Trust of the Righteous," 140–43
*Mishkan Tefillah,* 290, 304
Mishnah, 12, 28, 29, 48, 55, 65, 79, 81–83, 108, 159–60, 165–66, 226, 246, 259, 297–98, 346–49, 357
*Mishneh Torah,* 88–89, 174
*mitzvot,* "commandments," 44–46
*Mizmor LeTodah,* "A Psalm of Thanksgiving," 20–21
modern liberal movements, 97, 290, 304
modern prayer books, 176, 212, 220
*Modim DeRabbanan,* "The Thanksgiving (Blessing) of Our Rabbis." See *HaTov Shimkha U'Lekha Na'eh LeHodot,* "Your Name is "Goodness"
*Moment Magazine,* 156
monotheism, 31–32, 36, 211, 233, 237
Mordecai, Rabbi Avraham, 215
Mordechai of Lechovitz, 139
Moses, 69–72, 86–88, 95–96, 279–93, 313–15, 331–34
*Musaf Amidah,* 205, 291, 294–307, 298n464, 328–29, 346, 350–51, 357–58
mystical meaning of *Lekhah Dodi,* 233–38; refrain of *Lekhah Dodi* in the mystical interpretation, 233–35; sample verse of *Lekhah Dodi* in the mystical interpretation, 235–37
mystics, 309

*Naḥeim,* "Remembering Jerusalem on T*isha B'Av,*" 144–48, 147nn221–22, 150–51
name of God, 348
name of God in the first line of the *Shema,* 32–33
Naropa University, 212–13
Nash Papyrus, 28–29
nature, 55–56, 307, 360
Navahrudak Yeshivah, 187–88
*nefesh,* "soul," 221, 224, 225
negative theology, 213
*neḥamot,* "consolations," 175–76
Neḥunia ben HaKaneh, R., 246
The New English Bible, 242
*Nishmat Kol Ḥai* "The Breath of All," 259–67, 261n415
Nondual Judaism, 36–37
non-Jews, 3–7, 135–40, 143, 180–83, 208–12
non-mystical meaning of *Lekhah Dodi,* 227–32; refrain of *Lekhah Dodi* in the non-mystical interpretation, 227–30; verses of *Lekhah Dodi* in the non-mystical interpretation, 230–32
non-Orthodox prayer books, 6, 345
Normal Mysticism, 42
*notein haTorah,* "The Giver of Torah," 71
*Nusaḥ Bavel,* "The Babylonian Rite," 82
*Nusaḥ Eretz Yisrael (Ha'Atik),* or "The (Old) Palestinian Rite," 82

*Nusaḥ Eretz Yisrael HaKadum,* "The Ancient Palestinian Rite," 49

*One God Clapping* (Lew), 35
Orthodox movement, 43, 66–67, 139, 160, 210, 303–4, 335, 342, 349, 355

paganism, 235
Palestinian rite, 49, 82, 87, 96n145, 114n169, 258, 328
Palestinians, 131
Palestinian Talmud, 82, 124, 145–48, 163–64, 163n244, 181, 182n280, 182n283, 295
*Parashat Ha'Azinu,* 297, 306
Passover, 339–40, 357–58, 361
Passover *Seder,* 259
Patriarchs, 20, 58–59, 95–97, 314, 358
Paul addressing the Galatians, 4–5
peace, 165–70
people of Israel, 152, 169, 301–2
*Pesaḥ,* 173, 257, 330
*Peshitta,* 242
*Pesukei DeZimra,* 8–27, 219–20, 259–62; *Ashrei* (Psalm 145), 22–23; *Hodu L'YHVH Kir'u Vishmo,*"Prayer from when David brought the Ark to Jerusalem," 19–20; *Mizmor LeTodah,* "A Psalm of Thanksiving," 20–21; outline of, 15–17; Psalm 91, 26–27; Psalm 149, 23–24; Psalm 150, 25–26
piety, 10–11
pilgrimage holidays, 173
Pinḥas, Rabbi, 20
polytheistic religions, 208, 235
post-biblical Judaism, 32, 152
post-talmudic era, 2n6, 13, 94, 164, 191–92, 197
praise of God from a non-human source, 275, 277
*Prayer is a Place* (Tickle), 93–94
Priestly Blessing, 166–68
prostration, 184–86
Prouser, Joseph H. 71n109
Psalm 6, 186–87
Psalm 19:15 *(Va'Ani tefillati),* 74, 335
Psalm 20, 189
Psalm 29, 85–86
Psalm 33:5, 133–34
Psalm 91, 26–27
Psalm 92, 226, 227, 239–40, 278
Psalm 93, 239–40
Psalm 99, 222
Psalm 119, 117–18
Psalm 145, 12, 22–23, 189
Psalm 146, 106
Psalm 149, 23–24
Psalm 150, 14, 25–26, 262
Psalms, Book of, 8, 12–16, 22, 25, 117, 223, 331–32, 336n517. See also *Pesukei DeZimra*
Ptolemy II of Egypt, 242
public fasts, 297–98
*Purim,* 178–84

Rabban Gamaliel II, 136–38
rabbinic and biblical wording, 309–10
Rabbinic Judaism, 152, 291
Rabbinic Literature, 28–29, 48, 79, 85, 94, 95, 107, 144, 180–81, 192, 229, 230, 237, 246, 247, 250, 280, 308
Rabinowitz, Louis, 11n21
*Raḥeim,* "Have Mercy," 145–48
Rambam, 79n120, 88–90, 126n189, 151–52, 159–60, 174, 213, 349, 373
Rashi, 4, 14, 136, 239, 255–57, 280–81, 314, 348–49, 348n541, 351
Rav, 164, 181, 332
Rava, 50–51, 193–94
Reconstructing Judaism Movement, 31–32, 66, 73, 99, 139, 145, 155, 158, 161, 168, 169, 179–80, 249, 258, 325, 330, 335, 342, 349, 355, 359
redemption, 91–93
reenactment, first line of *Shema* as, 33–34
Reform movement, 43, 45–46, 66, 73, 99, 130, 139–40, 145, 158, 161, 176–77, 179, 249, 290, 304, 325, 342, 355, 359
repentance, 114–15
repetitions, 252–53
return, 129–32, 133
*Retzeh,* 173
righteous converts, 140–43

*Rofei Ḥolei Amo Yisrael,* "Healer of the Sick of his People Israel," 122–26
Rosenbaum, Rabbi Jay, 351
*Rosh HaShanah,* 116–17, 203–10, 333, 350
*Rosh Ḥodesh,* 219–20, 275n441, 337
Rosh Yeshivah, 187–88

Saadia Gaon, Rav, 14, 54, 168n253, 240n371
sacrifices, 159–62, 185, 294–307
Sages, 163–64, 168, 185, 192, 228–29, 331–32
Sages of the Talmud, 107, 337
salvation, 151–57
Sambatyon river, 354, 357
II Samuel 24:14, 187
Saposh, Rabbi Pinḥas (Pinky), 60–61
Sarah, 102–3
"Satisfy us through your goodness," *Sabenu mituvekha,* 246–47, 251
*Sattan* in Jewish tradition, 64
Schachter-Shalomi, Rabbi Zalman, 212–13, 340
Schechter, Solomon, 81–82
Scheinberg, Robert xix, 79n121, 168n253
Schneerson, Rabbi Menachem, 155
second blessing after the *Shema* (evening), 63–65
Second Temple Period, 2n6, 14, 32, 107
Second Vatican Council, 214
*Seder Olam,* 15n31, 19–20
*Seder Rav Amram,* 174, 178, 248, 268n425, 312
*Sefat Emet* ("The Language of Truth") (Rabbi Yehudah Aryeh Leib Alter), 215
*Sefirot,* 223, 233–38, 273, 273n439, 334, 386n558
self-censorship, 6, 135–36, 181–82, 208
Seligman Baer, Rabbi, 21
Sephardic rite: *Aleinu,* 209; *Al HaNissim,* "For The Miracles," 174–75; *Kedushah,* "Holiness," 106; *Musaf Amidah,* 301; *piyyutim,* 359; *Shomei'a Tefillah,* "Listener to Prayer," 158; *Taḥanun,* "Supplication," 186
Septuagint, 241–42
*Sha'ar HaKavannot,* "The Gate of Intentions," 218–19
Shabbat, 351; *Kabbalat Shabbat,* 218–40; *Minḥah,* "Afternoon," Service, 308–15; *Musaf Amidah,* 294–307; Psalms 92 and 93, 239–40; as the sole possession of Israel, 280, 288–90, 292–93; Torah Service, 74See also *Ma'ariv,* "Evening" service; *Shaḥarit,* "Morning," Service
Shabbatai Tzvi, 155
Shabbat Evening *Amidah,* Part 1, 240–44
Shabbat Evening *Amidah,* Part 2, 244–52; "Accept our rest," *retzeh vimenuḥateinu,* 245–46, 248–50; "Grant our portion in your Torah," *VeTen ḥelkeinu beToratekha,* 245–46, 250–51; "Satisfy us through your goodness," *Sabenu mituvekha,* 246–47, 251; *VeTaher libeinu l'ovdekha be'emet,* "Purify our heart to serve you in truth," 247–48, 251–52
*Shaḥarit,* "Morning," Service, 27–28, 78, 259–93; *Aleinu,* 203–15; *Amidah* for Shabbat Morning, 252–53, 279–93; *Amidah* of *Shaḥarit,* 291, 295–307, 359; *Birkhot HaShaḥar,* 2–8, 65; blessings surrounding the *Shema,* 48–65; *Eil Adon,* "God, the Master," 267–77; *Kaddish,* "Holiness" or "Sanctification," 191–203; *Kedushah,* "Holiness," 109; *Kedushah DeSidra,* "The *Kedushah* of the Torah Lesson," 189–91; *La'Eil Asher Shavat,* "God Who Rested," 277–79; *Naḥeim,* "Remembering Jerusalem on Tisha *B'Av,*" 145–48; *Nishmat Kol Ḥai* "The Breath of All," 259–67; Priestly Blessing, 166–68; *Taḥanun,* "Supplication," 184
*Shalom Rav,* "Abundant Peace," 165–68
*Shavuot,* 173, 330, 336, 339, 352–57
*Shekhinah,* "Presence," 219, 224, 234–38
*Sheli'aḥ Tzibbur,* 262
*Shema,* 27–67; blessings surrounding, 48–67, 93; first blessing after the, 61–63; first blessing before the, 49–55, 103, 334; first line of, 30–39; first paragraph of, 39–42; introduction, 27–30; *Pesukei DeZimra,* 8, 13–14, 17–18; second blessing after (evening), 63–65; second blessing before the, 57–61; second paragraph of, 42–45;

third blessing after (evening), 65–67; third paragraph of, 44–48; *V'Ahavta* paragraph, 39–42, 57–60; *V'Haya Im Shamo'a* paragraph, 42–45
*Shema* and Its Blessings, 240
Shemini Atzeret, 350, 357–62
*Shibbolei HaLekket* (Tzedekiah ben Avraham), 314
Shimon, Rabbi, 55, 194
*Shirat HaYam*, "The Song at the Sea," 62
*Shivata*, 358
Shmuel ben Meir, Rabbi, 31
*Shomei'a Tefillah*, "Listener to Prayer," 157–58
*Shomer Yisrael*, "Guardian of Israel," 186, 187
Shore-Wittenberg, Rabbi Sally, 75
*Shoshanat Ya'akov*, "The Lily of Jacob," 180–81
*Shoveir Oyvim U'Makhni'a Zeidim*, "Breaker of enemies and Humbler of the arrogant," 135–40
*Shulḥan Arukh*, 21, 147, 147n222, 181, 186, 257
*Siddur Ḥasidei Ashkenaz*, 269
*Siddur Lev Shalem*, 175, 290, 305
*Siddur Rav Saadia Ga'on*, 147n221, 174, 178, 205, 248, 312
*Siddur Sim Shalom, A Prayerbook for Shabbat, Festivals, and Weekdays*, 174–75
Silverman, Ian, 286n449
Simḥat Torah, 60–61, 150, 350
*Sim Shalom*, "Grant Peace," 90, 165–68, 170
Sinai, 71–75
*Siyyum*, 192
sleep, 65
spices, 318–21
State of Israel, 131–32, 168
stewardship, 43–44, 360
successful week, 321
*Sukkot*, 173, 330, 336, 339, 346–51, 358

*Taḥanun*, "Supplication," 184–88, 184n287
*takhlit*, "end-goal," 243
Talmud, 2–3, 8–14, 9n19, 25, 26–27, 28–29, 51, 56, 62, 63, 80, 85–86, 90, 127, 135–36, 153, 192, 211, 226, 228–29, 230, 241, 246, 256, 259, 260n410, 297, 306, 316, 331–33
Tannaim, 85, 316
Tannaitic era/literature, 28, 79, 81–83, 107, 228, 245, 253
*Targum*, 352–55
Ta-Shma, Israel M., 2n6
*Tefillat Geshem*, "The Prayer for Rain," 350, 357–62
*Tefillat Tal*, "The Prayer for Dew," 357–62
*tekhelet* ("blue" or "violet") fringes, 44–48
*temei'im beyad tehorim*, "[you delivered] the impure into the hands of the pure," 175–77
Ten Commandments, 28–30, 31, 230, 236, 279–86, 286n449, 352–53
Ten Lost Tribes of Israel, 354
testimony, first line of *Shema* as, 34–35
Thales, 4
thanksgiving, 20–21, 88–90, 174n260
theurgy, 193–203
third blessing after the *Shema* (evening), 65–67
third paragraph of *Shema*, 44–48
Thirteen Attributes of God, 68, 74, 331–35n514
Three Pilgrimage Festivals, 74, 323–45, 359
Tickle, Phyllis, 93–94
*Tiferet*, 233–38
*Tikkunei Shabbat*, "Arrangements (of prayers) for Shabbat," 220–21, 224
*Tisha B'Av*, 144–48, 150–51, 311
Torah, 58–59, 61, 120, 138, 149, 159, 173, 184, 190, 197–99, 246, 250–51, 281–89, 299–300, 304
Torah scroll, 70–75
Torah service, 68–75
Torah study, 192, 308–11
*Tosafot*, 90, 174, 174n260, 182n280, 348–49, 351
*Tosefta*, 177, 184
Tractate *Soferim*, 13–14, 173, 173n259
translating the first line of the *Shema*, 30–32
translation of the Bible, 1917, 30–32, 242
translation of the Bible, 1962, 30–31, 242
Tsadok, Rabbi, 253–54

*V'Ahavta* paragraph, *Shema*, 39–42, 57–60
*v'al hamilḥamot*, "because of the battles," 175, 177

*VeHasi'einu,* "Grant to us," 327–30
*VeHu Raḥum,* "(God) the Merciful," 186
*VeShamru* passage, Exodus, 279–86, 291
Vespasian, 186
*VeTaher libeinu l'ovdekha be'emet,* "Purify our heart to serve you in truth," 247–48, 251–52
*V'Haya Im Shamo'a* paragraph, *Shema,* 42–45
Vital, Rabbi Ḥayyim, 218–19, 334n514

weekday *Amidah,* 78–188; *Al HaNissim,* "For The Miracles," 170–84; biblical verses, 85–86; *Boneh Yerushalayim,* "Builder of Jerusalem," 143–51; *Go'eil Yisrael,* "Liberator of Israel," 117–22; *Ha'Eil HaKadosh,* "Holy God," 101–11; *HaMaḥazir Shekhinato LeTzion,* "Restorer of His Presence to Zion," 159–62; *HaMevareikh Et Amo Yisrael BaShalom,* "The Blesser of Peace to His People Israel," 165–70; *Ḥanun HaMarbeh Lislo'aḥ,* "God Who Graciously and Abundantly Forgives," 115–17; *HaRotzeh BiTeshuvah,* "Desirer of Repentance," 114–15; *HaTov Shimkha U'Lekha Na'eh LeHodot,* "Your Name is "Goodness," 162–65; *Ḥonein HaDa'at,* "Gracious Giver of Knowledge," 112–13; how the 18-blessing *Amidah* became a 19-blessing *Amidah,* 81–83; as a literary whole, 83–95; *Magein Avraham,* "Shield of Abraham," 95–98; *Matzmi'aḥ Keren Yeshua,* "Grower of the Horn of Salvation," 151–57; *Meḥayei Hameitim,* "Reviver of the Dead," 98–101; *Mekabeitz Nidḥei Amo Yisrael,* "Gatherer of the Dispersed of his People Israel," 128–32; *Melekh Oheiv Tzedakah U'Mishpat* King, "Lover of Righteousness and Justice," 133–34; *Mevareikh HaShanim,* "Blesser of the Years," 127–28; *Mish'an U'Mivtaḥ LaTzadikim,* "Support and Trust of the Righteous," 140–43; as a pattern of personal and communal blessings, 90–91; as praise, needs, praise, 86–88; as praise, needs, thanksgiving, 88–90; *Rofei Ḥolei Amo Yisrael,* "Healer of the Sick of his People Israel," 122–26; *Shoveir Oyvim U'Makhni'a Zeidim,* "Breaker of enemies and Humbler of the arrogant," 135–40; *Taḥanun,* "Supplication," 184–88; titles of the 19 blessings, 78–79; as a unified statement on redemption, 91–93
wickedness, 135–40
windows, 56–57
wine, 318–19
Wise, Rabbi Isaac Mayer, 46
women, 4–6

Ya'akov, Rabbi, 145–46
Ya'akov ben Asher, Rabbi, 21
*Ya'aleh VeYavo,* "May we be remembered," 326–27, 328, 330
Yannai, Rabbi, 228
Yasa, Rabbi, 163
*Yehallelukha,* "May They Bless You," 259
Yehoshua, Rabbi, 80
Yehoshua ben Korḥah, Rabbi, 29–30
Yehoshua ben Levi, Rabbi, 27, 193
Yehudah, Rabbi, 194, 346–49, 348n541
Yehudah HaNasi, Rabbi, 255–56
Yeshivat HaMivtar, 187–88
Yishmael, Rabbi, 204
*Yishtabaḥ,* "May (Your Name, God) Be Blessed," 8, 16, 259
*Yizkor,* "May God Remember," 340–45
Yoḥanan, Rabbi, 56, 194–95
*Yom HaAtzma'ut,* Israel Independence Day, 170
*Yom Kippur,* 116–17, 205, 208, 302n467, 333, 350
Yossi, Rabbi, 9–10n19, 11n21, 194–95, 295–306
Yossi ben Ḥalafta, Rabbi, 9n19, 195
Yossi ben Rabbi Yehudah, Rabbi, 255

Zenger, Erich, 337n519
Zionism, 130, 144
Zippor, Moshe Ben Eliezer, 349, 351
Zohar, 72–74, 158, 190–91, 223–24, 334
Zulai, Menahem, 282
Zunz, Leopold, 215

## About The Author

Jeffrey Hoffman graduated with a double major in Hebrew and Judaic Studies from The State University of New York at Albany. He received an M.A., Rabbinic Ordination, and a Doctorate of Hebrew Literature (D.H.L.) in Liturgy from The Jewish Theological Seminary. He spent three of the years working on those degrees in Jerusalem where he also studied at The Hebrew University and at Yeshivat HaMivtar. Hoffman spent 23 years serving as a congregational rabbi in Vancouver, B.C. and Upper Nyack, NY. He is the editor of *Siddur Tisha B'Av* published by The Rabbinical Assembly, the co-author of *Karov L'Chol Korav – For All Who Call: A Manual for Enhancing the Teaching of Prayer*, and the author of many articles and reviews. He has taught liturgy to rabbinical and cantorial students at The Academy for Jewish Religion (pluralistic) for many years, and also at The Jewish Theological Seminary (Conservative), Hebrew Union College-NY (Reform), and the Aleph Ordination Program (Renewal), and has served as a guest lecturer at Yeshivat Chovevei Torah (Orthodox).

## Recent books from ***Ben Yehuda Press***

**Judaism Disrupted: A Spiritual Manifesto for the 21st Century** by Rabbi Michael Strassfeld. "I can't remember the last time I felt pulled to underline a book constantly as I was reading it, but *Judaism Disrupted* is exactly that intellectual, spiritual and personal adventure. You will find yourself nodding, wrestling, and hoping to hold on to so many of its ideas and challenges. Rabbi Strassfeld reframes a Torah that demands breakage, reimagination, and ownership." –Abigail Pogrebin, author, *My Jewish Year: 18 Holidays, One Wondering Jew*

**The Way of Torah and the Path of Dharma: Intersections between Judaism and the Religions of India** by Rabbi Daniel Polish. "A whirlwind religious tourist visit to the diversity of Indian religions: Sikh, Jain, Buddhist, and Hindu, led by an experienced congregational rabbi with much experience in interfaith and in teaching world religions." –Rabbi Alan Brill, author of *Rabbi on the Ganges: A Jewish Hindu-Encounter.*

**Liberating Your Passover Seder: An Anthology Beyond The Freedom Seder**. Edited by Rabbi Arthur O. Waskow and Rabbi Phyllis O. Berman. This volume tells the history of the Freedom Seder and retells the origin of subsequent new haggadahs, including those focusing on Jewish-Palestinian reconciliation, environmental concerns, feminist and LGBT struggles, and the Covid-19 pandemic of 2020.

**Duets on Psalms: Drawing New Meaning from Ancient Words** by Rabbis Elie Spitz & Jack Riemer. "Two of Judaism's most inspirational teachers, offer a lifetime of insights on the Bible's most inspired book." – Rabbi Joseph Telushkin, author of *Jewish Literacy.* "This illuminating work is a literary journey filled with faith, wisdom, hope, healing, meaning and inspiration." –Rabbi Naomi Levy, author of *Einstein and the Rabbi.*

**Weaving Prayer: An Analytical and Spiritual Commentary on the Jewish Prayer Book** by Rabbi Jeffrey Hoffman."This engaging and erudite volume transforms the prayer experience. Not only is it of considerable intellectual interest to learn the history of prayers—how, when, and why they were composed—but this new knowledge will significantly help a person pray with intention (*kavanah*). I plan to keep this volume right next to my siddur." –Rabbi Judith Hauptman, author of *Rereading the Rabbis: A Woman's Voice.*

**Renew Our Hearts: A Siddur for Shabbat Day** edited by Rabbi Rachel Barenblat. From the creator of *The Velveteen Rabbi's Haggadah*, a new siddur for the day of Shabbat. *Renew Our Hearts* balances tradition with innovation, featuring liturgy for morning (*Shacharit* and a renewing approach to *Musaf)*, the afternoon (*Mincha*), and evening (*Ma'ariv* and *Havdalah*), along with curated works of poetry, art and new liturgies from across the breadth of Jewish spiritual life. Every word of Hebrew is paired with transliteration and with clear, pray-able English translation.

**Forty Arguments for the Sake of Heaven: Why the Most Vital Controversies in Jewish Intellectual History Still Matter** by Rabbi Shmuly Yanklowitz. Hillel vs. Shammai, Ayn Rand vs. Karl Marx, Tamar Ross vs. Judith Plaskow... but also Abraham vs. God, and God vs. the angels! Movements debate each other: Reform versus Orthodoxy, one- two- and zero-state solutions to the Israeli-Palestinian conflict, gun rights versus gun control in the United States. Rabbi Yanklowitz presents difficult and often heated disagreements with fairness and empathy, helping us consider our own truths in a pluralistic Jewish landscape.

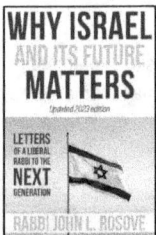

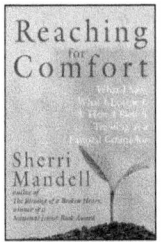

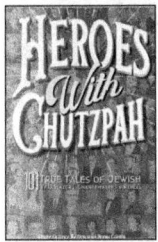

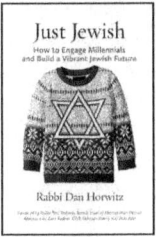

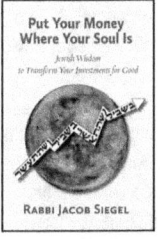

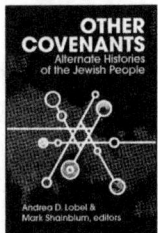

# Reflections on the weekly Torah portion from ***Ben Yehuda Press***

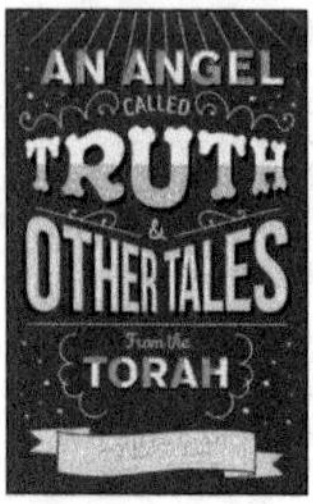


**An Angel Called Truth and Other Tales from the Torah** by Rabbi Jeremy Gordon and Emma Parlons. Funny, engaging micro-tales for each of the portions of the Torah and one for each of the Jewish festivals as well. These tales are told from the perspective of young people who feature in the Biblical narrative, young people who feature in classic Rabbinic commentary on our Biblical narratives and young people just made up for this book.

**Torah & Company: The weekly portion of Torah, accompanied by generous helpings of Mishnah and Gemara, served with discussion questions to spice up your Sabbath Table** by Rabbi Judith Z. Abrams. Serve up a rich feast of spiritual discussion from an age-old recipe: One part Torah. Two parts classic Jewish texts. Add conversation. Stir... and enjoy! "A valuable guide for the Shabbat table of every Jew." –Rabbi Burton L. Visotzky, author *Reading the Book.*

**Torah Journeys: The Inner Path to the Promised Land** by Rabbi Shefa Gold. Rabbi Gold shows us how to find blessing, challenge and the opportunity for spiritual transformation in each portion of Torah. An inspiring guide to exploring the landscape of Scripture... and recognizing that landscape as the story of your life. "Deep study and contemplation went into the writing of this work. Reading her Torah teachings one becomes attuned to the voice of the Shekhinah, the feminine aspect of God which brings needed healing to our wounded world." –Rabbi Zalman Schachter-Shalomi.

**American Torah Toons 2: Fifty-Four Illustrated Commentaries** by Lawrence Bush. Deeply personal and provocative artworks responding to each weekly Torah portion. Each two-page spread includes a Torah passage, a paragraph of commentary from both traditional and modern Jewish sources, and a photo-collage that responds to the text with humor, ethical conscience, and both social and self awareness. "What a vexing, funny, offensive, insightful, infuriating, thought-provoking book." –Rabbi David Saperstein.

**The Comic Torah: Reimagining the Very Good Book.** Stand-up comic Aaron Freeman and artist Sharon Rosenzweig reimagine the Torah with provocative humor and irreverent reverence in this hilarious, gorgeous, off-beat graphic version of the Bible's first five books! Each weekly portion gets a two-page spread. Like the original, the Comic Torah is not always suitable for children.

**we who desire: Poems and Torah riffs** by Sue Swartz. From Genesis to Deuteronomy, from Bereshit to Zot Haberacha, from Eden to Gaza, from Eve to Emma Goldman, *we who desire* interweaves the mythic and the mundane as it follows the arc of the Torah with carefully chosen words, astute observations, and deep emotion. "Sue Swartz has used a brilliant, fortified, playful, serious, humanely furious moral imagination, and a poet's love of the music of language, to re-tell the saga of the Bible you thought you knew." –Alicia Ostriker, author, *For the Love of God: The Bible as an Open Book.*

**Eternal Questions** by Rabbi Josh Feigelson. These essays on the weekly Torah portion guide readers on a journey that weaves together Torah, Talmud, Hasidic masters, and a diverse array of writers, poets, musicians, and thinkers. Each essay includes questions for reflection and suggestions for practices to help turn study into more mindful, intentional living. "This is the wisdom that we always need–but maybe particularly now, more than ever, during these turbulent times." –Rabbi Danya Ruttenberg, author, *On Repentance and Repair.*

# Jewish spirituality and thought from ***Ben Yehuda Press***

**The Essential Writings of Abraham Isaac Kook.** Translated and edited by Rabbi Ben Zion Bokser. This volume of letters, aphorisms and excerpts from essays and other writings provide a wide-ranging perspective on the thought and writing of Rav Kook. With most selections running two or three pages, readers gain a gentle introduction to one of the great Jewish thinkers of the modern era.

**Ahron's Heart: Essential Prayers, Teachings and Letters of Ahrele Roth, a Hasidic Reformer.** Translated and edited by Rabbi Zalman Schachter-Shalomi and Rabbi Yair Hillel Goelman. For the first time, the writings of one of the 20th century's most important Hasidic thinkers are made available to a non-Hasidic English audience. Rabbi Ahron "Ahrele" Roth (1894-1944) has a great deal to say to sincere spiritual seekers far beyond his own community.

**A Passionate Pacifist: Essential Writings of Aaron Samuel Tamares.** Translated and edited by Rabbi Everett Gendler. Rabbi Aaron Samuel Tamares (1869-1931) addresses the timeless issues of ethics, morality, communal morale, and Judaism in relation to the world at large in these essays and sermons, written in Hebrew between 1904 and 1931. "For those who seek a Torah of compassion and pacifism, a Judaism not tied to 19th century political nationalism, and a vision of Jewish spirituality outside of political thinking this book will be essential." —Rabbi Dr. Alan Brill, author, *Thinking God: The Mysticism of Rabbi Zadok of Lublin.*

**Return to the Place: The Magic, Meditation, and Mystery of Sefer Yetzirah** by Rabbi Jill Hammer. A translation of and commentary to an ancient Jewish mystical text that transforms it into a contemporary guide for meditative practice. "A tour de force—at once scholarly, whimsical, deeply poetic, and eminently accessible." —Rabbi Tirzah Firestone, author of *The Receiving: Reclaiming Jewish Women's Wisdom*

**Enlightenment by Trial and Error: Ten Years on the Slippery Slopes of Jewish Mysticism, Postmodern Buddhist Meditation, and Heretical Flexidox Spirituality** by Rabbi Jay Michaelson. A unique record of the 21st-century spiritual search, from the perspective of someone who made plenty of mistakes along the way.

**The Tao of Solomon: Finding Joy and Contentment in the Wisdom of Ecclesiastes** by Rabbi Rami Shapiro. Rabbi Rami Shapiro unravels the golden philosophical threads of wisdom in the book of Ecclesiastes, reweaving the vibrant book of the Bible into a 21st century tapestry. Shapiro honors the roots of the ancient writing, explores the timeless truth that we are merely a drop in the endless river of time, and reveals a path to finding personal and spiritual fulfillment even as we embrace our impermanent place in the universe.

**Embracing Auschwitz: Forging a Vibrant, Life-Affirming Judaism that Takes the Holocaust Seriously** by Rabbi Joshua Hammerman. The Judaism of Sinai and the Judaism of Auschwitz are merging, resulting in new visions of Judaism that are only beginning to take shape. "Should be read by every Jew who cares about Judaism." —Rabbi Dr. Irving "Yitz" Greenberg.

www.ingramcontent.com/pod-product-compliance
Lightning Source LLC
Chambersburg PA
CBHW050158240426
43671CB00013B/2171
* 9 7 8 1 9 5 3 8 2 9 6 0 3 *